aje

Bagages

laim 7-16

e

e Bagagem

»   »

LONELY PLANET

BLUE LIST.

THE BEST IN TRAVEL 2008

MELBOURNE ✿ OAKLAND ✿ LONDON

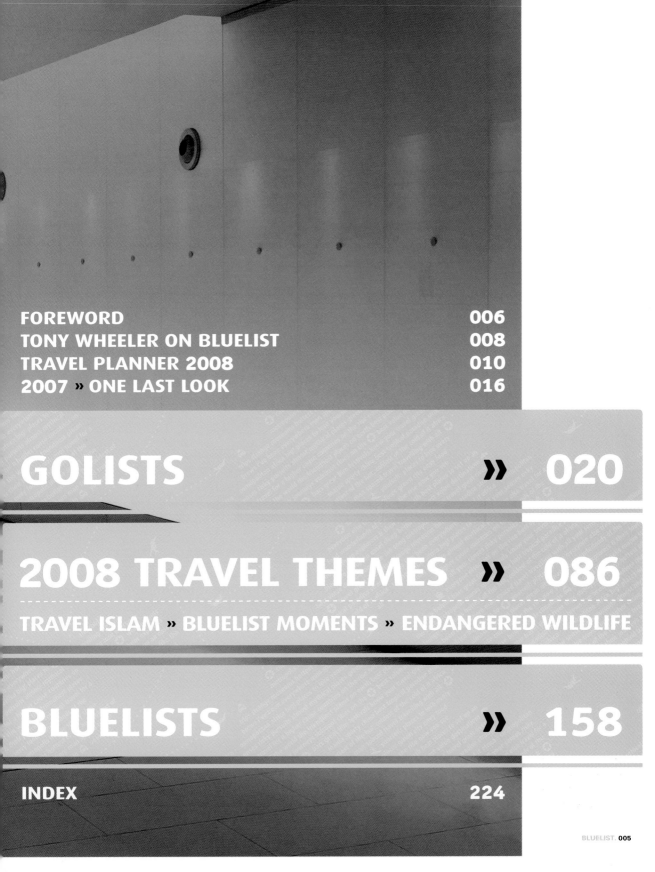

By Roz Hopkins
Publisher, Lonely Planet

FOREWORD

Last year we noted that Bluelist had shifted from a focus on recommending travel experiences to a conversation about travel, and this year we've seen the volume turned up as more and more travellers join in, contributing their Bluelists online, in print and on the television. Now in its third year, we're sure that our unique Bluelist annual will spark the imaginations of new and experienced travellers who are driven to share, recommend and promote the world's best travel experiences.

Our 2008 conversation begins as we reflect on the events which shaped the traveller space in the year gone and check whether our own predictions stacked up. Make up your own mind as you flip through the retrospective, 2007: One Last Look.

Then, put on your 2008 goggles and dive into this year's set of Golists – our 30 picks for destinations in 2008. This time around we take you on a journey to Africa's last frontier, cool down in an Armenian snow dream and catch jungle fever in the Bolivian Amazon. We also rediscover some of North America's Arctic charm and pull back the covers on Europe's smallest gems. Whatever your preference for 2008, these are the places to lock into your travel radar.

In the same vein as last year's Dark Tourism feature, the next section of the book zooms in on themes we believe will soon hit the traveller landscape. This time around we couldn't stop at one, and our trio of themes expresses a good mix of the ideas bouncing around among the die-hard travellers at Lonely Planet. This year's special theme, Travel

Islam, grew from a desire to discuss travel to a region sometimes misrepresented by Western media and, at the same time, share a conversation with one of the world's most travelled cultures. We hope that you will be as inspired by the result as we are.

Our second themed section, Bluelist Moments, is inspired and created by you, the traveller, and captures your best travel experiences as seen through the lens. Endangered Wildlife, the last of our themes, is a yearly planner to the best places to see endangered animals in their natural habitat. We hope that this feature will offer some new and surprising ways to be involved with the preservation of our planet and satisfy any lingering monkey obsessions.

A trusty collection of Bluelists makes up the final section of the book. In 2008, we suggest that you test your temperature at the hottest and coldest corners of the globe, get a taste of zero G in the world of space travel or spend time with the world's friendliest people – the choice is yours.

Lastly, I'm pleased to say that as Bluelist 2008 hits the market, the conversation has moved far beyond the bookshelf. In 2007, Bluelist videos were screened on Current TV in the US and the first Bluelist series was aired on a national network across Australia in June 2007. That's not to mention the 8000-plus Bluelists (submitted in word and video format) posted by travellers on our website…

This year, I urge you to explore the many faces of Bluelist. Enjoy, share, and take it all in – but don't forget to leave your own mark.

By Tony Wheeler
Cofounder of Lonely Planet

TONY WHEELER ON BLUELIST

My annual Bluelist review is a chance to look back – what I have done and where I have been during the last year – and forward – what I hope to achieve in the next 12 months. And perhaps a look sideways: what really interesting new travel possibilities have popped up?

If travelling more sustainably is going to become an increasingly important part of our travel experience then walking is the very best way to travel. The carbon emissions are certainly lower than just about any other form of travel. During the year I managed to fit in a couple of classic walks. There was the English Coast to Coast Walk, a two-week, 300km stroll up and down through the Lake District and then across the North York Moors and Yorkshire Dales. We followed the Wainwright Way although at times, such as when the weather was truly English, we were inclined to call it 'Wainwright's Revenge'.

Another week was spent on a repeat visit to Australia's most famous walk, the Overland Track in Tasmania. The Overland Track runs from Cradle Mountain more or less due south to Lake St Clair and includes numerous interesting side trips off the main route. I walked the track with a group of friends about 15 years ago, toting camping equipment and a whole week's food supplies. This time Maureen and I and another couple did it the comfortable way, staying at the Cradle Huts where not only are your meals provided, they even include wine every night!

A highlight of the travel year was an entry in the Plymouth–Banjul Challenge, an eccentrically English event which requires competitors to nurse an elderly vehicle from England to Gambia in Africa via France, Spain, Morocco, Mauritania and Senegal. Our 18-year-old Mitsuibishi sailed through with no more trouble than a puncture in Morocco, although we did spend some time digging it out of the sand when we traversed a stretch of the Sahara. The key point in the competition is not how fast you get there, but what your vehicle fetches at the finish line. All finishers are auctioned off with the money going to Gambian charities. Our faithful Mitsu that cost just UK£350 in England fetched UK£700 in Banjul.

Africa seems to have featured in my itineraries regularly in recent years. At the beginning of 2005 I could only claim to have visited eight of Africa's 50-odd countries. Today I'm up to 21. Tanzania is my most recent African discovery and my visit there included another place with a magical travel name: the island of Zanzibar. It makes a nice addition to other magical African names such as Marrakesh and Timbuktu. My Tanzania visit also included a magical climb: with a group of friends I made it to the top of Mt Kilimanjaro, which at 5896m is Africa's highest peak.

Every visit to Africa I'm reminded how remarkably easy and simple African travel tends to be. It's not quite what you'd expect from a glance at the newspaper headlines, is it? Of course there are also plenty of places in Africa which do indeed present a real challenge. Of all the books on the Lonely Planet publishing list it's our Africa guidebook which I regard as the real standard-setter when it comes to going a step or two further than anyone else. With every edition it's inevitable there is a handful of countries we don't cover, but never more than a handful. For the current edition I was delighted when our intrepid French writer-researcher Jean-Bernard Carillet (I wrote a scuba-diving guide to Tahiti and French Polynesia with Jean-Bernard a few years ago) sent an exultant email to his editor: 'Somaliland covered!' He went on to claim that 'Somaliland is no longer a "lost territory" for Lonely Planet'.

Apart from the Tasmania walk, my home country travels in Australia included a swim with the whale sharks off Ningaloo Reef near the small town of Exmouth in Western Australia. It was almost a homecoming because this was where Maureen and I arrived in Australia, on a yacht out of Bali, back in 1972. We wrote the first Lonely Planet guidebook a few months later. A visit to the spectacular Kakadu National Park with its beautiful waterfalls, stunning Aboriginal rock art, long list of bird life and king-size crocs was another highlight of our Australian travels. And a long overdue one.

The business side of my travel year included author tours in Britain, Canada, China, Italy, Southeast Asia and the USA, either for *The Lonely Planet Story* in its various guises (it's titled *Unlikely Destinations* in the USA, *Once While Travelling*

in Australia, and in Chinese I can't even pronounce it) or for *Bad Lands*, my account of travels along George W Bush's Axis of Evil. Of course there were some great travel moments interspersed amongst the business, but the best would have to be when an Italian journalist offered to show me Rome in the most authentic manner, from the back of his Vespa motor scooter. A lazy weekend in Paris included a visit to the finest museum of the year, the new Musée de Quai Branly, with its fantastic collection of indigenous art just a stone's throw from the Eiffel Tower.

Talking about the nine countries which feature in *Bad Lands* I often commented on the extraordinary friendliness and interest I encountered in that most staunchly Islamic nation Iran. Inevitably I would look out at my audience and see somebody nodding in agreement; they'd been there too, they'd had the same experience. Naturally my thoughts have been turning to other 'bad lands', the candidates to include if I get around to writing *Bad Lands II*. At the moment Syria, Israel-Palestine, Congo-Zaire, Somalia, Zimbabwe and Haiti top the list of contenders.

Other possibilities for next year? Well perhaps some of the unaccomplished tasks from previous years' Bluelists will finally earn a tick over the next 12 months. After all, one day I have to ride the Trans-Siberian and get to Yemen, and not just make excuses.

TRAVEL PLANNER 2008

JANUARY

☼ SUNDANCE FILM FESTIVAL » USA

Pack your bags and thermal underwear and head for wintry Park City, Utah for the annual Sundance. Featuring the best indie films that the US of A has to offer plus an array of overseas offerings, Sundance hits the screens for 10 days in the middle of January; see pp182–3.

☼ FESTIVAL NACIONAL DE DOMA Y FOLKLORE » ARGENTINA

Hop on your high horse and join the stampede to the tiny town of Jesús María, just north of Córdoba, where experts in the equine from every quarter assemble in early January to celebrate and demonstrate their gaucho prowess; see pp66–7.

☼ MIMOSA FESTIVAL » MONTENEGRO

Head for Hercog Novi, where the blossoming of the mimosa in this attractive walled town has been celebrated with gusto since the winter of '69. The festival runs from late January through to March, with the bulk of the blooming business and associated action taking place in February; see pp30–1.

☼ KING PULANKA » NICARAGUA

Commemorate the glory days of the Miskito kings at King Pulanka, a festival in which parades, dancing and plenty of drinking are enjoyed all over Nicaragua's remote Región Autónoma del Atlántico Norte (RAAN); see pp54–5.

☼ FESTIVAL NACIONAL DE FOLKLORE » ARGENTINA

Hear the latest and greatest in Latin American rhythms and Argentine folk music during the nine days of this festival featuring local and foreign stars of today and tomorrow. This acclaimed annual festival takes place in late January in the town of Cosquín, northwest of Córdoba; see pp66–7.

FEBRUARY

☼ BERLINALE » GERMANY

Grab your popcorn and get to the German capital for what is undoubtedly one of the world's foremost film festivals. Massive crowds flock to this top-notch line-up of premiere screenings held each year in early February; see pp182–3.

☼ GWAZA MUTHINI » MOZAMBIQUE

Make your way north of Maputo to the town of the Marracuene – scene of a famous 1895 battle against the colonial rule – where the fallen are commemorated every February in spirited celebrations; see pp32–3.

☼ TET » VIETNAM

Get set for Tet, the Vietnamese New Year, when the partying persists for about a week from 7 February. It's particularly popular with lowlanders who've moved to the mountains in the country's north; see pp50–1.

☼ COSQUÍN ROCK » ARGENTINA

Say yes to tinnitus and join young and not-so-young Argentinian lovers of music in the cultural capital Córdoba for the big beats and festival vibe that make Cosquín Rock, well, rock; see pp66–7.

☼ PUNAKHA DOMCHOE » BHUTAN

Learn a thing or two about deception as the ancient capital of Punakha comes alive for five days from 11 February. Amid much dancing the festival reenacts the 17th-century Bhutanese sleight of hand that fooled a Tibetan army into leaving empty-handed; see pp26–7.

MARCH

☼ PARO TSECHU » BHUTAN
Book early if you're wanting to catch a glimpse of Bhutan's biggest festival of masked dance, Paro Tsechu – it's immensely popular. The festival runs from 17 to 21 March, with the highlight performances at the hillside Rinchen Pung Dzong (literally 'fortress on a heap of jewels'); see pp26–7.

☼ WINTER MUSIC CONFERENCE » USA
Sample your beats beachside in Miami in March, when the world's largest electronic music festival, the Winter Music Conference, presents top DJs from around the world for a week of partying that culminates in a supersized Saturday session at Bicentennial Park; see pp74–5.

☼ FIESTA OF CAMELLIA » MONTENEGRO
Learn just how much the Montenegrans love their camellias when the flowers take centre stage for three weeks from 25 March. This festive floral fling begins with a reenactment of the 1780 day when the first seeds arrived from Japan; see pp30–1.

☼ FROZEN DEAD GUY DAYS » USA
Compete in a coffin race or try the 'Frozen Dead Guy' flavoured ice cream at what is possibly the only festival inspired by the plight of the cryogenically frozen. Treat yourself and head to Nederland, Colorado in the middle of March; see pp42–3.

☼ SNOW RODEO » USA
See off the winter blues by getting to Essex, Montana, where every March the town hosts its annual rodeo in the snow. If you've always dreamed of roping a goat or racing a barrel in the snow then this is your big chance; see pp44–5.

APRIL

☼ TRENTO FILM FESTIVAL » ITALY
Descend the Dolomites and make tracks for Trento in late April for the city's film festival. Winning an award here is to scale the summit of cinematic achievements – if your film is about mountain-climbing, exploration and adventure, that is; see pp182–3.

☼ GENOCIDE REMEMBRANCE DAY » ARMENIA
Watch as a nation remembers its past – a solemn procession leads from the capital, Yerevan, to the memorial at Tsitsernakaberd Hill on 24 April, the day when Armenians all over the world commemorate the victims of the Armenian Genocide; see pp24–5.

☼ RALLY ARGENTINA » ARGENTINA
Take a trip to Córdoba if you like your motorsport airborne and sideways, as the city hosts the Argentinian event of the World Rally Car Championship from 25 to 27 April; see pp66–7.

☼ MISIONES DE CHIQUITOS » BOLIVIA
Cruise into Santa Cruz and the nearby Jesuit Mission Towns when they play host to this international festival of Baroque and Renaissance music. The event starts 24 April and runs until 4 May; see pp40–1.

☼ MALAYSIAN GRAND PRIX » MALAYSIA
Get your motor running and join the revheads headed for Sepang International Circuit in early April, when a 45-minute (nonracing) drive south of Kuala Lumpur will get you to the Formula One circus at the Malaysian Grand Prix; see pp52–3.

TRAVEL PLANNER 2008

MAY

✪ CANNES FILM FESTIVAL » FRANCE
Make the A-list of film festivals (and places to be seen) top of your list. Cannes' festival is for the film industry, with few public screenings, but there's a galaxy of stars in town for the duration of the drama and visitors can bask in the radiated glow and witness the red-carpet arrivals; see pp182–3.

✪ ESPÍRITO SANTO » AZORES
Join in the jovial proceedings as these Atlantic islands get into the spirit for Espírito Santo, or Pentecost, with every village hosting festivities of one sort or another, including plenty of feasting, processions, music and even street bullfights; see pp38–9.

✪ KHAU VAI LOVE MARKET » VIETNAM
Set your heart aflutter on 1 May, when the love market opens for business in the town of Khau Vai in northwest Vietnam. The locals have been swapping wives and husbands and finding matches for lonely hearts for over 100 years; see pp50–1.

✪ BALSAMICO È » ITALY
Treat your tastebuds to tastings of Modena's most famous product when the city hosts its annual festival in honour of balsamic vinegar. There are exhibitions and events across town from mid-May to early June; see pp62–3.

✪ DRAGON BOAT FESTIVAL » MALAYSIA
Savour the spectacle as traditional dragon boats – up to 10m long and with 20 proud paddlers – battle it out at various festivals all over the Malaysian peninsula. One of the best is Penang's international event, which has been a highlight of the local calendar since 1971; see pp52–3.

JUNE

✪ CHELSEA FLOWER SHOW » ENGLAND
Sample the scents at the grounds of the Royal Hospital, where 11 acres of blooming gardens are the perfect place for some olfactory ogling. The Chelsea Flower Show, an annual celebration of the English garden, has been happening here since 1913; see pp214–15.

✪ TELLURIDE BLUEGRASS FESTIVAL » USA
Box up the banjo and head to Telluride, Colorado to join the biggest names in bluegrass for this immensely popular festival featuring camping and jam sessions under the enormous Colorado sky. Get in quick, as the tickets sell out well in advance; see pp42–3.

✪ FES FESTIVAL OF WORLD SACRED MUSIC » MOROCCO
Treat your ears and your soul to a celebration of spiritual music from all cultures when Fez welcomes one and all to this famous annual festival. There are performances for over a week, starting the first Friday in June; see pp70–1.

✪ TYNEDALE BEER FESTIVAL » ENGLAND
Soak up the suds in the Northeast England town of Corbridge, where the Tynedale Beer Festival brings out the best of local and borrowed brews for a mid-June session; see pp48–9.

✪ INDEPENDENCE DAY » SAMOA
Set sail for the South Pacific where dancing, feasting, frivolity and fun abound as the Samoans celebrate their gaining of independence on 1 June, and in true Samoan style, party on the following day; see pp60–1.

JULY

☼ SOUND SYMPOSIUM » CANADA

Find your way to Newfoundland to experience sound installations and concerts conducted in unusual venues around the capital, St John's. The Sound Symposium marks its 25th anniversary in style over 11 days from 3 July; see pp46–7.

☼ VARDAVAR » ARMENIA

Pack your raincoat if you plan to be in Armenia on the third Sunday in July (20 July 2008); Vardavar is a national festival involving the random soaking of strangers with water; see pp24–5.

☼ MILAMALA FESTIVAL » PAPUA NEW GUINEA

Visit the land of the tuber, the Trobriand Islands, where the annual yam harvest is celebrated with song, dance and plenty of yamming it up at the Milamala Festival; see pp34–5.

☼ SALMON FESTIVAL » CANADA

Make for Grand Falls-Windsor in the middle of July for outdoor music concerts, plenty of partying and dancing and even a craft fair. Be sure to sample the delicious local salmon; see pp46–7.

☼ CARNIVAL OF SAN IGNACIO DE MOXOS » BOLIVIA

See three days of fiesta fun with dancing, processions, colourful costumes and enchanting music as the rainforest village of San Ignacio de Moxos celebrates its patron saint. It all begins on the last day of July; see pp40–1.

AUGUST

☼ NATIONAL DAY » MALAYSIA

See out the month in style with parades and festivals to mark Malaysia's national day, 31 August. Celebrations take place all over the country, with the biggest bash being in the capital, Kuala Lumpur; see pp52–3.

☼ HERCEG NOVI FILM FESTIVAL » MONTENEGRO

Enjoy the summer days and nights in the great outdoors at this open-air festival of feature films. All screenings are in the historic walled seaside town of Herceg Novi on Montenegro's Adriatic coast; see pp30–1.

☼ STOCKTON INTERNATIONAL RIVERSIDE FESTIVAL » ENGLAND

Take to the streets in the first week of August for what is possibly the UK's largest celebration of street art and performance. The action unfolds in the Northeast England town of Stockton-on-Tees; see pp48–9.

☼ EMANCIPATION » NICARAGUA

Expect parades with flashy floats and plenty of dancing on 28 August when the annual commemoration of the end of slavery is celebrated with gusto by the Afro-Caribbean communities in the Región Autónoma del Atlántico Norte (RAAN); see pp54–5.

☼ ROYAL ST JOHN'S REGATTA » CANADA

Gather your crew and get to Quidi Vidi Lake, Newfoundland for North America's oldest continuous sporting event. Held on the first Wednesday of the month, the regatta still pulls in the crowds as it has done ever since the first oars were dipped in 1825; see pp46–7.

TRAVEL PLANNER 2008

SEPTEMBER

✪ TORONTO INTERNATIONAL FILM FESTIVAL » CANADA
Have your say at a film festival of the people where the People's Choice Award is the most esteemed prize. Toronto attracts over 300,000 cinephiles to its 350-odd screenings, and the festival's reputation continues to grow; see pp182–3.

✪ GREAT AMERICAN BEER FESTIVAL » USA
Drop into Denver for the annual celebration of the suds that boasts the world's biggest selection of brews available at the one place at the one time. As 2400 beers into three days doesn't go, the tough part is choosing which free shots to sample; see pp42–3.

✪ TEUILA FESTIVAL » SAMOA
Top off your trip at Samoa's top event, the annual Teuila Festival. This week of cultural celebration features longboat races on Apia Harbour, a Samoan-size serving of food and music, sports, a floral parade and, of course, the crowning of Miss Teuila; see pp60–1.

✪ RAINDANCE FILM FESTIVAL » ENGLAND
See the best of British as London hosts the UK's premier indie film fest, with heaps of documentaries and short films joining feature-length flicks in competition for the Film of the Festival award; see pp182–3.

✪ GOROKA SHOW » PAPUA NEW GUINEA
Join around 100 tribes from all over PNG as they travel to the town of Goroka in the Highlands to partake in the year's biggest *singsing* (festival). This cultural celebration with music and dance is your top chance to see and experience tribal culture; see pp34–5.

OCTOBER

✪ SEMAINE CRÉOLE » RÉUNION
Leave the continents behind and head for a little piece of France in the Indian Ocean in October, where Créole culture is the focus of a week's festivities celebrating the influences that have shaped Réunion; see pp56–7.

✪ CARNIVAL » USA
Choose your costume and get involved in the annual Carnival capers when Miami shakes its moneymaker for two weeks in the lead-up to a massive street parade on 31 October; see pp74–5.

✪ DÍA DE LA HISPANIDAD » NICARAGUA
Enjoy a slice of Spanish culture, food and entertainment in Central America as Nicaragua's Spanish-speaking community celebrates its heritage on Spain's national day, 12 October; see pp54–5.

✪ DIVALI » RÉUNION
Celebrate the Hindu festival of Divali in late October with the Indian communities in the main cities along Réunion's east coast. Tradition dictates several days of parades and the exchanging of gifts; see pp56–7.

✪ GLACIER JAZZ STAMPEDE » USA
Hear jazz in its various guises at this annual music festival in Flatheathead County, Montana. Performances are staged at four venues over four days in the town of Kalispell; see pp44–5.

NOVEMBER

☼ ONE TAKE FILM FESTIVAL » CROATIA
Forget the fadeouts and celebrate the continuity when the Croatian capital Zagreb hosts a festival of films shot in a single take. The festival runs for three days from 21 November; see pp182–3.

☼ MARCH TO PEACE & TRANQUILLITY » PHILIPPINES
Trek up to the new summit of Mt Pinatubo on 30 November with the local people as they commemorate the dramatic eruption in 1991 that blew away the top 300m of the peak and left a caldera in its place; see pp202–3.

☼ JAZZ IN RIADS FESTIVAL » MOROCCO
Feel the jazz rhythms resonate throughout the oldest of Morocco's Imperial cities, Fez. Performances take place in some of the fabulously restored traditional houses in and around the medina; see pp70–1.

☼ H'MONG NEW YEAR » VIETNAM
Keep an eye on the fields to know when the H'mong people of northwest Vietnam are about to break into celebration, as the date is determined by the end of the rice harvest. It's usually late November or early December; see pp50–1.

☼ THESSALONIKI INTERNATIONAL FILM FESTIVAL » GREECE
Catch the latest works from new directors at this 10-day festival in mid-November. Over 150 films are screened, with the international competition restricted to the first or second film by the director; see pp80–1.

DECEMBER

☼ CENTENARY OF THE MONARCHY » BHUTAN
Don't think you missed it – Bhutan's festivities in honour of its monarchy are pencilled in for 17 December 2008. True, it's a year after the actual achievement, but the lamas deemed it to be a more auspicious time to celebrate the milestone; see pp26–7.

☼ ART BASEL MIAMI BEACH » USA
Enjoy a fine fusion of music, art, architecture and film at this annual festival, the sister show of the famous event in Basel, Switzerland. Exhibitions are located all over the city's Art Deco District; see pp74–5.

☼ DIMITRIA FESTIVAL » GREECE
Take a trip to Thessaloniki to see the city's major festival, which honours the city's patron saint, draw to a close after three months of theatre, music, dance and cultural events; see pp80–1.

☼ CHRISTKINDLMÄRKTE » AUSTRIA
Wrap up in your winter woolies and hit the streets of Vienna for the city's famous Christmas markets. Be sure to sample the *Glühwein*, a spiced-up warm red wine drink that guarantees some seasonal cheer; see pp82–3.

☼ KING MANGO STRUT » USA
Strut to the neighbourhood of Coconut Grove in Florida on the last Sunday of the year for this particularly wacky and satire-laden street parade that's determined to keep true its slogan, 'Putting the nut into Coconut Grove since 1982'; see pp74–5.

By Craig Scutt
Writer

2007 » ONE LAST LOOK

FROM ECO-EVERYTHING TO VOLCANO TOURS, SKYWALKS TO SPARTAN SIX-PACKS, THIS IS HOW THE YEAR IN TRAVEL UNRAVELLED.

A NEW DIRECTION

Seven is the magic number and without doubt 2007 was another magical year for travel.

The year's watchword was sustainability. Climate change dominated global headlines and the repercussions were felt in every industry, including travel, in which 2007 was all about the ascendance of ecotourism and responsible travel. While some governments continued to debate the impacts of climate change, others took action.

In an effort to preserve the natural habitat of the southern islands, Thailand's government designated vast swathes as national scenic areas and national parks. The Vietnamese announced a $US50 million ecotourism project would be built over 574 hectares close to the world-renowned mountain resort at Dalat. And the new Caribbean island resort of Jade Mountain proved that ecological design doesn't have to mean a reduction in comfort by creating a refuge for 'eco-hedonists' that features enormous private pools and panoramic views – without the distraction of telephones, air-conditioning or high-definition television.

A SECOND HELPING

Bluelist 2007 was only the second title in the fledgling Bluelist series and it already seems like a veteran. When we started Bluelist the idea was to create a book that would spark the imaginations of new and experienced travellers alike. We wanted to reach out to people who share our passion for exploration and adventure. Even better, we wanted to create a book that could help you to reach out too. We're stoked at how you, our fellow travellers, have embraced the Bluelist concept by endorsing it with your own ideas and suggestions.

TALK ABOUT TOP PICKS

Between the covers, Bluelist 2007 had five gourmet sections bursting with travel treats. First up was your own Top 11 Hot Picks. This was a list of the most popular countries as voted for by 33,000 individuals from 170 countries. We reckon that makes it one of the most authoritative independent travel surveys ever undertaken, although we stopped short of asking the *Guinness World Records* for confirmation.

Australia came in at number one and 2007 proved to be a top year for girls and boys down under. After another epic New Year's Eve fireworks show in Sydney, Australia hosted the swimming world championships in Melbourne and gave travelling fans something to write home about after romping to victory in the cricket world cup. Australia Zoo honoured the memory of its founder, crocodile hunter Steve Irwin, who died in September 2006, by progressing his plans to create an AU$100 million safari experience. Visitors will be able to ride through landscapes reminiscent of Africa, Southeast Asia and North America, each populated with exotic animals found in that region. The expansion will be created over 135 hectares of land excised from Queensland's Beerwah State Forest.

Looking north, last year saw arguments about land and animals raging in Canada, which was voted in at number seven. Inuit leaders in the western area of Nunavut's Hudson Bay challenged a report by the Canadian Wildlife Service that stated there were less than 1000 bears left in the region. Inuit elders said an increase in 'close encounters of the bear kind' indicated there were too many bears and demanded an increase in the quota to be culled during the annual harvest. Meanwhile, more than 2000 barely sane swimmers spent the year trying to get warm again after voluntarily plunging into the freezing grey water of English Bay on New Year's Day. The 87th annual swim, organised by the Vancouver Polar Bear Swim Club, proves Canada didn't win its votes by lacking in absurdity.

Across the border in the USA, public opinion was divided after the Hualapai tribal council declared the Skywalk open for business. Perched on the rim of the Grand Canyon, the Skywalk is the world's first cantilever glass walkway and is suspended over 1220m above the canyon's floor. For US$25 visitors get to gasp at the view through the glass floor as the walkway extends 21m over the rim. Labelled a 'desecration' by one former superintendent of the Grand Canyon National Park, the Skywalk operated from dawn to dusk in 2007, catering to more than 200,000 visitors at the Hualapai's 760-sq-km reservation.

Meanwhile, a surge of interest in Spartan culture generated by bloodthirsty blockbuster *300* added to Greece's appeal in 2007. You nominated the birthplace of democracy as the 10th-hottest spot last year. Thanks to *300*, phalanxes of males around the world hit the gym in search of a six-pack while dreaming of marching across the Evrotas Valley to the mountain pass at Thermopylae, where King Leonidas and 300 Spartan warriors made their heroic last stand against the Persians in 480 BC.

As the ancient ruins of Greece can attest, time inevitably sees even the toppest of dogs knocked off their mantle. While this year throws up new lists of hot spots, there's no denying that last year's hot spots are still hotter than a pyroclastic flow.

LIGHT IN DARK PLACES

Oddly enough pyroclastic flows featured in the most controversial section of Bluelist 2007. Our coverage of Dark

KEEPING FAITH IN TRYING TIMES:
WOMEN PRAY INSIDE THE IMAMAIN
AL-HASSANAIN MOSQUE IN SOUTHERN
BEIRUT, LEBANON.

Tourism sparked debate in chat rooms and media around the world. One forum contributor asked, 'If two and a half million people are willing to take a tour around former Nazi concentration camps in Poland each year, why doesn't the South African government set up tourist attractions based on the remnants of concentration camps used by the British against the Boers?' Others suggested dark tourism was needlessly voyeuristic and should be banned.

We thought it was interesting that the most positive responses to Dark Tourism came from representatives of the places we featured.

Gerry Lennon, chief executive at the Belfast Visitor & Convention Bureau, said it was 'very satisfying' that the city infamously plagued by 'the troubles' had made it into Bluelist. With over six million people visiting Belfast annually it's clear that it's not only dark tourists warming to the city's charms.

Belfast wasn't the only Dark Tourism destination to make positive headway in 2007. After decades of calamity Beirut is finally booming without the sound of gunfire. The town centre that was once little more than a mountain of rubble is flourishing, with new banks and businesses open for trade. Nondark visitors can walk among magnificent architectural relics spanning 5000 years of culture. In years to come Beirut may once again be more famous for its Al-Omari, Emir Assaf and Emir Munzir Mosques, and the Roman columns in Nejmeh Square, than for its dark past. The Paris III donor conference saw US$7.6 billion pledged to help rebuild and restructure the Lebanese economy, and the city's developers have been working hard to revitalise the region, with plans to create an extended coastline, new residential areas, and recreational zones arranged around a central park.

Sadly, not all the countries featured in Dark Tourism are nearing the light at the end of the tunnel. Sudan made headlines in early 2007 when Google Earth launched its software feature that allows users to zoom in on the country's embattled Darfur region. The project was spearheaded by the United States Holocaust Memorial Museum and highlights 1600 villages ravaged by the ongoing conflict between the Sudanese government and militia forces.

In 2007 there was no shortage of places to entice dark tourists. The International Committee of the Red Cross listed its 10 largest humanitarian aid operations in 2007 as taking place in Sudan, Israel and the Occupied and Autonomous Palestinian Territories, Iraq, Afghanistan, the Democratic Republic of Congo, Colombia, countries covered by the Moscow regional delegation, Somalia, Ethiopia and Sri Lanka. Unless you're going to these places to help, it's clear that the respectful thing to do is stay away.

Another grim spot travellers were warned about last year was Bolivia's Yungas region. This area of treacherous curving roads about a hundred kilometres northeast of the capital, La Paz, is regarded as the most deadly road in the world. Whether it's the high traffic density or simply the erratic nature of Bolivian driving we don't know, but the road continues to claim lives. During the

2007 Easter weekend alone accidents along the Yungas Hwy claimed eight lives and left 30 seriously injured.

Dark tourism isn't just about being dark. Human ingenuity is such that silver linings can be found on even the blackest clouds. The Caribbean island of Montserrat, which we briefly featured in Bluelist 2007, is using income from the influx of tourists lured by the dark side to rebuild its community.

Nature has given Montserrat a pummelling in recent decades. Two volcanic eruptions and Hurricane Hugo rendered Plymouth, the island's capital, uninhabitable and 8000 islanders had to leave home on a permanent basis. With its once-plush hotels knee-deep in volcanic ash and the ever-present threat of another eruption, you'd think the place would be completely deserted. But Montserratians are tough cookies. In 2007 they turned disaster into profit by offering adventurous travellers tours to the Volcano Observatory and also providing 'unofficial guides' to explore within the exclusion zone – the area around Plymouth that is officially off-limits. Returning locals are now working to construct a new capital in the hills around Brades.

LISTS WITH A TWIST

A much-talked-about segment of Bluelist 2007 was the 40 featured lists written by our team of writers and travel authors offering tips on everything from Best Travel Adventure Ideas to Best Destinations After a Break-up. And there were a number of updates that could have been made as the year progressed.

Spook hunters can now add New Delhi to their list of paranormal destinations after two UFOs were spotted near the Indian prime minister's residence. The Indian Air Force failed to account for the weird blips that appeared on radar for more than three minutes over Safdarjung. Meanwhile, seekers of obscure festivals should head to Saudi Arabia for the hotly contested camel beauty pageant, which in 2007 featured 1500 long-legged spitting beauties. The ladies in question proved so attractive that special 'chastity belts' were needed to prevent lusty male camels from mounting them.

GO DAMMIT!

Sometimes a place is so cool you just have to pack your bags and go there. That's what last year's GoList section was all about. Among the many cool places featured, by far the most chilled is Antarctica. The world's southernmost and fifth-largest continent was put under a CGI spotlight in 2007 with the release of Oscar-winning animated movie, *Happy Feet*. This heart-warming tale about a tap-dancing penguin also had a strong environmental message calling for action to preserve Antarctica. Throughout 2007 scientists stepped up their warnings that unless we take action to reduce emissions of greenhouse gases we will have to bear the brunt of global warming. Seeing as

Antarctic ice makes up 70% of the planet's fresh water, causing it to melt may not be such a good idea.

In 2007 Honduran environmentalists spoke out about unsustainable development in another GoList favourite, the bird paradise of La Mosquitia. Visitors flock to the 'protected' sanctuaries around Tela and on the Swan Islands to observe over 700 bird species. There have been increasing calls for development of a more responsible tourism that avoids polluting the bird's habitat; unchecked, pollution will eventually cripple the region's main draw card.

Similar warnings were given in Madagascar, where oil mining commenced for the first time in 2007 and where environmental mismanagement has long been rife. Luckily the Tetik'asa Mampody Savoka (TAMS) conservation project continued its work to reestablish corridors of forest between Madagascar's national parks, which contain more tree species than any other site in Africa.

Bluelist 2007 also trumpeted the remote charms of China's Xinjiang region. It seemed no sooner had we done so than the Chinese police raided a suspected terrorist training camp near the Pamir Plateau, close to the borders with Afghanistan and Pakistan. It was alleged that 18 suspected members of the East Turkestan Islamic Movement were killed and another 17 detained.

STOP, COLLABORATE...

Bluelist 2007 was a collaborative project among people who love travel. Scattered throughout the book were lists selected from those posted to the Lonely Planet website. Picking which ones to print from more than 4000 submissions was a daunting task. Even harder was the job to select four overall winners for the Bluelist 2006 competition.

In the end we chose Dov Quint, Sylvia Dubery, Lisa Burns and Baxter Jackson. In 2007 they had the time of their lives exploring and blogging about Morocco's fabled pink city of Marrakesh under the watchful eye of Lonely Planet aficionados Alex Leviton and Paul Clammer.

Maybe this year it will be you? ◎

GOLISTS

»

COOL DOWN IN AN ARMENIAN SNOW DREAM, CATCH JUNGLE FEVER IN THE BOLIVIAN AMAZON OR TAKE A JOURNEY TO AFRICA'S LAST FRONTIER. GET INTO GOLISTS AND LOCK THESE COUNTRIES, REGIONS & CITIES INTO YOUR 2008 TRAVEL AGENDA.

GOLISTS

024
ARMENIA
COUNTRIES

026
BHUTAN
COUNTRIES

028
ERITREA
COUNTRIES

030
MONTENEGRO
COUNTRIES

032
MOZAMBIQUE
COUNTRIES

044
**GLACIER
NATIONAL PARK,
USA**
REGIONS

046
**NEWFOUNDLAND
& LABRADOR,
CANADA**
REGIONS

048
**NORTHEAST
ENGLAND**
REGIONS

050
**NORTHWEST
VIETNAM**
REGIONS

052
**PENINSULAR
MALAYSIA**
REGIONS

064
**CHENGDU,
CHINA**
CITIES

066
**CÓRDOBA,
ARGENTINA**
CITIES

068
**DAMASCUS,
SYRIA**
CITIES

070
**FEZ,
MOROCCO**
CITIES

072
**MATSUYAMA,
JAPAN**
CITIES

034
**PAPUA
NEW GUINEA**
COUNTRIES

036
YEMEN
COUNTRIES

038
AZORES
(PORTUGAL)
REGIONS

040
**BOLIVIAN
AMAZON**
REGIONS

042
**COLORADO,
USA**
REGIONS

054
**RAAN,
NICARAGUA**
REGIONS

056
RÉUNION
(FRANCE)
REGIONS

058
**TIWI ISLANDS,
AUSTRALIA**
REGIONS

060
**APIA,
SAMOA**
CITIES

062
**BOLOGNA,
ITALY**
CITIES

074
**MIAMI,
USA**
CITIES

076
**MUMBAI,
INDIA**
CITIES

078
**PUNTA DEL DIABLO,
URUGUAY**
CITIES

080
**THESSALONIKI,
GREECE**
CITIES

082
**VIENNA,
AUSTRIA**
CITIES

ARMENIA

POPULATION 3 MILLION ◎ **VISITORS PER YEAR** 400,000 ◎ **CAPITAL** YEREVAN ◎ **NUMBER OF HISTORIC MONUMENTS** 40,000
◎ **LANGUAGES** ARMENIAN, RUSSIAN ◎ **UNIT OF CURRENCY** ARMENIAN DRAM (AMD), PRICES QUOTED IN EURO (€)
◎ **COST INDEX** HALF-LITRE OF BEER IN A BAR, €5 (US$6.60); HOTEL DOUBLE/DORM PER NIGHT, €95/15 (US$127/20); SHORT TAXI
RIDE, €10 (US$13.3); INTERNET ACCESS PER HOUR, UP TO €3 (US$4); SAUNA, UP TO €10 (US$13.30)

NOAH'S PARK

Armenia is Europe's easternmost oddity – an ancient Christian nation tucked up in a mountainous maze east of Turkey. Formerly part of the USSR, Armenia had a horrible 20th century but since 2000 the economy has been booming. Tourism is still fairly small-scale but is bounding ahead – up from barely 80,000 visitors in 2000 to 400,000 this year. History nuts battle mountain tracks to the finest medieval monasteries, trekkers scale 4000m-high peaks, nature buffs search for the ultra-rare Caucasian leopard, and everyone enjoys the potent local brandy, finely ground coffee and the easy-going what-the-heck tempo of daily life. Armenia is one of history's great survival stories – sliced up and cut down by its enemies for centuries. Its historic symbol, Mt Ararat, has for 90 years lain just inside Turkey's borders. Armenians remember their tragic past, but rejoice that the country where Noah planted the first vineyard is still around to enjoy a new vintage every year.

INTERNATIONAL CAPITAL

Armenia's biggest asset is its diaspora, which is pouring in money from every part of the world to revive the ancient, long-downtrodden homeland. Armenians from Brazil run Latin techno nights, French men and women revitalise the Ararat Valley's wine industry, farmers from California chip in to modernise agriculture, businessmen from Beirut run IT and communications start-ups and anybody with a few million to spare and an eye on the afterlife renovates a monastery or builds a chapel. The influx is giving the once-drab capital Yerevan a cosmopolitan edge; French bistros, Russian saunas, Lebanese bakeries, Australian backpacker hostels, Italian fashion houses and Middle Eastern carpet emporiums.

FESTIVALS & EVENTS

◎ Armenia's most solemn day is 24 April, a day to commemorate the victims of the Armenian Genocide. A solemn procession leads from Yerevan to the memorial at Tsitsernakaberd Hill just outside the capital.

◎ Vardavar – the national day of randomly drenching strangers with water – takes place on the third Sunday in July.

◎ The Blessing of the Holy Chrism ritual at Echmiadzin, Armenia's Vatican, is performed by the Catholicos (head of the Armenian Church) once every seven years. In 2008 it will be held on 28 September.

HOT TOPIC OF THE DAY ✴

Elections. Armenia gets a new president in 2008, and everyone wonders if the usual standards of democracy will be applied for once. The odds that powerful defence minister Serj Sargsyan will win are extremely short.

THANKS TO A LITTLE HELP FROM OUTSIDE, LIFE'S
SWEET AGAIN IN ARMENIA – THESE BEES AND
HIVE WERE AN AID-PROGRAMME DONATION.

DEFINING EXPERIENCE

⚙ Keeping up with a round of toasts at a country banquet, for which any excuse – say, the arrival of a foreigner – is a sufficient excuse to clear the table and set up the homemade brandies and fruit liqueurs. Follow the toastmaster in clinking glasses to friendship, family and something poetically melancholy (Armenians love the emotional stuff) like the deepest, most tear-jerking memory you keep locked up in your heart. Dry your eyes and make a toast of your own.

LIFE-CHANGING EXPERIENCES

⚙ Lighting a candle in the rock-hewn chapels of Geghard Monastery, where the holy lance from the crucifixion of Jesus was hidden for centuries.

⚙ Puzzling over the age and purpose of Zorats Karer, Armenia's mysterious megalithic Stonehenge.

⚙ Surrendering to cries of 'Gnoom! Nstek!' ('Come! Sit!') at one of the traditional family-run barbecue restaurants.

⚙ Marvelling at randomly sited Soviet-era relics – brooding WWII soldiers in bronze, giant eagles in orange volcanic rock and vast cinematographer's resorts.

⚙ Learning about the pagan Yezidi herders on the slopes of Armenia's highest peak, Mt Aragats, in the Lesser Caucasus mountains.

⚙ Munching on marijuana-seed Christmas cake.

RANDOM FACTS

⚙ The best apricots on the planet thrive here, and they are a native species (prunus armeniaca).

⚙ Armenia's most brutal stew, khash (brown, runny and made from cow's feet) is a winter's breakfast ritual that is always accompanied by vodka. In truth, it can only be consumed with vodka.

⚙ Traditionally, the only person not allowed to attend an Armenian wedding ceremony is the mother of the bride.

⚙ The heaviest book in the world, the Homilies of Mush, is preserved in two halves at Yerevan's Institute of Ancient Manuscripts, the Matenadaran.

MOST BIZARRE SIGHT

⚙ A semipagan matagh, or animal sacrifice. Many monasteries have special sacrifice altars upon which chickens and livestock (male only) are dispatched by priests to bless events such as baptism.

– Richard Plunkett

BHUTAN

POPULATION 810,000 ◌ **VISITORS PER YEAR** 13,500 ◌ **CAPITAL** THIMPHU ◌ **LANGUAGE** DZONGKHA ◌ **UNIT OF CURRENCY** NGULTRUM (NU) ◌ **COST INDEX** MANDATORY DAILY TOUR COSTS, US$200 PER PERSON; BOTTLE OF RED PANDA BEER, NU80 (US$2); INTERNET ACCESS PER HOUR NU60 (US$1.50); BLESSING FROM REINCARNATED LAMA, FREE

THE LAST SHANGRI-LA

Bhutan, the 'Land of the Thunder Dragon', is without doubt one of the world's most unusual countries. The last surviving great Himalayan kingdom has long turned its back on the rest of the world, favouring Buddhist compassion over Western capitalism and prioritising Gross National Happiness over Gross National Product.

ALL CHANGE

Yet change is afoot. In 2008 the country will not only crown a new king, Jigme Khesar Namgyal Wangchuck, but will also hold its first ever democratic elections and also celebrate the centenary of the founding of the monarchy. Workers have been preparing the site of Changlimithang in the capital Thimphu for lavish celebrations, which are expected to last throughout the year.

THE TOP-DOLLAR DESTINATION

If you fancy timing a visit with the celebrations, bear in mind that Bhutan strictly controls the number of tourists entering the country by enforcing a US$200 per day minimum tour charge. There's no such thing as a cheap trip to Bhutan! Still, with its towering fortresslike dzongs and other gorgeous monasteries, intact Tibetan culture and pristine Himalayan environment, Bhutan offers an opportunity to glimpse that rarest thing, a truly different way of living. And that's priceless.

DEFINING EXPERIENCES

◌ Hiking on pilgrim paths through tropical forest to a remote monastery, following pilgrims as they touch sacred rocks and perform sin tests, before heading back to your hotel for a traditional hot-stone bath and filling meal of *ema datse* (chillies and cheese) and red rice.

◌ Sharing a cup or two of home-brewed barley beer with a festival crowd and being teased by an *atsara* (clown) during a traditional masked dance, as cymbals crash, trumpets boom and masked dancers whirl around you in a riotous blur of colour.

RECENT FAD

◌ Über-luxury hotels such as the Amankora, Uma and Zhiwaling are popping up all over the country, attracting celebrities, royalty and the super-rich. This is Nepal for the jet set.

HOT TOPIC OF THE DAY ✪

The current hot potatoes are the rate of modernisation (too fast? too slow?) and the abdication of the much-loved King Jigme Dorji Wangchuck, in preparation for the country's upcoming shift to democracy.

TODAY THEY PRAY, BUT BHUTAN'S NEXT GENERATION WILL DECIDE THE COUNTRY'S FUTURE VIA THE BALLOT BOX.

FESTIVALS & EVENTS

- The Punakha Domchoe sacred festival is one of the most dramatic in the country, and will be celebrated from 11 to 15 February 2008.

- The spectacular Paro Tsechu, the country's most popular masked dance festival, will take place in Paro 17 to 21 March 2008. You'll need to book your hotel and air ticket months in advance for this one.

- Celebrations marking the centenary of the Bhutanese monarchy are slated for 17 December 2008. (The milestone was reached in 2007 but Bhutan's high lamas felt it to be an inauspicious year for celebrations.)

LIFE-CHANGING EXPERIENCES

- Hauling yourself up the mountainside to the 'Tiger's Nest' at Taktshang, probably the world's most spectacularly sited monastery.

- Hiking through lush forests of bamboo, past lonely *chortens* (Buddhist stupas) to a remote hermitage to receive a blessing from a reincarnate lama.

- Trekking for days over high mountain passes, past views of sacred Mt Jhomolhari, into the remote lands that are home to the iconic bamboo-hatted people of Laya.

- Spinning prayer wheels and shuffling past 7th-century religious treasures at the oldest temple in Bhutan, Jampey Lhakhang.

- Holding your breath as your Land Cruiser swings past bottomless drop-offs at the sheer Namling Cliffs, along the wild roads of eastern Bhutan.

- Simply savouring your brief time in a land largely untouched by the modern world.

RANDOM FACTS

- Not only the act of smoking but also the sale of tobacco is illegal in Bhutan (as are plastic bags and MTV).

- Television arrived in Bhutan in 1999.

- In 2002 Microsoft developed a special Dzongkha font for Windows.

- Bhutan has one set of traffic lights.

MOST BIZARRE SIGHT

- Exterior house walls and entryways decorated with giant painted penises that are symbols of the drunken, promiscuous 15th-century lama Drukpa Kunley.

- Otherworldly monks dressed in maroon robes transcribing ancient Buddhist texts into computers, or Bhutanese noblemen dressed in traditional Tibetan-style tunics and Argyle socks sending text messages on their ultramodern mobile phones.

– Bradley Mayhew

ERITREA

POPULATION 4.6 MILLION ⊙ **CAPITAL** ASMARA ⊙ **LANGUAGE** TIGRINYA ⊙ **UNIT OF CURRENCY** ERITREAN NAKFA (NFA), PRICES OFTEN IN US$ ⊙ **COST INDEX** MACCHIATO, NFA2 (US$0.15); BOTTLE OF ASMARA BEER, NFA8 (US$0.60); HOTEL DOUBLE PER NIGHT, NFA270-440 (US$20-35); LITRE OF PETROL, NFA33 (US$2.50); SOUVENIR T-SHIRT, NFA58 (US$4.70)

AFRICA'S BEST-KEPT SECRET

It's been dubbed the 'North Korea of Africa', which does not bode well. According to the US-based Committee to Protect Journalists, Eritrea is the only country in sub-Saharan Africa not to have a single private media outlet and there are at least 15 journalists held incommunicado there in secret detention centres. In recent years the regime has controlled the whole economy. The result? This tiny nation in the Horn of Africa remains cut off from the outside world. With such a reputation it's no surprise it has fallen below many travellers' radars.

. The truth is, there's a brighter side. Here's the paradox: Eritrea might have one of the toughest regimes in East Africa, but for travellers it's certainly one of the most welcoming countries on the continent, with virtually no hassle, extremely courteous people (including officials), a sense of harmony and a strong culture. This is where the sad comparison with North Korea ends. The gates are wide open to curious visitors, who feel very safe and welcome as long as they don't interfere with politics. Although the country faces hardships, it remains one of Africa's most peaceful and secure destinations. Open gates and open arms: the time to visit is now, before this secretive country is let out of the bag and is back on everyone's itinerary.

FORZA ASMARA

Arriving in the capital Asmara, foreigners feel as though they are setting foot on another planet. Very few cars in the streets. Very few people in the shops. Very few buyers at the markets. Deserted streets at night. At first sight, this is no wonderland. But scratch the surface and you'll soon realise that Asmara is a diamond of a capital, with lots of good surprises up its sleeves: peaceful neighbourhoods, pavement cafés with vintage Italian coffee machines, cheery pizza parlours, tantalising pastry shops, a relaxed pace of life…you'll feel like you've been transported to a southern Italian town. And there's the fabulous architecture, with a portfolio of Art Deco buildings dating from the era when the Italians colonised the country. Whatever the hardships, Eritreans have not lost their appetite for life, as testified by the daily ritual of *passeggiatta*: every evening between 5pm and 7pm the whole city promenades up and down the main avenue and the adjacent streets to see what's new, catch up with friends and hear the latest gossip. Terraces and cafés fill up with chattering locals sampling a cappuccino. You're in a Fellini film!

HOT TOPIC OF THE DAY ✦

The demarcation of the border with Ethiopia and the never-ending dispute between the two countries. The question that haunts the minds of Eritreans is: when are we going to be at peace with our neighbour?

FABULOUS TRUMP CARDS

There's huge potential for tourism in Eritrea. Who has ever heard of Massawa, a coastal city that's almost a carbon copy of Zanzibar? And the pristine reefs off the Dahlak Archipelago, far from the overexploited dive sites in Egypt? And the surreal landscapes of Dankalia, one of the most inhospitable (but accessible) areas on earth? When the border conflict with Ethiopia is settled this fascinating country will unveil itself. Meanwhile, a little bit of curiosity pays off handsomely.

DEFINING EXPERIENCE

- Travelling to the ends of earth on a rickety old bus, destination the Marslike wasteland of Dankalia, and overnighting in an Afar village along the way, after having shared a wicked cup (or three) of palm wine.

FESTIVALS & EVENTS

- If there's ever a good time to be in Eritrea, it has to be for Timkat (Epiphany) on 19 January: jostle everyone else for views of the colourful processions. Priests are sexy in their full regalia.
- Meskel (Finding of the True Cross) is celebrated on 27 September; this two-day festival is the most colourful after Timkat. Bonfires are built, blessed and lit, with much dancing and singing taking place around them.

LIFE-CHANGING EXPERIENCES

- Speculating on Eritrea's mysterious past at Qohaito's ruins.
- Hiking upward to the monastery of Debre Libanos and confessing your sins in total seclusion.
- Enjoying the smug feeling of having the whole country to yourself!

RANDOM FACTS

- It is estimated that about 1000 Italians still live in Eritrea, mostly in Asmara.
- Approximately 300,000 Eritreans (male and female) serve in the army – about 6.5% of the population.
- Less than 1% of the country is covered in woodland, whereas a century ago the figure was estimated to be around 30%.
- Some 35% of the Eritrean population is nomadic or seminomadic.
- If you're caught changing money on the black market, the fine is Nfa2,000,000 (US$133,000).

– Jean-Bernard Carillet

MONTENEGRO

POPULATION 650,000 ⊙ **VISITORS PER YEAR** AROUND 4 MILLION ⊙ **CAPITAL** PODGORICA ⊙ **LANGUAGES** SERBIAN (OFFICIAL), CROATIAN, BOSNIAN, ALBANIAN ⊙ **UNIT OF CURRENCY** EURO (€) ⊙ **COST INDEX** NIKSICKO BEER, €2.50 (US$3.30); HOTEL DOUBLE PER NIGHT, €40 (US$53); SHORT TAXI RIDE, €3 (US$4); INTERNET ACCESS PER HOUR, €1 (US$1.30)

THE NEWEST COUNTRY IN THE WORLD

Dropping out of its union with Serbia in 2006, Montenegro has pounced upon its newly found freedom with zest, sending out news of its recent singlehood like a girl that's been in a rotten marriage for far too long. The country's top assets are its untouched natural beauty and gorgeous Venetian coastal towns, and though some have called it 'the new Croatia' (which, in turn, was 'the new Italy'), Montenegro has an edge of its own. The sultry curve of its coastline is irresistible, and the sparkle of the Adriatic's deep blue waters is as enticing to beach potatoes as the tall peaks of the snowy mountains are to activity-spurred travellers. The country's diverse ethnic make-up stirs those curious about Balkan culture – Montenegrins, Serbs, Croats and Albanians are all squeezed in with each other.

THE SMALLEST COUNTRY IN THE EUROPE

OK, it's isn't *the* smallest country in Europe, but it's among the top 10. Montenegro is perfect for those who want to explore independently and love the great outdoors in a compact size: hiking, mountaineering, rafting and swimming are within easy reach. And though Montenegro is touted as a summer destination, the winter is perfect for going up into Durmitor National Park, for skiing, snowboarding and, come springtime, rafting on the river Tara, inside Europe's deepest canyon.

ALL THAT GLITTERS AIN'T GOLD

Montenegro is also trying to appeal as a 'luxury destination', emphasising exclusive resorts, golf courses and multistar hotels, all intended to entice diamond-studded celebrities to the country's share of Mediterranean coast. But with its relaxed building regulations and a progress-at-all-costs attitude, coupled with a high level of government corruption, reports show that developers are already rendering Montenegro's 'sustainable development' motto redundant. So hurry up and enjoy the unspoilt nature while you still can.

DEFINING EXPERIENCE

⊙ Trekking in the mountains in the morning, before heading for a sandy beach in the afternoon followed by a night on the town – if you still have the energy.

HOT TOPIC OF THE DAY ✪

The EU. Will Montenegro become a member? Talks for the possible inclusion into the EU should take place before 2010.

RING THE BELLS: EUROPE'S NEWEST NATION HAS ARRIVED, WITH TOWNS SUCH AS CETINJE SHARING THEIR HISTORICAL, CULTURAL AND RELIGIOUS RELICS.

RECENT FAD

○ 'Casino Montenegro' appeared in the latest James Bond flick, an imaginary spot that took its inspiration from real Montenegro. The country's southernmost city of Ulcinj features in *The Brothers Bloom*, bookmarked for release in 2008 and starring Adrian Brody and Rachel Weisz.

FESTIVALS & EVENTS

○ Herceg Novi's Mimosa Festival is a big street party anticipating spring and celebrating the afforementioned fluffy yellow flowers, starting at the end of January and ending in March.

○ The three-week Fiesta of Camellia celebrates the day when, back in 1780, a Kotor sailor brought the seeds of the camellia flower to Montenegro from Japan. In 2008 the fiesta begins on 25 March: a crowd reenacts the day the sailor stepped off the boat with the seeds in his hands.

○ The Herceg Novi Film Festival is a week-long alfresco bonanza, held in the first or second week of August, depending on the organisers' whim. It provides a great opportunity to catch up with the former Yugoslavia's film talent.

LIFE-CHANGING EXPERIENCES

○ Swimming in the transparent waters of the Adriatic and eating fresh fish and seafood in Perast.

○ Climbing the many steps up to the mausoleum of Count Njegos on Mt Lovcen, and feeling dizzy as you take in the views over the surrounding sea of mountains.

○ Huffing and puffing up the stairs above Kotor town, and getting a bird's eye view of Kotor Bay, Europe's biggest fjord.

○ Hiking up Mt Durmitor and swimming in the cool waters of the mountain's lakes.

○ White-water rafting down the Tara River, inside Europe's deepest canyon.

○ Spending a night partying along with the Montenegrins and skinny-dipping at dawn.

MOST BIZARRE SIGHT

○ The tiny islet of Gospa od Skrpjela, an artificial island built by a shipwrecked sailor on top of a rock. It supports only a little church from 1630, built by the same sailor, who took a vow to build a church on the spot where he was saved. Each year on 22 July the citizens of nearby Perast throw stones into the water off the island, keeping up the tradition – and the island.

– Vesna Maric

MOZAMBIQUE

POPULATION 19.7 MILLION ☺ **CAPITAL** MAPUTO ☺ **LANGUAGE** PORTUGUESE (OFFICIAL) PLUS MANY LOCAL LANGUAGES ☺ **UNIT OF CURRENCY** METICAL NOVA FAMÍLIA (MTC), PRICES QUOTED IN US$ ☺ **NUMBER OF ELEPHANTS** IN NIASSA RESERVE: ABOUT 12,000 ☺ **COST INDEX** PLATE OF GRILLED PRAWNS, US$12; DAY DHOW SAFARI, US$45; INTERNET ACCESS PER HOUR, US$2

NEWS DOESN'T ALWAYS TRAVEL FAST...

You could be forgiven for confusing today's Mozambique with that perpetually struggling southeastern African country where socialist murals once dominated cityscapes, and war, flooding and other calamities seemed to be permanent headline features. But things have changed fast. Although most of the world hasn't yet caught on, Mozambique has quietly zoomed to the top of the charts as one of Africa's hottest new destinations, with an alluring mix of stunning beaches, a rugged bush interior and a pulsating Afro-Latino vibe.

AFRICA'S LAST FRONTIER?

A heady assertion, this, on a continent of constant surprises and almost boundless frontiers, but if anyone can stake a claim to the title it is Mozambique. And, it's this off-beat, undiscovered element, combined with a 2500km-plus coastline and a rapidly expanding tourism infrastructure that's drawing all the attention these days. In the far north, rugged Niassa Reserve ranks as one of the most challenging and least-trammelled wildlife-watching destinations to be found anywhere. East of here along the Indian Ocean coastline, several of the seductive Quirimbas isles are part of a pioneering ecotourism project mixing conservation and adventure tourism with some of Africa's finest luxury getaways. To the west, on the remote shores of Lake Niassa, there's top-notch community development and environmental conservation going on in the shadow of Nkwichi Lodge, an idyllic lakeside getaway.

RECENT FAD ✦

Adventurous and superluxurious bush-beach experiences for the well heeled.

NOT EVERYTHING IS NEW...

Some of Mozambique's attractions have been around for centuries. Ilha de Moçambique (Mozambique Island), for example, has been drawing visitors for at least 500 years, and partly as a result, it's a magical melting pot of a place where cobwebbed colonial-era buildings, graceful plazas and cobbled streets mix with squawking chickens, thatched-roofed huts and a lively fishing community. In recent years this Unesco World Heritage site finally began to get a face-lift and is more visitable than ever. Well down the coast near the country's southern tip is Maputo – one of southern Africa's liveliest capitals, with bustling sidewalk cafés, Mediterranean-style architecture and a renowned pub and club scene.

DEFINING EXPERIENCE

☺ Dining on grilled prawns and dancing to salsa music in Maputo before

being whisked off to the country's far north for a safari in the Niassa Reserve, followed by a few nights luxuriating on one of the island lodges in the Quirimbas Archipelago.

FESTIVALS & EVENTS

- Every February the small town of Marracuene, about 35km north of Maputo, commemorates those who died resisting colonial rule in the 1895 Battle of Marracuene. The festival, known locally as Gwaza Muthini, also marks the start of the season for *ukanhi*, a potent traditional brew.

- Every year, sometime between June and August, tiny Quissico, a town along the main highway north of Maputo, comes to life with the famed *timbila* (marimba) festival of the Chopi. Complex, fast-paced rhythms, lively lyrics and some spirited competitions between rival *timbila* orchestras are the order of the day.

LIFE-CHANGING EXPERIENCES

- Spending a few days at the beautiful Nkwichi Lodge in the community-owned conservation area of Lake Niassa's Manda Wilderness.

- Walking at dawn through the empty, cobbled streets of Ilha de Moçambique's Stone Town.

- Getting involved with one of the many children's projects in the country – ASEM and the orphanage run by Mother Teresa's sisters in Maputo are good places to start.

- Attending a Sunday morning church service and listening to the singing.

- Island hopping in the Quirimbas Archipelago or snorkelling around the islands of the Bazaruto Archipelago.

RANDOM FACTS

- The waters around Mozambique's Bazaruto Archipelago host East Africa's largest dugong population.

- Before finalising marriage arrangements, the matrilineal Lomwe-Makua peoples in north-central Mozambique require an exchange of services for the man to prove he can work.

- The Niassa-Selous corridor that spans the Mozambique–Tanzania border is the world's largest elephant range.

MOST BIZARRE SIGHT

- Giant coconut-eating land crabs on Rolas Island in the Quirimbas Archipelago. These nocturnal creatures – at up to 1m long, the world's largest arthropods – get their name from their proclivity for climbing coconut palms, shaking down the nuts and then prying the cracked shells open to scoop out the flesh.

– Mary Fitzpatrick

PAPUA NEW GUINEA

POPULATION 5.7 MILLION ⊙ **VISITORS PER YEAR** 75,000 ⊙ **CAPITAL** PORT MORESBY ⊙ **LANGUAGES** PIDGIN, MOTU (IN THE EAST), 870 MUTUALLY UNINTELLIGIBLE LANGUAGES, ENGLISH ⊙ **UNIT OF CURRENCY** KINA (K) ⊙ **COST INDEX** CUP OF COFFEE, K4 (US$1.40); SP LAGER 'BROWNIE' BOTTLE, K5 (US$1.75); HOTEL DOUBLE PER NIGHT, K180-700 (US$63-245)

THE LAND TIME FORGOT

In the 1930s the Leahy brothers walked into the PNG Highlands in search of gold. Instead they found the huge Waghi Valley and around 100,000 people who had no idea of the outside world – they thought the white-skinned prospectors were spirits of dead ancestors. While coastal people have had contact with missionaries and traders since the late 1800s, the Highlands did not really open up until the 1960s and '70s. Tribal warfare and cannibalism were rife throughout PNG until the 1930s, and even today parts of the Highlands remain virtually lawless and beset with tribal fighting.

THE REAL DEAL

Very few travellers go to PNG as it's an expensive and difficult place to get around. But this means that nothing is contrived for tourists and every experience is authentic – most people live much the way they have for thousands of years.

DEFINING EXPERIENCE

⊙ After you've attended an authentic Highlands *singsing* (festival) with thousands of others in traditional dress, retraced the steps of WWII Australian soldiers by walking the infamous Kokoda Track and sampled the world-class diving and snorkelling on offer, take a slow dugout canoe up the mighty Sepik River to visit towering *haus tambarans* (spirit houses), meet master carvers and sleep in one of the villages.

MOST BIZARRE SIGHT ✪

Koteka (penis gourds) are still *de rigueur* in many remote parts, as are decorative objects inserted through a pierced nasal septum.

FESTIVALS & EVENTS

⊙ Show off your tuber at the Milamala Festival in the Trobriand Islands in July. The annual yam harvest is celebrated with song, dance and, naturally, much discussion about yams.

⊙ The famous Goroka Show in September is the big *singsing* on the PNG social calendar. Thousands of people from all over the country head to Goroka to strut their stuff in traditional regalia and *bilas* (finery).

LIFE-CHANGING EXPERIENCES

⊙ Sitting shoulder-to-shoulder with locals, pigs and chickens in a bus riding up the Highlands Hwy from Lae or Madang on the north coast over the rugged Finisterre Range and up into the Highlands – one of the most spectacular razorback road journeys in the world.

⊙ Visiting the ghost town of old Rabaul – once the most beautiful town in the Pacific – levelled by the twin volcanic

...ER TIME, ANOTHER PLACE – FAR
...THE TOURIST TRAIL, THE HIGHLANDS
...NG'S MOST POPULOUS REGION.

eruptions of Mt Tuvurvur and Mt Vulcan in 1994. Mt Tuvurvur still rumbles and belches great plumes of smoke and ash into the sky.

- Riding a dinghy from Kokopo to the Duke of York Islands, seeing dugongs surface and manta rays leap into the air, to visit the steps of Queen Emma's mansion – the last vestige of her plantation empire at Mioko Island.

- Climbing the summit of 4509m-high Mt Wilhelm in the predawn twilight for spectacular sunrise views of both north and south coasts.

- Canoeing across Lake Kutubu – one of PNG's five national parks, its second-largest lake and the highest at 800m – home to countless butterfly species and birds of paradise.

- Riding a bicycle down the Boluminski Hwy along the north coast and staying in villages with easy access to beautiful, pristine coastal regions.

RANDOM FACTS

- On 2 July 1937, aviator Amelia Earhart and navigator Fred Noonan left Lae in PNG's north and flew off into oblivion.

- After the great American military machine left after WWII, cargo cults began to appear. People built runways for imaginary planes to deliver *kago* (material goods), and ritually mimicked military officers sitting at desks shuffling paper.

- Huli wigmen spend four years at hair school learning the finer arts of wig work.

HOT TOPIC OF THE DAY

- PNG has the Pacific's highest incidence of HIV infection – around 2% of the adult population, or 65,000 people. Poor health education and sexual promiscuity have led to an explosion of HIV infection, and poor understanding of HIV has coincided with a huge resurgence of witchcraft and black magic in remote areas.

– Rowan McKinnon

BLUELIST ONLINE

» HIGHLAND LOWDOWN

✪ MIXING IT IN THE TARI BASIN

BY // JEFFREYWILSON (422361)

The beautiful Tari Basin is one of the few valleys in the PNG Highlands that is relatively accessible. The town of Tari is where the modern world meets traditional Highland culture, resulting in an eclectic mix of huge human-hair wigs, feather headdresses and Osama bin Laden T-shirts.

✪ SHELLING OUT FOR THE LIFESTYLE

BY // CHERRY_BLOSSOM11 (427502)

A gathering of clans in Mt Hagen will have you asking 'Which planet am I on?' There's lots of tribal dancing and feathers in the wild and untamed Eastern Highlands – it's the frontier of the world. Around Goroka is the place for a lifestyle change: you've gotta love the idea of shells, pigs and feathers being used as currency.

✪ SAKSAK THE SAGO, YES OR NO?

BY // ESTHER GOLDSBY (427098)

The staple food in swampy PNG is the superstarchy *saksak* (sago). Just say no. Or at least take some spicy sauce to rescue your tastebuds if you think you'll be that desperate.

WWW.LONELYPLANET.COM/BLUELIST

YEMEN

POPULATION 21 MILLION ⊙ **VISITORS PER YEAR** 336,000 ⊙ **CAPITAL** SAN'A ⊙ **LANGUAGE** ARABIC ⊙ **UNIT OF CURRENCY** YEMENI RIYAL (YR) ⊙ **COST INDEX** CUP OF TEA, YR20 (US$0.10); HOTEL DOUBLE PER NIGHT, YR3000 (US$15); SHORT TAXI RIDE, YR100 (US$0.50); INTERNET ACCESS PER HOUR, YR200 (US$1); MACHINE GUN, YR60,000 (US$300)

OSAMA, YOU'RE SO YESTERDAY

It's on the TV, it's in the travel magazines and it's just beginning to turn tour company heads: at last Yemen is making news for all the right reasons. Of course it hasn't always been like this. Following the attacks of 9/11 Yemen was viewed with absolute fear and distrust by just about everyone and the country's already spindly tourist industry completely collapsed. But with Osama and his gang starting to look short of mates and all that fretting over the country becoming another Somalia proving unfounded, Yemeni tourism is finally feeling confident enough in 2008 to come back out to play.

CASTLES IN THE SAND

And what does this confident new Yemen have on her menu? Well, just for starters you can choose from mud-brick castles in the sand or formidable fortresses high up in the sky. Main courses consist of towering towns old enough to remember when Rome was but a twinkle in someone's eye and monstrous mountains terraced in fields of drugs that you chew like a camel. And for dessert how about some delicious Red Sea diving or an unlikely portion of quality surfing on the southern coast? Any meal tastes better when it's fresh, and right now Yemen, with its fruity slices of Africa and Arabia, is as fresh and tasty as a batch of strawberry tarts in a Parisian patisserie.

DEFINING EXPERIENCE

⊙ For a cab ride you'll never forget, how about grabbing a Kalashnikov or two and riding in a Bedouin 'taxi' over the bulging sand swells of the Empty Quarter to the far away palace of the Queen of Sheba?

RECENT FAD

⊙ Tossed out into the Indian Ocean, not far from the coast of Somalia, the otherworldly island of Suqutra is flavour of the month with travellers at the moment. It's got trees that bleed for the memory of dragons, cucumbers the size of small cars, a host of endemic birds, divine beaches and, best of all, the secret of eternal life, which, if you can find it, will save you a fortune on anti-ageing and wrinkle potions.

FESTIVALS AND EVENTS

⊙ Yemen doesn't go in for Glastonbury-style rock concerts or international sporting events too much and

MOST BIZARRE SIGHT ★

The mysterious Well of Barhut in eastern Hadramawt is a bottomless pit with walls made of poisonous scorpions and snakes. It's supposed to be the place to which fallen angels and the souls of infidels are sent for eternity.

DS WATCH OVER THEIR VILLAGE IN
TAINOUS YEMEN, WHERE ANCIENT WARRIOR
RE HAS EMBRACED MODERN WEAPONRY.

Ramadan (from 1 to 29 September in 2008) is about as racy as things get.

- Very rarely, the Qarnaw Tourism and Heritage Festival, which features fast and furious horse and camel races, is held in the desert province of Al-Jawf. Currently there's no word as to if or when the festival might be held in 2008.

LIFE-CHANGING EXPERIENCES

- Realising that succulent San'a is safer than your hometown.
- Contemplating life after a mouthful of the stimulant qat.
- Dancing with daggers at a tribal get-together.
- Trudging misty mountain trails in the 'deserts' of southern Arabia.

HOT TOPIC OF THE DAY

- He's led the nation since the '60s and has just been re-elected in free and fair elections, but with no obvious successor, the big question is what will happen when the ageing Ali Abdullah Saleh finally releases the reins of power?

RANDOM FACTS

- There are more weapons in private hands in Yemen than any other country not at war.
- 14,622,000 working hours are lost daily in Yemen to qat chewing.
- Yemen was the first multiparty democracy in Arabia as well as the only Marxist state.
- Nobody knows the name of the Queen of Sheba, who is said to have been the most beautiful woman who ever lived; she also had hairy legs and a cloven foot.
- Coffee comes from Yemen.
- Yemenis cannot make good coffee!

– Stuart Butler

AZORES (PORTUGAL)

POPULATION 244,000 ✪ **CAPITAL** PONTA DELGADA ✪ **LANGUAGE** PORTUGUESE ✪ **MAJOR INDUSTRIES** FARMING, FISHING ✪ **UNIT OF CURRENCY** EURO (€) ✪ **COST INDEX** BOTTLE OF ESPECIAL BEER, €1 (US$1.30); HOTEL DOUBLE PER NIGHT, €95 (US$127); THREE-HOUR WHALE-WATCHING TOUR, €50 (US$67); ADMISSION TO SUBTERRANEAN LAKE INSIDE FURNA DO ENXOFRE, €0.75 (US$1)

OLD EUROPE ATOP VOLCANOES

If you've heard the name but can't point to them on the map, you're in good company. The Azores has only recently gained much attention, and even those in the know aren't eager to let out the secret. The autonomous Portuguese archipelago, which lies some 1300km west of the European mainland, has spectacular rugged beauty, offering visitors a chance to explore one of Europe's most far-flung outposts. While beach isn't the lure – except for lovers of the black-sand variety – the lush scenery, whale-watching and tranquil village charm make for an uncommon sojourn on these idyllic islands.

Old-world traditions are alive and well on the nine islands of the Azores, with ox-drawn carts and farmers on horseback more commonly spotted than automobiles during a typical stroll across the countryside. Fishing villages, dairy farms and rolling vineyards dot the landscape, amid a diverse backdrop of flower-covered cliffs, pristine forests, sulphurous hot springs and otherworldly volcanic craters. Some believe the Azores are the remnants of the lost island of Atlantis, a once great nation of seafarers that sank in 9000 BC (according to Plato) leaving only scattered islands.

SUMMER DREAMING

Although the winter can be gloomy with chilly days of rain, when spring arrives Azoreans come out to celebrate, and festivals pack the summer months. Visitors are always welcome to join the Azorean revelry; they can also connect to island life by walking atop verdant cliffs above the azure sea, soaking in hot springs or taking a viticultural ramble through the islands' historic wineries, whose vineyards date back centuries.

DEFINING EXPERIENCE

✪ After a morning walk along rugged windswept cliffs, book a boat ride for the awesome sight of whales pounding across the Atlantic (seen from the safety of your small inflatable raft), then recover from the bumpy journey with a soak in a thermal bath; finish the evening at a cosy family-run restaurant, with fresh fish and *vinho verde* (green wine).

FESTIVALS & EVENTS

✪ Festa do Senhor Santo Cristo dos Milagres (the Festival of Christ of the Miracles), held on the Sunday five weeks after Easter, has long been São Miguel's biggest fest; streets in the

RANDOM FACT ✪

Of the 90 species of whales and dolphins in the world, 25 can be spotted in Azorean waters, including the great sperm whale.

NO SADDLE REQUIRED FOR THESE KIDS, HORSING AROUND ON FAIAL ISLAND, IN THE HEART OF THE AZORES.

capital Ponta Delgada are strewn with flowers over which passes a colourful priestly procession, and there's music and dance to enjoy in the evening. The date for 2008 is 27 April.

- Espírito Santo (Pentecost), seven weeks after Easter, is celebrated in every village on the islands and includes processions, brass bands, fireworks and feasting on sweetbreads, soups and other traditional plates; street bullfights often bring the festivities to a close. In 2008 you can join the festive spirit on 11 May.

LIFE-CHANGING EXPERIENCES

- Contemplating the twin lakes – one blue, one green – and the tiny village of Sete Cidades which are set against a backdrop of lush cliffs from the Vista do Rei (King's Lookout).
- Sharing bread, wine and cheese with a dairy farmer on the remote

lores, the westernmost island in the archipelago.

- Running for your life from a bull at the *tourada à corda* (street bullfight) on the island of Terceira.

MOST BIZARRE SIGHT

- Peering out the windows of a local café during a *tourada à corda*, when bulls are let loose on the streets to chase down courageous fools testing their mettle against the animal. In contrast to the bullfights of Spain, the bulls here are teased but at the day's end they are left unharmed – which is not always the case for the humans involved.

DEFINING DIFFERENCE

- The archipelago, which is comprised of the upper sections of volcanoes strung along the Mid-Atlantic Ridge, looks nothing like mainland Portugal. Seismic

activity and volcanic eruptions are as unpredictable as the weather, which can go from balmy to stormy in a matter of minutes. Indeed, locals often talk of having four seasons in one day.

REGIONAL FLAVOURS

- Azorean delights include fresh grilled fish and squid, octopus, *racas* (a kind of barnacle), lobster and *cavaco* (a type of crab). Local cheeses and wines along with abundant fruits, including pineapples that are grown in local greenhouses, complete the feast.
- At Lagoa de Furnas on the island of São Miguel you can watch how locals prepare meals at the famous *Cozido nas Caldeiras* – holes dug into the earth that serve as natural ovens, making use of the endless geothermal emanations from below.

– Regis St Louis

BOLIVIAN AMAZON

POPULATION 9 MILLION ⊙ **VISITORS PER YEAR** OVER 400,000 ⊙ **CAPITAL** LA PAZ ⊙ **NUMBER OF NATIONAL PARKS** 22 ⊙ **LANGUAGES** SPANISH, QUECHUA, AYMARA ⊙ **UNIT OF CURRENCY** BOLIVIANO (BS) ⊙ **COST INDEX** GLASS OF *CHICHA* (FERMENTED CORN OR QUINOA DRINK), 2BS (US$0.25); HOTEL DOUBLE PER NIGHT, 80BS (US$10); INTERNET ACCESS PER HOUR, 5BS (US$0.65)

IT AIN'T ALL IN THE ANDES

What do you think of when you hear the words 'rainforest' and 'the Amazon'? Bugs and mosquitoes, or jaguars, macaws and monkeys? Or do you envisage wild rivers surrounded by ferns and palms? And what about when you hear about Bolivia? For most people it's women wearing bowler hats, the high Andes and llamas, but the truth is – and pssst! don't spread the word too fast – the largest part of this wonderful country is covered in tropical rainforest. Bolivia may be among Latin America's poorest by economic measures, but it is one of the world's richest for plant and wildlife species. If you've never been to the rainforest, Bolivia's Amazon is a fantastic place to start, and the relaxed, hammock-swinging town of Rurrenabaque is the perfect traveller base. But tread carefully – and we don't mean for fear of stepping on a scary spider or snake (though that too). As you might imagine, tourism and wildlife don't gel too well, but they can coexist and become mutually helpful if we act responsibly. The best agent (and traveller) will not offer (or demand) guarantees of wildlife sightings or disturb and handle wildlife, will have good safety records and will take care not to leave rubbish in the forest.

WHERE IT'S AT

Madidi National Park may be the biggest, but east of Santa Cruz, Bolivia's second city, is Amboró National Park, a more accessible area with great trekking opportunities. To the north of Santa Cruz is Noel Kempff Mercado National Park, a hard-to-access region, with vast unspoilt forests that beckon the hard-core adventurer.

WANT MORE?

Yes, there is more to the Amazon than wildlife spotting and trekking, and fighting off the creepy-crawlies. Bolivia's indigenous communities are increasingly providing lodgings for visitors. Some make it part of the stay to show their traditional crafts and give a glimpse of their way of life, while not letting tourism impact greatly on their lifestyle. Then there's the slow pleasure of river travel, taken up only by those with bags of patience and carriage-loads of time. If you don't mind discomfort and a monotone gastronomic existence, with an adventure or three packed in, river travel can be the perfect way of getting to know the rainforest.

DEFINING EXPERIENCE

⊙ Walking through the thick rainforest, watching the sun's rays play with intricate spider webs, hearing trees rustle as monkeys hurl themselves between branches, seeing a hairy tarantula

HOT TOPIC OF THE DAY ★

Where to start? With Bolivia's controversial president Morales in power, there are more hot topics than ever: coca leaf production, gas nationalisation, rainforest logging, indigenous rights, you name it.

NOT A DROP IN SIGHT: CRUISING UP A RIVER OF WATER HYACINTH ON A TRIBUTARY OF THE RÍO BENI, BOLIVIAN AMAZON.

mother protect its little ones, and waving mosquitoes away from your face.

FESTIVALS & EVENTS

- The biennial 10-day music festival Misiones de Chiquitos starts at the end of April 2008, with performances of Baroque and Renaissance music in Santa Cruz and the Jesuit Mission Towns.

- The best festival of the rainforest in 2008 starts on 31 July: it's the three-day Carnival of San Ignacio de Moxos, where feathers, colours, chants and plenty of booze take over the tiny indigenous village.

LIFE-CHANGING EXPERIENCES

- Hearing the sound of the howler monkeys at dawn. You'll cherish the sound of your alarm clock thereafter.

- Hiking through the rainforest, with a guide to show you which tree to bang on for help if you're lost.

- Swimming in a lagoon, surrounded by friendly caimans.

- Relaxing on a hammock in dreamy Rurrenabaque.

DEFINING DIFFERENCE

- Unlike the besieged and pillaged Brazilian Amazon, Bolivia's rainforest is home to thousands of big and small species of wildlife, rare plants and undiscovered creatures. This is mostly thanks to Madidi National Park, which protects 1.8 million hectares of forest, thousands of colourful bird species, hundreds of scary reptiles and over 100 amphibians, some of which you're likely to spot midswim as you cruise up a river. The jaguar is sometimes glimpsed resting on a river bank at night, eyes aglow as a guide flashes a torch in his direction. Howler monkeys will wake you with their hollers at dawn, and funny bird noises will provide music at breakfast.

– *Vesna Maric*

COLORADO, USA

POPULATION 4.8 MILLION ⚙ **VISITORS PER YEAR** MORE THAN 6 MILLION ⚙ **UNIT OF CURRENCY** US DOLLAR (US$) ⚙ **LANGUAGES** ENGLISH (OFFICIAL), SPANISH ⚙ **COST INDEX** MIDRANGE HOTEL DOUBLE PER NIGHT, US$120; PINT OF LOCALLY BREWED BEER, US$3.50; DAY LIFT TICKET, US$80; RIDING THE COG RAILWAY TO THE TOP OF PIKE'S PEAK AND BACK, US$26

ROCKY MOUNTAIN HIGH

Colorado was cool with the college crowd long before MTV's cameras caught on. No, the seven strangers on the hit reality show The Real World weren't the first to discover Colorado's funky Rocky Mountain High. Their contemporaries have been flocking to the 'Centennial State' for decades to participate in a uniquely Colorado coming-of-age ritual: the act of ski bumming (definition: living in a mountain ski resort town, working in the service industry and riding as much fresh powder as possible in between).

And it's not just the college crowd: Colorado has been catching Californians, New Yorkers and Washingtonians faster than a fly fisher canhoist a rainbow trout from one of the state's wide glossy rivers. Simply said, Colorado is a great place to live and play, and locals pride themselves on a high quality of life. Where else can you spend the morning in an office, the afternoon on the mountain bike and the evening sipping a hopped-up, locally brewed beer at a brewpub with friends?

A REASON EVERY SEASON

Tourism and the military are among the state's major industries. Colorado sees more than six million visitors every year who spend more than US$7 billion during their holiday. In the winter it's all about the world-famous snow riding at the state's numerous ski resorts – in 2006 Colorado's resorts were American's 10th-most-popular spring-break destination. In summer, Rocky Mountain National Park, north of the ultracool, hippy college town of Boulder, attracts tens of thousands of people each year. They come to gawk at 4348m Longs Peak and the other craggy mountains viewed along the world-famous Trail Ridge drive. Other draws? Camping beside a mountain lake or staying on a working cattle ranch. Experiencing the Wild West of centuries past in the state's southwestern corner, where you'll find mysterious Mesa Verde National Park and perhaps even a UFO amid towering golden dunes in Great Sand Dunes National Park, America's newest.

DEFINING EXPERIENCE

⚙ Pondering life's riches from an inner tube ripping down the nearest bloated creek, from the back of a chestnut horse galloping across a field of flowers while singing John Denver's 'Rocky Mountain High', soaking in the buff at a natural hot springs or talking to a cowboy over pints of 'fat tire' while perched on a microbrewery bar stool.

FESTIVALS & EVENTS

⚙ The Telluride Bluegrass Festival, held in late June, sells out months in

RANDOM FACT

North American Aerospace Defense Command (NORAD) headquarters in hollowed-out Cheyenne Mountain, Colorado Springs, are now on 'warm standby' (ie mothballed): the missile monitors have surfaced and moved to regular offices.

advance and attracts the biggest names in the industry for a weekend of camping and outdoor jam sessions.

⊛ You won't want to miss the Great American Beer Festival, held in Denver in early September, which purportedly offers the largest selection of beer varieties of any such event. Brewers from around the country serve hordes of thirsty beer enthusiasts their mouth-watering hoppy ales and big porters.

RANDOM FACTS

⊛ Pikes Peak provided Katherine Lee Bates with the inspiration to pen the poem turned song 'America the Beautiful' – ride the famous cog railway to the top to see why.

⊛ Colorado has 54 'fourteeners' – mountains over 14,000ft (4275m) – and it is considered a coup d'etat to summit them all.

⊛ In Boulder the ATMs offer Nepalese as a language option – the city has a high concentration of people from Nepal and Tibet.

⊛ At almost 4000m, A-Basin is North America's highest ski resort.

LOCAL LINGO

⊛ 'Dude, it's a sick powder day, let's go catch some big air' is Colorado talk for going skiing. If someone asks you to try the local delicacy, Rocky Mountain Oysters, you might want to think twice as you'll be eating fried bull's testicles. Biking and beer drinking are statewide obsessions and both can involve single tracks and fat tires. If someone asks you if you'd like either of these while you're sitting at a pub, they're talking about beer; if they ask you while you're climbing aboard a bike they're talking narrow trails and the wheels you'll need to ride them.

– *Becca Blond*

GLACIER NATIONAL PARK, USA

LANGUAGE ENGLISH ✿ **MAJOR INDUSTRY** TOURISM ✿ **UNIT OF CURRENCY** US DOLLAR (US$)
✿ **COST INDEX** ROOM AT GLACIER PARK LODGE, FROM US$150; TENT SITE AT ONE OF GLACIER'S 13 NATIONAL PARK SERVICE CAMP GROUNDS, US$15-20; PARK ENTRANCE FEE PER VEHICLE, US$10; SHUTTLE SERVICE AROUND THE PARK, US$8-24

GRIZZLIES, GOATS & GLACIERS

Gorgeous Glacier National Park is Montana's guiltiest outdoor pleasure and an even better place to just get away. The park's rugged and desolate alpine terrain, a land where mountains were forged by prehistoric ice rivers, is home to 200 clear crystal lakes, 50 (sadly shrinking) glaciers and too many rushing waterfalls to count. Wildlife enthusiasts will have a field day in Glacier. Spotting animals is common: cougars, grizzlies, black bears and elks all roam freely. Most visitors tend to stick to developed areas and short hiking trails, but take some time to explore off-the-beaten path routes in this gem.

Despite being Montana's premier tourist attraction in the summer (in winter the park mostly shuts down), Glacier still feels empty. Preciously few miles of tarred road wind through Glacier's 4140 sq km of primitive landscape, but there are 1127km of foot and horse trails. And while most travellers choose to stick to the pavement and traverse Going-to-the-Sun Rd (it is pretty awesome), adventure addicts can easily strap on a pack and hit the great unknown. Getting off the road, and up against the soaring sedimentary peaks, is what Glacier's really all about and the best way to discover just how soul-soothing this ancient terra firma is. The sky seems bigger and bluer amid the wilderness mountaintops than anywhere else. The air is intoxicatingly crisp, fresh and scented with pine, and you're more likely to exchange hellos on the hiking trail with a shaggy, medium-sized brown bear that's sipping glacier water from an ice-blue lake than with another human being.

DEFINING EXPERIENCE

✿ Hiking past mama grizzly bear and her cubs on the famous Iceberg Lake trail in July, where the way is enclosed by stunning 900m vertical headwalls on three sides as it ascends through wildflower-strewn meadows to one of North America's most impressive glacial lakes.

FESTIVALS & EVENTS

✿ For a rodeo with a difference head to Essex, a town near the southern end of Glacier, where in March the annual Snow Rodeo sees would-be-cowboy competitors strutting their stuff – be it on skis or snow shoes.

✿ The annual Glacier Jazz Stampede in nearby Kalispell in October is a four-day, four-venue music festival featuring performances in various jazz styles from Dixieland to big band and swing.

RANDOM FACTS

✿ Although the USA's Glacier National Park and Canada's Waterton Lakes National Park

DEFINING DIFFERENCE ✪

Comprising the lower half of the Waterton-Glacier International Peace Park (the upper half is in Alberta, Canada), Glacier National Park was listed as a World Heritage site in 1995, in recognition of its diverse communities of plant and animal species.

evoke images of binational harmony, in reality each park is operated separately: entry into one doesn't entitle you to enter the other.

⊙ In 2003 some 15% of the park's acreage was scorched by wildfires.

⊙ The park is open year-round; however, most services are only open from mid-May to September.

⊙ Iceberg Lake was named in 1905 by George Grinnell, who saw icebergs calving from the glacier at the foot of the headwalls. The glacier is no longer active, but surface ice and avalanche debris still provide sizeable flotillas of bergs as the lake melts in early summer.

⊙ Scary fact? Scientists predict that if global-warming trends continue, all of the park's 50-odd moving ice masses will have completely melted by the year 2030.

– Susan Derby

BLUELIST ONLINE

BY // MICAH_REYNER (515447) & BRITSCH (513345)

» FINDING THE MIDDLE OF NOWHERE IN AMERICA

✪ GATES OF THE ARCTIC NATIONAL PARK, ALASKA
One of the last places in the United States that is largely untouched by civilisation. The park is crossed by meandering rivers, thick with Arctic wildlife, and ablaze with wildflowers in early summer...just be sure to bring lots of mosquito repellant.

✪ WISDOM, MONTANA
An hour's drive from the more heavily touristed Bitterroot Valley, Wisdom, a town with fewer than 300 inhabitants, is the population centre of the Big Hole River Valley. A starkly beautiful landscape of real cowboys, abandoned ranches, and rarely used trailheads.

✪ CRATERS OF THE MOON NATIONAL MONUMENT, IDAHO
A lightly visited park in Idaho, Craters of the Moon lacks the popularity of the neighboring national parks, but it is a unique sight in 'the lower 48', with lavaflows, cindercones, and no vegetation in sight.

✪ ISLE ROYALE, MICHIGAN
Smack in the middle of Lake Superior, Isle Royale is accessible only by seaplane or ferry. Home to wolfpacks, moose and the occaisional backpacker or park ranger, it's one of the few places east of the Mississippi in which one can feel truly immersed in the wilderness.

✪ SWAN'S ISLAND, MAINE
No booze, no stores, no movies: Swan's Island is not choc-full of creature comforts, but this remote island makes up for its lack of amusements with daily fresh lobster catches, a small-town culture and stunning ocean views.

✪ RURAL ROAD DINER, MONTANA
Listen to Native Americans and cattle ranchers discuss the difficulties and rewards of maintaining their livelihoods as you dig into your huckleberry pie. If there is a forest fire or rodeo nearby, take a stool next to the cowboys and firefighters, who will eagerly recount their death-defying careers. Just don't ask if veggie burgers are on the menu.

WWW.LONELYPLANET.COM/BLUELIST

NEWFOUNDLAND & LABRADOR, CANADA

POPULATION 509,000 ❂ **VISITORS PER YEAR** 500,000 ❂ **CAPITAL** ST JOHN'S ❂ **LANGUAGE** ENGLISH
❂ **MAJOR INDUSTRIES** FISHING, FORESTRY, OIL, GAS, MINING, TOURISM ❂ **UNIT OF CURRENCY** CANADIAN DOLLAR (C$)
❂ **COST INDEX** GLASS OF BEER, C$4.25 (US$4.00); B&B DOUBLE PER NIGHT, C$75 (US$70); FISH & CHIPS, C$7 (US$6.50)

THE ACCIDENTAL TOURIST ATTRACTION

Tourism to the Rock, as Canada's craggy, easternmost province is nicknamed, really only began about 15 years ago. That's when the codfishing industry pooped out, and locals had to find new ways to earn a living. 'Hmm,' they thought. 'We've got waters teeming with humpback whales and icebergs. We've got a couple of World Heritage sites, like Leif Ericson's Viking settlement at L'Anse aux Meadows and the sublime mountains and freshwater fjords at Gros Morne National Park. Maybe these are things folks would want to hike or kayak around, or just plain see?'

Damn right. Visitor numbers to Newfoundland & Labrador have slowly crept upward, but the province's remoteness (one has to ferry over wicked seas or fly into fog-swallowed airports to get there) keeps it off the beaten path. For now. Surely the cat's about to leap out of the bag on this otherworldly place, where ancient glaciers scattered boulders like marbles across the terrain, and where moose, puffins and caribou now roam as part of the odd provincial menagerie.

FAR FROM THE MADDENING CROWD

The province offers plenty of hiking, fishing or kayaking escapes where it will just be you, the local family who's putting you up for the night and the lonely howl of the wind. Try any of the wee fishing villages, called outports, that fringe Newfoundland's coast. Or break for The Big Land, aka Labrador, the wintry home of the Inuit. Many communities are so isolated they can be reached only by boat.

RANDOM FACT

In the early 1960s Newfoundland's capital St John's had more millionaires per capita than any city in North America, thanks to the booming codfish industry.

DEFINING EXPERIENCE

❂ A day spent kayaking through the spray of whales and hiking along the shore to view icebergs, followed by a night of eating fish 'n' brewis and partridgeberry pie, then tossing back a shot of rum and kissing a codfish to become an 'Honorary Newfoundlander'.

FESTIVALS & EVENTS

❂ The Sound Symposium celebrates its 25th anniversary in 2008 (3 to 13 July), with experimental concerts and sound installations at unusual venues around St John's, including WWII bunkers at Cape Spear (with crashing waves and whale spouts in the background).

❂ Supposedly held to honour the Atlantic salmon's annual migration, the mid-July Salmon Festival in Grand Falls-Windsor is really about chowing down on the mighty fish and partying hard at the outdoor concerts featuring big-name

VILLAGERS ON QUIRPON ISLAND, NEWFOUNDLAND, NEVER TIRE OF THE VIEW, AS A RANGE OF ICE MOUNTAINS DRIFT BY ON THE CURRENT.

performers such as Nelly Furtado, The Tragically Hip and Bryan Adams.

- Come the first Wednesday in August, the streets of St John's empty and stores close as people migrate to the shores of Quidi Vidi Lake where the Royal St John's Regatta hits the water. The rowing event began in 1825 and is the oldest continuously held sporting event in North America.

RANDOM FACTS

- Newfoundland was the only place in North America directly attacked by German forces during WWII. It happened when U-boats torpedoed the loading pier at Bell Island in 1942.
- The world's largest caribou herd (some 750,000 beasts) migrates across Labrador annually.

LOCAL LINGO

- Unique slang and colourful idioms pepper the language to the extent

that the province merits its own *Dictionary of Newfoundland English*. These are some examples: a 'nunny-fudger' is a person who dreams more of their upcoming dinner than the work at hand; 'scurrifungeing' means a thorough cleaning; 'whizgigging' is boisterous, silly laughing or being foolish; and a 'yaffle' is an armful of dried codfish.

REGIONAL FLAVOURS

- Get ready for a curious plateful. Meats include seal flipper (only for the brave!), caribou and moose. Fish 'n' brewis is a popular dish that blends salted fish, onions, scruncheons (fried pork fat) and a bizarre near-boiled bread. Local fruits such as the partridgeberry (cranberrylike) and bakeapple (apricot-meets-raspberry) stuff pies and jams. Screech is the infamous local rum.

– Karla Zimmerman

BLUELIST ONLINE

» THINGS TO FIND IN NEWFOUNDLAND

❂ L'ANSE AUX MEADOWS

Make the trek to the extreme north tip of the island – the only Viking site discovered in North America (so far). The low-key approach to the site has created an authentic experience – it's like going back in time 1000 years. Interpreters dress like Vikings (real beards, too) and visitors can play with, I mean handle, the replica weapons.

❂ HARD-TO-FIND FOODS

Cod tongues are found on many restaurant menus and are usually deep-fried but if eaten plain are like slimy oysters. With the collapse of the seal hunt, seal-flipper pie is harder to find; tender and tasty, it's an acquired taste for most.

❂ DISTINCTLY NEWFIE PLACE NAMES

Newfoundland has some of the best place names: Heart's Delight, Heart's Content, Dildo (stop giggling), Dildo Run Provincial Park (I said stop giggling), Witless Bay & Blow Me Down are but a few. They also have a penchant for naming any body of water a 'pond' regardless of its size. Western Brook Pond (a giant fjord) is an example.

WWW.LONELYPLANET.COM/BLUELIST

NORTHEAST ENGLAND

POPULATION 2.5 MILLION ⊙ **CAPITAL** NEWCASTLE-UPON-TYNE ⊙ **LANGUAGE** ENGLISH, GEORDIE
⊙ **MAJOR INDUSTRIES** PETROCHEMICALS, CARS, BIOTECHNOLOGY, ELECTRONICS ⊙ **UNIT OF CURRENCY** UK POUND (UK£)
⊙ **COST INDEX** BOTTLE OF NEWCASTLE BROWN ALE UK£1.90 (US$3.80); STOTTIE (LOCAL BREAD SANDWICH) UK£1.55 (US$3.10)

COALS TO NEWCASTLE

If your image of Northeast England is of coal mines and bad weather then it's time you forgot your preconceived ideas and discovered the most exciting, beautiful and friendly region in the whole of England. Stretching from the River Tees to the Scottish Border, the Northeast sees nine-million visitors annually, with overseas visitor numbers rising by 30% in the last seven years.

The regeneration of this once depressed – and depressing – area has been most obvious in the regional capital Newcastle and its neighbour across the River Tyne, Gateshead (a combination officially, if rather unsuccessfully, promoted as NewcastleGateshead). Beautiful 19th-century architecture now has a modern counterpart in the BALTIC centre for contemporary arts and the Sage music venue, while the legendary nightlife shouldn't be missed.

Away from the city the wildernesses of the North Pennines and Northumberland mean you can really get away from it all, stopping off to explore historical sights such as Hadrian's Wall and the medieval castles along the coast or, for more contemporary attractions, check out the new art gallery in Middlesbrough or the renovated quayside in Hartlepool.

DEFINING EXPERIENCE

⊙ In the region that gave railways to the world, it would be almost rude not to ride the train line from Darlington (where it all began in 1825), past Durham, with an amazing view of its cathedral and castle, on over one of Newcastle's seven Tyne-crossing bridges and then along the coast, passing several magnificent castles, to Berwick-upon-Tweed and the border.

FESTIVALS & EVENTS

⊙ Tynedale Beer Festival takes place in Corbridge in mid-June 2008, offering devotees the chance to sample over 70 local and national brews.

⊙ Stockton International Riverside Festival is an annual celebration of street performance that's held in Stockton-on-Tees during the first week in August.

⊙ The Great North Run is the most popular half-marathon in the world, with around 35,000 runners trying to make it all the way from Newcastle to the coast at South Shields. The event takes place every year around the end of September.

RANDOM FACTS

⊙ Berwick-upon-Tweed is the definitive border town, having changing hands between England and Scotland 13

RECENT FAD

It all started with the BALTIC in Gateshead and now the rest of the Northeast is discovering a love of art, with MIMA (Middlesbrough Institute of Modern Art) celebrating its first birthday in 2008.

COLOUR YOUR VISION WITH A CONTEMPORARY
TAKE ON TYNESIDE FROM THE VIEWING PLATFORM
AT THE BALTIC ARTS CENTRE, GATESHEAD.

times. Furthermore, the local team is still playing in the Scottish Football League, despite the town being south of the border.

- Northeast England, with a population of 2.5 million, produces as much CO_2 as the entire country of Bangladesh, which has 140 million people.

- Kielder Water in Northumberland is the largest manmade lake in Europe; it took two years and 200 billion litres of water to fill it.

- The Venerable Bede, a local 8th-century Benedictine monk, was responsible for popularising the use of AD (anno Domini) in dates. His bones are now buried at Durham Cathedral.

- Newcastle's famous Tyne Bridge was completed in 1928, nearly four years before its illustrious cousin, Australia's Sydney Harbour Bridge.

MOST BIZARRE SIGHT

- It's a bitterly cold Friday night in January but for Newcastle's hardcore hedonists this is still no reason to wrap up. Short-sleeve shirts and short-cut skirts are the uniform and unless you want to stick out from the crowd, brace yourself and leave your coat behind.

LOCAL LINGO

- Geordie is the nickname of both people from the Newcastle area and the dialect they speak. No-one knows for sure where the term comes from – it's something to do with the name George and connected either to local support for George II during a rebellion or to George Stephenson, inventor of a lamp used by the region's miners – but its vocabulary is as close to Old English as you'll hear today. Key phrases to use (and to try to understand) include 'Howay' (Come on, as in

'Howay the lads' when supporting the local football team); 'Why aye' (Yes, of course); 'Let's gan hyem' (Shall we go home?); and the ever useful 'Hadaway and shite!' (Go away!).

- A word of warning: the cities of Newcastle and Sunderland may be just a few miles apart and the accent may sound identical, but there's a fierce rivalry between them. A Sunderland inhabitant is called a Mackem – never, ever, call a Mackem a Geordie.

CLASSIC PLACE TO STAY

- For a room with a rather splendid cathedral view, Durham Castle is the destination of choice. Founded in 1072 and now a student residence, visitors can stay here during holidays, with doubles starting at a modest UK£50 (US$100). Or for a romantic splurge, book the castle's Bishop's Suite and sleep like a saint for UK£180 (US$360).

– Clifton Wilkinson

NORTHWEST VIETNAM

POPULATION 4.5 MILLION ⊙ **LANGUAGES** VIETNAMESE, H'MONG, DZAO, THAI ⊙ **MAJOR INDUSTRIES** HYDROELECTRICITY, TEA, COFFEE, TOURISM ⊙ **UNIT OF CURRENCY** VIETNAMESE DONG (D), US DOLLAR (US$) & THE GOOD OLD BARTER SYSTEM ⊙ **COST INDEX** HOTEL ROOM PER NIGHT, US$10; BOTTLE OF HALIDA BEER, US$1; H'MONG INDIGO-DYED TOP, US$5

COOLER MOUNTAINS, COOLER DESTINATION

Vietnam is a hot destination these days. But for most visitors, hot means just that, the hot and steamy lowlands of the coastal regions. Close your eyes and stick a pin in most itineraries through Vietnam and they'll involve a Hanoi and Halong Bay hit-and-run in the north, a quick dose of central culture in Hue and Hoi An and some shopping in Saigon. Fine, if you're happy to follow the crowd, but if you crave an adventure more than a holiday, it is time to chart a cooler course to the majestic mountains of the northwest.

A KALEIDOSCOPE OF COLOUR

Welcome to the roof of Vietnam. The landscape is a rich palette that provides some of the most spectacular scenery in Vietnam. Forbidding and unforgiving terrain for lowlanders, the mountains have long been a haven for an eclectic mix of hill tribes. Dressed in elaborate costumes, living as they have for generations, extending the hand of friendship to strangers, an encounter with the Montagnards is both a humbling and heart-warming experience.

RISE ABOVE THE FLOODS

For many visitors Sapa is *the* northwest, an atmospheric old hill station set amid stunning scenes of near-vertical rice terraces and towering peaks. However, the Vietnamese have discovered the beauty of their own backyard and are beginning to flood the area, quite literally when it comes to obsessive dam building. Get here now, before some places become overrun and others go underwater.

DEFINING EXPERIENCE

⊙ Ride a mighty Minsk motorbike through the mindblowing mountain roads of the Tonkinese Alps, the home of the hill tribes.

FESTIVALS & EVENTS

⊙ Tet (Vietnamese New Year) is the big one for all Vietnamese and can easily rumble on into a week-long celebration. Popular with lowland Vietnamese who have settled in the mountainous regions of the north, in the 2008 festivities start 7 February.

⊙ Khau Vai Love Market is speed-dating minority style. Original swingers, the good folk of Khau Vai in Ha Giang Province have been wife swapping, and husband swapping for that matter, for almost a century. Youngsters come to find a mate. Old

MOST BIZARRE SIGHT ★

The mad Sunday morning market in Bac Ha is the place to get your water buffaloes, pigs, horses and dogs, or bottles of the local firewater. Groups of Flower H'mong throng here early, decked out in hippy-trippy rainbow-braided velvet.

A SIGHT COMMON IN NORTHWEST VIETNAM, THIS DZAO WOMAN'S HEADWEAR, CALLED A *HONG*, COMPRISES AT LEAST SEVEN LAYERS OF COTTON SCARVES.

flames fan the dying embers of a lost passion. The love market occurs three months after Tet (1 May 2008).

○ H'mong people celebrate their very own New Year in late November or early December. The dates are somewhat nomadic because celebrations kick off at the end of the rice harvest.

HOT TOPIC OF THE DAY

○ Dammed if you do, damned if you don't, or at least that seems to be the government attitude towards this part of Vietnam. Hydroelectric plants are going in at an alarming rate, driven by an insatiable demand for power in the populous provinces of lowland Vietnam. And it's the minorities that are paying the price as the rest of the country rushes towards riches. Long an underclass, they'll soon be an underwater class,

as the only way to visit places like the Muong Lay valley in the next few years will be by submarine.

DEFINING DIFFERENCE

○ It's all about the fashion, darling. Lowland women might opt for the sweeping lines of the national dress, *ao dai*, in the city or the classic conical hat in the countryside. Men prefer Western dress in the cities, although some can't resist taking the pith, and donning a classic Ho Chi Minh hat. Not so in the forbidding mountain terrain of the northwest, where the people are clearly cut from a different cloth. Life is certainly colourful in this part of the world: choose from the striking reds of the Dzao, the enduring indigos of the Black H'mong or the blaze of colour that defines the Flower H'mong.

– Nick Ray

» TAKING YOUR TASTEBUDS TO HEAVEN IN HANOI

○ CHIM SAO

You're starving, especially if you've exercised with the locals. With Hoan Kiem Lake at your back, walk down Pho Hué for 1km till you reach the alley called Ngo Hué, look for the sign, take off your shoes and get ready for the ultimate sour fish hotpot.

○ BUN CHA

If you promise not to tell... At the end of tiny Pho Hang Manh in the Old Quarter, look for a ground floor storefront with ladies cooking, grab a seat and for US$1, pig out on the most unbelievable springrolls, beef patties, leafy greens and rice.

○ GARDEN CAFÉ

One second away from motorbike madness, tucked away on tiny Pho Hang Manh is the peaceful Garden Café, with possibly the best shrimp-stuffed fresh spring rolls and fruit shakes in Vietnam. There's no no need to hurry, as it's open till late at night.

PENINSULAR MALAYSIA

POPULATION 2.4 MILLION ◎ **LANGUAGES** BAHASA MALAYSIA, ENGLISH, MANDARIN, HOKKIEN, CANTONESE, TAMIL ◎ **NUMBER OF SULTANS** NINE ◎ **UNIT OF CURRENCY** RINGGIT (RM) ◎ **COST INDEX** LARGE BOTTLE OF TIGER BEER, RM10 (US$2.90); HOTEL DOUBLE PER NIGHT, RM100 (US$29); BOWL OF LAKSA, RM 5 (US$1.45); INTERNET ACCESS PER HOUR, RM3 (US$0.85)

THE PARTY'S NOT OVER YET

The hullabaloo over Malaysia's 50th birthday may have died down, but there's still plenty to celebrate over on the federation's peninsula. The big push to boost tourist numbers during the Visit Malaysia 2007 campaign has paid off, with improved facilities and infrastructure all round. And visitor arrivals are only set to increase. Air Asia, Malaysia's fast-growing budget airline, offers connections to the peninsula from as far afield as Bali and Yangon and plans to expand its network of flights in Southeast Asia.

NEW AND OLD

One of the peninsula's key attractions is its intriguing mix of new and old Asia. Home to the dazzling Petronas Towers, the country's capital Kuala Lumpur (known simply as KL) is Malaysia at its most dynamic, while down the road in Putrajaya – the nascent Federal Administrative Centre – impressive new architecture is setting the tone for the country's future. At the same time there's a growing awareness of the importance of preserving historic buildings, particularly in key heritage towns such as Malaka, and Georgetown on the island of Penang.

MAKING TRACKS

Getting around by train has become easier with the opening in late 2007 of a new high-speed rail service between KL and Ipoh, facilitating speedy access to the refreshingly cool Cameron Highlands. The peninsula's modern highway system makes driving a joy and it's possible to travel the 966km from Perlis in the far north to Johor Bahru at the southern tip in one smooth trip. But with a double coastline peppered with hundreds of serene beaches, not to mention scores of alluring islands, you'd be right not to rush. Now more than ever the peninsula is a place to wind down and take it easy.

DEFINING EXPERIENCE

◎ Sipping strong milky tea through a straw from out of a plastic bag, while squished next to cheroot-smoking female market traders and their bundles of fresh produce, as you travel aboard the 'jungle railway' – a rickety local line that runs from near Kota Bharu in the country's northeast to the town of Jerantut, the gateway to the magnificent national park of Taman Negara.

FESTIVALS & EVENTS

◎ Start the year in spectacular fashion enjoying the riotous celebrations

MOST BIZARRE SIGHT ✪

During the Thaipusam festivals held in Johor Bahru, Ipoh, Penang and Kuala Lumpur, you can see religious devotees pierce their skin with pikes and hooks, from which they hang milk pots, feather decorations and pictures of deities.

for Chinese New Year (firecracker anyone?) and the Hindu festival Thaipusam – notorious for its parade of devotees displaying some eye-wateringly painful, self-inflicted body piercings.

- In March the Sepang International Circuit resounds to the fuel-injected revs of Formula One's long-running Southeast Asian outing, the Malaysian Grand Prix.
- From May to June the competitors take to the waters at locations all over the peninsula for the Dragon Boat Festival, with the colourful spectacle best appreciated on the island of Penang.
- Parades and general festivities are par for the course during the National Day celebrations on 31 August; take a ringside seat for the action in the capital KL, then hang around for the city's annual shopping carnival in October.

LIFE-CHANGING EXPERIENCES

- Spending some time helping to monitor turtle landings, collecting eggs to transfer to hatcheries or releasing hatchlings at the Ma' Daerah Turtle Sanctuary.
- Taking a riverside bath with the resident elephants at the Kuala Gandah National Elephant Conservation Centre in Pahang.
- Watch the spectacular natural display of synchronised flashing from fireflies on the Selangor River.
- Catching your breath as you walk the skybridge spanning the void between the two Petronas Towers.
- Searching for a glimpse of the elusive Sumatran rhinoceros (not to mention the fabled 'big foot') in Endau-Rompin National Park.
- Digging into some delicious chicken wings, frog porridge or an amazing laksa at KL's bustling Jalan Alor hawker market.

RANDOM FACTS

- Malaysia is the first country in the world to have introduced passports embedded with microchips and biometric data.
- Over 60% of all software used by Malaysian businesses are reckoned to be illegal copies.
- Operating on a rotational cycle, each of Malaysia's nine sultans takes a turn as the country's head of state, serving as king for a five-year term (the current one is Sultan Mizan Zainal Abidin of the northeastern state of Terengganu).

HOT TOPIC OF THE DAY

- The need to improve both the standard of education and the reputation of Malaysia's universities – too many graduates are unable to find jobs.

– Simon Richmond

RAAN, NICARAGUA

POPULATION 314,000 ◎ **CAPITAL** BILWI (PUERTO CABEZAS) IS THE UNOFFICIAL REGIONAL CAPITAL ◎ **LANGUAGES** SPANISH, MISKITO, ENGLISH, SUMO-MAYANGNA ◎ **MAJOR INDUSTRIES** FISHING, TIMBER, MINING ◎ **UNIT OF CURRENCY** CÓRDOBA (C$) ◎ **COST INDEX** BOTTLE OF TOÑA BEER, C$14 (US$0.75); GUESTHOUSE TWIN ROOM PER NIGHT, C$120-400 (US$7-22)

THE WILD FRONTIER

The vast and rather untamed Región Autónoma del Atlántico Norte (RAAN) offers the hardy traveller a fabulous and adventurous contrast to the alluring but well-trodden western areas of Nicaragua. With a large indigenous population and a frontier feel – the Contra War landmines have largely disappeared, but the Colombian coke smugglers are still active – it's ripe ground for exploration, with great opportunities for off-the-beaten-track volunteering and ecotourism.

A REGION APART

This is part of La Mosquitía – the Mosquito Coast made famous by Paul Theroux and Harrison Ford, which takes its name from the Miskitos (although the biting insect also flourishes here) that live here, speaking their own tongue and living mostly from fishing and mining. Once ruled by Miskito kings under British protection, the region now has significant autonomy, with a separate judicial system. The land is largely indigenous-owned, and the various groups demarcate it for individual and community use. As well as the Miskitos, Sumo tribes live in remote upriver settlements, while the coastal population includes English-speaking Afro-Caribbeans.

WATER HIGHWAYS

Boats are the way to get around this largely flat region, which has large swathes of fairly impenetrable forest crisscrossed by hundreds of rivers that are essentially the region's roads. Houses rise on stilts to cope with the yearly floods. Most communities, especially those on the coast, get by on fishing as the waters are rich in prawns and lobster.

BOSAWÁS

The great jewel of the RAAN's interior is the Reserva de Biosfera Bosawás, a protected area that forms part of the Mesoamerican Biological Corridor, which theoretically will one day provide an unbroken chain of protected forest that will extend through the whole Central American isthmus. Accessing Bosawás isn't easy, and travel into the reserve is best done by river. The town of Wiwilí, on the Río Coco, is one entry point; there you can arrange boats and guides – definitely recommended in this zone, which still has landmines and antisocial characters left over from the Contra War. Another is San José de Bocay, from where you can access the semimythical caves of Belén de Tunowalan.

DEFINING EXPERIENCE

◎ Trying not to notice the water seeping into the Panga as you finish the last

REGIONAL FLAVOURS ✦

It wouldn't be the Caribbean without coconuts, and the local seafood is often exquisitely prepared. Look out for *rondón*, a delicious stew of fish or meat, but make sure no endangered turtles have been put in your lunch. *Gaubul* is a refreshing drink, blended from green banana and coconut milk.

4000 FISHERMAN, LOTS OF LOBSTER AND THE ODD
FLOATING BAG OF CONTRABAND COLUMBIAN COCAINE
– JUST ANOTHER DAY IN NICARAGUA'S MISKITO KEYS.

of the midday rum with your trusty fisherman, whom you hope is going to drop you safely off at some remote little island, where a local family's hammock, the lapping waters of the Caribbean, and the lobster you've caught today will be your rewards.

FESTIVALS & EVENTS

- The region's premier festival, King Pulanka, runs from 6 January to mid-February and commemorates the glory days of the Miskito kings; different communities compete in traditional dances and masked parades, and get plenty sloshed on *tualbi*, a fermented corn drink.
- Afro-Caribbean inhabitants celebrate the end of slavery on 28 August with Emancipation, a great party featuring exuberant dancing and gaudy floats.
- Día de la Hispanidad is a holiday on 12 October that's celebrated in style by the Spanish-speaking community, but is not particularly popular with the native Miskitos.

LIFE-CHANGING EXPERIENCES

- Volunteering in a remote Miskito or Sumo community; this is an untouched part of Central America that really needs the help.
- Persuading a lobster fisherman to take you in his rickety boat out to the fabulous Miskito Keys archipelago.
- Helping locals kick-start their communities and giving yourself a memorable adventure by making use of the primitive but well-meaning new ecotourism projects that are appearing in rural areas.

HOT TOPIC OF THE DAY

- The Sandinistas are back in power, but you won't find many people on the Río Coco who voted for them.

The infamous 'Red Christmas' of 1981 saw every town in the area razed by the Sandinistas in an attempt to forestall a pro-Somoza insurgency, creating thousands of refugees in the process. It hasn't been forgotten, so Ortega can't expect to be cut much slack here. Mind you, RAAN had big problems with the previous government too: calls for secession remain strong.

LOCAL LINGO

- While you'll get by OK with Spanish and English, many people speak only Miskito, a type of Creole with a fair smattering of Spanish- and English-derived words. Greet people with *naksa*, and if planning a hike in remote areas, the question *'danomite barsakei?'* asks about landmines. You'll be hoping to hear the answer *'apia'* (no)!

– Andy Symington

RÉUNION (FRANCE)

POPULATION 800,000 ☼ **VISITORS PER YEAR** 320,000 ☼ **CAPITAL** ST DENIS ☼ **LANGUAGE** FRENCH
☼ **UNIT OF CURRENCY** EURO (€) ☼ **COST INDEX** BOTTLE OF DODO BEER, €3 (US$4); CREOLE CURRY, €9 (US$12); HOTEL DOUBLE PER NIGHT, €40-80 (US$53-107); TANDEM FLIGHT PARAGLIDING IN ST-LEU €60 (US$80); CAR HIRE PER WEEK, €200 (US$267)

A VERY CHIK ISLAND

First, the bad news. Réunion faced a major health crisis in early 2006, a year which is considered an annus horribilis in the history of the island. The mosquito-borne Chikungunya virus hit this Indian Ocean island in late 2005 and by 2007 had infected about 266,000 people (almost one third of the population) since the outbreak of the epidemic. Chikungunya is named after a Swahili word meaning 'that which bends up', referring to the stooped posture of those affected. This crippling disease is not directly fatal but causes acute muscular and joint pain as well as high fever that can last several weeks, if not months. There's no vaccine or cure available. In reality, the whole region was hit, including Mauritius, the Seychelles, Comoros and Madagascar, but not on the same dramatic scale as Réunion.

Unsurprisingly, the epidemic had a negative impact on tourism in Réunion. Bookings were down by more than 60% in 2006 and early 2007.

BACK ON ITS FEET

Now, the good news. In an effort to kill off the problematic mosquito population, hundreds of people, including an array of army troops and firefighters, were mobilised and deployed on the island, spraying every potential risk zone with insecticide. Though not exactly environmentally friendly, this strategy paid off. By the middle of 2007 the 'Chik', as it's affectionately (well, almost) dubbed in Réunion, was eradicated, and the situation was considered to be back to normal, according to French health officials.

The time is ripe to (re)discover the phenomenal assets of this French island located between Madagascar and Mauritius. Réunion is home to several best-in-the-world experiences that very few people, aside from the French and a handful of travelati, know about.

Very few visitors have heard about its dramatic mountain terrain – so dramatic that Réunion was dubbed 'the Himalaya of the Indian Ocean'. 'The Hawaii of the southern hemisphere' would suit it fine too, with the Piton de la Fournaise (2632m) being one of the most active volcanoes in the world. This rumbling peak still pops its cork relatively frequently and in spectacular fashion, spewing lava down its southern and eastern flanks, and between eruptions it quietly steams and hisses away. A major eruption occurred in 2007, when lava flows reached the sea and added another few square metres to the island. The Réunionese are passionate about their volcano – and you will be, too.

HOT TIP

Take a helicopter or light aircraft tour of the magnificent cirques and the volcano to get an exhilarating and sensational view of the island's interior landscape. Most travellers rate such a trip as a highlight of their visit to Réunion.

AS IF LIVING ON AN ACTIVE VOLCANO WEREN'T
ENOUGH, RÉUNION HAS THREE CALDERAS
WITH FOLK LIVING IN THEM.

Outdoorsy types, take note: in 2007 part of the rugged interior was classified as a national park, which means increased opportunities and outdoor options on offer, including treks, abseiling and canyoning. Go now!

DEFINING EXPERIENCE

- Witnessing fiery-red molten lava flowing down to the shore and cascading into the ocean in the southeast – hair-raising!

FESTIVALS & EVENTS

- In January don't miss Mégavalanche, a thrilling mountain-bike descent on the flanks of the Le Maïdo.

- A week of cultural events focusing on Créole culture, Semaine Créole is held in October.

- Hinduism's answer to Christmas, Divali consists of several days of parades and presents in the main cities on the east coast of the island, home to an important Indian community. In 2008 Divali is in late October.

LIFE-CHANGING EXPERIENCES

- Pumping the adrenaline while abseiling in a canyon near Cilaos.

- Descending the steep Le Maïdo on a mountain bike at breakneck speed.

- Riding the left of St-Leu, one of the Indian Ocean's most thrilling waves.

HOT TOPIC OF THE DAY

- When is the next volcanic eruption? How close can we get to the lava flow?

RANDOM FACTS

- Réunion hosts one of the world's most challenging cross-country races, the Grand Raid. The pack leaders complete the 130km course in around 18 hours.

- The twisting inland road that connects the west coast to Cilaos has more than 400 hairpin bends.
  – *Jean-Bernard Carillet*

BLUELIST ONLINE

BY // SHEEN8R (507792)

» VOLCANIC VACATIONS: SUPER SOUPS, SUMMITS & SOUVENIRS

✪ FUEL UP FIRST

Some of the best food in Central America is cooked up in Antigua, Guatemala. Fuel up in the main plaza at Café Condessa, which serves amazing breakfasts and desserts. The Rainbow Reading Room (a restaurant/book store/internet café) has delicious lunches and dinners; try the thai coconut soup.

✪ IS THIS LEGAL…OR SAFE?

Shop around for an inexpensive guide that does group tours. The hike to Volcán Pacaya's rumbling crater takes about two sweaty hours. As you approach the choking lava spout, you might question the legality and safety of the whole matter. Don't worry…you're in Guatemala. Guides know escape routes down Pacaya's back side.

✪ A MOMENTO FOR MEMORIES

After the climb head to Chichicastenango, where Central America's largest indigenous market is the place to grab an elaborate bag, traditional poncho, or just some great photos. Watch your wallets, especially around friendly children. Don't be afraid to bargain, and remember that products tend to get cheaper towards the afternoon.

WWW.LONELYPLANET.COM/BLUELIST

TIWI ISLANDS, AUSTRALIA

POPULATION 2700 ◎ **VISITORS PER YEAR** 4000 ◎ **CAPITAL** NGUIU IS THE MAIN SETTLEMENT ◎ **LANGUAGE** TIWI ◎ **MAJOR INDUSTRIES** FORESTRY, FISHING, TOURISM ◎ **UNIT OF CURRENCY** AUSTRALIAN DOLLAR (A$) ◎ **COST INDEX** LITRE OF PETROL, A$2 (US$1.70); PIE & SAUCE, A$4 (US$3.40); BOTTLED WATER, A$3 (US$2.55); DAY TOUR, A$235-500 (US$200-425)

PUKUMANI POLES & GOAL POSTS

The Tiwi Islands – Bathurst and Melville – sit in a tight hug about 80km north of Darwin. Home to the culturally distinct Tiwi Aboriginal people, the islands embody the ancient culture and remoteness that fascinates people about Australia's Top End. But it's a unique interplay of the modern and traditional that draws visitors to this neck of Indigenous Australia. Art and football are unlikely bedfellows, but here they share an equal measure of talent and devotion. If you're lucky enough to visit, you'll be greeted with the sight of striking ironbark burial poles known as *pukumani* throughout the islands. These are one of the cornerstones of Tiwi culture. Along with bark paintings and ironbark sculptures, they are stained with natural ochre and have become synonymous with Tiwi art. Australian Rules Football may be a newcomer to Tiwi culture, but it's just as intrinsic as art. In the 60-odd years since the game was introduced it has become an outlet, opportunity and source of cultural pride, and the local lads have displayed the kind of innate talent only dreamed of on the mainland. In fact, some of the finest players in the national league herald from Melville and Bathurst Islands. They get plenty of practice: eight football teams and the sport's highest-participation level in Australia provides pretty fierce competition.

KEEPING THE CULTURE ALIVE & KICKING

Cultural enlightenment is reason enough to visit the Tiwi Islands, but the fact that you can only do so on a tour is the real kicker. Do we hear a protest from the fiercely independent voyager? Well, bear in mind that restricting visitors to tours is how the Tiwi people keep their home unadulterated: preserving cultural distinctiveness, traditional values and spirituality is far more important to this population than chasing the tourist buck. So why is now the time to get in on this bastion of Indigenous culture? Visitor numbers to the Northern Territory have exceeded the national average in recent years and further growth is on the menu. The maths gets pretty simple – more tourists getting in on the action means less seats on tours in the future.

DEFINING EXPERIENCE

◎ The Tiwi Grand Final, held at the end of March on Bathurst Island, is one of the highlights of the Northern Territory's annual events calendar. Every year thousands of spectators flood in from the mainland to watch the best of the Tiwis' sparkling skills and passion for football. If you can't make it to watch the islands' best two teams tough it

RANDOM FACT

Bathurst Island was the first point in Australia to be attacked by the Japanese in WWII. The Tiwi people played a vital role, capturing fallen Japanese pilots, rescuing allied pilots and guiding allied vessels through dangerous waters.

out for championship glory, then take in a match during the season, played from October to March.

FESTIVALS & EVENTS

- The Tiwi Grand Final is held at the end of March on Bathurst Island.
- The Tiwi Islands Annual Football Art Sale (yep, it coincides with the Tiwi Grand Final) is a huge family gathering and a rare opportunity for visitors to pick up a piece of Tiwi art at local prices.

LIFE-CHANGING EXPERIENCE

- The Australian Red Cross operates the Tiwi Islands Holiday Program twice a year in the settlements of Nguiu and Milikapiti, during which volunteers can spend two weeks working with the islands' youth. The aim is to alleviate the boredom local kids experience in between school terms, and volunteers engage in sport, craft, dancing and singing with them. The experience is

mutually beneficial and participants walk away with a deeper insight and appreciation of Tiwi culture than would be otherwise possible.

DEFINING DIFFERENCE

- As with all Aboriginal tribes, ceremonies are intrinsic to Tiwi culture. The two main ceremonial events performed here are the Kulama (yam) ceremony, and the Pukumani (burial) ceremony. The Kulama ceremony celebrates life and entails three days and nights of ritual singing, body painting, dancing and yam scoffing. The Pukumani ceremony is held six months after someone has died, and ensures the spirit goes from the living into the spirit world. The Tiwi believe that the dead person's existence in the living world continues until the completion of the ceremony, which culminates in the erection of a colossal ironbark *pukumani*.

– Justine Vaisutis

BLUELIST ONLINE

BY // SCOTTM_AT_LP (369821)

» SAYINGS YOU ONLY HEAR AT AN AUSSIE RULES MATCH

✪ CHEWIE ON YA BOOT!

This expression use to confuse me as a kid. Even as a five-year-old the physics didn't quite make sense. Could a piece of chewing gum on your boot make the ball stick, or at best deflect the ball from its intended goal? No, the magic is in the expression itself.

✪ BALL!

Only at an AFL match can you protest your displeasure with the umpiring by screaming the monosyllabic cry of 'Ball'. To the uninitiated this practice seems to only confirm beliefs that die-hard supporters lack any ability to put a sentence together and in the heat of excitement can only yell at the object the players are running after.

✪ MISS, MISS, COCKIES PISS

OK, maybe not so well known as other sayings but my family has a very successful history of making opponents miss goals with this chant. As a kid I assumed that Cockatoo urine must possess some mystical characteristics.

WWW.LONELYPLANET.COM/BLUELIST

APIA, SAMOA

POPULATION 40,000 ○ **VISITORS PER YEAR** 100,000 ○ **LANGUAGE** SAMOAN ○ **MAJOR INDUSTRIES** AGRICULTURE, TOURISM ○ **UNIT OF CURRENCY** SAMOAN TALA (ST) ○ **COST INDEX** 355ML BOTTLE OF DELICIOUS VAILIMA BEER, ST4 (US$1.50); HOTEL DOUBLE/DORM BED PER NIGHT, ST200/40 (US$75/15); SHORT TAXI RIDE, ST10 (US$3.80); INTERNET ACCESS PER HOUR, ST16 (US$6)

NOT TOO HARD. NOT TOO SOFT.

Samoa, with its laid-back, sleepy little capital city of Apia, is neither intensely touristy and resorty nor extraordinarily difficult and dangerous for travellers. You won't find Samoa crowded with thousands of tourists; nor are you going to have to get here by outrigger canoe, risking exotic jungle diseases while worrying from where the next coup is coming. Samoa lies somewhere in the middle of the Pacific Islands' tourism spectrum – interesting, singular and a bit off-beat, but still comfortable and fun.

GO LOCAL

The low-key, relaxed atmosphere of Apia encourages a similarly low-key travel itinerary. There's really no 'must see' destinations (and although locals will insist otherwise, the list of local 'highlights' is modest enough to remind you with a smile that this is no Disneyland or Queenstown). Instead, Apia rewards those who kick back, put down their camera and guidebook, and try to fit in. Spend your morning in church, or at sundown join the crowd sitting on the breakwater with a cool beer and takeaway food. At the local markets, instead of browsing the rows of carvings and T-shirts, *relax*: borrow a local newspaper, buy a plate of deep-fried goodies and sit down for a coffee in the 'locals' area. (Yeah, it's instant coffee, and it's baad, but it won't kill you just this once.)

DEFINING EXPERIENCE

○ Even if you're not a die-hard *Treasure Island* fan, it's worth taking a bus trip to Vailima, the grand old manor of Robert Louis Stevenson in the hills behind Apia. As brilliantly white as the starched clothes of a Samoan churchgoer, with a cheerily red roof and framed by the lush green of the surrounding hills, it's a handsome sight. If that view's not quite sufficient to take your breath away, the steep climb through verdant forest to the peak of Mt Vaea and Stevenson's tomb probably will. You can use the spectacular vista from the tomb – lush greenery, sprawling Apia township and the turquoise ocean beyond – as an excuse to rest for a long while before descending.

FESTIVALS & EVENTS

○ The long-running Marist Rugby Sevens competition sees local and international teams compete for the hotly contested

RANDOM FACT ★

There is no limit to team sizes in *kilikiti*, the Samoan version of cricket, so it's not unusual for a team of up to a hundred to play another of similar size.

DECKED OUT TO DANCE AT TEUILA FESTIVAL, AN EVENT INVENTED TO LURE TOURISTS THAT HAS BECOME A LOCAL FAVOURITE.

title at picturesque Apia Park. Taking place in late February, it's a very Samoan way to spend two days, and is loads of fun: it's hard not to enjoy the locals around you bursting suddenly and inexplicably into laughter several times a game.

- Samoa's independence from the ruthless Kiwi yoke of oppression is celebrated each year in early June; expect much feasting and dancing, and numerous sports events. (Kiwis are welcome.)

- The biggest festivities each year revolve around September's Teuila Festival, which features longboat and canoe races on the waters of Apia Harbour, dance competitions, food stalls loaded with local fare, games of *kilikiti* (Samoan cricket) and Samoan music.

RANDOM FACTS

- Renowned Scots novelist Robert Louis Stevenson died in Apia only five years after relocating here to recover from tuberculosis and generally poor health.

- Samoa (then called Western Samoa) was the first German territory to fall to the forces of Good King George in WWI.

- The Samoan moss spider, *Patu marplesi*, is hard to spot because it measures just 0.3mm and is the tiniest of the 35,000 species of spider currently known to exist.

BEST SHOPPING

- Apia's liveliest shopping experiences are to be found in the two markets: there's a level of bustle and noise that is almost un-Samoan in its busyness, but also plenty of quiet benches on which to sit and watch locals tackle the serious work of checkers or kava. Stock up on insanely colourful fabrics, a carved kava bowl of your own and a good, strong three-sided *kilikiti* bat, then finish off the shopping trip at the bookshop with Samoan-language copies of the local favourite *Treasure Island (O Le Motu O Oloa)* or the Bible *(O Le Tusi Paia)*.

CLASSIC PLACE TO STAY

- Fans of James Michener's *South Pacific* (or the Rodgers and Hammerstein version) should visit large, colonial Aggie Grey's Hotel on Apia's waterfront. It's Samoa's best-known hotel and one of the most famous in the entire Pacific. The late Aggie Grey – a famous local hamburger cook, hotelier and WWII entrepreneur – was the inspiration behind the Bloody Mary (though Michener stressed that 'only the good bits' came from Aggie). Even if you can't afford to stay, it's worth checking out the hotel's *fiafia* (dance performances) and feasts.

– Errol Hunt

BOLOGNA, ITALY

POPULATION 374,000 ✪ **VISITORS PER YEAR** 1.6 MILLION ✪ **LANGUAGE** ITALIAN ✪ **UNIT OF CURRENCY** EURO (€)
✪ **COST INDEX** CUP OF COFFEE, €0.90 (US$1.20); THREE-COURSE TRATTORIA DINNER, €20-35 (US$27-47); HOTEL DOUBLE/DORM
BED PER NIGHT, €110/16 (US$147/21); INTERNET ACCESS PER HOUR, €2 (US$2.65); MUSEUM ADMISSION, UP TO €4 (US$5.35)

SLOW FOOD FOR FAST TIMES

You'll need to leave your good intentions behind when you go to Bologna. Dubbed *la rossa, la grassa, la dotta* (the red, the fat, the wise), Italy's culinary capital is a city where calories add to the finger-licking fun and food fads are something that happen elsewhere. Yet, Bologna is far from trapped in its traditions. Its pristine medieval centre might scream history but its large student population and active gay scene ensure Italy's most cosmopolitan nightlife. And it's this mix of slow food and bright lights, of laid-back lunches and bohemian nights that's making Bologna one of Italy's hottest short-break destinations. That, and the fact that it's not Florence or Venice or Rome.

PORTICOES, PALAZZI & AN UNFINISHED CHURCH

Italy's heavyweight destinations have long held a virtual monopoly over the public imagination, but as European air fares continue to fall and the number of routes continues to rise, so the travelling public becomes ever-more adventurous. While Bologna isn't exactly off the beaten track, it's certainly less known than Italy's usual suspects.

Of course, there's more to Bologna than what it's not. The city boasts one of Italy's great medieval cityscapes – an eye-catching ensemble of red-brick *palazzi* (palaces), Renaissance towers and 40km of arcaded porticoes – and enough culture to excite without exhausting. Visit the world's largest unfinished basilica, Basilica di San Petronio, and Europe's oldest university; climb Torre degli Asinelli and admire frescoes in 15th-century churches, keeping just enough energy for a night on the tiles.

RED PASSIONS

La rossa (as much a political moniker as reference to Bologna's colourful buildings) has long had a reputation for left-wing militancy. Passions have cooled since students faced down tanks in 1977, but the city remains highly political. Italian PM Romano Prodi is from Bologna and the city is at the forefront of Italy's gay movement.

DEFINING EXPERIENCE

✪ Get in some people-watching on Piazza Maggiore and some deli-drooling in the picturesque alleyways of the Quadrilatero; climb the landmark Torre degli Asinelli, the straighter of Bologna's two leaning towers, and walk the animated arcades before an apéritif, some dinner and taking in a few late-night tunes in the orange university quarter.

FESTIVALS & EVENTS

✪ Solemn processions take to the city streets on the Saturday before the

HOT TOPIC OF THE DAY ✪

Students and takeaway owners are up in arms at a new law to cut down on boozing in the historic centre. Under the new edict, food shops and pizza takeaways are no longer allowed to sell alcohol for consumption off the premises between 10pm and 6am. The upshot is that a cheap beer on the piazza is no longer an alternative to the pub.

YES, THEY GAVE THE WORLD BOLOGNESE, BUT JUST LOOK WHAT THEY KEPT FOR THEMSELVES...

fifth Sunday after Easter (26 April 2008) and the following Wednesday and Sunday for the Celebrazioni della Madonna di San Luca, Bologna's main religious festival.

- From mid-May to earlyJune nearby Modena hosts Balsamico È, a series of exhibitions, events and tastings celebrating the city's famous vinegar.

- Techno, hip-hop, reggae and pop whip up the dance frenzy during the the Street Rave Parade in early July.

- Swing to a smoother beat during the Salotto del Jazz, a small-scale jazz fest organised by four venues in and around Via Mascarella. Concerts run from July to September.

RANDOM FACTS

- The world's longest portico, held aloft by 666 arches, connects a medieval gate in the southwest of the city to a hill-top sanctuary 3.5km away.

- Dating from 1088, Bologna's university is the oldest in Europe and the third oldest in the world.

- The clock at Bologna train station is stopped at 10:25am, the exact time that a bomb exploded on 2 August 1980, killing 85 people and injuring more than 200. Two Italian neofascists are today serving life sentences for the bombing.

CLASSIC RESTAURANT EXPERIENCE

- The full-on trattoria experience – think earthy, no-bullshit food, relaxed surroundings and a jovial host – is what Bologna does so well and exactly what you get at the Drogheria della Rosa on Via Cartoleria. Locals squeeze into this former pharmacy, its walls lined with wooden shelves, apothecary jars and bottles, to dine on Bolognese classics such as *tortellini in brodo* (stuffed pasta in broth) and sip on robust regional reds.

– Duncan Garwood

CHENGDU, CHINA

POPULATION 4 MILLION ✿ **VISITORS PER YEAR** 200,000 FOREIGNERS & SEVERAL MILLION DOMESTIC TRAVELLERS
✿ **LANGUAGE** MANDARIN CHINESE IF YOU'RE LUCKY, CONFOUNDING SICHUAN DIALECT IF YOU'RE NOT
✿ **UNIT OF CURRENCY** YUAN (Y) ✿ **COST INDEX** BOTTLE OF BEER, Y5 (US$0.65); DORM BED PER NIGHT, Y20 (US$2.60)

SLEEPY CHINESE BACKWATER GOES GLITZ

Long known for its laid-back locals and centuries-old teahouse culture, Chengdu is working on a second act as the dynamic, economic engine and cultural cornerstone of southwest China. Investment is pouring in (along with tens of thousands of people) and a construction boom is completely transforming the city; be sure to check out the futuristic new city-hall complex being thrown up south of town.

Whether you're looking for the traditional or modern face of China, Chengdu can rise to the challenge and makes 'now' one of the most exciting times to come take it all in.

'WELCOME TO MY CITY'

You'll be hearing that phrase a lot. Chengdu's mayor is pursuing the national 'Best Tourism City in China' award with a near religious fervour. He's had the city plastered with pro-tourism ads and in speeches and broadcasts has urged the population to learn English and help foreigners. The campaign has made Sichuan's capital one of the most traveller-friendly places in the country. Sleek, new red tourist buses run between the major sites, taxi drivers shyly try out English phrases, interesting new sights are constantly being developed and even the people who take your ticket are starting to smile and hand you your change instead of scowling and throwing it at you.

DEFINING EXPERIENCE

✿ Searing your tongue and crying for mercy (or just a glass of water) after tucking into one of Sichuan's classic chilli- and spice-laden disheshe not-to-be-found-anywhere-else taste combinations of this world-renowned cuisine are unforgettable and will eventually win you over – no matter how much it burned the first time around.

RECENT FAD

✿ Setting up your business here after getting fed up with high prices in Beijing and Shanghai.

FESTIVALS & EVENTS

✿ Chengdu's Lantern Festival lasts a month and starts during Chinese New Year celebrations (from the first to the 15th day of the first lunar month). Traditional paper and silk lanterns go up in certain city parks, and shows

RANDOM FACT ★

According to the principals of traditional Chinese medicine, Chengdu's trademark spicy foods combat people's 'internal dampness', which is believed to cause illness and be brought on by the city's humid and rainy weather.

featuring acrobats and Sichuan opera multiply throughout town.

LIFE-CHANGING EXPERIENCES

- Seeing the endangered giant panda up close. Whether you're five years old or pushing seventy-five, you'll turn into a drooling, cooing mess in front of these inexplicably captivating animals.
- Gossiping for hours amongst the locals in one of the city's numerous traditional teahouses.

WHAT'S HOT

- The nightlife. From freakily mammoth discos through to cool little clubs, Chengdu boasts the biggest and best selection in all of southwest China.

WHAT'S NOT

- Getting a taxi. On weekends it can take up to an hour to flag one down.

Locals gripe that the city has cut the number of cabs on the road despite the economic boom and the influx of people.

CLASSIC RESTAURANT EXPERIENCE

- Sichuan's snacks are legendary and eating them at Xiaohui Douhua, a neighbourhood restaurant on Xi Dajie, is a culinary thrill. Order like the regulars do (ie a *lot*) so as to sample as many flavours and textures as you possibly can. Don't head for home without trying the truly unforgettable sweet-and-spicy noodles or the exotic but exquisite ox throat with beef.

BEST SHOPPING

- Rub elbows with Buddhist monks at Chengdu's Tibetan market where you'll find anything and everything – from Tibetan clothing to cans of 'instant' yak-butter tea.

- Downtown's Qingshiqiao Market is the place to head for colour and bustle. Watch locals haggle over exotic plants, multicoloured songbirds and all manner of fish and household pets.

HOT TOPIC OF THE DAY

- The subway. Chengdu's first-ever massive, multilined subterranean transit system is slated to open in 2010, although a first line may be in operation as soon as 2008. The project is a huge source of local pride – the construction-caused traffic chaos isn't. Certain roads in and out of the city are sometimes open for as little as two hours per day (and the general public aren't necessarily warned ahead of time). Buses get cancelled at the last minute and many taxi drivers refuse trips to certain destinations for fear of getting stuck overnight on the city's outskirts.

– *Eilis Quinn*

CÓRDOBA, ARGENTINA

POPULATION 1.4 MILLION ☼ **LANGUAGE** SPANISH ☼ **UNIT OF CURRENCY** ARGENTINE PESO (AR$)
☼ **COST INDEX** CUP OF COFFEE, AR$3 (US$1); HOTEL DOUBLE PER NIGHT, FROM AR$45 (US$15); SOUVENIR T-SHIRT AR$12 (US$4); SHORT TAXI RIDE, AR$6 (US$2); INTERNET ACCESS PER HOUR, AR$2 (US$0.65)

STREETS AHEAD FOR CULTURE

There's no way you could call Córdoba a hidden gem. This is Argentina's second largest city, a place that has many of the charms of the capital and few of its drawbacks. Its long colonial history provides some stunning streetscapes and the large university population keeps the buzz on the streets lively.

Córdoba is the place to be for culture vultures. There's more contemporary art, independent film, theatre and live music going on here than you could possibly take in all on one trip. In recognition of this, Córdoba was named 'Cultural Center of the Americas' in 2006.

DEFINING EXPERIENCE

☼ After fuelling up on coffee and croissants at any of the excellent, hip little cafés around the Plaza San Martín, architecture nuts can easily fill a few hours taking in the glorious sights of Centro. If you're up for a movie, there's always an excellent selection of offbeat arthouse flicks at the Cine Teatro Córdoba, after which a stroll around the gorgeous French-designed Parque Sarmiento should clear your head. While you're down this way, don't miss the contemporary art on display at the Museo Caraffa. You'd better rest up at some point, though, because night time is when the city *really* comes alive, offering up everything from tango shows to reggae clubs to underground DJs. If you're a drinker you should try washing all this down with the city's favourite drink, Fernet. The aniseed spirit is usually mixed with coke and is guaranteed to give you a good night and a rough morning.

HOT TOPIC OF THE DAY ✪

FESTIVALS & EVENTS

☼ In early January the little town of Jesús María, just north of Córdoba, hosts the Festival Nacional de Doma y Folklore, a chance for jockeys and professional horse riders from all over the world to show off their skills.

☼ In late January the town of Cosquín, northwest of Córdoba, hosts the Festival Nacional de Folklore. It's a nine-day folk music extravaganza that has become an institution, featuring numerous established and emerging artists from all over the country and around the world.

☼ Catering to a slightly younger set than the folklore fun is Cosquín Rock, a festival held in mid-February. If you want to see how Argentines rock out, this is the place to be. Featured acts in the past have included Los Callejeros, Rata Blanca and Resistencia Suburbana.

The Festival Nacional de Doma y Folklore may keep the Argentine gaucho tradition alive, but animal rights activists call it cruel and inhumane – physically because riders often use whips and spurs, and psychologically because horses are made to perform complicated and dangerous feats in front of screaming crowds under harsh lights.

A CHANGE OF PACE FROM ALL THAT
...URE, HEAD FOR THE HILLS OF CÓRDOBA'S
...K YARD – UNPARALLELED PATAGONIA.

Córdoba is firmly placed on the World Rally Car circuit, and motorheads flock in every year in late April. In 2008 the rally is scheduled for 25 to 27 April.

LIFE-CHANGING EXPERIENCES

Going underground and checking out the maze of Jesuit crypts that run under the city centre.

Dancing the tango by starlight with hundreds of other couples on a Sunday night in the central Plaza San Martín.

Strolling beside La Cañada, a shady, café-lined stone canal that flows just a few blocks west of the Plaza San Martín.

RANDOM FACTS

After he was diagnosed as asthmatic, Che Guevara's family relocated to the cool, dry hill town of Alta Gracia, just out of Córdoba.

Córdoba is truly a university town: 12% of the population are students.

The Catholics are here, too, with 21 churches in the downtown area alone.

BEST SHOPPING

With so many students around, it's no surprise that there are plenty of outdoor markets around. The big bargains here are leather wares, hand-blown glass products, jewellery and ceramics. The following are some of the best regular markets:

Feria Artesanal – at Plaza Italia, Monday to Friday.

Feria Municipal de Artesanias y Manualidades – at Plaza Velez Sársfield, Wednesday to Saturday.

Feria Artesanal del Paseo de Las Artes – at the corner of Rodríguez and La Cañada, Saturday and Sunday afternoons.

– Lucas Vidgen

DAMASCUS, SYRIA

POPULATION 6 MILLION ✪ **VISITORS PER YEAR** WELL, I SAW A GUY IN SHORTS THE OTHER DAY, HE MUST'VE BEEN ONE... ✪ **LANGUAGE** ARABIC ✪ **UNIT OF CURRENCY** SYRIAN POUND (S£) ✪ **COST INDEX** BOTTLE OF LOCAL BEER, S£50 (US$1.00); BOTTLE OF IMPORTED WINE, S£400 (US$8); SHORT TAXI RIDE, S£40 (US$.80); HOTEL DOUBLE/DORM PER NIGHT, S£700/300 (US$14/6)

WHERE HAVE YOU BEEN?

Damascus is one of the world's oldest cities, although it looks nowhere near completion. In fact it just keeps collecting pieces of history, working whatever's new around what's left from previous eras. Historic sights aren't roped-off – you stumble upon them, such as the western gate of the 3rd-century Roman Temple Jupiter while you're shopping in Souq al-Hamidiyya. And in this enigmatic bazaar even the iron roof tells a story – those torchlight shafts of sunlight filtering through were made by French machine-gun fire in 1925. Even the sacred courtyard of the Umayyad Mosque, one of Islam's most significant, teems with activity. In Damascus, it's all happening on the streets. People make things and sell them. Spices are ground and sold from giant sacks, not little plastic packets. You want furniture? Get someone to make it for you. You need something special and the shopkeeper doesn't have it? He's probably already sent someone to get it from a guy he knows who does.

WE'VE BEEN HERE THE WHOLE TIME...

With Syria replacing Iraq (for obvious reasons) as a member of the 'axis of evil', Western tourists are thin on the ground. This is wonderful news for those who enjoy exploring a city without the telltale flags-in-the-air of tour groups. The World Heritage-listed Old City is a gem. It still retains the feel of a city of the 'Orient', with labyrinthine bazaars, narrow alleyways, medieval mosques and the echo of the muezzins' call to prayer.

HOT TOPIC OF THE DAY ✦

DEFINING EXPERIENCE

✪ Exploring the Old City: getting lost (easy to do) in Souq al-Hamidyya on your way to splendid Umayyad Mosque; inhaling the heady aromas of the spice souq; admiring Damascene architecture's stunning *tour de force*, Azem Palace; browsing the fascinating antique stores on Straight St en route to an Old City restaurant for lunch; and watching the dervishes whirl before a late supper at Elissar.

RECENT FAD

✪ Restoring Old City Damascene houses and opening boutique hotels. Locals are bemused by foreign visitors willing to pay up to a month's wages (in terms of local earnings) for a night at a hotel. That includes the approximately one million Iraqis who have made Syria their 'temporary' home, along with the 100,000-odd Lebanese who moved in during the summer of 2006.

Politics, always politics! The US speaker of the house and the EU foreign policy chief visited only weeks apart – is Syria coming in from the cold?

AT BAB AS-SAGHIR CEMETERY, DAMASCUS, IS THE 7TH-CENTURY TOMB OF MU'AWIYAH I, INSTIGATOR OF THE UNSTOPPABLE UMAYYAD DYNASTY THAT TOOK ISLAM TO THE WORLD.

FESTIVALS & EVENTS

- Islamic holidays (which move according to the Islamic calendar) are the time to visit – in the evenings the city comes alive.

- The Silk Road Festival (also held in other major Syrian cities) in late September celebrates Syria's long cultural history, with folkloric events, handicraft exhibitions and food festivals.

- Damascus International Film Festival, held in November and December every odd-numbered year, screens beautiful films from across the Arab world.

LIFE-CHANGING EXPERIENCES

- Axis of what? Syrians are some of the most hospitable people in the world. Be warned: accepting every invitation to take tea is a truly bladder-expanding experience.

WHAT'S HOT

- The opening of chic designer boutique Villa Moda on Straight St – it's leaving everyone wondering could this be the start of a Damascene renaissance?

WHAT'S NOT

- Some of the dubious 'restoration' in the Old City, as well as the ongoing lack of freedom of speech.

RANDOM FACTS

- While most assume Syria is an Islamic state, and the majority of Damascenes are indeed Sunni Muslims, it's a parliamentary republic of sorts.

- Syria's leader Bashar al-Assad is neither a Shia or Sunni but from the minority Alawite sect.

- Christians make up 10% of the population and a couple of hundred Jews live in Syria.

MOST BIZARRE SIGHT

- Women and their sheesha (waterpipe). Sure, women smoke sheesha in other Middle Eastern countries, but in Damascus they smoke it before, during and after meals, and often with a mouthful of food.

CLASSIC RESTAURANT EXPERIENCE

- Syrian cuisine is one of the most sophisticated in the world. Sample it at Elissar in a renovated old Damascene house. The place buzzes after 10pm when diners have taken their courtyard tables. Well-heeled locals happily puff sheesha between nibbling mezze and sipping arak, while an army of waiters work in sync to keep coals, food and drink refreshed. While the fine Syrian and French cuisine rarely springs surprises, the quality is sublime.

– Terry Carter & Lara Dunston

FEZ, MOROCCO

POPULATION 1 MILLION, OF WHOM 300,000 LIVE IN THE MEDINA ◎ **VISITORS PER YEAR** 340,000 ◎ **LANGUAGES** MOROCCAN ARABIC, FRENCH ◎ **MAJOR INDUSTRY** TOURISM ◎ **UNIT OF CURRENCY** MOROCCAN DIRHAM (DH) ◎ **COST INDEX** POT OF MINT TEA, DH5 (US$0.60); TAGINE, DH35 (US$4.20); GUIDE PER HALF DAY, DH200 (US$24); RIAD DOUBLE PER NIGHT, DH1000 (US$120)

SENSUAL FEZ

The medina of Fez is a sensual experience. Lying in a bowl of mountains to the northeast of the Ville Nouvelle, it's a journey back in time to an ancient city redolent with the sounds, sights and smells of a thousand years ago. Men hammer copper basins, donkeys plod down narrow streets, spice shops entice with heaps of cumin, coriander and turmeric, frankincense wafts around the tomb of the city's founder Moulay Idriss, and over it all, the muezzins sing out the call to prayer from 350 mosques. Down in the souqs, get out of the way when you hear 'balak!' – there could be an overburdened mule or a man with a cart of oranges. Step into the quiet of a 13th-century *medersa* (college) and gawp at the intricacy of carved plaster, massive cedarwood doors, finely worked wooden screens and elaborate mosaics.

TOURIST APPEAL

Morocco's tourism industry is booming. King Mohammed VI set a target of 10 million visitors by 2010; Fez expects a 10% to 15% increase in visitors in 2008. Plans are afoot to build large tourist facilities around the city, and, inside the medina, walking routes to promote spiritual tourism, with visits to saint's tombs and concerts of Sufi music.

DEFINING EXPERIENCE

◎ Venturing deep into the narrow alleyways of the medina, watched over by towering minarets bright with mosaics and arabesques, getting lost among the souqs selling everything from rose petals to camel's heads, kaftans and quail's eggs, then reclining on cushions in a pasha's palace to sample local cuisine, before retiring to the roof terrace of your riad to take in the views as the sun sets over the medina and the last call to prayer echoes across the city.

FESTIVALS & EVENTS

◎ In April the Fes Festival of Sufi Culture features debates, poetry readings and musical performances.

◎ April also sees chefs flocking to the city for the Fes Culinary Festival at Mokri Palace.

◎ Beginning the first Friday in June, the Fes Festival of World Sacred Music is a sublime celebration of world music.

◎ In September follow the Sufi brother-hoods deep into the medina during the Moussem of Moulay Idriss.

RECENT FAD ✪

Snapping up a riad or courtyard house for a song (from a little less than US$25,000).

In November the Jazz in Riads Festival features performances in traditional houses.

LIFE-CHANGING EXPERIENCES

Getting really clean in the hammam with the locals.

Breaking the fast in Ramadan with a bowl of *harira* (tomato soup), dates and hard-boiled eggs dipped in cumin.

WHAT'S HOT

Moroccan cooking lessons in a riad.

WHAT'S NOT

Odours from the city's tanneries.

MOROCCAN CUISINE

Fassi cuisine is renowned. Starters are a selection of subtly spiced cooked salads, or harira, a thick tomato soup with chickpeas and lamb. Next comes the pastilla, a pie stuffed with pigeon or chicken with almonds, sprinkled with sugar and cinnamon. Then there are tajines; whisk off the conical lid and taste chicken with preserved lemon, lamb with prunes or quails and quinces. Round off the experience with cinnamon-sprinkled sliced oranges and a glass of mint tea.

RANDOM FACTS

Today there are approximately 200 Jews living in Fez. Visit the Mellah, the old Jewish Quarter, to see its synagogue, cemetery and Andalusian architecture.

Having crossed the desert with camel-loads of silks and spices, weary merchants would stop at one of the 117 funduqs (caravanserais), stabling their beasts below and taking rooms around the balconies. There's a plan to renovate some of the funduqs to house craftsmen and cafés.

Many houses have huge cedar doors studded with nails and a stylised hand of Fatima that's intended to ward off the evil eye. Few windows on the outside keep the owner's wealth (and women) hidden from the curious.

BEST SHOPPING

Talaa Kebira and the souqs offer a wealth of souvenirs from dyed goatskin lamps to *babouches* (pointy-toed slippers) and jellabas, leather bags and carpets. Snap up a brass hand-of-Fatima doorknocker or a tasselled red fez. And remember, you're expected to bargain.

– Helen Ranger

MATSUYAMA, JAPAN

POPULATION 513,000 ⊙ **VISITORS PER YEAR** FOREIGN VISITORS ARE FEW AND FAR BETWEEN ⊙ **LANGUAGE** JAPANESE ⊙ **UNIT OF CURRENCY** JAPANESE YEN (¥) ⊙ **COST INDEX** ADMISSION TO MATSUYAMA-JŌ, ¥500 (US$4); HOSTEL DORM BED PER NIGHT, ¥3360 (US$27) BOWL OF SANUKI-UDON NOODLES; ¥400 (US$3.20); FINDING PEACE AND ENLIGHTENMENT, FREE

THE ORIGINAL TOURIST TRAIL

For over a millennium, *o-henrō* (pilgrims) have walked clockwise around Shi koku in the footsteps of the great Buddhist saint Kōbō Daishi (774 – 835), who achieved enlightenment on the island of his birth. Known as the '88 Sacred Temples of Shikoku', the 1400km journey is Japan's best-known pilgrimage and original tourist trail.

Before the publication of the first guidebook in 1685, pilgrims frequently disappeared forever in Shikoku's rugged and mountainous interior. Before the advent of modern conveniences such as weather forecasts, cellular phones and convenience stores, pilgrims frequently fell ill and perished along the journey. Nowadays, hardship is not a factor as *o-henrō* buzz around the island in air-conditioned vehicles while giving little thought to the trials and tribulations of the past. In recent years disenchantment with modern life has lead to an increase in the number of Japanese who strike out on foot in search of meaning and self-realisation.

LOST JAPAN

Like the rest of Japan, the provincial capital of Matsuyama is a land of contradic-tions – lightning-fast trains race alongside old ladies on bicycles while mountaintop shrines are illuminated by walls of vending machines. More than other destina-tions, however, Matsuyama serves up that elusive bit of lost Japan that that seems virtually absent everywhere else. The city is centred on Matsutyama-jō, one of the country's finest feudal-era castles, and is home to Dōgo Onsen Honkan, a storied public bathhouse, and Ishite-ji, one of the most famous temples on the pilgrimage. What's more, it's virtually undiscovered by foreigners, which means you may be the only *gaijin* (foreigner) around.

EXPLORING THE 88 TEMPLES OF SHIKOKU

If you have the time and the inclination, the best way to see and experience Shikoku is to journey around the 88 Sacred Temples. This is an opportunity to immerse yourself in old Japan, and to experience something utterly unique. The pilgrimage is considered nonsectarian, and some pilgrims aren't even Buddhists – just people in search of themselves. With the right attitude, the pilgrimage is as big an adventure today as it was in the past.

Allow 30 to 60 days if walking (de-pending on your fitness), two weeks to a month if you're on a bicycle and four to five days if making the circuit by motor-ised transport (though that would defeat the purpose of the visit).

RANDOM FACT

One point to remember: there are actually 89 temples. All pilgrims must travel back from Temple 88 to Temple 1 and complete the circle, for a circle is never-ending, just like the search for enlightenment.

DEFINING EXPERIENCE

⚙ After arriving in Matsuyama, wash your aching feet alongside other pilgrims in any of the historic foot baths that are scattered across the city. After 'wetting' your appetite for cleanliness, splurge on a first-class ticket to the Dōgo Onsen Honkan, which entitles you to a private relaxation room, a fine-cotton *yukata* (robe) and a post-bath snack of green tea and *dango* (sweet rice dumpling). Once you've washed away the hardships of being on the road, spend the afternoon climbing to the top of Matsuyama-jō, and praying with the Buddhist monks at Ishite-ji.

FESTIVALS & EVENTS

⚙ Making the circuit is in itself an event. As a foreign *o-henrō*, you will be viewed with equal parts awe and respect (and possibly a little suspicion), so don't be surprised if your arrival at some of the more rural temples causes a commotion. However, even if you don't speak Japanese, you'll be overwhelmed by local kindness.

⚙ Along the way remember to be respectful and to approach the journey with an open heart and mind. After all, in the words of Kōbō Daishi, 'Do not just walk in the footsteps of the men of old, seek what they sought'.

CLASSIC RESTAURANT EXPERIENCE

⚙ The island's most famous dish is *sanuki-udon*, a noodle renowned for its silky texture and *al dente* firmness. According to legend, udon was first brought to Shikoku from China in the 9th century by Kōbō Daishi himself. *Sanuki-udon* is traditionally served as *kake-udon* (noodles in hot soup), *zaru-udon* (cold noodles with dipping sauce) and *kama-age* (hot noodles with dipping sauce).

– Matt Firestone

MIAMI, USA

POPULATION 383,000 IN MIAMI; 90,000 IN MIAMI BEACH ✿ **VISITORS PER YEAR** OVER 10 MILLION ✿ **LANGUAGES** ENGLISH, SPANISH, HAITIAN CREOLE ✿ **UNIT OF CURRENCY** US DOLLAR (US$) ✿ **AVERAGE HIGH TEMPERATURE** AUGUST, 30°C; JANUARY, 23°C ✿ **COST INDEX** BOTTLE OF LOCAL BEER, US$5; GYROS IN SOBE, US$7; HOTEL DOUBLE/DORM BED PER NIGHT, US$145/24

BRINGING SEXY BACK

After simmering for years, Miami is totally hot through and through. Originally an Indian outpost ('Mayami' is Tequestan for 'sweet water'), the city has been turf to mobsters, rum-runners, and gamblers. Think...'Sexy Noir'. However, it was an adolescent then. Grown-up, built-up, and sexed-up, Miami has experienced its reckless youth. It ain't over it; it's just learned how to party right.

As the northern capital of the Latin world and the US gateway to Latin America and the Caribbean, Miami is really two cities. There's Thinking-Man's-Miami on the mainland, doing international finance and launching global design centres. Then there's Party-Girl-Miami Beach, getting tattooed, downing Mojitos, and shaking it 'til sun-up. Smart AND sexy? Yup, this tropical playground makes having a split personality hip. Call it Sexy Reinvented.

LOCATION, LOCATION, LOCATION

Miami's primo location – south enough to be eternally-warm, east enough to enjoy the Gulf Stream's sweet water and sweeter breezes – means adventure travel abounds: beyond the beaches you can see parasailers gliding past airboaters, deep-sea anglers and wreck divers. Back in town, restaurants and bars spill onto sidewalks, and world-class shopping abuts classier-still museums. Just wanna people-watch? Head to South Beach – excuse me, 'SoBe' – and you're guaranteed flesh...lots of flesh. Around here, bikinis, halters, and microskirts are for prudes.

It's not just real estate that makes Miami seductive. The 25- to 34-year-old demographic is the area's largest, and 67% of the population is Hispanic. Consequently, youthful Latin culture influences food (Mexican sushi anyone?), music (Latin rock bands aplenty) and attitudes (laid-back yet passionate). *Muy caliente*.

DEFINING EXPERIENCE

✿ Crossing from SoBe's pastel-drenched Art Deco District to Lummus Park Beach, the trendy place to catch rays, and seeing topless saline drones strutting past bronze beefcakes in banana hammocks.

FESTIVALS AND EVENTS

✿ Thump-thump with the planet's best DJs at the Winter Music Conference, the world's largest electronic music festival, spinning every March.

✿ During Carnival, the city shimmies-n-shakes for two hedonistic weeks,

RECENT FAD

Protests. Despite a reputation for superficiality, Miami speaks its mind. Students and janitors at the University of Miami recently staged sit-ins over poor benefits for cleaning crews, and farmworkers have started advocating for rights for illegal immigrants.

FOR CRUISING SOBE'S ART DECO DISTRICT LOOK NO FURTHER THAN A THREE-TONE '58 PACKARD – WITH WHITEWALL TYRES, OF COURSE.

culminating in a megaparade on that final October day.

- Each December Art Basel Miami Beach provides a dose of culture, mixing architecture, art, music and film.

- Ring out the year as the annual street parade, the King Mango Strut, syncopates (with kazoos and conch shells) for the Synchronized Briefcase Drill Team.

LIFE-CHANGING EXPERIENCES

- Swimming with frolicking dolphins at Miami Seaquarium.

- Sailing through the air with the greatest of ease at the Flying Trapeze School.

- Kayaking crystal-tipped waves along Key Biscayne.

RANDOM FACTS

- Only 26% of current residents were born in Florida.

- The first Burger King – known as Insta Burger King – opened here in 1954.

- Miami has seen snow once: 19 January 1977.

- Miami routinely ranks as the city with the worst road rage.

MOST BIZARRE SIGHT

- In Little Haiti the juxtaposition of ceramic Jesuses, life-sized voodoo priestesses and Little Haiti T-shirts will make you wonder if someone cast a spell on you.

CLASSIC RESTAURANT EXPERIENCE

- Afterglo's 'beauty cuisine' restores cellular health and reverses the effects of aging. Meals? Incredible. Staff? Informed. Plus, the first Saturday of every month features Erotic Party Night. With pole dancing, airbrush artists and fire twirlers, noshing nutritiously has never been so much fun.

BEST SHOPPING

- Into chain stores? Make a beeline to Lincoln Rd. Otherwise, Espanola Way has vibrant galleries and indie shops.

MOST UNUSUAL PLACE TO VISIT

- Jimbo's Place is a ramshackle bar fronting a lush bay. Cats, dogs and roosters dart among hipsters, models and bikers – all chugging $2 beers. Reportedly, squatters' rights have granted 80-year-old Jimbo ('The Friendliest Man on Earth') possession of the northeastern tip of Virginia Key and, despite the pleas from developers, the City refuses to kick him off.

HOT TOPIC OF THE DAY

- Affordable Housing. Attracting teachers and firefighters is tough, as Miami's cost of living is 38% higher than the national average.

– Willy Volk

MUMBAI, INDIA

POPULATION 17 MILLION ○ **LANGUAGE** ENGLISH, MARATHI, HINDI, GUJARATI ○ **UNIT OF CURRENCY** INDIAN RUPEE (RS)
○ **COST INDEX** LITRE OF BOTTLED WATER, RS12 (US$0.30); BOTTLE OF KINGFISHER BEER IN A BAR, RS80-120 (US$2-3); VADO-PAO
(FRIED POTATO FRITTER IN A SOFT ROLL WITH CHILLI-GARLIC CHUTNEY), RS30 (US$0.75); INTERNET ACCESS PER HOUR, RS30 (US$0.75)

A MANIC TEST OF YOUR TRAVELLER'S METTLE

Noisy, frantic, crowded and not for the faint-hearted, Mumbai has long been, to travellers at least, a city only Mother India could love. The City of Dreams has just been a gateway for many visitors on their way to somewhere just a bit calmer.

The business and Bollywood capital of the country has long been a city of contrasts, with some of the world's most expensive property sitting side-by-side with the world's most crowded slums. Growing economic strength and an expanding middle class has seen the city become noted for its sleek shopping, gourmet dining and swanky bars as much for grand colonial architecture including Chhatrapati Shivaji Terminus (the old Victoria Terminus, now commonly referred to as CST), the University of Mumbai, the High Court and an array of bazaars and temples.

With the film of *Shantaram*, Gregory David Roberts' epic novel set in the city, touted for release this year, Mumbai is set to reclaim the world's attention. Visit now for an experience as enthralling as any blockbuster.

DEFINING EXPERIENCE

○ People-watching at the Gateway of India before catching a boat to Elephanta Island to admire the ornate temple carvings; spending an afternoon watching cricket on Oval Maidan, backed by grand colonial architecture; strolling along the elegant curve of Marine Drive to Chowpatty beach at sunset and joining crowds of Mumbaiker families sharing *bhelpuri* – crisp, fried, thin rounds of dough mixed with puffed rice, fried lentils, lemon juice, chopped onion, herbs and chutney; and

finally sipping champagne cocktails at Dome, on the roof of the Intercontinental, and rubbing shoulders with the latest Bollywood stars.

FESTIVALS & EVENTS

○ Banganga Festival is a classical music festival held over two days early in January at the Banganga Tank on Malabar Hill.

○ Mumbai Festival celebrates the city's array of food, shopping and culture throughout January and includes cooking courses by some of the city's best chefs.

○ Pull out your best outfit for the Indian Derby held at Mahalaxmi Racecourse in February: it's the highlight of the racing year.

○ The Mumbai International Film Festival (MIFF) features short, documentary and animation films and provides a counterpoint to the city's usual chaotic offering; in 2008 the week-long festival starts on 3 February.

HOT TOPIC OF THE DAY ✪

Cricket and Bollywood, Bollywood and cricket, along with the new hottest bars, the eye-watering price of real estate, and traffic congestion and ambitious plans to combat it.

◌ Join millions for Mumbai's biggest festival, Ganesh Chaturthi, a celebration of the elephant-headed Hindu deity, which sweeps up the city for 10 days in August. Families gather in force to dunk their own Ganesh statues in the sea off Chowpatty Beach.

LIFE-CHANGING EXPERIENCES

◌ A visit isn't everyone's cup of chai, but finding out more about the people who live in the Dharavi slum gives a taste of another side to Mumbai life.

◌ Appearing in a Bollywood film as an extra, even if only for a split second, or learning the soundtrack by heart so you can sing along to the very latest hit.

RANDOM FACTS

◌ Daily commuter traffic passing through CST: 2.5 million people.

◌ Percentage of people living in slums: 55%.

◌ Number of Bollywood movies made since 1931: 67,000.

◌ Population density: 29,000 people per square kilometre.

◌ Proportion of Mumbai built on reclaimed land: 60%.

MOST BIZARRE SIGHT

◌ *Dhaba-wallahs* (lunchbox couriers) weaving through the chaos to deliver around 200,000 meals a day from homes to hungry office workers, using a sophisticated system of numbers and colours to distinguish the tiffin boxes.

CLASSIC RESTAURANT EXPERIENCE

◌ Bring a hearty appetite and discerning palate. Try Trishna for unfeasibly tasty seafood, Khyber for self-confident North Indian dishes, or enjoy creative European at atmospheric Indigo.

BEST SHOPPING

◌ Colaba Causeway is lined with a succession of stalls selling film pin-up posters, clothes and jewellery. Try Crawford Market for spices, fresh fruits and vegetables, Chor Bazaar for antiques and curios, Kemp's Corner for discount designer wear and Mangaldas Market for fabrics and silks.

CLASSIC PLACE TO STAY

◌ Most travellers will head for the many guesthouses in Colaba or more-up-market hotels near Juhu Beach. But no matter what your budget, it's worth taking a wander through the stunning lobby of the Moorish and Renaissance mix of the Taj Mahal Palace & Tower, imagining which room you'd pick and with whom you'd be staying.

– Sam Trafford

PUNTA DEL DIABLO, URUGUAY

POPULATION 650 ○ **VISITORS PER YEAR** BETWEEN 30,000 AND 50,000 ○ **LANGUAGE** SPANISH ○ **UNIT OF CURRENCY** URUGUAYAN PESO (UR$) ○ **COST INDEX** CUP OF COFFEE, UR$25 (US$1); HORSEBACK TOUR PER HOUR, UR$125 (US$5); SURFBOARD HIRE PER HOUR, UR$100 (US$4); INTERNET ACCESS PER HOUR, UR$50 (US$2)

THE OTHER PUNTA

Stuck way out near the Brazilian border, Punta del Diablo is indeed a wild place. A sleepy fishing village for most of the year, its sandy roads and tumbledown shacks are about as far as you can get from the bright lights and sophistication of Montevideo, in every possible way.

Not to be confused with the hedonistic Punta del Este to the west, *this* Punta has long been a favourite for vacationing Uruguayans looking to avoid the excesses of Uruguay's other coastal resort towns.

Like nearly all of Uruguay, Punta del Diablo is just starting to register on foreign visitors' radars. There's precious little development here, and certainly no high-rise hotels or resorts. The number of hotels can, in fact, be counted on one hand – most visitors come for a week or more and rent out a cabin, which can be anything from a humble fishing shack to an all-out luxury pad.

DEFINING EXPERIENCE

○ Grabbing a coffee and some croissants at any of the cute little cafés around town, then making your way down to the beach where you can pick your way around the rocky points while watching the waves crashing and the local fishermen hauling in the catch of the day that might just end up on your lunch plate. Come afternoon, it's time for a horseback tour out to the Parque Nacional Santa Teresa and its Portuguese-constructed fort, then heading back in town to enjoy more seafood from the dinner menu before hitting one of the little low-key bars or, if you want to keep it really real, follow the locals down to the beach for some star-gazing around a bonfire.

RECENT FAD

○ Uruguayan nature lovers have long been drawn by the natural charms of this area, and it's making its way onto the international map for the same reason – the big attractions here being Cabo Polonio, Laguna Negra and the Bosque de Ombúes, as well as the chance to watch the whales and birdlife.

FESTIVALS & EVENTS

○ Carnaval, celebrated in the week before Ash Wednesday (the first week of February in 2008), sees the normally sleepy streets of Punta del Diablo come alive with drummers, processions and scantily clad dancers.

○ Whale-watching season (July to November) is a chilly time to be at the

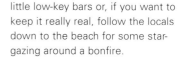

BEST SHOPPING

Calle de los Artesanos (Craft St) is a great place to pick up some locally made souvenirs any time of year, while in January and February artisans come from all over Uruguay and neighbouring Brazil and Argentina to display their wares.

beach, but worth it to catch a glimpse of one of these amazing animals.

LIFE-CHANGING EXPERIENCES

- Renting a surfboard and getting in the green room anywhere along the 10km coastline.

- Cruising the beach or going further afield – on horseback.

- Cozying up around a wood stove in the quiet winter months.

- Grabbing a line and tackle and heading down to the rocks to haul in a shark.

CLASSIC RESTAURANT EXPERIENCE

- Los Varales, perched on the hill overlooking the bay, is one of the best places to eat in town, with a great selection of truly fresh seafood, an atmosphere that's rustic and yet refined, but best of all are the excellent sweeping views looking out over the water.

CLASSIC PLACE TO STAY

- Hotel La Posada sums up all that is good about Punta del Diablo – the rooms are decorated in a beachy theme with plenty of seashells and driftwood scattered around. Paying a little more gets you one at the front, with big picture windows and panoramic views of the surf crashing below.

HOT TOPIC OF THE DAY

- Punta del Diablo – like many towns along this stretch of coastline – is caught up in the debate between development and heritage. Part of the town's charm is the fact that it's a rustic little fishing village, and locals argue that by 'beautifying' the area – tearing down little beachside fishing shacks to make way for more formal, modern structures – developers are actually doing away with one of the region's greatest attractions.

– Lucas Vidgen

BLUELIST ONLINE

BY // SHD (432629)

» MORE SOUTH AMERICAN JEWELS

✪ IS THERE A BETTER SIDE FOR A VIEW OF IGUAÇU?

The question: which side of the Iguaçu Falls should I visit? The answer: both. It's a small trip to make so you can see the panoramic beauty from both Brazil and Argentina. But beware the Brazilian coatis - they are amusing little food-jackers.

✪ BY FOOT, BUS OR DONKEY – HOW YOU SEE PERU IS UP TO YOU

Huaraz, Machu Picchu, the Amazon rainforest and unpredictable terrain; amazing people and kindness; guinea pigs and, of course, chickens. These are just some of the things Peru is made up of. The gateway to staying with an Amazonian tribe is Lima.

✪ SAMPLE SAMBA & SONG, BRAZILIAN STYLE

Rio is where the greatest show on earth meets the colours of the rainbow; where rattles, drums, whistles and flute fanfare keep you dancing through the night and across the beach by day. It's a city that inspires, energises, revives and loves life.

WWW.LONELYPLANET.COM/BLUELIST

THESSALONIKI, GREECE

POPULATION 608,000 ✪ **VISITORS PER YEAR** 1 MILLION ✪ **LANGUAGE** GREEK ✪ **UNIT OF CURRENCY** EURO (€)
✪ **COST INDEX** BOTTLE OF MYTHOS (LOCAL PILSNER), €3 (US$4); SOUVLAKI GYROS, €2 (US$2.65); FRAPPÉ (ICED COFFEE), €2 (US$2.65); HOTEL DOUBLE PER NIGHT, €60-150 (US$80-200); INTERNET ACCESS PER HOUR, €3 (US$4)

SECOND FIDDLE, FIRST RATE

By rights, Thessaloniki should have an inferiority complex. It just never gets top billing: it's regarded as little brother to Greece's sprawling capital, Athens, and during the Byzantine centuries was a poor cousin to imperial Constantinople. However, the locals are much too busy enjoying life to feel inadequate. Theirs is a spirited, energetic, forward-looking city (known affectionately as 'Thess'), a place with an urban vibe that effortlessly mixes venerable history with contemporary *joie de vivre*. Besides which, Salonikans know that their city is the cultural heart of Greece: it is the gateway to Mt Athos, the spiritual home of the Greek Orthodox Church, and was the birthplace of *rembetika*, the Greek musical equivalent of the blues.

GREEK BLUES – NOT HERE

In the 1920s Greek refugees from Anatolia created *rembetika* in the bordellos and hash dens of Thess. Their anguish fuelled a new musical idiom. You'll still hear the plaintive wail of bouzouki in many a Thess tavern of an evening, but melancholy has been replaced with an all-night exuberance enhanced by the largest student population in Greece, creating a nightlife that attracts dedicated partygoers from across Europe.

MEDITERRANEAN BLEND

Poised midway between Rome and Istanbul, Thess is one of those most clichéd of cities: a meeting point between continents. It once was home to large Turkish, Slav and Jewish communities, and even now wears its entrepôt status with ease while still managing to exhibit a potpourri of Mediterranean influences: Roman ruins can be seen protruding casually from Plateia Dikastirion, the verdant orange trees are reminiscent of Seville, the Ottoman *bedesten* are like a miniature Istanbul bazaar, and the elegant waterfront apartment buildings call to mind Nice.

DEFINING EXPERIENCE

✪ Wandering the Ottoman streets and enjoying the view from the Kastra neighbourhood, absorbing the Sephardic atmosphere of Molho bookshop, pondering icons in any of the Byzantine churches, heading for the White Tower on your evening waterfront promenade, then lighting out for *mezedes* (appetisers), ouzo and *rembetika* until sunrise.

RECENT FAD

✪ Thessaloniki doesn't have fads, just timeless pleasures. The day in Thess is unhurried: morning starts slowly, lunch

MOST BIZARRE SIGHT ✱

A museum devoted to Mustafa Kemal Atatürk, founder of modern Turkey – yes, in Thess. He was born in a house here in Apostolou Pavlou St in 1881.

FROM BIBLICAL MENTIONS TO BYZANTINE CHURCHES, CHRISTIANITY AND ITS ICONS HOLD HIGH OFFICE IN GREECE'S SECOND-LARGEST CITY.

is extended and convivial, and the *de rigueur* event for the evening is the promenade – an opportunity to see, be seen and catch up on gossip.

FESTIVALS & EVENTS

- The Thessaloniki Documentary Festival was conceived in 1999 as a way to document a new millennium of film making. It focuses on cultural and political films from across Europe and takes place in March.

- The Open Theatre Festival from June to September features ancient drama, European theatre and contemporary Greek plays in the Garden Theatre.

- The biggest event in the Thess calendar, the Dimitria Festival, named after Dimitri, the patron saint of the city, offers music, theatre and dance at venues throughout town from September to December.

- The Thessaloniki International Film Festival is held in November and is

the biggest film festival in southeastern Europe, highlighting the work of new and upcoming auteurs from the region.

LIFE-CHANGING EXPERIENCES

- Forgetting the Greek clichés of overtouristed islands and twee blue-and-white tablecloths – Thess shows the urbane and spontaneous side of Greek life.

- Fuelling an all-night tavern crawl with ouzo and listening to the music of the bouzouki.

- Traipsing out to the home of the Greek Orthodox church at Mt Athos (very sorry ladies, but this is a male-only activity).

RANDOM FACTS

- In some neighbourhoods you can still hear Ladino, the dialect of Spanish Jews, who were expelled from Spain in 1492.

- Isaac Carasso, who perfected the first industrial process for making yoghurt, was born in Thessaloniki in 1874.

CLASSIC RESTAURANT EXPERIENCE

- Don't pick just one place: head to the Ladadika district and take yourself on a tavern crawl, picking choice *mezedes* – pickled octopus here, stuffed peppers there, ouzo here, retsina there. *Kali orexi!*

HOT TOPICS OF THE DAY

- Thessaloniki bid for the 2008 World EXPO, but was pipped by Zaragoza. Ever optimistic, Thess is planning a bid for 2017.

- Will Thess have to stop partying all night? The Research Centre for Sleep in Athens says that Greeks are sleeping less than ever, and suffering for it.

– Chris Deliso

VIENNA, AUSTRIA

POPULATION 1.64 MILLION ○ **VISITORS PER YEAR** AROUND 4 MILLION ○ **LANGUAGE** GERMAN
○ **UNIT OF CURRENCY** EURO (€) ○ **COST INDEX** MELANGE COFFEE, €3 (US$4); WÜRSTELSTAND SAUSAGE, €3.20 (US$4.25); BOX OF MOZART KÜGELN (MARZIPAN CHOCOLATES), €7.50 (US$10); OPERA TICKET, €2-254 (US$2.65-337); U-BAHN TICKET, €1.50 (US$2)

IF IT AIN'T BAROQUE...

Poor Vienna. Caught like a fly in the amber of its self-created image – prancing horses, prepubescent choristers and simpering debutantes – for years it's been one of Europe's least fashionable city destinations. You won't hear the city fathers tearing their beards in despair over this – the Vienna Tourist Board's strict adherence to cliché make the city a favourite of Europe-in-Twelve-Days tour groups from around the world (and, it sometimes seems, beyond).

MORE THAN JUST SCHNITZEL

There's an undeniable fascination to a city that was once the centre of its known universe, where there still hangs in the air a slightly bemused breath of glory lost. But in the last few years a less dusty, more vigorous Vienna has begun to shake itself free from the heavy hand of the Habsburg legacy, and a younger, edgier city has emerged. The gallery complex MuseumsQuartier, opened in 2001, has established itself firmly as Vienna's cultural heart. Bold building projects such as Günther Domenig's T-Center show that the city isn't scared to take risks with modern architecture. And the Danube Canal, its banks a continually growing strip of bars and clubs, is the new flocking ground for hip young things. Old-fashioned, staid, a bit of a fuddy-duddy? We're here to tell you, Vienna is cool.

DEFINING EXPERIENCE

○ Skipping the big-ticket attractions of pogoing ponies and early Sunday morning adolescent sing-alongs and enjoying an anti-Vienna Viennese break: avoiding the baroque excesses of the Hofburg and Schönbrunn and tracking down Art Nouveau oddities out in the suburbs; forgetting schnitzel, as Vienna now has its own Michelin guide and options abound for trying 'new Austrian' cuisine; denying yourself the dirndl-shopping and instead trawling the side streets of the Innere Stadt for local designer boutiques; and foregoing Bach at the Staatsoper and heading for Flex to sample Vienna's thriving electronica scene.

FESTIVALS & EVENTS

○ All football eyes will be on Vienna as it cohosts Euro 2008. For the final on 29 June hordes of hyped-up, hopped-up followers will turn the city into one gigantic party. As German cities did during the FIFA World Cup in 2006, Vienna will feel like the centre of the universe.

○ Some 2000 performers, 22 stages, a massive festival area and zero admission cost all add up to make

RANDOM FACT ★

Vienna grows more wine within its boundaries than any other city in the world – you can taste it in the *Heurigen* (wine taverns) on the city's hilly outskirts.

PARTY TIME FOR THE SHARP END OF THE ARTISTIC AVANT-GARDE, VIENNA'S BALL SEASON IS ANYTHING BUT A SLOW WALTZ.

Donauinselfest (Danube Island Festival, 13–15 June) one of Europe's best open-air parties.

⚬ Kitsch gifts, hot mugs of *Glühwein* (mulled wine) and piles of *Kartoffelpuffer* (potato pancakes) – what's not to like? Vienna's legendary *Christkindlmärkte* run from mid-November to just after Christmas.

MOST BIZARRE SIGHT

⚬ It's a cliché, but one you can still see in Vienna today: a man in Tyrolean hat (complete with feather), green hunting jacket, lederhosen and knee-high socks, strolling down a street lined with international chainstores and mobile-chattering teenagers.

WHAT'S HOT

⚬ Support for the Green Party grows like weeds – in one Viennese district, Neubau, they hold over 40% of the state electoral vote. Not bad going

for the capital of a country that not so long ago had a suspected war criminal as president.

WHAT'S NOT

⚬ Vienna's mild-mannered bourgeoisie were finally driven to the streets recently by…dog poo. In all some 157,000 signatures were gathered in an attempt to force city officials to clean up the shit-strewn footpaths. The slogan, *Wien ist ein Hundeklo* (Vienna is a Dog's Toilet), rang sadly true – but as yet, nothing has been done to save residents from their nerve-racking evening strolls.

RANDOM FACTS

⚬ Six *Flaktürme* – monolithic, impervious defenses against air attacks – remain standing in Vienna. One of these WWII dinosaurs now houses, in an uncharacteristically whimsical gesture, an aquarium.

⚬ The Viennese fascination with death is evident in museums dedicated to undertaking, violent criminals, human anatomy, medical history – and not forgetting the new Museum of Contraception & Abortion – just to name a few. You have to wonder what native son Sigmund Freud would make of all this…

CLASSIC RESTAURANT EXPERIENCE

⚬ It's not a restaurant, not by a long shot. But the quintessential Viennese food experience is to prop up a traditional *Würstelstand* at the end – or in the middle – of a night out, take your pick from a dozen varieties of sausage, and ask for some ketchup to go with the *Senf* (mustard). Maybe grab a beer to wash it all down. Sometimes, tradition is best.

– Janine Eberle

GOLIST. » DESTINATIONS

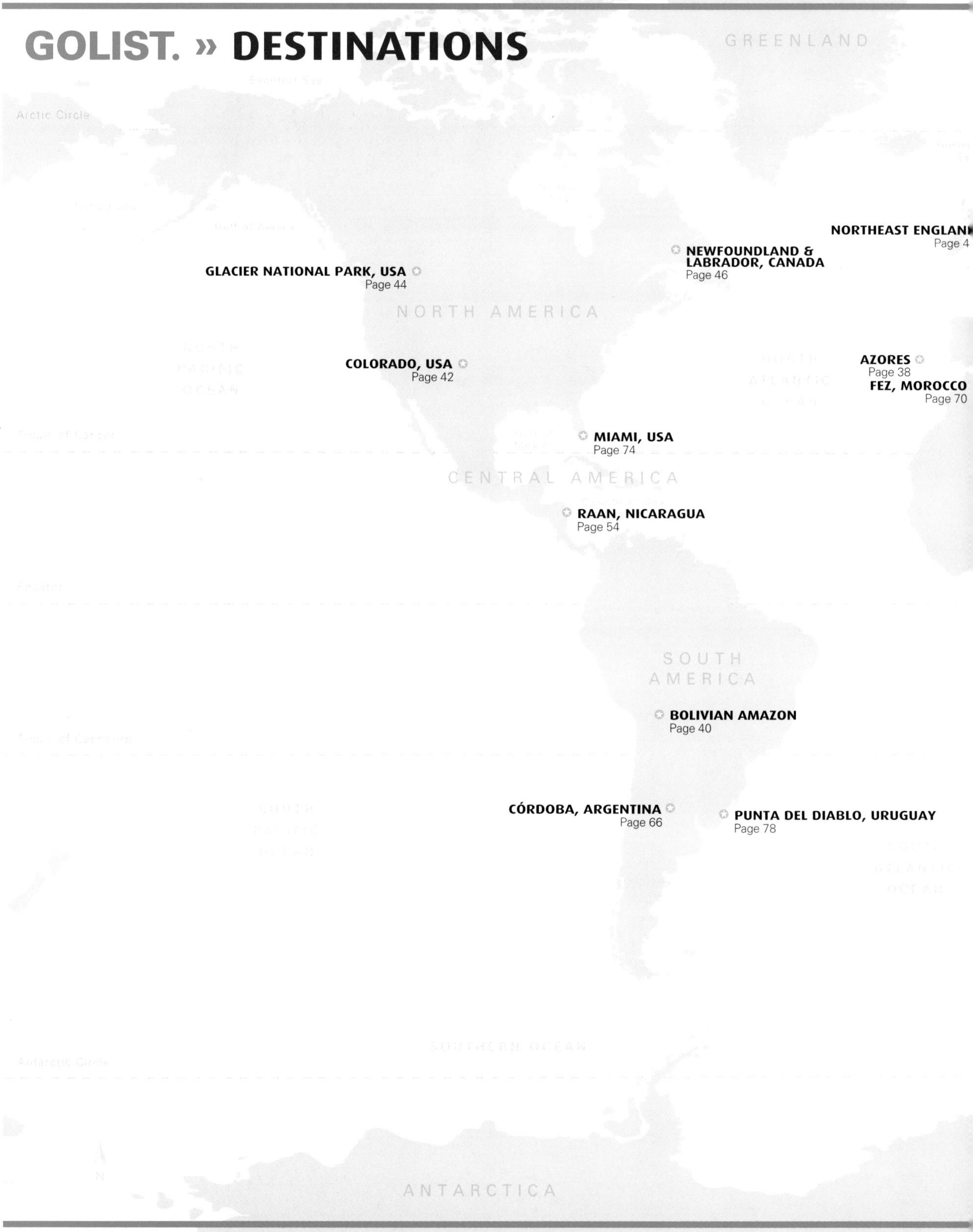
GREENLAND
Arctic Circle
NORTHEAST ENGLAND
Page 4
NEWFOUNDLAND & LABRADOR, CANADA
Page 46
GLACIER NATIONAL PARK, USA
Page 44
NORTH AMERICA
NORTH PACIFIC OCEAN
COLORADO, USA
Page 42
AZORES
Page 38
FEZ, MOROCCO
Page 70
MIAMI, USA
Page 74
CENTRAL AMERICA
RAAN, NICARAGUA
Page 54
SOUTH AMERICA
BOLIVIAN AMAZON
Page 40
CÓRDOBA, ARGENTINA
Page 66
PUNTA DEL DIABLO, URUGUAY
Page 78
SOUTHERN OCEAN
Antarctic Circle
ANTARCTICA

2008 TRAVEL THEMES

EACH YEAR, OUR THEMES SECTION ZOOMS IN ON INTERESTING APPROACHES TO TRAVEL. TAKE THE PLUNGE IN 2008 AND IMMERSE YOURSELF IN IDEAS BOUNCING AROUND AMONG THE DIE-HARD TRAVELLERS AT LONELY PLANET.

travel Isl

A JOURNEY THROUGH THE CULTURES & COUNTRIES OF THE ISLAMIC WORLD »

destination *Islam*

LOOK AGAIN

In the 19th century, when Victor Hugo described the whole of Europe as 'leaning towards the East', the Islamic Orient was considered the only destination of merit. It attracted travellers of all kinds – scientists, adventurers, aesthetes…and some perfect fools. These intrepid Europeans described countless exotic journeys, from pleasure cruises up the mighty Nile to camel-back treks across the stony plains of the Syrian desert. They also related tall tales, from Nile crocodiles that avoided eating Christians to Arabian ostriches that used their tail feathers as sun shades. Then, as now, to stay at home meant never knowing quite what to believe.

Travellers are an inquisitive lot who seek to use personal experiences to decide for themselves what's true and what's not. Turn on a TV or open a newspaper and you're bound to encounter caricatures that have been bandied around until they've asumed the guise of truth, and reports that seem designed to whip up public support for one cause or another.

Travel is a great way to debunk these myths and stereotypes. Given the current global and regional tensions, now's as good time a time as any to promote a reality check.

A visit to the Islamic world can be as rewarding today as it was 700 years ago, when Marco Polo roamed its realm from the ancient trails of the Silk Road to the busy ports of Sumatra. Its culture is vibrant and visible far beyond the boundaries of the nations that consider themselves Islamic. And with the hajj, or pilgrimage, as one of Islam's governing principles, travellers have an instant point of reference: they will be among people who know all about travel. From the cradle, Muslims are brought up to think of life as a spiritual journey, and throughout that life are looking forward to, planning, saving for and finally undertaking the big trip to Mecca.

A GLOBAL CULTURE

Hear the words 'Islamic world' and for many the Middle East springs to mind. This is hardly surprising, given that the region gave rise to Islam and is home to its holiest shrines. What may be more surprising is that the Arab heartland is but a relatively small part of the Islamic world. Today, some 50 countries, from Morocco to the Maldives, have predominantly Muslim populations.

Islam has also travelled slowly but surely into the heartland of its old rival, Christendom. It is now the fastest growing religion in many western countries, and there are large second-generation immigrant communities located throughout Europe, North America and Australia.

Thanks, or at least owing, to Borat Sagdiyev, the controversial faux journalist purportedly from Kazakhstan, there is a greater awareness that Islam has travelled east as well as west. In fact, Islam can be found in all the former 'stans' (Kyrgyzstan, Tajikistan, Turkmenistan, Uzbekistan) and as far east as China and Indonesia.

In addition to the living breadth of Islamic culture across the globe, there is also a strong Islamic legacy in non-Islamic lands. From the spice coasts of East Africa and Zanzibar, to the exquisite Moorish cities of Andalucía in Spain, the crescent still lingers over the horizon. Travellers are as likely to gain a sense of Islamic culture contemplating the symmetry of design at the gardens of the Alhambra in Spain's Granada as they are viewing the mosques, madrassas and minarets in Morocco, just over the Strait of Gibraltar.

countries of the crescent

While the crescent predates Islam, it has been the religion's principal symbol since 1453, when the Ottomans conquered Constantinople and adopted what was one of the city's enduring symbols. The moon is of great importance to Islamic countries as the Islamic calendar is based on the lunar cycle. The timing of Islam's two great festivals, marking the end of Ramadan and the culmination of the hajj (pilgrimage), is dependant upon the sighting of the new moon. Look for the crescent on top of a mosque: it indicates the direction of Mecca, towards which Muslims face when praying. The flags of 17 modern Islamic countries and territories feature the crescent, including these 10 destinations:

[TOP] » MERGING MALAY AND MODERNIST ARCHITECTURAL STYLES, MALAYSIA'S ENORMOUS SULTAN SALAHUDDIN ABDUL AZIZ SHAH MOSQUE IN SHAH ALAM FEATURES THE WORLD'S TALLEST MINARETS.

[LEFT] » TURKEY'S FLAG, DEPICTING A WHITE CRESCENT AND STAR ON RED, IS DERIVED FROM THE LATE OTTOMAN FLAG OF 1844; THE COLOUR SCHEME IS REVERSED ON THE FLAG OF TURKISH CYPRUS.

[RIGHT] » AFTER PRAYERS ON THE LAST DAY OF RAMADAN, CHINESE MUSLIMS BREAK THEIR FAST AT A CELEBRATION OUTSIDE THE MOSQUE.

✪ **BRUNEI** » Feel the call to prayer reverberate through the stilted walkways of the country's capital.

✪ **COMOROS** » Wander the cobblestone medinas of these sandalwood isles.

✪ **MALAYSIA** » Discover the hidden treasures of the Islamic merchants of Malacca.

✪ **MALDIVES** » Swim with Sultan Ibrahim fish around the Alps of the underwater world.

✪ **MAURITANIA** » Catch a camel caravan to Chinguetti, considered by locals to be a holy city.

✪ **PAKISTAN** » Trace the threads of Islamic design in Peshawar, Pakistan's carpet capital.

✪ **SINGAPORE** » Dine on halal (permitted) hawker food with a haram (forbidden) Tiger beer.

✪ **TUNISIA** » Imagine Ibn Battuta, Islam's famous traveller, trudging past Carthage.

✪ **TURKEY** » Watch pigeons circle the domes of the Blue Mosque – Islam's most beautiful.

✪ **UZBEKISTAN** » Find the 'spiced dainties' of Keats' 'silken Samarkand' in this city of treasures.

IN BRIEF
saudi arabia

✪ CONNECTION TO ISLAM »
Besides being governed according to Islamic law, the Kingdom of Saudi Arabia is keeper of the two holiest cities in Islam: Mecca, where the Kaaba is located; and Medina, where Mohammed set up the first Islamic state.

✪ LOCATION »
Saudi Arabia forms the greater part of the Arabian Peninsula, lying between the Red Sea and the Gulf.

✪ CONNECTION TO TRAVEL »
Saudi Arabia is host to millions of pilgrims each year, who come to perform the rituals at Mecca and Medina, particularly during hajj.

✪ ACCESS »
The easiest way to visit is as part of an organised tour. It's still hard for independent travellers to gain access, and it's almost impossible for single women.

✪ DRAWCARDS »
Fine ruins at Madain Saleh (almost a mini Petra); magnificent escarpment landscape around Riyadh; Aladdin's cave of antiquities in Old Jeddah; some of the best diving in the world in the Red Sea; stunning tribal architecture in the mountains of the Asir; strong African influence on the coastal plain; and, Saudi's biggest drawcard, the Empty Quarter – a vast, mostly uncharted sand desert that is home to the nomadic Bedu.

✪ VISITORS »
Though the modern state of Saudi Arabia only came into being in the 20th century, the territory has attracted numerous travellers over the centuries, including John Burkhardt, Richard Burton, Charles Doughty, TE Lawrence and Wilfred Thesiger.

[TOP] » TOURIST SPIN-OFF: THE WHIRLING MEDITATIONS OF THE SUFIS HAVE BECOME A SOUGHT AFTER SPECTACLE IN HOLIDAY DESTINATIONS SUCH AS CAIRO.

[LEFT] » GNAOUA PERFORMERS AND THEIR HYPNOTIC, BLUESY RHYTHMS, ACCOMPANIED BY A DANCING FRENZY OF SPINS AND FLIPS, ARE EVER POPULAR WITH THE CROWDS AT MARRAKESH'S DJEMAA EL-FNA.

[RIGHT] » OVER 2000 YEARS OLD, THESE ORNATE ROCK TOMBS ARE ALL THAT REMAINS OF MADAIN SALEH, A NABATAEAN CITY THAT STOOD AT THE MIDPOINT OF THE CARAVAN ROUTE FROM MECCA TO PETRA.

a world of wonders

For Muslims in Timbuktu and Tashkent, in New York and New Delhi, travel is one thing they have in common. Each year during hajj, over two million people make the journey to Mecca and play their part in one of the greatest annual migrations of people on earth. But regardless of your religious persuasion, whether you're seeking insights or wanting to see something spectacular, there's ample reason to visit the Islamic world, home to some of this planet's most treasured sights and experiences.

The mysteries of history await: the iconic pyramids of Giza, including the Great Pyramid, which is the only survivor of the ancient Seven Wonders of the World; the Roman ruins at the desert oasis of Palmyra, which for millennia was at the crossroads of Eastern and Mediterranean cultures; and Petra, the Nabataean city partially carved into red sandstone cliffs,

reachable only via a narrow gorge. And they're just starting points.

For mythical, untouched wilderness penetrating the Arabian Peninsula's Empty Quarter (Rub al-Khali), the majestic dunes of Africa's Sahara, or the inhospitable Taklamakan Desert of Central Asia continues to present a challenge to the adventurous, spirited traveller. And while these environments may be harsh, the local peoples – the Bedu, the Tuareg and the Uighurs respectively – are legendary for their hospitality.

There are plenty of places to watch daily life and be a part of business as usual, be it observing the nightly storytelling in Marrakesh's Djemaa el-Fna, detecting the aroma of cumin wafting round the twist of alley in Islamic Cairo, or being delighted by the brilliance of the saris and marigold garlands in Dhaka's Shankharia Bazar. Around any corner may lie that detail that truly makes your journey.

[LEFT] » SYRIA'S MUST-SEE, THE ANCIENT OASIS CITY OF PALMYRA ENDURES AS COLONNADES, FUNERARY TOWERS AND RUINED TEMPLES COVERING SOME 50 HECTARES OF DESERT.

[RIGHT] » STILL THE BIG QUESTION, EGYPT'S ARCHAIC MYSTERIES AWAIT YOUR INVESTIGATION – THEY'VE EVEN SWEPT THE DESERT FOR YOUR ARRIVAL.

top 10 Islam

The Islamic world covers some of the greatest treasures of the natural world as well as some of the finest gems of civilisation. Here's a top 10 of must-sees in no particular order as each is completely inspiring in its own way.

✪ HUNZA VALLEY (PAKISTAN)

Dressing the Karakorum Hwy with cherry blossom and apricots, tidy terraces, and suspension bridges that are suspended only in willing disbelief, this heartland of the north is the secret soul of Pakistan.

✪ BUKHARA (UZBEKISTAN)

Central Asia's holiest city, Bukhara boasts architecture spanning a thousand years of history, and a thoroughly lived-in old centre that has barely changed in two centuries. It is one of the best places in Central Asia for a glimpse of pre-Russian Turkestan.

✪ LAKE DAL (KASHMIR)

With the snow-capped Himalayas standing as distant sentinels, the lotus lakes near Srinagar are skimmed by flower-sellers punting gladioli, dahlias and lilies through the mirrored waters.

✪ GRANADA (SPAIN)

Dynamic and youthful, cultured and historic, the city of flamenco clambers up the hillside to the 14th-century Alhambra, the crowning glory not only of the town but of Islamic imperial architecture.

✪ OLD QUARTER SOUQS IN ALEPPO, MUTRAH & SAN'A (SYRIA, OMAN & YEMEN)

Coffee pots and copper plates, tanning hides and bales of wool, plastic trays and mosque clocks pile the alleyways of these garrulous, gossiping, grumbling organs of trade throughout the Islamic world.

(LEFT) » TAKE AN AROMATIC ADVENTURE THROUGH THE SPICE STALLS AT ALEPPO'S SOUQ, A DECIDEDLY UNTOURISTY MARKET THAT'S STILL THE MAIN CENTRE OF LOCAL COMMERCE IN SYRIA'S SECOND CITY.

(RIGHT) » SLOPING MUD WALLS PROTECT THE ARK, A ROYAL CITADEL IN THE HEART OF BUKHARA THAT NOW HOUSES SHOPS, EXHIBITS AND MUSEUMS.

[TOP] » PICK YOUR OWN APRICOTS AND SAVOUR THE VIEWS FROM MELISHKAR, ONE OF THE HIGHEST HABITATIONS IN THE IMPROBABLY GORGEOUS HUNZA VALLEY.

[LEFT] » HIRE A *SHIKARA* AND A FIND A FLOATING FLORIST SHOP ON LAKE DAL'S TRANQUIL WATERS, NESTLED BENEATH THE MISTY PEAKS OF KASHMIR'S PIR PANJAL MOUNTAINS.

[RIGHT] » THE DESIGN OF ALHAMBRA'S PALACE OF THE LIONS IS SYMBOLIC OF ISLAMIC PARADISE PARTITIONED BY FOUR RIVERS – THE FOUR WATER CHANNELS MEET AT A CENTRAL FOUNTAIN OF 12 MARBLE LIONS.

(TOP) » LITERALLY PUT ON A PEDESTAL BY ITS BUILDERS SO THAT ITS BACKGROUND IS ONLY SKY, THE TAJ MAHAL IS 'A TEARDROP ON THE FACE OF ETERNITY' ACCORDING TO INDIAN POET RABINDRANATH TAGORE.

(LEFT) » POSSIBLY CHARMED, DEFINITELY OBEDIENT, A SNAKE IS COAXED INTO AN OESOPHAGUS IN MARRAKESH'S DJEMAA EL-FNA.

(RIGHT) » EMPTY FOR A REASON: THE ONLY PERMANENT SOURCE OF DRINKING WATER IN THE EMPTY QUARTER IS THIS NATURAL SPRING AT UMM AL-HAYSH.

top 10 Islam

✪ BELLY DANCING (TURKEY)

Seductive and sensual, this ancient dance form refines the art of teasing and captures all the myths of the Orient in one muscle-clenching, hip-gyrating, bead-flashing curl of the torso.

✪ MINARET OF JAM (AFGHANISTAN)

The holy grail for travellers in Afghanistan, the 65m-high minaret was built in 12th century but was unknown to the Western world until the 19th century. It remains one of the world's most intriguing examples of Islamic architecture. In 2003 the minaret became Afghanistan's first World Heritage site.

✪ TAJ MAHAL (INDIA)

Although some Islamic sects prohibit the veneration of tombs, who could object to the peerless 17th-century Taj at Agra, built in loving memory of an adored wife, and coupled for eternity with its own reflection?

✪ MARRAKESH (MOROCCO)

Couched in the Atlas mountains, it has at its core Djemaa el-Fna, 'the greatest show on earth': a square ringed by orange-juice sellers, snake charmers, story tellers, spice shops and carpet vendors.

✪ EMPTY QUARTER (SAUDI ARABIA)

The Empty Quarter, attractive and repellent by the same measure, is crossed by the legendary Bedu; Thesiger claimed that this 'cruel land can cast a spell which no temperate climate can hope to match'.

[LEFT] » BELLY DANCING'S ORIGINS MAY LIE IN THE MIDDLE EAST, BUT THE TURKS HAVE MADE IT THEIR OWN.

[RIGHT] » THE MINARET OF JAM'S ISOLATION REMAINED MYSTERIOUS UNTIL EXCAVATIONS SHOWED THE SITE TO BE THE LOST CITY OF FIRUZKOH, THE GHORID CAPITAL DESTROYED BY THE MONGOLS AROUND THE 13TH CENTURY.

SPORT + ISLAM

WORK UP A SWEAT WITH SOME OF ISLAM'S MORE ACTIVE TRADITIONS

✪ CAMEL RACING (UAE)

This ancient desert sport has experienced a revival in recent years, with new tracks sprouting up across the United Arab Emirates. Both male and female camels are raced, although females can compete for twenty years, twice as long as males. One of the keys to success is the rider's weight, hence the practice of using young boys as jockeys. At a time when the country is rapidly modernising, camel racing opens a window onto the country's Bedouin past.

✪ BUZKASHI (AFGHANISTAN)

Buzkashi, which literally translated means 'goat grabbing', is a sporting legacy to the people of Afghanistan. The game is centred around a headless carcass of a goat or calf, placed between two teams of skilled horsemen. The aim of the game is to grab the carcass and then get it clear of the other players, pitching it across a goal line or into a target circle or vat. Only the most masterful players, the *chapandaz*, ever get close to the carcass. Play at your own risk: Afghani masters take the game very seriously.

✪ INTERNATIONAL WOMEN'S ISLAMIC GAMES (IRAN)

The Games is the only international women's sporting event that doesn't admit paparazzi. The fourth Games, which Tehran hosted in 2005, saw 1300 athletes from 43 countries competing in 18 events – from golf to athletics – before thousands of (mainly female) spectators. The aim of the Games is to integrate women's sports with the requirements of Islamic norms. Among the competitors expected to attend the next Games in 2009 are teams from Britain, Iran, Afghanistan and the USA.

✪ NO-RULES POLO (PAKISTAN)

Shandur Pass is an epic location for the world's highest polo match. Each summer a tent village springs up to service the crowds arriving for the equestrian spectacle that features teams from Chitral and Gilgit – two major mountain towns that are roughly equidistant from Shandur. Against a stunning backdrop of snowcapped mountains, the match, which is played with a minimum of rules, unfolds on a pitch 3700m above sea level – the crescendo of a unique cultural festival.

✪ 18 MUSLIM ELBOWS (CHINA)

Muslims displaced by Mongolian hordes in the 13th century settled in China's northern provinces, bringing fighting traditions that over the centuries have melded with traditional Chinese Wushu (kung fu). Migrants and Chinese converts to Islam kept these traditions alive, often in secret. A unique martial art, 18 Muslim Elbows consists of 18 sequences, based on 387 'forms'. It was considered lost until Master Ju Kui, born in 1896, was found by Wushu researchers in the 1970s.

FIGHTING OVER A CARCASS MIGHT GET YOUR GOAT, BUT FOR *CHAPANDAZ* PLAYING *BUZKASHI* IT'S ALL PART OF THE GAME.

THE ART OF ISLAM

BE PART OF ISLAM'S BUSY ARTS CALENDAR

✪ FAJR INTERNATIONAL FILM FESTIVAL (IRAN)

Billed as the Cannes film festival of the Middle East, FIFF is where cultures collide in a cinematic orgy of creativity. Held annually on the anniversary of the Iranian revolution, the festival is now in its 26th incarnation and has built up a solid reputation for its diverse programme. Arabic films are screened alongside those from Europe, Africa, Asia and the USA. Last year the best screenplay award in the Spiritual Cinema category was awarded to Polish scriptwriter Grzegorz Loszweski.

✪ UMM AL-FAHM ART GALLERY (ISRAEL & THE PALESTINIAN TERRITORIES)

When retired policeman Abu Shakra Said opened a gallery in the heart of his Arab-Israeli hometown, he was doing more than just indulging his passion for art. By purposefully curating exhibitions featuring contemporary artworks by Arab and Israeli artists, and displaying them side by side, he aims to provide a bridge between the local communities. The gallery has successfully attracted Israeli and international art lovers, including Yoko Ono, to visit the isolated Arab community.

✪ HIP-HOP ON ISLAM FM (ENGLAND)

More famous for colleges than trailblazing indie radio stations, the historic city of Cambridge currently hosts an audio revolution of mad hip-hop beats created from an Islamic

perspective. Launched early last year, Islam FM is streamed over the internet and is helping nurture grass-roots rappers worldwide, with a play list that includes everything from African rhythms and Hindi beats to Palestinian rap with Arabic overtones and edgy British flavas from the likes of Blakstone.

✪ CAPITAL OF ARAB CULTURE 2008 (SYRIA)

If any city can lay claim to being a capital of culture it's the Syrian capital. Founded more than 10,000 years ago, Damascus is the world's oldest continually inhabited city. This year it'll be rocked to its ancient foundations by a festival programme featuring Syria's best contemporary and traditional art, music, theatre, educational and scientific exhibitions. Organisers will

have their work cut out topping last year's hosts Algeria, who opened proceedings with a spine-tingling 500-strong 'choral extravaganza'.

✪ BEYOND THE PALACE WALLS

This touring exhibition features 200 of the most blindingly beautiful Islamic artworks that have literally been taken from 'beyond the palace walls' of the Winter Palace in Russia's St Petersburg. The collection includes intricate metalwork, geometrically astounding textiles, scintillating glasswork, and complex embroideries amassed over 1200 years (until the 19th century) from Egypt to China. Considered the cream of Islamic art, the collection was last displayed to coincide with Britain's 2006 Festival of Muslim Cultures.

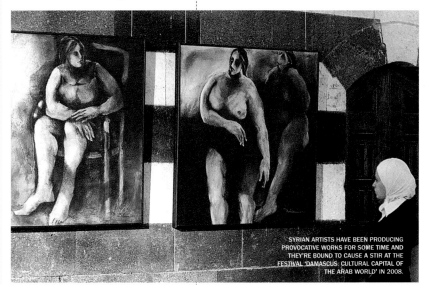

SYRIAN ARTISTS HAVE BEEN PRODUCING PROVOCATIVE WORKS FOR SOME TIME AND THEY'RE BOUND TO CAUSE A STIR AT THE FESTIVAL 'DAMASCUS: CULTURAL CAPITAL OF THE ARAB WORLD' IN 2008.

religion & culture

THE PROPHET

Islam was founded in the early 7th century by Prophet Mohammed, who was born around the year 570 in the city of Mecca (in modern-day Saudi Arabia). At the age of 40, disillusioned by the idolatry of the Meccans, he withdrew to a cave in the mountains in Mecca to contemplate a solution. According to Islamic tradition, it was here that the Angel Gabriel first visited him and revealed God's message. The revelations continued for the rest of his life.

Very little is known about the early years of Mohammed: his biography was written a century after his death and is not very revealing. In accordance with tradition he was sent to a Beduin wet nurse and lived among the Bedu. Difficult times followed: he was orphaned at six and adopted by his grandfather, who also died a short time later, whereafter he lived with his uncle. At a young age he began work as a trader attached to camel caravans but returned eventually to his home city of Mecca. Meanwhile, Mohammed's honesty, integrity and efficiency earned him the attention of a much older, wealthy widow called Khadijah, who soon took him on as her agent. Eventually the couple married and had four daughters and two sons, both of whom died in early childhood.

THE MEANING

The word 'Islam' means 'submission' and 'peace' with oneself, society and the environment, through conscious submission to the will of God.

The principal teaching of Islam is that there is only one true God, the same god as is worshipped by Christians and Jews. Muslims believe in the prophets, starting with Adam, including Abraham and Jesus, and ending with Mohammed; they don't believe that any of them were divine.

THE BOOK

Mohammed came from an oral tradition, and he memorised and repeated the revelations he received, which were recorded by his scribes. These revelations were collectively known as the Quran (meaning 'recitation' in Arabic), the holy book of Islam. The Quran was first compiled into book form by Abu Bakr in the first few years after Mohammed's death in 632. Muslims believe that it is the literal word of God, revealed through the sacred language of Arabic.

PORTABLE FAITH

From the outset, a creed that was based on a direct relationship with God, without intermediaries, might seem to have obvious appeal to the nomadic tribes of Arabia. Individual believers needed only to observe the Five Pillars of Islam in order to fulfil their religious duty, a fact true to this day. While some tribes offered fierce resistance, Islam's egalitarian message appealed to the poor and oppressed; later, various nations joined the faith, sometimes for political reasons.

INTO EUROPE

Muslim armies spread into Spain from North Africa in 711 and settled in Andalucía. Here they built great citadels and mosques, and entered into a mutually creative and mostly peaceful relationship with Christendom that lasted for seven centuries. The last Muslim monarch was ousted in Spain in 1492 – the year Columbus reached the Americas. The timing of the two events has come to represent the gradual waxing of Western imperialism and the equally gradual waning of Islamic imperialism.

The foray into Spain brought far more than Islamic rulers to Europe: Islamic culture helped bring about the Renaissance. The scholars of Muslim Spain translated the classical works of medicine, astronomy, chemistry, philosophy and architecture from Greek and Roman sources, lost to Europe in the Dark Ages, and thereby prompted the rebirth of the continent.

AND BEYOND

The supremacy of the Ottoman Turks in Europe began around 1326 and lasted well into the 17th century. Islamic culture flourished in an empire that stretched from Hungary to Libya. In the meantime, and throughout the course of the next four centuries, Islam also spread through word of mouth and by being the faith of powerful rulers. It reached well beyond the shores of Arabia and the Mediterranean – to India and the Indian Ocean, China and Indonesia.

In the 19th and 20th centuries, the Islamic world continued to grow through the migration of workers from continent to continent. Today, Islam is disseminated through the media aided by the growth in tourism to countries of the Islamic world such as Egypt, Jordan, Morocco, Tunisia and Turkey.

A TRAVELLER'S GUIDE TO
islamic vocab

Take the layman's guide to the most common Arabic names, words and phrases a traveller might encounter in the Islamic world:

✪ AL-HAMDU LILLAH »
The phrase 'All praise be to God' accompanies many references to the past.

✪ IN SHA' ALLAH »
The phrase 'God-willing' accompanies most references to the future.

✪ EID »
Meaning 'feast', eid refers to the holidays after hajj and Ramadan.

✪ HAJJ »
The annual pilgrimage of Muslims to Mecca falls 10 or 11 days earlier each year.

✪ IMAM »
Meaning 'model' or 'example', an imam is the leader of prayer in a mosque.

✪ MADRASSA »
Place of study, often attached to a mosque.

✪ MINARET »
Meaning 'lighthouse', it's a tower from which prayers are called.

✪ MUEZZIN »
Historically (before PAs took over) the person who makes the call to prayer from a minaret.

✪ QURAN »
The holy book of Islam, written in Arabic and often learnt by heart.

✪ RAMADAN »
The holy month of fasting: it falls in the ninth month of the Islamic calendar.

(ABOVE) » A STRING OF BEADS CALLED A SUBHA OR *TASBIH* IS USED WHEN RECITING A RANGE OF PRAYERS AND EXALTATIONS.

(OPPOSITE PAGE) » LEARNING THE LETTERS AND THE LESSONS. YOUNG BOYS TAKE QURAN CLASSES IN A TOWN IN SOUTHERN MAURITANIA.

(LEFT) » LOCALS TAKE THE TIME TO TALK BESIDE SÜLEYMANIYE, THE 16TH-CENTURY HILLTOP MOSQUE DESIGNED BY THE MASTERFUL MIMAR SINAN THAT'S A FEATURE OF ISTANBUL'S SKYLINE.

(RIGHT) » MUSLIM WOMEN ASSEMBLE FOR MORNING EID PRAYER AT PARANGKUSUMO BEACH OUTSIDE OF YOGYAKARTA IN CENTRAL JAVA, INDONESIA.

a question of cover

For travellers, perhaps the single most visible indicator of Islamic culture is clothing and the degree to which covering up is required when in public places. Here's a guide to how much skin is in.

BARING ALL
Long before the Brazilian became popular Muslims gave the 'zero' to the modern world, so don't be surprised to see it applied – in the steamy bathhouses of Turkey and Syria for example – but only among your own sex.

TOPLESS
Even in the most Westernised resorts in the most liberal Islamic regions, such as in the Maldives or on the beaches of Southern Turkey, topless means at most shirtless for men and swimsuit for women.

SHOWING A SHOULDER
In the tolerant, seen-it-all-before countries of Egypt and United Arab Emirates, showing a shoulder is seen as a bit daft in the heat of high summer. It also looks about as under-dressed as wearing a bikini to a shopping mall in the West.

NAKED KNEES
Modern and Western-leaning Bahrain and Qatar, Singapore and the cities of Malaysia and China are not shocked by knees – providing they come suitably hosed in stockings and a business suit for women and appear only on the golf course for men.

A BIT OF ANKLE
It's remarkable how seductive a bit of ankle can be when there's little else on show. Women travelling through Pakistan, Oman and Yemen, might want to bear that in mind before showing a shin in public.

DUSK AT MECCA'S AL-MASJID AL-HARAM, WHERE DURING HAJJ MUSLIMS PERFORM *TAWAF* BY CIRCLING THE KAABA ANTICLOCKWISE SEVEN TIMES.

FINGERS AND TOES

Some devout ladies of Islamic countries (especially Iraq, Saudi Arabia and Afghanistan) cover their feet with socks and wear gloves to drive (if they're permitted to drive). Take care not to follow suit or people will think you've got psoriasis.

FULL COVER

Bedouin ladies insist that the full, protective enrobing of the body for women was their idea and that it predates Islam. Besides, it covers a bad hair day and shabby traveller's clothes quite well. Only really needed in Saudi.

TO TOP IT ALL OFF

In every Islamic country, a hat, be it turban, cap, straw hat, baseball peak or yard of white cotton (Sudan) is the indisputable marker of gentility. Wear one of your own from home and you'll spend your travels swapping it for photos.

AFGHAN WOMEN WEARING BURQAS WALK BY THE MINARETS THAT MARK THE CORNERS OF BAIQARA'S LONG-GONE MADRASSA OF THE MUSALLA COMPLEX, HERAT.

the Islamic experience

A CHOICE OF CULTURES

Depending on where you go, Islamic culture might be something you hardly notice or the one thing that defines your travel experience. From determining opening hours for shop and businesses to dictating what you can wear on the street, what you can drink or where you're able to go, Islam's influence upon the local norms and laws is different everywhere you go. Here's a taste of what we're talking about.

BAHRAIN

Most of the population are Shiite Muslims, but some 40% of Bahrain's residents are non-Bahraini's or expats. Countless nightclubs and bars serve alcohol and social freedoms are on display on the streets of Manama.

MALAYSIA

Culturally diverse and dynamic, Malaysia has significant minority populations of Indians and Chinese: women aren't subject to strict purdah and cities feel international; it's in rural areas that Islamic culture comes to the fore.

BANGLADESH

The majority of the population are Sunni Muslims; purda is absent but religious customs make relationships between men and women very formal outside of the family. There's a relatively free press and people tend to voice their opinions.

EGYPT

While not strictly authoritarian in its manner, Islam permeates Egyptian life on an almost unconscious level, through dress, greetings and daily routine. There is a diverse and vocal free press. Friday mosque is well attended.

AFGHANISTAN

Daily life is strictly segregated and both sexes cover up in a land where the mosque and the family are the cornerstones of community. Hospitality is a point of honour, regardless of wealth: you will drink plenty of tea.

IRAN

The only Shiite regime in the world is governed by one, particularly strict interpretation of Islamic law. Women's rights are a hot topic in and out of the country. *Ta'arof*, the Iranian system of courtesy, means you will be well treated.

STOP THE BAD-MOUTHING

THINK AGAIN ABOUT DESTINATIONS SOMETIMES CONSIDERED 'UNSAFE'

✪ IRAN

After 9/11 everyone here hates Westerners. Or do they? Iranians might take a keen interest in politics and international relations, particularly when it comes to US foreign policy, but travellers venturing into Tehran can enter without fear. Avoid silly stunts like taking photos near nuclear power stations or trying to sneak into mosques and you'll make friends, not enemies. As many locals will tell you, 'We like Westerners, it's your governments we can't stand'.

✪ PAKISTAN

Pakistan's mountainous northern region is touted as the badlands. True, tribal law is dominant, but after enduring years of conflict the people here firmly aspire to peace. In recent decades millions of refugees have poured though the Khyber Pass from neighbouring Afghanistan, overcrowding provincial cities. Despite mounting social and political pressure, tribal warlords have been able to maintain sufficient order enabling hardy travellers to visit this remote part of the world.

✪ SAUDI ARABIA

Many see the country as synonymous with capital punishment. Whilst Saudi executioners did dispatch 86 people in 2006 (compared with 53 in the USA and an estimated 5000 in China) many death sentences (105) were also overturned. Muslim scholars, citing aspects of law known as the 'Pardon Provisions', work alongside a special 'Pardon Committee' to encourage victims, such as the family members of someone who has been murdered, to forgive and pardon criminals who are facing execution.

✪ SYRIA

Labelled an 'oppressive regime' by the Bush administration, Syria's cultural highs are hidden under a pile of politically motivated bad press. The country's Islamic recreational traditions may seem conservative when measured by Western standards – Damascus has only four main nightclubs – but once accustomed to the family-oriented way of life, it's easy to appreciate the gentle, caring nature of the people. Sitting at home, chatting, and being formally served treats like coffee and ice cream is also highly addictive.

✪ TURKEY

The most indiscriminately overused word Westerners use to describe Turkish men is probably 'sleazy', but is it fair? Every country has it's share of slimy Lotharios and Turkey's no exception, but as a rule the men here are polite and well intentioned. Trouble is, intimidating females who are travelling alone is an underhand technique some touts seem intent on using. Should you experience any bother, raise the alarm and a real (Turkish) man will be quick to step in.

MULLAHS AND STUDENTS MIX WITH THE STEADY FLOW OF PILGRIMS IN THE IRANIAN CITY OF QOM, FAMOUS FOR ITS MADRASSAS, OR COLLEGES.

HOLY CITIES

DISCOVER THE SACRED IN SOME OF THE WORLD'S MOST HISTORIC SPIRITUAL CENTRES

✪ MECCA (SAUDI ARABIA)

The city containing the Kaaba, Islam's holiest shrine, is so revered that its name has become a metaphor describing any site of special significance. As the destination for the world's largest pilgrimage, the hajj, Mecca is only accessible to Muslims. Around four million pilgrims, three times the number of permanent residents, visit the shrine each year. The magnificent buildings of the Al-Masjid al-Haram (The Sacred Mosque) can accommodate over 800,000 worshippers.

✪ JERUSALEM (ISRAEL & THE PALESTINIAN TERRITORIES)

emple Mount lie two of Islam's most revered monuments. The 7th-century Dome of the Rock marks the spot from which Muslims believe Mohammed ascended to heaven to receive the Islamic prayers. A magnificent 20m-diameter golden dome stretches over the Noble Rock where the event is said to have taken place. The nearby Al Asqa Mosque is Jerusalem's largest place of worship. Also sacred to Christians and Jews, the Dome of the Rock became headquarters for the Knights Templar during the 12th-century Crusades.

✪ KERBALA (IRAQ)

Home to over half-a-million people, Kerbala is one of Iraq's wealthiest and oldest cities. It is divided into two parts: New Kerbala contains the residential and administrative buildings; whilst Old Kerbala is where you'll find the shrine at the tomb of the revered Hussein ibn Ali, Mohammed's grandson by his daughter Fatima. The city grew up around the tombs of Hussein and his brother Abbas, who were martyred during the Battle of Kerbala in 680.

✪ CHINGUETTI (MAURITANIA)

Just getting to the Holy City of the Sahara is an act of faith involving an arduous crossing of the formidable western desert. Founded to serve caravans crossing the Sahara, Chinguetti once boasted 20,000 inhabitants. Today some 1500 people live there inside houses built from stone and dried mud. The old mosque dates from the 13th century. Its famous square minaret is capped by four *acroteria*, or pedestals, each topped with a stone ostrich egg.

✪ ISTANBUL (TURKEY)

In a metropolis that has over 500 mosques, the Mosque of Eyüp, lying just beyond the ancient city walls, has special significance for many Muslims. Built in 1485, it was the first mosque to be completed following the Ottoman conquest of Istanbul, then Constantinople, in 1453. The site is believed to mark the spot where Abu Ayyub al-Ansari, Mohammed's faithful standard bearer, died during the first Islamic assault on the city in 670.

IN THE AL-AQSA MOSQUE COMPOUND OF JERUSALEM'S TEMPLE MOUNT A PALESTINIAN GIRL PRAYS: THE GOLD-PLATED DOME OF THE ROCK IS IN THE BACKGROUND.

daily *life*

A WAY OF LIFE

As all Muslims will tell you, Islam is not just a religion for Fridays (Islam's holy day), it's a way of life. Equally, the Islamic world is not just a geographical accident, it's a dissemination of core principles. Inevitably, Islam means different things to different people. For Khalid, a Pakistani shopkeeper in Bradford, England, it means a daily compromise between 'having a drink with mates' and attending the mosque on Friday. For Ahmed, a Sudanese teacher working in Oman, it means juggling hard-earned cash among three wives. For Salma, an Iraqi Hajji newly returned from pilgrimage to Mecca, it means unity: 'We stand side by side, men, women, children, from East and from West, rich and poor and there are no distinctions'.

HAJJ - JOURNEY OF A LIFETIME

There is perhaps no other religion that embraces travel to the same extent as Islam. As one of the Five Pillars of Islam, all Muslims who are able are obliged to make their way to Mecca at least once in their lifetime. 'They shall come unto Thee on foot', states the Quran, 'and upon every lean beast, they shall come from every deep ravine that they may witness things profitable to them.'

At the beginning of the 20th century, when foot and lean beast were about the only method of reaching Mecca, only 10,000 pilgrims per year managed to reach the holy shrines of Mecca at the prescribed time of year. Today, stopover in Dubai airport during hajj and you can witness one of the greatest annual migrations of people in the world: some two million Muslims from 120 countries – Bahraini, American and Chinese, Kuwaiti, French and Malaysian – pour out of this and other airports in the region, many in the white, off-the-shoulder pilgrim robes that render all distinctions of race or nationality immaterial.

There is an Arab saying that 'a journey of a thousand miles starts with one step'. The harder the step, the more rewarding the journey. Ironically, while modern transportation has made it easier to reach Mecca, the sheer number of pilgrims trying to perform the necessary rituals brings its own difficulties: many faint, some die of exhaustion, occasionally tragedies occur in the overcrowding. But still the faithful keep coming, some choosing to perform the circumambulation of the Kaaba, the holiest shrine in Mecca, at the hottest time of day to gain the full reward of their effort.

This is nothing new. For centuries pilgrims have been drawn to Mecca not just in observance of their duty but as an act of attrition. Some (including a few intrepid impostors) have had less noble intentions, drawn to the journey out of camaraderie or even sheer curiosity. As the Saudi journalist Faiza Saleh writes, 'Spending a week...performing rituals more ancient than Islam itself, in the largest single gathering at one place for one purpose in the world, appeals more to the journalist than the Muslim in me'.

'a journey of a thousand miles starts with one step.'

Arab saying

(LEFT) » IN MODERN TURKEY LIFE ON THE LAND MAY BE MAINTAINING ITS TRADITIONS, BUT IN CITIES SUCH AS ANKARA THE LOCALS LIVE LIVES MUCH LIKE PEOPLE IN THE WEST.

(RIGHT) » FREE AS A BIRD, A COMPETITOR IN A LADIES' PARAGLIDING COMPETITION IN IRAN IS WATCHED FROM THE HILLSIDE BY HER COACH.

HIGH-PROFILE
converts to Islam

To convert, a believer only has to say the following words with conviction: 'There is no true god but God, and Mohammed is the Messenger of God'. Khadija, the Prophet Mohammed's first wife, was the first to put faith in her husband's revelations and therefore the first convert to Islam. Here's a few famous people who have uttered those words in recent years:

⊙ **HAIQA KAHN** » Formerly Jemimah Goldsmith. Daughter of the British billionaire Sir James Goldsmith. Converted after marrying the famous Pakistani cricket player, Imran Khan, when she was 21.

⊙ **HAMDAN EUBANK** » Formerly Chris Eubank. Former super middleweight world champion. Converted after beating Camilo Alocon at the Dubai Tennis Stadium in a light heavyweight boxing contest in 1997.

⊙ **QUEEN NOOR OF JORDAN** » Formerly Lisa Najeeb Halaby to a prominent Arab-American family but raised by Christian parents. Converted to Islam on marrying the late King Hussein of Jordan, a descendant of the prophet's line, in 1978.

⊙ **EL-HAJJ MALIK EL-SHABAZZ** » Formerly known as Malcolm X. Black-rights activist and religious leader who promoted brotherhood between blacks and whites. Joined the Nation of Islam in 1952. Converted to orthodox Islam after a pilgrimage to Mecca in 1964.

⊙ **MUHAMMAD ALI** » Formerly Cassius Clay. Three-time Heavy Weight Champion of the World. Joined the Nation of Islam in 1964. Converted to orthodox Islam in 1975.

⊙ **YUSUF ISLAM** » Formerly Cat Stevens. World-famous British pop singer. Converted to Islam in 1977.

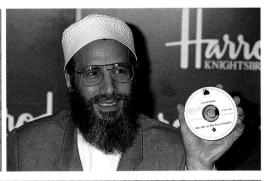

(ABOVE) » THE HANDPRINTS ABOUT THIS YEMENI BOY ARE A STYLISED FORM OF THE HAND OF FATIMA, A SYMBOL SAID TO BRING BLESSINGS AND AVERT EVIL.

(LEFT) » THE BIGGEST SINGLE GATHERING ON THE PLANET, THE ARRIVAL IN MECCA OF TWO MILLION HAJJ PILGRIMS NEEDING FOOD, SHELTER AND TRANSPORT CREATES LOGISTICAL CHALLENGES EACH YEAR.

(RIGHT) » IN 2006 YUSUF ISLAM, FORMERLY CAT STEVENS, RETURNED TO HIS MUSICAL ROOTS WITH HIS FIRST POP-STYLE OFFERING IN 28 YEARS.

5
the five pillars of Islam

1. SHAHADA – ISLAM HEARD
Shahada is a profession of faith: 'There is no God but Allah and Mohammed is his Messenger'; it is pronounced in the call to prayer.

There is no greater welcome to the world of Islam than through the call to prayer, issued from loudspeakers on mosque minarets. In the crowded cities of Cairo, Karachi and Kuala Lumpur, it seems to vibrate across the frantic, discordant hum of human activity like a tuning fork, bringing all those that hover under its resonance into eventual harmony.

2. SALAT – ISLAM SEEN
This refers to ritual prayer, offered five times a day, every day of the year. Prayer times are at sunrise, noon, mid-afternoon, sunset and night (usually 1½ hours after sunset). Ritual ablutions are performed before prayer.

Sometimes on international flights you'll see businessmen, freshly washed and in suit and socks, unfurl a prayer mat from a briefcase and proceed in the ritual prostrations towards Mecca (the direction of which is often shown by a crescent on the in-flight entertainment system). In the practised movements of submission and devotion, with the head covered by a cap, turban, headscarf or veil, is a unity of purpose that's expressed by every Muslim, five times a day, throughout the Islamic world.

3. ZAKAT – ISLAM FELT
Islam insists on practical generosity through the giving of alms. Muslims must give a portion of their wealth (one-fortieth of a believer's property) to those in greater need. The recognition that there's always someone in greater need is a comfort and an education.

One of the joys of passing through many devoutly Islamic countries (like Saudi Arabia, Oman, Malaysia and Brunei) is in leaving your groceries in the car park and finding them safely stowed for you on your return. Islam expects a high standard of moral integrity and generosity of spirit, not just a generosity of pocket. Those touched by it won't forget it.

4. RAMADAN – ISLAM TASTED
It was during the month of Ramadan that Mohammed received his first revelation in the year 610. Muslims mark this special event each year by fasting from sunrise until sunset throughout the month of Ramadan. During the fasting hours, Muslims must abstain from eating, drinking, having sex or smoking. The idea behind the fast is to bring people closer to Allah via spiritual and physical purity.

Ramadan can seem like an inconvenience for the traveller: restaurants are closed, eating (where permitted) is cloistered behind screens, drivers are as irritable as camels and no-one wants to work. But there are unexpected pleasures in Ramadan: water after drought

is particularly delicious, and when the sun goes down and the prayers are said, the party begins. Think honey-dipped, sesame-seeded, date-filled, sugary, buttery, ghee-laden, cinnamoned and nutmegged spicy delicacies – the ultimate fast-breakers.

5. HAJJ – 'THE PERFUMES OF ARABIA'
Every Muslim capable of doing so (whether physically or financially) is expected to perform the hajj, or

DECORATED HOUSE OF A MUSLIM AWAY PERFORMING HAJJ.

pilgrimage to Mecca, at least once in their lifetime. For a pilgrimage to qualify as a 'true' hajj it can only be performed during a few specific days of the Muslim year. After the hajj, all past sins are forgiven.

There's no need to lower the tone by referring to the assault upon the nasal organs inflicted by two million people in 45°C heat in too-close proximity – though plenty of travellers have noted exactly that. Think instead of the famous fragrance upon which the city of Mecca was founded. Gifted by wise men to babes (according to the Bible), and by queens to kings (Queen of Sheba to King Solomon), harvested from the barks of ugly trees in the mist-swirling magic of Dhofar, southern Oman, and used to this day by all major religions in their most sacred rituals, it is of course frankincense. If you're in the Arabian portion of the Islamic world, don't return home without some.

THE AROMATIC RESIN FRANKINCENSE.

travel *Islam*

SOME PRACTICAL DOS + DON'TS.

	TRUE IN MOST CASES	BUT THERE ARE ALWAYS SOME EXCEPTIONS...
CLOTHING 	For men, it's considered impolite to show upper arm, chest or lower leg in public. For women, wearing an *abeyya* (cloak) and *hejab* (headscarf) is a requirement in Saudi Arabia and Iran, and when visiting a mosque.	In hotels (outside the lobby area) and on the road in the wilds, no-one minds seeing shorts and a T-shirt. Wearing local dress and headwear, however, especially in the Middle East, is not appreciated. Outside hotels, women should never show their shoulders, cleavage, knees or thighs in public but, except in Saudi Arabia and Iran, they do not need to wear an *abeyya* or *hejab*. In fact, in many places it is interpreted as meaning that you are a Muslim. And as you probably won't have folded your *hejab* properly, they'll assume you're not a very good Muslim!
ALCOHOL 	In all countries, alcohol is considered haram (forbidden) for Muslims. In some countries (such as Saudi Arabia, Kuwait, Brunei and in parts of United Arab Emirates) the prohibition extends to all residents and travellers as well.	Other than in 'dry' countries, alcohol is as much part of the local culture as anywhere else. Even in parts of the Middle East, spirits such as the arak (aniseed brandy) and locally produced beers are consumed by Muslims and it's acceptable for visitors to follow suit. During Ramadan, alcohol may be unavailable or restricted to room service.
SMOKING 	During Ramadan you can't be seen to smoke during the day. Smoking pot (or taking drugs of any kind) is illegal in all Islamic countries.	Tobacco is a way of life in many Muslim countries – in Indonesia they even grow the stuff. Smoking comes in many shapes and sizes: roll-ups in Bangladesh, clay pipes in western China, cigars in the Gulf. The most fun way to smoke in Middle Eastern countries is to sit cross-legged on a carpet, puff on a communal water pipe of peach-flavoured tobacco and share stories.
TOUCHING 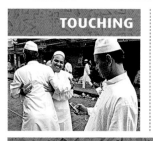	Many devout Muslim men will not shake hands with women; many Muslim ladies prefer not to shake hands with men. Public displays of affection are usually frowned upon.	Greetings across the Islamic world usually involve a lengthy asking after each other's health and families (but men shouldn't ask after wives and daughters). As for shaking hands, it's best to take your cue from your host and grasp whatever's offered. This can sometimes be a wrist if hands are wet. You'll note that while Muslim men and women usually refrain from holding hands in public, that doesn't stop women walking arm in arm, and men (including soldiers) walking hand in hand too.

MOSQUE VISITS

Many mosques are not open to non-Muslims. The holy cities of Mecca and Medina are not open to non-Muslims either.

Many exquisite mosques around the world are happy to show their treasures to non-Muslims under certain conditions: shoes must be removed (bring socks for burning summer surfaces); women must cover up (often a cloak and headscarf is provided); the Quran must not be touched; and opening hours (usually outside of prayer time and not on a Friday) must be observed.

CONVERSATION

Muslims are often offended (or at least bewildered) if you say you don't believe in God. Sex shouldn't be talked about between women and men. Avoid saying 'you' in politics if you mean 'your government'.

As anywhere in the world, these topics of conversation carry the potential for causing an international incident. That said, if handled diplomatically, you may be surprised at how frank Muslims (alarmingly so among married women) are about all three subjects. According to the Quran, all 'people of the book' (ie Jews and Christians) should be given respect for believing in the same God.

VISITING HOMES

In many traditional Islamic homes, seating is on the floor (hence the importance of the carpet and cushions and the need to remove shoes).

Islamic culture is so widely dispersed around the world it's almost impossible to generalise about what behaviour is appropriate if you're asked to someone's home. If seating is on the floor, bear in mind that for most Muslims the soles of the feet are offensive, so if the cramp in the knees gets too bad, shift to the other side or get up. Hitting someone with a shoe is a grave insult.

EATING

Cutlery in many Islamic countries is considered as unhygienic and unnatural. Eating is with the right hand, involving scooping, dipping with bread and otherwise fully involving with food. The left hand is NEVER used – it's kept for ablutions.

No-one minds a jot if you can't master the difficult art of rounding rice into balls and shovelling them into the mouth with the kind of neat, elegant refinement required. In fact, many hosts would rather you didn't even try: use a knife and fork and save everyone the embarrassment of the mess you're going to make. If you do try, then make sure you know your left from your right. Food across the Islamic world is often served from shared dishes, and no-one will want to dip into a dish you've had your left hand in. By the by, for the same reason, it's very impolite to give anything to a Muslim using your left hand.

GIVE + TAKE

It's polite in many parts of the Islamic world to refuse something offered at first. It's also polite to accept gestures of hospitality, the 'bread and salt' given to travellers.

Each country has its own tradition governing the number of times you need to refuse a gift. You don't need to worry too much about how many times, just be aware that it would be rude to grasp it with both hands and tear off the paper! Unwrapping is usually done in private. Avoid admiring portable things (a necklace or a vase), or you may make your host feel obliged to give it to you. In some parts of the world, they may even interpret it as casting an 'evil eye', bringing a curse to the owner. Coffee or tea is often offered to travellers (in souqs, before buying a carpet, in remote villages) and even if you don't drink it, it's hard to refuse these gestures politely. If you're invited to someone's home, take a small gift – but avoid flowers, which often have a funereal association.

mighty mosques

All Muslim men are required to attend mosque on a Friday and hence the mosque has become one of the most distinctive physical features of the Islamic world.

The first mosques were modelled on the Prophet Mohammed's house. To this day the basic plan in providing a safe, cool and peaceful haven for worship has changed little: there's the open *sahn* (courtyard), the arcaded *riwaq* (portico), and the covered, often domed, *sahat al salah* (prayer hall). A vaulted niche in the wall is called the mihrab; this serves to indicate the qibla, or direction of Mecca, towards which Muslims must face when they pray. The minbar, or pulpit, is traditionally reached by three steps. The Prophet is said to have preached from the third step. Abu Bakr, his successor, used the second step. The exact number of steps varies from mosque to mosque, but most imams stand or sit near the top when preaching the Friday sermon.

Superb mosques can be seen in Istanbul (Turkey), Isfahan (Iran), Islamabad (Pakistan), Samarkand (Uzbekistan), Xian (China), Bandar Seri Begawan (Brunei), Afghanistan, Egypt and the old cities of Morocco. Some of the most spectacular are the mud mosques of the Sahara – like the Djenné Mosque in Mali.

Some mosques significant in the history of Islam are listed on the opposite page.

ISLAM'S FIRST FORAY INTO MONUMENTAL ARCHITECTURE, DAMASCUS' 8TH-CENTURY UMAYYAD MOSQUE STANDS ON THE SITE WHERE ARAMEANS BUILT A TEMPLE SOME 3000 YEARS AGO.

DOME OF THE ROCK AND AL-AQSA MOSQUE

WHERE
JERUSALEM, ISRAEL & THE PALESTINIAN TERRITORIES
DATE
691

The golden dome stands over the rock on Temple Mount – the probable site of the Holy of Holies in the Temple of Solomon. The rock is alleged to be the point from which the Prophet Mohammed ascended to heaven in the Night Journey, carried by the Angel Gabriel. The Knights Templar turned the sanctuary into a church after the Crusades, but it was returned to Islam when Saladin recaptured Jerusalem.

GREAT UMAYYAD MOSQUE

WHERE
DAMASCUS, SYRIA
DATE
705

One of the largest and oldest mosques in Islam, and the last resting place of Saladin. It is significant to both Muslims and Christians who come to worship at the shrine of St John the Baptist (revered as a prophet in Islam), whose head was allegedly found during mosque excavations. The mosque has the distinction of being the first mosque to be visited by a pope (John Paul II in 2001).

MEZQUITA

WHERE
CÓRDOBA, SPAIN
DATE
755

Built as a mosque under an Islamic Arab caliph Abd-ar Rahman I, using Christian labour, it is now a cathedral. The building's chequered identity is made even more complicated by the history of its construction. Christians conscripted to the task were free to worship their own religion on site during the building process; attracted by this spirit of compromise, many allegedly converted to Islam.

IBN TULUN MOSQUE

WHERE
CAIRO, EGYPT
DATE
877

One of the oldest and most beloved mosques in Egypt, commemorated on the back of the Egyptian five pound note. It could be seen as a symbol of triumph in the face of adversity, as it was built by the son of a Turkish slave who rose to become Governor of Egypt. Architecturally, it is renowned for a unique spiral staircase.

ALMOHAD MOSQUE

WHERE
SEVILLE, SPAIN
DATE
1167

Started life as an important mosque but is now one of the largest cathedrals in the world. This remarkable building is considered an important landmark in the history of Gothic and baroque architecture. It is notable for its Giralda (bell tower), which is almost 100m-high and was originally designed as a minaret, with ramps wide enough for the muezzin to ascend on horseback.

MESJID AGUNG

WHERE
DEMAK, INDONESIA
DATE
1466

Built in Demak, a district of Java, the Mesjid Agung (Great Mosque) is one of the oldest mosques in the Far East. The great carved wooden doors are known as the 'Doors of Thunder', on account of the motifs, including an open-mouthed animal, which are said to be representative of thunder.

GLAM ISLAM

INDULGE IN SOME OF THE REGIONS GREAT EXTRAVAGANCIES

✪ DAHAB DIVING (EGYPT)

Its name, meaning 'gold' in Arabic, was given to the palm-fringed bay because of the glistening sands that seem to roll out of the desert into the Red Sea. The tranquil coastal town started out as a sleepy Bedouin fishing village before being 'discovered' by hippies in the late '70s. Now a hub for windsurfers and divers, Dahab's greatest treasures are its chilled-out atmosphere and plethora of spectacular marine life and coral reefs offshore.

✪ MARINA MALL (KUWAIT)

Its neoclassical Spanish architecture has made Marina Mall in Abu Dhabi an icon of contemporary sophistication and the modern jewel in Kuwait's cultural crown. Boasting over 300 designer stores and heaps of flamboyant water features (always impressive in the middle of a desert) the mall's shopping zones are linked to restaurants in the adjacent Marina Crescent by a 100m-long, air-conditioned footbridge, which affords seriously breathtaking views across the exclusive beachside suburb of Salmiya.

✪ BAHRAIN PEARLS (BAHRAIN)

Historically, pearls and the Persian Gulf go hand in hand. As one of the world's great pearling centres, Bahrain's natural bounty has secured its place on the Glam Map. For centuries, breath-hold divers launched into the deep, clear waters, braving sharks and jagged reefs to harvest the oysters. Even though the supply of natural pearls has sharply declined, the government enforces a ban on 'cultured' pearls to preserve the quality of it's ancient heritage.

✪ SOUQS OF DOHA (QATAR)

Wandering along the narrow laneways lined with stores selling anything from gold and pearls to bejewelled daggers and jellabas is both relaxing and an epic sensory assault. The sound of constant haggling reverberates against the ancient stone walls whilst the scent of leather and spices diffuses beneath fabric-covered rafters. The main souq is Souq Waqif, which was the original weekend market for Bedouins coming into town to trade wool and meat for staple goods.

✪ DUBAI SHOPPING FESTIVAL (UNITED ARAB EMIRATES)

If you're born to shop then DSF will be your idea of paradise. The annual, month-long shopping and cultural extravaganza attracts over three million visitors, who descend on Dubai to browse over 2300 participating retail outlets. The festival's permanent home is the Mall of Arabia (the biggest mall on earth) inside the epic Dubailand entertainment precinct, which upon completion in 2020 will cover 3 billion sq metres. Expect fashion shows, fireworks, freakin' everything, OK?!

RETAIL-FUELLED TOURISM, NOT OIL, IS POWERING THE UNITED ARAB EMIRATES' FLAGSHIP OF DUBAI: IN THE 45 DAYS OF THE DUBAI SHOPPING FESTIVAL OVER $US2 BILLION IS SPENT.

The earth has a new centre.
The Dubai Mall
دبــــي مـــول
www.thedubaimall.c

POP ISLAM

TUNE INTO ISLAM'S MORE MODERN SOUND WAVES

✪ SALMAN AHMAD (PAKISTAN)

After training as a doctor, the lead guitarist for Pakistani rock outfit Junoon – described by Q magazine as 'one of the biggest bands in the world' – committed his life to music as, in his own words, 'It was the most powerful expression of peace I could find'. A former UNAIDS ambassador and recipient of a Unesco award for 'outstanding achievements in music and peace', Ahmad is revered as Pakistan's answer to Ireland's Bono from U2.

✪ NANCY AJRAM (LEBANON)

As a teenager Ajram shot to fame by winning the popular TV music competition Noujoum Al-Moustakbal (Stars of the Future). Since then the 25 year old has released four albums selling over four-million records in Lebanon alone and is already ranked the third best-selling female Lebanese artist of all time. Described in the Los Angeles Times as 'that most effervescent of Arab sex kittens', Ajram represents a new breed of Arabian pop artists.

✪ THE KORDZ (LEBANON)

Since their debut at the Beirut Beer Festival in 1992, the goatee-sporting indie rock quintet has electrified locals with their blend of heavy riffs, disarming melodies and Arab-meets-West wall of sound. The Kordz cite influences from Bob Marley to Alice in Chains and fuse traditional sounds like the single-stringed rababa with Metallica-style power chords. For years international success has been on the horizon: perhaps 2008 will finally be the year of The Kordz.

✪ FUTURE ARAB SUPERSTAR

The best thing about Future Arab Superstar (the Arab world's version of the global Pop Idol phenomenon) is that archived footage from previous years is available online. That means not only can you check out previous winners, such as Saudi Arabia's Ibrahim El Hakami and Jordan's Diana Karazon, now among their country's biggest pop artists, you can also amuse yourself by watching some of the 'less promising' aspirants from the earlier rounds. Cringeworthy, but great entertainment all the same.

✪ SULIS CINTA RASUL (INDONESIA)

She recorded her first album at nine years of age and within weeks had become a household name throughout Indonesia. The multiplatinum-selling 18 year old now has millions of fans worldwide. Cinta Rasul's speciality is the spiritual power ballad, which she often belts out as a duet with Haddad Alwi, who's also her shalawat (songs of praise for the Prophet) teacher. To date her biggest hit has been 'Love for the Messenger', which she recorded in 2005 accompanied by Australia's Victoria Philharmonic Orchestra.

PAKISTANI BAND JUNOON HAVE RIDDEN THEIR VERSION OF SUFI ROCK TO THE TOP, WITH ALBUM SALES TO THE TUNE OF OVER 20 MILLION.

Islam around the corner

For many people, their first encounter with
the Islamic world is likely to be in their own
neighbourhood. In the last few decades, large numbers
of Muslims have settled in the West, especially in
Europe, either attracted by economic opportunities or
to escape strife in their home countries.

European countries may be the most evident
but they are not the only non-Islamic countries that
Muslims call home. In the far west of China, in the
province of Xinjiang, after days crossing the Buddhist
fringes of the Tibetan plateau, a traveller will suddenly
come across the dusty town of Turfan, with its
hollyhocks and mud-brick minarets. Then there are
the surprise communities of Omanis on the Eastern
shores of Africa and in the spice island of Zanzibar,
while perhaps the most surprising Muslim enclave is
marooned in an outpost of Suriname in South America.

As such, almost wherever you live or wherever you
go, the opportunity is there to engage with Islamic
culture. Near mosques you'll often find an array of
restaurants, cafés, shops and public spaces that
carry a distinctly Islamic flavour. There are museums,
galleries and cultural centres devoted to Islamic culture
where you can learn more about the history, customs,
beliefs and practices of Islam and its followers. Your
local bookstore or record shop is another place to get a
taste of what the culture has to offer.

So next time you head out the door for a trip across
town or continents, be sure to grab your curiosity
and a little of that universal currency, good will, and
take the next step on your own journey of a lifetime.

[TOP] » DIVISIVE ISSUES AND DEDICATED
FOLLOWERS: SUPPORTERS OF
CONTROVERSIAL MUSLIM CLERIC ABU
HAMZA AL-MASRI TOOK FRIDAY PRAYERS
TO NORTH LONDON STREETS AFTER HE WAS
EJECTED FROM FINSBURY PARK MOSQUE.

[LEFT] » WHEN IN ROME...MUSLIM WOMEN
AT THE SUNDAY ANGELUS PRAYER IN ST
PETER'S SQUARE, THE VATICAN.

[RIGHT] » KNOWING WHEN TO HOLD 'EM
IS A SKILL HONED MOST EVENINGS IN THE
UIGHUR OLD TOWN NEIGHBOURHOODS OF
YARKAND, ON THE SILK ROAD IN CHINA'S
XINJIANG PROVINCE.

MUSLIM COMMUNITIES IN NON-ISLAMIC COUNTRIES

PLACE	LOCAL ATTRACTIONS	INFUSED WITH ISLAM
FRANCE	The largest Muslim communities are in Paris, home of the Seine, the Eiffel Tower, the Louvre and many great monuments of Christendom.	Invited to take up residence after their brave support in WWI, many Algerians settled around Paris, numbering tens of thousands by the 1930s. Now there are over 1.5 million Algerians living in France. It hasn't always been an easy cohabitation. One Muslim writes of his recipe for survival: 'Respect yourself. Don't complain. Keep your kids on the straight and narrow. Know where you come from. Practice solidarity'.
ITALY	The gondalier city of Venice boasts a strong Islamic presence – Palazzo Ducale and Basilica di San Marco are full of the Serenissima's Eastern treasures.	The modern day Moors of Venice are to be seen either selling handbags on the Rialto over the Grand Canal or trading more successfully as Gentlemen of Verona in the surrounding areas of Northern Italy. There are 825,000 Muslims in Italy today (about 1.4% of the population) who are mainly from various parts of Africa.
NETHERLANDS	Cities like Amsterdam may become majority Muslim cities in the next few decades: travellers looking for the red light district may have to settle for tulips!	With 5.8% of the population being immigrant Muslims (nearly one million people), the recent tensions between the Islamic and local community following the death of a film maker in 2004 is a challenge in a country that epitomises freedom of speech. Immigrants include many Muslims from former Dutch colonies such as Suriname (especially in Den Haag) and Indonesia.
SPAIN	Barcelona is in parts like a modern Meknès – edgy, grand, independent and full of architectural statements, such as Gaudi's famous cathedral.	There are one million Muslims in Spain – about 2.8% of the population, and of these about 6000 are converts from Christianity, looking perhaps for a foundation for much of their cultural inheritance. Immigrants, many of whom have settled in Barcelona, are mostly from Morocco, joining their families after several decades working in Spain's tourist sector.
CANADA	The capital of Canada, Ottawa, neighbours two 'must-sees': Toronto, of Blue Jays baseball fame, and the world-renowned Niagara Falls.	The first Muslims who immigrated to Canada were the Wahab family from Lebanon who settled in 1903. Today there are about 60,000 Muslims in the Ottawa area alone; the population was boosted considerably by Somali refugees fleeing conflict in their own country during the 1980s and 1990s.

population *Islam*

50 NATIONS WITH THE LARGEST MUSLIM POPULATIONS*

INDONESIA
86% OF TOTAL POPULATION
- **CAPITAL** JAKARTA
- **ISLAMIC POPULATION** 202 MILLION
- **POPULATION** 234.7 MILLION
- **OFFICIAL LANGUAGE** BAHASA INDONESIA

PAKISTAN
97% OF TOTAL POPULATION
- **CAPITAL** ISLAMABAD
- **ISLAMIC POPULATION** 159.8 MILLION
- **POPULATION** 164.7 MILLION
- **OFFICIAL LANGUAGE** URDU

INDIA
13% OF TOTAL POPULATION
- **CAPITAL** NEW DELHI
- **ISLAMIC POPULATION** 151.4 MILLION
- **POPULATION** 1130 MILLION
- **OFFICIAL LANGUAGE** HINDI

BANGLADESH
83% OF TOTAL POPULATION
- **CAPITAL** DHAKA
- **ISLAMIC POPULATION** 124.9 MILLION
- **POPULATION** 150.5 MILLION
- **OFFICIAL LANGUAGE** BENGALI

EGYPT
90% OF TOTAL POPULATION
- **CAPITAL** CAIRO
- **ISLAMIC POPULATION** 72.4 MILLION
- **POPULATION** 80.4 MILLION
- **OFFICIAL LANGUAGE** ARABIC

TURKEY
99% OF TOTAL POPULATION
- **CAPITAL** ANKARA
- **ISLAMIC POPULATION** 71.1 MILLION
- **POPULATION** 71.2 MILLION
- **OFFICIAL LANGUAGE** TURKISH

NIGERIA
50% OF TOTAL POPULATION
- **CAPITAL** ABUJA
- **ISLAMIC POPULATION** 67.5 MILLION
- **POPULATION** 135 MILLION
- **OFFICIAL LANGUAGE** ENGLISH

IRAN
98% OF TOTAL POPULATION
- **CAPITAL** TEHRAN
- **ISLAMIC POPULATION** 64.1 MILLION
- **POPULATION** 65.4 MILLION
- **OFFICIAL LANGUAGE** PERSIAN

MOROCCO
99% OF TOTAL POPULATION
- **CAPITAL** RABAT
- **ISLAMIC POPULATION** 33.4 MILLION
- **POPULATION** 33.8 MILLION
- **OFFICIAL LANGUAGE** ARABIC

ALGERIA
99% OF TOTAL POPULATION
- **CAPITAL** ALGIERS
- **ISLAMIC POPULATION** 33 MILLION
- **POPULATION** 33.3 MILLION
- **OFFICIAL LANGUAGE** ARABIC

AFGHANISTAN
99% OF TOTAL POPULATION
- **CAPITAL** KABUL
- **ISLAMIC POPULATION** 31.6 MILLION
- **POPULATION** 31.9 MILLION
- **OFFICIAL LANGUAGE** AFGHAN PERSIAN

SAUDI ARABIA
100% OF TOTAL POPULATION
- **CAPITAL** RIYADH
- **ISLAMIC POPULATION** 27.6 MILLION
- **POPULATION** 27.6 MILLION
- **OFFICIAL LANGUAGE** ARABIC

SUDAN
70% OF TOTAL POPULATION
- **CAPITAL** KHARTOUM
- **ISLAMIC POPULATION** 27.6 MILLION
- **POPULATION** 39.4 MILLION
- **OFFICIAL LANGUAGE** ARABIC

IRAQ
97% OF TOTAL POPULATION
- **CAPITAL** BAGHDAD
- **ISLAMIC POPULATION** 26.7 MILLION
- **POPULATION** 27.5 MILLION
- **OFFICIAL LANGUAGES** ARABIC, KURDISH

ETHIOPIA
33% OF TOTAL POPULATION
- **CAPITAL** ADDIS ABABA
- **ISLAMIC POPULATION** 25.2 MILLION
- **POPULATION** 76.5 MILLION
- **OFFICIAL LANGUAGE** AMHARIC

UZBEKISTAN
88% OF TOTAL POPULATION
- **CAPITAL** TASHKENT
- **ISLAMIC POPULATION** 24.5 MILLION
- **POPULATION** 27.8 MILLION
- **OFFICIAL LANGUAGE** UZBEK

YEMEN
100% OF TOTAL POPULATION
- **CAPITAL** SAN'A
- **ISLAMIC POPULATION** 22.2 MILLION
- **POPULATION** 22.2 MILLION
- **OFFICIAL LANGUAGE** ARABIC

CHINA
1.5% OF TOTAL POPULATION
- **CAPITAL** BEIJING
- **ISLAMIC POPULATION** 19.8 MILLION
- **POPULATION** 1322 MILLION
- **OFFICIAL LANGUAGE** MANDARIN

RUSSIAN FEDERATION
13% OF TOTAL POPULATION
- **CAPITAL** MOSCOW
- **ISLAMIC POPULATION** 18 MILLION
- **POPULATION** 141.4 MILLION
- **OFFICIAL LANGUAGE** RUSSIAN

SYRIA
90% OF TOTAL POPULATION
- **CAPITAL** DAMASCUS
- **ISLAMIC POPULATION** 17.4 MILLION
- **POPULATION** 19.3 MILLION
- **OFFICIAL LANGUAGE** ARABIC

MALAYSIA
60% OF TOTAL POPULATION
- **CAPITAL** KUALA LUMPUR
- **ISLAMIC POPULATION** 15 MILLION
- **POPULATION** 24.8 MILLION
- **OFFICIAL LANGUAGE** BAHASA MALAY

TANZANIA
35% OF TOTAL POPULATION
- **CAPITAL** DODOMA
- **ISLAMIC POPULATION** 13.8 MILLION
- **POPULATION** 39.4 MILLION
- **OFFICIAL LANGUAGES** SWAHILI, ENGLISH

SENEGAL
94% OF TOTAL POPULATION
- **CAPITAL** DAKAR
- **ISLAMIC POPULATION** 11.8 MILLION
- **POPULATION** 12.5 MILLION
- **OFFICIAL LANGUAGE** FRENCH

MALI
90% OF TOTAL POPULATION
- **CAPITAL** BAMAKO
- **ISLAMIC POPULATION** 10.8 MILLION
- **POPULATION** 12 MILLION
- **OFFICIAL LANGUAGE** FRENCH

NIGER
80% OF TOTAL POPULATION
- **CAPITAL** NIAMEY
- **ISLAMIC POPULATION** 10.3 MILLION
- **POPULATION** 12.9 MILLION
- **OFFICIAL LANGUAGE** FRENCH

TUNISIA
98% OF TOTAL POPULATION
- **CAPITAL** TUNIS
- **ISLAMIC POPULATION** 10.1 MILLION
- **POPULATION** 10.3 MILLION
- **OFFICIAL LANGUAGE** ARABIC

SOMALIA
100% OF TOTAL POPULATION
- **CAPITAL** MOGADISHU
- **ISLAMIC POPULATION** 9.1 MILLION
- **POPULATION** 9.1 MILLION
- **OFFICIAL LANGUAGE** SOMALI

GUINEA
- **CAPITAL** CONAKRY
- **ISLAMIC POPULATION** 8.4 MILLION
- **POPULATION** 9.9 MILLION
- **OFFICIAL LANGUAGE** FRENCH

85% OF TOTAL POPULATION

 AZERBAIJAN
- **CAPITAL** BAKU
- **ISLAMIC POPULATION** 7.6 MILLION
- **POPULATION** 8.1 MILLION
- **OFFICIAL LANGUAGE** AZERBAIJANI

93% OF TOTAL POPULATION

 KAZAKHSTAN
- **CAPITAL** ASTANA
- **ISLAMIC POPULATION** 7.2 MILLION
- **POPULATION** 15.3 MILLION
- **OFFICIAL LANGUAGES** KAZAKH, RUSSIAN

47% OF TOTAL POPULATION

 BURKINA FASO
- **CAPITAL** OUAGADOUGOU
- **ISLAMIC POPULATION** 7.2 MILLION
- **POPULATION** 14.3 MILLION
- **OFFICIAL LANGUAGE** FRENCH

50% OF TOTAL POPULATION

 CÔTE D'IVOIRE
- **CAPITAL** YAMOUSSOUKRO
- **ISLAMIC POPULATION** 6.8 MILLION
- **POPULATION** 18 MILLION
- **OFFICIAL LANGUAGE** FRENCH

38% OF TOTAL POPULATION

 CONGO, DEMOCRATIC REPUBLIC OF
- **CAPITAL** KINSHASA
- **ISLAMIC POPULATION** 6.6 MILLION
- **POPULATION** 65.7 MILLION
- **OFFICIAL LANGUAGE** FRENCH

10% OF TOTAL POPULATION

 TAJIKSTAN
- **CAPITAL** DUSHANBE
- **ISLAMIC POPULATION** 6.4 MILLION
- **POPULATION** 7.1 MILLION
- **OFFICIAL LANGUAGE** TAJIK

90% OF TOTAL POPULATION

 LIBYA
- **CAPITAL** TRIPOLI
- **ISLAMIC POPULATION** 5.8 MILLION
- **POPULATION** 6 MILLION
- **OFFICIAL LANGUAGE** ARABIC

97% OF TOTAL POPULATION

 JORDAN
- **CAPITAL**
- **ISLAMIC POPULATION** 5.7 MILLION
- **POPULATION** 6.1 MILLION
- **OFFICIAL LANGUAGE** ARABIC

94% OF TOTAL POPULATION

 **CHAD**
- **CAPITAL** N'DJAMÉNA
- **ISLAMIC POPULATION** 5.3 MILLION
- **POPULATION** 9.9 MILLION
- **OFFICIAL LANGUAGES** FRENCH, ARABIC

53% OF TOTAL POPULATION

 **FRANCE**
- **CAPITAL** PARIS
- **ISLAMIC POPULATION** 4.8 MILLION
- **POPULATION** 63.7 MILLION
- **OFFICIAL LANGUAGE** FRENCH

7.5% OF TOTAL POPULATION

 **PHILIPPINES**
- **CAPITAL** MANILA
- **ISLAMIC POPULATION** 4.6 MILLION
- **POPULATION** 91.1 MILLION
- **OFFICIAL LANGUAGES** FILIPINO, ENGLISH

5.0% OF TOTAL POPULATION

 TURKMENISTAN
- **CAPITAL** ASHGABAT
- **ISLAMIC POPULATION** 4.5 MILLION
- **POPULATION** 5.1 MILLION
- **OFFICIAL LANGUAGE** TURKMEN

89% OF TOTAL POPULATION

 **KYRGYZSTAN**
- **CAPITAL** BISHKEK
- **ISLAMIC POPULATION** 4 MILLION
- **POPULATION** 5.3 MILLION
- **OFFICIAL LANGUAGES** KYRGYZ, RUSSIAN

75% OF TOTAL POPULATION

 **UGANDA**
- **CAPITAL** KAMPALA
- **ISLAMIC POPULATION** 3.7 MILLION
- **POPULATION** 30.3 MILLION
- **OFFICIAL LANGUAGE** ENGLISH

12% OF TOTAL POPULATION

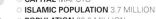 **SIERRA LEONE**
- **CAPITAL** FREETOWN
- **ISLAMIC POPULATION** 3.7 MILLION
- **POPULATION** 6.1 MILLION
- **OFFICIAL LANGUAGE** ENGLISH

60% OF TOTAL POPULATION

 MOZAMBIQUE
- **CAPITAL** MAPUTO
- **ISLAMIC POPULATION** 3.7 MILLION
- **POPULATION** 20.9 MILLION
- **OFFICIAL LANGUAGE** PORTUGUESE

18% OF TOTAL POPULATION

 GHANA
- **CAPITAL** ACCRA
- **ISLAMIC POPULATION** 3.6 MILLION
- **POPULATION** 22.9 MILLION
- **OFFICIAL LANGUAGE** ENGLISH

16% OF TOTAL POPULATION

 CAMEROON
- **CAPITAL** YAOUNDÉ
- **ISLAMIC POPULATION** 3.6 MILLION
- **POPULATION** 18.1 MILLION
- **OFFICIAL LANGUAGES** FRENCH, ENGLISH

20% OF TOTAL POPULATION

 MAURITANIA
- **CAPITAL** NOUAKCHOTT
- **ISLAMIC POPULATION** 3.3 MILLION
- **POPULATION** 3.3 MILLION
- **OFFICIAL LANGUAGE** ARABIC

100% OF TOTAL POPULATION

GERMANY
- **CAPITAL** BERLIN
- **ISLAMIC POPULATION** 3.1 MILLION
- **POPULATION** 82.4 MILLION
- **OFFICIAL LANGUAGE** GERMAN

3.7% OF TOTAL POPULATION

UNITED STATES OF AMERICA
- **CAPITAL** WASHINGTON
- **ISLAMIC POPULATION** 3 MILLION
- **POPULATION** 301 MILLION
- **OFFICIAL LANGUAGE** ENGLISH

1.0% OF TOTAL POPULATION

OMAN
- **CAPITAL** MUSCAT
- **ISLAMIC POPULATION** 3 MILLION
- **POPULATION** 3.2 MILLION
- **OFFICIAL LANGUAGE** ARABIC

93% OF TOTAL POPULATION

OFFICIAL ISLAMIC COUNTRIES NOT LISTED
ALBANIA
BAHRAIN
BENIN
BRUNEI
COMOROS
DJIBOUTI
GAMBIA
GUINEA-BISSAU
GUYANA
KUWAIT
LEBANON
MALDIVES
QATAR
UNITED ARAB EMIRATES

*RANKINGS MEASURED IN TERMS OF SIZE OF MUSLIM POPULATION (NOT PERCENTAGE OF POPULATION). ALL FIGURES ARE APPOXIMATIONS.

BLUELIST.
MOMENTS »

IN 2007 WE ASKED YOU, THE LONELY PLANET
TRAVEL COMMUNITY, TO ENTER OUR ONLINE PHOTO
COMPETITION. WELCOME TO BLUELIST MOMENTS
– YOUR BEST TRAVEL RECOMMENDATIONS
CAPTURED ON CAMERA.

DEVJIT ACHARYA

» PREDAWN AT THE PUSHKAR CAMEL FAIR, INDIA

Every year some 200,000 people converge on the town of Pushkar in Rajasthan for this annual fair, bringing with them 50,000 camels and cattle. Everyone is busy selling and buying animals and the process involves a lot of bargaining – it's so chaotic that you can't even stand and talk to people for too long. I got up at about 3am so I could take some shots of the camels at dawn. On the way to the grounds, I stopped by a stall for a cup of tea, and that's when I took this photo. I found the entire composition so appealing – it was such a contrast to the hectic daytime, with everyone so calm as they waited for the sun to rise.

ASHWIN KUMAR

» SUNSET AT BROKEN HILL TRAIN STATION, AUSTRALIA

I love travelling by train. During my journey through the Australia I made the *Indian Pacific* railroad trip from Perth to Sydney and was awed by the visually stimulating landscape. After travelling for two days in the outback and visiting towns in the middle of nowhere, we got out to stretch our tired legs at Broken Hill, New South Wales. The sunset generated wonderful hues, and the seemingly never-ending string of train carriages caught my eye. This photograph tries to capture that moment; the beauty of man-made elements juxtaposed against nature and the ephemeral feeling of never having to end a journey.

ERIC CABAHUG

» LANDING AT CAMIGUIN'S WHITE ISLAND, PHILIPPINES

My trip to Camiguin did not start as I'd imagined. Dark clouds were looming when I missed my ferry, and it was night and raining when I reached the resort. The electricity was down, and it just kept raining. The following morning was still cloudy and I was worried that my trip to White Island – a sand bar in the shape of a crescent moon a few hundred metres off the shore – wouldn't be possible. But the boatman said it was safe, so off we went in a blue pumpboat. As I set foot on the island the sun peeked through the clouds, kissing the white sands and lighting the wavy blue waters around me. Just as I'd imagined.

SAYAN CHOWDREY

» BOATMEN CARRYING CORACLES AT HOGENAKKAL, INDIA

At Hogenakkal, which means 'smoking rocks', the Cauvery River plunges down over the rocks creating a beautiful mist at the bottom of the waterfall. Our boatman took us to the very base of the falls. Time froze as the angry water thundered all around us and the world spun round and round in a haze of mist and spray. This photo shows the boatmen carrying their coracles up the cliff to the waiting customers. I feel it shows something of their indomitable spirit and also their skill in providing tourists like me with an experience to remember forever.

KIERAN BALL

» MORNING FOOTBALL AT SALAR DE UYUNI, BOLIVIA

It was really cold early in the morning, so we had on our handmade llama-wool hats and socks. Of course I had my football with me – I'd taken it everywhere I'd been throughout Latin America, as it's a great way to make friends with the locals. The giant Uyuni salt pans are are not only one of the most amazing landscapes on the planet, they also make a football pitch of epic proportions. I took this photo while kicking my ball around. It seemed like a good study of shapes and colours, but more importantly it represented countless unforgettable experiences in one of my favourite countries.

BLUELIST. » MOMENTS

GIL MOSES

» HORSESHOE BEND OF THE COLORADO RIVER, USA

Were we in the right spot? My friend had promised me a breathtaking site – so where were all the tourists? A short drive from Page, Arizona on Hwy 89, we came to a small dirt lot with not a single parked car. A sign read '¾ miles to scenic view. Take nothing but pictures, leave nothing but footprints'. We walked to the rim but there was no view in sight, so we hiked down the dirt trail. The view was hidden until the last step. We stood in silence. Far below, the Colorado River reflected the colours of sun and sky. Birds flew up from inside the canyon and whooshed passed us. It was an awe-inspiring moment.

JOEL DOUSSET

» WASHING GOMATESHVARA'S FEET AT SRAVANABELAGOLA, INDIA

We were visiting the famous 17.5m-high monolithic statue of Gomateshvara, which stands on top of a hill near Sravanabelagola in Karnataka. Gomateshvara is a Jain deity, and every morning the statue's feet are washed with water, milk and saffron. The women in the photo were there for a pilgrimage and were allowed by the priest to enter the holy restricted area. The way they were touching the feet was quite remarkable, as were the contrasting colours of their robes and flesh as they honoured the grey granite. As a ray of sunlight penetrated the shade...I felt that here was art, right under my eyes.

MARIE BRYAN

» STORMY SKIES OVER THE TRAVERTINES AT PAMUKKALE, TURKEY

When I first arrived at the travertine (calcium carbonate) shelves and pools at Pamukkale, I had despaired of getting a really interesting photo – my tour guide had dropped me off at the end of the formation where all the tourists were. So I walked away from all the people, taking photos all the way. It was only when I got to the far end that I could see that the light and the clouds and the luminescence of the travertines might yield something wonderful – if only I was up to the challenge! This photo was the result.

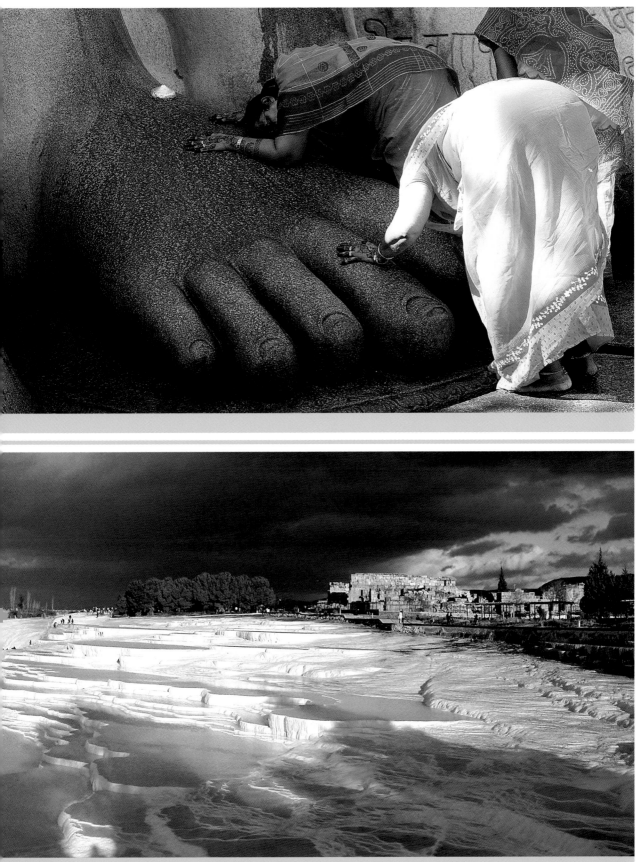

PETE CHESHIRE

» BREAKFAST AT LAKE LOUISE, CANADA

All that I'd read about the turquoise waters and the glacial backdrop couldn't quite prepare me for Lake Louise in Alberta. It's a beautiful place: during the day its perfect for canoeing and kayaking; in the evening the chateau is lit up like a fairy tale. But the time to catch it at its most tranquil and peaceful has to be just as dawn is breaking. We decided to take our breakfast down to the lake at very first light, and this picture was an attempt to capture that moment. The waters were absolutely still – a flawless mirror reflecting the surrounding mountains, trees and glacier. Simply stunning.

MAXENCE TOMBEUR

» SHOOTING POOL AT NAM-TSO, TIBET

In Tibetan Nam-tso means 'Heavenly Lake', which is a good name given the breathtaking scenery. At 4718m it's the highest salt-water lake in the world, lying in one of the windiest and coldest areas of Tibet. *Drokpas* (nomads) who live there wear capes for protection against the sand and dust. I was there in March and the lake was still frozen; it can get down to –40°C at night. Around the lake there's almost nothing, just a few tents for travellers who want to spend the night…and a pool table! Playing pool with *drokpas* in such conditions and in such an incredible setting is not the kind of experience you can readily forget.

ENDANGERED
WILDLIFE

SEE SOME OF THE WORLD'S MOST-ENDANGERED ANIMALS IN THEIR NATURAL HABITATS

GO » KOMODO NATIONAL PARK, INDONESIA

AN EQUATORIAL WONDERLAND, REPLETE WITH GIANT PREHISTORIC REPTILES, BIZARRE PLANT LIFE & TURBULENT GEOLOGICAL FEATURES – ALL SET IN A CORAL SEA AT THE MEETING POINT OF TWO GREAT OCEANS.

WHERE Komodo National Park includes three major islands: Komodo, Rinca, and Padar, as well as numerous smaller islands, situated at the centre of the Indonesian archipelago between the islands of Sumbawa and Flores. The park encompasses an area of 1817 sq km (of which marine areas constitute 67%), with extensions proposed that would bring the total up to 2321 sq km.

WHY Established in 1980 to protect the endangered Komodo dragon, the park's significance was recognised when Unesco designated it a World Heritage site and a Man and Biosphere reserve in 1986. The park's focus has since expanded to include all terrestrial and marine environments in the region.

Sitting where two continental plates – the Sahul and Sunda plates – collide, the region is home to volcanoes, frequent tremors and upthrusting coral reefs. For eight months a year there is little or no rainfall and lack of fresh water is a major problem for both local communities and for the animals of the islands. It is an arid landscape with a limited variety of plants that have adapted to the dry climate and frequent fires. At the same time cloud forests can be found on mountain tops and ridges.

The park's islands host an exchange of flora and fauna between the Indian and Pacific Oceans and the area is one of the richest marine environments in the world. Along with abundant marine reptiles and mammals, the park is also home to over 1000 species of fish, 70 species of sponges and over 260 species of reef-building corals.

[TOP] » HARMONIOUS HUES AND INTRICATE FORMS GRACE THE CORAL SEA WATERS AROUND THESE ARID ISLES IN THE INDONESIAN ARCHIPELAGO.

CONSERVATION OPPORTUNITIES

With the local human population having grown by 800% in the past 60 years and 97% of the villagers dependant on fishing for their livelihood, there is a significant and growing threat to the region's marine ecosystems. Since 1995 the organisation Nature Conservancy has been working on a strategy to make the park financially self-sustaining, including developing a grassroots fish-farming industry that engages local fishermen in sustainable fishing practices. All park fees paid by visitors go directly into a conservation fund.✿

✪ YELLOW-CRESTED COCKATOO

WHAT The yellow-crested cockatoo *(Cacatua sulphurea)*, also known as the lesser sulphur-crested cockatoo, is a familiar sight due to its prevalence in the pet trade. While this regal bird is highly valued as a pet for its brilliant white feathers and elegantly curled yellow crest, nothing compares to seeing one in its native habitat. Found in forests on just a few islands from Bali to East Timor, this 35cm-long cockatoo feeds on a diet of seeds, nuts, fruits and buds. Like other members of the parrot family, it lives many years and is capable of complex vocalisations.

STATUS Populations of these beautiful birds have declined more than 80% in three generations due to collection for the pet trade and the impact of rampant logging. Now extinct on many islands and close to extinction on others, this bird is critically endangered in its native habitat.

✪ KOMODO DRAGON

WHAT It's hard to deny the allure of a prehistoric lizard that weighs upwards of 166kg and has the power to take down and kill a full-grown water buffalo. Not surprisingly, the Komodo dragon *(Varanus komodoensis)* looms large in the imagination of the local people, who revere it as a mystical ancestor. Attaining lengths of 3m, the dragon is the islands' top predator and every living animal is its potential prey, including humans. The bite of the dragon is rightly feared because its saliva contains toxic microbes that cause death from blood poisoning within days. Fortunately, Komodo dragons have a preference for dead animals, and use their uncanny sense of smell to find carrion up to 11km away.

STATUS With a world population of around 3000, it would appear at first glance that the Komodo dragon is not among the world's most threatened creatures. It has been recently noted, however, that out of this total there are only 350 breeding females and the entire population hinges around the survival of these important members. Even within the park, Komodo dragons have recently been rendered extinct on the island of Padar.

GO » ALAK'I SWAMP, HAWAII, USA

SEARCH FOR THE MOST ENDANGERED PLANTS & ANIMALS IN THE NORTHERN HEMISPHERE WHILE TRAMPING THROUGH A PRIMEVAL, FOG-ENSHROUDED SWAMP IN ONE OF THE RAINIEST PLACES ON EARTH.

WHERE In the summit crater of the six-million-year-old volcano that dominates the Hawaiian island of Kaua'i lurks the inhospitable 40-sq-km Alak'i Swamp, one of the most pristine ecosystems left in the Hawaiian Islands. Officially designated the Alak'i Wilderness Area, this place is better known to indigenous Hawaiians as the site where Pele, the goddess of fire, left an imprint when she stomped her foot into oozing lava.

WHY This virtually impenetrable thicket of stunted trees and waist-deep bogs was until quite recently explored only by biologists and hog hunters, and largely ignored by everyone else. A newly constructed wooden boardwalk now allows access into the murky heart of this utterly unique wetland, considered the highest and largest high-elevation swamp in the world.

Come for glimpses of this unique environment's incredibly rare birds and flowers, but expect to encounter rain and fog – the Alak'i gets up to 760cm of precipitation each year and visitors are likely to have the feeling of walking in clouds for much of the time. Whatever you do, don't wander off the boardwalk: not only does your presence endanger this incredibly fragile ecosystem, but some of the swamp's explorers have disappeared and never been found, so it's definitely not a place in which you want to get lost.

(TOP) » BETWEEN ALPINE SWAMPS AND DOLPHIN PODS, KAUA'I FINDS ROOM FOR THE COASTLINE OF NA PALI.

CONSERVATION OPPORTUNITIES

Of 71 native birds known from the Hawaiian Islands, 24 are extinct and another 32 are critically endangered; while 120 species of plants are represented by fewer than 20 individuals each. For some of these species, the Alak'i Swamp is their most important remaining stronghold. Unfortunately the 'o'o bird, whose tuffs of yellow feathers once adorned the capes of Hawaiian royalty, has not been seen since 1984. Current restoration efforts include removing invasive plants and constructing fences to keep out extremely destructive introduced pigs. ✪

SEE »

✪ PUAIOHI

WHAT The diminutive puaiohi (*Myadestes palmeri*), a native thrush, is little more than a dusky brown bird with pink legs. It inhabits fern- and sedge-covered streambanks in the heart of the Alak'i Swamp, where it eats the purple berries of the native 'olapa plant. Rarely seen because it hides in such dense vegetation, it is sometimes heard giving a song that is said to sound like the squeaking of a metal wheel in need of lubrication.

STATUS Numbering fewer than 25 only a few years ago, the exceedingly rare puaiohi, like all native birds in Hawaii, faces the twin threats of shrinking habitat and introduced competitors. Having evolved in a tropical paradise, these birds do not easily tolerate competition from exotic species or the alteration of habitats by humans.

The death blow for many of these birds was the arrival of disease-carrying mosquitoes and avian malaria in the early 1820s. In one experiment 90% of a group of native birds died after a single mosquito bite, and humans have aided the spread of mosquitoes by clearing forests.

Though puaiohi numbers have rebounded to around 300, thanks to an intensive captive breeding programme, their survival is not yet guaranteed.

✪ 'I'IWI

WHAT If you hike the trails of the Alak'i Swamp in search of rare birds, you will almost certainly be accompanied by the scarlet 'i'iwi (*Vestiaria coccinea*; pictured below). Although five of Alak'i's native birds became extinct during the 20th century, the outrageous 'i'iwi has held on and continues to draw stares of awe from visitors. One of the world's most beautiful birds, its jewelled feathers once adorned the capes of Hawaiian royalty.

If Hawaii could be defined by any group of animals, it would be the honeycreepers that arrived three million years ago and diverged into 50 distinctive species. Each honeycreeper had its own lifestyle, and pollinated specific flowers that also plunged into extinction as each honeycreeper disappeared one by one. Fortunately, the 'i'iwi is still around to visit its favourite flower, the ohia, whose red blossoms, shaped like a shaving brush, fill native forests in February.

STATUS Though doing better than many other native Hawaiian birds, the 'i'iwi is approaching extinction on several islands. Its population remains fairly robust on Kaua'i largely due to the protection provided by Alak'i Swamp.

GO » CAT TIEN, VIETNAM

ONE OF SOUTHEAST ASIA'S PREMIER WILDLIFE DESTINATIONS, A JUNGLE WILDLAND OF ELEPHANTS, RHINOS, & MORE THAN 40 OTHER ENDANGERED SPECIES.

WHERE Cat Tien National Park is located at the south end of the Truong Son Mountain Range, a mere three hours' drive from Ho Chi Minh City. This 742-sq-km park spans a full range of habitats from flat-topped highlands to lowland rivers.

WHY Established in 1978, Cat Tien was catapulted onto the international stage with the finding of a Javan rhinoceros in 1989. Thought extinct in mainland Southeast Asia for over 40 years, the rediscovery of such an important 'mega charismatic' animal is considered one of the most spectacular finds of the past century. Now in the limelight, Vietnam has since expanded the park's boundaries and is making an effort to protect this incredibly valuable species.

Recent biological surveys continue to reveal new species in the park and surrounding region, including an astounding five species of large mammals previously unknown to science: four species of deer and antelope, and a new primate. Most of these have never been seen alive in the wild by scientists, and more is known about the moon than these elusive creatures.

Even though Cat Tien was hit hard by chemical defoliants during the American War, it's remarkable how many big trees survived and how well the habitats have recovered. As one measure of the area's global significance, Unesco added the park to its list of biosphere reserves in 2002.

CONSERVATION OPPORTUNITIES

When Vietnam set aside a special rhino reserve in 1992 it designated the surrounding forest a 'new economic zone'. So many settlers have since moved into the area that undisturbed rhinoceros habitat has diminished 85% since 1990. Remarkably, the World Wildlife Fund and other groups decided to educate local villagers about conservation and the value of their resources rather than angering people by relocating them. Although human pressure continues, villagers now take a lot of pride in their wildlife.

SEE »

✪ JAVAN RHINOCEROS

WHAT Imagine a lumbering giant that weighs 2000kg hiding in a small, densely populated country that had much of its vegetation destroyed during the American War. It is nothing short of a miracle, so it's no surprise that biologists were dumbfounded when a freshly killed Javan rhinoceros *(Rhinoceros sondaicus)* showed up in a Vietnamese market in 1989.

Unlike their African cousins, rhinos of Southeast Asia live in dense rainforests and are rarely observed. In fact no scientist has ever seen one of Vietnam's rhinos alive in the wild, though they have been photographed with remote cameras.

STATUS The Javan rhinoceros is one of the rarest mammals in the world. Only 50 survive in a park in western Java, so the discovery in Vietnam sent shockwaves through the scientific community and international media. Even more amazing is that Vietnam's rhinos appear to be a different subspecies. It is thought that there are five to 10 living in Cat Tien and their chances for survival are very slim.

✪ SIAMESE CROCODILE

WHAT Crocodile-skin boots or belts in the marketplace have to come from somewhere, and in Southeast Asia the source has long been the 3m-long Siamese crocodile *(Crocodylus siamensis)*. Hunted to virtual extinction in the wild, this formerly abundant freshwater crocodile no longer plies languid rivers and swamps between Myanmar and Borneo.

Fortunately, hardy hikers can now venture from Cat Tien park headquarters to see a newly established population at the wetlands of Bau Sau, 16km away. At night look for their fiery-red eyes by spotlight.

STATUS The discovery in 2005 of a nest of baby Siamese crocodiles in southern Laos raised hopes that this species might still survive in the wild. Efforts are underway in Cat Tien National Park and also in Thailand to reintroduce the creatures to their natural environment, using populations taken from crocodile farms.

GO » MANAS, INDIA & ROYAL MANAS, BHUTAN

ONE OF THE WORLD'S PREMIER BIODIVERSITY HOT SPOTS SURROUNDED BY UNPARALLELED NATURAL SPLENDOUR, WITH STUPENDOUS OPPORTUNITIES FOR VIEWING ELEPHANTS, RHINOS & TIGERS.

WHERE Manas and Royal Manas National Parks (391 sq km and 658 sq km respectively) straddle the Bhutan–India border where the eastern Himalaya massif plunges spectacularly into the swampy plains of Assam.

WHY Taken together, these two contiguous parks form the vibrant core of the majestic eastern Himalaya ecosystem, one of the richest biological sites in the world because it lies at the junction of the Indian, Ethiopian, and Indochinese biogeographic regions.

Intact forests still cover an impressive 92% of Bhutan's Royal Manas, while India's Manas National Park was designated a World Heritage site by Unesco in 1985. The area is home to some of the most substantial populations of tiger, rhino and elephant in all of Asia, as well as 22 other globally endangered species.

The extreme relief of this region, from alpine peak to lowland marsh in a matter of miles, creates homes for an astounding range of plants and animals, including some only recently discovered. Wildlife viewing opportunities are especially well developed in Manas National Park.

India's Manas National Park is just now rebounding from the tragic period from 1988 to 1993 during which a separatist group in Assam raided the park and destroyed infrastructure, leaving the park open to rampant poaching. Disgruntled local villagers continue to be one of the primary threats to long-term conservation of the park. Across the

[TOP] » ANTI-POACHING PATROLS STRIVE TO MAINTAIN THE BEST PRESERVED OF ALL EASTERN HIMALAYAN HABITATS, BHUTAN'S ROYAL MANAS.

border in Royal Manas, the presence of Indian insurgents and poachers continues to act as a drain upon limited resources.

CONSERVATION OPPORTUNITIES
In one innovative project, video shot in Royal Manas is shown on national television in Bhutan each Friday evening as part of an attempt to promote awareness of wildlife and conservation. At the same time, staffing levels and budgets for the two parks are woefully inadequate. ◌

SEE »

✪ PYGMY HOG
WHAT Would you travel halfway around the globe to see a pig? You might if it were the pygmy hog *(Sus salvanius)*, a diminutive creature that is one of the unexpected stars of Manas and Royal Manas parks. Standing 20cm to 30cm high at the shoulder and weighing about 8kg, the pygmy hog was thought extinct until rediscovered in 1971. Wildlife aficionados in the know rank it high on their list of must-see Indian animals. Unfortunately, efforts to protect this wonderful animal lack the public support given to Bengal tigers and Indian rhinos.

STATUS Critically endangered with only 100 to 150 left. The captive breeding programmes of the Pygmy Hog Conservation Program (PHCP) may be all that stands between survival and extinction.

✪ GOLDEN LANGUR
WHAT When a golden langur *(Presbytis geei)* stares down at you with its delightful black face peeking out from a ruff of golden-yellow fur, you realise that you are seeing one of the world's most beautiful monkeys. Discovered in 1955, this slender-limbed langur is found only in a small triangle of tropical forest in northern Assam and nearby Bhutan.

STATUS Numbering under 5000 and living in small isolated colonies, the langur is significantly threatened by illegal logging and poaching in India. Fortunately, most langurs live in Bhutan, where they can readily be observed and may well have a better chance of survival.

GO » KAA-IYA DEL GRAN CHACO, BOLIVIA

SECOND IN SIZE ONLY TO THE AMAZONIAN RAINFOREST, THIS VAST REGION OF DRY SCRUB FOREST IN THE ARID RAIN SHADOW OF THE MIGHTY ANDES IS HOME TO GIANT ARMADILLOS, JAGUARS, CHACOAN PECCARIES & MANED WOLVES.

WHERE Kaa-Iya del Gran Chaco National Park occupies some 34,000 sq km of southern Bolivia along the nation's border with Paraguay. Officially established in 1995, the area is thought to be the largest national park in South America.

WHY Gran Chaco is an inspiring example of pure community-based grassroots conservation at its finest. Despite their humble circumstances, local indigenous peoples came up with the idea for the park, organised their own management committee, and somehow convinced the Bolivian government to set the land aside despite overwhelming opposition from logging, mining and other industry groups. It is now the only park in the Americas, and one of the few in the world to be established and administered by indigenous peoples.

The habitat the park protects, the Chaco forest, is second only to the Amazon in terms of size, but it has more species of mammals than any other site in the entire Americas. Many of the plants and animals that are representative of the area are endemic due to their adaptations to the arid climate. The dry scrubland areas typically receive an annual average rainfall of less than 300mm.

Potential visitors to the region should be aware that the Kaa-Iya del Gran Chaco National Park is remote with a capital 'R' and at last count no tour groups had yet visited the area.

This is definitely not a place for folks looking for a picnic, or for those who are requiring hand-held treatment.

CONSERVATION OPPORTUNITIES

The park's indigenous managers have found an innovative, if controversial, way to sustain the park. An agreement reached with the owners of the Bolivia–Brazil pipeline that crosses the park sees monies paid by the oil and gas companies go into a trust fund that pays for park operations.

SEE »

✪ CHACOAN PECCARY

WHAT The Chacoan peccary (*Catagonus wagneri*), the largest of the three peccary species, was originally described from fossil remains and presumed long extinct until it was 'discovered' by a scientific expedition to the Chaco in 1972. As is often the case, local peoples already had extensive knowledge of this widely hunted animal and were the ones who taught scientists to recognise it. Weighing as much as 40kg, and running in groups of four to 10 animals, the peccary survives in the most arid reaches of the Chaco by eating cacti and licking mineral salts from ant mounds.

STATUS One best guess is that around 5000 Chacoan peccaries remain, although hunting, the conversion of Chaco forest to Texas-style ranches in Paraguay and the spread of an unidentified disease are all taking a toll.

✪ GIANT ARMADILLO

WHAT Having the appearance of a prehistoric turtle covered in an armour of chain mail, the giant armadillo (*Priodontes maximus*; pictured below) is one strange-looking mammal. Reaching as much as 50kg, it is the undisputed king of the world's 20 armadillo species, while its stout covering means it has few predators other than humans. During the day they sleep in burrows, coming out at night in search of ant and termite mounds that they demolish in a single sitting. Virtually nothing is known about how giant armadillos live, but if they are like other armadillos they are among the few mammals in the world that mate face-to-face.

STATUS Much of the giant armadillo's habitat is rapidly being destroyed. The species is listed as globally endangered, and is thought to be in danger of extinction. Many farmers still kill giant armadillos on sight, due to the erroneous belief that they cause damage to crops.

GO » BORJOMI-KHARAGAULI, GEORGIA

PRISTINE MOUNTAIN FORESTS – SO MAGNIFICENT THEY WERE ONCE PROTECTED BY RUSSIAN ROYALTY – FAMOUS TODAY FOR THEIR RHODODENDRONS, AUTUMNAL COLOURS & MANY RARE ANIMALS.

WHERE Situated in central Georgia in the Lesser Caucasus, Borjomi-Kharagauli National Park was officially inaugurated in 2001 as the first national park in the Caucasus Mountains. Covering 850 sq km, Borjomi-Kharagauli stretches from subtropical broadleaf forests to alpine meadows and is one of the largest national parks in Europe.

WHY Protection of the forests of the Lesser Caucasus began when feudal lords set these wildlands aside as their personal hunting grounds in the Middle Ages. In the 19th century, Russian royalty became so enamoured with the region that they made it their favourite summer residence and forbade trespass or hunting without permission. Through this long succession of caretakers the forest endured in its original primeval condition and is today one of the largest tracts of undisturbed forest left in Europe.

Animals whose populations have diminished elsewhere in Europe persist here in healthy numbers, and the Caucasus are also rich in rare species. A full 20% of the mammals and 25% of the plants here are found only in the Caucasus and nowhere else – the highest rate of endemicism of any temperate forest in the world – while the northern part of the park has a flora that has existed continuously for nearly 60 million years.

The hardest part about Borjomi-Kharagauli could be deciding when to visit and on what to focus. From April to May the lower forests dazzle with blooming rhododendrons, while mountain meadows

[TOP] » ROUGHING IT AMID RAINBOWS, RAVINES AND RARE ENDEMIC FLORA AND FAUNA IN THE CAUCASUS MOUNTAINS, GEORGIA.

host flamboyant wildflower displays from June to August. By October the hills are ablaze with autumn colours, and in winter the local mountains are a premier skiing destination. Surrounding the park are villages dating back to the 1st century AD that are famous for their hospitality and ancient traditions.

CONSERVATION OPPORTUNITIES
The World Wildlife Fund and Dutch Molecaten Group have joined forces to include Borjomi-Kharagauli in its Protected Area Network (PAN). This network of European parks seeks to promote nature protection through the development of sustainable tourism.

SEE »

✪ CAUCASIAN LEOPARD
WHAT You wouldn't expect to see a leopard in the mountains of Europe, but then again few people realise that these large spotted cats once roamed throughout Europe. Like other leopards throughout the world, the Caucasian leopard *(Panthera pardus ciscaucasica)* has been relentlessly persecuted, but it figures prominently in the traditional folklore and mythology of the Caucasian region.

STATUS Even though the country's rugged mountains and wild lands seem to offer safe refuge, leopards were last seen in Georgia in 1954. Local villagers reported seeing big cats in the 1990s; biologists found tracks in 2003 and have recently sighted a leopard. Perhaps coincidentally, a leopard was photographed in neighbouring Armenia for the first time ever in 2005, raising hopes that this distinctive subspecies might survive.

✪ CAUCASIAN CHAMOIS
WHAT The Caucasian chamois *(Rupicapra rupicapra)* is an exceedingly agile, goatlike creature that inhabits rugged rocky terrain from the European Alps to the Caucasus Mountains of Russia. Weighing upwards of 50kg, it is capable of graceful 2m-vertical and 6m-horizontal leaps that carry it from rock pinnacle to pinnacle. In the winter their brown-to-grey hair grows 10cm to 20cm long, offering some protection from the fierce mountain environment. In the summer chamois may be seen browsing in alpine meadows.

STATUS Once common, the Caucasian chamois is hunted throughout its range, and populations have dropped precipitously in the past 20 years. Unfortunately, their decline has accelerated even further in the last two to three years and no-one knows what is killing them. Fewer than 25 are left in the Lesser Caucasus (including Borjomi-Kharagauli), although thousands remain in the Greater Caucasus of Russia.

JUL

GO » NORTHEAST GREENLAND, GREENLAND

NATURE & WILDERNESS ON A SCALE SCARCELY COMPREHENDIBLE TO THE HUMAN IMAGINATION, OFFERING BREATHTAKING ISOLATION IN A LAND OF GIANT ICEBERGS, GLACIERS, POLAR BEARS, MUSK OXEN & NORTHERN LIGHTS.

WHERE Occupying the entire northeast quarter of the world's largest island, Northeast Greenland National Park comprises a staggering 972,000 sq km, larger than France and Great Britain combined. The park was established in 1974, added to Unesco's list of biosphere reserves in 1977 and expanded to its present size in 1988.

WHY More than just the largest park that no-one has heard of, this is in fact the largest park in the world. Though visited by a handful of scientists and the occasional expedition, there are only 40 residents – it's about as isolated as you can get.

A dramatic natural spectacle is the reward for visitors who've made the journey to these remote parts. Sheer cliffs soaring 1500m out of the ocean, gigantic icebergs and more shades of blue and white than you can

imagine combine to guarantee an experience that lingers long in the memory and calls you back again and again. And then for one brief window in the middle of its short summer the place comes alive with breeding seabirds, whales, gleaming white arctic foxes, and other remarkable creatures.

While the interior of Greenland is buried under an icefield so massive that it bows the centre of the island downward some 300m, the coastline presents rugged peaks and cliffs that twist around countless fjords of stunning beauty. Landing sites are hard to come by, so

most visitors sail along the coastline on the lookout for whales, walruses, narwhals and polar bears.

CONSERVATION OPPORTUNITIES

Although a place so large and wild seems untouchable, Greenland's massive ice cap is melting in our warming climate. The entire ecosystem, in fact the entire fate of our entire planet, hangs in the balance, but for those who act now there's still time to see Greenland in its full splendour.

SEE »

◎ BOWHEAD WHALE

WHAT Count yourself lucky if you ever see a bowhead whale *(Balaena mysticetus)*. Also known as the Greenland right whale, a name that comes from it being the 'right' whale to hunt, the slow-moving bowhead was hunted to near extinction before being protected. The 55-tonne bowhead follows the edge of the ice pack through the seasons, eating 1800kg a day of the smallest organisms in the ocean. Insulated from the frigid waters by a layer of blubber more than 50cm thick, this is the only baleen whale that lives year-round in the Arctic.

STATUS Although 8000 to 9000 bowhead whales survive in the world, they are subdivided into smaller populations or stocks that occupy specific geographic areas. The Spitsbergen stock that roams between Greenland and the Norwegian island of Spitsbergen is critically endangered, and would be considered extinct but for eight that were seen off the northeast coast of Greenland between 2000 and 2004.

◎ POLAR BEAR

WHAT The majestic top carnivore in the arctic ecosystem rules its icy kingdom with a certain swagger and undeniable grace. Whether loping along in a casual trot or swimming across the open ocean, the polar bear *(Ursus maritimus)* fears no creature, not even humans. Despite being uncommon in the park, their arrival is unpredictable and tour guides are required to carry high-calibre rifles at all times. Exquisitely adapted for the arctic cold, these 500kg to 600kg bears have thick blubber and special translucent fur that appears white because of the way it refracts light. Against the ice, the polar bear can be invisible except for its black nose, which it reputedly hides behind its paw when stalking prey.

STATUS You see them in zoos and you see them on posters, you see their images so often that it's hard to imagine a world without them. Along with melting ice, however, the bears are sliding towards extinction before our very eyes. Under consideration for being listed as endangered in the US, polar bears are suddenly dying of starvation and other causes as their icy world melts away.

GO » GURVAN SAIKHAN, MONGOLIA

DINOSAUR BONES, VAST SAND DUNES & SUNSET-COLOURED CANYONS ON THE NORTHERN EDGE OF THE GOBI DESERT – HOME TO CREATURES RANGING FROM SNOW LEOPARDS TO CAMELS.

WHERE Situated in southern Mongolia where the eastern end of the Altai Mountains are swallowed by the Gobi Desert. Established in 1993, then expanded in 2000 to its current size of 27,000 sq km.

WHY Although the Gobi Desert, one of the greatest deserts in the world is known for its gigantic sand-dune systems, the Gobi Gurvan Saikhan protects an unexpected mix of habitats ranging from grassy steppe to marshes and salt flats. The park itself is named for the Gurvan Saikhan, literally the 'Three Beauties' – the mountain ridges that comprise the eastern tail of a range that stretches eastward from Russia.

This part of the Gobi is renowned as the site where the first fossilised dinosaur eggs were discovered in the 1920s. The region's fabulous fossil sites continue to yield many amazing dinosaur remains including examples of Velociraptor, easily the best known dinosaur in the world due to its prominent role in the movie *Jurassic Park*.

Travellers are just as likely to visit the park for the Khongoryn Els, an improbably vast dune system that 'sings' eerily as its sands shift.

Its bleak appearance is deceptive, as this park protects a very high diversity of plants and animals. Out of 620 species of flowering plants found within the boundaries of the park, 38 species are endemic to the region, and eight of the park's 52 species of mammals are endangered.

[TOP] » BACTRIAN CAMEL CARAVANS ARE STILL THE PREFERRED MODE OF TRAVEL OVER THE 'SINGING' SANDS OF THE KHONGORYN ELS.

CONSERVATION OPPORTUNITIES

The park is home to over 1100 families that live a subsistence pastoral lifestyle dependent on domesticated animals. With a national goal of protecting 30% of Mongolia, which amounts to a doubling of the current area of land under protection, this ancient lifestyle could be threatened. The challenge Mongolia faces today is to find a viable way to protect both local traditions and the wildlife.○

SEE »

✪ BACTRIAN CAMEL

WHAT The two-humped camel, better known as the Bactrian camel *(Camelus ferus bactrianus)*, is famous among travellers. Domesticated over 4500 years ago, this unparalleled pack animal was the lifeblood of the ancient Silk Road because it can carry 270kg loads for nearly 200km at a stretch. Bactrian camels may also go months without water and can tolerate everything from freezing cold to blistering heat. Their long eyelashes and sealable nostrils help protect them from blowing sand.

STATUS While there are nearly two million domesticated Bactrian camels in the world, wild camels are critically endangered. It is estimated that a mere 950 remain in remote areas of Mongolia and northwest China. These wild camels help serve to preserve the species' original behaviours, which would otherwise be lost.

✪ SNOW LEOPARD

WHAT It's difficult to imagine how easily the snow leopard *(Panthera uncia)* camouflages itself in plain view. Even nomadic herdsmen who work every day in the snow leopard's habitat have rarely seen this animal and tell many legends about its supernatural powers. The leopard's gorgeous 12cm fur is smoky-grey with black rosettes and blends perfectly among rocks and snow. To help it catch wild sheep and goats, this cat has an extraordinarily long tail that provides balance and long back legs that enable it to make great leaps.

STATUS With pelts fetching very high prices on the black market, and its remote habitat being invaded by herdsmen and livestock, the snow leopard struggles for survival. Numbers declined to 1000 in 1960, but they have climbed back to over 3000 in recent years due to international attention. Often living in the rugged mountains of contested border regions, the snow leopard is extremely difficult to study and poorly understood.

GO » BLACK RIVER GORGES, MAURITIUS

LEGENDARY HOME OF THE EXTINCT DODO, NOW ONE OF THE DENSEST
CONCENTRATIONS OF CRITICALLY ENDANGERED PLANTS & ANIMALS IN THE WORLD.

WHERE Black River Gorges lies in the southwest corner of Mauritius, an isolated island in the Indian Ocean some 900km east of Madagascar. Established in 1994 and only 66 sq km in size, this national park is located on the island's Central Plateau and includes waterfalls, gorges and breathtaking views.

WHY Part of a cluster of islands that arose from undersea volcanoes eight to 10 million years ago, Mauritius was home to hundreds of unique plants and animals that evolved in utter isolation. Foremost among these species was the 23kg flightless pigeon known as the dodo that became extinct when the Dutch settled this lonely outpost in the 1600s. To this day, introduced weeds and predators continue to wreak havoc on the island's fragile ecosystems.

Black River Gorges National Park protects nearly all that's left of Mauritius' indigenous forests and wildlife – among the most imperilled in the world. A number of plant and animal species are represented by less than a dozen individuals each, and uncounted species went extinct before they were even discovered. Only nine native birds of Mauritius survive, and all of them might be expected at Black River Gorges.

Though easily accessed and popular among tourists who want to see a little bit of nature, the incredible importance of this park is probably overlooked by most visitors.

[TOP] » IT LOOKS SO FINE FROM AFAR, BUT BIODIVERSITY ON MAURITIUS IS STILL UNDER THREAT FROM DOMINANT INTRODUCED SPECIES.

CONSERVATION OPPORTUNITIES

Despite the sad story of Mauritius' wildlife, there have been some remarkable successes achieved due to concerted conservation efforts. Current programmes include the fencing off and weeding of conservation management areas that are scattered around the island. With reduced pressure from invasive species occurring in these areas, it is hoped that native species can flourish once again.

✪ PINK PIGEON

WHAT Given that this is Mauritius, home of some the world's most endangered animals, you can bet that that soft cooing in the trees isn't coming from an ordinary pigeon. In fact it is the pink pigeon (*Nesoenas mayeri*), the rarest pigeon in the world. Pale grey and tinted with a gorgeous pink flush, these pigeons can be seen flying in small flocks around the wet forests of Black River Gorges National Park. Pink pigeons feed on flowers, fruits, and buds, and will now come to supplemental feed put out by scientists. New fledglings from captive breeding programmes have recently been introduced into the flocks of adult birds.

STATUS Like the other animals of Mauritius that evolved in the absence of predators, the pink pigeon is very tame and extremely vulnerable to the predations of introduced black rats, monkeys and mongooses. By 199 there were an estimated 10 pink pigeons left in the wild and captive breeding remained the species' last hope for survival. Today, there are an estimated 350 pigeons in the wild and a healthy captive population in zoos around the world.

✪ MAURITIUS KESTREL

WHAT A small, finely striped falcon, the Mauritius kestrel (*Falco punctatus*; pictured below) is the sole remaining endemic raptor of Mauritius. Inhabiting forested areas, it seeks a diet of geckos, insects and small birds. Unlike many other birds of prey, the kestrel nests in tree cavities.

STATUS In 1974 the Mauritius kestrel was declared the world's rarest bird because there were only four left. The epic story of how this species was brought back from the brink of what seemed certain extinction is one of the 20th century's most inspiring conservation successes. Despite international attention and efforts, the programme suffered numerous setbacks and the first viable egg was not collected for captive rearing until 1979. From this meagre beginning, the recovery programme has grown until today there are about 800 Mauritius kestrels roaming the forests of Black River Gorges National Park. It is thought that populations of this kestrel never reached very high numbers because repeated volcanic eruptions keep altering their habitat over millions of years.

梵鐘閣

OCT

GO » JIRISAN, SOUTH KOREA

VISIT ANCIENT BUDDHIST TEMPLES IN THE LARGEST PARK IN SOUTH KOREA WHILE HIKING WILDERNESS TRAILS SET AMONG FLAMING RED & ORANGE MAPLES, VALLEYS, WATERFALLS & VISTAS OF ENDLESS MOUNTAINS RIDGES.

WHERE Jirisan National Park is situated in the southeast corner of South Korea at the southern end of the mountain ranges that divide the Korean Peninsula into eastern and western regions. Established in 1967 this is South Korea's first national park, and at 470 sq km it is the nation's largest.

WHY Seen from many angles and revered for its summit views, Mt Jirisan is considered one of the three most important mountains of South Korea. With a rich cultural history that stretches back thousands of years, Mt Jirisan translates as 'perceive the truth' because visits to the mountains will reputedly make a wise man out of a fool. Ready access to spiritual powers may account for the fabulous assortment of ancient temples and religious monuments scattered throughout this mountainous wilderness.

In late autumn, however, Jirisan National Park evokes a different kind of pilgrimage as people come to wander amongst the park's psychedelic displays of autumn leaves. Visitors may also hike the park's many vista points to gaze in awe at views of endless mountain ridges spilling off into the misty distance.

Few visitors realise that this virgin wilderness is also one of South Korea's premier strongholds for endangered wildlife. The last tiger was observed here in 1944 and wolves are probably now extinct in the park, but a remnant population of bears was recently rediscovered and other species hang on by a thread.

(TOP) » A SENSE OF BALANCE RESONATES THROUGH JIRISAN, WHERE THE PURSUIT OF ENLIGHTENMENT AND THE PERSISTENCE OF THE ENVIRONMENT SHARE A NATURAL ACCORD.

CONSERVATION OPPORTUNITIES

It is said that South Korea is just beginning to recognise the potential value of protecting wilderness and wildlife and encouraging ecotourism. Bird-watchers, for instance, will find that information on finding the country's birds is generally lacking, and information on other animals may be even harder to track down. Ecotravellers with a strong interest in wildlife have an opportunity to draw attention to the importance of these resources.✪

SEE »

✪ MUSK DEER

WHAT This small deer tips the scales at just 17kg, but has the unfortunate distinction of producing one of the most valuable animal products in the world. Musk from the glands of the male deer is worth three times its weight in gold and is an ingredient in 400 Chinese and Korean traditional remedies. In the wild, musk deer *(Moschus moschiferus)* lead solitary lives and follow well-established trails that they mark by rubbing their musk glands against trees and rocks. Males are further distinguishable in having 8cm canine teeth that project from their mouths.

STATUS Villagers can earn the equivalent of US$70 from a single male deer, a veritable fortune in many countries, so hunting of musk deer has reached rampant levels. In one Nepalese valley a scientist counted 500 to 600 snares per sq km; these snares are set to catch male musk deer but kill just as many females and juveniles. Populations have decreased sharply in South Korea and national parks may be their only hope for survival in the short term.

✪ ASIATIC BLACK BEAR

WHAT Like its American cousin, the Asiatic black bear *(Ursus thibetanus)* has a fondness for many types of food, readily climbs trees and is widely misunderstood. Nicknamed the 'moon bear' for a white moon-shaped crescent on its chest, this 100kg creature occupies many types of habitats across Asia. It can be found from Afghanistan to Japan, though in response to human pressure it has become largely reclusive in much of its range.

STATUS Killed throughout Asia for its gall bladder and paws, which are said to have special medicinal properties, the black bear is rapidly becoming endangered. Despite national protection in South Korea, the last black bear was observed in the mid-1980s. After one was accidentally filmed in Jirisan National Park in 2000, a renewed search discovered tracks and scat. It is now thought that between 20 and 30 remain in Korea, and part of the park has been set aside as a bear preserve.

GO » BALE MOUNTAINS, ETHIOPIA

THE LARGEST ALPINE AREA IN AFRICA IS A SURPRISING LANDSCAPE OF HIGHLY ENDANGERED ANIMALS, ALPINE LAKES, WATERFALLS, DEEP GORGES & DRAMATIC PEAKS SOARING ABOVE THE ARID AFRICAN PLAIN.

WHERE Perched in the highland mountains of southeastern Ethiopia, the 2200-sq-km Bale Mountains National Park was created in 1970. The park is divided into two major parts by the spectacular east–west running Harenna Escarpment.

WHY Alpine habitats are rarely associated with Africa, and under the double whammy of global warming and human intrusion the alpine zone of Africa could soon be a faint memory. The small, isolated pockets of alpine habitat scattered across the continent are like an archipelago of islands being drowned in a rising sea – the already endangered plants and animals are in desperate straits.

Despite being listed as one of the 34 most important biodiversity hot spots in the world, the Ethiopian highlands and associated habitats are on the brink of collapse. Bale Mountains National Park embodies many

of the problems facing the region, as the park has never been formally gazetted and human settlement and livestock are widespread within the park. The highlands are among the most densely populated agricultural areas in Africa and overgrazing is a serious problem.

Although the park is under a lot of pressure, this remarkable landscape is also the last stronghold for an array of animals endemic to Ethiopia. Amid opportunities for unsurpassed mountain walking and horse trekking, visitors will be treated to views of Ethiopian wolves, blue-winged geese and giant mole-rats. During

the northern winter, a fantastic number of waterbirds visit the park's numerous alpine lakes and marshes.

CONSERVATION OPPORTUNITIES

The resources of Bale Mountains National Park have suffered significant damage during 15 years of serious neglect and deficient funding, but in 2004 the Frankfurt Zoological Society made a 10-year commitment to help secure the long-term future of the park. Part of their work includes supporting tourism development and the training of local guides.

SEE »

✪ MOUNTAIN NYALA

WHAT It is amazing that this large (150kg to 300kg) magnificent antelope was unknown before 1910. Standing over 120cm at the shoulder – its regal appearance accentuated by a towering rack of deeply spiralled horns – the mountain nyala *(Tragelaphus buxtoni)* is found only in the wet, high-elevation woodlands and heath forests of the Bale Mountains. Here it lives in small, secretive herds that often remain in dense cover during the day.

STATUS Once hunted so extensively that they learned to avoid humans at all costs, the mountain nyala of Bale Mountains National Park have grown more confident in recent years and can be readily observed, especially in open areas around Lake Ziway. Estimates of how many nyala remain range from less than 1000 to over 4000, with some observers saying that they are in immediate danger of extinction and others saying that the animals should be hunted to keep them from overpopulating their limited habitat. Everyone agrees, however, that mountain nyala populations can rise and fall abruptly and need to be closely watched.

✪ ETHIOPIAN WOLF

WHAT With a weight somewhere between 10kg and 20kg it's no surprise that the midsized Ethiopian wolf *(Canis simensis)* has been variously called a jackal, fox and wolf. Wandering alpine grasslands in search of small mammals, this bright reddish, lanky wolf is best observed in the Bale Mountains as it hunts its favourite food, the giant mole-rat. Unlike other wolves, the Ethiopian wolf is a solitary creature while hunting, but it gathers in packs when defending territories.

STATUS Restricted to a few isolated mountain outposts, the Ethiopian wolf is now finding its last strongholds being invaded by livestock, villagers and disease-bearing domestic dogs. Perhaps 400 remain, making this the rarest member of the dog family in the world, and one of the world's rarest animals. Over half their number were to be found in Bale Mountains, but recent wildfires and disease have had a serious impact this population.

GO » SHARK BAY, WESTERN AUSTRALIA

EXPLORE THE WORLD'S LARGEST & RICHEST EELGRASS BEDS, SWIM AMONG 14,000 DUGONGS & MARVEL AT STROMATOLITE ALGAE COLONIES THAT ARE AMONG THE OLDEST FORMS OF LIFE ON EARTH.

WHERE Located 800km north of Perth, Shark Bay is an area the size of Wales with less than 1000 people living along 1500km of sweeping coastline. This Unesco World Heritage site covers 23,000 sq km and includes numerous reserves and protected islands.

WHY Home to diverse marine life and endangered land animals, Shark Bay sits at the meeting place of tropical and temperate waters and is one of the world's most important marine sanctuaries. Its vast eelgrass beds are extremely rich and support an exceptionally abundant and diverse variety of marine invertebrates. In turn, the protected waters provide vital breeding and nursery habitats for a fantastic number of marine animals including 6000 sea turtles, several types of whales, more than 300 species of fish and the greatest concentration of dugongs in the world.

Shark Bay is one of the richest and most significant terrestrial environments in Australia. Sitting at the junction of three major climatic zones, and the transition zone between two major botanical provinces, it has a mind-boggling array of plants and animals living in specialised communities. Nearby islands and peninsulas, long isolated from the outside world, provide refuge for 26 species of endangered mammals, including six that were once widespread on the mainland but are now reduced to single populations.

One of Shark Bay's most bizarre features is an abundant gathering of stromatolites, cauliflowerlike

[TOP] » SAVAGED BY THE INDIAN OCEAN, DIRK HARTOG ISLAND SERVES AS THE BARRIER THAT MAKES POSSIBLE THE UNIQUE MARINE REFUGE OF SHARK BAY.

growths of algae whose lineage stretches back 3.5 billion years. Stromatolites at Hamelin Pool are over 4000 years old and are a valuable example of what life on ancient earth once looked like.

CONSERVATION OPPORTUNITIES

In an attempt to stem the extinction of several Australian species, Project Eden is actively restoring habitats and native animals in the Shark Bay region. Fencing off the 1050-sq-km Peron Peninsula and removing introduced species from the enclosed area should give the entire ailing ecosystem a chance to recover.

SEE »

✪ BANDED HARE-WALLABY

WHAT Looking somewhat like a funky cross between a miniature kangaroo and a large rat, the banded hare-wallaby *(Lagostrophus fasciatus)* is named for its harelike hopping and its grizzled, faintly banded appearance. Weighing around 1.7kg, these nocturnal marsupials live in social groups and nest beneath very dense thorn scrub, which helps to protect them from predators as they scamper back and forth along narrow paths. Despite living in an arid region, they secure all of the moisture they need from the rather unpalatable-looking grasses and vegetation upon which they feed.

STATUS Formerly widespread across southwest Australia, the banded hare-wallaby was last seen on the mainland in 1906. It is thought that clearing of native vegetation for agriculture, coupled with the introduction of cats and rabbits, led to their precipitous decline. If it weren't for two small colonies that survived on Bernier and Dorre Islands in Shark Bay they would probably be extinct. An attempt to reintroduce them to a third island in 1970 failed due to predation by cats, but new plans for reintroducing them to safer areas are in the works.

✪ DUGONG

WHAT It takes a serious stretch of the imagination to conceive how this soft beanbag of a creature inspired homesick sailors to concoct those legends of mermaids. Sporting a whiskered, pouty face and dolphinlike tail, the 250kg to 300kg dugong *(Dugong dugon)* moves languidly through shallow tropical waters in search of eelgrass, its primary food. This diet is the reason for the common nickname 'sea cow' and helps explain this mammal's low-energy lifestyle. The long-lived dugong reaches sexual maturity between the ages of nine and 17 years, and females give birth every three to seven years. These marine herbivores never come to land and rise to the water's surface only to breathe.

STATUS Once widespread in tropical and subtropical oceans, dugong populations are declining rapidly and are now vulnerable to extinction even with fairly universal protection. Destruction of eelgrass beds, pollution and some hunting pressure partly account for this poorly understood decline. The 14,000 dugongs at Shark Bay afford an opportunity to witness and study an intact, healthy population in the hope of learning how this remarkable animal might be better protected.

BLUELISTS

THEY'RE BACK – ANOTHER COLLECTION OF BEST TRAVEL EXPERIENCES TO WHET THE APPETITE. FROM THE HEART OF METROPOLIS MANIA TO THE WORLD'S STRANGEST MUSEUMS, THESE ARE OUR TOP PICKS OF THINGS TO SEE AND DO IN 2008.

BLUELISTS

162
BEST-VALUE DESTINATIONS

164
NOW YOU SEE THEM… NOW YOU…

166
EXPLORERS & THEIR JOURNEYS

168
'I'VE BEEN EVERYWHERE, MAN…'

170
CITIES ON THE RISE

182
GREAT FILM FESTIVALS

184
TROPICAL PARADISE

186
FRIENDLIEST COUNTRIES

188
SPORTY CHINA

190
LIKE THE SONG?

202
VOLCANO!

204
KNOW YOUR TRAVEL

206
SLEEP BEHIND BARS

208
RISKY PURSUITS

210
SPACE TRAVEL

172

FIVE PLACES TO
LOSE YOURSELF/
LOSE EVERYONE

174

THE BEST OF
COSMOPOLITAN
AFRICA

176

GREAT RIVER TRIPS

178

BEST BREWS

180

COUNTRIES ON
THE RISE

192

FOOD
WONDERLANDS
OF THE WORLD

194

METROPOLIS
MANIA

196

COLDEST/HOTTEST

198

ALMOST MYTHICAL
PLACES

200

GREEN CITY ENVY

212

TRAVEL FOR A
HIGHER CAUSE

214

TRAVEL WITH ALL
YOUR SENSES

216

BIG!

218

STRANGE
MUSEUMS

220

WINNERS' LISTS
2008

BEST-VALUE DESTINATIONS

BEST VALUE DOESN'T MEAN CHEAPEST! IT'S A CASE OF BANG FOR YOUR BUCK & THESE ARE OUR PICKS FOR GETTING THE MOST FROM YOUR HARD-EARNED.

✪ DOMINICAN REPUBLIC

The DR packs a huge punch. On the one hand, it's your typical tropical island paradise with pure-white beaches, oh-so-blue waters and oodles of palm trees. On the other hand, it boasts a rugged mountain interior with ample opportunities for first-class wildlife discovery, rafting and hiking. And the locals like to hang loose, too, holding surfing championships with all the attendant hoopla, block parties galore, and two annual Carnival extravaganzas. If none of that satisfies, check out the capital, Santo Domingo: with its faded, Spanish-colonial and Art Deco architecture, it's like Cuba without the rhetoric.

✪ ETHIOPIA

Beautiful Ethiopia offers the chance to step back in time, as befitting a country known as the 'Cradle of Civilisation' (in Addis Ababa's National Museum are the three-million-year-old remains of 'Lucy', one of humankind's earliest ancestors). Ethiopia is the home of remarkably well-preserved traditions (the north is filled with Christian monuments dating back to the 4th century AD), a legacy of its status as the only African nation to avoid colonisation. It also boasts diverse ecosystems – deciduous forest, evergreen forest, desert scrub, wetlands, grasslands – and there are plenty of hiking opportunities in the country's rugged mountains.

✪ LAOS

Laos is unique in its region – its relative isolation from foreign influence means travellers are in for a remarkably well-preserved slice of traditional Southeast Asian culture, everywhere from the fertile lowlands of the Mekong River valley to the rugged Annamite highlands. And now, with the opening of the border to central Vietnam, southern Laos – previously the remotest place in the region – is easier than ever to get to. Laos is studded with ancient temples and monasteries, and ecotourists are also in for a treat, with tremendous caving and kayaking opportunities in the country's large, unspoiled forests.

✪ NICARAGUA

Nicaragua, Central America's largest country, has been curiously ignored by the tourist hordes thus far. But relax – the war's over, even if outsiders' perceptions haven't changed. Discerning travellers with a thirst for adventure know that the country's protected parks and nature reserves, massive black volcanoes and tracts of rainforest are perfect for trekking. Others will just appreciate the scenery, including the atmospheric Spanish colonial towns. The beaches are superb, too, with plenty of surfing and diving spots, and all of it is easy on the wallet.

✪ SYRIA

For history buffs and lovers of atmospheric locations alike, Syria delivers the goods – the Egyptians, Phoenicians, Assyrians, Persians, Greeks, Romans, Mongols, Ottomans and French are just some who've left their imprint on the country. Think of Syria as a vast open-air museum, with stunning ruins and magnificent castles; Bosra, possibly the world's best-preserved Roman amphitheatre; Aleppo, with its covered, stone-vaulted souqs, extending for 10km; and Damascus of course, probably the world's oldest continuously inhabited city.

✪ UKRAINE

After a long, bitter and very bloody period of Russian occupation – and the appalling disaster that was Chornobyl – you'd be forgiven for thinking Ukraine needed time to heal. But, although the scars are still fresh, the country is infected with an enthusiasm that's rapidly rubbing off on travellers. What's on offer? Cheap food and drink, the frenetic capital Kyiv, wonderful trekking through the Carpathian Mountains, with its rich and exotic wildlife; Gothic and Byzantine architectural wonders; the Crimean coast by the Black Sea…you can even kit yourself out in protective clothing and take a tour through the Chornobyl power station itself, perfect for lovers of haunted, post-apocalyptic landscapes.

✪ URUGUAY

The meat in a geographical sandwich between Latin American behemoths Brazil and Argentina, Uruguay just quietly goes about its business. A respite from the hustle and bustle of Buenos Aires and Rio, Uruguay charms travellers with its wonderful colonial towns, lovely beaches and peaceful, unspoiled natural beauty. Hiking, horse riding, fishing, biking and whale-watching are just some of the pursuits on offer. If you do need something more, shall we say, 'cosmopolitan', there's always Punta del Este: this renowned beach peninsula is in party mode 24/7, year-round, attracting socialites and celebrities from all over Latin America.

✪ ICELAND

Chilly Iceland is a tourist hot spot, due largely to its striking natural features: majestic glaciers, empty black-sand beaches, hot springs, geysers, active volcanoes, ominous peaks, massive lava deserts…and, in summer, a sun that never seems to set. This is the land of classic photo opportunities. It's also got a storied history and folklore tradition and a renowned, and eclectic, modern music scene centred on Reykjavik, a vibrant, friendly city that contains some of northern Europe's best bars. For more physical pursuits, whale-watching, swimming and fishing are popular, and there's also the chance to – wait for it – go diving.

✪ JAPAN

Hit Tokyo's clubs, bars, karaoke rooms and restaurants for full-tilt sensory overload. Or just wander the streets: there's always something to do in Tokyo, and not all of it involves great wads of cash. The sheer energy of the city's consumer culture can provide days of entertainment, but there are pockets of tradition, from small backstreet noodle shops and *onsen* (hot springs) to little old ladies in traditional dress. The streets and alleyways are teeming with worlds within worlds, and you'll never be short of eye candy, whether it involves girls dressed as Little Bo Peep or boys dressed as Edward Scissorhands.

✪ COSTA RICA

Costa Rica is unique in turbulent Latin America. It's leading the way in its conservation policies, with around 27% of the country protected, ensuring that the lush jungles are teeming with monkeys, lizards, frogs, and all manner of exotic birds and insects. It's also got awesome surfing and terrific beaches, a swag of huge national parks and volcanoes, and fantastic hiking and rafting opportunities. Plus the people are friendly (it's the only Latin American country with no army), the coffee's outstanding, and, off Cocos Islands, there's some of the world's best diving.

[TOP] » GEOTHERMALLY HEATED WATER FROM 2KM UNDERGROUND GENERATES GRINS AS WELL AS ELECTRICAL POWER AT ICELAND'S BLUE LAGOON.

[LEFT] » EYES UP: TOKYO'S HARAJUKU SHOPPING DISTRICT IS A WEEKEND HANG-OUT FOR *ANIME*-INSPIRED GOTHS AND PUNKS.

[RIGHT] » FOR THIS NOCTURNAL TREE FROG FROM COSTA RICA, RED EYES ARE ALSO A DEFENCE AGAINST DAYTIME PREDATORS.

NOW YOU SEE THEM...
NOW YOU...

THESE DESTINATIONS DEMAND OUR ATTENTION & CARE & THEY ALSO HAPPEN TO BE SOME OF THE MOST AMAZING SITES TO HAVE ON YOUR ITINERARY. VISIT NOW, TREAD LIGHTLY.

✪ TUVALU

Tiny Tuvalu has the misfortune to be a flat chain of atolls and islands in the middle of a rising ocean, with its highest 'peaks' rising to little more than 5m above sea level. It's remote – around 1000km north of Fiji – quintessentially Pacific, and is slowly disappearing beneath the rising sea levels being created by global warming. Some forecasts suggest Tuvalu may go the way of Atlantis within decades, and evacuation plans for the 11,600 residents have already been mooted. If you want to see Tuvalu before it becomes purely a divers' destination, there are flights and boats from Suva, Fiji.

✪ TIMBUKTU, MALI

Propped against the Sahara Desert, this legendary town of Islamic scholarship may one day be no more than the foundations for a sand dune. Encroaching sands from the Sahara knock on Timbuktu's famously decorative doors, creating desertification that's destroyed vegetation around the town, choked the water supply and weakened buildings. In 1990 Unesco placed Timbuktu on its List of World Heritage in Danger, citing the need to consolidate the Dyingerey Ber Mosque and improvement of terrace rainwater drainage systems. It was removed from the danger list in 2005, but the Sahara isn't about to go away.

✪ VENICE, ITALY

The world's most romantic city won't seem so quite so dreamy when it's breathing through an aqualung. Like Tuvalu, rising oceans threaten the city of canals, though for the Venetians this is not new; they've been battling floods ever since the city's creation in the 5th century. This time, however, the problem may be terminal. Sporadic flooding has become as regular as buses, and even the slightest rise in ocean levels has the potential to turn St Mark's Square into St Mullet's Square, despite endeavours such as the MOSEs Project, which plans to use floodgates to hold back high tides.

✪ BABYLON, IRAQ

The war in Iraq has claimed many victims but few as ancient as Babylon. Just 90km south of Baghdad, the biblical city is the most famous of Iraq's many ancient sites, celebrated for the magnificent (and supposedly apocryphal) Hanging Gardens, one of the Seven Wonders of the World. Parts of the city were reconstructed by Saddam Hussein in an attempt to forever link his name to that of another famous Babylonian leader, King Nebuchadnezzar II – but since 2003 foreign forces based in Babylon have been accused of damaging the fragile site, including the famous palace of Nebuchadnezzar.

✪ LUXOR TOMBS, EGYPT

In the Nile Valley of Upper Egypt, the grandeur of the temples of ancient Thebes sits comfortably alongside the bustling town of Luxor. Here, the Valley of the Kings, the Luxor Temple and a host of other antiquities have helped make Luxor Egypt's greatest attraction after the Giza Pyramids. But for how long, given that the rising water table is now threatening the temples' very foundations? The spread of agriculture and irrigation (especially of thirsty sugar cane) along the Nile has seen the water table rise several metres. This water has been absorbed by the temples' porous sandstone, leading to its disintegration. The race is on to save them.

✪ THREE GORGES, CHINA

At 6300km in length, China's Yangzi is the world's third-longest river. Between the towns of Fengjie, in Sichuan, and Yichang, in Hubei, it threads through three incredible gorges, flowing between distinct rock formations and stunning cliffs. The Three Gorges (Qutang, Wu and Xiling to give them their correct names) stretch over 200km, and now come to an abrupt conclusion at the Three Gorges Dam near the end of Xiling Gorge. Get aboard a cruise now to experience one of China's great moments in natural design because by 2009, when the mega-project dam is completed, the gorges will be consigned to history.

✪ PANAMA CANAL, PANAMA

While the Panama Canal itself is under little threat, its usefulness as a shipping route may be. To its north, running below Iceland and Greenland and across the top of Canada and Alaska, is the fabled Northwest Passage, long a Shangri-la of shipping. For sailors, it would offer the chance to knock off up to 7000km from shipping routes, if only it wasn't so ice-choked. Enter global warming. The melting ice pack in the Passage has scientists and sailors pondering the prospect that these waters may yet become a viable shipping route, at the expense of the Panama Canal.

✪ AMAZON FOREST, SOUTH AMERICA

Covering around six million sq km in Brazil, Peru, Ecuador, Colombia and Venezuela, the Amazon is the world's largest tropical forest and the 'lungs of the planet', but deforestation has claimed around 15% of the forest; in 2004 alone, around 26,000 sq km – an area larger than Sicily – was lost to logging and farming. In 2005 and 2006 the deforestation rate almost halved, with an area three times the size of France now protected from development in Brazil, but the Amazon is still very much a punctured lung.

✪ SNOWS OF KILIMANJARO, TANZANIA

Receding glaciers are a familiar tale around the world, but there's a more haunting ring to it when it's Hemingway's famous snows of Kilimanjaro that may disappear. In the past century, Kili's resilient skull cap of ice, all but straddling the equator, has receded by more than 80%. Some forecast the glaciers on Africa's highest mountain disappearing entirely by 2020 and, with it, one of Africa's classic images. It won't be the end of the ever popular climb on Kilimanjaro, but it will be like eating cake without the icing.

✪ GREAT BARRIER REEF, AUSTRALIA

As if the Great Barrier Reef didn't have enough problems, what with sediment pouring out from Queensland rivers, and the occasional ship running aground atop the reef. To that you can add a familiar demon: global warming. The world's largest reef, stretching more than 2000km along Australia's east coast, is hotting up. Amid rising ocean temperatures the reef has experienced two mass coral bleaching incidents in recent years, with up to 90% of the reef losing its colour. Experts warn that the reef may be almost gone by 2050 if the Pacific keeps heating up.

(TOP) » SMOKING RAINFOREST NEAR MARABA, BRAZIL – SOON TO BE A RANCH.

(BOTTOM) » ALTHOUGH CONSIDERED VULNERABLE, THE AFRICAN BUSH ELEPHANT HAS A BETTER CHANCE OF SURVIVAL THAN THE SNOWS CROWNING KILIMANJARO.

EXPLORERS & THEIR JOURNEYS

FOLLOW THE LEAD OF SOME OF THE WORLD'S BRAVEST EXPLORERS & BLAZE
A TRAIL OF YOUR OWN.

⭐ ERIK THE RED, BRATTAHLID, GREENLAND

Outlawed in Iceland in the 10th century, Erik the Red sailed west into unknown waters and discovered
Greenland. On his return from exile three years later he encouraged Icelandic settlers across to the new
land, setting up in the southwest at Brattahlid, where the first church in the western hemisphere was later
established. Now part of a Unesco World Heritage site, only the foundations of the original church remain,
next to the current church. There's also a fireplace from Erik the Red's own manor house. Brattahlid is
situated across a fjord from the southern town of Narsarsuaq, which has an international airport.

⭐ MARCO POLO, SILK ROAD, CHINA TO TURKEY

In 1264 two Venetian brothers, Niccolo and Maffeo Polo, journeyed overland through Asia to Beijing.
Seven years later, at the Pope's request, they did it again, only this time Niccolo took his son Marco.
Seventeen years in Kublai Khan's court and one book later, Marco Polo's name is now synonymous with
the Silk Road, an ancient network of trading routes across Asia that has been resuscitated as evocative
traveller favourites. Originally linking the Chinese city of Xi'an to Istanbul or Antakya, any journey between
these centres today will mean time spent on the Silk Road and amid its connections with Marco Polo.

⭐ DAVID LIVINGSTONE, VICTORIA FALLS, ZAMBIA & ZIMBABWE

Synonymous with African exploration, David Livingstone began surveying the Zambezi River in 1852 (19 years
before he'd famously meet a fellow called Stanley). Three years later he would become the first explorer to sight
Victoria Falls, a waterfall so mighty it's considered one of the seven natural wonders of the world. There's plenty
on offer at 'the smoke that thunders' to make you feel like a modern-day adventurer – rafting, bungy jumping,
jetboating – or you can explore beyond for more Livingstone links. The Tanzanian town of Ujiji on Lake Tanganjika
is where Henry Stanley found the missing Livingstone, and Livingstone died by Lake Bangweulu in Zambia.

✪ JAMES COOK, QUEEN CHARLOTTE SOUND, NEW ZEALAND

To see James Cook's hometown, visit Whitby on the Yorkshire coast. To see the place where he felt most at home, visit Queen Charlotte Sound on the frayed north coast of New Zealand's South Island. In suitably titled Ship Cove, Cook anchored five times, staying a total of around 100 days (and where he is celebrated today with an elephantine monument). Offshore you can climb to the summit of Motuara Island and a plaque commemorating the spot where Cook raised the Union Jack to claim British sovereignty over New Zealand. Nearby there's accommodation in Endeavour and Resolution Bays, named for Cook's ships.

✪ ERNEST SHACKLETON, SOUTH GEORGIA

The story of the Ernest Shackleton's Endurance Antarctic expedition is one of the enduring survival epics. When the Endurance was crushed by pack ice, most of the crew was left on Elephant Island while Shackleton and two crew members sailed 1300km to South Georgia. Here, they trekked on frostbitten feet across the mountainous island for 36 hours to the whaling station at Stromness. For Antarctic-bound visitors to South Georgia, re-creating the trek has become an adventure as memorable as the encounters with emperor penguins and elephant seals. Pay final homage to the Irishman at his burial place at Grytviken whaling station.

✪ CHRISTOPHER COLUMBUS, SPAIN & DOMINICAN REPUBLIC

Like Columbus himself, those travellers in quest of the remains of the world's most famous explorer have traditionally had to range across the globe, with his burial place claimed by both the Dominican Republic and the Spanish city of Seville. DNA testing in 2006, using the remains of Columbus' brother Diego, has reduced the travel bill, suggesting that the bones inside a tomb in Seville Cathedral are those of Columbus. If you want a second opinion (and the Dominicans will happily give you one), head for the 210m-high Columbus Lighthouse in Santa Dominigo, containing a tomb that also supposedly holds Columbus' remains.

✪ FRANCIS DRAKE, PLYMOUTH, ENGLAND

The most famous of the Elizabethan seafarers, Francis Drake is best remembered for a single apocryphal event. Legend has it that he was warned of the approaching Spanish Armada while playing bowls on Plymouth Hoe, but he chose to finish his game before sailing out to defeat the Armada. Bogus though the story may be, Plymouth isn't about to let the truth get in the way of a good tourist attraction. Today, a statue of Drake stands atop a 5m-high plinth on Plymouth Hoe, beside a bowling green. In nearby Buckland Abbey, which was once Drake's home, you'll find more reminders of Sir Francis, including reputedly his ghost and accompanying hell hounds.

✪ BURKE & WILLS, INNAMINCKA, AUSTRALIA

In one of the original Australian battles of outback versus man, it was outback that won, with the overland explorers Robert O'Hara Burke and William Wills dying in the desert along Cooper Creek. Having crossed the country from Melbourne to the Gulf of Carpentaria the pair perished near the site of present-day Innamincka, and though they are now buried in Melbourne, the sites where they died are still marked beside the creek. Nearby is the Dig Tree, engraved with the phrase 'DIG 3FT NW', marking the position where a cache of food was left for the expedition.

✪ VASCO DE GAMA, KOZHIKODE, INDIA

Among history's great seafarers, Vasco de Gama was the first to establish an ocean route between Europe and India, rounding Africa's Cape of Good Hope in the 15th century and nosing his boat into the subcontinent near the modern-day city of Kozhikode (Calicut). The landing heralded the beginning of Portuguese colonisation in India, and is remembered today by a nondescript plaque near the landing site at Kappad Beach. Trace de Gama's journey in reverse, to Portugal, and you'll find his tomb in the Jeronimos Monastery in Belem – he died in Cochin in India, but his remains were later exhumed and returned to Portugal.

✪ LEWIS & CLARK, OMAHA, USA

In 1803 President Thomas Jefferson enlisted Meriwether Lewis and William Clark to find a river route to the Pacific, in North America's uncharted west. In little more than two years the pair travelled around 6000km, crossing from near St Louis to the mouth of the Columbia River in Oregon. Today, their remarkable journey is remembered in the Lewis & Clark National Historic Trail, the 6000km route that's administered by the National Park Service. The trail crosses through 11 states and around 100 sites related to the expedition. The trail headquarters are in Omaha, Nebraska.

'I'VE BEEN EVERYWHERE, MAN...'

A BRAGGERS' GUIDE TO THE BEST TRAVEL BOASTS, GLOATS, MYTHS & LEGENDS.

✪ TRAM HOPPING, AUSTRALIA

Some travellers consider fare evasion on public transport to be a God-given right. And nowhere are they able to exercise this 'right' more than in Australia's tram capital, Melbourne. Trams have operated in the city since 1885 but it was recently estimated more than A$1 million in revenue is lost every day due to fare evasion. The irony is that in Hong Kong, where trams convey an average of 231,000 passengers daily, an advanced ticketing system has virtually eliminated fare dodgers – the system was designed by Australians.

✪ PROFESSIONAL BEGGING, CHINA

On your travels you'll almost certainly hear rumours of professional beggars hobbling into chauffeur driven limousines at the end of a long day spent pretending to be skint. Less dramatic is hearsay contending that many beggars have been offered government aid but would rather hold out their hands to strangers. A government report on the coastal city of Guangzhou, north of the Pearl River delta, found 80% of beggars were 'professional'. But if you're unsure whether you can afford to spare any change, remember that more than 90 million Chinese must survive on less than US$1 a day.

✪ UPGRADES

Every flight has more first-class hopefuls vying for an upgrade than there are reclining seats to fit them into. We've all heard of the 'failsafe' techniques – from wearing a tie, slipping the attendant a few loose notes, to pretending to be a celebrity in disguise – but what is the real likelihood of moving into the champagne and caviar set sans charge? Actually, close to zero. Most airlines' rules of conduct state that upgrading anyone without specific permission from a supervisor or from the Captain (in emergencies) is a sackable offence.

✪ BLUFF ETIQUETTE

Your mate has just returned from their round-the-world trip. You're gathered round the projector admiring their snaps, awestruck by their vivid recollection of adventures when suddenly you notice a flaw. Perhaps they've said Timbuktu is in Asia or maybe you doubt Jennifer Aniston was in Bolivia at the time their supposed rendezvous took place. Whatever your suspicion, it is polite and respectful that before you call their bluff you should check your facts first using the internet. With an estimated 7.3 million new pages of information added every day, the web is the ultimate bluff-callers tool.

✪ TREASURE SEEKING, CANADA

There's nothing like the promise of loot to inspire treasure-transfixed travellers to trek to a faraway island. In 1795 teenager Daniel McGinnis discovered a 'money pit' on Oak Island, Nova Scotia. He was convinced pirate treasure was buried in the log-lined pit, and so began over 200 years of treasure hunting that's revealed an ingenious system of booby traps, false beaches and tantalising glimpses of the treasure that still remains buried hundreds of feet deep. Wannabe Captain Jack Sparrows should be warned that four men died in 1959 while trying to excavate the gold.

✪ ROMANCING

Travellers don't have to go to Paris or Venice to find their mojo. Statistically speaking, your chances of getting frisky 'on the road' are pretty hot. This year airlines around the world will convey almost 5 billion passengers. Couple that with the fact that every year sales of romance fiction generate nearly US$1.5 billion and you don't have to be Eric von Lustbader to realise that the odds of hooking up are surely in your favour. And regardless of how you rate your chances make sure you take along a few rubber raincoats, just in case.

✪ HIKING ROUTE 66 FOR KICKS, USA

On the Road, Jack Kerouac's legendary Beat novel, has inspired generations of hikers around the world. The story features two young men hiking along Route 66 in a speed- and whiskey-fuelled search for the American Dream. The legendary highway is the 4000km grey ribbon tying Chicago to California. With the film version of *On the Road* slated for release next year, 2008 could be the last chance to pursue Kerouac's literary ghost before a wave of newly inspired Route 66ers come looking for their kicks.

✪ WASTED TALES, INDIA

Any travel tale that starts with 'When I was in Goa' is bound to end with 'we were wasted, man'. Sitting serenely between the Western Ghats and the Arabian Sea, Goa's beaches host the infamous Full Moon Party that has given rise to more tales of student-traveller decadence than Woodstock spawned hippies. Funnily enough it was the hippies that 'founded' the Goan party scene back in the '70s. If you squint your eyes and peer through the psychedelic waves generated by the trance tunes you'll notice a lot of them never left.

✪ MILE-HIGH CLUBBING, USA

Until recently the idea of fornicating at 5000 feet was a lot more appealing than the reality of squirming around inside a cramped and poorly sanitised airplane lavatory. But thanks to Georgia pilot Bob Smith, amorous would-be clubbers can do it in comfort for less than US$300. Smith's Piper Cherokee is fitted out with a mattress and curtain so privacy is assured. The pilot says he has flown everyone from couples in their teens to swingers in their sixties. Hopefully, he remembers to change the bed sheets.

✪ BROKEN SPECTRE

For thousands of years anyone lucky enough to witness this extraordinary optical phenomenon probably thought they were in the presence of God or undergoing their own spiritual rebirth. That's because the spectator is confronted with an image of their shadow surrounded by a halo of light, usually around the head. The phenomenon mostly occurs near mountain peaks when the air is moist and the sun is low. The name owes its provenance to the Brocken, which at 1141m is the highest peak in the Harz Mountains that straddle the German province of Saxony-Anhalt.

(TOP) » FULL BORE AT FULL MOON: TRIPPERS, TRAVELLERS, SADHUS AND STUDENTS DANCE TO TRANCE AT ARAMBOL, GOA.

(LEFT) » THERE ARE MORE COMFORTABLE PLACES TO JOIN THE MILE-HIGH CLUB.

(RIGHT) » HOLY HALO OR HOCUS-POCUS: BROKEN SPECTRE PHENOMENON OBSERVED NEAR CAIRNGORM, EASTERN SCOTTISH HIGHLANDS.

CITIES ON THE RISE

OUR TOP PICKS FOR TRAVEL AROUND THE '08 CORNER.

✪ HELSINKI, FINLAND

Cold Helsinki is sooooo hot right now, with its cutting-edge design and music scenes, its affordability (by northern European standards), its chilled Nordic good looks…and its status as the host of the 2007 Eurovision Song Contest (some may argue that last point). Yes, Helsinki has the lot: old-world culture (a plethora of museums and galleries), new-world hedonism (bleeding-edge cafés and clubs), and future-forward cool (there's even a non-Finish band named Architecture in Helsinki, for all you 'twee pop' freaks).

✪ OLOUMOUC, CZECH REPUBLIC

Lying roughly midway between Prague and Warsaw, Oloumouc has naturally been overshadowed by its flashy, more muscular neighbours. But if you prefer the silent, contemplative type, then get off the train here. With a population of around 100,000 and a flavourful history, Oloumouc delivers for the discerning city hopper, with Baroque architecture, a peaceful air, grand old cobblestone streets, cheap beer and sleepy good times. You've probably heard this about all Slavic cities on the rise, but think 'Prague before tourism'.

✪ PALM SPRINGS, USA

If location's your thing then Palm Springs is king, surrounded as it is by the Colorado Desert and the eye-catching San Jacinto Mountains. Meanwhile, connoisseurs of '70s moustaches know that Sonny Bono was the former mayor and the founder of the Palm Springs International Film Festival, a popular, pre-Oscars event that really packs 'em in. Even more niche is the city's reputation as the spiritual home for 'clothing optional' tourism (that's 'nudist resorts' to you, chief): well, at least the climate's right for getting your kit off, and because it's a desert city, Palm Springs doesn't have pesky mosquitoes, which means no painful welts you-know-where.

✪ PANAMA CITY, PANAMA

Panama hats, the Panama Canal… Panama has always been a burr on the collective consciousness. And now its capital lays claim to being an up-and-coming tourist hot spot, as confirmed by none other than 'Brangelina', the famous two-headed celebrity monster that visited the city recently (taking in the shops and investment opportunities, primarily). But if you prefer a bit more under-the-radar meat and a little less Hollywood tinsel to your travel recommendations then strap these on for size: lush rainforest on the city's perimeter; 16th-century ruins; the grand colonial district; and, of course, the vibrant Latin vibes.

✪ SIGHISOARA, ROMANIA

This exceedingly well-preserved medieval fort town (it's World Heritage-listed by Unesco) sits in the heart of Transylvania, its famous citadel dating back to the 12th century. Mmmmmm – you can cut the history with a knife, so thick and rich is it. The surrounding mountainside landscape adds green splendour to the proceedings, but Sighisoara has impeccable 'dark tourism' credentials, too: it's the birthplace of Vlad the Impaler, better known to you and I – and all his victims – as Dracula. Watch out for garlic on the menu.

✪ GUANGZHOU, CHINA

Guangzhou has always been one of China's economic miracles, with its bustling population of six million working hard to ensure post-Mao prosperity. But in recent times it's become a tourism leviathan, too. Why? It's got a few thousand years of history on its side manifested in ancient architecture and traditions, plus green scenery and renowned Cantonese cuisine. And now there's also a ramped-up infrastructure, with a few hundred billion yuan being pumped into improving facilities in preparation for the city's hosting of the 2010 Asian Games.

✪ SÃO PAULO, BRAZIL

Bryan Ferry once sang 'You're so sheer / you're so chic' and he may as well have been crooning about São Paulo, which impresses with its nests of boutiques, galleries and eateries. You won't see everything – this is the world's third-largest metropolis – but you will see plenty. São Paulo has long played second fiddle to Rio, but with its blend of European and Latin influences, it's now screaming up the hipster charts. Actually, chic and São Paulo go way back – Chic the band, that is, whose track 'São Paulo' is a super-smooth lounge ballad. Style never dates, so who needs Rio?

✪ MARSEILLE, FRANCE

France's oldest city is shaking off its former rep as a rough-and-ready Mediterranean coastal town for a stake in the golden dawn of discerning tourism. The 1998 World Cup gave all of this a super kick-off and now Marseille is capitalising on the exposure to smarten up its act and present a stellar forward line to the world: all that history, embodied in architecture and tradition; fashionable music and niche films; a punchy multiethnic population; and the Med location. But of course.

✪ TRIPOLI, LIBYA

Libya?! Bet that raised a few eyebrows out there in Reader Land…but you read right. What's more, Tripoli, Libya's capital, is rapidly becoming one of Northern Africa's biggest draws – against the odds, given that Colonel Gaddafi, Libya's dictator, has made a career out of alienating the country from the rest of the world. But now that tensions have eased and sanctions have been lifted, tourists are flying in to Tripoli, with the capital's ancient medina and unbeatable coastal location providing the flypaper.

✪ PHNOM PENH, CAMBODIA

Phnom Penh, Cambodia's largest city and its capital, has a superviolent past that virtually everyone knows about. But today its charming, if crumbling, French colonial architecture and its Cambodian tradition combines with newfound optimism and a bustling new riverside precinct to push the Khmer Rouge further and deeper into the past. With economic growth comes the requisite hotels, bars and restaurants, and Phnom Penh certainly delivers these, but with a tangy Southeast Asian twist. Food's good, too.

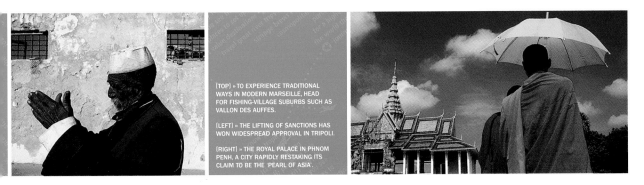

[TOP] » TO EXPERIENCE TRADITIONAL WAYS IN MODERN MARSEILLE, HEAD FOR FISHING-VILLAGE SUBURBS SUCH AS VALLON DES AUFFES.

[LEFT] » THE LIFTING OF SANCTIONS HAS WON WIDESPREAD APPROVAL IN TRIPOLI.

[RIGHT] » THE ROYAL PALACE IN PHNOM PENH, A CITY RAPIDLY RESTAKING ITS CLAIM TO BE THE 'PEARL OF ASIA'.

FIVE PLACES TO LOSE YOURSELF

OUR PICKS FOR THE BEST PLACES TO REVEL IN A LITTLE ANONYMITY.

✪ MUMBAI, INDIA

For anyone who's ever wanted to get lost in the crowd, Mumbai presents the ultimate opportunity. With 17 million residents and counting – on track to becoming the world's most populated city – you'll be hard-pressed to find a bigger, more seething mass of humanity. Dive in from any street corner to whip your senses silly: hear traffic horns honk and wedding bands boom by, smell vendors frying sweet-sour *bhelpuri* then taste its chillied heat, see dreamy Bollywood stars pout from omnipresent movie posters, and feel the monsoon rains that pour down and soak the whole chaotic scene.

✪ DUBAI, UNITED ARAB EMIRATES

Brash, flash and flush with cash, Dubai is quick to suck visitors into its audacious vortex. Want to snow ski, but it's 40°C outside? Head to the mall, where they're making fresh powder on the indoor, black-diamond-grade slopes. Running out of beaches to soak up the sun? The city built artificial islands that rise from the sea to supply more waterfront. Add spiralling skyscrapers, gold-, spice- and camel-stuffed souqs, and marble-floored designer shopping centres, and just try not to get swept up in the crackling, can-do current of this desert oasis.

✪ JERUSALEM, ISRAEL & THE PALESTINIAN TERRITORIES

In the search for saviours and prophets among the tangled stone streets and tunnel-like passageways of Jerusalem, it's easy to forget what century it is. Jews, Muslims and Christians all hold the city sacred. Pilgrims pour in to pray and leave wishes folded into the Wailing Wall's massive crevices, kneel at Jesus' tomb in the Holy Sepulchre and contemplate Mohammed's heavenly ascent at the gold-plated Dome of the Rock. Sing-song prayers ricochet through the ancient corridors, as they have for more than 2000 years, transporting visitors back in holy history.

FIVE PLACES TO LOSE EVERYONE ELSE

OUR PICKS FOR THE BEST PLACES TO GET AWAY FROM IT ALL.

✪ ALEUTIAN ISLANDS, USA

Aside from wee native villages, small military installations and a couple of fishing ports, it'll pretty much be you and the seabirds enjoying the volcanoes and 160km/h winds that lash the Aleutians. This chain of treeless, lava-scarred islands juts nearly 1800km into the stormy North Pacific, with the westernmost tip practically in Russia. The islands' remoteness landed them the dubious honour of being a nuclear testing site in the 1960s and '70s. The best way to visit is via the state-run ferry, which makes the five-day journey from the Alaska mainland a few times per month in summer.

✪ TUAMOTUS, FRENCH POLYNESIA

The coral atolls of the Tuamotus are the world at its Robinson Crusoe simplest. Because little can grow or feed on the sparse soil (besides palm trees), the landscape is left to the trade winds, blue-green lagoons and huge sky, under which you can almost feel the world turning. The archipelago's residents live scattered throughout the atolls and make their living from black-pearl farming, fishing and preparing copra (the dried meat of the coconut). Access is primarily via outrigger canoe.

✪ KHONGORYN ELS, MONGOLIA

To reach these lonely sand dunes in southern Mongolia, you'll have to trek over steppes and deep into the Gobi Desert. It's a leg-taxing slog up the 200m-high hills, but once at the top you'll have the world – or at least a big, bald portion of it – to yourself. A quick spin north, south, east and west reveals nothing but coppery sand. The only sound is the grains 'singing', a resonant hum that vibrates all around. The only accommodation is a *ger* (felt tent of the local nomads) pitched under fat stars streaking across the heavens above.

✪ GUANGZHOU, CHINA

Disappear into the cacophonous markets of this freewheeling port city for indelible sights and scents. The opium trade may be long gone, but exotic items still fill the cramped stalls: zebra testicles, deer antlers and snakes floating in liquor bottles. Need to strengthen your kidneys? Try the seahorse tonic. Liver ailment? The bear gall-bladder bile will fix it. Jade bracelets, stone Buddhas and silk trousers line more shelves. The relentless pace continues at mealtime. Dim sum is king in Guangzhou, and cart after steaming cart wheels by bearing fried taro puffs with crab, sesame balls and barbecued pork.

✪ MEXICO CITY, MEXICO

The 2200m altitude isn't the only thing that will make your head spin. The world's se-condmost mega of megacities has picked up quite a few people since the Aztecs did their sacrifice thing here. These days it'll be you and 18 million of your closest amigos sharing the air and taxis to explore the mash-up of museums, monuments, plazas, monasteries, murals, galleries, colonial buildings, shrines, religious relics and – whew! To catch your breath, toss back a tequila in one of the hundreds of elbow-to-elbow cantinas.

KEEPING THE PRE-COLUMBIAN RITUALS ALIVE, CONCHEROS DANCERS AND MUSICIANS SET THE TONE IN MEXICO CITY.

✪ KULUSUK, GREENLAND

This village of just 300 people clasps to Greenland's rocky east coast above a glisten-ing, iceberg-strewn sea. A wide belt of field ice surrounds the area, making Kulusuk very isolated both from the rest of Greenland and the rest of the world. The easiest way in is by plane from Iceland; it lands on a runway shared occasionally with polar bears. Days are devoted to fishing and seal hunting in the local fjords, dog sledding or watching icebergs drift by, while nights are given over to the polychromatic aurora borealis that saturates the sky.

✪ FOULA, SCOTLAND

They didn't film a movie titled *The Edge of the World* here for nothing. Located more than 160km off Scotland's northeast tip in the ice-cold waters of the North Sea, tiny Foula in the Shetland Islands is Britain's most remote inhabited island. Its denizens consist of 30 locals who raise sheep, and a Shetland pony herd that roams the hills. Visitors should pre-pare to settle in for a spell, as the frequent storms and gale-force winds that batter Foula can keep boat and plane departures land-locked for weeks at a time.

A LONG WAY FROM HOME COMFORTS IS A GOOD PLACE TO LOOK FOR A LITTLE PERSPECTIVE.

THE BEST OF COSMOPOLITAN AFRICA

CELEBRATE AFRICA & SUBMERGE YOURSELF IN SOME OF THE WORLD'S MOST SURPRISING CITIES.

✪ KAMPALA, UGANDA

Unexpectedly sophisticated, diverse and globally aware, Kampala pulled itself up by its bootstraps after Idi Amin wrecked it with civil war. Now its economy is a continental tiger, and the city sports a contagious buzz and bustle. Modern buildings have popped up all over the place and old, dilapidated ones are being renovated. The young, forward-thinking vibe is spurred by Makerere University, which remains a top centre of learning in Africa; its students drive the energetic nightlife scene. Kampala's sizable Asian population adds an international dimension.

✪ WINDHOEK, NAMIBIA

Guys in lederhosen clink steins of sweet beer, juicy slow-cooked sausages scent the air, and oompah bands get the crowd dancing like chickens. Sounds, smells and tastes like Oktoberfest in Deutschland, right? Actually, we're thousands of miles away in Windhoek, Namibia's small capital, and an odd outpost of German culture left over from colonial days. The prosperous, garden-filled ambiance differs radically from Africa's other towns, and Windhoek remains the continent's only place to carve into an authentic schnitzel.

✪ MINDELO, CAPE VERDE

Set around a moon-shaped port, Mindelo is Cape Verde's answer to the French Riviera, complete with cobblestone streets, candy-coloured colonial buildings, yachts bobbing in the harbour and cigarette-smoking celebrities such as Cesaria Evora calling the place home. The steamy days are given over to cafés where locals indulge in a glass of beer, read the newspaper and buy their lottery tickets. The sultry nights hot up around 11pm, when the townsfolk pour out into the main plaza, bands fire up the Latin rhythms, and the all-night bumping and grinding begins.

✪ ANTANANARIVO, MADAGASCAR

Cheerily-coloured Tana (the city's less-tongue-tying nickname) is perhaps Africa's most un-African city. Cobbled streets wind up steep, rocky hills past wooden houses with painted shutters. Purple jacaranda trees blaze to life and rain nectar onto the heads of skipping children and strolling couples. Church spires soar skyward. Tearooms brim with tea, coffee, hot chocolate and cream-plumped pastries. Come night-time, residents swarm out to hear jazz at the local cabarets or get down to Malagasy chart hits at the clubs.

✪ DAKAR, SENEGAL

Raw, chaotic and utterly electrifying, Dakar epitomizes urban Africa. It shines brightest at night – late at night, well beyond midnight. That's when the city's devoted, music-loving public suit up in their gladdest rags and make a beeline to the nightclubs of Youssou N'Dour or Thione Seck, international stars who rock locally when they're not touring the world, or any of a hundred other clubs. As the percussive rhythms and swooping vocals gain momentum throughout the wee hours, the Dakarois shake, shimmy and sweat until sunrise.

✪ ACCRA, GHANA

It's the weekend and time to go to a beach party in Ghana's seaside capital. The stars glitter over the palm-fringed sand. The sound of waves rolling in from the Atlantic can be heard beneath the throbbing reggae music that the DJs spin. Party-goers chow down on fried plantain chunks sprinkled with salt, ginger and cayenne pepper, and cool down with a Guinness. It's Africa at its easiest, mon. Meanwhile, swish ocean-view resorts continue to sprout as the city preps to host the African Cup of Nations football (soccer) fest.

✪ LIBREVILLE, GABON

Hoist a glass of French champagne and toast this city that resembles Miami Beach more than a major African capital. High-rise hotels ascend from the Atlantic-kissed beaches, glassy office buildings wheel and deal oil, flashy cars speed down the wide boulevards, and a sharp-dressed crowd fills the fancy shops and restaurants. Just to prove the point, prices are big-time cosmopolitan as well: Libreville is one of the world's most expensive cities. The hard-partying locals try to forget the fact by getting together for a beer or the aforementioned champagne.

✪ MARRAKESH, MOROCCO

The city's name conjures exotic images of snake charmers, fire-eaters and magic-carpet sellers. And indeed, they're here, enchanting carnival-like crowds in the old town's square. But just one shaded boulevard away is Gueliz, the Art Deco new town that resembles a mini Paris (if orange trees were perfuming the Champs Elysées). Well-coiffed matrons walk their dogs along the streets, couples sip *café au lait* at breezy bistros, and mobile-phone-mad youth queue for the latest Hollywood blockbusters at the neon-lit cinema.

✪ MAPUTO, MOZAMBIQUE

Tropical enough to be in Brazil, colonial enough to be on the Mediterranean, Maputo mashes it up to make one of the continent's most happy-go-lucky cities. By day folks swill espresso at sidewalk cafés, by evening they toss down spicy tiger prawns at beachside restaurants, by night they slurp *caipirinhas* (sugarcane-based brandy, lime, sugar and ice) to pumping salsa and jazz at the bars. Palmy sunbathing beaches, flame-tree-lined avenues and myriad markets round out the picture, which is particularly exceptional given Maputo's recent war-torn past.

✪ ALEXANDRIA, EGYPT

This confident Mediterranean city of cafés and promenades has drawn Alexander the Great, Caesar and Napoleon, among other luminaries. Perhaps, like today's inhabitants, they enjoyed sauntering down the Corniche, the long curving sea-front, to enjoy the cool breezes. Or maybe they wanted to soak up a place as steeped in literature as it is tea. Once home to the world's greatest library, Alexandria rises again with its sleek, modern recreation of the classical repository, which has reading rooms stepped over 14 terraces and a vast rotunda with space for eight million books.

(TOP) » THE HEART OF MARRAKESH'S MEDINA, DJEMAA EL-FNA IS CALLED 'THE GREATEST SHOW ON EARTH', AND THE FOOD AIN'T HALF BAD, EITHER.

(LEFT) » PARK YOURSELF AT COSTA DO SOL, MAPUTO'S BEACHSIDE PLAYGROUND.

(RIGHT) » IF READING'S NOT YOUR THING, THE BIBLIOTHECA ALEXANDRINA ALSO BOASTS SIX ART GALLERIES, THREE MUSEUMS, TWO PERMANENT EXHIBITIONS AND A PLANETARIUM.

GREAT RIVER TRIPS

RIDE THE RAPIDS OR DRIFT DOWNSTREAM ALONG SOME OF THE PLANET'S FINEST WATERWAYS.

✪ PADDLING THE WILDERNESS WATERWAY, USA

The Florida Everglades are a watery labyrinth designed by a god who clearly enjoyed a spot of canoeing. Paddling the Everglades' every bend could occupy a lifetime, which makes the Wilderness Waterway as much a relief as an adventure. This 159km paddling route threads along the Everglades' western edge, winding through the 10,000 Islands and briefly into the Gulf of Mexico. Campground and camping platforms are no more than 15km apart, and you'll share your journey with alligators, dolphins and manatees. If you need a canoe or kayak, they can be hired in Everglades City. Expect to paddle for about nine days.

✪ FELUCCA ON THE RIVER NILE, EGYPT

The classic of classics…a tiny felucca on the world's longest river, leaving behind the souqs of Aswan and cruising on the current towards Kom Ombo, Edfu or Esna. Feluccas can deliver their passengers a very personal Nile, with the lateen-rigged boats typically carrying between six and eight people. Nights are spent aboard the felucca (bring a sleeping bag) or camping on an island in the Nile: felucca trips to Kom Ombo involve one night out, while sailings to Esna mean four days and three nights on the Nile. Feluccas are big business in Aswan, and you won't have trouble finding a captain and boat.

✪ RAFTING THE FRANKLIN RIVER, AUSTRALIA

Though Tasmania's Franklin River isn't far from the city of Hobart, it remains among the world's most remote and pristine rafting waterways. Once you launch from below the Lyell Hwy, you're all but committed to eight days and 100km of rough-and-ready river travel until the Franklin finally spits your inflatable raft into the Gordon River. Blanketed by the impenetrable forest of the Word Heritage-listed Tasmanian Wilderness, the journey morphs from the haunting stillness of the Irenabyss to the fury of the 5km-long Great Ravine, which boils with invitingly named rapids such as the Cauldron, Thunderush and the Churn.

JETBOATING THE SHOTOVER RIVER, NEW ZEALAND

For high-octane thrills in a high-octane city, head for Queenstown on New Zealand's South Island, where one of the signature activities (among a smorgasbord of adventures) is jetboating the Shotover River. Through the river's steep-sided canyons, jetboats skim past the rock walls, fishtailing and throwing themselves into 360-degree spins. It's 30 minutes that's like a drug-induced dance on water, deep in the mighty Middle-earth scenery of the Southern Alps – Tolkien geeks may recognise the Shotover as the Ford of Bruinen, if they can look beyond the spinning bow of the jetboat, that is.

✪ CANOEING THE BOWRON LAKE CIRCUIT, CANADA

Set beneath the Mowdish and Cariboo Ranges, Bowron Lake Provincial Park offers one of the world's finest canoe journeys. The renowned canoe circuit in British Columbia crosses through 10 lakes and paddles along three rivers in its 116km course. The circuit takes between six and 10 days, and numbers are strictly limited, so paddling reservations are essential. A shorter (three to four days) alternative is the West Side return route from Bowron Lake to Unna Lake. The circuit can be paddled from mid-May to mid-October; September is considered the best month because of the vivid displays of autumn colour.

✪ NARROWBOATING, ENGLAND

With more than 3000km of navigable canals and rivers, England is the ideal place for a bit of leisurely canal boating.

You can hire your own narrowboat and play skipper, or you can have somebody else do all the work on a hotel boat. Popular narrowboating canals include the Kennet and Avon Canal, running between the Rivers Thames and Avon; and the busy Llangollen Canal, which crosses from England to Wales and has a reputation as the most beautiful canal in Britain. Across the Channel, in France, the World Heritage-listed Canal du Midi that flows between Toulouse and Sète is another classic among the canal crazy.

✪ DUGOUT CANOE ON THE SEPIK RIVER, PAPUA NEW GUINEA

Flowing more than 1000km from its source in the PNG highlands to the Bismarck Sea, the mighty Sepik River is navigable for much of its length. Motorboats ply most of the trade routes along the river, but for visitors the most popular and most redolent mode of river travel is by dugout motor-canoe, puttering between villages on the Middle Sepik or among its lakes and tributaries. The best place to arrange Sepik travel is in Wewak, while on the river itself you'll be able to find motor-canoes for hire at Ambunti, Pagwi and Angoram.

✪ CRUISING THE VOLGA, RUSSIA

Europe's longest river is a prime destination for the cruise crowd, with ocean-style liners as large as the Kremlin barging their way along the Volga. Cruises typically operate between St Petersburg and Moscow (though neither city is actually on the Volga), or extend further downstream to Volgograd, the city once – and more notoriously – known as Stalingrad.

Ports of call along the way usually include Uglich, a town perched like an onion-domed fairytale above the river; and the island of Kizhi, with its World Heritage-listed Kizhi Pogost featuring Russia's finest wooden buildings.

✪ SAILING THE NIGER RIVER TO TIMBUKTU, MALI

It's an unusual highway into the desert, but sailing up the Niger River to near the legendary Timbuktu is one hell of an entrance. Passenger boats operate on the river in the high-water season between August and mid-December, and you can expect five very crowded days getting between Koulikoro and Korioumé (18km from Timbuktu). For relative comfort there are also pinasse (motorised canoes). Laden with either cargo or tourists, pinasse depart from the city of Mopti and take around three days to reach Korioumé. Pack a sleeping bag for the cold nights spent on board or on the river bank.

✪ TUBING THE NAM SONG, LAOS

The Laotian town of Vang Vieng sits among an inspiring landscape of limestone spires, and is best viewed from the reclining position floating atop a tractor tyre inner tube on the Nam Song. This idle pastime is so pleasurable it has become a staple on Southeast Asia's backpacking circuit. Tubing trips usually involve a 3km scenic float, made even more enjoyable by the presence of several bars on islands and beaches en route. As idyllic as it sounds, keep a clear head, for there's the occasional horror story; in times of high water, rapids along the Nam Song can be quite daunting.

BEST BREWS

HAVE A COLD ONE COURTESY OF THE WORLD'S FINEST BEER HEADQUARTERS.

✪ YUENGLING, USA

David G Yuengling in Pottsville, Pennsylvania established North America's oldest brewery as the Eagle Brewery in 1829. It was changed to the family name in 1873 after David was joined by his son Frederick. During prohibition Yuengling had to manufacture 'near beer' products or face closure. When the government ban on alcohol ended in 1933 the brewery celebrated by producing Winner Beer and promptly shipping a truckload to the then president, Franklin D Roosevelt. You can congratulate the Yuengling's descendants in person by visiting one of their two breweries, either at Pottsville or Tampa, Florida.

✪ MUSSEL INN, NEW ZEALAND

New Zealand's remotest boutique micro-brewery is two hours from the town of Nelson on the South Island. Apparently there is a signpost, but it's far easier to spot by the cars parked nearby. Beer is an integral part of life at the Inn. The owners once used it to eradicate furry pests by offering a 'beer bounty' to cull possums taking over the Onekaka countryside. The offer of a free handle of beer or cider for every possum tail encouraged locals to eradicate over 5000 of the critters.

✪ MONSTEIN, SWITZERLAND

Après-ski there can be nothing better than getting 'pon high and supping a brew at the most elevated brewery in Europe. The village of Monstein perches at over 1600m, on the edge of a picture-postcard forested valley. The ancient site dates back to the 14th century and is accessed via a scenic trip on a vintage bus from the nearby township of Davos. As if the charms of the mountain village weren't enough, the tour ends in a vaulted cellar with beer, cheese and a platter of air-dried beef.

✪ GUINNESS, IRELAND

If you don't know what it is that makes the Guinness Brewery Ireland's number one visitor attraction then you must be under 18. The syrupy black nectar is so good the Guinness executives are almost forgiven for touting a brewery tour that doesn't actually let you into where Guinness is brewed. The action takes place in the Storehouse, an architect's wet dream that features a gigantic pint glass, which if it were filled to he brim would hold a modest 14.3 million pints of the black stuff. Delicious.

✪ TOKYO MICROBREW BEER FESTIVAL, JAPAN

In beer circles microbreweries are the new black. And in Japan the rising popularity of the microbrew, or *ji-biru*, which translates as 'regional beer', has given rise to a four-day festival where the public can sample ales produced by more than 50 brewers and toast the health of the industry. The coolest thing about this festival is that after deciding which brews you like best, you can make arrangements to travel around Japan visiting the breweries in situ.

✪ RED TOWER, TURKEY

Named after the massive octagonal Seljuk Kizilkule (Red Tower) that rises over the coastal city of Alanya like a dominatrix wearing 12-inch stilettos, the brewery has adopted the brewing traditions of the Reinheitsgebot – the German 'purity' law that says beer must be made using only three ingredients: barley, hops and water. While many believe this old brewing code was invented as a way to ensure Bavarian brewers in the 16th century paid their taxes, these Turkish brewers reckon it makes for the 'finest, freshest beer possible'.

✪ BIRKENHEAD, SOUTH AFRICA

Have a chat with the owners of the first brewery estate in the southern hemisphere and you'll soon be in no doubt that this lot are complete beer nerds. Thankfully, all the talk about incrementally increasing temperatures during the mashing process is justified by the end result. And because it is situated in the shadow of the Klein River Mountains in South Africa's awesome Western Cape, a trip to Birkenhead will satisfy the eyes as well as the beer buds.

✪ CASCADE, AUSTRALIA

Hailed by beer lovers as the 'Jewel in the South', Australia's oldest brewery looks a lot like a castle. This may be because an Englishman, Peter Degraves, built it in 1824. With Mount Wellington soaring high in the background, the brewery's magnificent setting in South Hobart is exactly where you would expect to find a king quaffing down ales. The tour takes you round the fully operational brewery and includes a trip through the museum plus a walk through its popular Woodstock Gardens. As with all brewery tours, remember to wear flat-soled, covered shoes or you'll be barred.

✪ WEIHENSTEPHANER, GERMANY

In 1040 a bunch of Benedictine monks were hit with a bolt of divine inspiration. Their plan was simple: brew beer and sell it. The rest, as we know, is history. Tucked away in leafy Bavaria, the world's oldest continually operated brewery churns out 200,000 hectolitres of liquid gold every year. A visit to this part of the world is an eye-opener if only so you can absorb the undiluted passion Bavarians have for beer. When they tell you it is the 'fifth element' they are definitely not taking the piss.

✪ STAROPRAMEN, CZECH REPUBLIC

Like much of Prague, the brewery has adapted its centuries-old buildings to meet the burgeoning curiosity of visitors to the historic city. The tour kicks off in the state-of-the-art visitor centre with a film about how beer is made before a live demonstration in Brew House Number One. It's all pretty educational, but just when you think your brain is about to pop you'll be ushered into the depths of the brew house and invited to taste your fill of beers – poured from special rapid-fire taps.

(TOP) » FIRST THINGS FIRST – THE CASCADE BREWERY WAS COMPLETED A YEAR BEFORE THE COLONY OF VAN DIEMEN'S LAND WAS OFFICIALLY RECOGNISED.

(LEFT) » ONLY AT BAVARIA'S GASTHOF OBERBRAU CAN YOU DOWN A DRAFT 'POPE BEER', AS POPE BENEDICT XVI WAS BORN NEXT DOOR.

(RIGHT) » DIY BREWERY TOURS: MANY OF PRAGUE'S OLD BEER HALLS, SUCH AS U FLEKU, BREW THEIR BEERS ON THE PREMISES.

COUNTRIES ON THE RISE

OUR TOP PICKS FOR TRAVEL AROUND THE '08 CORNER.

✪ MONTENEGRO

Forget any notions about the spectacular Dalmatian Coast starting and ending in Croatia. The ragged limestone coast that has sold a thousand sailing dreams continues south from Dubrovnik, crossing the border into the new nation of Montenegro. Here you'll find the dramatic village of Kotor on the shore of Europe's southernmost fjord, the postcard-perfect old town of Budva and the stunning and exclusive island of Sveti Stefan, connected to the mainland by a causeway. Add to this the 1.3km-deep Tara Canyon, a sleeper favourite among rafters, and it's no wonder that Croatia's shine is beginning to light up Montenegro.

✪ BOSNIA & HERCEGOVINA

The war is 13 years gone, and only the plasterwork still tells the story. Mostar's Old Bridge across the Neretva River has been rebuilt; the smell of coffee and ćevapčići (minced meat) again floats through Sarajevo's Turkish-styled Baščaršija bazaar; the Catholic faithful still crowd Međugorje; the rafts are back in the rivers; and the walking trails have re-opened. Bosnia & Hercegovina is clearly back in business, and there's much to like about it. In Sarajevo you'll find one of Europe's most welcoming cities, while poke into the crannies of the mountain landscape to find town beauties such as Mostar, Trebinje and Stolac.

✪ COLOMBIA

More often in the headlines than on tourist itineraries, Colombia's dawn is breaking, with this lively nation offering one of the few remaining chances to get off South America's rutted gringo trail. The gulf between Colombia's reputation and its welcome is not the only contrast that's worth experiencing, for here you'll find vibrant cities and virgin national parks, or swim pristine reefs by day and dance salsa by night. Visitor numbers have shot up in the last three or four years, but that's only by Colombian standards. This is still a land where you'll see more locals than tourists.

✪ LIBYA

With a new bunch of international pariahs on the scene, Libya is out of the figurative desert. Geographically it's a different tale, with the Sahara covering around 95% of the country. It's here, like in no other Saharan country, that you'll find readily accessible scenes of windswept desert dunes, punctured by stunning massifs such as Jebel Acacus. Too much desert? Then head for the Mediterranean – Libya has one of the longest of all Mediterranean coasts – or experience the grand Roman city of Lepis Magna or the Greek city of Cyrene. For a city of Libya's own creation, Tripoli is among the most appealing in North Africa.

✪ URUGUAY

Pinched between Argentina and Brazil, Uruguay has tended to be overshadowed by both, though its quiet charms are finding a newly appreciative travelling audience. The capital, Montevideo, comes down somewhere between crumbling and contemporary, while for many visitors there's an easy taste of Uruguay at postcard-perfect, World Heritage-listed Colonia del Sacramento, just a short ferry ride across the Rio de la Plata from Buenos Aires. Within South America, which accounts for about 90% of Uruguay's visitors, this country's beaches are legendary, nowhere more so than the glitz and glamour of Punta del Este.

✪ NEPAL

The trekking Shangri-la is back in vogue, thanks to the signing of a peace agreement between the Nepali government and the rebel Maoists at the end of 2006. A decade of conflict had all but destroyed Nepal's once-thriving tourism industry, leaving twitchy trekkers pining for lost glimpses of Everest, Annapurna and Makalu, as well as the boisterous respite to be found in the lanes of Kathmandu's Thamel district. If the peace holds, Nepal will undoubtedly become one of the world's most fashionable destinations once again, and while much has changed, the country's major draw card – its mountains – has not.

✪ OMAN

Welcome to a corner of the Middle East nobody has stereotyped. Staring across the Arabian Sea towards India, Oman combines 2000km of untrammelled coastline with an interior filled with classic Arabian desert scenes: wet-and-wonderful wadis, a sea of dunes in the Wahiba Sands, and some of the Arabian Peninsula's finest mountains in the Western Hajar. Part of Oman's appeal is its ease of access, with the capital, Muscat (home to one of the Middle East's most evocative souqs) just a short hop from stopover-central Dubai. Though Oman is no longer a travel secret, there's still time to get here before the crowds do.

✪ SOUTH KOREA

Ignore the dodgy neighbour to the north and you'll discover the next big thing in Asian travel on the Korean Peninsula. South Korea's capital, Seoul, buzzes with infectious energy, and history and religion jostle for space in the south. Yet it might not be the culture vultures who ultimately drive South Korea's rising fortunes – it may be the outdoorsy types, with the country's spectacular national parks finally coming to visitor notice. Around 70% of the country is mountainous, and the country's 20 national parks offer endless hiking opportunities.

✪ ZAMBIA

What Zimbabwe has forfeited through bad press, Zambia has gained. The two countries share the prize possession of Victoria Falls, and where once the smoke thundered loudest in Zimbabwe, that country's troubles have lured people across to Zambia instead. What they're discovering is more than a waterfall, with Zambia also considered to be one of the finest wildlife-watching destinations in Africa. Travel here retains a raw, *Out of Africa* edge, far beyond the gentrifying effects of tourism, which is in itself a good reason to visit.

✪ GREENLAND

Even for the traveller who has been everywhere in Europe there's usually still Greenland outstanding, though many are now beginning to correct this. This Greenland that's predominantly white (and named by Eric the Red) presents a face of towering sea cliffs and an interior that's sagging beneath the burden of a 3000m-thick sheet of ice. For most travellers a visit to the world's largest island is all about iceberg-choked Disko Bay, while those who just want to say they've been there, can settle for a day tour flying from Iceland to the southern Greenland town of Kulusuk.

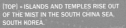

(TOP) » ISLANDS AND TEMPLES RISE OUT OF THE MIST IN THE SOUTH CHINA SEA, SOUTH KOREA.

(LEFT) » A RAFT OF HIPPOS IN ZAMBIA: AFTER WALLOWING ALL DAY, ADULTS EAT UP TO 65KG OF GRASS EACH NIGHT.

(RIGHT) » AS DUSK FALLS AN INUIT HUNTER SETS AN IGLOO ALIGHT IN NORTHWEST GREENLAND.

GREAT FILM FESTIVALS

TAKE A RED-CARPET TOUR TO SOME OF THE WORLD'S EMERGING & MORE FAMOUS FESTIVALS.

✪ TORONTO, CANADA

From its beginnings in 1976 as a simple highlights package from other film festivals, the Toronto International Film Festival has grown to become the most prestigious celluloid shows in North America – some critics have rated it second only to Cannes on the international calendar. In 2006 over 300,000 people attended screenings of around 350 flicks, and past winners of the coveted People's Choice Award include *Whale Rider*, *Strictly Ballroom* and *Hotel Rwanda*. Passes and coupon sales for the purchase of multiple tickets for the September festival open in July, while individual sales begin just a few days before the event.

✪ PORTABLE FILM FESTIVAL

Like films but hate travel and frocked-up starlets on red carpets? Then the Portable Film Festival is for you, requiring nothing more than a bit of computer savvy. This is a festival of short films downloadable to laptops, video iPods, Playstation Portables and the like, with films competing for two prizes: one judged by the submitting film makers and the major prize voted for by the online audience. The festival, held at the uncommon address of www. portablefilmfestival.com, was inaugurated in 2006, with around 70 films selected from more than 250 entries.

✪ RAINDANCE, ENGLAND

Britain's premier independent film festival is held across the last week of September and the first week of October, with screenings at the Cineworld cinemas in Haymarket and the Trocadero Centre. Specialising in films from first-time directors, it screens around 80 feature films and 150 short films and documentaries, with each production vying for the simply titled Film of the Festival award. Festival passes allow access to all screenings, plus associated festival parties (and a free umbrella!). Raindance movies that have gone on to grander things include *Memento*, *The Blair Witch Project* and *Pulp Fiction*.

✪ ONE TAKE FILM FESTIVAL, CROATIA

Forget about the clapboard reminding you that you're up to take 36 of scene 17, because to enter this festival your entire film needs to have been shot in a single take – editing is a dirty word at the One Take Film Festival. First held in 2003, the biannual festival is held in the Croatian capital Zagreb in November, with its programme spread across three days. Films of any genre can be submitted, and there is no restriction on running time for submitted films – imagination and battery life are the only limits.

✪ TRENTO, ITALY

Parked below the Italian Dolomites, Trento is the city that spawned the burgeoning generation of mountain and outdoor film festivals (Banff, Kendal, Taos, Dundee etc). First held in 1952, the Trento Film Festival is a showcase of mountain, adventure and exploration films – both feature films and documentaries – and is held across 10 days in late April and early May. The roll call of winners reads as a who's who – at least of the mountain world – featuring epic tales from Everest, K2, Fitz Roy and Kangchenjunga. Expect to see a few celebrities of the mountaineering world in attendance, even if they lack some of the glamour of a Hollywood hunk.

✪ BRING YOUR OWN FILM FESTIVAL, INDIA

Puri beach is not one of India's palm-backed, sun-soaked strands, making it a better place to watch films than work on a tan. Each February since 2004 it has provided the sandy seats for the curiously named Bring Your Own Film Festival, an egalitarian gathering to which anybody, from anywhere, can submit a flick. There's no competition, no awards, no selection criteria, and the beach screenings go till late in the night – think Woodstock with an Orissan accent. Film makers at BYOFF range from the established to the unknown, with each given the same platform to showcase their work.

✪ BERLINALE, GERMANY

One of the world's largest and most esteemed film festivals, the Berlinale screens around 350 movies across two weeks in February. Most films shown at the festival are premieres – either European or world – with more than 180,000 tickets sold, making it among the highest-attended film festivals in the world. Movies at the Berlinale vie for prizes in five categories, from the big-ticket Competition section to the art-house Panorama, with the top prize – the Golden Bear (the Jack Nicklaus of awards) – going to the best feature film. Past Golden Bear winners include *The Thin Red Line* and *Sense and Sensibility*.

✪ CANNES, FRANCE

The world's most prestigious film festival is an event arguably more famous than Cannes itself, and as chic as its Côte d'Azur backdrop. Held each May, it's limited to film-industry workers, with very few public screenings. Amid a host of awards, plus a few 'out of competition' screenings, the top prize is the Palme d'Or (Golden Palm), of which past winners include *Apocalypse Now*, *Dancer in the Dark* and *The Pianist*. Despite the lack of public events, celebrity spotting is high on the visitor agenda – try the red-carpet entrance to screenings at the Palais.

✪ TROPFEST, AUSTRALIA

Forget Hollywood's crocodile-fighting image of the land Down Under – Australia is the proud owner of the world's biggest outdoor short-film festival. In 2007 Sydney's open-air Domain screened 16 finalist films to an audience of more than 150,000, a feat made possible via simultaneous satellite screenings to other capital cities and regional areas around Australia. With a seven-minute run limit, entries must have had no prior public screenings and should contain the Tropfest Signature Item, which for 2008 is '8' – interpreted in any way you choose.

✪ SUNDANCE, USA

Behind its veneer of Mormons and jaw-dropping desert landscapes, Utah has managed to create the United States' largest festival for independent film makers. Named for the nearby ski resort owned by Robert Redford (who was the festival's inaugural chairman), the festival is held in Park City, with some screenings in Sundance itself. Started as a way to lure more movie makers to Utah, it now showcases around 100 feature-length movies – most of them premieres – each January, offering skiing by day and screenings by night. Cult classics such as *Clerks*, *Reservoir Dogs* and *Napoleon Dynamite* have premiered here.

(TOP) » THE ACTION STARTS BEFORE THE CURTAIN RISES, WITH THE RED-CARPET ARRIVALS FOR A PREMIERE SCREENING AT CANNES.

(LEFT) » WITH OVER 700 ENTRIES WHITTLED DOWN TO 16, OVER 45,000 SYDNEYSIDERS DESCEND ON THE DOMAIN FOR THE OPEN-AIR TROPFEST FINALE.

(RIGHT) » A SUNDANCE IN WINTRY PARK CITY IS A POPULAR STOPOVER FOR THOSE ON THEIR WAY TO HOLLYWOOD.

TROPICAL PARADISE

ENDLESS SUMMERS, COCONUT TREES & WHITE BEACHES – THESE ARE THE PLACES WHERE THE POSTCARD IS REAL.

☆ ATIU, COOK ISLANDS

This particular Cook Island has got all the tropical gear: deserted beaches, bluest water, whiter-than-white sands. But it's also got that little bit extra, with a clutch of famous, multichambered limestone caves tucked away in thick jungle on the coral coastal plains surrounding the island. Some of the caves were used for burials, which means there are human bones about, but relax: Atiu's vicious warrior history is long gone. Nowadays, Atiu is also a mecca for ecotourists, with more flora and fauna than you can shake a pair of binoculars at.

☆ RANGIROA, FRENCH POLYNESIA

A coral atoll beyond compare, Rangiroa (the world's second-largest coral atoll) is about as languorous and remote a place as you'd care to find. Most come here for diving, but what on Earth is wrong with just lazing around on the beach and sipping a cocktail or three? There's also a huge lagoon that's more like a massive inland sea, sure to add to your expanded consciousness and sense of perspective – even the name 'Rangiroa' means 'vast sky'.

☆ KUNA YALA, PANAMA

Look up 'tropical paradise': there'll probably be a picture of the Kuna Yala archipelago alongside. These small islands (also known as the San Blas Islands) are part of the semiautonomous territory of the Kuna people and feature palm trees, gorgeous beaches, thatched huts and timeless charm. Big business hasn't gained a foothold because the Kuna rule the roost, with a series of laws laid down to preserve the natural environment. That means no ugly hotels spoiling the view and no package tourism polluting the vibe, but plenty of uninhabited islands to explore.

CAPE TRIBULATION, AUSTRALIA

This World Heritage-listed, biodiverse region in the state of Queensland deserves to be on your radar for so many reasons. Gorgeous beaches and ancient rainforest that extends right to the water, fringing reefs, wild and beautiful animal and plant life, rock pools, mangrove boardwalks and a backdrop of breathtakingly rugged mountains are the main ingredients. Then there's the Great Barrier Reef, just 40 minutes offshore. Now you understand – it's a totally unique part of the world.

GILI ISLANDS, INDONESIA

These three beloved islands, northwest of Lombok, have all the essentials: coral reefs, stunning beaches, pristine water, superb fishing and snorkelling opportunities, and friendly locals. According to lore, there's also a magic ring around the island that makes it impossible to leave. Go on – test it out. If you can defeat that, then the tuna steaks, plentiful local beer and the complete lack of cars and motor vehicles of any kind might accomplish what magic failed to.

CAPE VERDE

This archipelago of 10 volcanic islands off the Senegal coast has long been a byword for 'mystery'. A strange amalgam of West African rhythms and Portuguese colonialism, Cape Verde is now succumbing to tourism, with the government planning to aggressively market all that sunkissed splendour. But tread carefully: with its unspoiled coastlines and uninhabited beaches, the archipelago may sound inviting, but it also shields a fragile ecosystem; you'll be sharing space with many species of animals unique to the Cape.

FERNANDO DE NORONHA, BRAZIL

This sparsely populated archipelago off Brazil's northeastern coast is famous as a diving destination, with dolphins, shipwrecks and psychedelic coral all available for underwater viewing. Not only that, but the islands play host to the Western Atlantic's largest colony of tropical seabirds, a fact that's sure to raise the pulse of twitchers everywhere. There aren't that many facilities here, but the trade-off is that you have the islands pretty much as they have been for the last 500 years, with only some ex-Portuguese ruins providing clues to past life.

LALOMANU, SAMOA

Mmmmmm, thank God for the South Pacific and more sea, sand and sun than any person can cram into a lifetime. This time it's Samoa's turn, with Lalomanu beach on 'Upolu turning out to be the perfect spot for first-class swimming and snorkelling. If you want to stay, sleeping in open beach fales (huts) can impart the sense that you're doing it in some kind of authentic, beachy, tropical-island style. A kind of paradisiacal virtual reality for jaded Westerners, then? If you like, locals will argue the toss. Lalomanu is what it is, and the sunsets just have to be seen to be believed.

SAN ANDRÉS & PROVIDENCIA, COLOMBIA

If you like your tropical paradises 'Caribbean' flavoured, then you should probably visit this little-known haven, with its swashbuckling English, Jamaican and pirate history. There's a big Rastafarian influence around these parts; we're sure you don't need us to tell you the attendant treasures of such a culture. What we will tell you, though, is that beautiful beaches, coves, caves and swimming holes combine with native architecture and lots of reggae, rum and cocktails to provide sensual delights.

TULUM, MEXICO

Make no mistake, Tulum is one of the world's premier beaches, with 7km of the finest powder sand, perfect blue water ripped straight out of your dreams, and the beach's famous, unpowered, cabana-style accommodation all along the coastline. Not only that, but backing onto Tulum is something amazing: the ruins of a 6th-century Mayan walled city (tulum is the Mayan word for wall), possibly the most majestic backdrop of any beach in the world.

FRIENDLIEST COUNTRIES

TIME AFTER TIME, THESE ARE PLACES WHERE THE WELCOME IS WARM.

✪ FIJI

Fiji is one of the most coup-ridden countries on the planet, yet its citizens are generally considered to be the 'friendliest people on the planet'. And why not? They've got plenty to smile about – lush islands, kaleidoscopic reefs, cobalt sea, a wealth of marine life, world-class diving, romantic coastlines, awesome cuisine – and they love to spread the love around. Fijians have a rep for helping all travellers feel welcome, thereby allowing you to uncover the best from this sprawling group of islands. Just don't talk politics.

✪ INDONESIA

It's hard to make generalisations about a country that contains so many different cultures…still, a cliché you'll hear often is that 'Indonesian' people greet foreigners with open arms. Fact is they do, but the media limelight is stolen by the knack of their law-enforcement officers for welcoming drug dealers and bomb makers in an altogether different ritual. Word of advice: if you travel to the beautiful island of Bali, leave the ecstasy at home, otherwise diplomatic relationships with other countries will be strained, foreigners might not be so welcome anymore, and you'll make fools of us for including Indonesia on this list.

✪ VIETNAM

Vietnam's another country inextricably caught up in Western images and stereotypes: napalm death; tormented American soldiers; assassins hiding in the rice fields; the whirr of helicopter blades like the Grim Reaper's scythe. But Vietnam put all that behind it a long time ago and is now on a huge drive to become the new 'Asian' tiger economy. Not even the rampant threat of bird flu can dim the people's appetite for friendliness and hospitable greetings to travellers.

✪ SAMOA

What's this? Samoa reckons they have 'the world's friendliest people'? Hmmm, trouble is there's no ratifying body for such a claim, meaning the Samoans have to contend with the challenge of Fiji, which also self-applies the title. OK, enough: let's settle this with a Googlefight. A Boolean search for the phrase 'Fiji world's friendliest people' garners 36,500 hits; the phrase 'Samoa world's friendliest people' reaps 21,000. Sorry, Samoa, the interweb has spoken, although readers can rest assured that your beautiful country harbours lovely and warm people who will leave a deep and lasting impression on them.

✪ THAILAND

Southeast Asia's most-visited country is bound to offer up a welter of stereotypes and clichés. Here are some of them: dazzling islands and beaches; lush and balmy weather; great shopping and great food; the 'France of Asia'; lady boys. Here's another one: 'world's friendliest people'. Gawd, not another contender (see Fiji and Samoa). But yes, the Thai people's gracious hospitality does indeed take some beating. Why bother trying to analyse why the Thais are so easygoing and incredibly quick to smile? They just are and that's all there is to it.

✪ SCOTLAND

Forget Begbie in the film *Trainspotting* – Scotland's becoming the destination for visitors to the British Isles, winning out over dog-eat-dog London. The Scots have survived English invasion, brutal weather and the pain of having the world's worst goalkeepers. This fighting spirit against insurmountable odds has left them with an extroverted, buoyant demeanour and a blackly humorous nationalism (you'd want to see the funny side after witnessing some of those goalies). Naturally, this attitude rubs off on travellers – Scots are so loyal they want you to share in the good stuff, too.

✪ TURKEY

It's a shame that for such a long time the Western world's image of Turkey revolved around the brutal drug-smuggling film Midnight Express – as an advertisement for a nation, it rates slightly below Chornobyl. Thankfully, we've all moved on from that and we can now report that the Turkish people actually have an unsurpassed reputation for hospitality. With their heavenly cuisine, dreamy coastline and spectacular historical sites, the Turks know there's no reason to be secretive.

✪ IRELAND

Centuries of turmoil, conquest and famine – and subsequent immigration – have certainly taken their toll on the Irish: it's left them with a deliciously dark sense of humour and a welcoming attitude towards strangers. That famous ability of the Irish – to find craic (fun times with convivial company) in boom or bust times – means you're always in for a treat. These days, after the end of the 'Troubles', a cautious optimism reigns supreme, infecting the land once again with the sense that anything's possible.

✪ USA

Blamed for the coming of World War III, the Anti-Christ, Bon Jovi, Tom Cruise, Michael Jackson, rampant street crime, and noise pollution through overloud talking, Americans just take it all in their stride – they know there's no such thing as a 'typical Yank', so you can just stuff your stereotypes in a sack, mister! Americans may be patriotic and love their country but so are all the nationals on this list – they'll invariably welcome you and help you get the best out of the US, and all they ask in return is for you to leave your shoe bomb at home.

✪ MALAWI

Whereas other African nations are beset by deadly tribal war and internecine fighting, Malawians describe them-selves as 'the friendliest people in Africa' living in the 'warm heart of the continent'. Anyone who's visited will know that the rare (for Africa) cohesion of the country's ethnic groups is solid evidence for this, as is the people's propensity to welcome you into their homes as well as their nation. Malawi is small, poor and without a lot of facilities, but with a greeting like that who needs Western-style comfort?

[TOP] » IN IRELAND GREAT CRAIC IS NEVER HARD TO FIND, WITH A PUB FOR EVERY 250 ADULTS, TO BE SURE.

[LEFT] » THE NAKED COWBOY'S STILL DOING HIS THANG AT TIMES SQUARE, NEW YORK.

[RIGHT] » DON'T JUST STAND THERE – KIDS BUSTING MOVES IN A REFUGEE CAMP IN MALAWI.

SPORTY CHINA

SOME OF CHINA'S BEST SPORTING TRADITIONS WON'T BE REPRESENTED AT THE OLYMPICS, SO TAKE THE TIME TO BE A TRUE TRAVELLING SPECTATOR.

✪ TIAOBAN

Also known as seesaw diving, *tiaoban* requires prodigious balance and bravery. The two participants (often women) mount a wooden springboard on a pivot like a seesaw, and take their places at either end. The first player jumps down, launching her opponent on the opposite side skyward. The airborne player then spins or back-flips before landing on the seesaw and sending her rival in the air. The players go higher and higher with each rebound, trying to out-do the other and win the crowd's approval. The contests usually are held during the Dragon Boat Festival.

✪ FIREWORK CATCHING

Imagine: instead of mum telling you to stay away from lit fireworks, she encourages you to get right under and catch them for this team sport. A small iron ring swaddled in red ribbon is attached to a firework and shot over the playing field. Two eight-member sides then rush out to grab it and throw it to their teammates – without it being intercepted – as they make for a basket at the field's end. Once a team scores a point, another firework is launched and the scrum begins anew. The game is played in two 20-minute halves.

✪ STILT BALL

Ostensibly it is similar to football (soccer), except all 10 players (five per team) are wobbling high above the ground on stilts, which they use to dribble, pass and whack the ball down the field and into the opponents' goal. Anyone whose feet touch the ground is suspended, leaving the arena to wait in the 'penalty box' for two minutes. In some regions of China there is a related, smaller-scale sport in which each be-stilted team is comprised of a husband and wife.

✪ SILK-BALL THROWING

Played between boys and girls at harvest time, this sport goes beyond good exercise – it's also a way to court that hottie you've been eyeing all season. First of all, everyone suits up in their finest threads. Players then take the field, with males lining up on one side of the field and females on the other. The teams then toss silk balls back and forth, with individuals aiming for their beloved. Each ball is handmade by the females using intricate embroidery. If either side drops the ball, that entire side is required to perform a song or dance.

✪ BASKETBALL

It's not the game Yao plays in the NBA, but a more literal version of the sport. The basket is just that, a woven, picnic hamper-esque receptacle, and each player carries one on his back. A bag of sand constitutes the ball. Otherwise, the rules are the same: five players per team run around and try to score by shooting the ball into the opponents' basket (or baskets, as the case may be, with the added twist that what players are aiming for is constantly moving). Another difference: less bling and fewer sideline babes in the Chinese game.

✪ STRAW BALL

According to legend, a local fisherman brought home a good catch. But his wife complained, 'The fish have big holes in their skin made by your spearing fork!' So the husband practiced his aim by forking bundles of straw. The exercise morphed into a game vaguely akin to volleyball. Two three-person teams stand on a court that's divided into eight zones. One team hand-serves a straw ball, to be received with a wooden fork by the other team. The side that fails to spear it withdraws to the next zone and loses one point when the ball gets dropped in the end zone.

✪ TUG-OF-WAR

People throughout China have been trying to yank each other over the centre line for close to 2000 years. Back then, tug-of-war was a contest between neighbouring villages. The main rope had multiple branches so up to 100 people could join in the game, fired up by the sound of beating drums. While the primal rhythms are now gone, the sport continues to be popular, not only as an exercise of strength, but also as one of team-building and group cooperation.

✪ YAK RACING

This sport is a Tibetan specialty and usually takes place during the Ongkor harvest festival. Owners adorn their shaggy bovines' heads with red flowers and their backs with ornamented saddles. The yak jockey swings atop the animal and lets his whip fly as he urges the creature toward the finish line. While the mammoth yaks are surprisingly sure-footed, they can also be disobedient and stop in the middle of the track, refusing to budge. Less amusing to spectators is when they charge toward the audience.

✪ MONGOLIAN-STYLE WRESTLING

Long a revered pastime in Mongolia – Genghis Khan supposedly used it to decide which soldiers to recruit and officers to promote – this theatrical style of wrestling takes place outdoors on a grassy field. The contestants enter wearing leather boots, necklaces of silk ribbons and cowhide waistcoats. They start by performing a dance that imitates a fierce animal such as a tiger or eagle. Then the smackdown ensues. There are no weight classes or time limits, just man against man throwing, tripping and lifting until one gets the other to touch the ground with any body part other than his feet.

✪ DRAGON-BOAT RACING

Dragon boats are – get this – boats carved and painted to look like dragons. About 20m long with the front resembling the beast's fiery open mouth and the rear shaped like its scaly tail, the bold-coloured vessels hit the water during the annual Dragon Boat Festival, an event held across China on the fifth day of the fifth lunar month. Teams of 20 or more paddlers, including a gong beater and a drummer, send each boat slicing through the waves spurred by the rhythmical beating. Zong zi, the festival's traditional gooey rice-ball snack, provides the oarsfolks' power.

[TOP] » TIBETAN RACING YAKS ARE ON THE SMALL SIDE COMPARED TO THEIR WILD COUSINS, WHO STAND UP TO 2M TALL AND WEIGH UP TO A TONNE.

[LEFT] » PRO-WRESTLERS TAKE NOTE: MONGOLIAN WRESTLERS SHAKE HANDS AND SALUTE EACH OTHER BEFORE AND AFTER A BOUT.

[RIGHT] » THE DRAGON BOAT FESTIVAL COMMEMORATES THE PATRIOTIC POET QU YUAN, WHO DROWNED ON THE DAY IN 277 BC.

LIKE THE SONG?

HITCH A LYRICAL RIDE WITH SOME OF MUSIC'S GREATEST TOUR GUIDES & SEE WHAT ROCKED THEIR WORLDS.

✪ PORTOBELLO SHUFFLE (1972; PINK FAIRIES)

Visit the Portobello Rd in Notting Hill, London, today: there's the famous antique market, sure…plus a whole lot of affluent fashionistas prancing around with oversized sunglasses and huge handbags hanging off shoulders like cancerous lumps sprung from the bowels of evil capitalism itself. But back in the early '70s, this strip was quite a different beast, home to anarcho-hippie-proto-punk tribes Hawkwind and the Pink Fairies, the latter singing in this ode to two-fisted freedom, 'Roll out of your seats / Get out in the streets / There's a new day a-comin''. It was all a long way from Hugh Grant, a few weddings, and a funeral.

✪ LIFE ON MARS? (1972; DAVID BOWIE)

Do the lyrics bear any relation to Earth's red-tinged neighbour? Well, Bowie sings of 'America's tortured brow' and how Mickey Mouse has 'grown up a cow'; about his mother, his dog, 'and clowns'; and 'sailors fighting in the dance hall'… Not really a lot of convergence, considering that Mars is a barren rock that supports no discernible life. Although to be fair, the 'Is there life on Mars?' chorus was probably a call to colonise the Red Planet and make a fresh go of it. Yes, probably – this is one obtuse song.

✪ HIROSHIMA MON AMOUR (1977; ULTRAVOX)

Original Ultravox lead singer John Foxx had a fixation with the writings of JG Ballard and the films of Alain Resnais, and combined them in this anomie-infested new-wave classic. The lyrics are based on Resnais' eponymous 1959 film, in which a Japanese man and a French woman have a love affair in post-war, bomb-ravaged Hiroshima. Backed by an ultraminimal, metronomic drum machine and vaporous synths, Foxx imbues the lyrics with an unmistakeable Ballardian sheen, meditating on a future that's 'fused like shattered glass' and the pain of communicating 'like distant stars'.

✪ ECHO BEACH (1980; MARTHA AND THE MUFFINS)

When one-hit wonders Martha and the Muffins sang about 'Echo Beach, far away in time', many people wondered how to get there. But Echo Beach – at the time – didn't exist, being the band's idealised version of an untainted haven far away from the urban rat race. Since then, though, Echo Beach has become the name of a San Franciscan club and a tourist park in Lakes Entrance, Victoria, Australia. Are they like the song? Well, the latter has a beach. Interestingly, 'Hiroshima Mon Amour', also on this list, features the line, 'Riding out to echo beach'.

✪ UNION CITY BLUES (1980; BLONDIE)

Blondie's title song for the 1980 noir film *Union City*, about brain-eating paranoia in the eponymous industrial town, captured the tenor, with Debbie Harry (who also starred) singing 'What are we gonna do?' in a precise summation of the film's humid sexual heat. There are nine conurbations called Union City in the USA; this one's the New Jersey version. Is it like the town? Maybe, maybe not.

The film and the song are set in the 1950s, which would seem to indicate things have moved on, but Ms Harry once worked as a dancer in Union City, so all bets are off.

✪ KIDS IN AMERICA (1981; KIM WILDE)

Ah Kim Wilde, the early '80s, one-and-a-half-hit wonder with big hair, singing about dirty windows, cars and cities rushing by, being alone 'and wondering why', heat and 'searching for beats in a dirty town', people living for something called a 'music-go-round', sprawling suburbia 'from east coast to California', and a subsequent musical new wave a-coming kick-started by American kids. Hmmmm, as a poet of modern America, we'll give her five out of 10 and a homework assignment to rewrite clichés in her own words. As a prophet of new musical styles, she sucks eggs: Beyonce and co ain't no edgy 'new wave'.

✪ SHE CREATURES OF THE HOLLYWOOD HILLS (1973; IGGY & THE STOOGES)

This X-rated song – in which Iggy Pop taunts all the women who ever done him wrong, plus all the managers who ever screwed him over, while cataloguing the sexual, pharmaceutical, physical and psychological abuse he willingly puts himself through to make it in rock 'n' roll – is by all accounts fairly accurate with regards to the notoriously cannibalistic showbiz scene that is modern-day Hollywood. In the song's live incarnations, Stooges' guitarist James Williamson would end 'She Creatures' with brainmelting squalls of feedback, as if death

✪ 30 SECONDS OVER TOKYO (1975; PERE UBU)

You know Tokyo: lots of neon, weird subcultures, girls dressed as Little Bo Peep, boys like asexual androids, manga, skyscrapers alive with embedded vid screens, mobile phones… Then what the hell were Pere Ubu on about when they sang, 'Toy city streets crawling through my sights / sprouting clumps of mushrooms like a world surreal / this dream won't ever seem to end / and time seems like it'll never begin'? Well, it's a pilot's-eye view of Tokyo unfolding beneath the belly of a fearsome American warplane as it begins its descent to open a can of whoop-ass on WWII Japan.

[TOP] » JAPAN'S SUBCULTURES SURFACE TIME AND AGAIN IN WESTERN POP MUSIC: MEET LITTLE BO-PEEP AND MADAME LASH.

[BOTTOM] » BEACH GIRLS: BREAKING HEARTS AND INSPIRING SONGS OF UNREQUITED LOVE THE WORLD OVER.

✪ GIRL FROM IPANEMA (1964; STAN GETZ & ASTRUD GILBERTO)

This one's all about a tall, tanned, young, lovely, completely self-assured girl walking on by at the beach at Ipanema, a southern district of Rio de Janeiro in Brazil, with a slinky bossa nova rhythm that immediately conjures up sexy Latin good times. Is that what you can expect to find on the same beach today? Yeah, definitely: whole websites are devoted to tips for males hoping to impress the flocks of tall, tanned, young, lovely, completely self-assured girls walking on by 24/7.

✪ DEATH VALLEY '69 (1984; SONIC YOUTH & LYDIA LUNCH)

This noise fest, all detuned guitars and fiery menace, pits the blackhearted Ms Lunch against the Youth, champions of off-kilter alternarock. It's ostensibly, obliquely about Charles Manson and his Family, who were holed up in the Barker Ranch in the appropriately named Death Valley National Park at the time of their arrest. 'Deep in the valley / in the trunk of an old car / in the back of a Chevy' sing the Sonic Lunch: it's all downhill from there.

FOOD WONDERLANDS OF THE WORLD

DREAMING OF CHOCOLATE RIVERS, CANDIED DOGS & YOUR OWN TROUPE OF OOMPA LOOMPAS? VISIT THE PLACES WHERE FOOD FANTASIES COME TRUE.

✪ BEN & JERRY'S ICE-CREAM FACTORY, USA

You can pretend you're on the tour to learn about the company's socially responsible business practices (use only natural ingredients, buy them from local family farms). But let's face it: you're really at this factory in Vermont for the dreamy ice-cream samples swirled with fudge chunks, toffee bars, brownie batter and chocolate chip-cookie dough. Would it not be the world's greatest job to ensure quality control of the 55-gallon (208L) fudge tank or proper blending of the peanut-butter-filled pretzels into their vanilla malt base? Ice-cream fanatics have been known to weep onsite.

✪ YELISEYEVSKY, RUSSIA

Fit for hungry tsars, this grand 1901 Moscow food hall drips with crystal chandeliers and Art Nouveau stained-glass windows, with plenty of gold and marble tossed in for good measure. The edibles and drinkables are even more opulent. Beluga caviar and champagne? Check. Smoked salmon and vodka? Yep. Siberian meat dumplings and cognac? Got it. Salamis, cheeses and more vodka? Here. And what about dessert, say jam-filled gingerbread and Belgian chocolates? Yeliseyevsky has it all.

✪ PASEO DE LA PRINCESA, PUERTO RICO

Energetic kids, amorous couples and old men clacking dominoes get their fill along this San Juan promenade that runs beneath moss-draped walls. Food carts with coloured awnings proffer candy apples, cotton candy and other sugar-fuelled sweets to young ones, while older gents sip rich coffee and chomp golden-fried, seafood-stuffed yucca dough at outdoor tables. Cold drinks are the paseo's specialty, with folks trying to beat the heat by gulping fruit-sweetened shaved ice, pineapple-juice-and-coconut-milk piña coladas (sans rum) and maví, a tree-bark cider served frosty from wooden barrels.

✪ HERSHEY'S CHOCOLATE WORLD, USA

Yes, it's geared mostly to youngsters with its animated films of singing Hershey Bars and Reese's Cups wearing top hats. That doesn't mean adults won't have ample opportunity to act like kids in the candy shop. Chocolate World is, after all, a Pennsylvanian tribute to the making of some of America's finest sweets – crisp wafery Kit Kats, tooth-destroying caramel Milk Duds, cool tingling Peppermint Patties and roast-peanut-infused Nutrageous bars. The *pièce de résistance* for chocoholics: gaping at shelves of 5lb (2.3kg) Hershey Bars in the onsite chocolate emporium.

✪ MERCADO DE LA MERCED, MEXICO

Those who elbow through this cramped, four-block span of marketplace in Mexico City are rewarded with tastes from all over the country. Traditional eats include dark and chewy cactus paddles (aka nopales), normally gobbled raw or cooked in stew; fresh white cheese; and an array of atomically hot chillies – all of which vendors generously offer samples. In addition to explosive flavours, multihued *piñatas* and bright wool blankets dangling from the stalls ignite the Mercado into a festival of colours.

✪ SPICE MUSEUM, GERMANY

The scent tickles your nose as soon as you enter this Hamburg establishment. It's sweet, peppery, astringent and licoricey all at once. As you step over creaking floorboards and approach the individual burlap bags scattered throughout the warehouse, the aromas begin to focus. First marjoram, mint and nutmeg, then cinnamon, sage and fennel. The olfactory paradise continues, with 50 different spices to sniff along with exhibits explaining five centuries of spice history. The aphrodisiac spices (hello, cloves and coriander!) make for particularly good inhaling.

✪ BRAMAH MUSEUM OF TEA & COFFEE, ENGLAND

Exotic teas and roasting coffee waft out waves of caffeine from the onsite café, which helps put you in the mood while browsing drink-making devices (decorative ceramic pots, presses etc) that date back to the 1650s, as well as maps and diagrams explaining the great beverage trade routes that brought tea here to London and elsewhere in Europe from the Far East and Africa. Fragrant teas boiled include rose-petal-scented congou from China, orange pekoe from Sri Lanka, sharp green sencha from Japan and sweet jasmine from India. Coffees brewed come from Indonesia, Ethiopia and Kenya, among other far-flung locales.

✪ TSUKIJI FISH MARKET, JAPAN

The smell is, er, not so fresh, but the flurry of commerce, led off by the 5:30am Tokyo tuna auction, is a sight to behold. Heaps of big fat slippery blackfin, bluefin, bigeye and longtail tuna, some weighing 300kg, lie on rows of ice alongside poisonous blowfish, scallops and sea cucumbers. Motorized carts whiz down the aisles, workers scurry around with clipboards and seafood-stuffed cartons, band saws hack through the giant tuna, and the slicing, scaling and sectioning of fish carries on apace. Once you've seen it, go eat it at the sushi bars along the market's edges.

✪ CHANDNI CHOWK, INDIA

Get ready to graze through the sweets and savouries of this 350-year-old bazaar in Delhi, attached to the Red Fort of Mughal Emperor Shahjahan. Crunch into a buttery, pistachioed *sohan halwa* dessert, then mix it up in the ol' taste buds by downing a cone of spicy fried potato sticks. Vendors sell mounds of *masalas* (spice mixes), tubs of *paneer* (fresh cheese), towers of mangoes and bins of candied fruits. Thirsty from bargaining over the din? Quench with a *thandai*, a milk, sugar, almond, cardamom and crushed ice concoction. When you're ready to bust, wave down a rickshaw to wheel you home.

✪ MUSTARD MUSEUM, USA

It's a teeny building in the tiny Wisconsin town of Mt Horeb (that's OK, no one else has heard of it either), but it packs more mustard than you can shake a ballpark's worth of hot dogs at – 4600 jars, to be exact. There's horseradish mustard that'll singe your nose hair, orange rind and espresso mustard that'll wake up your corned beef sandwich and sweet, bubbly champagne mustard that'll make your pork chop giggle. Antique tins and other items of great mustard historical importance line the shelves. 'Condiment counselors' spread samples at the back mustard bar.

[TOP] » SUPERSIZED SUSHIMI: TSUKIJI FISH MARKET SELLS SOME 2500 TONNES OF SEAFOOD EVERY DAY.

[LEFT] » SYRUP GETS A TWISTING AT THE HANDS OF A SWEET MAKER IN DELHI.

[RIGHT] » WISCONSIN'S GREAT WALL OF MUSTARD.

METROPOLIS MANIA

JUMP INTO SOME OF THE WORLD'S MOST INCREDIBLE URBAN MACHINES.

✪ ISTANBUL, TURKEY

Here's trouble: Istanbul (population 10 million) sits on the site of a vicious fault line that has coughed up lethal earthquakes. The most recent, in 1999, caused massive loss of life as a result of a densely packed population and the fact that large swathes of housing development – built in haste to accommodate the city's rapid growth – were flimsy constructions. Geologists predict another major disaster some time within the next few decades, throwing into sharp relief the need for megacities to somehow grow megabrains and do some serious thinking about the consequences of rampant development.

✪ MEXICO CITY, MEXICO

Chiming in with 22 million people, Mexico City can't help but represent both poles of the megacity experience. Let's get the bad out of the way: the pollution here is extraordinary, a brown shell hanging over the city like a geodesic dome from hell. Then there's the suffocating poverty, the corruption, the slums, the alarming crime rate. But then again, there's the justly famous museums, the vibrant music, the zesty arts scene, the remarkably well-preserved sense of history. In short, this is one hell of a complex megacity.

✪ MUMBAI, INDIA

Mumbai (population 17 million) means Bollywood; endless shopping malls; unbelievable pollution; crass commercialism; cricket and more cricket; food, food and more food; chai; writhing, snarling, totally unpredictable traffic jams; buzzy street scenes; intoxicating nightlife; humidity like a hammer; grinding slums; beggars; luxurious spas; sacred cows; Kingfisher beer; the Ganesh Festival and a few million revellers out on the streets at once; incubator of dreams for countless Indians... Well, this is a book of lists.

✪ SEOUL, SOUTH KOREA

Repeatedly flattened by conflict (the Japanese and Manchu attacks of the 16th and 17th centuries and the Korean War more recently), Seoul (population 23 million) has bounced back to become a shrine to modern life, with high-rises, big business and freeways galore. But now it's greening up, planting over three million trees since 1998, developing the US$200 million Seoul Forest, and reinvigorating its public-transport system to wean residents off their car addiction. Given the 21st-century forecast of more and more megacities worldwide, Seoul is far and away the exemplar in how to give a damn.

✪ KARACHI, PAKISTAN

Although the port city of Karachi (population 15 million) has become increasingly affluent and urbanised, it has suffered from frequent outbreaks of cholera, emphasising the way in which megacities magnify pain alongside pleasure. Still, Karachi is Pakistan's cultural centre, a city with a rich sense of history and a multiethnic community. It's rapidly becoming an Asian tourism hot spot, with the markets, bazaars and cricket the major drawcards, as well as the nearby beaches.

✪ TOKYO, JAPAN

Tokyo, inspiration for dystopian science-fiction flick, *Blade Runner*, was once described by William Gibson as 'the global imagination's default setting for the future'; Greater Tokyo, the world's biggest megacity (population 35 million), has swallowed up nearby cities including Yokohama and Kawasaki. It's a beast of a place, a living, breathing organism constantly reinventing itself and generating hyperaccelerated fashion, design, technological prowess...plus attendant health problems, pollution, traffic-driven nightmares. Track its transition from the diminutive 'Tokyo' to the untameable 'Greater Tokyo' and you are in fact tracking Japan's speed-of-light rise – and subsequent decline – as an economic superpower.

✪ MOSCOW, RUSSIA

If you like your megacities cold, then don't pass up Moscow (population 11 million) – the average temperature here is just 5°C, meaning three times more energy is needed to heat the place than your average Asian megacity. And that means a terrible time for the environment. Here's hoping the Russian government can get cracking and cook up some sustainable solutions, but in the meantime you all know what Moscow's good for: history, culture – all the basic essentials.

✪ BANGKOK, THAILAND

It may be a megacity – huge (population 12 million), modern, increasingly Westernised – but Bangkok still retains a somnambulant village air…albeit one that's continually disrupted by the ever-present thrum of megatraffic and meganightlife. Still, Bangkok, unlike Mexico City and Mumbai, has gone some way to controlling its pollution. But enough of that: Bangkok is also surprisingly historical. Before you know it, your nostrils will be twitching from incense rather than smog as you stumble upon a temple in the thick of it all.

✪ NEW YORK, USA

OK, this is where it all began: New York was the first city to bust the 10-million-people barrier, somewhere in the late '40s, kicking off the megacity trend that continues apace, worldwide, in the 21st century (today NY's greater metropolitan area has doubled to 19 million people). There's not that much to utter about Noo Yawk that hasn't been kicked to death by numerous go-rounds in Woody Allen (lite) and Martin Scorsese (dark) movies, suffice to say that there's a lot of dog shit on NY pavements because there's a hell of a lot of dogs.

✪ SHANGHAI, CHINA

Possibly the world's fastest-growing megacity, Shanghai (population 18 million) was voted 'most exciting city in the world' by *Time* magazine, a far cry from its old rep as crucible of the sleaziest vice this side of Miami. Yes, it's exciting if you like the smell of big finance. But scintillating Shanghai is also tops for sophisticated, big-city life including the best of art, cutting-edge architecture and fine cuisine. Then there are the crumbling remnants of Shanghai's decadent colonial past, plus temples, gardens and bazaars. Megacity madness! Plus, it's the birthplace of author, JG Ballard, and for many that's recommendation enough.

[TOP] » ARTERIAL ART: BY NIGHT BANGKOK'S ELEVATED HIGHWAYS BIND THE CITY IN A GOLDEN NETWORK.

[LEFT] » TIMES SQUARE, CENTRE OF THE KNOWN UNIVERSE, DOESN'T HAVE SIGNS, IT HAS 'SPECTACULARS'.

[RIGHT] » FOR A 350M-HIGH BIRD'S EYE OF SHANGHAI, RIDE THE ELEVATOR TO THE 'SPACE MODULE' AT THE ORIENTAL PEARL TOWER.

COLDEST

PUT ON YOUR THERMALS & FOLLOW THE MERCURY AS LOW AS IT CAN GO.

✪ VOSTOK STATION, ANTARCTICA

Located near the South Geomagnetic Pole, and at the lofty height of around 3500m above sea level, the Russian research station at Vostok is perpetually cold, but never more so than on 21 July 1983, when it registered the coldest recorded air temperature on the planet: –89.2°C. The key geographic feature around Vostok is Lake Vostok, one of the world's largest lakes, buried beneath around 4km of glacial ice and itself colder than all other lakes on earth. With the enormous ice mass above, the lake remains unfrozen at around –3°C.

✪ EUREKA, CANADA

Forget sea changes and try an ice change to the Arctic weather station that has been called the world's coldest inhabited place. The Eureka research base on Canada's far-northern Ellesmere Island, which straddles the 80th parallel, was created as a weather station in 1947 and boasts an average annual air temperature of around –20°C. In winter it's about 20°C cooler still. For visitors to Eureka, the low temperatures are matched only by the high price of getting here. To add this chilly nowhere land to your travelling resumé you need to fly in from Resolute – factor on about US$20,000 for the airfare.

✪ OYMYAKON, RUSSIA

It seems only fitting that a place with a reputation as ferocious as Siberia should also claim the dubious honour of recording the northern hemisphere's coldest air temperature. In the republic of Yakutia, around 350km south of the Arctic Circle, the village of Oymyakon slipped to the numbing frostiness of –71.2°C in 1926, an event that seems to be remembered with unusual fondness, given that a plaque in the village commemorates the occasion. Expect a long day of rugged driving from Yakutsk, around 800km to the west, if you plan to pay homage to this mercury marvel.

HOTTEST

AS THE PLANET TURNS UP THE HEAT, TAKE A TOUR OF THE GLOBAL HOT SPOTS.

✪ DASHT-E LUT, IRAN

History tosses up its hottest and coldest places, but modern times strongly favour the remarkable desert of Dasht-e Lut in southeastern Iran as the roasting capital. In 2004 and again in 2005 this plateau desert recorded the planet's highest surface (as opposed to air) temperatures of the year, cracking the 70°C barrier. Coupled to the heat, the Dasht-e Lut vies with Chile's Atacama Desert for the title of world's driest spot, and across a large area of the central Lut not a single creature survives, not even bacteria. The desert's east has great visitor potential, with a vast area being composed of classic wind-sculpted dunes rising to heights of 500m.

✪ DEATH VALLEY, USA

An uninviting name with an inviting infrastructure, California's Death Valley has recorded the second-highest air temperature on record, reaching 56.7°C; in midsummer it averages around 47°C and is the driest place in the USA. Hardly the environment in which you'd expect to find hiking trails, resorts, and a bewilderingly green golf course lined with palm trees. Yet, through the heat haze and the coyotes, they are not mirages. Ringed by mountains, Death Valley plunges to 86m below sea level at Badwater, making it the lowest point in the western hemisphere, which helps explain the heat.

✪ BANGKOK, THAILAND

Crowned as the planet's hottest city by the World Meteorological Organization, Thailand's capital Bangkok has an annual mean air temperature of around 28°C (as a comparison, 'hot' Brisbane has an annual mean air temperature of around 20°C). The months form March through to May are the hottest time of the year, when the smog-saturated city swelters in 34°C days and swims through 90% humidity. In cooler December the mercury creeps down to 31°C and the barometer to, um, 90% humidity, so that even on the best Bangkok day conditions can only be described as rather uncomfortable.

DENALI, USA

In the alpine world, frostbitingly cold conditions are a fact of life, yet one mountain stands above all others as the most arctic on the planet. Denali, or Mt McKinley, the highest peak in North America, has long been considered the coldest mountain on earth, with winter air temperatures plunging to around –40°C. To experience the full frostiness of this Alaskan peak you must be a mountaineer – the 6194m mountain is mostly climbed by the West Buttress – but you can ponder it from slightly warmer locales with a visit or backpacking trip through Denali National Park.

ULAANBAATOR, MONGOLIA

Perched on the Mongolian steppe, around 1300m above sea level, Ulaanbaator has been called the world's coldest capital city, and it does indeed pack a winter punch: in January the average maximum air temperature in the city is a frigid –16°C. But with the city's rush towards modernisation in recent years, there are more and more ways to escape the Ulaanbaator chill. You can warm your digits and your mind inside the city's impressive collection of museums – be it a camel museum or a museum about political persecution – or seek out the body heat of 500 monks in Gandantegchinlen Khiid, Mongolia's largest monastery.

MAKING IT THROUGH THE ULAANBAATOR WINTER CAN BE HARD YAKKA, EVEN FOR A WILD, HAIRY LOCAL.

DALLOL, ETHIOPIA

At Dallol, in the Denakil Depression in northern Ethiopia, Africa dips to a depth of 116m below sea level, and the mercury soars towards the heavens. Dallol has the highest average air temperature in the world, calculated at 34.4°C across a six-year period in the 1960s. If that's not hot enough for you, head across the salt plain to the Dallol volcano, the lowest volcano on earth, where in the event of an eruption things could heat up an extra few hundred degrees.

AL-AZIZIYAH, LIBYA

Drive about 40km south from the Libyan capital Tripoli and you come to a place of climatic royalty. In the city of Al-Aziziyah, on 13 September 1922, the world experienced its hottest air temperature ever recorded: 57.8°C. What's surprising in this Sahara-carpeted country is that Al-Aziziyah is not at the heart of the world's most famous desert – it's less than an hour by car from the Mediterranean Sea, a handy tonic if the mercury ever again spikes towards record levels, which it hasn't shown signs of doing.

SAHARAN HEAT WILL HAVE YOU LOOKING FOR LAKES IN THE SEA; THEY'RE OUT THERE, HIDDEN IN THE DUNES OF THE UBARI SAND SEA, LIBYA.

ALMOST MYTHICAL PLACES

PACK YOUR COMPASS, READING GLASSES & IMAGINATION FOR A JOURNEY TO SITES OF MYTH & LEGEND.

✪ ZANZIBAR, TANZANIA

Just the name 'Zanzibar' conjures images of harem girls giggling behind gauzy veils, carved wooden doors opening to spice-filled rooms and other images from *The Thousand and One Nights*. Only in this case, they're not fiction. Zanzibar grew into a powerful city state between the 12th and 15th centuries, sending ships laden with slaves, gold, ivory and wood to Arabia and beyond. Eventually the Sultan of Oman moved his court here – 100 concubines and eunuchs included – and started Zanzibar's famous clove plantations. He's long gone, but an Arabic influence and the scent of sweet spice still lingers over the sultry island.

✪ EL DORADO, COLOMBIA

Veiled behind vine-draped trees deep in the Amazon jungle gleams a dazzling kingdom of gold. Or so the story goes. When the Spanish conquistadors caught wind of El Dorado (literally 'The Golden One') after washing up on Colombia's shores in the 1500s, they scattered like frenzied piranhas to find it. They began in the Andean highlands, and whacked through the forests of Peru, Venezuela and Guyana over the next two centuries in their savage quest. No one ever found the fabled city, perhaps because it has the ability to retreat from unworthy seekers.

✪ VALLEY OF THE KINGS, EGYPT

On the west bank of the Nile River, across from the city of Luxor, lies the final resting place of Egypt's pharaohs. You know the guys – Ramses the Great, Tuthmosis, and the funkiest pharaoh of all, King Tut. They ruled between 1500 and 1000 BC, pooh-poohing pyramids for elaborate tombs carved into the valley's rocky hills. More than 60 chambers have been unearthed so far, containing mummies in gilt sarcophagi, bejewelled statues and a curse that lands on those who dare disturb the graves. Visitors remain undeterred, as the valley ranks as one of Egypt's top attractions.

✪ YS, FRANCE

Celtic Princess Dahut asked her dad, King Gradlon, to build her a city by the sea. Ys sprung up, and to protect it from the high waves, the king built a dyke around it. The sole entrance was through a brass gate, and only Gradlon had the key. Meanwhile Dahut, taking advantage of her new digs, chose a different lover every night and had him killed afterward. Eventually a demon outwitted her, persuaded her to steal the key, and opened the gate. Ys flooded, and everyone drowned except Gradlon. The ruined city lies beneath the bay at Douarnenez, now a popular beach town in Brittany.

✪ TROY, TURKEY

Fans of mythology will recognize Troy as the old stomping grounds of folks like Hector, Paris and Helen, as well as one giant wooden horse. The city was ground zero for the Trojan War, sparked when Paris kidnapped Helen from her kingly husband in Greece. The Greeks ganged up and sailed straight over to Troy, determined to kick ass. And they did, especially after Odysseus Trojan Horse idea. Modern-day visitors can tromp around the walls, temples and ruins at the area, also known as Truva, in Turkey's northwest corner.

✪ KARAKORUM, MONGOLIA

Genghis Khan set up house here in the mid-13th century, then headed out to conquer half the world. Karakorum was his Mongol capital and became known as the Empire of the Steppe. Alas, the glory didn't last long – about 30 years, in fact – and then the city was destroyed. Current visitors will need to muster serious imagination to envisage the great walls and gates that once encircled the place. Many bits were incorporated into the nearby Erdene Zuu monastery's long white walls and 108 stupas.

✪ CARTHAGE, TUNISIA

Located on the outskirts of modern Tunis, Carthage was a city-state superpower and the archenemy of Rome during the 3rd century BC. Its might came from a killer navy of Phoenician ships that patrolled the Mediterranean Sea, and an army of elephants that marched over mountains with a military commander named Hannibal. Despite being dubbed 'the shining city', Carthage couldn't hold on for long. The Romans stormed in and razed it, ultimately building their own city on the site. It's their baths, houses, cisterns and basilicas that visitors see today.

✪ TIMBUKTU, MALI

A byword for 'place that's way the hell out there', Timbuktu earned its reputation early on as the terminus of a rich trade route linking West Africa and the Mediterranean. All you had to do to get your gold, slaves and ivory north (or salt to come south) was join a camel caravan and plod for months across the Sahara through sand-storms, blazing heat and insanity-inducing isolation. It's still a mighty trek to reach Timbuktu, and though salt caravans continue to pass through led by blue-clad Tuaregs, the city only hints at its 15th-century grandeur of wealthy merchants and mosques.

✪ AVALON, ENGLAND

King Arthur rests on the enchanted isle of Avalon, sleeping off the wounds accrued during a lifetime of knights, crusades, sorcerers, Round Tables and magical swords. As Britain's 'once and future king', it is said he will return wielding Excalibur and the Holy Grail to unite his country when it needs him most. Today the modern town of Glastonbury spreads over the site where Avalon once floated. True to its mystic roots, it attracts free spirits who come to buy crystals, consult with psychics, lick vegan ice-cream cones or attend crop-circle symposiums.

✪ SHAMBHALA, TIBET

The kingdom of Shambhala hides somewhere deep within the snow-stained peaks of the Himalayas. An en-lightened, peaceful 'Pure Land' of Buddhist lore, it can be reached only by individuals who have racked up the appropriate karma. Explorers in the past century have set out to find Shambhala in Tibet, which is also where James Hilton placed it in his novel *Lost Horizon* (under the name of Shangri-la). Since no one has yet discovered the kingdom, perhaps the next best thing is the town of Zhongdian on the China–Tibet border. It was renamed Shangri-la in 2001, claiming to be the place's inspiration.

(TOP) » A TUAREG NOMAD BY THE 13TH-CENTURY SIDI YAHIYA MOSQUE, TIMBUKTU.

(LEFT) » THE IMPOSING RUINS OF GLASTONBURY'S 14TH-CENTURY ABBEY... AND THAT'S JUST THE KITCHEN.

(RIGHT) » GUIHUA LAMASERY IS BUT AN HOUR'S WALK FROM SHANGRI-LA, OR 5KM FROM ZHONGDIAN, DEPENDING ON YOUR KARMA.

GREEN CITY ENVY

SOME OF THE BEST GREEN TRAVEL EXPERIENCES CAN BE FOUND IN THE URBAN JUNGLE. DON'T MISS THESE.

✪ BEST GREEN NIGHTCLUB

Off_Corso in Rotterdam, the Netherlands, has taken a step toward becoming the world's first sustainable dance club. Responding to statistics that say clubs use 150 times the energy that normal households use, even though clubs are open only three nights per week, Off_ Corso hosts dance parties where revellers groove under energy-efficient LED lights, drink organic beer and can buy free-trade designer jeans and clothing onsite. Future concepts include energy-generating dance floors that power the lights, and toilets that flush with rainwater, or possibly even dancers' captured and recycled sweat.

✪ BEST GREEN SLEEP

It seems a million miles from the urban world, but Wenhai Ecolodge technically is on the outskirts of Lijiang, China (population: one million plus). Its distance comes from the lengthy hike visitors must undertake to reach it: five hours up a mountain through pine, oak and rhododendron forests. Owned and operated by community families, the 12-room lodge is equipped with solar panels, bio-gas equipment, water purifiers and a greenhouse. Villagers take turns cooking traditional-style vegetarian meals for guests. The lodge donates 10% of profits to conserving nearby Wenhai Lake and its woodlands, which are threatened by logging.

✪ BEST GREEN TOUR

It might seem odd, even voyeuristic, to treat the impoverished townships of Cape Town, South Africa, as a tourist attraction. But to gain any kind of appreciation for South African reality, you have to visit them. It's also another way of supporting local, black-owned businesses directly. Tour companies like Daytrippers bring visitors into the townships to meet residents, drink a sorghum beer at the local shebeen, visit village herbalists and craft shops and even attend a church service (on Sunday tours). Company profits go toward building much-needed daycare centres in the community.

✪ BEST GREEN CAR RENTAL

OK, we're jumping the gun here because the hydrogen-powered Honda FCX, the first real-world zero-emission car, isn't easily available so far. Sure, a smattering of FCXs zip along the roads in Tokyo, Los Angeles and New York, but since the cars are not yet mass produced they cost a lot (a few years ago rentals ran more than US$7500 per month). They're also difficult to fuel, as hydrogen stations – needed to power up the fuel cell that serves as the car's battery – aren't widespread. Some day, though, it'll be a green dream ride come true…

✪ BEST GREEN FOOD MARKETS

The bountiful supply of regional organic markets makes it impossible to pick just one, so we'll just reel off a few of our farmers favourites: East London's Spitalfields Market sells rare-breed meats and air-dried hams in addition to its fruit-and-veg arsenal. Amsterdam's Noordermarkt adds organic cheeses, olive oils, whole grains and spiced pestos to its sustainable-goods mix. And in Melbourne, Australia, the twice-weekly CERES Market stocks the area's mother lode of eco-friendly products, including locally roasted almonds, organic pastries and booze and biodegradable citrus-based cleaners.

✪ BEST GREEN BUILDING

In San Francisco the new California Academy of Sciences is expected to be the largest and most visited green building in the world when it opens in late 2008. Its standout feature is its roof, one of the planet's largest 'living' roofs, planted with 1.7 million beach strawberries, miniature lupins, poppies and other Northern California foliage that serve as a natural insulator and absorb rainwater. Solar cells supply clean energy (about 5% of the Academy's needs) and prevent the release of greenhouse gas emissions.

✪ BEST BIKE-AROUND TOWN

You thought we were going to say Amsterdam? It's a good one, but we're putting our money on the flatter, less congested, but equally bike-path crossed city of Copenhagen. The city is so two-wheel supportive that it places 2000 free white bikes in 110 specially designed stands throughout the central city. Anyone can go up and deposit the required coins (about US$3), and then use the bike as long as needed within city limits. When finished, cyclists return their bikes to any stand and it returns their money. Voila, pollution-free transport made easy.

✪ BEST URBAN GREEN SPACE

Stanley Park is Vancouver's sweet garland, a 404-hectare forest of cedar, hemlock and fir wafting green just a few blocks from the glass skyscrapers, big business and high finance of this prosperous modern metropolis. On a sunny day it seems all of Vancouver is here cycling or jogging through the woods. Meadows, lakes, cricket pitches and lawn bowling greens are interspersed among the trees, but it's the beaches around Stanley Park's perimeter – where visitors might see a seal or bald eagle – that make it a particularly wild urban refuge.

✪ BEST GREEN THEATRE

Redmoon Theater in Chicago puts on performances in parks, streets and other public spaces using found objects for costumes, scenery and musical instruments. The company involves community members both young and old who participate as set designers and performers, working side-by-side with Redmoon's professional artists. The collaborative productions focus on timeless themes of love, death, hope and friendship, and are presented in Redmoon's trademark dreamy, whimsical fashion using fanciful masks, giant puppets, stilt walkers and live music.

✪ BEST GREEN MUSEUM

Everything in the ingenious City Museum in St Louis, USA, is made from recycled industrial castoffs; even the building itself had a prior life as a shoe factory. The museum's 20 resident artists continually transform the exhibits using new found objects. They reach no further than municipal borders for their materials, incorporating items like old chimneys, salvaged bridges, construction cranes, miles of tile and two abandoned planes into futuristic funhouse structures that visitors can climb on, crawl through and walk over.

[TOP] » HUNTING BIRDIES AT VANCOUVER'S STANLEY PARK – JUST NOT THE BALD EAGLES.

[LEFT] » TAKING THEATRE OUT OF THE THEATRE, REDMOON PERFORMANCES HIT THE PARKS.

[RIGHT] » THE JEWEL FROM THE JUNKYARD, ST LOUIS' CITY MUSEUM.

VOLCANO!

LET THE LAVA FLOW THROUGH YOUR VEINS AS YOU SALUTE SOME
OF THE WORLD'S MOST ERUPTIVE ROCKS.

⍟ WHAKAARI (WHITE ISLAND), NEW ZEALAND

White by name, but black by nature, White Island has been in almost constant eruption for
the last three decades. Sitting in the Bay of Plenty, the island marks one end of the highly active
Taupo Volcanic Zone, which also includes the volatile Mt Ruapehu and the geothermal fields of
Rotorua, and though the latter is one of New Zealand's premier tourist attractions, the ever-changing
colours and fury of White Island are arguably more impressive. The island can be visited by boat or
helicopter from Whakatane, and once ashore at Crater Bay you'll witness an array of volcanic features.

⍟ PARICUTIN, MEXICO

Three hundred kilometres west of Mexico City, Paricutin is one of the youngest mountains on earth, and a
volcano so unusual it quickly earned a place among the seven natural wonders of the world. During WWII
an eruption suddenly began in the middle of a cornfield, with a 410m-high cinder cone rising from the
earth, and lava flows covering an area of about 20 sq km (engulfing two villages). Today there's the surreal
sight of a church spire poking above the solidified lava – all that remains of the two villages. You can climb
Paricutin and visit the spire from the town of Angahuan.

⍟ HEKLA, ICELAND

Once believed to be the entrance to hell, Iceland's most famous volcano has shown watch-setting
punctuality in recent times, boiling over pretty much every 10 years – its schedule calls for another eruption
in 2010. Located around 70km east of Reykjavik, its name means Hooded One, referring to the mountain's
perpetual cap of cloud. The 1491m peak makes for a comfortable climb when it's inactive, and rewards
walkers with a heated crater ringed by a snow-capped summit. If you venture here in winter, there are even

✪ RABAUL, PAPUA NEW GUINEA

The PNG island of New Britain is a constant bubble of geothermal activity, and in 1994 twin volcanoes erupted around Rabaul, a town many travellers considered to be the finest in the Pacific. Set inside a caldera, Rabaul had always flirted with danger, but in this two-pronged erosion the entire town collapsed beneath ash, leaving behind a strange, black wasteland. Today, the port continues to function, and there's a modicum of activity in the town, even as the Tuvurvur volcano still issues the occasional smoke signal. For a surreal volcanic experience you need do no more than wander the town, most of which is buried beneath your feet.

✪ MT ST HELENS, USA

Once a classic symmetrical volcano, Mt St Helens showed a disdain for geometry on 18 May 1980 when an eruption blew around 400m off its peak and created a 1.5km-wide crater on its north side. Though much life has returned to the peak, the devastation is still clear, and the mountain continues to steam, with a new lava dome growing inside the crater. Around the mountain a number of hiking trails highlight the volcanic landscapes, while climbers wanting to attain the summit must obtain a permit. There's no technical climbing involved, but most of the ascent is through loose pumice fields and over chunks of lava.

✪ SOUFRIÈRE HILLS, MONTSERRAT

A volcano with true bang, the Soufrière Hills ended four centuries of dormancy in explosive fashion in 1995, blowing away one third of its own height and rendering the Caribbean holiday island of Montserrat almost uninhabitable. The geothermal belches calmed over the following decade, prompting even the re-opening of the airport, but in January 2007 the volcano erupted again, shooting out a cloud of ash that smothered both the island and its re-emerging tourism industry. If you make it to the island, the crater is off-limits but the Montserrat Volcano Observatory on its slopes is open to visitors.

✪ MT PINATUBO, PHILIPPINES

In 1991, after around 600 years of dormancy, Mt Pinatubo, on the Philippine island of Luzon, produced one of the greatest volcanic jolts of the 20th century, shooting ash and rock 40km into the sky and decapitating almost 300m of its own summit and leaving a 2.5km-wide caldera in its place. The new summit is accessible to hikers – the climb begins from Santa Juliana, 40km from Angeles – and is also the scene of a virtual pilgrimage on 30 November each year, when the annual Pinatubo trek – the so-called March to Peace and Tranquillity – commemorates the eruption.

✪ GUNUNG BROMO, INDONESIA

In eastern Java sits a caldera 10km wide, covered by a sea of sand and punctured by a trio of volcanic cones. Steaming among them is Gunung Bromo (2392m), a volcano within a volcano, shadowed by Java's highest mountain, the highly active Gunung Semeru. As a grandstand to this remarkable scene, Bromo is one of the most remarkable outings in Southeast Asia. Most hikes to Bromo follow the Probolinggo approach, with the walk beginning atop the crater wall at Cemoro Lawang, crossing the Sand Sea for a sunrise spectacular atop Gunung

✪ HAWAII VOLCANOES NATIONAL PARK, USA

Hawaii Volcanoes National Park is a huge preserve containing two active volcanoes and terrain ranging from tropical beaches to the subarctic Mauna Loa summit. The park's centrepiece is the steaming Kilauea Caldera, at the summit of the planet's most active volcano. Amid a landscape of craters and cinder cones, hills piled high with pumice, and hardened oceans of lava, you can pay rare witness to flowing lava. Here, the fluid lava mostly oozes and creeps along, and at the end of the Chain of Craters road you can follow a walking trail to witness the active flow entering the sea.

KNOW YOUR TRAVEL

FADS, TRENDS OR HERE TO STAY? GET A HANDLE ON DIFFERENT WAYS TO EXPERIENCE THE WORLD.

❂ PERPETUAL TOURISM

A rolling stone gathers no moss, as the saying goes, and some travellers take the concept to heart. These souls (often sandal-clad) remain on the road for vast stretches of time, moving from one exotic locale to the next, and keep no fixed residence. Some call it wanderlust, others call it evading the taxman – it depends on your income bracket. One thing's for certain: the sense of freedom and feeling of lightness that come with constant motion can be giddily addictive.

❂ HEALTH TOURISM

Ever since Roman times, folks have sought out the healing waters of specially designated baths for their R&R. By the 19th century, health tourism had exploded, especially at European spas near thermal hot springs and sanatoriums high in the mountains. It's still big business today, with pampering and wellness doled out worldwide, be it resorts around the mineral-rich Dead Sea that immerse visitors in healing mud baths; the geothermal waters of Rotorua, New Zealand, that soak away muscle aches; or the springs near Sivas, Turkey, where doctor fish nibble away skin conditions like psoriasis.

❂ LITERARY TOURISM

A gent named William Shakespeare and a little town called Stratford-upon-Avon launched this genre, which focuses on places associated with authors and their writings. Destinations range from historical (say Karen Blixen's farmhouse outside Nairobi, the basis for her memoir *Out of Africa*) to sights that are a bit more colourful (New York City's White Horse Tavern, where poet Dylan Thomas downed the 18 whiskey shots that killed him). Even places where literary connections are tenuous get in on the action. (Anyone up for Horton Bay General Store in Charlevoix County, Michigan, where Ernest Hemingway sat on the porch?)

❂ ARMCHAIR TOURISM

Sometimes the best travel adventures are the ones experienced from home, in your chair, with a nice cuppa steaming tableside and a plump pillow propping up your feet. Because, while it's exciting to read about Redmond O'Hanlon's tramp through the Congolese forest in *No Mercy*, the flesh-eating ants and spear-toting pygmies probably wouldn't be that fun experienced in person. Ditto for Alexandra David-Neel's eight-month trek over the snow-swamped Himalayas disguised as a male beggar in *My Journey to Lhasa*. At times it's OK to travel vicariously, safe from the world's blizzards and spears.

❂ INDUSTRIAL TOURISM

Sure, museums, temples and other cultural sights are the main things visitors go to see when they explore a foreign city. To get the full picture of a place though, you also need to see where and how its people work. For instance, you'll walk away with a deeper understanding of Rotterdam – the city's current economic situation and its historic role in global trade – if you visit its container port. Touring the Airbus factory in Toulouse or the Harley Davidson factory in Milwaukee provides similar insight (plus it's just plain cool to sit on a vintage motorcycle).

❂ ATOMIC TOURISM

It's niche travel, to be sure, but for certain people the missiles and explosion sites of atomic history fire up their interest. They hit the highway to visit places like Las Vegas' Atomic Testing Museum; Chantilly, Virginia for the Udvar-Hazy Center (home of the *Enola Gay*, the plane that dropped the bomb on Hiroshima); and Los Alamos, New Mexico for missile-filled museums (in the town where scientists developed the A-bomb during the Manhattan Project). Of course Hiroshima and Nagasaki, Japan, are on any atomic tourist's must-see list, as are testing sites throughout the western USA and Pacific Ocean islands.

❂ ECOTOURISM

Ecology tourism goes by many stage names (green, sustainable and responsible tourism, to name a few) and comes in many forms. Perhaps it's an Amazon tour where you sleep and eat manioc in local families' huts. Perhaps it's a Maori-owned New Zealand whale-watch boat that tracks the behemoths' breeding patterns while taking you out to view them. No matter what shape the journey takes, true ecotourism adheres to three principles: tread lightly on the environment, immerse in the local culture, and create a positive economic benefit for the local community. Follow these, and your eco-karma will take you far.

✪ POP-CULTURE TOURISM

No surprise that the king of pop-culture tourism is the King himself, aka Elvis Presley. Fans have been making the pilgrimage to Graceland, his shag-carpeted, fake-waterfalled house, for 30 years. They get to weep at the music icon's poolside grave, then buy a Jailhouse Rock toenail clipper at the onsite store. Not all pop-culture sites endure like Elvis; film-oriented sites can be particularly fickle. Whereas once there were as many Lord of the Rings tours as hobbits in Hobbiton, fewer visitors now come to New Zealand panting to see Middle-earth's sites.

✪ HERITAGE TOURISM

By gaining an appreciation of a destination's past, visitors can better undertand its present and guide its future. That's the basis of heritage tourism, a booming travel sector that has an entire United Nations governing body dedicated to it. Unesco currently protects 830 cultural and natural World Heritage sites. These include the Taj Mahal palace in India, Angkor's jungly temples in Cambodia, the churches of the Chiloé Archipelago in Chile and the Viking settlement at L'Anse aux Meadows in Newfoundland, Canada (which has the added bonus of costumed docents who spin fleece and forge nails in sod huts).

✪ MEDICAL TOURISM

As costs and waiting times for medical procedures rise in places like the USA and Western Europe, many folks are jetting off to distant lands to get the job done. In the market for a nose job? Consider South Africa, where you can get a new schnoz for a fraction of the Western price – and a free trip to see lions and elephants (yes, the term 'medical safari' has entered our lexicon). Bangkok rakes in medical tourists for sex-change surgeries, India for everything from heart-valve replacements to molar extractions.

(TOP) » ELVIS HAS LEFT THE BUILDING: OUTDOOR MOVIES AT GRACELAND RUN NONSTOP DURING ELVIS WEEK.

(LEFT) » BEASTS OF BURDEN BEFORE THE MUGHAL MASTERWORK, THE TAJ MAHAL.

(RIGHT) » LETTING THE DIAGNOSIS DETERMINE THE DESTINATION, MANY WESTERNERS ARE DECIDING THEY CAN'T AFFORD TO STAY AT HOME.

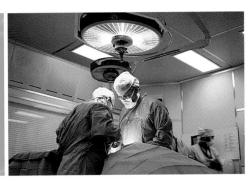

SLEEP BEHIND BARS

FOR A SLEEP OF A DIFFERENT KIND, BOOK YOURSELF A NIGHT OR TWO IN THE SLAMMER.

✪ NAPIER PRISON BACKPACK-ERS, NEW ZEALAND

As New Zealand's oldest prison, the Napier facility locked up convicts from throughout the country, including mass murderers, drug barons, gang members and the criminally insane. Inmates had the special opportunity to attend Rock College, ie they were marched to the quarry next door and forced to break the stone and build the walls that kept them imprisoned. Guests nowadays can tour the hanging yard (where locals used to pay a shilling to watch executions take place), sleep in converted cells and get a mug shot taken as a memento of their time in the clink.

✪ BREAKWATER LODGE, SOUTH AFRICA

The original prison housed long-term male convicts who were put to work construct-ing Table Bay's breakwater (hence the lodge name). Little remains of this former hard-core Cape Town joint, other than the building's imposing turrets and the Tread-mill displayed onsite. No, the latter is not part of the facility's gym. Rather, it was a nasty punishment consisting of a staircase that rotated when prisoners stepped on it. If they slacked off, the machine's revolving planks lacerated their shins. No worries about such hardships now – the modern hotel is entirely un-slammerlike, located where the wardens once lived.

✪ MALMAISON OXFORD CASTLE, ENGLAND

It may have been a stark Victorian prison between 1870 and 1996, but the days of bread and water are long gone. The own-ers have returned this Oxford property to its regal roots (the jail was once a castle owned by William the Conqueror more than 900 years ago), and swaddled it in mod, boutique-hotel luxury. Each of the current rooms occupies the space of three former cells, providing a bit more elbow room than the inmates got (they were sardined three per cell). They also missed out on the satellite TV, power showers and DVD players.

✪ LANGHOLMEN HOTEL, SWEDEN

Langholmen is the name of a 1.4km-long, 400m-wide island in the middle of Stockholm where Sweden's largest prison was plopped. Initially a spinning house (the lockup for naughty women), it soon welcomed criminals of all types into the confines of its thick walls. Guests today sleep in the original cells, but they're now bright, airy and sans bars. Groups want-ing to get in the convict groove can pay extra to role-play a stint in jail, complete with striped uniforms, a series of tasks to undertake, and guards to bribe to win freedom (celebrated with drinks at the local pub).

✪ JAIL BACKPACKERS, AUSTRALIA

Mt Gambier's joint may have been small (it accommodated just 30 prisoners), but it hosted plenty of action while incarcer-ating men and women between 1864 and 1995. Inmates spent lots of time in the games yard playing tennis, though not because they loved the sport.

It seems many of them had friends out-side the jail walls who would slyly throw over marijuana-stuffed tennis balls, the fruits of which prisoners enjoyed back in their cells. Visitors today sleep in those same cells, and can examine the murals prisoners painted (under the influence?) on the courtyard walls.

✪ JAILER'S INN, USA

This wee county jail in Kentucky did its time from 1819 through 1987. Now converted to a B&B, the 76cm-thick stone walls come in handy as noise buffers. Five of the six rooms are flowery, four-poster-bed, claw-foot-bathtub types. The sixth room, the Cell, provides the novelty of sleeping in a pair of prison bunk beds while Elvis (via a poster) watches protec-tively over you. Breakfast is served in the courtyard where prisoners worked crush-ing limestone. It doubled as the county gallows, which is why some guests claim the place is haunted and hear strange footsteps thumping about.

✪ LÖWENGRABEN JAIL HOTEL, SWITZERLAND

For the felons confined here through until 1998, the magical Alps backdrop must have softened the blow of being in the Big House. The simple rooms retain their barred windows and original chunky wooden doors, complete with food-tray slots, from their former lives as cells. The onsite Club Alcatraz draws Lucerne's good-time seekers. After a few drinks, it's fun to devil mum with a call of 'Hi. I'm in jail' and mean it – but for once without needing bail money.

✪ OTTAWA JAIL HOSTEL, CANADA

Formerly the Carleton County Jail, a maximum security holding facility for 110 years, this place is infamous as the site of Canada's last public hanging. Patrick James Whelan was convicted of murdering journalist and politician Thomas D'Arcy McGee, and was strung up from the onsite gallows in front of 5000 spectators. Convicted on circumstantial evidence, Whelan maintained his innocence to the bitter end. That's why his spirit remains restless, they say, and roams the jail, often startling current guests in their barred-door cells by perching at the end of their beds.

✪ CELICA HOSTEL, SLOVENIA

Celica means 'cell', and this was indeed a former military prison in Ljubljana abandoned only after Slovenia's independence and the departure of the Federal Yugoslav Army. The barbed wire and graffiti-covered exterior look intimidating, but it's all vibrant, hip hostel inside. More than 80 Slovenian artists transformed the first-floor cells into individual works of art, designing each room in its own theme ranging from traditional Slovenian to modern Finnish to meditative to Hollywood. Bars still slam shut in front of the doors and block the windows, so you never forget where you are.

✪ KAROSTA PRISON, LATVIA

It's billed as 'unfriendly, unheated and uncomfortable', and considering guests receive verbal abuse by uniformed guards and a single piece of stale bread for dinner, Karosta delivers as advertised. The Nazis, Soviets and Latvians used the property in Liepāja as a military detention facility, where wardens specialised in breaking the human spirit right through until 1997. Today's lodgers get the full treatment: cold damp cells, rusted water taps, thin mattresses and flimsy blankets that must be made to military standards (or else punishment ensues). It's all play acting, but still creepy knowing that for others Karosta was no game.

[TOP] » GALLOWS FOR SHOW AND GHOSTS FOR HOSTS AT THE OTTAWA JAIL HOSTEL.

[LEFT] » PRESIDENTIAL SUITE: FIDEL CASTRO'S CELL AT PRESIDIO MODELO, CUBA, IS AS HE LEFT IT WHEN RELEASED IN 1955.

[RIGHT] » NO CREATURE COMFORTS IN KAROSTA PRISON, THE PLACE FOR THOSE SEEKING PUNISHMENT.

RISKY PURSUITS

GET YOUR ADRENALINE GOING WITH TRAVEL'S MOST EXHILARATING EXPERIENCES.

✪ WORLD'S MOST DANGEROUS ROAD, BOLIVIA

In 1995 the Yungas Hwy between the Bolivian capital La Paz and the town of Coroico went from being a simple deathtrap to a risk-takers' nirvana when the Inter-American Development Bank officially crowned it the world's most dangerous road. Bending and twisting, the narrow gravel track supports swarms of trucks, their wheels precariously pendent over 1000m drops – little wonder that an average of 26 vehicles disappear into the void each year. Into this has stepped an emerging adventure industry, with mountain bikers now commonly jostling among the trucks and the carnage. Bike hire is available in La Paz.

✪ SURFING CORTES BANK, USA

In the endless quest for big-wave surfing, it's appropriate that some of the mightiest waves on the planet are as difficult to reach as they are to ride. The Cortes Bank is a submerged mountain chain, around 170km offshore from San Diego, with many of its peaks just a few metres below the surface of the Pacific Ocean. In 2001 a group of board-riders journeyed here to find waves beyond belief – one surfer rode a wave 20m high (the tallest wave ridden in the world that year), losing his board in the explosion that is a Cortes breaking wave.

✪ FREE DIVING

Hold your breath and swim as deep underwater as you can go…that, in a crude nutshell, is free diving. Wearing slick wetsuits, extra-long flippers and no air tanks, the art of free diving is to plunge as far below the water surface as is humanly possible. Some free divers can hold their breath for up to nine minutes, and in 2005, using a weighted sled, Belgian Patrick Musimu dived to a record depth of 209.6m. At such limits it's unsurprising that free diving has claimed lives, most famously that of world-record holder Audrey Mestre in the Dominican Republic in 2002.

✪ TRAVEL TO THE DARIÉN GAP, PANAMA

In the pantheon of lawless places, the Darién Gap, sprawling across the junction at which North America becomes South America, holds a special spot. It's a land where the cloud forest and the human activity are so wild that even the Pan-American Hwy from Alaska to Tierra del Fuego has never been able to get through. Here, as Panama morphs into Colombia, the lands are frequented by Colombian paramilitaries, drug traffickers, poachers, guerrillas and bandits, a volatile and violent mix that only seems to be part of the attraction for the few visitors who venture beyond the frontier town of Yaviza and into anarchy.

✪ SWIM WITH ORCAS, NORWAY

As you pile out of the boat in Tysfjord, it might help your state of mind if you think of the creatures below as orcas rather than killer whales. In this chilly notch in the Norwegian coast, 250km north of the Arctic Circle, visitors come to don wetsuits and swim the seas beside the misnamed killer whales (they're actually dolphins), which grow to around four times the size of an average person. The motto isn't quite 'If the cold doesn't kill you, the orcas might', but tell that to your brain as you enter the sea.

✪ VISIT CHORNOBYL, UKRAINE

Somehow, visits to the scene of the world's most infamous nuclear accident haven't quite hit the big time, but that hasn't stopped a steady flow of visitors from treading through the Chornobyl ruins. Several travel agencies in the Ukraine capital Kyiv offer day trips to the site, where you can wander through the reactor information centre, among the abandoned vehicles used in the clean-up, and into the deserted streets of Pripyat, where workers and their families used to live. For good measure, there are giant catfish to see in the river, though you'll be assured that their size has nothing to do with radiation.

✪ SAIL AROUND CAPE HORN

South America's southernmost tip parts one of the most notorious stretches of ocean on the planet. Here, as the Pacific and Atlantic Oceans meet in Drake Passage, the waters are a soup of white caps, wild winds and even a few rogue icebergs. The Cape's usefulness as a trading route is largely gone, but its appeal to the hardy sailor is undiminished. Around-the-world yacht races sail through, as do other yachties seeking (and sometimes regretting) the challenge of this maritime equivalent of scaling Mount Everest.

✪ STORM CHASING IN TORNADO ALLEY, USA

In the USA's so-called Tornado Alley, stretching between the Rocky and Appalachian Mountains, an average of around 1000 tornadoes strike each year, with winds up to 500km/h destroying crops and homes and killing people. Instead of running from the storms, as reason would dictate, there are some people who sprint to them to witness the undeniable beauty of a twister. Using satellite radar imaging, the tornado chasers tour the Alley, swirling from twister to twister – the good news is you can join them if you wish, for there are now several tour companies offering tornado-chasing holidays.

✪ WALKING SAFARI AMONG LIONS, ZIMBABWE

On the shores of Lake Kariba in northern Zimbabwe, Matusadona National Park protects an area of land where many animals resettled after the Zambezi River was dammed to create Lake Kariba in the 1950s. Wandering its torpedo grass plain is one of Africa's greatest concentrations of lions, a creature usually considered among the least desirable of walking companions. In Matusadona, however, walking safaris to see lions are the prize visitor ticket, and for a bit of extra 'fun' you can even camp out on the plain among your furred friends. Stay close to the man with the gun.

✪ BASE JUMP AT VOSS, NORWAY

An acronym for Building, Antenna, Span and Earth, BASE jumping involves throwing yourself (with a parachute) off fixed objects such as bridges, mountains and cliffs. In many parts of the world, it's considered so dangerous that it's been banned – there have been an average of around four BASE-jump deaths a year since 1981 – but in the southern Norwegian town of Voss it's actively encouraged during Extremesport Week, an event held each June. BASE jumpers in Extremesport Week leap from the 350m-high Nebbet cliff, plunging towards the fjord below. Scary, but scenic.

(TOP) » ABOUT TO GET TWISTED IN TORNADO ALLEY, USA.

(LEFT) » EXTREME READING IN ZIMBABWE'S MATUSADONA NATIONAL PARK.

(RIGHT) » GO JUMP OFF A CLIFF – IN THIS CASE IT'S NEBBET (THE BEAK), NORWAY.

SPACE TRAVEL

FIRE UP THE JET PACK, SUCK IN SOME THIN AIR, GET A TASTE OF ZERO G – IT'S TIME TO MAKE A GIANT LEAP INTO THE FUTURE OF TRAVEL.

✪ ARECIBO RADIO TELESCOPE, PUERTO RICO

The Arecibo Observatory houses the world's largest radio telescope, a beautiful structure (a work of art to many) featuring a huge, spherical reflector dish, 300m in diameter, composed of 40,000 perforated aluminium panels embedded into the surrounding jungle. Suspended by cables alomst 140m above is a 900-tonne platform housing an extremely complicated system of antennas and units for focusing radio waves received from deepest space. It's all far too complex to do justice to in 100 words. The telescope features in the films GoldenEye and Contact. Thankfully, it is open to the public (or at least an observation platform is).

✪ VERY LARGE ARRAY, USA

Like Arecibo, the VLA in New Mexico is also featured in Contact, as well as in 2010 (sequel to 2001) and Independence Day – all films about alien contact. Jon Bon Jovi even filmed a music vid here (some reckon he's a bit alien, too). The VLA consists of 27 radio antennas, each 25m wide, arranged in a Y-shape, with one arm of the array extending 21km. Each antenna can be moved to various positions on locomotive tracks and the output of the entire array synchs together, effectively functioning as one super-antenna with an area of 36km. You can visit it – listen out for ET (or Bon Jovi).

✪ STAR CITY, RUSSIA

If you were a civilian visiting here a few decades back, you might have been shot or detained indefinitely, for Star City,

Russia's cosmonaut-training complex, was strictly off-limits while the Cold War was yet to thaw. These days you can book a tour to Star City, which has its own shopping centre, post office and train station. While you won't be able to peer in at the cosmonauts' living or training quarters, you will be able to visit the awesome Space Museum, with its 20,000 exhibits including space suits, space vehicles and assorted Gagarinalia.

✪ JIUQUAN SATELLITE LAUNCH CENTRE, CHINA

This gargantuan launch facility, 1500km from Beijing in the remote Gansu province, is where most Chinese space vehicles leave Earth. The centre's huge – about 3000 sq km – and, China being China, is strictly off-limits to nonrocket types. Still, you can visit Jiuquan, the small town it takes its name from. It's in the desert, but because of the whole space infrastructure, it's not as primitive as other isolated Chinese towns. And it boasts thoroughfares with names like 'Space Road', so you know you're in the right place.

✪ RSC ENERGIA SPACE MUSEUM, RUSSIA

The RSC Energia Corporation built the Salyut and Mir space stations, the Soyuz rockets and numerous other extraterrestrial vehicles – the backbone of the Soviet space fleet. Now they've put this exceedingly rich history on display in Moscow, showcasing everything from rusting descent modules to gleaming satellites and massive booster stages. The '60s selection is surely the best, featuring

those exotic, grandiose, bulbous designs that seemed a million light years away from NASA's functional hardware. Marvel at how three cosmonauts squeezed into a space the size of a closet; lie down on Mir's bunk beds and dream of Mars.

✪ INTERNATIONAL SPACE STATION, LOW EARTH ORBIT

The ISS has been inhabited since 2000 and was assembled in space; construction is ongoing. A joint project between the USA, Russia, Japan, Canada and the European Space Agency, the ISS promises to usher in a new age of spacey cooperation (although China threatens to scupper everything if they continue to blow up satellites in orbit). Do you want to visit? Then shell out US$20 million like Dennis Tito, the world's first space tourist, who spent seven days, 22 hours and four minutes aboard this box in the sky.

✪ TANEGASHIMA SPACE CENTER, JAPAN

No, it's not the complex where Ernst Stavro Blofeld launched his secret rocket fleet, only to be foiled by James Bond. In fact, Japan has a legal space programme plan and Tanegashima is a vital cog in that, mainly used for satellite launches. Located on Tane Island, 100km south of Kyushu, the centre is open to the public, except when Japan's space agency is shooting complicated hunks of metal into the air. Visit the launch complexes and interact with the wonderful full-scale simulacra of the Japanese Experiment Module (the actual version will be embedded inside the International Space Station in 2008).

✪ PALOMAR OBSERVATORY, USA

High on Palomar Mountain, at an elevation of 1800m to avoid light pollution, the Palomar Observatory in San Diego is simply spectacular – as large as Rome's Parthenon. It's almost as beautiful as the Parthenon, too, with a classic design dating from the 1930s. The Observatory houses the world's once-largest telescope, the 5.1m Hale Telescope, operated chiefly by computers now rather than humans. These days the observatory is chiefly used to track near-earth asteroids and is open to the public daily.

✪ KENNEDY SPACE CENTER, USA

Located on the famous Cape Canaveral in Florida, this is the grandaddy of all space facilities, the launch pad for the *Mercury*, *Gemini* and *Apollo* programmes, as well as the various space shuttles. Remember masses of spectators gleefully cheering on astronauts ascending to the heavens; the *Challenger* shuttle falling to the sky to the horror of those watching…that's all Kennedy. You too can witness history: select a launch date and park beside the highway a few miles away for free views. Or pay to get inside the VIP visitor's area on the cape for the ultimate view.

✪ BAIKONUR COSMO-DROME, KAZAKHSTAN

Fans of Borat may laugh, but Kazakhstan has at least one genuine tourist attraction: the Baikonur Cosmodrome, still under lease to the Russians. This is the world's oldest facility for launching space vehicles (Gagarin blasted off here) and has been a backdrop in *Star Trek* and William Gibson stories, among others. Join a tour and geek out at the obligatory space museum, as well as seeing the facilities where rockets are prepared and the actual rockets themselves.

(TOP) » BEFORE PALOMAR'S HALE TELESCOPE – 'THE BIG EYE' – OPENED, ITS 5.1M PERSPEX MIRROR WAS POLISHED CONTINUOUSLY FOR 13 YEARS.

(BOTTOM) » NASA'S FIRST FUNCTIONAL SPACE SHUTTLE *COLUMBIA* HEADS FOR THE HEAVENS.

TRAVEL FOR A HIGHER CAUSE

MAKE YOUR OWN PILGRIMAGE TO SOME OF THE WORLD'S GREAT SPIRITUAL SITES.

✪ SOURCE OF THE GANGES, INDIA

The River Ganges is Hinduism's holiest river, beginning in the Himalayan peaks of Uttar Pradesh and spilling out into the Bay of Bengal more than 2000km later. For Hindus, the source of the Ganges is a holy of holies, and many thousands make the pilgrimage to its source near Gangotri. To join them requires a trek of 24km from Gangotri, threading through Himalayan valleys to Gaumukh, where you'll find the trickle of water that will flow on to become one of Asia's major rivers. Pilgrims perform *darshans* (offerings) as near as possible to the point where water flows from the ice wall beneath the terminal moraine.

✪ MT KAILASH, TIBET

As the source of several of Asia's mightiest rivers, including the Ganges, Karnali and Indus, it's little surprise that the Tibetan peak of Mt Kailash is revered in a number of religions. To circuit holy Kailash is a pilgrimage for Buddhists, Hindus, Bonpos, Jains and, more recently, trekkers. The most ardent pilgrims walk the 52km circuit in a day, while the truly pious prostrate themselves around the mountain, lying down with arms outstretched, then standing and lying down again at the point that their hands reached. The journey to Kailash is itself an epic worthy of being called a pilgrimage, so allow time for this remarkable trek.

✪ MEĐUGORJE, BOSNIA

On 28 June 1981 six youths in the Bosnian mountain village of Međugorje claimed to have seen an apparition of the Virgin Mary. Instantly, a place of pilgrimage was born, complete with bus tours and an unholy number of souvenir stands. The Virgin is said to still appear at Međugorje, bringing messages to the world, delivering them through the original six 'visionaries' – three of them see the apparition daily. For a Međugorje vision of your own, begin in the famed bridge town of Mostar; Međugorje is a mountainous 30km away.

✪ SHASHEMENE, ETHIOPIA

With Rastafarianism founded on the belief that Ethiopian emperor Haile Selassie is an African Messiah, it's unsurprising that a Rasta community has taken root in Ethiopia. Around 240km from Addis Ababa, Selassie himself granted land in the town of Shashemene to Jamaican Rastafarians in the 1960s. It was first settled by 12 Jamaicans but the community has now grown to number hundreds. In the late 1970s the most famous Rasta of all, Bob Marley, visited Shashemene, and in recent years his widow has talked of relocating his remains here, which would indeed turn this southern town into a site of rock and Rasta pilgrimage.

✪ MASHHAD, IRAN

With a name that translates as The Place of Martyrdom, Mashhad is sacred to Shiites as the place where the 8th imam and direct descendant of the Prophet Mohammed, Imam Reza, died in 817. Each year more than 15 million Shiite pilgrims visit the city in eastern Iran, which literally radiates out from Astan-e Qods-e Razavi, the site of the Holy Shrine. The busiest pilgrimage times are around the Iranian New Year (21 March) and a dedicated pilgrim season from mid-June to late July. Non-Muslims are not permitted into the Holy Shrine itself, though there are three attached museums that can be visited.

✪ 88 TEMPLE CIRCUIT, JAPAN

On the Japanese island of Shikoko there are 88 temples, a number equal to the evil human passions as defined by the Buddhist doctrine. If you want to free yourself from every one of these passions in a single hit, you can do so by completing the 88 Temple Circuit. Traditionally the 1500km route was walked, even though there's a space of more than 100km between a couple of the temples. In modern times, however, it's become just as acceptable to complete the 88 Temple Circuit by tour bus – who said the gods weren't modernists? The circuit begins in Tokushima and most pilgrims go clockwise.

✪ ADAM'S PEAK, SRI LANKA

In the highlands of Sri Lanka there is a mountain that's all things to all religions. Depending on your spiritual persuasion, the indent on the summit of Adam's Peak is either the place at which Adam first set foot on earth, or a footprint left by Buddha, Shiva or St Thomas. Small wonder the track to the summit is like an ant trail in the pilgrimage season (December to May). Secular pilgrims will find the view alone worthy of the journey: on a clear day it stretches to the Sri Lankan capital, Colombo, 65km away.

✪ GOLDEN TEMPLE, INDIA

Resting against the India–Pakistan border, the city of Amritsar has a golden heart, with the Golden Temple, the holiest site in Sikhism, dominating the city. Glowing in the hot Punjabi sun, the temple is as golden as its name suggests, and sits in the middle of the holy Amrit Sarovar pool, which lends its name to the city. Pilgrims bathe in the pool, and amble clockwise around its marble edges, while the temple kitchen by the eastern entrance spoons out free meals to pilgrims and tourists alike. Visitors are welcome to join the faithful in and around the temple.

✪ MT ATHOS, GREECE

Known as the Holy Mountain, Mt Athos is a self-governing community of 20 Eastern Orthodox monasteries sprinkled around the slopes of 2033m-high Mt Athos on Greece's Chalkidiki Peninsula. A strict entry-permit system applies: 100 Orthodox pilgrims and 10 non-Orthodox visitors are allowed in at a time; only men over 18 years of age can visit; permit applications from non-Orthodox visitors must be made at least six months ahead; and *diamonitiria* (permits) usually allow stays of just four days. The Holy Mountain is reached by boat, and you then walk between monasteries, each of which contains a guesthouse.

✪ SANTIAGO DE CAMINO, SPAIN

One of the great Christian pilgrimages is to the tomb of the apostle St James in the Spanish city of Santiago de Compostela. It's a journey of such spiritual note that it has been named Europe's Premier Cultural Itinerary and is also listed on the Unesco World Heritage register. The Camino begins in Roncesvalles, on the French border, and covers 783km to the Atlantic coast. Cycling and horseriding are considered appropriate forms of pilgrim transport, but most people walk the route, wandering between an extensive system of *albergues* (refuges or hostels), spending around one month as a modern pilgrim.

(TOP) » CROSS THE GURUS' BRIDGE TO REACH THE GOLDEN TEMPLE AT AMRITSAR.

(LEFT) » FOUNDED IN 963, MEGISTI LAVRA IS THE OLDEST MONASTERY AT MT ATHOS AND HAS 37 CHAPELS AND 15 TOWERS.

(RIGHT) » HIGH IN THE MOUNTAINS OF SPAIN, A BRONZE STATUE OF A PILGRIM MARKS THE WAY TO SANTIAGO.

TRAVEL WITH ALL YOUR SENSES

SOME OF THE BEST TRAVEL EXPERIENCES DEMAND YOUR COMPLETE SENSORY ATTENTION.

✪ INNER EAR

If you adore quietude then take a trip to Minneapolis. Here you'll find the quietest room on earth as designated by the Guinness Book of Records. Engineers measured the interior of the Orfield Institute's anechoic chamber to be negative 9.4 decibels. It's so quiet that after 30 minutes inside you begin to hear your heartbeat and your lungs pumping. Any longer and you start tripping. NASA uses the chamber to test astronauts. If would-be space pilots can maintain their train of thought despite their aurally inspired hallucinations then they are one step closer to outer space.

✪ SMELL THE ROSES

Give your hooter a break from city smog and serve it the nasal equivalent of your favourite cordon bleu cuisine. Since 1913 London's Chelsea Flower Show has traditionally heralded the start of the English summer. Set in the grounds of the Royal Hospital designed by 17th-century architect Sir Christopher Wren, the blooms blossom over 11 magnificent acres. With some flowers, such as the Rosa 'Princess Alexandra of Kent' emitting three distinct fragrances during its life cycle (from a tea scent as a young flower, developing to lemon, and ending as blackcurrant), the show is a veritable smorgasbord of good scents.

✪ TASTE OF EDEN

No two sets of taste buds are the same, which means everyone's taste is different. But that's of zero concern to the folks who run the annual Salt Lake Fall Fair on Salt Spring Island that lies across the Strait of Georgia, south of Vancouver. One of the highlights of the two-day event is the keenly contested Best Tasting Apple competition. The title is awarded to the apple variety that proves its worth by kick-starting the biggest taste frenzy in the most mouths. It's the competition guaranteed to sort the Granny Smiths from the Pink Ladies.

✪ ANGELIC RUSH

Cultural anthropologists have documented the powerful emotional impact that natural phenomena such as waterfalls can have on both humans and chimpanzees. Apparently they emit a kind of energy that primates find enticing. In which case the Salto Angel Falls in Venezuela's Canaima National Park will have us all going ape as we absorb the energy generated by the world's highest waterfall. After flowing along the flat-topped mountain of Auyantepui, water plunges 979m down a vertical cliff. The falls, known by local Indian tribes as Churún Merú, are accessed by an energising hour-long trek through the jungle.

✪ DEAD SEA SERENITY

It is the world's biggest flotation tank-cum-health spa. For two thousand years people have come here in search of vitality. The traditional way to enjoy a Dead Sea experience is to coat yourself in the mineral-rich black mud found along the shore before floating around on your back like an upturned turtle. Because it is the lowest place on earth (417m below sea level), the Dead Sea area has a uniquely high barometric pressure, which means there is something intangible about the place that makes you feel blissfully alive.

✪ GARDEN OF TRANQUILLITY

When it comes to creating sensory calm only a gorgeously surreal array of plants will do. Australia's Hunter Valley Gardens is unique in the southern hemisphere. The 12 themed gardens are like doors of perception, and simply entering them will expand your mind. Imagine Salvador Dali meets Edward Scissorhands and you might have some idea what to expect. The Garden's manager, Bill Creedon, reckons twilight is the best time to enjoy the gardens, and a visit then will induce a sense of both natural serenity and effortless peace.

✪ HOT STUFF

How hot is too hot to handle? The hottest temperature ever recorded was a barmy 57.8°C at the Al-Aziziyah weather station in Libya on 13 September 1922. Since then California's Death Valley has consistently ranked as the world's hottest spot, with average daily summer temperatures exceeding 40°C. In such heat extremes the body sweats like mad in an attempt to cool down. But sweat requires water, and that's something neither Al-Aziziyah nor Death Valley have much of. Hence it's probably not just a coincidence that desert, dehydration and death all begin with the letter 'd.'

✪ HOWLER MONKEYS

These guys do exactly what their name suggests and then some. The pint-sized loudmouths (the largest Howlers stand at just 1.2m tall) howl blue murder high up in the jungle canopies of Brazil, Argentina, Paraguay and Bolivia. It is customary for them to compete for 'decibel space', which involves making a racket most humans would find unbearable. Despite their diminutive stature Howlers are the loudest land animals. Only blue whales, the largest creatures on the planet, can make more noise.

✪ SENSORY ASSAULT

Arriving in Delhi for the first time is the sensory equivalent of jumping out of a plane straight into a typhoon. In a city of 13 million people, 2.7 million cars, and a large portion of India's 100 million mobile phones, Delhi is bursting with life on every street corner. Even the places you'd think might offer refuge from the urban mayhem, such as the sprawling National Museum, will blow you away with its collection of almost 200,000 artefacts spanning 5000 years of Indian culture. Intense.

✪ SEEING BLIND

Everest is the world's highest mountain. Reaching the summit is the ultimate test of a climber's abilities that involves scaling ice waterfalls and battling gale-force winds. In 2001 Erik Weihenmayer met Everest's challenge. In doing so he became the first blind person to stand on the Roof of the World. He now leads blind, partially sighted, and sighted students along the Inca trail in Peru. In his book *Touch the Top of the World*, Weihenmayer says, 'Life is a never-ending process of reaching out into the darkness and you never know what you're going to find'.

[TOP] » THESE LOUDMOUTH AMERICANS ARE AUDIBLE UP TO 5KM AWAY.

[LEFT] » TEST THE NERVES ON OLD DELHI'S MAIN DRAG, CHANDNI CHOWK.

[RIGHT] » REMEMBER, IT'LL ALL BE DOWNHILL ON THE WAY BACK.

BIG!

SIZE MATTERS! PAY HOMAGE TO MASSIVE MONUMENTS BUILT WITH A TOUCH OF THE BIZARRE.

✪ BIG BANANA, AUSTRALIA

Coff's Harbour's ferrous-concrete banana – 13m long, 5m high and 3m wide – has been hailed as a national icon; then again, it's also been voted 'the most bizarre and grotesque tourist attraction in the world'. The adjoining park offers ice-skating, a snow slope and other 'attractions'. Kids will love it, banana freaks will make a beeline for the over-stuffed gift store, while cynics and the easily bored will make like a banana and split. This monstrosity actually started the craze for 'Big Things' in Australia, in 1964. Just so you know who to blame or praise, as you like.

✪ RODINA MAT, RUSSIA

The Rodina Mat ('Motherland') statue in Volgograd (formerly Stalingrad) is a terrifying, awe-inspiring sight. This stainless-steel female form, a literal representation of Mother Russia in full flight, commemorates the 'heroes of the Stalingrad Battle' in WWII. Its gigantic scale places it among the world's largest statues, weighing in at a rather hefty 8000 tonnes and with a height of 85m. Another thing: Mother, her mouth twisted with rage, wields a 33m-long sword – on this evidence, we reckon she'd kick the placid Statue of Liberty's butt.

✪ SWORDS IN ROCK, NORWAY

These three, 10m-tall bronze swords embedded in Norwegian rock at Stavanger are certainly an imposing sight, with a magnificent fjord as backdrop, but it's not

a monument to King Arthur. Rather, they commemorate the Battle of Hafrsfjord in 872, significant for the fact that it united Norway as a single kingdom under the leadership of the legend known as Fairheaded Harald. The largest sword represents the winning king, while the two smaller ones symbolise the losing kings; the Stavanger artist Fritz Røed designed the monument, and the swords were cast in Italy.

✪ PADRÃO DOS DESCOBRIMENTOS, PORTUGAL

Here's another huge slab of concrete that's thoroughly deserving of your attention. By the Tagus River in Lisbon, it's 52m high and is carved in the shape of the prow of a Portuguese caravel. What does it all mean? Well, it's a tribute to the Portuguese and their Age of Exploration, that golden time during the 15th and 16th centuries when Portuguese explorers boldly set forth and forged new trading routes to destinations far and away all across the globe. Carved into the tip of the prow are the likenesses of 30 of Portugal's heroes of the age, including Vasco da Gama, Ferdinand Magellan and King Manuel I.

✪ USHIKU AMIDA BUDDHA, JAPAN

OK, this baby in Ushiku Arcadia reigns supreme – at 120m high, it's the largest statue in the world. Some stats tell the story: the statue itself is 100m high, and the base is 10m high, as is the platform.

The body itself consists of 6000 bronze plates, and there's an observation platform at a height of 85m set in the Buddha's chest. One of its fingers is 7m long. Altogether the Buddha is three times the size of the 'puny' Statue of Liberty, so there!

✪ WORLD'S LARGEST AMISH BUGGY, USA

'Amish tourism' hasn't really grabbed the travel industry by storm, although the town of Berlin, Ohio – right in the heart of the Amish Country Byway – is doing its best to change that. Berlin is the home of the 'world's largest cuckoo clock' and used to be the home of the 'world's largest wheel of cheese' until it got eaten. Its other 'big thing' is the world's largest Amish buggy, weighing in at 545kg and measuring over 3m tall and nearly 4m wide. That thing sure could haul a lotta Amish!

✪ BIG BEAVER, CANADA

The rodent known as a 'beaver' has huge buck teeth and a huge, flat tail. Now, imagine one of the little buggers nearly 4m high and made of fibreglass (or whatever they make these big things out of) – that's a lot of teeth and a lot of tail. The Big Beaver is on Highway 401, in Odessa, Ontario. It's a 'metaphor for Canada', according to Beaver Tales Magazine (yes, such a publication exists). Unfortunately, the beaver boffins don't explain why, so we can only assume that Canada has teeth and a tail (we're not touching the 'rodent' aspect).

✪ WORLD'S LARGEST BUFFALO, USA

This North Dakotan sculpture of an American bison may be 8m tall, 14m long, over 60 tonnes in weight, but nevertheless it is anatomically correct; you can see it and all its bits from the interstate highway I-94. There are websites devoted to this thing, including one that claims in a huge, multicoloured font that 'JAMESTOWN HAS ACHIEVED **MAXIMUM BUFFALOSITY**'. Indeed: Jamestown's nickname is 'The Buffalo City' and near the statue is the National Buffalo Museum, plus herds of real, live, substantially smaller buffaloes.

✪ BIG KIWI FRUIT, NEW ZEALAND

The town of Te Puke touts itself as 'the world's kiwi-fruit capital' – with its warm climate and fertile soil, it couldn't be anything but. Accordingly, it's built a giant representation of the furry brown berry known as the 'kiwi fruit' to rub it in to other pretenders to the title. Jump on a KiwiKart and tour the kiwi-growing surrounds, before returning to marvel once again at this giant, green, circular sculpture sticking out of the ground. OK, we get it – Te Puke's kiwi fruit rules.

✪ ATOMIUM, BELGIUM

Atomium is far more aesthetically pleasing than some of the other big things here (we're talking about you, Big Banana). Built for the 1958 Brussels World Fair, it's simply awesome, its design replicating the structure of an iron-crystal molecule at a magnification of 165 billion times. The aluminium-clad steel structure features nine spheres at a diameter of 18m each, joined by tubes with a diameter of 3m each; the entire kit is 102m high and over 2400 tonnes. There's a restaurant in the top sphere and scientific exhibitions, chiefly about 'peaceful uses of atomic energy', in the others.

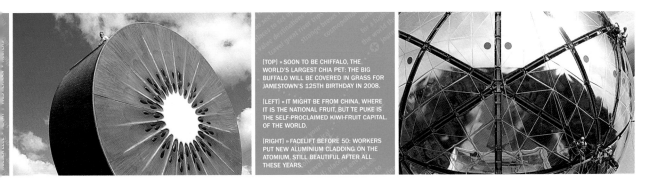

[TOP] » SOON TO BE CHIFFALO, THE WORLD'S LARGEST CHIA PET: THE BIG BUFFALO WILL BE COVERED IN GRASS FOR JAMESTOWN'S 125TH BIRTHDAY IN 2008.

[LEFT] » IT MIGHT BE FROM CHINA, WHERE IT IS THE NATIONAL FRUIT, BUT TE PUKE IS THE SELF-PROCLAIMED KIWI-FRUIT CAPITAL OF THE WORLD.

[RIGHT] » FACELIFT BEFORE 50: WORKERS PUT NEW ALUMINIUM CLADDING ON THE ATOMIUM, STILL BEAUTIFUL AFTER ALL THESE YEARS.

STRANGE MUSEUMS

THE BEST OBSESSIONS BECOME COLLECTIONS – TAKE A PEEK AT SOME OF THE MORE ECCENTRIC ARRAYS TO MAKE IT BEHIND GLASS.

✪ GRUTAS PARK DRUSKININKAI, LITHUANIA

Also known as 'Stalin World', Grutas Park in Druskininkai is a blackly humorous, deeply ironic museum-cum-theme park dedicated to the Soviet occupation of Lithuania, featuring a sculpture garden with statues of former Soviet identities, plus recreations of Gulags including electrified fencing and wooden guard towers. There were plans to herd visitors in via a cattle truck on a railway track, but this was defeated after fierce public disapproval. There are occasional re-enactments in which, according to the *Guardian*, 'Soviet pioneers sing paeans to the dignity of work; Stalin waves his pipe and delivers tedious speeches; and Lenin sits on a bank fishing.'

✪ MUSEUM OF BAD ART, USA

With the motto, 'Art Too Bad to be Ignored', this Massachusetts museum's collection of over 250 pieces includes paintings and sculptures with grossly misaligned perspectives, bodies with arms that look more like thighs, and the most garish colours this side of Ken Done. As the museum promises, this is truly 'exuberant art by people who sometimes don't have a clue what they're doing'. Some of this stuff has been donated, some of it has been fished out of garbage cans, but all of it stinks to high heaven.

✪ HAIR MUSEUM, TURKEY

Galip Körükçü is a Turkish potter who decided to collect as much hair from women all over the world and open a hair museum. The idea was to raise awareness for his ceramics course by dreaming up the most hair-brained scheme imaginable so that people would remember his name. Housed in a cave in Avanos and featuring over 16,000 samples of women's hair hanging from the walls and roof, this hair lair resembles a serial killer's den more than anything, especially when Mr Körükçü puts on his apron and gets his scissors out (predictably, he has a full head of hair).

✪ INTERNATIONAL TOWING HALL OF FAME & MUSEUM, USA

Towing is a serious business indeed, as anyone who's witnessed Australia's rabid towing firms fighting for crash scraps will attest. This museum in Chattanooga is proof, too, with its mission statement to 'preserve the history of the towing and recovery industry, to educate the children of the world, and all of society, about said industry, and to honor those individuals who have made significant changes, and have dedicated precious time throughout our industry'. Anyone'd think there was a war on or something. Come here and see all the trucks and tow bars you can handle.

✪ SULABH INTERNATIONAL MUSEUM OF TOILETS, INDIA

Commodes, the john, the throne, dunnies, the porcelain bus…it's all here and more, with numerous exhibits detailing toilet design all over the world, from squat-and-shit styles to more regal gold-plated numbers. 'Join the sanitation crusade', this New Delhi museum exhorts; see if you could hold on while attempting to follow the numerous steps required in the 'code for married people: an elaborate drill for defecation prescribed in the most respected Aryan scripture Manusmriti Vishnupuran'. Remember to wash your hands afterwards.

✪ MUSEUM OF CRUTCHES, AZERBAIJAN

The renowned health resort town of Naphthalan is known for its healing qualities – oil extracted from the land is supposed to cure all manner of ills. Accordingly, Naphthalan boasts the world's only museum devoted to old crutches. All were supposedly left behind by sick people who came here and were suddenly cured, Monty Python style, therefore requiring their aids no longer. Take the test: break your leg before visiting, bathe in the oil, and then see what happens.

✪ BRITISH LAWNMOWER MUSEUM, ENGLAND

Some say the craftsmanship of Qualcast hand mowers will never be matched by powered mowers, let alone unpowered ones; others swear blind by the Allen Scythe TS with its smooth Villiers Mk25 four-stroke 256cc engine; and then there are those who can only get off on the sight of a mighty Dennis 1-2633 Bradbury four-stroke 500cc mower in full flight. Rub shoulders with all these freaks at the British Lawnmower Museum in Southport, where the exhibits include 'Lawnmowers of the Rich and Famous' (including Prince Charles's), the Fastest Mowers in the World and the world's first solar-powered robot mower.

✪ PARIS SEWER MUSEUM, FRANCE

Prepare yourself: the 'galleries' of the Musée des Egouts de Paris are actually disused sections of Paris' sewage system (fans of Hugo's Les Misérables will know what to expect). The smell is unbelievable, and let that be a warning – you can't completely eradicate over 100 years of crap. Exhibits include photographs, maps…and stuffed sewer rats. As a bonus, you can actually walk around on walkways a few metres above flowing, flushing waste from the stinky Parisians above ground. There's a souvenir shop, too, that sells giftwrapped turds…just kidding.

✪ MEGURO PARASITOLOGICAL MUSEUM, JAPAN

Truly, this really takes the cake – coloured beakers and test tubes lines the walls, each containing a different human or animal parasite. Yes, that's right: tapeworms, hookworms, larvae. Plus detailed anatomical maps showing the life cycle of parasites in the abdomen and nether regions, and gruesome medical photos showing the real-life consequences of infection. If that doesn't satisfy, the souvenir shop can sell you parasite-themed T-shirts and key rings. This Tokyo museum's publicity claims it's the perfect place for lovers on a date – if you're dating David Cronenberg, perhaps. Warning: avoid curry before visiting.

✪ ICELANDIC PHALLOLOGICAL MUSEUM, ICELAND

You'll be cock-a-hoop after visiting this place, with its collection of phalluses from animals and humans; the museum claims that 'phallology is an ancient science', something that a chap like John Holmes would certainly agree with. From the outside this museum in Husavik is dainty and old-fashioned, but inside is a world beyond belief, with over 150 penises and penile parts of all sizes mounted, stuck and glued to the walls, hanging from the ceiling, and illuminated in glaring light. Be careful: some of these could have your eye out. Needless to say, no touching is allowed.

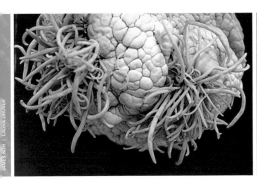

[TOP] » FOR A WHIFF OF HISTORY, FORGET THE LOUVRE AND TOUR THE SEWER.

[LEFT] » A PARTICULARLY GNARLY BRAIN PARASITE AWAITS YOU AT TOKYO'S MEGURO MUSEUM.

[RIGHT] » THE WEIRD AND WONDERFUL WORLD OF PENISES AT HUSAVIK'S PHALLOLOGICAL MUSEUM.

BY THE SEAT OF YOUR PANTS...LITERALLY

✪ ONE, TWO, THREE...COOL RUNNINGS

Sitting down never quite feels the same when you're being hurtled down the Olympic bobsleigh track in Lillehammer, Norway at speeds of up to 120km/h (pictured left). Screaming won't stop this tin machine – well, it might if you can muster a squeak, but if you can maintain consciousness remember to hang on tightly, keep your head down and hold on – to your bladder.

✪ A QUICK WAY TO EAT SAND

One piece of advice. Lift the front of your board. Do this when sand tobogganing on Moreton Island and you won't get a free teeth whitening or exfoliating treatment. Sitting and sliding on sand has two benefits. A soft landing and a smooth ride. The con – you have to climb a 70m-high sand dune to make the ride doable. The record: 21 times in one hour.

✪ RIDING MELINDA

Exotic Asian elephants with names such as Lupcik, Seng Wong and Senggigi will carry you through the lush surroundings of the Balinese Elephant Safari Park. Pity my trunk-bearing transport was called Melinda, which according to my guide meant 'something in English'. They paint, perform, parade and let you pet them. Animals lovers – this may just be paradise.

TRAVEL THE SOLAR SYSTEM

✪ MERCURY

The side of Mercury that faces the sun can reach temperatures exceeding 420°C, while the dark side remains −1800°C. To experience this extreme contrast, drive up to the Liard River Hot Springs in British Columbia. Surrounded by snow for much of the year, the naturally steaming waters will tickle the senses of any earth-bound creature.

✪ VENUS

Much of Venus' surface has been shaped by volcanic activity. To see our own planet reshaping itself, take the trip to Hawaii's Volcanoes National Park. Imagine yourself trapped on Venus and contemplate the awesome power of the universe as you stand in the red glow of Kilauea's lava flows.

✪ MOON

The moon has been visited by a few travellers, but most of us can only dream of getting so far away. The desert near Nazca, Peru, offers trekkers a sprawling, barren landscape with an extra-terrestrial twist. Some theorists contend that ancient animal-shaped geoglyphs found there, known as the Nazca lines, were carved by aliens.

✪ MARS

Hitch along the desert highways of Utah amid the red Martian landscapes of the American southwest. Sandwiched by Canyonlands and Arches National Parks, the town of Moab is heaven for mountain bikers and rock climbers. If you prefer to keep your feet on the ground, the desert terrain alone will give the feeling of walking on Mars.

✪ JUPITER

Island hoppers in the Philippines will testify that the country's famed sunsets rarely disappoint. Head to the coasts of Mindoro and hire a boat to take you out. As the sun slowly melts into the South China Sea, turning the sky and the ocean into innumerable shades of red, imagine you're on a tiny raft, lost on our solar system's largest planet.

✪ SATURN

Saturn's illuminated rings have fascinated human beings for centuries. Down here, rainbows have the ability to provide us with a smile-inducing visual display. To see these splendid rings of colour, traverse the African jungles to Victoria Falls. The mist that rises from this thundering waterfall creates the perfect conditions for a rainbow.

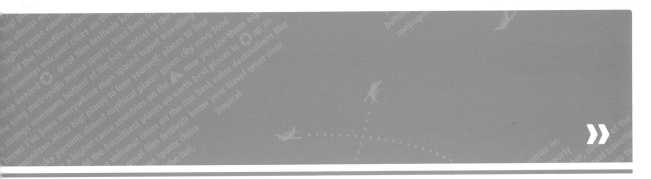

✪ RUN, JUMP, SIT, FLY

A leisurely jump off an Austrian alp is refreshingly stressless when you have no idea you are about to jump off an Austrian Alp. Paragliding will have you soaring above hills that appear alive, giving you a bird's eye view of the world before landing you smoothly on the back-up parachute that was your seat in the air. Breathtaking.

✪ SIT & SIP

Romance has reached its peak when you find yourself sitting in a gondola, sipping champagne and kissing your loved one under glorious Italian bridges in Venice. Heck, its even romantic when you find yourself alone in a gondola and are forced to 'take photos' when those bridges appear – just to cover up for your lack of a partner.

✪ THE BIG MAN IN RED

Sure your parents lied to you as a child, but believing in Santa Claus for the day is completely forgivable when you visit his office at the Arctic Circle border town of Rovaniemi, in the Finnish Lapland. See the real man himself, tug his beard, compliment him on his reindeer-skin boots and do some decoration shopping!

✪ LISA BURNS

I'd describe myself as a joker, never too serious and always willing to make someone smile. My family is known for its ability to pack up and move, having relocated 36 times at last count (not for any suspicious reasons). I'm a photographer at the Tangalooma Wild Dolphin Resort. On a typical day I snap people sand tobogganing at 40km/h, riding quad bikes and feeding the wild dolphins at sunset. My fave destination is Japan: no other place can make you feel as tall or as foreign, and I'm yet to visit a country with people more welcoming or willing to befriend you.

✪ URANUS

The sky of Uranus is a bright spectrum of blue and green clouds. If you would like to gaze skyward at something similarly spectacular, pack your warm gear and head north to Fairbanks, Alaska, for a view of the aurora borealis. Watch in amazement as our own atmosphere puts on a light show that will have you questioning whether or not you are actually still on planet earth.

✪ NEPTUNE

The planet Neptune gets its blue colour from methane gas in its atmosphere. Earth's mostly blue colour comes from its vast liquid oceans. Fly, or swim, to the islands of Thailand in the tropical waters of the Andaman Sea – diving there among some of the most pristine coral reefs in all of Asia can make you wonder what else lurks in our own unexplored ocean depths.

✪ PLUTO

In order to experience Pluto's frigid surface, head to Greenland to see some of its truly surreal glacial landscape. Bundle up your gear and go north in the winter, when the sun disappears for several months. Look up to the heavens and locate a bright star in the perpetual night sky. You can pretend that it's our own sun, shining down on you from far away as you sit on Pluto, the far-flung dwarf planet of the solar system.

✪ DOV QUINT

I was born and raised in Brooklyn, NY. My first life-changing travel experience was as a volunteer, helping to build a primary school in eastern Ghana and renovating a Jewish cemetery in Ukraine. After studying international business in Hong Kong I explored every corner of that island, and travelled all around China, Japan and south-east Asia. I'm ready to travel to almost any country in the world. The place I'd most like to go right now is South America. The whole continent seems to have great natural beauty and such diverse culture.

WINNERS' LISTS 2008

X-FILES TRAVEL

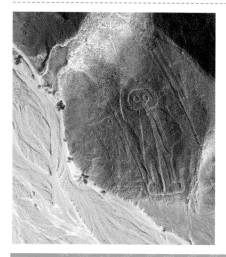

✪ A FLIGHT PATH TO THE STARS

Venture to the Plains of Nazca just south of Lima, and behold the ancient flight paths to the stars. Among the many lines, discernable only by taking a flight overhead, are giant pre-Incan figures of animals: a condor, a hummingbird, a tarantula, and most enigmatic of all, a humanlike figure with a helmet resembling a modern-day astronaut (pictured left).

✪ ANCIENT ASTRONAUTS

Wonder at the similarities between the crypt stone found among the Mayan ruins in Copan and the cockpit position of modern-day astronauts. With their hands on their flight equipment and their eyes on the control panel, both the ancient carving and latter day cosmonauts lie in the same position ready for takeoff. Coincidence?

✪ CAVE SIGHTINGS

Ponder the implications of the millennia-old cave drawings of humanlike figures in suits and headgear at Val Camonica in Northern Italy. You may conclude that primitive man's obsession with otherworldly visitors make Fox Mulder and Von Daniken's theories on alien intervention seem not only plausible, but probable as well.

GROWING OLD GRACEFULLY

✪ TOLLUND MAN

Forget cryogenics, a bog is the best bet if you want to keep hold of your youthful looks. Tollund Man (pictured left) has a complexion that's still as smooth as the day he was garrotted and tossed in a bog. Well, admittedly he may be a bit leathery and distorted these days, and he does look a bit grumpy from his long sleep (of around 2000 years in a bog in Silkeborg, Denmark).

✪ GINGER

Ginger is one of the stars of the British Museum. The oldest and most famous fossilised human form, he lies in a foetal position in a sandy pit that's been reconstructed to look like the one in which he was preserved. He was named for the straggly remains of his ginger hair, but his skin is remarkably ginger too.

✪ MUMMIFIED MONK

One man's 'remarkably well preserved' is another man's creepy corpse. On Ko Samui, at Wat Khunaram, a venerated monk who died over 30 years ago sits in his saffron robes. His flesh is grey and crumbling and he wears a pair of sunglasses to hide his hollow eyes. Nearby you can walk to the waterfall at Na Muang and watch as the monkeys climb for coconuts.

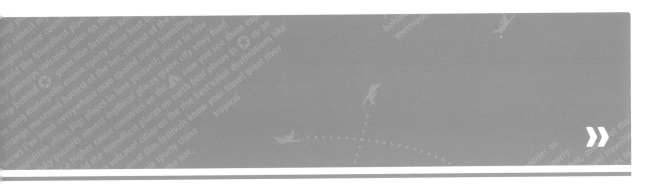

✪ VISITORS FROM ANOTHER TIME

Befriend Bedouins of North Africa and they might guide you through the shifting sands of time to cave paintings at Tassili. Gazing upon the ancients' version of mankind's *The Martian Chronicles*, remember that if there were time travellers, as the drawings seem to indicate, they're with us, even now.

✪ STARGATE

Step into the confines of the Great Pyramid at Giza to see what's not seen. Unlike the Valley of the Kings, where the final resting place of the gods is adorned with the inscriptions from the book of the dead, the tomb of Khufu, builder of the only remaining wonder of the ancient world, is incongruously bare. A tomb or a stargate?

✪ BAXTER JACKSON

For fun, I like to ride my skateboard around Cairo. When I skate through my neighbourhood of Maadi, most Egyptians say, 'Meya, meya'. I'm an ESP teacher. I don't actually have ESP but I do have a specialised group of students (Egypt Air pilots) who need English for the very Specific Purpose of aviation communication. My fave destination is Sacramento, California. I always seem to go back there for some reason or other. Friends, family and the abundance of skateparks might have something to do with it. The place I most want to go is Brazil – I wanna learn Brazilian Jujitsu and Caopeira.

✪ MUMMIFIED MONKEY

Slipping away from the boring guided tour we were on in Cairo we were drawn to a little monkey that was huddled in a glass case at the top of the main staircase. He's kind of cute and kind of hideous at the same time and makes a change from the pay-as-you-go mummies of kings and queens.

✪ ROSALIE LOMBARDIO

Die young, stay pretty. Little Rosalie looks like a beautiful wax doll in her ribbons and lace, amongst the gallery of Palermo's finest dead under the Chiesa dei Capuchin. Her skin is still plump and pink and she looks like she is just about to wake from her 100-year slumber. No wonder they call her 'Sleeping Beauty'.

✪ MICHELANG DA CALIANISSETTA

All right, so he's just a head. But it's a fine head with a shelf of its own and at least he's opted out of the undignified competition to be the best dressed corpse in Palermo.

✪ SYLVIA DUBERY

I come from Anglesey, which is an island off the coast of North Wales, the most beautiful place in Britain. I love walking in the Welsh mountains but I prefer the downhill bits to the up. My Mastermind specialist subject would be the life and work of the Brontes (Gothic romance, windswept moors, Yorkshire – what more could you ask for?). My perfect travel destination would include volcanoes, ruins, temples and beautiful beaches. The next places I would love to visit are Vietnam and St Petersburg.

INDEX

ENJOYED THE BOOK? »

DIVE INTO THE BLUELIST COMMUNITY – ONLINE, ON THE TV AND IN
PRINT – AND BE A PART OF THE WORLDWIDE TRAVEL CONVERSATION.

★ GET YOUR FINGERS CLICKING...

Post your travel recommendations
on our Bluelist website at
www.lonelyplanet.com/bluelist

★ BE SEEN ON CURRENT TV

If you're reading this from the US, check
out the Bluelist program on Current TV.
Wherever you are in the world, upload
your own video to the Current TV website
(www.current.tv/make/vc2/bluelist) and
be in the draw to have your footage
picked for tv broadcast.

SHOUT ALL ABOUT IT WITH MOVING PICTURES

Upload your own Bluelist videos at www.lonelyplanet.tv

If your Bluelist makes it to the Lonely Planet picks, we'll buy it from you for US$500.

TAKE A DETOUR...

Lonely Planet also hosts a dedicated Bluelist Australia website. Choose from a wide variety of true blue travel tips of what to see and do in the land of plenty. Visit www.lonelyplanet.com/bluelistaustralia for more information.

AND LET US KNOW WHAT YOU THINK

www.lonelyplanet.com/surveys

BLUELIST[3] (blu₁list) *v.*
to recommend a travel experience.

ACKNOWLEDGEMENTS

PUBLISHER Roz Hopkins

ASSOCIATE PUBLISHER Chris Rennie

COMMISSIONING EDITORS Ben Handicott, Rachel Williams

DELIVERY MANAGER Jenny Bilos

PROJECT MANAGER Adam McCrow

IMAGE RESEARCHER Craig Newell

DESIGNER Mark Adams

LAYOUT DESIGNER Mik Ruff

DESIGN MANAGER Brendan Dempsey

COORDINATING EDITOR David Carroll

ASSISTING EDITORS Sasha Baskett, Stephanie Ong

MANAGING EDITOR Geoff Howard

PUBLISHING ADMINISTRATOR Jessica Boland

PRE-PRESS PRODUCTION Gerard Walker

PRINT PRODUCTION MANAGER Graham Imeson

Bluelists written by Andrew Bain, Craig Scutt, Karla Zimmerman and Simon Sellars.

WITH MANY THANKS TO
Adam Stanford, Alex Fenby, Amanda Canning, Brice Gosnell, Bridget Blair, Clifton Wilkinson, Ella O'Donnell, Emily Wolman, Errol Hunt, Fayette Fox, Fiona Buchan, Frank Ruiz, Greg Benchwick, Heather Carswell, Heather Dickson, Imogen Hall, Imogen Young, Jane Thompson, Janine Eberle, Jason Shugg, Jay Cooke, Jennye Garibaldi, Judith Bamber, Kalya Ryan, Kathleen Munnelly, Kerryn Burgess, Lucy Monie, Marg Toohey, Marina Kosmatos, Meg Worby, Michala Green, Myriam Cotterell, Nic Lehman, Nick Wood, Paula Hardy, Piers Pickard, Rebecca Chau, Sally Schafer, Sam Trafford, Simone McNamara, Stefanie Di Trocchio, Suki Gear, Tashi Wheeler and William Gourlay.

Special thanks to Waleed Aly for his work on Travel Islam.

LONELY PLANET
BLUE LIST.
THE BEST IN TRAVEL 2008

LONELY PLANET BLUELIST 2008
November 2007

PUBLISHED BY
Lonely Planet Publications Pty Ltd
ABN 36 005 607 983
90 Maribyrnong St, Footscray,
Victoria, 3011, Australia

lonelyplanet.com

Printed by SNP Security Printing Pte Ltd
Printed in Singapore

PHOTOGRAPHS
Many of the images in this book are available for licensing from Lonely Planet Images.
lonelyplanetimages.com

ISBN 987-1-74179-195-2

© Lonely Planet 2007
© Photographers as indicated 2007

LONELY PLANET OFFICES
AUSTRALIA – Locked Bag 1, Footscray, Victoria, 3011
Phone 03 8379 8000 Fax 03 8379 8111
Email talk2us@lonelyplanet.com.au
USA – 150 Linden St, Oakland, CA 94607
Phone 510 893 8555 Toll free 800 275 8555
Fax 510 893 8572 Email info@lonelyplanet.com
UK – 72-82 Rosebery Ave London EC1R 4RW
Phone 020 7841 9000 Fax 020 7841 9001
Email go@lonelyplanet.co.uk

BLUELIST COVER IMAGES Jlsohio istock » Akivi istock » Gizmo istock » Simonmack istock » Lisegagne istock » Kjell Sandved Photolibrary
Peter Adams Photolibrary » Raphotography istock » Stwief istock » Kayglobal istock **INSIDE COVER IMAGES** James J Bissell Photolibrary

A RESPECTABLE TR...

Philippa Gregory is an established ... ...oadcaster for radio and television. She ... ...n eighteenth-century literature from th... ...f Edinburgh. She has been widely praise... ...rical novels, including *Earthly Joys* and *A Resp... ...de* (which she adapted for BBC television), as wel... ...her works of contemporary suspense. *The Other Boleyn Girl* has been adapted for BBC television and is now a major film, starring Scarlett Johansson, Natalie Portman and Eric Bana. Philippa Gregory lives in the North of England with her family.

Visit www.PhilippaGregory.com for more information and www.AuthorTracker.co.uk for exclusive updates about Philippa Gregory.

By the same author

The Wideacre Trilogy
WIDEACRE
THE FAVOURED CHILD
MERIDON

Historical Novels
THE WISE WOMAN
FALLEN SKIES
*A RESPECTABLE TRADE
EARTHLY JOYS
VIRGIN EARTH

Modern Novels
MRS HARTLEY AND THE GROWTH CENTRE
PERFECTLY CORRECT
THE LITTLE HOUSE
ZELDA'S CUT

Short Stories
BREAD AND CHOCOLATE

The Tudor Court Novels
*THE OTHER BOLEYN GIRL
*THE QUEEN'S FOOL
*THE VIRGIN'S LOVER
*THE CONSTANT PRINCESS
*THE BOLEYN INHERITANCE

* Also available on HarperCollinsAudio

Harper
An imprint of HarperCollins*Publishers*
77–85 Fulham Palace Road,
Hammersmith, London W6 8JB

www.harercollins.co.uk

This paperback edition 1996
14

First published in Great Britain by
HarperCollins*Publishers* 1995

A catalogue record for this book
is available from the British Library

ISBN-13: 978 0 00 647377 4
ISBN-10: 0 00 647377 7

Typeset in Linotron Janson and Medici Script by
Rowland Phototypesetting Limited
Bury St Edmunds, Suffolk

Printed and bound in Great Britain by
Clays Ltd, St Ives plc

PHILIPPA GREGORY

A Respectable Trade

HARPER

This book is dedicated to the children of Sika village, in The Gambia, and to all the peoples of Africa, wherever they are today.

Chapter One

Mehuru woke at dawn with the air cool on his outstretched body. He opened his eyes in the half-darkness and sniffed the air as if the light wind might bring him some strange scent. His dream, an uneasy vision of a ship slipping her anchor in shadows and sailing quietly down a deep rocky gorge, was with him still.

He got up from his sleeping platform, wrapped a sheet around him and went quietly to the door. The city of Oyo was silent. He looked down his street; no lights showed. Only in the massive palace wall could he see a moving light as a servant walked from room to room, the torch shining from each window he passed.

There was nothing to fear, there was nothing to make him uneasy, yet still he stood wakeful and listening as if the coop-coop-coop of the hunting owls or the little squeaks from the bats which clung around the stone towers of the palace might bring him a warning.

He gave a little shiver and turned from the doorway. The dream had been very clear – just one image of a looped rope dropping from a stone quayside and snaking through the water to the prow of a ship, whipping its way up the side as it was hauled in, and then the ship moving silently away from the land. There should be nothing to fear in such a sight but the dream had been darkened by a brooding sense of threat which lived with him still.

He called quietly for his slave boy, Siko, who slept at the

foot of his bed. 'Make tea,' he said shortly as the boy appeared, rubbing his eyes.

'It's the middle of the night,' the boy protested and then stopped when he saw Mehuru's look. 'Yes, master.'

Mehuru waited in the doorway until the boy put the little brass cup of mint tea into his hand. The sharp aromatic scent of it comforted him. There had been a stink in his dream, a stink of death and sickness. The ship which had left the land in darkness, trailing no wake in the oily water, had smelled as if it carried carrion.

The dream must mean something. Mehuru had trained as an obalawa – a priest – one of the highest priests in the land. He should be able to divine his own dreams.

Over the roofs of the city the sky was growing paler, shining like a pearl, striped with thin bands of clouds as fine as muslin. As he watched they melted away and the sky's colour slowly deepened to grey and then a pale misty blue. On the eastern horizon the sun came up, a white disc burning.

Mehuru shook the dream from his head. He had a busy day before him: a meeting at the palace and an opportunity for him to show himself as a man of decision and ambition. He put the dream away from him. If it came back he would consider it then. It was a brilliant cream and white dawn, full of promise. Mehuru did not want such a day shadowed by the dark silhouette of a dreamed ship. He turned inside and called Siko to heat water for his wash and lay out his best clothes.

In the Bristol roads – where salt water meets fresh in the Bristol channel – the slaving ship *Daisy* paid off the pilot who had guided her down the treacherously narrow Avon gorge and cast off the barges which had towed her safely out to sea. She put on sail as the sun rose and a light wind got up, blowing from the west. Captain Lisle drew his charts towards him and set his course for the Guinea coast of Africa. The

cabin boy had laid out a clean shirt for him and poured water
for him to wash. He poured it back into the jug, holding the
china ewer carefully in grubby callused hands. It would be
two months at least before they made landfall in Africa and
Captain Lisle was not a man to waste clean water.

Cole and Sons,
Redcliff Dock,
Bristol.

Monday 15th September 1787

Dear Miss Scott,

*I write to you Direct on a delicate matter which Perhaps
should best be addressed to his lordship. However since I
have not Yet his lordship's Acquaintance, and since you indicated to me that you have to make your Own Way in the
World, perhaps I May be forgiven for my Presumption.*

*I was Delighted to meet you at my Warehouse when you
applied for the Post of Governess, but your Family
Connexions and own Demeanour convinced me that I could
Never think of You as an Employee of mine. It was that
Realisation which prompted me to draw the interview to a
Close.*

*I had an idea Then which I now Communicate to you:
Namely that I wish that I might think of you as a Wife.*

*Some might say that as a Bristol Merchant I am overly
Ambitious in wishing to Ally myself with your Family. But
you say Yourself that your circumstances do not permit the
Luxury of Choice. And tho' I am in business – 'in Trade' as*

I daresay his lordship might say – it is a 'Respectable Trade with Good prospects.

You will be Concerned as to the House you would occupy as my wife. You saw Only my Warehouse apartment and I assure you that I am moving Shortly, with my Sister who will remain living with Me, to a Commodious and Elegant house in the best Part of town, namely Queens Square, which his lordship may know.

As to Settlements and Dowry – these certainly should be Arranged between his lordship and myself – but may I Assure you that you will find me Generous if you are Kind enough to look on my Proposal with favour.

I am Sensible of the Honour you would do me, Madam, and Conscious of the Advantage your connexion would bring me. But may I also hope that this Proposal of mine will Preserve you from a lifetime of employment to which your 'Delicate talents and Aristocratic Connexions must render you unfit?

I remain, your most obedient servant,

Josiah Cole.

Josiah sprinkled sand on the letter with a steady hand and blew it gently away. He rose from his chair and went to the high window and looked down. Below him were the wharves and dark water of the Redclift dock. The tide was in and the ships were bobbing comfortably at the dockside; a steady patter of sound came from their rigging, rattling in the light freezing wind. There was a heap of litter and discarded bales on the Coles' empty wharf, and mooring ropes were still coiled on the cobbles. Josiah had seen his ship *Daisy* set sail on the dawn tide. She should be at sea by now, with his hopes riding on her voyage. There was nothing that he could do but wait. Wait for news of *Daisy*, and wait for the arrival of his second ship, the *Lily*, labouring slowly through the seas from the West Indies, heavy with a cargo of sugar and rum. His third ship, the *Rose*, should be loading off Africa.

Josiah was not by nature a patient man, but the job of a merchant in the Trade with only three little ships to his name had taught him steadiness of purpose and endless patience. Each voyage took more than a year, and once a ship had sailed from his dock he might hear nothing from her until she returned. He could do nothing to speed her, nothing to enrich himself. Having provisioned and ordered *Daisy* and watched her set sail, there was nothing to do but wait, gazing down at the rubbish slopping on the greasy water of the port. The distinctive smell of his ships – fearful sweat and sickness overlaid with heady alcohol and sugar – hung around the dockside like an infected mist.

Josiah's own clothes were lightly scented; the hair of his wig and his hands were impregnated. He did not know that throughout Friday's interview with Miss Scott she had been pressing her handkerchief to her face to overcome the acrid smell of the Trade, overbearing in his little room above the warehouse and never stronger than when a ship was in dock.

He glanced at the letter in his hand. It was written very fair and plain, as a man of business writes when his orders must be understood and obediently followed. Josiah had never learned an aristocratic scrawl. He looked at it critically. If she showed it to Lord Scott, would he despise the script for its plain-fisted clarity? Was the tone too humble, or was the mention of the Queens Square house, which he had not in any case yet bought, too boastful?

He shrugged. The stubborn ambition that had brought him so far would carry him farther – into social acceptance by the greater men of the city. Without their friendship he could not make money, without money he could not buy friendship. It was a treadmill – no future for a man. The greater men ran the port and the city of Bristol. Without them Josiah would forever cling to the side of the dock, to the side of the Trade, like a rat on a hemp rope. Miss Scott and her uncle Lord Scott would open doors for him that even his determination could not unlock . . . if she so desired.

Frances opened Josiah's letter and re-read it for the tenth, the twentieth time. She tucked it into the pocket of her plain gown and went down the vaulted marble-floored hall to his lordship's study. She tapped on the door and stepped inside.

Lord Scott looked up from his newspaper. 'Frances?'

'I have had a reply,' she said baldly. 'From the Bristol merchant.'

'Has he offered you the post?'

She shook her head, pulling the letter from her pocket. 'He makes no mention of post or pupils. He has offered me marriage.'

'Good God!' Lord Scott took the letter and scanned it. 'And what do you think?'

'I hardly know what to think,' she said hesitantly. 'I can't stay with Mrs Snelling. I dislike her, and I cannot manage her children.'

'You could stay here . . .'

She gave him a quick rueful smile, her pinched face suddenly softening with a gleam of mischief. 'Don't be silly, Uncle.'

He grinned in reply. 'Lady Scott will follow my wishes. If I say that you are our guest then that should be an end of it.'

'I do not think that I would add to her ladyship's comfort, nor she to mine.' Her ladyship and her three high-bred daughters would not welcome a poor relation into their house, and Frances knew that before long she would be fetching and carrying for them, an unpaid, unwanted, unwaged retainer. 'I would rather work for my keep.'

His lordship nodded. 'You're not bred to it,' he observed. 'My brother should have set aside money for you, or provided you with a training.'

Frances turned her head away, blinking. 'I suppose he did not die on purpose.'

'I am sorry, I did not mean to criticise him.'

She nodded, and rubbed her eyes with the back of her hand. Her ladyship would have fluttered an embroidered handkerchief. Lord Scott rather liked his niece's lack of wiles.

'This may be the best offer I ever get,' Frances said abruptly.

He nodded. She had never been a beauty, but now she was thirty-four and the gloss of youth had been worn off her face by grief and disappointment. She had not been brought up to be a governess and her employers did not treat her with any particular consideration. Lord Scott had found her first post, but had seen her grow paler and doggedly unhappy in recent months. She had replied to an advertisement from Cole and Sons thinking that in a prosperous city merchant's house she might be treated a little better than in a country house of a woman who delighted to snub her.

'What did you think of him as a man?' he asked.

She shrugged. 'He was polite and pleasant,' she said. 'I think he would treat me well enough. He is a trader – he understands about making agreements and keeping them.'

'I cannot write a contract to provide for your happiness.'

She gave him her half-sad rueful smile. 'I don't expect to be happy,' she said. 'I am not a silly girl. I hope for a comfortable position, and a husband who can provide for me. I am escaping drudgery, I am not falling in love.'

He nodded. 'You sound as if you have made up your mind.'

She thought for a moment. 'Would you advise me against it?'

'No. I can offer you nothing better, and you could fare a lot worse.'

Frances stood up and straightened her shoulders as if she were accepting a challenge. Her uncle had never thought of courage as being a woman's virtue but it struck him that she was being very brave, that she was taking her life into her own hands and trying to make something of it.

'I'll do it then,' she said. She glanced at him. 'You will support me?'

'I will write to him and supervise the contract; but if he mistreats you or if you dislike his life I will not be able to help you. You will be a married woman, Frances, you will be his property as much as his ships or his stock.'

'It cannot be worse slavery than working for Mrs Snelling,' she said. 'I'll do it.'

Mehuru, dressed very fine in a long embroidered gown of indigo silk and with a staff in his hand carved with Snake, his personal guardian deity, strolled up the hill to the palace of Old Oyo with Siko walking behind him.

It was yet another full meeting of the council in two long months of meetings. The Alafin – the king – was on his throne, his mother seated behind him. The head of the military was there, his scarred face turning everywhere, always suspicious. The council, whose responsibility was for law and enforcement throughout the wide federation of the Yoruba Empire, was all there; and Mehuru's immediate superior, the high priest, was on his stool.

Mehuru slipped in and stood at the priest's shoulder. The debate had been going on for months; it was of such importance that no-one wanted to hurry the decision. But a consensus was slowly emerging.

'We need the guns,' the old soldier said briefly. 'We have to trade with the white men to buy the guns we need. Without guns and cannon I cannot guarantee the security of the kingdom. The kingdom of Dahomey, which has traded slaves for guns, is fast becoming the greatest of all. I warn you: they will come against us one day, and without guns of our own we cannot survive. That is my final word. We have to trade with the white men for their armaments, and they will take nothing from us but slaves. They will no longer buy gold nor ivory nor pepper. They will take nothing but men.'

There was a long thoughtful silence. The Alafin, an elected monarch, turned to the head of the council. 'And your view?'

The man rose to his feet and bowed. 'If we capture our own people, or kidnap men from other nations, we will be ruined within a generation,' he said. 'The strength of the kingdom depends on its peace. A nation which trades in slaves is in continual uproar, making war on individuals, on other nations. And we will never satisfy the white men's need for slaves. They will gobble us up along with our victims.'

He paused. 'Think of our history,' he continued persuasively. 'This great nation started as just one town. All the other cities and nations have chosen to join with us because we guarantee peace and fair trading. We *have* to keep the peace within our borders.'

The king nodded, and the queen, his mother, leaned forward and said something quietly to him. Finally he turned to the chief priest, Mehuru's superior. 'And your final word?'

The man rose. His broad shoulders, thickened by a cape of rich feathers, obscured Mehuru's view of the court and their serious faces. 'It is a sin against the fathers to take a man from his home,' he began. Mehuru knew that his vote was the result of months of meditation and prayer. This was the single most important meeting that had ever been held. On it hung the future of the whole Yoruba nation, perhaps the future of the whole continent of Africa. 'A man should be left free with his people unless he is a criminal. A citizen should be free.'

Mehuru glance l around. The faces were grave, but people were nodding.

'It is a sin against the Earth,' the chief priest pronounced. 'In the end it all comes back to the Earth, the fathers, the ancestors, and the gods. It is a sin to take a man from his field. I say we should not take slaves and sell them. I say we should protect the people within our borders. They should be safe in their fields.'

There was a long silence. Then the king rose to his feet. 'Hear this,' he said. The old women who had the responsibility for recording decisions of the council leaned forward to hear his words. 'This is the decision of the council of the Yoruba kingdom and my command. Slave trading with white men of any nation shall cease at once. Kidnap of slaves within our borders is forbidden. There shall be no safe passage for white men or their agents when they are on slaving hunts. Other trade with the nations of white men such as gold, ivory, leather goods, brassware and spices is allowed.'

There was a murmur of approval and the king seated himself again. 'Now,' he said with a rueful smile, 'we have the policy – all we have to do is to enforce it while black slavers hammer at our western borders and white men's ships cruise up and down our coastline in the south.'

Mehuru leaned forward and whispered to the high priest. The man nodded and rose to his feet. 'The Obalawa Mehuru has made a suggestion,' he said. 'That we of the priesthood should send out envoys to the country and the towns to explain to the people why it is that we are turning away from this profitable trade. Already some cities are making handsome fortunes in this business. We will have to persuade them that it is against their interests. It is not enough simply to make it illegal.'

The king nodded. 'The priests will do this,' he said. 'And we will pass the orders down to the local councillors, from our council down to the smallest village.' He shot a little smile at Mehuru. 'You can organise it,' he said.

Mehuru bowed low and hid the look of triumph. He would travel to the far north of the Yoruba kingdom, he would speak in the border towns and convince people that slaving was to be banned. He would serve his country in a most important way, and if his mission was successful he would make his name and his fortune.

'I am honoured,' he said respectfully.

Chapter Two

≈≈≈

Whiteleaze,
nr Bath,
Somerset.

Thursday 25th September 1787

Dear Mr Cole,

I am Honoured and deeply conscious of the Compliment you pay me in your kind letter and your Proposal.

I was indeed Surprised at the Abrupt termination of our interview before you had explained my Duties or introduced my Pupils; but now I understand.

It gives me great Pleasure to accept your Offer. I will be your wife.

My Uncle, Lord Scott, will Write to you under a separate cover. He tells me he will Visit Bristol shortly to give himself the Pleasure of your Acquaintance, and to Determine the Marriage Contract, and date of the ceremony.

Please convey my Compliments to your Sister Miss Cole. Your obdt servant,

Frances Scott.

Josiah tapped on the door of the parlour and entered. His sister was seated at the table, the company books spread before her. A small coal fire was unlit in the grate, the room was damp and chill. Her face was pale. Only the tip of her nose showed any colour, reddened by a cold in the head. She was wearing a brown gown with a black jacket and little black mittens. She looked up, pen in hand, as he came in.

'I have a reply from Miss Scott.'

'She has assented?'

'Yes. His lordship himself is coming to Bristol to draw up the marriage contract.'

'I hope it serves its purpose,' Sarah Cole observed coldly. 'It will cost a great deal of money to keep a wife such as her.'

'She will have a dowry,' Josiah pointed out. 'If nothing from her father then her uncle, Lord Scott, is likely to dower her with something.'

'She will need a larger house, and a carriage and a lady's maid.'

Josiah nodded, refusing to argue.

'Her tastes will be aristocratic,' Sarah said disapprovingly.

'It is a venture,' Josiah replied with a small smile. 'Like our others.'

'In the Trade we know the risks. Miss Scott is a new kind of goods altogether.'

Josiah's quick frown warned her that she had gone too far. As his older sister, responsible for him throughout their motherless childhoods, she still retained great power over him; but Josiah could always call on the prestige of being a man. 'We must take care not to offend her,' he said. 'She will find our business very strange at first.'

'She was prepared to come here as an employee,' Sarah reminded him.

'Even so.'

There was a brief irritated silence. Brother and sister waited for the other to speak.

19

'I'm going to the coffee house,' Josiah said. 'I shall see if anyone is interested in coming into partnership with us for the *Lily*. She is due home at the end of November; we need to buy in trade goods and refit her.'

Sarah glanced at the diary on her desk. 'She set sail from Jamaica this month, God willing.'

Josiah tapped his large foot on the wooden floorboards for luck. The modest buckle on his shoe winked in the light. 'You have the accounts for the *Lily*'s last voyage to hand?'

'You had better seek a partner without showing them. We barely broke even.'

Josiah smiled. His large front teeth were stained with tobacco. 'Very well,' he said. 'But she is a good ship and Captain Merrick is usually reliable.'

Sarah rose from her desk, crossed over to the window and looked down. 'If you see Mr Peters in the coffee house we are still waiting for his money for the equipping of the *Daisy*,' she said. 'The ship sailed two weeks ago and he has not yet paid for his share. We cannot extend credit like this.'

'I'll tell him,' Josiah said. 'I will be home for dinner.' He paused at the door. 'You do not congratulate me on my engagement to be married?'

She did not turn from the window, and her face was hidden from him. He did not see her look of sour resentment. Sarah's marriageable years had slipped away while she worked for her father and then for his heir, her brother, screwing tiny profits out of a risky business. 'Of course,' she said. 'I congratulate you. I hope that it will bring you what you desire.'

Siko was unwilling to leave the city of Oyo. He was a city boy who had sold himself into slavery with Mehuru when his parents died. He had thought that with a young man whose career was centred on the court he would be safe from the discomfort of farming work and rural life. He was deeply reluctant to venture out into the countryside, which he regarded as a dangerous place inhabited by wild animals and surly peasants.

'For the last time,' Mehuru said abruptly. 'Finish packing and fetch the horses or I shall sell you to a brothel.'

Siko bowed his head at the empty threat and moved only slightly faster. He was confident that Mehuru would never ill-treat him, and indeed he was saving money to buy his freedom from his young master as they had agreed.

'Should we not take porters and guards?' he asked. 'My brother said he would be willing to come with us.'

'We will be travelling along trading routes,' Mehuru said patiently. 'We will be meeting porters and guards on the trading caravans all along the way. If there is any danger on the roads we can travel with them. I am on an urgent mission, we are travelling at speed. You would have us dawdling along the road and stopping at every village.'

'I would have us stay snug in the city,' Siko muttered into a saddlebag. Aloud he said: 'We are packed, sir, and ready to leave.'

Mehuru nodded to him to load the bags and went into his room. In the corner were his priestly things, laid out for meditation. The divining tray made out of beautifully polished wood indented with circular cups filled with cowrie shells, the little purse filled with ash, a cube of chalk, a flask of oil. Mehuru picked them up one by one and put them into a soft leather satchel, letting his mind linger on them and calling for vision.

Nothing came. Instead he saw once more the prow of a ship, rocking gently on clear tropical waters. He could see a shoal of small fish nibbling at the copper casing of the wooden hull, something he had never seen in waking life. Again he smelled the heavy sickly smell of sugar and sepsis.

'What does it mean?' he whispered softly. 'What does it mean?'

He shuddered as if the day were not pulsing with heat, as

if he could feel a coldness like death. 'What does it mean, this ship?' He waited for an answer but he could hear nothing but Siko complaining to the cook about the prospect of a journey and the chattering of a flock of glossy starlings, gathering on the rooftop, their deep blue feathers iridescent in the morning sun.

He shrugged. No ship could endanger him; his journey lay northwards, inland. To the north were the long rolling plains of savannah country, an inland river or two, easily forded or crossed by boat, and then even further north – at the limits of the mighty Yoruba kingdom – the great desert of the Sahel. No ship could be a threat to him, he was far from the coast. Perhaps he should see the ship as a good omen, perhaps it was a vision of a slaving ship which would no longer be able to cruise casually off the coast of his country and gather in his country's children as greedily as a marauding hyena.

Mehuru picked up his satchel of goods and slung it over his shoulders. Whatever the meaning of the vision, he had a job to do and nothing would prevent him. He bundled his travelling cape into a neat roll and went out into the brilliant midday sunshine. The horses were waiting, and the great city gates set deep into the mighty walls of the famous city of Oyo had been open since dawn.

'So!' he said cheerfully to Siko. 'Off we go!'

The quayside coffee shop was on the opposite side of the river from Josiah's dock, and so he took the little ferryboat across and tossed the lad who rowed him a ha'penny. The coffee shop was the regular meeting place for all the merchants of Bristol from the finest men to the smallest traders. When Josiah pushed open the small door his eyes smarted at the strong aromatic smell. The place was thick with tobacco smoke and the hot familiar scent of coffee, rum, and molasses. Josiah, with his hat under his arm, went slowly from table to table, seeing who was there. All of the merchants were known to him, but only a few did business with him regularly. At the best table, farthest from the damp draughts from the swinging door, were the great merchants of Bristol, in fine coats and crisp laundered linen. They did not even glance up when Josiah said 'Good day' to them. Josiah was not worth their attention.

He nodded politely in their direction, accepting the snub. When he was nephew by marriage to Lord Scott they would return his greeting, and he would be bidden to sit with them. Then he would see the cargo manifests which were spread on their table. Then he would have a chance at the big partnerships and the big trading ventures. Then he would command their friendship, and have access to their capital for his own ventures. They would invite him to join their association – the Merchant Venturers of Bristol – and all the profits and opportunities of the second-greatest provincial city in Britain would fall open to him.

'Josiah!' a voice called. 'Over here!'

Josiah turned and saw a table crowded with men of his own class, small traders who shared and shared again the risks of a voyage, men who scrambled over each other for the great prizes of the Trade and yet who would be wiped out by the loss of one ship. Josiah could not reject their company. His own father had been an even lesser man – trading with a fleet of flat-bottomed trows up and down the Severn: coal from Wales, wheat from Somerset, cattle from Cornwall. Only at the very end of his life had George Cole owned an ocean-going ship and she had been a broken-down privateer which had managed one voyage for him before she sank. But on that one voyage she had taken a French trading ship, and claimed all her cargo. She had shown a profit of thousands of pounds and the Cole fortune had been made, and the Cole shipping line founded. George Cole had put up his sign 'Cole and Sons', and bequeathed the business to his son and daughter. They had made it their life's work to expand yet further.

Two men seated on a bench moved closer to make space for Josiah. Their damp clothes steamed slightly in the warmth and there was a prevailing smell of stale sweat and wet wool.

'Good day,' Josiah said. He nodded at the waiter for coffee and the boy brought him a pot with a cup and a big bowl of moist brown lump sugar.

'You did well on the *Daisy* then,' the man who had called him commented. 'Prices are holding up for sugar. But you get no tobacco worth the shipping.'

Josiah nodded. 'It was a good voyage,' he said. 'I won't buy tobacco out of season. I'll only take sugar. I did well on the *Daisy* and we turned her around quickly.'

'Do you have a partner for your next voyage?' the man opposite him asked. He spoke with a thick Somerset accent.

'I am seeking a partner for the *Lily*. She will be in port within two months.'

'And who commands her?'

'Captain Merrick. There is no more experienced master in Bristol,' Josiah said.

The man nodded. 'D'you have the accounts for her last voyage?'

Josiah shook his head, lying with easy fluency. 'They are with the Excise men,' he explained. 'Some trouble over the bond last time. But the *Daisy* is a better example in any case. She was fresh into port and showed a profit of three hundred pounds for each shareholder. You won't find a better breeding-ground for your money than that!'

The man nodded. 'Could be,' he said uncertainly.

Josiah dropped two crumbling lumps of thick brown sugar into his coffee, savouring the sweetness, the very scent of the Trade, and signalled for a glass of rich dark rum. 'As you wish,' he said casually. 'I have other men that should have the offer first, perhaps. I only mentioned it because of your interest. Think no more about it.'

'Oh no,' the man said quickly. 'What share would you be looking for?'

'A quarter,' Josiah replied coolly. He looked away from the table and nodded a greeting at another man.

'And how much would that be?'

Josiah seemed to be barely listening. 'Oh, I couldn't say . . .' He shrugged his shoulders. 'Perhaps a thousand pounds each, perhaps nine hundred. Say no more than nine hundred.'

The man looked rather dashed. 'I had not thought it would be so much . . .'

Josiah turned his brown-stained smile on him. 'You will not regret it being so much when it shows a profit of twenty or thirty per cent. Eh?'

'And who will be the ship's husband? You? You will do all the fitting and the orders?'

'Myself,' Josiah said. 'I always do. I would trust it to no other man. But I should not have troubled you with this. There is Mr Wheeler now, I promised him a share in the *Lily*.'

'No, stay,' the man protested. 'I will take a share, Josiah. I will have my share in her.'

Josiah nodded easily. 'As you wish, Samuel.' He held out his hand and the other grasped it quickly. 'Come to my warehouse this afternoon, and bring your bond. I will have the contract for you.'

The man nodded, half-excited and half-fearful. He rose from the table and went out. He would be busy from now until the afternoon scouring the city for credit to raise his share.

'I had not thought he had nine hundred pounds to outlay,' one of the others remarked. 'You had best see your money before you sign, Josiah.'

Josiah shrugged. Despite himself, his eyes strayed to the table at the top of the room. The men had called for a pie, a ham and some bread and cheese for their breakfasts. They were drinking port. They were joking loudly, and their faces were flushed. They did not have to haggle over some small man's life savings to finance a voyage. They carved up the profitable voyages among themselves, they shared the profits from the docks – even the barges that plied up and down the Avon paid them a fee, the little ferryboat and even the lighthouses paid them rent.

'I have some news,' Josiah said abruptly. 'I am to be married.'

There was a stunned silence at the little table.

'To the niece of Lord Scott of Whiteleaze,' Josiah went on. 'His lordship will be calling on me soon and we will settle the marriage contract.'

'My God! Josiah!' one exclaimed.

'Wherever did you meet the lady?' one of the others asked. The rest simply gaped.

'She called on us,' Josiah lied convincingly. 'She knows a friend of my sister's. They were at school together.'

The men could hardly find words. 'I had thought you would be a bachelor forever!' one of them said.

'And with Sarah to keep house for you! I never thought you would marry.'

'I was waiting for the right lady,' Josiah said precisely. 'And for my fortunes to be on such a rise that I could offer her a proper position in life.'

The men nodded. The news was too staggering to be taken in all at once. 'I had not thought he was doing *that* well,' one of the men muttered.

'I shall move from the warehouse,' Josiah said. 'I shall take a new house for my wife.'

'Where will you live?'

'I shall buy a house in Queens Square,' Josiah said. Again

he glanced toward. the top table. The men there owned Queens Square outright; it had been built by the Corporation, to their design. They could choose whether or not to sell to him. Money alone could not buy him into their neighbourhood; but with Lord Scott's niece on his arm he would be welcomed in the elegant brick-faced square. Josiah would call them 'neighbour' and his new wife would visit their wives.

The men at the table nodded. 'And the lady . . .'

'Shall we return to business?' Josiah asked with a small triumphant smile. 'I think that is enough about the lady who is to be Mrs Cole.'

They nodded, as impressed by the triumph of his marriage as by his quiet dignity.

'About this voyage of the *Lily*,' one of them said. 'I think I'll take a share after all. Will his lordship be coming in with us?'

Josiah smiled slightly. 'Oh, I should think so,' he said.

Mehuru's mission was going well. He went from town to town and even stopped at the councils of the larger villages as he worked his way north-west across the great rolling plains of the Yoruba nation. The villagers knew that he was talking nothing more than sense. For all the profits that could be made from the slave trade – and they were beyond the dreams of most farming communities – there were terrible stories, garbled in the telling, of rivers where no-one dare fish and woods where no-one could walk. Whole villages were desolate, hundreds, thousands of women and children abandoned and starving in fields which they could not farm alone. It was a blight spreading inland from the coast, a plague which took the young men and women, the fittest and the strongest, and left behind the ill, the old, and the babies.

This plague of slavery worked unlike any other. It took

27

the healthy, it took the adventurous, it took the very men and women who should command the future. The guns and gold and fine cloth could not repay Africa for the loss of her brightest children. It was the future leaders who were bled away, along the rivers, down the trade routes.

'This is where it stops,' Mehuru said firmly in one town council after another. 'One nation has to refuse. One nation has to throw up a wall and say that it must end here. Otherwise what will become of us? Already the trade routes running north are unsafe, and the wealth of this nation depends on our trade. We send our leather goods, we send our brassware, we send our rich luxuries north, across the Sahel Desert to the Arab nations, and we buy our spices and silk from them. All our trade has always been north to south, and now the slavers are cutting the routes.

'The coastal forests and plains are becoming deserted. Who will fish if the coast is abandoned? Where shall we get salt if the women cannot dry it in the salt pans? Where shall we get food if we cannot farm? How can a country be strong and safe and wealthy if every day a hundred, two hundred men are stolen?'

The men in the village councils nodded. Many of them showed the profits of the slave trade with ragged shirts of cotton woven in Manchester, and guns forged in Birmingham. But they were quick to notice that the vivid dyes of the cottons bled out after a few washings, and the guns were deadly to the users as well as to the victims when they misfired. No-one could deny that the slave trade was an unequal deal in which Africa was losing her brightest sons in exchange for tatty goods and shoddy wares.

Mehuru worked his way north, persuading, cajoling. He and Siko became accustomed to riding all day and camping out at night. Siko grew deft at building small campfires for cooking when they were out in the open savannah. The young man and the boy ate together, sharing the same bowl, and then rolled themselves up in their cloaks and slept side by side. They were fit and hardened by exercise and quietly companionable. Every time they stopped for Mehuru to tell the village elders of the new laws they heard more news, and all of it bad. The trade goods were faulty, the muskets blew to pieces the first time they were fired, maiming and killing. The rum was poisonous, the gold lace and smart hats were tawdry rubbish. Worse than that, the white men were establishing gangs of African brigands who belonged to no nation and followed no laws but their own whim, who cruised the rivers and seized a solitary man, a child playing hide and seek with his mother, a girl on her way to a lovers' meeting. There could be no rule of law where kidnappers and thieves were licensed and paid in munitions.

Some of the coastal nations now dealt in nothing but slaves. They had turned from a rich tradition of fishing, agriculture, hunting and trading, to being slaving nations, with only men to sell, and gold to buy everything they might need. Nations of brigands, terrible nations of outlaws.

And the white men no longer kneeled to the kings of the coastal nations. They had built their own stone castles, they had placed their own cannon in their own forts. Up and down the rivers they had built great warehouses, huge stone barns where slaves could be collected, collected in hundreds, even thousands, and then shipped on, downriver, to the forts at the river mouth. There was no longer any pretence that the African kings were permitting the trade. It was a white man's business and the African armies were their servants. The balance of power had shifted totally and completely. The white men commanded all along the coast by the power of the gun and the power of their gold.

The more Mehuru heard, the more certain he became that the Yoruba states were right to stand against slavery. The wickedness of slavery, its random cruelty, no longer disturbed him as much as the threat to the whole future of the continent which was opening before him like a vision of hell: a country ruled by the gun for the convenience of strangers, where no-one could be safe.

'If slavery is such a bad thing,' Siko said one night as they lay together under the dark sky, 'I suppose you'll be setting me free as soon as we get back to Oyo.'

Mehuru reached out a foot and kicked him gently. 'You buy yourself out as we agreed,' he said. 'You've been robbing me blind for years anyway.'

He smiled as he slept; but in the night, under the innocent arch of the sky, he dreamed of the ship again. He dreamed of it cruising in warm shallow water, its deck misshapen by a thatched shelter, the sides shuttered with nets. In its wake were occasional dark, triangular fins. There were sharks following the ship, drawn through the seas by the garbage thrown overboard, and by the promising smell of sickness and despair. They could scent blood and the likelihood of death. The prow sliced through the clean water like a knife into flesh, and its wake was like a wound. Mehuru started awake and found that he was sweating as if he had been running in terror. It was the ship again, his nightmare ship.

He woke Siko. It was nearly dawn, he wanted the company of the boy. 'Let's go and swim,' he said. 'Let's go down to the river.'

The boy was reluctant to get up, warning of crocodiles and hippos in the river, and poisonous snakes on the path. Mehuru caught the edge of the boy's cloak and rolled him out.

'Come on,' he said impatiently. He wanted to wash the dream away, he wanted to play like a child in the water and then run back and eat porridge for breakfast. They had camped in the bend of a river and slept on the dry bank. Mehuru left his things by the embers of last night's fire and jogged, half-naked, to the river. Siko trotted behind him, still complaining. The coolness of the morning air cleared his head, he could feel his breath coming faster and the dark ominous shadow of the ship receding.

Ahead of them was the river, fringed with trees, the tall nodding heads of the rhun palm making a continual comforting clatter as the dried leaves pattered against each other. He ran between an avenue of locust bean trees, the broad gnarled trunks on either side of him, the fluttering feathery leaves brushing the top of his head. He could see the river, the green water gleaming through the thick undergrowth. A flock of plantain eaters swooped overhead, pied birds calling coop-coop-coop in a melodic chatter, and brightly coloured parrots flew up as Mehuru and Siko ran easily side by side. Mehuru's feet scrunched on white sand and he was pausing to catch his breath and to check the water for crocodile or hippo when he saw, from the corner of his eye, a shadow launch forward and in the same moment he was buffeted by a blow which flung him to the ground.

He struggled to get his arms free but he was winded and helpless under the weight of his attacker. He heard another man running forwards and saw a club rising above him and he cried out in terror, 'Siko! Run! Run!' as the blow crushed his head and flung him into fragments of darkness.

His last thought, as the dark shape of the nightmare ship rose up in his mind to blot out the sunlight and the gleam of the green water, was that he, of all people, should have known how far inland the slavers might have come.

At Mrs 'Daley's house,
'Dowry 'Parade,
the Hot 'Well,
'Bristol.

11th November 1787

'Dear 'Frances,

I am 'Writing this before I leave for London as I Know
you would want to Know at once my thoughts on Mr Josiah
Cole.

I find him a Plain and simple Man, on whose 'Word I
think we can Rely. I have had sight of his Company books
and he seems to be well-established, tho' he is not a member
of the Merchant Adventurers nor of the Africa Company,
which is a regret to him. However, the 'Friends you can bring
may 'Rectify the Omission.

He was Not demanding as to your 'Dowry and we have
settled matters to our Satisfaction. I have taken a Share, on
your behalf, in the cargo of one of his ships, the 'Daisy, which
is loading off Africa in this Month. Another of his ships, the
Lily, came into port while I was there and I watched the
unloading of his 'Wealth in the 'Form of Sugar and 'Rum. It
is a 'Risky business, but highly profitable. I have no
Hesitation in believing that you will be well Provided for during your Marriage; and if 'Widowed, you will 'Enjoy an
adequate jointure. 'We have Agreed that there is no haste for
the Marriage and since you have to complete your contract
with Mrs Snelling, and he hopes to 'Buy a house Suitable for
his new 'Family, we have fixed it for the month of July next

year. It is Not what your father would have wished, but I Agree with you that it is the best you can Anticipate.

As to the Pupils you were to teach, he made no Mention of them, except as a Scheme he had in Mind for later. My principal concern was your Sister-in-law, Miss Sarah Cole, who does not Seem to welcome the Match. However, you will have Dealt with more Intractable domestic situations at Home and with Mrs Snelling.

I shall be home within the Sennight, and will drive over to Mrs Snelling's house to discuss the matter with you then.

Yours,

Scott.

Mehuru regained consciousness with an aching head and flies buzzing about the blood on his temple. His arms were bound behind him and his neck was lashed into a forked wooden brace with rough hemp twine. At his side was Siko, whimpering pitifully, his neck-brace paired with Mehuru's so that they were bound together like some misshapen yam which sprouts a twin. They were whipped to their feet and then directed down the river path to where their captors had hidden their boats. Every stumble Siko made tore Mehuru's neck and knocked him from his stride. They fell together in a helpless embrace and were whipped until they stood again. Only when they fell into a slavish head-bowed shuffle could they move forward, and even then both their necks were rubbed through bruises into bleeding sores. 'I am sorry, sir, I am sorry,' Siko wept. 'I am sorry.'

'It is I who am sorry,' Mehuru said only once as they struggled to their feet. 'I brought you far from your home and mine, I should have taken more care. I did not know that they had come this far inland.'

He did not finish his thought: that it was not only Siko whom he had failed. If the slavers were raiding this far inland then the whole of Africa was open to them and Mehuru could not send a warning. 'The gods only know what will be the end of this,' he said to himself. He was worried for the Yoruba kingdom and for its plan to boycott the slave trade. He did not yet know enough to fear for himself.

Siko wept like a little child, but Mehuru stayed calm. He knew that while they were within the borders of the Yoruba states his authority would be recognised. The men who had captured them were ignorant violent peasants of the worst sort. Mehuru tried to speak to them in all the African languages he knew but they answered him only with a threatening wave of a cudgel. He decided to wait until they reached their base camp. As soon as they reached their master, Mehuru would explain who he was and they would be released. In his more optimistic moments Mehuru thought what an excellent anecdote this would make back at the court, and what a hero he would seem: fighting slavery and personally endangered.

It took three days walking downriver to where the slavers' boats were waiting, and at every halt the slavers went out and hunted down another man, another woman, another little child. Mehuru's opposition to the slave trade had been theoretical; but when he saw the women sick with fear and the children too terrified to weep he knew that he hated the Trade and would be against it all his life. Then he longed to be back at court – not only to boast of his escape, but to add his voice to the counsels against slavery. He had heard it named as a sin but when he saw the whipping and the casual brutality, he understood for the first time in a comfortable leisured life what a mortal sin could mean.

And he was afraid – if the slavers had penetrated this far to the north and east then how far might they yet go? Africa was a massive continent, rich with people living well on fertile soil. Slavers using the river routes could penetrate deep and deeper into the very heart of nations. Mehuru had been in the borderlands of the Yoruba kingdom but even so, he was thousands of miles from the coast. How far would the slavers go for their Trade? What would it take to stop them?

They were twenty in all by the time they were loaded into the boats to travel downriver. They were made to kneel on the floor of rough wooden canoes, still bound neck to neck. The sun burned down on their heads, and where the lashes of the whip had cut the flies crawled and feasted. With hands lashed tightly behind him Mehuru felt the skin of his back cringe at the touch of the insects, the little minute trampling of their feet against his eyelids, the probe of their tongues into the gash on his face. The men paddled the canoes out into midstream and caught the smooth fast current, but the flies were not blown away. They followed like a haze, tempted by the smell of fearful sweat and open wounds.

The heavily laden canoe slipped past green thickly wooded banks like a dream, rocking only slightly as the men held it in the centre of the river. Sometimes the water was so wide that you could hardly see from side to side, sometimes it narrowed and Mehuru looked longingly at the banks. The sun beat down on them, the boat rocked them like a cradle. The heat haze danced on the banks and the flies buzzed around their heads. Mehuru thought of the silent progress of his ship, his nightmare ship, and its wake of sharks and the stink which hung around it in his dream.

On the fifth day they rounded a bend in the river and saw before them a large stone building, which could only have been built by white men with their strange desire for block shapes and their disregard for the contours of the land. It was nothing more than a cube, with little slits for windows, the roof steeply thatched. Before it, sticking out into the river, was a wooden jetty which led to a stone quay. Behind it was a cluster of huts, a poor slovenly place

35

with no women to keep it tidy and no men to farm the land.

Mehuru thought that here at least he would find someone who would see sense and release them. He was anxious for Siko, who had stopped weeping and was now like a man drugged. The boy sat in the boat in silence, his eyes downcast on the green water, and neither the pain of the neck-brace nor the discomfort of sitting in the heat of the midday sun prompted him to speak. His eyes had gone blank with fear, he would not eat. Mehuru wanted them both to be released promptly, before the boy fell sick. He readied himself to demand to see whoever was in charge.

But there was no-one on the landing stage. There was a big iron gate in the massive stone wall and their boat was simply unloaded with shouted commands and whipped in through the gate. The men ignored Mehuru's demand to see their master and pushed him into the entrance vestibule with the rest. When the outer gate clanged shut behind them, another was opened before them and they stumbled into a massive stone chamber ten times as big as the largest barn. A group of men pushed them into line and chained them, quickly and efficiently, with the chain running through their manacles, and fastened each end to rings set into the stone-work of the wall. Mehuru noted the clumsy cast-iron man-acles and chains, nothing like the light well-crafted metal of his own people. But it was good enough to hold him, to hold them all.

Time passed. He tried to count the dawns with marks on the dirt in the floor but there was no space, they were packed too close, and every day another couple, another dozen of new captives were added. The food was scanty and often bad. Many people were sick, vomiting into the slop pail, or voiding uncontrollably on to the earth floor. The smell was dreadful. There was no water for washing and no change of clothes. Mehuru banked down the flickering panic at his own degradation. He refused to let the dirt and the humiliation touch him, and he spoke encouragingly to Siko.

'This is a mistake,' Mehuru said. 'They should not have taken us. When someone in authority comes I will tell them who I am. A Yoruban envoy cannot be so treated. When they realise who I am they will let us go.'

Siko did not reply. He would not look at Mehuru.

When new men and women were brought in Mehuru tried to speak to the jailers. Every time one of them came within shouting distance he called out to him, first in Yoruban, then in Dahomean, then in Mandinka: 'Tell your master that I am an obalawa of Yoruba, on the king's business. Tell him the king will pay a high ransom for me. Tell him I demand to speak with him!'

They did not understand, or they would not listen. Mehuru knew he must be patient and wait until he could speak to their leader. Then he would be released and he could demand that Siko be returned to him. His main fear was that they would try to keep Siko when they released him; and Mehuru's duty to his slave, to offer complete protection in return for complete obedience, would be threatened.

He let himself worry about Siko, he let his concern for Siko be the principal, the only thing in his mind. While he could think of himself as a master, as a man of property with obligations, he could pretend that he did not belong in the nightmare storehouse, soiled with his own mess, with dirty hands and matted hair. He thought his sanity depended on him remembering that he did not belong there, that he was not a slave, he was a Yoruban envoy on a mission for the Alafin himself.

After about a month in which conditions in the storehouse grew worse and worse, there was a gathering, like some nightmare market. A new boat, a white man's boat, had come upriver from the coast, bringing two white men. Mehuru readied himself to explain to the men that he must be released. All of the captives were dragged one at a time from

37

their prison and brought out to a white man, who lolled on a chair under a tree.

It was Mehuru's first sight of a white man, the race that was destroying his country. He had expected a towering demon or an impressive god – not this dirty weakling. His skin was pale, his clothes were grey and foul and the stink of him as he sweated in the sunshine was so bad that he could even be smelled above the stench from the storehouse. The man was wet all the time. He lounged on a chair in the shade but he did not sit still and consider his purchases. He shifted all the time in his seat, getting hotter and hotter and his terrifying pallor went an even more frightening flushed red colour and all his face grew shiny and wet with sweat.

When they pulled Mehuru forward by a twitch on the rope around his neck he was so shocked by the corpse face of the man, and the disgusting thick clumps of stubble hair on his chin and at the open neck of the dirty shirt, that for a moment he could barely speak. But then he drew himself up to his full height and looked the man in the eye.

'I am an envoy of the Yoruban federation,' he said clearly. 'I must be released at once or there will be severe reprisals.' He repeated the sentence first in Portuguese, the language of the slavers, and then in all the African languages he knew. 'I demand the release of my personal servant and my own freedom,' he said.

The white man turned his head to one side, coughed and spat a gob of infected yellow phlegm. He nodded to a second white man who stepped forward. Mehuru forced himself not to flinch; the man was rancid with the stink of drink and a sharp acrid smell of old sweat. Mehuru breathed in through his mouth and repeated the speech again in Portuguese.

The white man did not even reply. He put his filthy hands in Mehuru's face and pulled back his lips to see his teeth. Mehuru jerked back, and staggered over the chains at his ankles.

'How dare you!' he cried. At once two of the African slavers seized him from behind and held him in an unrelenting grip.

'Let me go!' Mehuru shouted. He bit off his panic and spoke clearly in Portuguese. 'You are making a serious mistake,' he said urgently. 'I am an envoy for the Yoruba federation.'

The white man nodded to the guard to hold him firmly, leaned down and pulled aside Mehuru's loincloth. He pulled back the foreskin of his penis to see if he were infected, and then nodded at the guard to make him bend over, to see if the flux had left blood on his anus.

Mehuru's outraged shout was stifled in his throat. When he felt the dirty hands on him he choked with shame. Siko was watching him, his eyes wide with horror. 'It's all right,' Mehuru called in hollow reassurance. 'We will get to their leaders and explain.'

It was bravado, not courage. That night when Siko had wept himself to sleep and was lying with his limbs twitching with dreams of freedom, Mehuru sat quietly, dry-eyed and horrified. The fingerprints of the white men burned on his skin, the recollection of their washed-out stares scorched his memory. They had looked at him with their pale eyes as if he were nothing, as if he were a piece of meat, a piece of Trade. They looked at him as if he were a nobody, and Mehuru thought that in their horrible transparent eyes he had seen the death of his individuality. He thought that if he lost his sense of who he was, of his culture, of his religion, of his magic power, then he would be a slave indeed.

Only the god, Snake, was with him in that long desolate night. Mehuru called on him to save him from the men who were as white as ghosts, and the Snake god laughed quietly in his long throat and said, '*All men are dead men, all men are ghosts.*' Mehuru did not sleep that night, though he was weary through to his very bones.

The next day the chosen hundred were herded into canoes

39

and taken down the river. Mehuru no longer depended on his powerful status as a representative of the Alafin of Yoruba. He kept a sharp lookout instead for a chance to escape and run, run like a slave, for freedom.

But even that could not be done. Not on the river journey, not when they were unloaded on the beach at the coast. The slavers had done this too often. Mehuru saw that they were practised in the handling of many angry, frightened people. They never came within reach, they whipped them into line with long whips from a distance. Mehuru kept watching for a chance to order the whole line of them to run – run in a great line towards the market place of the town – and in the confusion find hammers to shear the chains, and spears to kill and then scatter. But there were too many too lame to run fast enough, and too many little children crying for their mothers, chained in the line.

He waited, pretending obedience and waiting for his chance. They were herded through the little village at the mouth of the river and down to the wide white-sand beach where boats, white men's boats, were drawn up with the waves washing around their keels.

When he saw the ship, the great ship, bobbing at anchor beyond the white breakers, his heart sank. It was the ship of his dreams come for him at last. The hot humid wind which blew steadily on shore brought the smell of death as clearly as if he could already hear the widows crying. Mehuru stared at the water around the ship and saw the swift movement of a shark's fin – just as he had seen it in his dream. He looked at the prow which he had dreamed slicing so easily through the water and knew that it would cut through miles of seas. Even the rope of his dream was stretched out tight, as the ship bobbed on her mooring. It was all as he had known it.

Mehuru embraced despair then. The ship had been coming for him for months, he had seen it set sail, he had seen it arrive off his own coast, and now here it was at last, waiting for him. He closed his eyes as a man will close his eyes in death and let them herd him, like a sacrificial goat, on board.

Chapter Three

Frances Scott, now Frances Scott Cole, closed the door of what was to be her bedroom and looked around her. It was a plain room bereft of any trimming or prettiness. The bed was a massive four-poster in dark heavy wood and had a small table beside it. The wash jug and ewer stood on another matching side table. There was a chest for her clothes and a mirror on the wall. It had been Josiah's; now he would use the adjoining room, except for the nights when he might choose to sleep with her.

The room smelled. The whole house stank of the mid-summer garbage of the dock. Only in a rainstorm or at high tide would the air smell clean to Frances, who had not been brought up on these fetid river banks.

Josiah still had not bought his house on Queens Square; but he had promised to find a house soon. As the date of the July wedding drew near, Frances had agreed to live for the first months of her wedded life over a warehouse on the Bristol quayside.

The room was in half-darkness. Only a little cold moonlight found its way in through the casement window, obscured by the brooding cliff which towered over the back of the house. Even at midday the room would be dark and damp. Frances put her candle down on the bedside table, went over to the mirror and unpinned her hair. Her reflected face looked impassively back at her. She had been a pretty child but that had been many years ago. She was thirty-five now and no-one would mistake her age. Her forehead was lined, around her mouth were the downward lines of discontent. Her pale skin was papery and dry, around her dark eyes were slight brown shadows. She suffered from delicate health, inherited from her mother who had died of consumption. Her great beauty was her dark hair which showed no grey. She looked what she had been only yesterday – a lady clinging on to fragile social status, of uncertain health, unmarried, impoverished, and ageing fast.

But now it was all changed. Frances smiled slightly and picked up her silver-backed hairbrush. She was a married woman now and an entirely new life was opening up before her. It seemed like a hard choice – matrimony at thirty-five – when many women were matrons already with a family around them. But anything was better than being a governess in a state of genteel servitude. Anything was better than watching her place move inexorably down the dining table until one day she would be asked to dine in the nursery with the children, and disappear from polite society altogether. It had been a hard choice, but in the end no choice at all.

Frances started to plait her hair in a thick hank, ready for bed. The wedding dinner had been better than she could have hoped. Lord Scott had been as kind as always, although his cold unfriendly wife had cast a cool shadow over the proceedings. Frances had dreaded that Josiah would be rowdy and jolly but the evening had been as dignified as a funeral. Only Sarah and Josiah represented the Cole family so Frances's other great fear – that there would be dozens of vulgar relations emerging from the Bristol woodwork – was stilled. The dinner had been well cooked, a little lavish for just the five of them. The wines – as you would expect in Bristol – had been excellent.

Frances had sat at the foot of the table in the tiny airless parlour and smiled without flinching. Everyone at the table knew that marriage to such a man as Josiah was not her first choice. Everyone at the table knew that she had no choice. The coldness in her heart was reflected in the cool serenity of her face.

Her calm had been threatened only once. When Lord Scott took her hand on leaving he had whispered to her: 'God bless you my dear, it's the best thing you could have done ... considering.' This tactful acknowledgement that she was orphaned and penniless sent a shiver through her. 'I will pray it goes well for you,' he said.

There would be nothing he could do for her if it did not. Frances was owned by Josiah, body and soul. She had promised to obey him till death.

'But it will go well for me,' she whispered. She tied her nightcap under her chin and crossed the cold floorboards to the bed. She had wept the night her father died. She had wept the first night that she had slept in a strange house, far from the country vicarage, and far below the genteel status of the vicar's only daughter. She had raged then against the unfairness of a life in which a woman is dependent completely on a man. A woman who lacks a father must find a husband. Frances had not married when she should have done, in the brief bloom of her youth. She had aimed too high and her father had been too proud. He had not understood that a man, any man at all, was better than spinster hardship. Her father's death abandoned Frances to loneliness and to poverty and to the unending slights of the life of a governess.

She got into the broad bed, and rested her head on the plain linen pillow. She would not cry tonight. She was a wife and she had a dinner table of her own, even though it was only a little table and pushed to one side in a tiny parlour. The rest of her life would be spent accommodating her desires to her husband's fortune. If Josiah rose in the world she would rise with him; if he did not she must bear it with patience and be glad to have found such a haven as this little house. She pulled the covers over her shoulders as if the coldness in her spirit had chilled her very skin, despite the sultry night air. She felt as if tears or feelings would never touch her again. She was heartbroken and exhausted by heartbreak; and she mistook it for the calmness of old age.

There was a tap on the door between Josiah's room and her own and her husband came in, carrying his candle. He was wearing a plain linen nightshirt. He set the candle down on the bedside table and stood, looking at her. He was clearly at a loss.

'I hope you enjoyed the dinner,' he said awkwardly.

Frances nodded. 'Thank you,' she said in her cool level voice.

Josiah's feet in Moroccan leather slippers shuffled on the wooden floor. He looked intensely uncomfortable. 'The wines were good,' he volunteered.

Frances nodded.

There was silence. Frances realised that Josiah was painfully embarrassed. Neither of them knew how a husband claimed his marital rights. Neither of them knew how a wife consented. Her dry little cough rose up in her throat and she cleared her throat.

'It's quite late now,' Josiah remarked.

Frances turned back the covers. 'Will you come to bed, husband?' she asked, as coldly civil as if she were offering him a dish of tea.

Josiah flushed scarlet with relief. 'Thank you,' he said. He stepped out of his slippers and slid into bed beside her. They lay side by side for a moment, taking care not to touch each other, then Josiah leaned over and blew out both candles. Under cover of the sudden darkness he reared on top of Frances and pulled her nightdress out of his way. Frances lay still underneath him with her eyes closed and her teeth gritted. It was a duty which had to be done. Josiah fumbled awkwardly for a few moments and then he exclaimed in a whisper and moved away.

45

'It's no good,' he said shortly. 'I have drunk too much wine.'

Frances opened her eyes. She could see only the silhouette of his profile. She did not know what she was supposed to do.

'It does not matter,' he said, consoling himself rather than her. 'It will come right in time. There is no need for us to hurry. After all, we neither of us married for desire.'

There was a long, rather chilling silence. 'No,' Frances acknowledged. 'Neither of us did.'

'Good morning, ma'am,' a voice said, and the curtains rattled on the brass rail as the maid drew them back and tied them to the bed posts.

Frances stirred and opened her eyes. The maid who had waited at the dinner table last night was standing before her with a small silver tray bearing a jug of hot chocolate and a warm pastry. Frances sat up and received the tray on her knees.

'Thank you.'

The maid dipped a curtsey.

'Master said to tell you that he is gone out early,' she said. 'But Miss Cole expects you in the parlour as soon as you are dressed. She is there already.'

Frances nodded. She waited for the maid to leave the room and then bolted the food and gulped down the hot chocolate. She sprang from the bed and went over to the ewer of water to wash her face. Then she paused, remembering her new status. She was no longer the governess who had to hurry downstairs for fear of keeping the mistress waiting. Frances smiled at the thought and poured water into the bowl. She washed her face and patted it dry, enjoying the sense of leisure. Her clothes for the morning were laid out on the heavy wooden chest: a linen shift, a morning dress in white muslin, embroidered at the hem, with a frivolous silk apron to denote Frances's intention of domestic work.

The dress was new. Lady Scott had given Frances whole bolts of fabric when the marriage contract was signed. Her entire wardrobe had been renovated and improved with gifts from her cousins and her aunt. Frances knew it was the last thing Lady Scott would ever do for her and she accepted the old gowns and yards of silk with nothing more than polite gratitude. Her husband would have to provide for her new clothes, and there was an allowance of pin money laid down in the marriage contract. Frances would never again darn and re-darn her silk stockings.

She slipped on the shift and turned as there was a tap on the door and the maid came in again. Frances sat at the dressing table and brushed her hair in steady sweeps of the silver-backed brushes, and the maid helped her plait it into two braids and pin them up on her head with a pretty scrap of lace for a cap. The woman was slow and not very skilful. She dropped the hairbrush.

'I am sorry, Mrs Cole,' she said awkwardly. 'I don't usually work as a lady's maid.'

'Does Miss Cole have her own maid?'

'She dresses herself.'

Frances hid her surprise. She had never heard of a lady dressing herself, she wondered how Sarah managed with the small covered buttons at the back of a gown. Even as a governess Frances had borrowed a maid to do her hair and help with the fastenings. For the first time Frances had a glimpse of her tumble in status. The maid shook out the morning dress and held it for Frances to put on, fastening the two dozen mother-of-pearl buttons up the back of the dress, and tied the ribbon of the apron. Lastly she set out the little insubstantial slippers of pink silk.

'Shall I show you to the parlour, ma'am?'

'Yes,' Frances said.

47

She followed the woman down the stairs. It was a dreadfully dark poky house, she thought, sandwiched between one large warehouse and another, with its front door giving directly on to the dock and its back door into a yard overhung by the glowering red sandstone cliff. The cliff was part of the building; the warehouse carved into its overhanging walls. The storerooms extended into caves deep inside it, running back for miles in a red sandstone labyrinth.

It was no house for a lady. It was crashingly noisy with the rolling of barrels on the cobbles of the quay. Costers and hawkers shrieked their wares, screaming to make themselves heard over the bawled orders on the unloading ships. Frances did not know if Josiah had a carriage and she did not know if she would be allowed to walk along the quayside outside her front door without endangering her reputation. She had a fine line to tread as the niece of a lord but the wife of a man whose house was no larger than a shop.

Bristol was not a genteel city; it was all port and no town, quaysides and no pavements. Every other street towards the town centre was a bridge with a river running beneath it. The town centre itself was crammed on the banks of the river with masts of sailing ships overtopping the chimneys, and the prows of the boats almost knocking on the doors. When the tide was full the boats rocked and bobbed and sailors in the rigging could see into bedroom windows and shout bawdy comments at the housemaids. When the tide was out the ships were dumped on the stinking mud of the harbour bottom and the garbage from the boats and the sewage from the town gurgled sluggishly around them.

The maid paused before the dark wooden parlour door, tapped lightly and stood aside. Frances turned the door handle and went in. Sarah Cole rose from her seat at the table, her face unsmiling under a plain morning cap.

'No need to knock,' she said coldly. 'You are the mistress here now.' She put her hand on a great ring of keys on the

48

table. 'These are the household keys. My brother has told me to offer them to you, if you wish to take the housekeeping into your own hands.'

Frances hesitated, and Sarah Cole gestured to an ominous pile of dark-backed ledgers. 'Also the housekeeping books,' she went on. 'I think you will find them in order. I present them to my brother once a month for his signature. That will now be your task.'

'Gracious,' said Frances weakly.

The stern face of the older woman gleamed with pride. 'It has been my life's work to make this house run as smoothly as our trading company. The company books are no better than the household ones. I do them both.'

'He must be very grateful to you,' Frances said tentatively.

Miss Cole's face was stern. 'There is no reason why he should be,' she replied. 'I was doing my duty and protecting my fortune, as I trust you will do. It was my task to run the business and the housekeeping, for both my brother and for my Papa, for all these years ever since Mama died. Now it is my duty to hand the housekeeping accounts over to you.'

Frances went to the table and opened a ledger at random. It was written in perfect copperplate script:

'To Mr Sykes, butcher ... £3. 4s. 6d.' Beneath it was another entry, and another and another for page after page.

Frances turned the pages. They fluttered with the petty cash of many years. 'I have never done accounts,' she confessed. 'In my father's house it was done by the cook. I merely checked the totals at the end of each month. I am afraid I don't know how to do them.'

Miss Cole raised an eyebrow. 'You must have been badly cheated,' she said.

'Oh, no! Cook had been with us since I was a baby. She was devoted to my father and to me. She would not have cheated us. She was like one of the family.'

Miss Cole shrugged. 'I do not know about grand houses,'

she said. 'I am a trader's sister and a trader's daughter. I do not have servants who are one of the family. I check their work and if I see an error then I sack them.'

'It was hardly a grand house. It was a little country vicarage on Lord Scott's estate.'

'I was born in a collier's cottage,' Miss Cole said sharply. 'I think your country vicarage would seem very grand to me.'

Frances paused. This woman would be her daily companion; when they moved house she would move too. They would live together, they would meet every day for the rest of their lives. She forced herself to smile. 'There is much I do not know about your life and your business,' she said. 'I hope you will teach me, Miss Cole, and help me to fulfil my side of the bargain and be a good wife to your brother.'

The woman's face was stern. 'I do not know what bargain you have made. I do not know why he wanted a wife, and such a wife as you.'

Frances blinked at the woman's abrupt honesty. 'Well, this is frank speaking indeed!'

Sarah nodded. 'I speak as I find. I am a simple trader's daughter.'

'You did not wish him to marry?' Frances ventured.

'Why should I? We have lived together and worked side by side on the company for years. We have made it grow from one ship to a fleet of three. We have trebled our business and our profits. And now Josiah wants a town house, and a smart lady for his wife. But who is to pay for this? Are we to spend our money on houses rather than ships? What return will they make? What return will you make?'

Frances snatched a little breath. She could feel her heart pounding with embarrassment at the other's plain speaking. 'Really . . . Miss Cole . . .'

'You asked and I answered you,' the woman said stubbornly.

Frances put her hand to her throat. 'I hope you will not be my enemy,' she whispered.

Sarah Cole looked at Frances's white face and shrugged. 'What would be the sense in that?' she said. 'It is a business arrangement, after all. But you should not try to manage my account books if you do not understand them.'

'Would you prefer to do them?' Frances asked. 'Until I have learned how things are to be done? Would you prefer to go on as you have been, and I will watch you and study your ways?'

'I think that would be best if it is your wish.'

'I have no desire to push you from your place,' Frances said hastily. 'Nor cause any quarrel in this house.'

'You don't look the quarrelsome type,' Sarah said with grim humour.

Frances suddenly flushed as she smiled. 'Indeed I am not! I cannot bear quarrels and people shouting.'

Sarah nodded. 'I see. You suffer from sensibility.'

Frances, who had never before heard it described as a disability, gave a shaky little laugh. 'It is how I was brought up,' she said.

'Well, I am not a lady, and I thank God for it,' Sarah said. 'But I will try to make allowances for you. You have nothing to fear from me. Now I will show you around the house,' she continued, rising to her feet. 'You have seen only this parlour and your bedroom so far.'

There was not much to see. The parlour was on the first floor. It ran the length of the house, overlooking the quay at the front and overshadowed by the cliff at the back. There was a small dining table and six hard chairs where Miss Cole worked during the day and where breakfast was served at mid-morning, dinner at mid-afternoon, and supper in the evening. There was a fireplace with two straight-backed chairs on either side. There was Miss Cole's workbox. The walls were washed with lime, empty of any pictures or

51

ornament and the floorboards were plain waxed wood, with a thin hearthrug before the fire.

Josiah's office, the next room, was even plainer. It also overlooked the quay but it did not even have curtains at the windows, just forbidding black-painted shutters. His desk was set before the window to the left of the fireplace, a big wooden captain's chair before it. There was a chair by the fire and a small table beside it. There were three maps hanging on the walls. One showed the south coast of England, one the west coast of Africa, little more than a wriggling coastline and a completely empty interior, and the third was a navigation chart of the shoals and currents around the islands of the West Indies. Nothing else. Frances, looking in through the door of the spartan room, wondered what the Coles did for amusement, where they entertained their friends. There was nothing in either room to indicate anything but a life dedicated to work.

Miss Cole gave a longing glance out of the window before she turned away. On the quayside immediately below, the Coles' ship the *Rose* was unloading. Sarah Cole would rather have been entering profits into the ledger.

On the floor above the parlour were the bedrooms. Josiah and Miss Cole had bedrooms facing the dock; Frances's room was quieter, at the back, sheltered by the red sandstone cliff. If she opened her window and leaned out she could look down to the cobbled backyard outside the kitchen door, hemmed in by high warehouse walls, and beyond them, the twisting little streets which ran from the dockside up to the church on the peak of the hill: St Mary Redclift. On her left was the towering height of a lead-shot tower. To her right, overtopping the church spire, was the fat kiln-shaped chimney of the glassworks. All day there was ceaseless noise: the crash of the metalworks, and the roar and rattle of the furnaces. The sour toxic smell of lead haunted the Backs.

Above this floor was the attic bedroom for the servants

and the linen and storeroom. Miss Cole showed Frances the bare poverty of the rooms with quiet pride and then led the way down the stairs to the front door and hall.

The hall was hopelessly dark, the only light seeping through a grimy fanlight over the front door. At the end of the corridor at the back of the house was the door to the kitchen. They could hear someone pounding dough on a board and singing softly. In all the shaded, sombre house, it was the first happy sound.

At the sound of Miss Cole's footstep the singing stopped abruptly, and the pounding of the dough became louder and faster.

Sarah Cole opened the door to the kitchen and ushered Frances in. 'This is your new mistress, Mrs Cole,' she said abruptly, surveying the kitchen. The cook – floured to the elbows – bobbed a curtsey, and the upstairs maid, Brown, rose from the table where she had been polishing silver and glasses. A little hunchbacked girl came in from the backyard wiping her hands on a hessian apron and dipped a curtsey, staring at Frances. Frances smiled impartially at them all.

'The cook is Mrs Allen. The maid is Brown. Mrs Allen discusses the menus with me every week and shows me the housekeeping books.' Sarah shot a sideways glance at Frances. 'You should be there when we meet. I take it that Monday afternoon will still be convenient?'

'Perfectly,' Frances said politely.

The little scullery maid had not even been named to Frances.

'You can get on with your work,' Miss Cole ordered them brusquely and led the way from the kitchen, through the poky little hall and up the stairs to the parlour.

She seated herself at the table and drew one of the ledgers towards her. She took up a pen. Frances, rather at a loss, seated herself on the narrow windowseat and looked down on the quay.

53

The tide was in and the foul smell of the mud had lessened. The sunshine sparkled on the water of the dock and quicksilver water lights danced on the ceiling of the parlour. The quayside was crowded with people selling, loading and unloading ships, hawking goods, mending ropes, and caulking the decks of outbound ships with great steaming barrels of stinking tar. The Coles' own ship, the *Rose*, was still unloading her goods, the great round barrels of rum and sugar were piled on the quayside. The intense stink of a ship of the Trade wafted up to Frances and even penetrated the house: sugar, sewage, and pain. As she watched, she saw Josiah slap one of the barrels for emphasis and then spit on his palm and shake hands on a deal with another man.

Sarah's pen scratched on the paper. The room was stuffy and hot, the windows closed tight against the smell and noise of the quayside.

'I should like to go out,' Frances said after a while. 'I should like to walk around and see the city.'

Miss Cole lifted her head, her finger on the page to keep her place. 'Brown will have to go with you. You cannot walk on the quayside alone.'

Frances nodded and rose to her feet. 'Very well.'

Sarah shook her head, not taking her eyes from the book. 'Brown is working in the house now. You will have to wait until afternoon. You can walk then.'

There was a short silence.

'I see Mr Cole down there on the quayside,' Frances said. 'May I go down to him?'

Sarah dragged her attention from her work again. 'He is engaged in business. He would have no time for you, and the men he is dealing with are not those he would wish you to meet. They are not gentlemen. You will have to be patient. You are no longer a lady of leisure,' Miss Cole volunteered spitefully. 'You cannot act on whim.'

54

'No,' said Frances, turning her attention back to the quay-side, 'I see that I cannot.'

Most of the sailors had been paid off and had left the ship but the captain and one other man, his hair tied back in a greasy little plait, were watching the sailmakers pulling the ragged canvas out of the lockers and spreading it on the dockside. Josiah inspected the worn sails and nodded his agreement as the sailmakers bundled it on a sledge, took up the ropes and started to tow it away. Frances watched him from her vantage point above him, a curiously foreshortened view as if he were not a powerful man in a man's world, but a little man, struggling to cope.

'It is strange to see your money being made,' she remarked thoughtlessly and then flushed with embarrassment. 'I beg your pardon! I spoke without thinking.'

'It is not strange to me,' Miss Cole said. She did not take offence as Frances had feared. 'I have lived in this house most of my life. I have waited for our ships to come in and I have known what profit or loss they made on every voyage. Since I was a child of nine I have cared for nothing else. That one you see there, the *Rose*, has done well for us.'

'What a pretty name,' Frances said.

Miss Cole showed her thin smile. 'All our ships have flower names since our first one, a captured French merchant ship called *Marguerite*,' she said. 'That means *Daisy* in French, you know. We have three ships: the *Rose* which you see here, the *Daisy* which should be at the West Indies, and the *Lily* which was in port a few months ago and should be loading off Africa, God willing.'

'You say that they "should be" . . . do you not know where they are?'

'How should I know? I know when they set sail and I know when they are due, but between their destination and their home port is the most vast and dangerous ocean. We have to wait. The largest part of being a merchant in the Atlantic

Trade is waiting, and keeping your counsel while you wait.'

'Have you ever sailed with them?'

'No-one of any sense would sail to Africa,' Miss Cole replied. 'It is a death-trap.'

'Do you sail nowhere else?'

Miss Cole turned from the window and went back to her work. 'There is nowhere else,' she said irritably. 'What other trade is to be had?'

'I don't know,' Frances said foolishly. 'I thought perhaps you might sail to India, or to China.'

'This is Bristol,' Miss Cole explained patiently, as one might speak to a child. 'This is the heart of the sugar trade. We trade to the West Indies and to the Americas. It is on this Trade that my father made his fortune and on this Trade that we will make ours.'

'Only sugar?'

'There is no more profitable business,' Miss Cole said firmly. 'The Trade is supreme.'

'But so uncertain . . .'

'We trust in our abilities,' Sarah said piously. 'And we are all of us in the merciful hands of God.'

They did not know themselves to be in the merciful hands of God. They seemed very far from any god. They lay very close together, stacked side by side like logs in a woodpile. When the ship rolled they rolled hard one way, bumping and bruising, and then when it pitched back, they rolled again. When the ship reared up over a massive wave and crashed down it was as if they had been packed on their naked backs in a rough wooden case and dropped, over and over again. Within a day they were bruised from the planking, within a week the skin was rubbed away. When the sea was heavy the water poured in through the gratings on the deck into the hold where they lay, and the slop buckets overturned and sewage washed around them. They were not fed during bad weather and those that were not vomiting from seasickness or already dying from typhus went hungry. When the sea was calm they were ordered up on deck, staggering under the bright uncaring sky, and made to wash and dry themselves, sharing a soiled piece of cloth. A man watched them rinse out their mouths with vinegar and water and spit through the netting into the huge waves which rolled unstoppably towards the little ship, coming from the far horizon, as high as hills. It was a nightmare, a long unbelievable nightmare, which got worse and worse every day.

At first Mehuru had thought that the crew were ghosts, that he had died at sight of the ship and that this was some long punitive afterlife. The crew's skin was so pallid and their eyes were empty of colour or warmth. He could not at first accept their dreadful ugliness. They did not look like men and they did not act like men. They behaved as if they were a different species from Mehuru, from Siko, from the two hundred men they had on board. They prodded at them with sticks, they whipped them with casual cruelty. They never looked in their faces, they never met their eyes. There was something so cold and unnatural in their indifference that Mehuru felt his very soul wither and shrink from them. These could not be men. No man could treat another man with such chilling indifference.

The Snake god's counsel was bleak on the voyage and the farther he went from his home, the fainter and fainter grew the voice until Mehuru had to face the dreadful prospect of losing his guide. He had no magic to bring him back, the gods go where they will, and Mehuru could make no offering. He had no pet snake to feed, he had no smoke to please the god, or bones for it to play with. All he could do was dream that he was making pleasures for the god and give him the thoughts of his mind. So he lay in the pitching blackness with his back rubbed raw against the sweating planks of the hold, the filth of the bilges washing around him, and made in his mind a perfect flower, a flower from the hibiscus bush, bright scarlet, frilled as silk. Then he pictured a jewelled snake and brought the flower to the snake in a bowl of white clay studded with tiny blue stones.

The three images were almost too much for him: the brilliant snake, the perfect flower, and the white bowl with the blue pattern. In the sodden sweaty torture of the black hold with people dying around him, Mehuru shut his eyes and summoned three perfect forms: god in a flower, god in an animal, and god in a man, guiding his hands to work with clay and with little blue stones.

There was no way to measure time in the darkness. Mehuru woke sometimes and thought perhaps he had died and that the Yoruban belief that you stay near to the people you loved, watching over them, was all wrong. The afterlife was a perpetual rolling and pitching, heat and smell, and the horror of being pushed against sickly men, unable to help them, and no emotion but hatred for their rough bumping against you, and hunger for their share of food.

Sometimes the sailors opened the hatches and bawled down into the darkness for the captives to come out. The sunlight hurt their eyes but they had to stand on deck and one of the sailors would beat a drum while another cracked a whip. Mehuru looked at them in utter wonder. The sailors wanted them to dance. As obedient as idiot children, with the guns all around them and the whips cracking out the time, they shuffled and hopped while others were ordered to clean out the hold and throw the dead and dying over the side. Mehuru sank deep inside his mind while his body hopped and pranced.

If the dancing were to keep them healthy Mehuru could not think why they were fed so poorly. If their jailers wanted them fit, Mehuru could not think why they let so many sicken for lack of water in the unbearable heat of the hold. They lowered buckets filled with stale warm water and bad yams which crawled with insects. Never enough water, never enough food. They had loaded about two hundred men and elsewhere in the ship they were keeping women and little children, perhaps another hundred of them. On Mehuru's shelf alone, five had already died. One had flung himself over the side, two had sickened, one had been whipped too hard and never came back to the hold and the last one had sealed his lips from food and water and had watched the others eat every day while he starved himself to death. Mehuru's imagination could not stretch to the scale of it. It never occurred to him that more than three hundred of them had been shipped but that only two hundred and forty or so were expected to survive. It was not necessary that they should all survive. It was a process so large as to be industrial. Mehuru had no concept that his life could be written off as wastage.

He started to dread the arrival of the bucket of food for only then, when they were ordered to gather around and share ten to a bucket, eating with their dirty hands, could he see how many of them were sickening to death. They were the ones who did not struggle and claw at each other to get to the food. Mehuru set himself the task of fighting for his share and then giving half of it to the neighbour on his right. He did it as an exercise, a discipline, not an act of love. He thought he would never love anyone, ever again.

When he had eaten, and the slowly dying man beside him had mumbled on his slabber porridge, Mehuru would shut his eyes and try to build a picture of a perfect tiny snake as an offering for the god.

He knew that his mind was going when the snake became very bright and easy to find. The snake became more important than the ship, more vivid than the clammy touch of the dying man beside him. The snake opened his mouth and sang to him as Mehuru felt his skin grow wet with sweat and his mind shift and slide away from the darkness. He knew he should stay in his waking mind and guard Siko; but he had not seen Siko, except for a glimpse on deck, since they had set sail. He knew he had failed in his duty to him. He knew he was guilty of a mortal sin in taking the boy into danger. But he could not keep himself alert, he could not stay on guard. As they went farther and farther west Mehuru sank into a deep deathly indifference.

He could not tell how long they had been sailing, but when they came on deck to dance there were more limp bodies thrown overboard, and there were fewer who could dance each time. Mehuru looked around idly for the children, the little ones who had been loaded on the ship as round as berries and as dark and shiny as the sacred wood of the iroko tree. They were thinner and many of them were sick, but worst of all was the way the bright life was draining from them. They no longer cried like desperate fledglings for their mothers, they were lost children. Whether they lived or died there would be a gap in their spirits which nothing would ever replace. How would they respect their fathers, and how love children of their own, if their most powerful memory was being abandoned to despair?

He thought that about forty had died, and two crewmen as well, when the sound of the ship changed one night. Then came urgent noises of running on the deck overhead, and abrupt commands and anxious shouts and then the great rolling yaw of the ship ceased, ceased at last, and he heard the roar as the anchor chain sped out through the housing and the ship thrust a claw into the ocean bed and dragged herself to a standstill. They were brought up on deck as if to be ready for dancing, but then they were manacled, arms to legs, and chained from one neck to another. The captain, even whiter than before and thinner from the voyage, looked at each shivering black man or woman or little child before he waved them into the line and had them locked on to the chain. A few, a very few, he waved to one side under guard of a sailor who held a musket easily at their heads. Mehuru thought of the unreliability of the muskets on sale in Africa and thought it might be worth taking the chance and rushing the man. But when he looked around to see where he might run he felt sicker than he had felt in the whole long voyage. For they were not off the coast of Africa any more. Wherever they had come to, it was a land he had never seen before.

The last of his courage went out of him then and when the captain waved him to the little group he went as weakly as the children who were already chosen. The last time he saw Siko was when the boy hobbled obediently to the long chain and bowed his neck to the collar. Mehuru tried to find a voice to call to him, to wish him well, to promise to return to find him if he possibly could. He was dumb. Siko looked at him, a long look of reproach and despair, and Mehuru could find no words at all. He dropped his gaze and turned away and when they were ordered back down into the hold he went without looking back. When they chained him back on a strangely empty shelf he held his hands out for the manacles on his wrists like a foolish trusting child.

A great longing for his home, so painful that he thought he would die of it, sickened him to his very core. He lay in the darkness, refusing to open his eyes, refusing to take food. The little group was kept together in the hold, twenty of them. Two other men manacled with leg-irons like himself chained on the shelf, and five women with neck-irons and long chains so that they could move more freely, but not reach the men. The smallest children were allowed to go free; two of them could barely walk. The other children aged from four years to adolescence wore light chains from wrist to wrist and ankle to ankle.

One of the women called to Mehuru to eat, but he turned his head from her and closed his eyes. The smallest toddler struggled through the slurry which washed around the floor to bring him a bowl. Mehuru saw fresh fruit – the first he had seen in the long two months of the voyage – but he did not allow himself desire. He would not eat. He had been robbed of his home, he had been robbed of his people. He had been robbed of his servant and robbed of his duty to provide for him. He had been robbed of his life. He would live no more.

Days passed, and still the ship did not sail. They were ordered on deck and made to build a little shelter against the sun. They were kept there like hens in a pen, lying on straw. They laboured below to clean out the mess of two hundred men, stalled like animals for nearly sixty days. They baled out the excrement and the filth and then the master of the ship went below with his handkerchief over his face and lit pastilles of camphor which smoked all day and all night and still could not drown the stench.

Mehuru would not speak. He ate a little rice every day and drank some of the fresh sweet water. When the women asked his name or the men touched his hand in companionship and shared mourning he turned his head away. Nothing should tie him to life.

The sailors lived on board and worked during the day, loading the ship and making it ready for another voyage. They had long idle periods when they came and took the women away. The women came back bruised and sometimes bloodstained, with their heads in their hands. Mehuru, chained hand and foot, turned his head away from the horror in their faces.

One woman did not come back at all, and after that the sailors were forbidden to touch them. The little children missed her, she had played with them and fed them and sung them songs. Without her they were a little more lost. One little girl sat beside Mehuru for the greater part of every day and banged her head gently against the deck. Mehuru lay with his eyes shut, the deck echoing beneath his head like a drum to the steady thud of the little girl's head against the planks.

62

The master came back on board and the ship was ready to sail, only half-loaded with large kegs of sugar and rum. The little girl disappeared, they took her away one day, but still Mehuru could hear the thud thud thud of her head on wood. It beat like a heart, it drummed like an accusation.

He closed his eyes and refused to eat rice. He drank only water. He felt himself floating away. There was none of the right things that an obalawa should have around him, and he could not warn his fathers that he would need their help in crossing over. He thought his tree that held his spirit had bent in some storm and was perhaps breaking, and he prayed for it to fall so that his spirit might flow out of it and he might die.

Mehuru readied himself to join the ones who had to die sitting down with their eyes staring out into the darkness. He feared he would not find his fathers, dying thus. Only the Snake god had seen him with his huge shiny eyes and would know where his son had been stolen far away across the great seas.

Chapter Four

～⁓⁓⁄

Josiah came into his house for a pint of porter and a slice of pie at midday and Frances was waiting for him at the top of the stairs.

'I should like to go out for a walk,' she said. 'But Brown cannot escort me in the mornings.'

Josiah was absorbed in business, a missing hogshead of tobacco – a great round barrel packed with whole sweet-smelling dried leaves – and he looked at her as if she were an interruption, a nuisance. 'I meant to get you a carriage,' he said absently. 'You cannot walk along the dockside.'

'So I understand,' Frances said. 'But I wish to go out.'

He sighed, his mind still on the *Rose* and the question of missing cargo. 'Perhaps we can hire a carriage.'

'Today?'

'I am very busy,' he replied. 'And troubled over this ship. There is an entire hogshead of tobacco unaccounted for, and the captain can give me no satisfactory explanation. I shall have to pay Excise tax on it as if I had it safe in my bond, as well as carrying the loss.'

'I am sorry to hear that,' Frances said politely. 'Where would I hire a carriage?'

Josiah broke off with a sudden short bark of laughter. 'You are persistent, Mrs Cole!'

Frances flushed at his use of her new name. 'I am sorry,' she said. 'At home I always walked in the gardens in the

64

morning. My health is not very strong, as you know, and the day is fine and I wanted to go out.'

'No, it is I who am at fault. I have not provided for you as I should have done,' Josiah apologised. 'I will hire a carriage for you myself and I will drive with you this afternoon and show you the sights you should see.'

'If it is no trouble . . .'

'It is an interruption to my work,' he said frankly. 'But I should have provided you with some amusement. Can you not do sewing or painting or something of that nature?'

'Not all day.'

'No, I suppose not.' Josiah thought for a moment, and then nodded at her and headed towards his office.

'At what time shall I be ready for the carriage?' Frances called after him.

'At two,' he said. 'Tell Brown to go around to the coachyard and hire a coach, a landau or something open.' He nodded to her again and shut the door firmly in her face. Frances waited a moment and then went back to the parlour.

Miss Cole's place was empty, her ledger open at the accounts of the *Rose*. Frances leaned over the chair and saw the meticulous march of figures down the page, showing the purchase of petty goods for small sums. Sixpence for gold lace, threepence each for small knives, fourpence each for brass pots. She shrugged. She could not imagine how Miss Cole could bear to spend the day on these trifling sums, nor what difference they made to an enterprise of any size. She did not know what a trading ship sailing to the Sugar Islands would want with gold lace or small knives. Frances returned to her seat in the window and waited for two o'clock.

The coach was prompt; it was standing at the door as Frances came down the stairs wearing a large picture hat crowned with two fat feathers. She had changed into a walking dress: a greatcoat dress with a wide collar and caped sleeves.

65

Mindful of the plainness of Sarah's attire, Frances was rather relieved to find only Josiah waiting for her at the door, and Sarah shut up in the parlour.

'I was afraid you would have forgotten,' she said. 'Did you find your tobacco?'

'The planter in Jamaica cheated us, or made a mistake,' Josiah answered. 'And the captain had it wrong on the cargo manifest. They were loading in a hurry. I had ordered him to make haste, it was the last of the new crop, and this is what comes of it.'

'I am sorry to hear it,' Frances said uncertainly. She felt she should condole with him, as one would to a man who has suffered a loss. But her training to avoid the vulgar topic of money was too powerful.

'I shall write to the planter and send the letter by *Rose* when she sails,' Josiah decided. 'Within fourteen or fifteen months she will be back in port again and it should be set right.'

'Gracious,' Frances said.

'And I will carry the loss for the whole of that time,' he said irritably. 'Just as I have to offer credit to the planters for two years at a time.' He looked at her and his frown cleared. 'This means nothing to you. Let me take you for a drive.' He handed her up the little step into the carriage. Frances unfurled her parasol against the bright summer sunshine and tipped the shade over her face.

'Go to Queens Square first,' Josiah ordered the driver. 'This is where I propose we should buy a house,' he explained to Frances. 'We have to go round through the old town, but pay no attention to the dirt and the noise. Queens Square is very smart indeed.'

The carriage moved forward, jolting on the cobbles, sailors and dockers begrudgingly giving it room. The street sellers eyed Frances's fine clothes and one girl, hawking watercress from a tray, turned her head and spat on the ground.

They drove down the Back Lane, the overhang of the houses above their heads so close that the streets were in permanent twilight, in a fog of foul air. The sun shone in a brilliant stripe down the centre of the street but the houses and the foul-smelling middens were in dank shade. Great wooden beams over their heads braced apart the houses on opposite sides of the street, which looked as if they were ready to topple together. The broad gutter in the centre of the road was an open drain, thick with slops, mud and garbage, stinking in the heat, breeding swarms of fruit flies. People swore as the carriage lurched past, splashing them with slurry. The horses scrabbled to find their footing on the greasy stones and the carriage bumped and dipped; the road was almost impassable. Frances was afraid that the horses would founder. She gripped her parasol a little tighter and held one gloved hand to her face, trying to block out the evil stink of the lane.

Every doorway, every archway was an entrance to a workshop. There were woodcarvers and sempstresses, there were coopers and workers of metal. There was a wigmaker who also drew teeth, there was a small dingy apothecary shop doing a roaring trade in laudanum and neat opium. Every other house seemed to be a ginshop, every third house was a brothel. It was a mediaeval city of timbered overhanging houses suddenly crowded to bursting point with small dangerous industries.

Frances, who had spent all but two of her thirty-five years in the country vicarage, stared in horror from one ominously dark doorway to another. The white-faced occupants stared back at her, and someone shouted an insult at the carriage and threw a handful of mud.

'It is rough,' Josiah conceded. 'Bristol is a city of labour, my dear, not leisure.'

'How can people bear it?'

He gave a snort of laughter. 'This is a prosperous street,

my dear. If I showed you the colliers at Bedminster *then* you would see something to shock you. They live like animals in their own filth and no person of any wealth goes near them. They live in a world of their own, without parson or magistrates – totally outside society, totally without law.'

Towering on the hill above them, in abrupt contrast to the clutter of roofs below it, was the ornate highly decorated church of St Mary Redclift at the head of a soaring flight of stone steps. But they turned away from the spire and back towards the city, passing over the bridge.

'It would have been quicker to go across the river by the ferryboat,' Josiah explained. 'Queens Square is directly opposite my dock. When we have our house I will take a boat over every day. The lad will row me over for a ha'penny each way.'

'I am sure these streets cannot be healthy,' Frances said. She tried to keep the dismay from her voice.

'They are pestilential, madam!' Josiah exclaimed. 'If you are not killed by some fool setting fire to your house, or felled by someone dropping something on you, or poisoned by some manufactory, you will be destroyed by cholera or typhoid or both. The foul water and the summer sun are a fatal combination.'

'I wonder that your family chose to live here,' Frances said faintly.

Josiah laughed shortly. 'We did not choose! We were not in a position to choose! We bought what we could, where we could. My father bought the warehouse and dockside from his profits as a privateer and that was where we lived. We were glad enough to have a business to run and premises to call our own.'

'He was a privateer?'

Josiah nodded and then laughed abruptly at her shocked face. 'Don't look so aghast, Mrs Cole, he was a privateer, not a pirate! He had a letter from the Crown licensing him to attack French shipping. He took out his one leaky old boat and captured a French brig. That was our first chance. She was called the *Marguerite*. We paid our dues to the Crown and kept her and traded with her. It was the founding of our fortunes, the founding of our trading line. When she sank we called our next boat *Daisy* after her.'

Frances nodded. The carriage rolled on to a wooden bridge. Looking down, she saw the water rich with waste. Litter, garbage, excrement, and all the flotsam and jetsam of a busy port bobbed around the pillars of the bridge on the rising tide. The carriage bumped along the quay on the northern side of the river and then the road ahead opened out with sudden surprising grace. There was an avenue of young plane trees ahead, their broad leaves still fresh. There was a smooth green lawn in the centre of the square, there was a proud statue of a man on a galloping horse. The stink from the river was less strong, and the noise of the Backs was left behind them.

'Queens Square,' said Josiah with satisfaction. 'As good as any Crescent in Bath, eh?'

He was exaggerating, it was not as good as Bath. It lacked the easy regularity of those fine terraces, it lacked their confident scale. Part of the square was built in the golden stone of Bath but part of it was red brick, and the profile of the roofs and the detail on the houses was idiosyncratic – each house an individual. But it was a well-proportioned square lined with young trees, divided into four by long avenues running north to south and east to west. At the centre of the square the paths crossed and the statue made a handsome centrepiece. The houses were new; some looked like London houses in smart red brick with pointings of white mortar and corners of white stone. At the east end was an elegant large building flanked by two wings in thick yellow stone: the Custom House.

The carriage drew up before the first house in the southwest corner, one of the biggest and most imposing in the square. 'This is where we shall live,' Josiah announced. 'This is where I have been aiming for years.'

Frances looked at him in surprise. She had never before heard of a man desiring anything more than to stay in the position to which he had been called. She had heard men complain of the decline of manners; but never to seek change. Her father had preached that it was God's will for a man to remain where he was born, a good Christian stayed where God had been pleased to put him. Josiah was the first man in her experience to express an ambition – to want something more than what he had been given. It was a revolutionary doctrine.

'You have been aiming for it?'

'My father was born on an earth floor in a hovel,' Josiah said. 'No more than a peasant. My sister in a collier's cottage, a coalminer's daughter. I was born on a stone floor in a warehouse. My son will be born in a proper bed, in a proper house. My family is on the rise, madam. Before the century is out we will be known as gentry. We will have a country house and a carriage. This is but a step on our way; not our final destination.'

Frances flushed at his mention of a son but Josiah had no idea that he was indelicate. He pointed to the grand house, the best house on the square, three red-brick storeys high with little attic windows let into the roof. Long white stone columns ran the length of the windows on each storey; above each window was a carved face. The double doorway was large and imposing, flanked by more pillars. Stone-carved gateposts and wrought-iron railings shielded the front of the house and emphasised its importance. 'This is it, Mrs Cole. This is our house-to-be. I happen to know that it is coming up for sale and I shall bid for it, you may be sure. And I shall have it. No-one will outbid me, cost what it will. It is generally known that you and I are wed. It is generally known that

I am looking for a town house to establish my family.'

Frances looked around the square, trying to imagine what it would be like to live there. A curtain in a front parlour beside them twitched and dimly she saw a woman step back from the window. It would be a little community, ingrowing and inbred. There would be small feuds and long memories. Frances did not mind. She had lived in a country village, dependent on the good will of the lord, her uncle. She knew how small communities worked.

'We should drive on,' she said gently to Josiah. 'We will be noticed if we stay here any longer, looking.'

'So?'

'These people will be our neighbours,' she explained. 'We wish them to have an agreeable impression of us.'

He was about to argue but she saw him hesitate and then he nodded. 'You know best, Mrs Cole,' he agreed. 'You are the one to teach me. It shall be as you wish. Now, is there anywhere else you would like to see?'

'I don't know the city at all,' Frances said. 'I have never visited here. I had some friends who drove out to a picnic and looked at the Avon gorge. They told me it was sublime.'

Josiah leaned forward and gave the order to the driver. 'We can go and look at the gorge,' he said. 'You will not think it so sublime when you understand what it costs me in barge charges. We can drive to the Hot Well at the foot of the gorge. I have a particular interest in it.'

The carriage turned out of the square and bumped along yet another dockside beside another river.

'This is the Avon again?' Frances asked.

'The River Frome,' Josiah corrected her.

'It is as if we live on an island,' Frances said. 'Surrounded by water.' She nearly said, 'foul water'.

'The old city was a defensive site ringed by the two rivers, the Avon and the Frome – like a moat,' Josiah told her. 'Now it is all docks.'

They waited for the drawbridge ahead of them to be dropped and then the carriage bowled over the wooden planks and turned left, away from the docks.

Frances looked ahead as for the first time the city seemed something more than a dockside slum. The pretty triangle of College Green was before them, with two churches on their left. The College church was an imposing building with the Bishop's Palace behind it. Frances heard birdsong – not the irritable squawk of seagulls, but the summery ripple of a blackbird's call. Looking up, she saw swallows and housemartins swooping and wheeling around the cathedral.

The thick foliage of the elms threw dark green shadows over the road and as they drove up the steep hill the air grew fresher and cleaner and the sun shone brightly on the new buildings.

'Oh, if we could only live up here!' Frances exclaimed. Set back from the track were occasional terraces of houses in soft yellow stone, built in the style that Frances liked – plain regular and square.

Josiah shook his head. 'It's a whim. One or two people are building here but no true merchant will ever move away from the city. The river is our life blood. Clifton is too far to go. It is country living – not city dwelling at all. There are people buying land and putting up houses but it will never be the heart of the city. We will always live along the river banks, that is where the city always has been. That is where it always will be.'

At the top of the hill they forked to the left, skirting a high hill and dropping down towards the river again.

'But if we had a carriage you could drive down to your work,' Frances observed, her voice carefully neutral. 'And these are handsome houses, and very clean air. I love to breathe clean air and my health needs it.'

Josiah shook his head. 'It is a whim,' he repeated. 'It will pass and those men who have bought land and built will have

72

bankrupted themselves. Take my word for it, my dear, Park Street is beyond the limit of the city and Clifton will never be more than a little out-of-the-way village.' He craned his head to see a ship in the dry dock. 'The *Traveller*,' he said with quiet satisfaction. 'I heard she was badly holed. That will put Thomas Williams's nose out of joint.'

Ahead of them the river widened out and started to form sinuous curves between banks of thick mud. Dark woodland reared up from either side of the banks and then broke up around the lower reaches of white cliffs of limestone which towered above them. The little road clung to the side of the river, following the curve of the bank overhung by the cliffs. It was spectacular scenery. Overhead seagulls wheeled and cried and dropped down to dive for little fish. A small fishing smack slipped downriver, moving fast on the ebbing tide, her sails filled with wind. The air was salty and clean, damp with the smell of the sea. A flat-bottomed trow crossed from one side to another and passed a ferryboat rowed by a man bright as a pirate in a blue jacket with a red handkerchief tied on his head.

'Sublime,' Frances said. It was Lady Scott's favourite word of praise. 'This is wonderful scenery, Mr Cole. So romantic! So wild!'

Josiah tapped the driver on the back with his stick and the man stopped the carriage. 'Will you walk, my dear?'

The driver let down the step and Frances got down from the carriage and took Josiah's arm. 'Above is the St Vincent's rock,' he said. 'It's quite an attraction for people who love scenery.'

Frances craned her neck to look upwards at the high white cliffs with wild woodland tumbling down. 'I never saw anything more lovely. You would think yourself in Italy at least!'

Slowly they walked along the little promenade which clung to the side of the river, tucked in beneath the cliff. An avenue of young trees had been planted in a double row to shade the road and form an attractive riverside walk. Ahead of them to their right was a pretty colonnade of shops set back from the river in a curving half-circle, lined with small pillars so that the customers could stroll under cover, admiring the goods on sale, on their way to and from the Hot Well Pump Room. It was as pretty as a set of dolls' houses, a dozen little red-brick shops in miniature under a colonnade of white pillars.

Frances and Josiah walked along the flagstones, looking in the shop windows at the fancy goods and the gloves and hats, and the crowded apothecary shop. There was a small circulating library which also sold stationery and haberdashery goods.

'This is Miss Yearsley's library!' Frances exclaimed.

'Who is she?'

'Why, Anna Yearsley, the poetess, the milkmaid poet! Such a natural unforced talent!'

Josiah nodded at the information. 'I have not had much to do with poetesses,' he confessed. 'Or milkmaids. But I know about her library. This is a new building, all brand new, and she will be paying a pretty sum in rent. The Merchant Venturers have spent a fortune to make this the most fashionable place in Bristol.'

'I believe my uncle stayed at the Hot Well when he visited you,' Frances said. 'In Dowry Parade. He spoke very highly of the lodging house but he said it was dear.'

Josiah nodded. 'Whoever takes it on will have to charge a fortune to recoup his investment. Not just these shops but the spa itself has recently been improved. These trees are new-planted. For years the place has been open to anyone – you can take a cart from the city for sixpence to come here, and drink the water for free. Any tenant who takes it on will have to charge more and exclude the common people. A successful spa must be for the fashionable people only, don't you think? Will you take a glass of the water? I am sure you do not need it for your health but you might enjoy the experience.'

They walked towards the Pump Room which stood on the very edge of the river, its windows overlooking the water and the Rownham woods on the far side of the bank. Josiah paid an entrance fee and they went in. The place was busy. A string quartet positioned in a corner of the room played country dances. Invalids advertised their ill health with yards of shawls and rugs across their knees, but there were others, whose visit was purely social, flirting and laughing in the corners. A few people promenaded self-consciously up and down the length of the rooms, stopping to greet friends, and staring at the new arrivals.

Frances straightened her collar where it fell elegantly at the neck of her walking gown, and held Josiah's arm. He seemed to know no-one. No-one stopped to speak to them, no-one hailed him.

'Do you have no friends here?' she asked after they had walked the length of the room. They paused before the fountain of the spa. Josiah paid for a glass of water and the woman pocketed the coin and poured a small glass for Frances. It was light-coloured and cloudy, sparkling with little bubbles.

'My friends are working traders, not pleasure-seekers,' Josiah said. 'They will be at their warehouses at this time in the afternoon, not dancing and walking and drinking water. How does it taste?'

Frances took an experimental sip. 'Quite nice,' she said cautiously. 'Bland, a little like milk. And quite hot!'

'Very strengthening!' the woman at the fountain asserted. 'Especially for ladies. Very effective for skin complaints, stomach complaints and the lungs.'

Frances blushed at the frankness of the woman's language, and forced the rest of the glass down. 'I would not care to drink it every day.'

'Many people do,' Josiah replied. 'Some of them are prescribed a glass every couple of hours. Think of the profit for the tenant in that! Many come and stay for weeks at a time to drink it. And it is cried all around the city and sold like milk at the back doors. And bottled and sent all around the country. A very good business if one could afford to buy in.' He took her arm and walked her back down the length of the Pump Room. 'How does it compare to the Pump Room at Bath, in your opinion?' he asked. 'I have a reason for my interest.'

Frances thought for a way to tell him that would not seem offensive. 'Of course it is smaller,' she began carefully. 'And very much prettier. The scenery is wonderful, much better than Bath. But Bath has more ... Bath is more ... established.'

'Only a little place but I think it will grow,' Josiah said as they left the Room. 'But I am glad you like it. I am glad you like the rocks of the Avon gorge even if you do not like the taste of the water.'

'One could not help but admire it,' Frances said. The carriage had followed them down to the Pump Room; she took the driver's hand and stepped in. 'I am a great admirer of fine landscape.'

'Do you draw or paint?' Josiah asked her.

'A little,' Frances said. 'I should like to come to try my hand at drawing this scene.'

'So you shall,' Josiah said. 'You shall hire the carriage whenever you wish and my sister will drive with you. You shall teach us how to enjoy leisure, Mrs Cole. And we will teach you about business!'

'I shall be happy to learn,' Frances said. The carriage turned back towards the city and to the dark little house by the noisy quay filled with the stink of the harbour. 'I shall be happy,' she repeated firmly.

Chapter Five

Josiah's attempts to buy the house at 29 Queens Square were not at first successful. The building was owned by Mr Stephen Waring, a Merchant Venturer and a member of the Corporation of the city. He was building a grand new house halfway up Park Street in a new road to be called Great George Street. Josiah approached him as he sat in the coffee house with his brother-in-law – another Merchant Venturer – on one hand and his cousin standing behind him.

'Good day,' Josiah said. He tried not to sound deferential but he could hear the hint of inferiority in his voice – a tinge of Somerset, a trace of servility. He sounded like a man who had been born on the floor of a warehouse. 'Good day, Mr Waring.'

The man looked up. 'Cole?'

'I wonder if I might speak with you on a matter of business?' Josiah's plain three-cornered hat was in his hand. He felt himself turn it, and tap the points, like a servant fidgeting before a master.

'Yes?'

Josiah glanced at the other men. They were staring at him with open curiosity. No-one made any movement away from the table, they did not even trouble themselves to turn aside. His business would have to be done before them all.

'I am interested in your house in Queens Square,' he said. 'I understand that you may be selling it? I am newly married and my wife . . .'

The man laughed gently. 'I do not think you would like it, Cole,' he said. 'It is the wrong side of the river for your little warehouse, and you would find my neighbours very poor company.' He smiled at his brother-in-law and turned his back on Josiah. The meeting was concluded.

Josiah flushed with embarrassment. There was nothing he could do but sketch a bow and go back to the table where he usually did his business, with the smaller traders and the unemployed captains. They had been watching him; everyone in the coffee shop had seen him rebuffed. Josiah pulled out a chair and seated himself, trying to look jaunty and hide his mortification. 'I have mentioned my interest in the house at Queens Square to Mr Waring,' he said to the table generally. 'I shall write him a letter with my offer.'

'He's a warm man,' Captain Legge warned. 'I've heard that he paid more than two thousand pounds for his new house off Park Street.'

Josiah blinked. 'That is a new house though,' he objected. 'New built and according to his specifications. The house in Queens Square must be nearly seventy years old!'

'And his father and the rest of the landlords made profits enough in the first year!' a small merchant commented. 'The leases on those houses were an extortion. Many a tenant was ruined in the first year if he was not a member of the Merchant Venturers, who had insiders' terms.'

Another trader nodded. 'How convenient it was that the Corporation chose to build in brick when the Waring family owned the brickyard,' he remarked slyly.

'That'll do,' Josiah said swiftly, glancing towards the top table where Mr Waring had summoned one of the masters of his ship and was examining a cargo manifest. 'The Corporation of Bristol and the Merchant Venturers have together brought this city to the highest prosperity. We all know that.'

'It's joining them that's the challenge, eh, Josiah?'

Josiah Cole flushed. 'Gentlemen,' he said. 'My future plans

are my own concern, I think. Now, I heard that you were interested in my sugar, Mr Williams. Shall I send you a sample?'

Frances was seated at the parlour table, the ledgers of the company spread before her. Sarah was teaching her the business, showing her the books of the ship *Daisy* due home in December.

'This page shows the cost of fitting out a ship,' Sarah explained patiently. 'See, here is every item, and along the line,' her finger traced the row of ink dots, 'here is what it cost. At the foot of the page is the total cost.'

'I see,' said Frances wearily. Outside the window the *Rose* was being fitted with new ropes and newly mended sails. There was a continual bellow of orders and screams of quay-side sellers. They had a pulley rigged on the mast which screeched every time it took the weight of a load, and then the crew started a chant to help them pull the ropes together. The sun burned in at the parlour window and the reflected light on the ceiling danced a dizzying ballet. The tide was coming in and the filth and sewage which had been draining downriver was now washing up and down the quayside wall. The wind blowing up the gorge brought the acrid stink of burning lime from the Clifton woods to mingle with the pervasive smell of Bristol: boiling fat for soap, smoke from the furnaces. The window was tightly shut as usual. The parlour was hot and stuffy, the sun beating in through the glass of the panes. Frances had a headache; she sat very still and straight and did not complain.

'So the total cost of repairing and fitting out the ship was £907. 2s.'

Sarah Cole nodded. 'Correct. On the next page we show the trade goods supplied.'

Frances passed her cool fingers over her eyelids. 'What are all these names?'

'These are our four partners. Merchants and tradesmen who joined with us for this voyage. Here you see that they supply the trade goods themselves. Here is a cutler – he supplied the knives and forks and tin dishes. We show the goods and the value of them. Here is a haberdasher. He supplied cloth and lace and some hats. The other things, some beads, Italian blue beads, and the guns, we bought direct. The other partners supplied the money to buy them.'

Frances looked down the page. There were many things listed but the greatest quantity of money had been spent on muskets, Bonny muskets at nine shillings each, gunpowder and flints. 'What a lot of guns,' she said.

'They are the most popular trade goods,' Sarah Cole said. 'And a great cost to us. They can only be bought from Birmingham and no Birmingham firearm maker will come in with us as a partner. They are quick enough to make a profit from us but they will not share the risk. Now, Frances, can you see how much it cost to send out the ship?'

Frances looked wearily to the foot of the page. The shifting light in the room seemed to be beating on her eyes. 'Yes, £5692. 16s. od,' she said. 'What a great deal of money!'

'Now you see!' Sarah exclaimed. 'Now you begin to understand. This is why I don't want a grand house. This is why I don't keep a carriage. I daresay Lord Scott himself could not find such a sum, and find it three times every two years! Every time we send out a ship!'

'I don't know,' Frances said unwillingly. 'I have never learned about money before.'

Sarah smiled in triumph. 'Well, you are a merchant's wife now,' she said. 'It is right that you should know where the money comes from. When you hire the carriage or want a new silk dress it all has to be paid for.' She smoothed the pages lovingly with the flat of her hand. 'It all comes from here.'

She turned the page. 'Now this is the record for the transactions in Africa,' she went on. 'I compose the books when the captain shows me his log on his return. See here: purchased over six months on the Africa coast – three hundred and twelve – at an average of fourteen pounds each. Wastage on voyage – sixty-two. Price in Jamaica, average fifty pounds each. First profit – £12500, minus the cost of buying – £8132.' She waited for Frances to speak.

'Very profitable,' Frances said.

'Apparently so,' Sarah said sourly. 'From this profit we buy sugar, tobacco and rum to the cost of £4830. We extend credit to the planters to the cost of £1750, and we pay off half of the crew at a cost of £130.' She ran her finger down the columns, Frances followed it with her eyes. All she could see was the neat fingernail and the black-ink numbers spooling away.

'Now you see,' Sarah Cole went on. 'When the ship comes into port she has to pay for a pilot up the Bristol channel, and then another pilot up the Avon. She has to pay a fee to every lighthouse, she has to pay a fee for the new bridge, she has to pay the rowing boats to tow her up the gorge, she has to pay a fee to the mayor and to the quay warden, and a docking fee.'

'Gracious,' Frances said weakly.

'No wonder the Liverpool merchants steal our trade,' Sarah Cole muttered to herself. 'They sail straight into a deep-water dock with cheap quay rates. No wonder they build bigger and bigger ships.' She turned her attention back to Frances. 'So, can you see the profit which is made at the end of the voyage?'

Frances looked wearily at the final page. 'Here, £2513.'

'Divided among the partners – five partners including ourselves,' Sarah prompted.

Frances looked at the final figure. 'That's £502 each.'

Sarah Cole nodded at her, waiting for some response.

'After all that work and worry?'

'And we own the ship and keep the warehouse, and allow credit to the planters in Jamaica and all the other costs that the partners do not see,' Sarah added.

'It does not seem very much for us when you put it like that,' Frances said.

Sarah got up from the table and went over to the window. 'It's a good profit on a two-year investment for the partners,' she said. 'For a little man with little savings it is good business. But the scale of it is not big enough for my brother now. He can double his money every five years on these figures, but he wants to advance in six months, by tomorrow. I do not see how we are to do it. I show you these figures because you should know our business, but you can see for yourself that we are not making the profits we need.'

'Why not?'

The woman shrugged. 'Rising prices all around us. It costs more and more to repair and equip a ship. The price of sugar is falling as more and more planters increase their land and grow a bigger crop each season. The American war made it dangerous even for civilian shipping and increased the cost of insurance. The French can import their own sugar from their own colonies, and now they are selling in England. I heard that a man is finding a way to make sugar from vegetables called beets. When they make sugar from carrots we are ruined indeed.'

She stepped towards the table and shut the ledger gently, passing her hand over the ship's name, *Daisy*, engraved on the front of the leather-bound book. 'The Liverpool merchants have ships twice the size of the *Daisy*,' she said. 'And they do the trip in half the time. That means they can make four times our profits. Just think of it! Twice the amount of trade in half the time!

'The big Bristol merchants are members of the Royal Africa Company and they do not have to wait off the coast, trading up and down at all the little stations, buying here and selling there. They anchor at a Royal Africa Company fort and they load food and water that is waiting for them, and the Trade that is ready and waiting for them. They halve the loss of life for the crew because they are away from West Africa within a month, while we delay for six months gathering cargo.

'When they arrive in the West Indies they have an agent waiting on the quayside to greet them. He has already bought the cargo for loading, he has already arranged the sales. He has agreed prices while they were still at sea. They deal with the best planters and they have contracts arranged. When they give credit to the planters they bring home bills which are honoured in London at once, by the planter's agents, as soon as they are presented. So they get their money within the quarter. But *we* have to give credit and then wait until our ship is in the West Indies again, sometimes as long as two years before we are paid! The people we trade with do not have a London agent. They are the smaller planters, and they demand credit from us. It is no business for the little men any more.'

'Yet Josiah seems so confident,' Frances demurred.

Sarah's face was grim. 'Yes,' she agreed. 'He is very confident. He sees sugar in the storerooms of the Redclift, his bond is filled with tobacco and rum. He can see the gold coming in from one little sale after another, and he is down on the quayside doing as well as other little traders. But I spend my day with the books and I can see that the profits are slowly falling as the costs rise. The world is changing and we will have to change too.'

'My uncle thought that Josiah was a prosperous man,' Frances protested, clinging to hope.

Sarah shrugged her shoulders. 'What would he know?' she said disrespectfully. 'I imagine he has never seen a set of accounts in his life. He would see his rent rolls and nothing more. But I have spent my life with these books and I can read them as you would read a novel. And I can see that each voyage out, and each voyage back, is less and less successful. It costs more every day, the risks are greater all the time.'

'What can we do?' Frances asked. 'Can't we build a bigger ship? Or take up a different trade?'

Sarah Cole measured Frances. 'No,' she said with a little smile. 'We can never leave the Trade. It is the only thing we know. It is the foundation of our fortunes and it is our inheritance. Whatever anyone says, I will never countenance that we leave the Trade. We must stay with it – but do it in a new way.'

'What way?'

'We import slaves direct,' Sarah said very softly. 'We bring black slaves into England. We put a black slave in every household in England. We call them Scott slaves – named in honour of you – and we make our fortune.'

There was a loud crash from the quayside as something was dropped, followed by half a dozen shouts. Neither woman heard them.

'What?'

'We ship slaves already,' Sarah said sharply. 'You saw the accounts with me. You saw the figures. You saw that we bought three hundred and twelve on *Daisy*'s last voyage, you read it yourself. You saw wastage on voyage – sixty-two, you knew that meant that sixty-two of them had died during the passage. You saw how they sold in Jamaica – they went for fifty pounds each. My idea is to bring a sample of them on to England. To train them here to be house servants, to sell them for households in England. Isn't it the fashion?'

'Yes,' Frances said slowly. Lady Scott had a little black boy to carry her fan and run her messages, and every lady in London had a black maid or a handsome black footman to ride behind the carriage, and a little black girl to play with the children. But all the slaves that Frances knew had been imported singly from the West Indies, brought over by

84

returning planters, sold by slaving captains. 'Can you train them in large numbers, and sell them in large numbers?'

'Why not?' Sarah demanded. 'It was done in the past. In the last century people imported slaves direct from Africa. I have heard of a Liverpool merchant who has imported a dozen this year. They take up little space on the ship coming home from the Sugar Islands, and they will sell in England for eighty or ninety pounds each. But if our slaves could become known for their manners and their training, we could command an even greater price.

'You shall teach them. They are the pupils you would have had, if you had come to us as a governess. Now you will take a profit rather than a wage but they will still be your work. They will be famous for their smartness and their training, and that will be your job.'

'I'm not sure . . .' Frances said.

'You can have no objection,' Sarah said coldly. 'You knew we were Bristol merchants. You accepted the Trade well enough when it took place at a distance. You came for a job with us.'

'I did not know I was to be governess to slaves . . . Josiah never said . . .'

'You can have no objection though. You knew where our wealth was earned.'

'I have no objection,' Frances said. 'Of course I have none. I know that it is a good thing to take the Africans away from their paganism and to teach them godly work and religion.'

'And they are not humans, not as we understand humans,' Sarah reminded her. 'They are animals. They cannot speak unless we teach them; otherwise they just grunt and moan. They are not fully human.'

'Oh,' Frances said. 'I had not realised. I have never had much to do with them. Lady Scott has a nigger pageboy, but I have never seen one fully grown.'

85

'So you will teach them?'

Frances nodded. 'I only hesitated because I do not know if I can. I have taught children, but they were human children. I wouldn't know how to teach niggers.'

Sarah nodded grimly. 'Then let me tell you, Sister, that you had better find a way to teach them. This will be the saving of our Cole and Sons and its key to the future. If we can train and sell slaves then we can make a fortune big enough to satisfy Josiah's ambition, and to pay for Queens Square. If we do not, it will not be Queens Square for you, you will stay here forever, beside the filthy water of the dock – cold and damp in winter, deadly in summer.'

There was a long silence. Frances could feel herself becoming breathless and put her hand to the base of her throat to steady her pulse. 'You are not exaggerating?' she confirmed. Her little cough rose up and choked her for a moment.

Sarah waited until she had her breath back. 'The bottom is slowly falling out of the Trade,' she said. 'If, in a few years, our Bristol partners can get a better return in land and building, or in shops, or in importing cotton to Manchester, they will no longer put their money with us. Then we will not be able to send out ships at all and our investment – in our ships, in our warehouse, in the quay – will be thrown away. We have put so much money into the Trade that we *have* to trade, and we have to make the Trade pay.'

'I will try, Sarah, I will try my best to teach them.'

Sarah smiled a wintry smile. 'You were a governess, weren't you?' she asked. 'You replied to our advertisement for a governess? We planned all along that you should teach them. But now instead of working for a wage you are working for yourself. You shall be their teacher and you shall recommend them to their places and give them a character. You will make this plan work for us. You will earn the new town house. You want it, don't you?'

Frances looked around the tiny parlour and breathed the tainted air. 'Yes,' she said. 'Of course I do.'

Chapter Six

Josiah came in for his dinner in the mid-afternoon in thought-ful silence. Frances, new to his moods and weary herself from Sarah's long lessons with the account books, sat at the foot of the table and said nothing. Her cough was troubling her. She sipped water, trying to choke it back. Sarah waited until the tablecloth had been taken away and a decanter of port set at Josiah's hand before she asked:

'Trouble?'

He raised his head and smiled. 'Oh! Nothing. I have been all day seeking proper insurance for *Rose*. Ever since the *Zong* case it has been more and more difficult.'

'The *Zong* case?' Frances asked.

'Business,' Josiah said dismissively.

'She should understand it,' Miss Cole pointed out. 'It is her business too now.'

'Oh aye, you're probably right,' Josiah agreed. 'The *Zong* case, my dear, took place half a dozen years ago and concerned the good ship *Zong* which is still in dispute with the insurers.'

'Why?' Frances asked.

'Well, it is a long story, but basically the *Zong* ran short of water while sailing to Jamaica. There was much illness on board and the captain took the decision to pitch a quarter of the cargo overboard.'

'What cargo?' Frances asked stupidly.

'She does not understand,' Miss Cole said.

'It is simple enough,' Josiah said briskly. 'The captain of the *Zong*, fearing that a large number of his four hundred and seventy slaves would die of thirst, had them thrown into the sea to drown.'

Frances looked from Josiah's face to his sister's. 'To save the drinking water?'

Josiah allowed himself a small sly smile. 'Well, that is what the captain claimed. However, while they were in the midst of these kindly killings, it came on to rain and it rained for two days.'

Miss Cole hid a little laugh behind her hand.

'And the good ship *Zong* docked with full casks of drinking water in Jamaica.'

The two of them smiled at Frances, expecting her to understand the joke. She shook her head.

'It was a fraud,' Miss Cole said impatiently.

'The captain was lying,' Josiah explained. 'See here, Frances, he had a bad batch of slaves, very sick, dying on him, dropping like sick flies. Slaves who die of illness are a cash loss – a loss to the traders; but slaves drowned at sea are paid for by the insurance. Captain Luke Collingwood had the neat idea of slinging all the sick men and women over the side and claiming for them on the insurance.'

'He drowned them for the insurance money?'

Josiah nodded. 'In three batches, over three days as I remember. A hundred and thirty-one altogether.'

'And they say the big Liverpool shippers are better,' Miss Cole crowed. 'You never heard of a Bristol captain cheating like that.'

'He did not cheat, Sister,' Josiah reproved her. 'He ran his ship at a profit. Lord Mansfield himself sat in judgement and ordered a retrial.'

'The captain was tried for murder?' Frances asked.

The look the two of them turned on her was of blank incomprehension. 'Lord, no!' Josiah shook his head. 'It is no

89

crime to kill slaves. This was a civil matter. The insurers refused to pay out. They argued that slaves are insured only against accident, not against deliberate drowning. They won the first round in the courts and then it went to appeal. Lord Mansfield sat on the appeal, I remember. He said that it was exactly the same as if horses had gone overboard, and that the owners should be insured against their goods going into the sea for whatever reason.'

Miss Cole nodded in mild triumph. 'He said that slaves are property, Lord Mansfield himself said they were the same as horses.'

'But it has left us with great difficulties,' Josiah went on. He rubbed his hand across his face and his boyish exuberance suddenly drained away. 'Because his lordship ruled that all slaves lost at sea are to be paid for by the insurance, there is a fear that all captains running at a loss will simply drown their slaves and claim for them. The insurers do not trust us. I have spent all day trying to find someone to insure a cargo of slaves for me, and they put in so many requirements and conditions that it is hardly worth insuring at all.'

Sarah looked anxious. 'We dare not sail without insurance,' she said. 'What if the ship were to go down and we were to lose all? Or a slave revolt? Josiah, we *must* insure.'

'I know! I know!' he snapped. 'But now they will only insure against rebellions. They will not compensate for sickness, or for slaves who suicide. If a slave is whipped to death they will not compensate. If a slave starves himself to death they will not compensate. If they kill themselves what can I do? I cannot carry such losses.'

Sarah was grave. 'Someone must insure us.'

Josiah shrugged his shoulders crossly. 'They are all in a ring. If I could break into the Merchant Venturers then I could share my insurance with them. On the inside they all insure each other. It is the little fish left on the outside which bob about trying to snap at trifles. If I could get inside the Company then I would be safe.'

He broke off and looked at Frances, his mood lightening. 'We can do it, I know we can do it. With the house at Queens Square and with you, Mrs Cole, to give me some presence in the world, we will get there. We have been trading for two generations, we are respectable Bristol merchants. They will invite me to join, they must invite me to join soon.'

'It is an old trade,' Frances said. 'Respectable.' She was thinking of the ship in the drizzling rain. The one hundred and thirty-one men and women thrown over the side into the heaving water, clinging to the ropes and screaming as they went overboard, bobbing in the wake of the ship as it ploughed on without them, trying to swim after it in the buffeting waves, and then seeing, on the edge of their vision, a dark scythe-like fin as it came straight towards them, slicing through the water.

'*Rose* is nearly ready to sail,' Sarah said. 'We have to have insurance within the week. And we are still two partners short.'

'I will get it,' Josiah promised. 'I will get it in time, and partners for the voyage as well. I cannot have her sitting on the dock eating up my money doing nothing. I will get insurance for her and partners too. Trust me, Sarah, I have never failed before.'

Josiah was trying, but the mood of the city, as sensitive as a flock of little wading birds which scavenge at the edge of the sea, was against him. There was a whisper around Bristol that Josiah was losing his sure touch. He was spending too much time with his new wife, he was seen driving in a hired carriage to the Hot Well, to the Clifton Down. He was negotiating to buy a house on Queens Square. They said he wanted to be a man of leisure, soon he would be too grand to drive a hard bargain. The small traders who haunted the quayside coffee shops with their savings to invest wanted to place their gold with a man who knew the value of money as they did. They wanted a man who admired the chink of a hundred hard-won guineas in a little purse. They suspected Josiah of soaring too high for them. They did not know that he was trapped in the gulf between the two worlds of the hardest city in Britain. The great men, the Merchant Venturers, had no place for him. Their wives might murmur that the new Mrs Cole had been Miss Scott and niece to Lord Scott and long to be her friend; but the new Mrs Cole was seen only at church and she attended St Mary Redclift, not the more fashionable cathedral on the north side of the river, on College Green.

They could not call on her in that dreadful little house on the dockside. The drive to the front door alone was more than most of the ladies could stomach. They sent their footmen to leave their cards, but they did not call in person, and Frances, reading the signs quite correctly, knew that she must wait until they moved into the big house in Queens Square.

At the end of the week Josiah decided to take a gamble. He would send *Rose* out with insurance only for goods. No insurer would cover him for shipping slaves. Josiah was too desperate for profits to wait. He threw down his hat, took Captain Smedley by the arm as they walked along the quayside and thrust him towards the ship.

'Go!' he exclaimed. 'And sail her as if she were your own. I tell you honestly, Captain Smedley, we have to see a mighty profit on this sailing, and we are taking a mighty risk.'

The captain nodded. 'I am ready. I will join her at the Kingsroad, when the pilot has brought her down the channel. I will do my best for you, Mr Cole, as I always have done.'

'There will be a note for you in your cabin.' Josiah's face was hungry. 'We may need to bend the law a little on this voyage, Captain Smedley. You would have no difficulty with that, I take it.'

'As long as the ship and my crew are safe . . .'

Josiah nodded. 'Keep the ship safe, whatever you do. I will see her set sail on the tide at dawn tomorrow. And your orders will be on your chart table in your cabin.'

The captain stooped and picked up Josiah's hat, and returned it to him with a smile. 'Cover your head, Mr Cole, I shall see you in the Merchant Venturers' Company yet.'

Josiah bared his brown teeth. 'Please God,' he said tightly.

Next morning Josiah was up early waiting on the quayside in thick cold fog. *Rose* was loading her final stores, extra boxes of trade goods carried swiftly and efficiently from Josiah's warehouse: crate after crate of Birmingham muskets with flints and shot and gunpowder. Josiah was pouring munitions into Africa, to feed their need of guns.

Captain Smedley was not aboard; he would join the ship at Kingsroad anchorage, when the pilot had guided her down the Avon gorge, with the rowing boats towing her. Josiah wrote one final letter of instructions to him and left it in his cabin.

4th September 1788

On this Trip above all Others I must stress that we have to show a Profit. To this End select the Very best Negroes you can find; but do not Delay too long off Africa. Ship Women and young children and Pack them very Close. I want you to carry as many as Six Hundred. The Extra deaths in passage will be paid for by the Extra profit in taking So many.

On this voyage, on this one Voyage only, you are to Go straight to the Spanish colonies and sell the slaves There, for Bullion. The papers to cover this Voyage make No mention of the Spanish colonies, and you will 'Destroy this letter when you have 'Read it. I know that this is Smuggling and you will see a Bonus on your 'Return. 'This will be the only 'Time I will ask you to 'Trade with the Spanish, and I will 'Reward your Success. Buy what Sugar they offer, provided it is of Good quality, but take No notes of Credit. I want nothing but Gold and Sugar. Do not 'Fail me, Captain Smedley – Ship as many as you can find and 'Pack them 'Tight!

The *Rose* was rocking temptingly on the tide, the waves slapping the quayside. The pilot came aboard as Josiah watched the barges attaching their lines.

'Take care now,' Josiah said under his breath. The ship was uninsured for the middle voyage and would be perilously overloaded. He dared not tell Sarah; he hardly dared acknowledge to himself what he was doing.

The dockers slipped *Rose*'s moorings and the rope snaked through the green water and was hauled up to the ship. The rowing boats moved slowly forward and the towing ropes sprang out of the water and quivered tautly, shedding drops of silver water along their length. There was the silent, precious moment as the ship hesitated, as if she could not believe that she were free, freely in her element after weeks of being tied to land, then slowly, almost reluctantly, the *Rose* moved away from the dockside and gathered speed as she glided down the channel towards the heights of the Avon gorge.

'God speed,' Josiah said under his breath. She was under-capitalised on this trip. She was financed by himself and only three other small partners. He had taken three shares to himself and the others had only one share each. He had borrowed to buy the extra trade goods, he owed more than a thousand pounds on her. She was undercapitalised and underinsured. Josiah had no choice but to send her outside the law to sell to the Spanish plantations. It was a risk he had never taken before; but the Spanish would pay highly and in bullion. Josiah was sailing very close to the wind. 'God speed,' he said.

As if to justify Josiah's belief in his luck, that very day, when the sun had risen, showing red through the smoke from the lead shot tower, Mr Waring took breakfast with his wife and finally decided to sell the house in Queens Square to the Coles. Mrs Waring had heard from the bishop's wife herself that the new Mrs Cole was the daughter of the Reverend John Scott who had held the living at Claverton Down. Stephen Waring was frankly incredulous that a Miss Scott should marry a man such as Josiah, and sleep above a sugar store, but Mrs Waring was more acute. 'I daresay if Josiah Cole is good enough for Lord Scott he is good enough to buy our house,' she remarked archly. 'And I daresay, Mr Waring, that you can name your price if Mr Cole has to provide a good house for his new wife.'

Mr Waring said nothing but when he retreated to his office he wrote a note to Josiah naming a price for the house that was high enough to discourage any but the most eager.

If Josiah had been a regular at the top table of the coffee shop, he would have known that other houses in Queens Square were about to come on the market. If Josiah had been acquainted with the wealthy men of the city, he would have been in no hurry to snap up 29 Queens Square when 18 and 31 would be on the market within the month. The richest merchants were moving from the square; the city centre was becoming too noisy, too dirty and too crowded for them. Their wives had ambitions to be ladies of leisure, they did not want a parlour which also did service as an office.

Park Street was paved almost to the crown of the hill and on either side of the street elegant town houses in pale honey stone were springing up. The first few houses in Great

George Street had been sold and others were planned. The astute men were buying up land all around Great George Street, and on either side of Park Street, and architects were drawing plans for elegant terraces to rise one above the other all the way up the hill. Mr Waring was discreetly negotiating, through an agent, for land even farther from the dockside. He did not share Josiah's love of the city centre. Mr Waring was interested in Clifton.

Queens Square was falling from fashion and the prices would slide as soon as it became apparent. Mr Waring opened the paper again and added a note along the bottom.

> *I can Offer you this house at This price for a Week Only, Mr Cole. I have had a Pressing enquiry from Another man to Whom I must reply within Eight days.*

He folded the paper over, dropped red wax on it, and pressed his seal on it.

Thoughtfully he took up another page.

> *Dear Tom,*
>
> *Oblige me by Keeping your house Off the market for a Week. I have a Buyer for mine and I do not want him Distracted.*

He scrawled his initial and sprinkled sand over the note, rang for a footman to deliver them both, and went through to the parlour.

'I think you should call on Mrs Cole, my dear,' he said to his wife. 'Warehouse or no warehouse, I think she would reward an acquaintance. And certainly, I shall be happy to do business with her husband.'

Chapter Seven

'We have to rise,' Josiah said to Sarah, Stephen Waring's note in his hand. 'We have to move in the circles where capital is available. The little men are growing wary of risk and the bigger men want only large investments. You are right, the Trade is in a temporary decline. It will boom again – we have seen it come and go – and we have to ride out these doldrums. There are great chances in this city if we can but grasp them. We have to move in the circles of those that know.'

Sarah was pale with anxiety. 'We had only three partners for *Rose*,' she said. 'And she will not be home until late next year. *Daisy* will not be in until this December. We cannot overextend ourselves, Josiah. Mr Waring's price is far too high for that house. We are carrying too great a risk on the *Rose*, and too much of our capital is tied up in her. We cannot buy a new house as well.'

'Then we must borrow,' Josiah said determinedly. 'Another house might not come vacant for months, even years. You know how sought-after that address is, Sarah. I have been waiting for a house for nearly a year. We have to buy it now, we dare not wait. We have to borrow.'

Sarah shook her head. She feared debt more than anything in the world. 'Is there nothing left from her dowry?' She nodded to the room above the parlour where Frances was lying down, sick with a headache, her curtains drawn against the noise of the streets near her window and the smell from the middens in the backyards.

'No, it was all invested in *Daisy*.'

'Please God that she comes in safe with them and we see a profit.'

Josiah bowed his head. 'Please God,' he said.

The Vessle Daisy,
at St Kitts.

15th August 1788

Dear Mr Cole,

I send this Letter to you by the Bristol ship Adventure which is leaving Port tomorrow, to Announce that I have arrived Safely in St Kitts, Praise God.

Tomorrow I shall arrange for the Sale of the majority of the Slaves who are generally Good in health and Well in appearance. Prices seem to be Lower than at my Last Visit but you can be Assured I shall do my Best.

According to your Instruction I have reserved Twenty slaves for your use. Three men, Five women, Four infants, Four girls and Four boys. I will bring them Home as you Instructed and will indeed take Care that they have Blankets as they may be Weakened by Cold.

I will Seek other Cargo tomorrow but I Fear we may be Disappointed this Late in the Season. Be Assured however That I will do my best as Per your Instructions.

With God's Will I shall Complete my business here within the Month and set sail for Bristol as Soon as may be

Possible. I hope to convey my respects to you in person in the month of December 1788.

Your obdt servant,

Capt. William Lisle.

Josiah placed the letter before Sarah. She threw her needle-work to one side and snatched it up.

'Where did you have this?'

'From the master of the *Adventurer*. He had a good cross-ing. The letter is dated August, it has taken him only six weeks to get home. He does not speak well of the trade in St Kitts.'

'What does it say about the slaves?' Sarah scanned the letter quickly and then looked up. 'Twenty,' she said. 'And as I ordered, children, and he has even brought infants.'

'Infants?' Frances was at the table, making entries into the household ledger. A pile of bills was under a paperweight, and she was ticking them off as she entered the petty sums.

'If I could have bought babes in arms I would have done,' Sarah declared. 'They are bound to learn the quickest, and you have the more work from them.'

'Oh,' Frances said. 'When will they arrive?'

'January at the latest,' Josiah replied. 'It takes more than a month to load the ship in the West Indies, and then he will have to come home through the autumn storms. Please God they will make safe landfall by Christmas.'

'We will be in the new house by then,' Frances said. The end of the summer had brought an end to the dreadful smell of the dock and the continual fear of cholera and typhoid in the old town; but autumn wind and rain meant that Frances was confined even more to the little parlour. She suffered painful claustrophobia from the small rooms and low ceilings of the little house. It would never be anything more than a warehouse with rooms tacked on the side; the fireplaces were inadequate and the constant smoke made Frances cough and cough. The rainy weather made driving a rare pleasure, and she could not walk out among the dockside workers. She spent every day in the cramped parlour with Sarah, unless she chose to sit alone in her unheated bedroom. Nobody called at the little house on the quayside. No-one invited them to any parties. Nothing would breach the Coles' loneliness and isolation until they moved into Queens Square. 'Surely we should be in the new house by then!'

Josiah glanced at her. 'I am sorry for this delay,' he said. 'It is all the fault of Mr Waring. I have paid the deposit we agreed but his builder is taking longer than he promised and Mr Waring's new house is not yet ready. He has been delayed by the weather. We are all waiting on each other.'

'We would have been hard pressed to pay the whole in any case,' Sarah pointed out. 'If we do not move until after *Daisy* comes in, we will have her profits to go towards the final payment.'

'Another two or three months!' Frances exclaimed involuntarily.

Sarah looked at her sharply. 'This house was a palace to my mother. I have always been proud to live here.'

Frances bit her lip. In the four months of her marriage she had learned that Sarah was defensive about their home. 'I did not mean to be impolite,' she said carefully. 'But I should like to be able to walk out of doors, and the noise from the quay is very disturbing. We will have no society until we move.' She glanced at Josiah. 'It was part of the agreement,' she reminded them. 'When Josiah first wrote to me, he promised that we would live in Queens Square.'

'She is right,' Josiah said fairly. 'And Queens Square is our side of the bargain. We will move as soon as we can and, if need be, I can find the money, with or without the *Daisy*.'

'You mean borrowing,' Sarah snapped.

'I mean forward selling,' Josiah said steadily. 'I can sell *Daisy*'s cargo while she is still at sea and complete the payment for the Queens Square house with the money.'

'It is a risk,' Sarah said. She glanced at Frances, hoping for support. 'If the ship sinks then we have to carry the loss and repay the buyers of the cargo. I am sure Frances would not want us to take such a risk just for her benefit.'

Frances gave Josiah a demure smile. 'If you think it is worth the risk, Husband, then I must follow your judgement. And if it ensures that we get the house . . .'

'Very wifely,' Sarah commented acidly.

'As soon as Mr Waring is ready to leave I will complete the sale and we shall move to Queens Square,' Josiah declared, closing the subject. 'But I am glad to have heard that Captain Lisle is well. The *Daisy* always was a lucky ship. God speed to her as she sets sail!'

When the *Daisy* was ready to leave, the little shelter that they had made on her deck was dismantled, and the slaves returned to the hold. Mehuru was not strong enough to stand, he lay on the dirty straw and watched the others hold out their hands for manacles and their feet for leg-irons.

The sun shimmered on the blue water, the quayside of St Kitts wavered before his dazed eyes. The dark green terraced hills melted slowly into the low beautiful grasslands of his home. Mehuru thought that soon his body would release its tenacious grip on life. Soon the pain would be over. Soon he would be home. If the gods were kind to him, if his ancestors sought his soul, he would be home and lying on the breast of the kindly fertile earth of Africa once more.

The captain, watching them as they were chained and sent below, noticed for the first time that Mehuru's skin and muscles were wasting away.

'What the devil is ailing him?' he demanded. 'Is he sick?'

They watched him when the food came and saw that he

lay, his face turned away. Then they came and bolted an iron mask around his head with a funnel going into his mouth. Twice a day they poured scalding soup down his throat. The first day Mehuru felt nothing, he was floating and gliding down the sweet river of his home. But that night he was tortured with pain as his shrunken stomach griped on the food. Next day he felt the spiteful heat of the soup, burning his throat and his mouth. The third day he fought them, but they got it down despite his struggles. The fourth day they took the mask off and he knew he was hungry. He came back from his journey into darkness and he heard Snake's voice counselling patience and wisdom. He knew himself to be wiser for having risked everything. He tried to find within himself some power as a survivor, as a living ghost, since all his power as a man, even as a human being, had been stolen from him.

The ship set sail. Mehuru felt himself rolling on his shelf again and wondered if he was to spend the rest of his life in half-darkness with the wash of waves pouring through the grating, longing for his home and forever in exile. He would not fast again, he could not bear the grip of the white men and the sharp evil pain as the boiling soup threatened to drown him. Instead he ate his share of the common pot of food.

It grew bitter, colder than any weather Mehuru had known before. When they were ordered on deck to dance Mehuru could not recognise the sea, could not recognise the sun. The waters were a deep sullen grey, the wind had a smell behind it which was icy cold. He could not comprehend where the sun had gone, it seemed to be walking farther and farther away and it was losing its heat and strength. Every day it grew smaller and paler. Mehuru thought that the ship was sailing into permanent night. When the shadow of the grating moved across the floor of the hold the squares of sunlight were insipid and pale. Through the grille he could see the sky veiled, slurred with clouds. He had never seen a sky so thick. Even in the rainy season at home the storm clouds would suddenly part and the sun would burn through. He and one of the other men lay close together for warmth. Mehuru missed the others who had gone. They seemed very few in the echoing hold, and they were fearful and could not comfort each other.

One of the infants became sick. They thought she was dying of the cold. Mehuru saw that as the sun sickened and grew weaker the child sickened too. There was nothing they could do for her. She cried a little, very pitifully, and then died while a woman held her and rocked her. When Mehuru brought the little body up on deck for burial they took her roughly from him and tossed her over the side. Her arms and legs flew up as she went over and Mehuru had a heart-stopping moment when he thought she cried out. But the ship plunged down into the deep grey waves and her little black head bobbing in the water was hidden from him.

Days stretched beyond counting, weeks, and then months. They took the flux – dysentery – and one of the men died and another of the infants. The weather was too stormy for them to dance on deck, and besides they were all growing weaker. Mehuru wondered if they would sail on and on until they were all dead. When they were called up to empty the waste pail, two of the boys slipped through the nets hung around the rigging to keep them on board and flung themselves into the sea. Mehuru felt shame at their loss. He should have given them hope, he should have given them a reason to live. But there was no hope and there was no reason to live.

The bucket of food grew more and more stale but it did not rot. Unbelievably it was too cold for that to happen. Then in the night Mehuru felt the rhythm of the heaving ship steady and change. He heard the yell of the men dropping the sails. There was a long time of rocking gently as if they were anchored, and then a new jerky movement as the ship was taken into tow.

Mehuru waited in the darkness of the hold, listening for any clues which might tell him what was happening on deck. Once again he heard the urgency of the ship nearing port and the growing noise of a quayside. The others woke, the women clutching each other in fear, the children whimpering. There was a foul sour smell of dirt, like an old midden. It penetrated even to the fetid hold of the slave ship. There was a dreadful noise of people shouting, and a screech of machinery working. Mehuru gathered his blanket around his shoulders and trembled a little with cold and fear. Then the grating was lifted off, they were ordered on deck, and they climbed out unsteadily and stood, shivering in the cold, looking around them.

They could see little for it was not yet dawn and there were only a few lanterns lashed to the rigging and to the side of the ship. A chain was passed along their line, linking one neck collar with another, and they were ordered to walk down a ridged bridge of wood to the quayside. Mehuru, his insteps flinching from the cold hard cobbles, touched ground for the first time in six months. He had never felt freezing stone before, he could not believe the ache of coldness in the high arched bones of his feet. They whipped him and the others with light biting blows on his shoulders and his back, and they shouted at him, as men shout when they herd cattle. The cold air in his face and the cold hardness beneath his feet told Mehuru that he had arrived into some dreadful exile in the land where all the men were dead men; and Snake alone knew what they wanted of him.

Mehuru breathed deep, three, four times, of the icy dirty air, and tried to hold down his panic. Before him was a high building with no lights showing and arched doorways like gaping mouths leading to storerooms. A small door at the side of the building opened at their approach and they were ordered into a hallway, through another door into a kitchen. The warmth and the smell of cooking gave him a sharp pang of homesickness, but then a blow on his back forced him forward and they were through the kitchen before he had time to look around.

At the far end of the kitchen there was a stout wooden door standing open and four steps cut downward into rock. Mehuru and the others stumbled down, their chains jerking at each other's necks as they were pushed roughly into line around the walls of the room. It was part cellar, part cave. Mehuru saw a couple of old barrels of wine, and a rack which had once held bottles. Hammered into the soft red sandstone of the walls were new iron rings to hold their neck chains, and anchor points for their shackles. A new man, a stranger, whose clothes smelled of the land and not of the sea, came along the line, bolting each of them against the wall, and kicking clean straw around their cold feet. He took up the lantern and surveyed them carefully, like a good groom checks a stable before he leaves it for the night, and then he walked from the cave, taking the lantern with him. They heard the door at the head of the steps slam on the light and warmth of the kitchen, and they were left alone, buried alive in the damp cave, in the dark.

Then Snake spoke softly to Mehuru, and said one word to him:

'*Despair.*'

Frances learned that the *Daisy* had docked at dawn when Sarah sent a message with her breakfast tray asking her to come to the parlour as soon as she was dressed. The long anxious wait for the ship was over, and Frances's work was about to start. She dressed in a plain grey gown and wore her plainest cap, but she did not resent the slide back into governess work. The winter days in the little house on the quayside were very long, it was dark by four o'clock and too cold to drive out. The sides of the dock were lined with ice every morning and the smoke from the glass furnaces hung like a fog over the house. There was no birdsong, only the cry of seagulls, and only the frozen cold cobbles of the quay to watch. There were none of the amusements that Lady Scott and the Whiteleaze ladies took for granted, no walks in the winter shrubbery, no afternoons in the glasshouses.

Frances could remember an annual competition with her father to see the first snowdrops in the hedge at the bottom of the rectory garden. She could hardly bear a winter with no prospect of flowers, nor trees coming slowly into bud. She had read more novels than she could remember, she had sketched the view from the parlour window a dozen times: the shelf of the Coles' quay in the foreground, the gibbet profile of the Merchant Venturers' crane on the opposite side of the dirty river, the forest of masts, and the blank square face of the warehouse opposite. She had completed more darning and hemming than she would have believed necessary; and still there were hours to fill in every day.

The move to Queens Square would have diverted her, but Mr Waring still had not vacated the house. To Josiah's mounting anger he found that he had agreed to a high price for a house in a square where other properties were now coming on the market, and he was not even in possession of it.

Frances straightened her cap and went down the stairs to the parlour. Brother and sister were waiting for her.

'*Daisy* has docked with a good cargo of sugar and rum and the first consignment of your slaves,' Josiah beamed at her. 'I have a list here of them.'

'*My* slaves!' Frances exclaimed.

'They were bought with your dowry and will be trained and named by you,' Josiah said. 'They should certainly be your slaves and indeed, my dear, Sarah is right in thinking that they will command a better price if they are known to be your own.'

'We hoped to have twenty,' Sarah said. 'The losses have been very bad, I shall have words to say to Captain Lisle. He has delivered only thirteen.'

Josiah handed her the list. Frances read:

'Two healthy men
'Four healthy women
'Two boys aged seven and sixteen years
'Three girls aged between seven and fourteen years
'Two infant boys aged two and five years.'

'I did not expect them all to survive,' Josiah said. 'Remember, Sarah, that although we lose twenty in a hundred crossing the Atlantic, another twenty-five in a hundred die in the first year on the plantations. We must prepare ourselves to lose even more during the first year here.'

'Still, it is an excellent mix,' Sarah said. 'I particularly wanted young children. They are easier to train and the fashion is for very young black pages.' Her eyes were shining, she was smiling. Frances had never seen her look so animated.

'How long will it take you to teach them to speak English?' Josiah asked Frances. 'They know none as yet. But that is all to the good, isn't it? They will have no rough accents, they have not learned the patois of the Islands. They will speak pure English if they are so taught, won't they?'

Frances laughed, catching their enthusiasm. 'I believe so. But I know nothing about niggers. And whether they can learn quickly or slowly I will not know until I have seen them. Where are they now?'

'The ship docked in the night and I had them unloaded and stored in the cellar,' Josiah said. 'I had it cleared out and some straw put down on the floor. I thought it best that they be kept there until they are trained to stay in the house without chains. It is safe, there is only one stout door that leads into the kitchen. Will you teach them here, in the parlour?'

'Yes,' Frances said. She looked around the room. 'But there are too many of them. I cannot teach them all at once. I will have just six for my first lesson and then the others in the afternoon.'

Sarah looked displeased. 'Speed is essential,' she said. 'The sooner they are trained the sooner they can be sold.'

'I have to have some time to get used to them,' Frances said.

'She is right,' Josiah agreed kindly. 'She needs to become accustomed. I have taken on a good man, my dear, who has handled slaves on the Sugar Islands. He is an experienced driver. His name is John Bates and he will feed them and clean them, and muck them out and beat them for you.'

'We can go and look at them now,' Sarah said eagerly. She was animated, her pale cheeks had two spots of red.

Josiah smiled. 'I saw them when they were unloaded, so I shall leave you to inspect them on your own. I have to go to my work, but I look forward to hearing your progress this evening.' He nodded to Sarah but he took Frances's hand and bowed low over it. 'If you can accomplish this I will be obliged to you,' he said formally. 'Our fortune depends on it.'

Frances shifted uneasily. 'I will do my best, Josiah,' she promised.

'I ask nothing more,' he said, and left the room.

Frances stood by the window and looked down, watching Josiah's dark three-cornered hat moving among the labourers on the dockside unloading the *Daisy*.

'What a long way they have come,' she said. 'And what a terrifying voyage it must have been. All the way from Africa to the West Indies, and then all the way to England, in rough seas and sometimes becalmed, in heat and in cold weather. How frightened they must have been.'

'Oh, I doubt it,' Sarah Cole said. 'They do not feel as we feel, you know. And they do not understand things as we do. Even now they probably do not realise that they are far from home, and never going home again.'

Chapter Eight

Cook was standing by the kitchen table in offended silence. Brown was washing the second-best china dishes at the sink. She turned when Sarah and Frances came in and dipped a curtsey. The scullery maid backed away, her head down, wiping her dirty hands on her hessian apron.

Miss Cole nodded at them and led the way past the table to the massive door in the wall, bolted top and bottom and secured with a lock. Hanging by the door was a heavy key on a ring. Sarah lifted it down and turned it in the lock. Then she slid back the bolts.

'Have they been fed?' she asked. It was as if she were enquiring about the welfare of carriage horses.

'Yes, Miss Cole.' The kitchen maid bobbed. 'And Bates has taken out the slop pail.'

Miss Cole nodded and beckoned Frances to follow her. Frances went towards the doorway and then hesitated. Ahead was a narrow passage-like cave, carved from the dark red sandstone of the cliff, illuminated by the horn lantern which Sarah hung high on a peg hammered into the soft stone.

At its highest the roof of the tunnel was only about six feet; Frances could see the scrape marks of the picks and shovels where the cellar had been hollowed out from the cliff. The floor was bumpy, rutted in parts by the rolling of barrels of sugar and wine. A heavy acrid smell wafted towards her. A smell of old long-stored wine, and a new smell of men and women left for months in their own dirt, a smell of degradation and despair. She recoiled but Miss Cole took hold of her arm and drew her forward.

'This is where the money comes from to buy your embroidered morning dresses,' she said sharply. 'Money has to be earned in this world. This is how we earn ours. It's a good trade and an honest trade.'

'It was just the smell . . .'

'The ships smell worse than this and we send our sailors out in them. The lead works poison their workers and yet your uncle buys their shot. You have been hidden from the real things, the dirty things, Sister. But now you are the wife of a man who makes his living by the sweat of his brow, whose hands are dirty at the end of the day. And I am proud of it. I don't want to be a lady who knows nothing of the real world. I am ready to earn my daily bread.'

Sarah's face was exalted in the flickering light. Frances pulled her arm away. 'I am ready to play my part,' she said with simple dignity. 'I have taken a share in the prosperity of this family. I am ready to work, Sarah, and I was never a lady of leisure. You need not lecture me.'

'Good,' Sarah said briefly, and led the way, sure-footed down the familiar passage. As Frances followed, the smell of sweat and grief and infection grew stronger.

'There!' Sarah said avidly. 'Look at them! And in good condition too! I shall pay Captain Lisle a bonus!'

Frances blinked, trying to accustom her eyes to the darkness. The tunnel had widened into a circular cave, lined with silent people. She could dimly make out the gleam of the candlelight on shining eyes and there was a soft chink of a chain as someone moved. She had a sense of a mute crowd, filling the small cellar. They were chained like dogs to each other, and to rings in the walls. Each man, each woman, each child had a light iron collar bolted around their necks and above this shackle their faces were dulled with pain, weary with hopeless grief. She could see stains of pus on the collars where the blisters had gone septic, and bloodstains where they had worn their necks raw.

One ring on the neck collar held the chains for the manacles on the hands, another ring held the chain which roped them together in pairs, the links passing from behind their heads up to bolts on the walls. Their feet were in heavy leg-irons locked to the floor. The place smelled of excrement and the sweet sickliness of diseased flesh. Frances clamped a hand over her mouth to hold back the nausea and above it her face was white as a cave-fish in the gloom, her eyes as black as theirs.

None of them looked at her. None of them cared enough to look at her. Those whose eyes were open stared blankly at the space before them, or looked down at their feet, skin puckered from standing barefoot in the mulchy straw. Mostly they were sitting on the stone bench cut out of the wall of the cave, leaning against the wall, their heads tipped back against the damp stone with their eyes tight shut.

Frances found her breath and whispered: 'My God!'

Miss Cole looked at her pale face. 'What is it?'

'I did not know,' Frances said. She looked around the cellar at the thirteen black faces still as heartbroken statues in the shadows. The cruelty of the Trade suddenly opened before her, like a glimpse of hell beneath her feet. 'I did not know,' she said.

Miss Cole nodded briskly as if that confirmed her poor opinion of Frances. 'Well now you do,' she said, and turned to go up the steps again.

Frances started to follow her, but then she froze. She had a strange feeling of being observed. She felt it so strongly it was as if someone had put a warm hand on the nape of her neck. She spun around, forgetting the roughness of the floor, and had to put her hand on the damp wall to steady herself.

One of the slaves was looking at her. His skin was black, as dark as the skin of a ripe grape, his nose flared, his mouth a sculptured perfection. His cheeks were scarred with curious blue lines drawn in intricate patterns on his cheekbones. The same pattern was etched like a headband around his forehead. He had been standing with his head thrown back against the wall, the blank look of all the captives in his eyes. But something about her had drawn his attention, and his head had come up, the chain attached to the collar around his neck chinked. His eyes met hers.

He looked at her as if he knew her. She felt a jolt – as tangible as a light slap in the face. She had a strange falling sensation as if she were about to faint. The moment seemed to last for a long long time as she stared at him and he looked back at her.

'Come along, Frances.' Miss Cole's voice was spinster-sharp.

Frances did not move. She stared at the man. He stared impassively at her.

Miss Cole came back a few steps to see what had attracted Frances's attention. 'Oh, you are looking at his tattoos, are you?' she said. 'Grotesque, isn't it? And pagan. One of our captains told me that the ones who wear those tattoos are the wizards and priests of their pagan beliefs. He would have talked with the spirits and foretold the future.' She laughed one of her rare laughs. 'He couldn't have been a very good fortune-teller!'

Frances looked at him. His face was still impassive.

'Do they not understand English at all?' she asked.

'They'll have to learn,' Miss Cole said, holding open the door at the end of the passage. Frances turned unwillingly and walked away from the man. 'The whip is all the language they know now.'

Frances paused at the doorway and looked back at him. She longed to touch him, just lightly, a soft touch with her fingertip on the inside of his wrist where his black skin was soft.

He turned his head to watch her go, until all he could see was the hem of her grey gown and the shadow of the closing door.

The door at the head of the passage closed abruptly, shutting out the daylight and the sound of voices. The slaves were left in darkness.

Mehuru leaned his head back against the damp wall again and closed his eyes.

He did not despair. The Snake's counsel was ambiguous, not always to be obeyed. Like all gods he teased with false knowledge. Mehuru kept his mind turned inward and waited for the earth under his feet to stop rocking. One of the women was crying but the children were shocked and silent. They looked to Mehuru to advise them, to speculate about what would happen next. The smallest of the children was not yet three and he watched Mehuru's face with the large trusting eyes of a baby. Mehuru shook his head and looked away from the child. He did not know what would happen. He could be of no comfort to anyone.

In a little while the door opened again and the man brought them loaves of strange-tasting bread, slices of cooked meat that tasted like old dry beef, and some hard good fruit with a green skin and white sweet flesh. There was clean sour-tasting water to drink in a pan.

After a short time the man came back and made them stand, and prepared them to walk in a line. Mehuru did not look for a chance to escape. He realised he was defeated. He did not know where he was, he had never even heard of a place where the air itself was cold and grey and smelled of smoke and dirt. He could not run when he did not know where he should go. So he followed like one of the children in his pitiful obedience. The man had two pistols stuck into his belt and a long thick horsewhip in his hand, they had no chance against him. They lined up like herded cattle, and did as they were bid, straggling along the tunnel and up the four shallow steps into the warmth and poignant normality of the kitchen.

They were not allowed to linger. There was a lad waiting for them who steered them out of the kitchen door into the backyard. Mehuru was so afraid that they were going back to the ship and on another long dreadful journey that he did not look around him at first but watched his bare cold feet creeping slavishly on the cold cobbles; a man no longer, but a trained animal.

'Get on, you!' the man said gruffly, and tugged at Mehuru's chain. They were in a cobbled yard surrounded by high red-brick walls. Ahead of them and on each side were the glowering bulks of the warehouses with barred small windows. Mehuru gazed up and up the grim facade. He had seen stone buildings before, the city of Oyo had higher walls and greater buildings than this, but he had never seen such functional ugliness before. The blank redness of the walls held his eyes. He was afraid the stones had been coloured with blood.

The man shouted at him and Mehuru was pulled forward to the pump in the centre of the yard. The lad worked the pump until the water gushed out into a bucket and the big man threw buckets of water at their heads and mimed to them that they should wash themselves with a block of soap. The water was icy and tasted bitter. The soap stank of ashes from old fires and the fat of pigs. Mehuru shivered miserably and hastened to do as he was ordered.

Two of the women seemed paralysed with fear; they were certain they were being washed for the white men to eat them. They thought they would be safer if they remained dirty. They held tight to their loincloths and ducked away from the buckets of water. In the end the lad poked them with a pitchfork and laughed as they flinched between the icy water and the sharp prongs. He licked his lips at them and the slave driver guffawed when he saw how they looked to the manacled men for help. The two men looked back at them in passive misery, wishing they were blind.

One by one they washed and then rubbed themselves dry on the same rough cloth. Then the back door of the house opened and the scullery maid brought out clothes for them, tittering at their naked discomfort. The lad, tiring of the jest, pulled the clothes on one of the boys and left the rest to guess how the breeches should fit. The women kept their hands spread over their genitals, their dark faces blushed even blacker with shame. The lad grinned and slid a curious finger between one of the women's clenched buttocks.

Mehuru spoke softly to her and she disengaged herself with a slow speechless dignity. The lad glanced at Mehuru, his eyes drawn to the blue tattoos on his forehead and cheeks.

'What you staring at?' he asked aggressively, gesturing with the pitchfork. 'What you looking at, you beast, you?'

'Is it now?' Mehuru asked Snake curiously, in the quietest corner of his mind. 'Will he spear me and kill me now?'

Snake kept his silence.

Mehuru dropped his eyes to the ground and the lad put the pitchfork down, oddly dissatisfied. 'I hate them,' he said to the driver. 'Let's get them out of the yard and back into the cellar.'

John Bates shook his head. 'They're to go upstairs,' he said. 'The new mistress is teaching them to talk English, if she can. Then they go into service.'

The lad looked at them. 'They can talk?' he asked incredulously. He stepped closer to Mehuru. 'Can you talk?' he shouted into his face.

Mehuru flinched at the spittle. He had no idea at all what the young man was shouting at him. The young man stuck his tongue out at Mehuru.

'Got a tongue?' he shouted. 'Can you speak to me?'

A sigh of pure terror went through the others at the sight

116

of that startlingly red tongue poking out from the obscene pink lips.

'Gently,' Mehuru said to the others in his own language. 'Be still.'

'He made a noise!' the lad said, delighted. 'Say some more, Animal! Say something more!'

Mehuru looked down into the face of the young man. The scaly grey-green eyes looked up at him curiously. The ghostly dreadful skin was speckled with spots of brown as if the youth had some strange sickness.

'Come on,' said John Bates the slave driver, weary of the lad's interest. 'You must have seen enough niggers before.'

'Not straight from Africa I haven't,' the lad replied. 'I've seen them when they're tame, from the Sugar Islands. I've never seen them straight from Africa. They eat each other, don't they?'

'They wouldn't eat you,' Bates said. 'Too smelly by half. Come on now, let's get them in.'

They split them into two groups by pushing them into place and prodding them with the pitchfork. One group they left chained in the yard but Mehuru, two women, two little boys and one youth they chained and led towards the kitchen door. Mehuru turned back to the other group, shivering in the coldness of the wind.

'The gods be with you,' he said.

The other man looked after him. 'May we meet again, in a better place,' he said.

They shuffled into the kitchen, stooping to accommodate the weight and cutting edges of the neck-irons. Mehuru looked more vulnerable in the ill-fitting breeches and shirt than in his own loincloth. It had not been thought worth while to buy them shoes so the new breeches ended just below the knee and he was barefoot. The women were wearing cheap gowns which reached their ankles.

Frances and Miss Cole were waiting for them in the hall.

117

When Frances saw them she drew a quick breath of surprise. Close at hand she was struck at once by the tiny frailty of the little children. Their smocks and breeches were far too large for them, their little black necks were coldly exposed by the broad scoop of the collars. The smallest boy was about two, she thought, and the one who stood beside him and watched her with enormous black eyes was no more than five. They both looked at her solemnly, unwaveringly, with the open faces of children whose experiences of cruelty and loss have not yet wiped out the early memory of love. They were still capable of hope.

'They don't smell so bad now, ma'am,' John Bates said loudly. 'Will you have them in the parlour?'

'Yes, take them upstairs,' Miss Cole said. 'Are they safe?'

'Quiet as dead rats,' John Bates assured her cheerfully.

'We'll keep them chained for the first lesson,' Miss Cole decided nervously. She walked down the line as they stood, their eyes fixed on the ground. They trembled slightly as the ghostly woman went by.

'Come along then,' she said, and turned for the staircase to the upper floor. John prodded the woman at the head of the chain, and they followed her, their lips compressed tight so they did not cry out in their terror. Only the widening of their eyes revealed that they were afraid, and the slight sheen of sweat on their faces.

Frances watched each one as they went past her. The two women looked as if they had suffered the most. Their skin was lighter and they clung together; both were scarred on the back, and one had an unhealed cut on her cheekbone. They were followed by one awkward ungainly youth who tried to keep a courteous distance from them but was dragged forward by the shortness of the chain. Frances made herself look away and stepped back to let the line go by her. She did not look up again, not even when she heard the thud of someone struck with the butt end of a whip.

'He was lagging, ma'am,' Bates explained cheerfully.

Miss Cole led them up the narrow stairs to the little parlour. When the line walked into the room they hesitated, and did not know what to do. Miss Cole pulled out a chair but then could not bring herself to touch the leading woman to guide her to her seat.

'Bates,' she said shortly. He put a broad red hand on the woman's shoulder and thrust her into a seat. Then the other woman and the youth perched on the very edge of the hard chairs and looked at Miss Cole and Frances with eyes which were blank with terror. The little boys had to be lifted up on their chairs. John Bates stepped back from the table and set himself with his back against the door, two pistols stuck in his belt, and his whip held across him.

'Sit at the head of the table, Frances, and start their lesson,' Miss Cole ordered.

Mehuru kept his head down, but he noted the tone of command, and he saw that the young white woman obeyed.

Her looks were horrible. She was as smooth and as pale as polished ivory. But the worst thing about her was her hair, which was as long and as thick as weeds in the river and was piled upon her head with trails of it coming down around her shoulders and curling like water weed around her face. Unpinned it must stretch down to her buttocks like some dreadful smooth cloth. Her eyes were as dark as his own but she moved like one of them, with small steps and a hunched body as if she hated herself, as if she were trying to hide her breasts and her belly.

She was bony and small, like an ugly child. He scanned her body and saw the uselessness of her narrow pelvis and the skinny buttocks. She was too thin, a man could not embrace her and roll her over and over on the ground. She would not seize a lover and take him with laughter. She would not shout joyfully at the approach of pleasure. He thought of his woman at home and how he would thrust his shoulder against her open mouth to muffle her singing cries when she opened her legs wide to him. This ghostwoman knew nothing of this, could learn nothing of this. She moved as if she had denied herself of pleasure for many years, as if she had never known lust, as if she had never known desire. She held herself like a criminal, not like a woman at all.

Mehuru suddenly realised that she was looking at him, and feared that his thoughts were showing on his face. He flushed quickly and looked away from her.

Chapter Nine

Frances drew a breath. She seated herself gingerly in the chair at the head of the table. Sarah went to the windowseat and gazed avidly at them all. 'Go on,' she said impatiently. 'Teach them something!'

The noises from outside the window were very loud. Josiah was auctioning his sugar on the quayside, Frances could hear his excited shout as the bids went higher.

'Go on,' Sarah said.

Frances looked down the table. The children were whimpering softly, each stretching out for the woman seated beside him. Only Mehuru was looking at her, with his strange judging gaze. As their eyes met he slightly inclined his head. It was as if he had given her some permission. She felt an unexpected sense of humility before him. She looked at him more closely. His forehead was lined with raised tattoos showing dark blue against his black skin. Around his mouth there were half a dozen blue circles that drew the gaze to the wide sensuality of his lips. His eyes were dark and unfathomable. His nose was broad and flat. His skin was perfectly black and smooth. Frances wanted to touch him, to feel that he was real.

She dragged her eyes from his face and tapped the table with the flat of her hand. 'Table,' she said quietly.

They looked at her in silence. They were all of them frozen with fear.

She slapped the table again. 'Table,' she repeated more firmly.

Miss Cole glared irritably at her across the bowed black heads. 'They clearly don't know what you mean,' she said. 'You must make them speak.'

Frances drew a breath and paused. She did not know what to do.

'Begging your pardon, ma'am, *he* can speak.' John Bates pointed with the butt end of his whip at Mehuru. 'Spoke in the yard when the lad asked him to make a noise. Him with the drawings on his face.'

Frances looked at Mehuru. 'Say: table,' she said, without much hope. 'Tay-bull.'

'Day-bull,' Mehuru said.

Frances jumped. He had a pleasant confident voice, the voice of a man who is accustomed to being heard. She was as surprised as if the table itself had said its name to her. She had not expected him to speak – she had not expected him to have this strong clear baritone.

'Yes,' she nodded.

'Make the others say it!' Miss Cole came forward from the windowseat, her flat breasts heaving with excitement. 'Make them say it too! Make them all say it!'

'Now you.' Frances pointed to the woman seated at the foot of the table. She slapped the wood and looked at her. 'Table,' she said.

With the tip of his fingers the young boy pattered out a message on the table top in the ancient language of drumming. 'What?' the rhythm asked urgently. 'What?'

'Speak,' Mehuru tapped back. He glanced round the table and nodded at the frightened faces. 'Speak,' his fingers tapped again. It was not the warm-skinned talking drums of home which could send messages for miles and miles across country, but it was still a little power, a little secret they had left.

'Stop that!' Miss Cole snapped with instant anger. 'Make the next one speak.'

122

Frances pointed at the woman again, and slapped the table with her hand. Her palm made a sharp unkind sound after Mehuru's seductive drumming. 'Table,' she said.

'Day-bull,' the woman replied in a voice as low as a whisper.

'Yes!' Miss Cole's shrill excitement frightened them all. They shot scared looks at Mehuru, who had his eyes fixed on the wooden shiny surface.

'Make them all say it!' Miss Cole commanded. She was standing at the foot of the table, her sallow cheeks burning with two pink spots. 'Make them speak!' she cried.

'Table,' Frances said. 'T . . . t . . . table.'

'Day-bull,' they repeated.

Mehuru was watching Frances though she did not know it. His eyes were still turned down to the table top, and he was watching the inverted reflection of her pale face in the polished surface.

'Day-bull,' he said with the rest; but in his head he called for Snake.

Snake would know who this ghostwoman was and what she wanted with them. He called for Snake and begged him for sight. As if from a distance, Snake chuckled in his long throat and said: '*Sight is easy*'. Then Mehuru saw this woman with her hair in a thick plait lying in a high bed with a great many white covers. She was lying on her back and her face was wet with tears. Mehuru sensed her coldness and her loneliness. He thought that he had never in his life known a woman with so much power – power over him and all these others – and yet such passivity that she should lie like a stone and grieve for nothing.

She was defeated and fearful, a woman who had thrown away her power. She was a fool who had chosen to know nothing. She had closed her eyes to her own feelings. She had denied her own nature. All she had left was the cold shell of her body and – weep-weep-weep – a constant flow of tears.

The light in the room and the covers on the bed were very cold and white. Mehuru knew it was this land, but not, he thought, exactly this time. Snake hissed a laugh in his head and said: '*What does time or place matter to you? You who are imprisoned in the here and now?*'

'Day-bull,' Mehuru repeated with the others. Day-bull? What did she mean, day-bull? Did she mean wood, or the sort of wood it was? Did she mean the polish which made the wood shine? Did she mean the name of the woodcarver? Or the god of woodcarvers? Did she mean the feel of the wood under her palm, or the noise it made when she slapped it so?

Frances looked down the table and saw Mehuru frown even as he repeated the word. She suddenly flushed with her sense of helplessness. If she could not teach them to speak then the experiment would be abandoned and they would be sent to the plantations. No-one lived long working on the sugar crop. A quarter of them would die before their first year was out, half of the rest would not live more than four years.

That was why the slavers went crossing and re-crossing the wide reaches of the Atlantic seas, pouring men and women and children into the plantations which ate them up as surely as they crushed sugar cane. They worked so hard, they lived so poor, that they could not even breed to replace the dead. Children died before they could reach adulthood. Women died before they could give birth. Men died before they could lie with a woman and give her a child. Every month, every week, every day, new slaves had to be captured and shipped and sold. Without them the plantations would collapse and the English people would have no sugar, tobacco, cotton or rum.

Frances had spent her life among events which never rose above the trivial. Now suddenly, she was responsible for the survival of thirteen people, and one of them a man who sat as if he were wrapped in a cloak of magic. She turned quickly to the sideboard.

'Glasses,' she said, showing them two wine glasses.

'Classes,' they repeated.

'Knives, forks, spoons,' she said, laying them down on the table.

They babbled the words in panic, she had gone too fast. One of the little children started to cry. Miss Cole was still standing at the foot of the table, her colour high, her breath coming quickly.

'That one,' she said abruptly, pointing to Mehuru. 'The man with the marks on his face. He understands the most, he is watching.'

The meaningless repetition of words died away into silence. 'Find out his name,' she demanded. 'You can teach him, then he can explain to the others in their own tongue.'

Frances turned towards Mehuru. She could smell his fear like smoke.

She put her hand on the base of her throat.

'Frances,' she said. 'Frances.'

Then she pointed at him. Mehuru gulped.

'France-sess,' he repeated. He felt as if he had a thrashing animal trapped in his brain. What did she mean now, France-sess? Was that the word for woman? Or for throat? Was it the word for thirst? Or for the scared thumping of his heart which he felt as he put his hand there, mirroring her action?

'Not you! You fool! Her!' Miss Cole said irritably, watching him gesture to himself and say 'Frances'. His dark eyes snapped towards her as if he were waiting for an attack but did not know which woman would spring first.

'I am Frances,' the young one said quickly. She pointed to the older woman. 'Miss Cole.' Mehuru noted the dislike in her voice. She pointed at the white man with the whip who had thrown water over them and laughed when the woman was assaulted. 'John Bates,' she said.

Mehuru nodded, he understood: they were names. He had four names. He gave her his public name, which anyone could use without summoning his soul or harming him. He put his hand on his chest and looked her in the eyes. 'Mehuru,' he said.

Frances's black eyes gazed at him, and widened. She leaned forward a little closer, as if to hear him better. She put her hand to her throat and felt beneath her fingers her own rapid pulse.

'Frances,' she said again. Then she reached out across the table and put her hand on Mehuru's chest. He could feel the light touch of her fingers tremble as she touched him.

'Mehuru,' she said.

Her small white childlike face looked into his. 'Mehuru?' she asked, seeking confirmation. She could feel the warmth of his chest through the thin linen shirt. She could smell the scent of his newly washed skin. The tattoos on his face were fine delicate lines of blue. The skin beneath his eyes was faintly blue too with fatigue and sorrow. His eyelids slanted upwards, his eyes met hers. He was as wary as a trapped animal.

'Mehuru,' she said lingeringly.

A ripple of fear ran through them all. A new depth of terror went through them like hot wind through the grasslands. They heard the tone of a woman speaking to her beloved.

Mehuru heard it too. He lowered his eyes to avoid her penetrating, horrible gaze.

'Mehuru,' he said obediently. 'France-sess.'

Miss Cole was exultant. She would have kept them all day in the shadowy parlour, learning new lessons. But Frances refused.

'They'll be getting tired,' she objected. 'And I am weary. We've done enough for today.'

Miss Cole nodded unwillingly. 'Bates, you must keep them

chained in their groups so we do not muddle them up,' she ordered. 'Bring these particular ones to do another lesson tomorrow.'

Frances bowed her head. Mehuru held himself with weary alertness. The two white women were talking together but their voices were cold with dislike. The older one had the sharp tone of command but the younger one had power too. The man at the door called Johnbates was their servant. Mehuru had given orders in his own world and he knew the tilt of a head which was ready to bow. Johnbates might be dangerous, but he was only a cipher for the women.

'Take them back to the cellar,' Miss Cole said to John.

Mehuru shot a swift look at Frances and met her slanty dark eyes. Her skin coloured and Mehuru stared, fascinated, as a deep red blush rose up from the white fichu at Frances's throat to colour her whole face. 'Red as frangipani,' Mehuru thought. 'Red as a tongue.'

Frances cleared her throat. 'They should not go back in the cellar where it is so cold and dark and dirty,' she said. 'Not now they are washed and have clothes on.'

Miss Cole was looking out of the window, relishing her sense of achievement. 'What?'

'We should teach them to keep clean,' Frances said. She found herself tapping some secret reserve of female cunning, the skill which says one thing while thinking another. 'Now we have washed them, and dressed them, they should not go back into a dirty cave in the dark.'

Miss Cole turned from the window in surprise. 'Why not?' she asked.

'Because they will only have to be washed again, and because they must learn how to keep clean, and sleep in beds, and wear proper clothes,' Frances reasoned. 'They should have a light. They should have proper food on plates. They should have a clean floor, and benches to sit on.'

'But they're slaves!' Miss Cole protested.

Frances slyly bobbed her head. 'I am sorry. I did not understand,' she lied. 'I thought they were to be trained as servants.'

Miss Cole opened her mouth to argue and then hesitated. Frances was right. It could not be too early to start training them in the standards of a proper Christian household. And they could clean the cave themselves.

'You, Bates,' she said abruptly. 'Take them back to the cave and get them to muck it out. Scrub it clean and put down some matting on the floor. Get some benches for them to sit on, and put a lantern high on a hook for light.'

'They should be unchained,' Frances added. She stretched out her hand towards Mehuru's clenched fists, touched the manacle on his wrist. Mehuru froze as if some unknown animal were brushing against him.

'Not yet, not yet,' Miss Cole said nervously. She looked around at the impassive black faces. 'Not until they are a little more tame.'

'I could give them some linen to go around the manacles,' John offered from the doorway. 'That'd stop them bleeding into their shirts. Help with the smell too. The sores get filled with pus if they wear irons for too long.'

'That will do,' Miss Cole said, revolted. 'Make whatever arrangements are necessary, Bates. Take these back and bring the others for their lesson this afternoon. And then bring these back tomorrow morning.'

The driver nodded and stepped to one side. Mehuru watched him carefully, saw the little bow towards the old woman and the more shallow nod to the younger one. So the old one was the senior, as he had thought. He rose from his chair and saw the old one flinch back from his height and strength.

The others followed him, on their feet and walking with their painful shuffle from the room. They crowded at the top of the stairs, finding the narrow wooden steps frightening.

Mehuru touched his mind with the wisdom of Snake: '*All skin sheds at last*', and went down, like a ghostman, one foot after another, his body erect. The others followed his lead. Frances watched the top of Mehuru's head until he was out of sight in the kitchen and she could hear the rising litany of complaint from the cook.

'Now,' Miss Cole said coldly, masking her pleasure, 'there is an hour left before noon. I suggest that you apply yourself to the housekeeping accounts.'

Frances turned demurely. 'Yes, Sarah,' she said.

They went back together to the parlour. Miss Cole laid out the bills and the ledger, and directed Frances to the pen in the standish. Frances nodded, sat down at the desk and pulled the ledger towards her.

Miss Cole drew up a chair at Frances's elbow and watched the downward march of figures in the columns.

'Very well.' She gathered her sewing basket and announced that she would leave Frances alone with the ledgers. 'You will want to study them, I expect.'

Frances nodded, saying nothing. But as soon as Miss Cole shut the door she pushed the books to one side and laid her face on the coolness of the polished wood.

She felt very strange, as light-headed as if she had drunk some young fresh wine. The room no longer seemed stuffy or oppressive, the sparkle of the sunlight on the ceiling seemed to promise a bright wintry day, the noise of the working quay was cheerful. She felt as if she were a girl again, as if she were young and hopeful. In her early days when her mother had been alive Frances had been a pretty, petted, optimistic child. Under the cold carapace of her adult disappointments her spirit stirred, as if it might warm and come alive again. She sat very still for long moments, feeling her sense of inexplicable elation. She did not know why she suddenly felt as if joy were possible. She did not know why the air seemed a little cleaner and the house less oppressive.

'Mehuru,' she said thoughtfully to the open pages of the ledger.

She did not think about where he had come from. She had no notion of an Africa before the coming of the British, of a huge continent populated by a complex of different peoples and kingdoms, of trading and barter stations, of caravans of goods which crossed from one nation to another; of men and women, some living like peasants working the land, some living in towns and cities and working in industries, some established in hereditary kingdoms seated on thrones of gold and ivory and living like gods.

She had no interest in the slaves as people who had come from a living and potent culture. She felt powerful beside the black slave in a way she had never felt powerful before. She had always been a young woman in a world where male power was absolute. For the first time in her life she was able to look at a man and know that she could command him. For the first time in her life she could be a woman who could find and take her own power, and make a difference in her world. If she were clever and cunning she could keep him from death on the plantations. She nodded and felt her lips curve upwards in a smile. 'I can save his life,' she said softly. 'And he has to obey me.'

She rose from the table and went to the mirror above the fireplace. She almost expected to see the face of the girl she had been when her mother had been alive and her father had been prosperous and happy. She looked for that round-faced confident girl and was surprised to see the reflection of the drawn thin woman who gazed back at her.

But her eyes were very bright.

The lantern-lit cellar glowed a dusky red. The walls, quarried out of the ruddy sandstone, were red as brick, the lamplight reflected an ominous carmine glow on the faces of the slaves as they gathered around Mehuru. They were still all chained one to another, and the last one at each end was fastened to the wall. Mehuru – whose uncle was a blacksmith, a sacred worker in iron – was looking over the chain for faults in the metal. Sometimes, if iron was cooled too quickly it became brittle and could shear as easily as stone could chip. He looked at each link in the uncertain light of the tallow candle. Each slave stood waiting patiently in turn. Mehuru shook his head.

'The chain is perfect,' he said in his own tongue. For the two women who were from another nation and did not understand him, he put both fists together to indicate strength and shook his head sorrowfully. They nodded.

'We will have to wait until they release us before we can escape,' he said.

The others nodded solemnly. 'D'you know where to run, Obalawa?' one of the women asked. She bent her head a little as she addressed him, in the instinctive respect of a woman to a man; and that of a mere mortal to one who speaks with the gods.

'No,' Mehuru admitted honestly. 'I have no sight here. I am blind like you. I am lost like you.'

A shiver of disappointment ran through them. The women groaned softly. The two Fulani women looked from one anxious face to another, trying to understand what was being said. Mehuru resisted the temptation to smile at them, to reassure his own people. He could offer them only false comfort, and in this pit in the ground he did not want to play at magic.

'I have no power here,' he said. 'I have lost it, just as the sun has lost its heat. I know no more than you. At home I was a priest with the ear of the gods, I was high at court with the ear of the king. Here I have to learn to be nothing. I am not a man, I am a slave. I know nothing more than any one of you.'

'If we walk,' one of the women suggested, 'if we walk with

the afternoon sun on our right we will get home. D'you remember, in the great ship after we lost the others, the afternoon sun was always to the left? We must walk south.'

'If there is land,' the other man, Kbara, warned. 'It may be water everywhere. It was many days sailing, remember; weeks and months at sea. Who would make that journey if they could walk? Who would build a ship like that unless they had to? These people have horses and carriages. If there was land they would have gone by land. Perhaps we have come from our world to this one by a great sea of time.'

Instinctively they looked to Mehuru – he knew the mysteries of one world and another, he should know.

Mehuru shook his head. 'I do not know,' he said. 'It will be enough for me if we can get away from this house and from these people. And from that woman,' he added very low.

'Somewhere there must be real people,' Kbara said desperately. 'They cannot all be white. They eat food, somewhere there must be real people planting crops and herding animals. They must be people like us working the earth. They eat meat, there must be herdsmen like the Fulani.'

Mehuru nodded. 'Perhaps.'

'At least they have given us clothes and water and now a light,' one of the women said hopefully. 'They cannot mean to eat us, can they? They would have started by now, wouldn't they?'

'I don't think they will eat us,' Mehuru said carefully. 'I think they are teaching us to speak their language for a reason.'

The others nodded. 'For what?'

'To serve them,' Mehuru suggested. 'If we ever had a slave from far away we would teach him our tongue.'

The younger woman shrank back against the wall in distaste. 'To serve them!' she exclaimed. 'To cook their food and clean their houses and touch them, and endure their smell and the coldness of their eyes! I could not do it!'

Mehuru looked at her and his face held a world of sorrow. 'I think they will teach us to do all that, and worse,' he said.

Then he turned from the circle around the candle and squatted down with his face to the damp wall of the cave, rested his head against the cold stone and let himself long for the heat and the scents of Africa.

Chapter Ten

Josiah sent a message from the coffee house that he would be bringing guests home for dinner, a gentleman and his daughter. Brown brought the news to Frances as she was lying down on her bed, resting after her lesson with the second batch of slaves. Frances pinned on her cap and hurried down to the parlour.

'We will dine at five,' Miss Cole said. 'I have already sent out to the pastrycook's for some puddings and ordered Cook to make a special dinner. Since you were resting again I thought I should make the preparations. I did not wish to disturb you. Are you ill again? Is it your cough this time, or your headache?'

'Neither,' Frances said. She felt well for the first time since coming to the little house by the foul-smelling river. 'I feel very well.'

Sarah raised her thin eyebrows. 'I am glad to hear it. You may take your tea now, in the parlour if you wish,' she offered. 'I have no time for it this afternoon. I am going to see Cook again and then to my room to change.'

'I shall change too,' Frances said obediently as she followed Miss Cole out of the parlour and up the narrow stairs to the second-floor bedrooms. 'Who are our guests? Did Josiah say?'

'Sir Charles Fairley and his daughter,' Sarah said. 'I met Sir Charles when he visited England before but I do not know Miss Fairley. He is a very important man in Jamaica and a good customer to us. We buy our sugar from him and he pays a top price for slaves. His demand for slaves is almost beyond our ability to meet.'

'He has such large estates?' Frances asked.

'His use is very rapid,' Sarah answered carefully. 'He gets through slaves quicker than any other planter.'

Frances nodded. She was starting to recognise the euphemisms of the Trade.

'There is no need to wear anything too fine for dinner,' Sarah said waspishly as she reached the door of her room. 'Our guests know me and they know my brother as respectable traders, not gentry. I have only one evening dress in dark silk – I shall be wearing that. If you have anything simple it would be appropriate.'

'I have a sack dress in grey silk,' Frances said carefully.

'That sounds very suitable,' Sarah replied.

Frances nodded, went into her bedroom and shut the door. She saw her own smile in her dressing-table mirror. She looked pretty and girlish and naughty. 'I will *try* to be as ugly as a boot,' she said to the mirror. 'To keep you in countenance, Sister-dear.'

Frances and Miss Cole waited in the parlour for their guests, sitting either side of a large fire. Miss Cole was resplendent in an evening dress of dark blue silk with a small half-train. Frances had chosen a gown of grey watered silk with grey silk gloves. It was high-waisted with a long sweeping skirt and a loose panel at the back like a train. The sleeves were white silk trimmed with grey velvet, very fine. Brown had spent an hour with the hot curling tongs trying to make Frances's hair into ringlets which were supposed to cling around her face, but had settled in the end for a soft wave rather than the tight corkscrew curls dictated by fashion. Against the sheen of the silk Frances's skin was warm cream. Miss Cole eyed her without pleasure.

135

'I think we should sew while we wait for our guests,' she said.

Frances took a cambric handkerchief from her workbox and started hemming it with small even stitches. The two women sat in silence. Then they heard Josiah open the door and the sound of footsteps on the stairs. Frances put her work away and rose to greet the visitors.

Sir Charles entered the room first, his daughter behind him. He was a large red-faced man, his broad chest and stomach bursting against his brilliantly embroidered waistcoat. Dark knee breeches encased fat thighs, his high white stock was wrapped tightly around multiple chins, his blue coat was lined with sable which made him even more bulky.

'So this is the bride!' he said jovially to Frances after he had greeted Miss Cole with a kiss on her hand.

Frances dropped a small curtsey and let him clasp her hand in his two moist palms and then kiss it.

'Oh, Papa!' Miss Fairley exclaimed languidly in a strange rich accent.

'Here, Miss Cole, this is my daughter Honoria that you've heard me tell so much about, in England at last!' he said to Sarah. He turned to Frances. 'I am honoured to present my daughter to you, Mrs Cole.'

Frances curtseyed to the girl. She was pale and slim, wearing a silk gown of icy white which drained her mousy hair and pale face of what little colour she had. She had a shawl of silver tissue around her shoulders and large pearls at her neck and in her ears and on her wrists. She had a second shawl of warm white wool trailing from her right shoulder as if she feared they would not have heated the room.

'Honoured,' she said coolly. Her rich accent was oddly at variance with her strictly conventional dress.

Josiah Cole came in behind his guests. 'Sit down, Sir Charles,' he said. 'What will you have to drink? Dinner will be served shortly.'

'I'll take a glass of rum and water if you have any of my own excellent barrels in the house.' The fat man winked at Frances. 'That's the worst of the Sugar Island life, Mrs Cole. You get a taste for all of it. The sunshine, the drinks, the company. You should come on a visit. We'd make you very welcome, wouldn't we, Honoria?'

The girl gave the smallest of nods. 'There's very little society for ladies,' she said, her voice lilting with the rhythm of the Sugar Island speech.

'But the weather!' Sir Charles took his glass from Brown. 'I tell you, I have not been warm since I set sail.'

'It has been very damp,' Miss Cole observed. 'I sometimes think December is the worst month of the year, always cold and often wet.'

'I am spoiled, Miss Cole, and that is the truth. If I came in midsummer I should still feel a chill.'

Frances sipped a glass of ratafia. The scullery maid hovered in the parlour doorway and whispered to Brown, who stepped forward and whispered in turn to Josiah Cole.

'Dinner is served,' he said. 'You must take us as you find us, Sir Charles. You know we are simple merchant people. We dine on the table, here in the parlour. Will you sit here, sir? And Miss Honoria here?'

They took their places. Frances, who had dined all her life at a table which never seated less than twelve, tried not to feel snubbed by Honoria's rude stare around the cramped room.

Brown took up a position at the door and collected the dishes from the scullery maid who could be distantly heard pounding up the stairs, carrying the hot and heavy platters. Josiah looked down the table to Frances with an uneasy glance, and she felt a sudden pity for his discomfort. He knew it was not being done correctly, but not how it should be done. Frances smiled at him and his face lightened at once.

137

'Are you well, Mrs Cole?' he asked. 'Have you had an enjoyable day?'

'I am very comfortable,' Frances assured him. She saw Sarah's glance of surprise at her determinedly bright tone. 'I am very comfortable indeed.'

'I am sorry not to be served by your slaves,' Sir Charles observed. 'Josiah has been telling me that you have a dozen of them in training.'

'They will not be ready for some months,' Josiah said. 'My wife is teaching them to speak.'

Honoria turned on Frances a look of pale disdain. '*You* are breaking slaves?'

Frances nodded defensively. 'Yes.'

'It's a man's job at home,' Sir Charles said abruptly. 'On my plantation the old hands train the new ones. This is a man's job that you have given to your wife, Cole.'

'She has the help of a driver, and besides they are no trouble. We have only two men and the rest are women and small children.'

Brown circled the table serving soup from a large tureen. Frances recognised the best silver brought down from the storeroom for the occasion.

'It's not the wit that's required but the whip!' Sir Charles exclaimed. He laughed, a deep satisfied laugh. 'Did you hear that? Not the wit but the whip!'

Miss Cole tittered agreeably, Josiah smiled.

'They're like children,' Sir Charles explained. 'They can remember nothing unless it is beaten into them. And their spirits are surly and defiant. On my plantation we have a beating in the stocks every day. In the fields they are whipped as they work; but at least once a day I have one whipped in the stocks. And I have the blacksmith brand them at the forge, oh! time after time, and sometimes slit their tongues for insolence. I wear myself out trying to devise punishments which will serve as an example to the others, and yet not

138

injure them so badly that they are spoiled for work or re-sale.'

'So stupid,' Miss Honoria said languidly in her high sweet voice. 'They are so stupid.'

'What's your death rate now?' Josiah asked.

Sir Charles shrugged. 'I suppose of our two hundred we lose about fifty or sixty a year. They hardly breed at all. We lose women in childbirth all the time, and the babies are often born dead. When I hear of men preaching that the trade in slaves should stop I wonder how they would have me run my plantation? How else can sugar be grown?'

Josiah nodded and signed to Brown to pour more wine. 'It's ignorance,' he said. 'And fashion. It'll pass. It's a few young prating clergymen and a couple of members of Parliament trying to make their career. Methodists and radicals! It will blow over. It's nothing more than a few grubby radicals stirring up bad feelings and signing petitions. The leaders of this country know the profits that the Trade brings, and they like to take sugar in their tea. We won't be driven by the mob.

'Look at Bristol! Before the Trade it was a little town; nothing to what it is now. The fortunes made in this town are a monument to slavery. And Liverpool has been built on the back of the Atlantic trade. Every day they build another great house or another town hall. People know where their interests lie. This is a milksop agitation, it will pass.'

'I hope so,' Sir Charles said heavily. 'I cannot tell you how alarmed we get when we hear the fools agitating and complaining. What of this Wilberforce, and his bill?'

Josiah scowled and poured himself another glass of wine. 'It comes before Parliament this May,' he said. 'But we are all prepared. Our men will call for more evidence and adjourn the reading, it can be adjourned forever they tell me. The great men of the Trade in Liverpool and London and here are all ready to act in concert and their pockets are well-lined. I don't think that a handful of clergymen and some ignorant working men can stand against them. There's not one member of the Houses of Parliament that does not have an investment to protect. They will hardly vote themselves out of business.'

'I pay two members a pension direct,' Sir Charles said. 'To guard my interests. But it makes me so angry when I hear of these radicals. They know nothing about the Trade. They know nothing about our difficulties. Every visitor we've ever had to Clearwater Plantation has gone away convinced that we are working the land in the only way possible. You can't get white labourers, and all the Indians are dead now – not one of them lasted beyond the first few years of our arrival. How are we supposed to manage? And what would the slaves be doing in Africa? Hunting each other and burning each other alive! We have saved them from the most foul paganism and taught them work and discipline. Why I could tell you some tales . . .'

'Papa!' Honoria murmured.

'I beg your pardon,' Sir Charles said. 'My daughter is delicate in her tastes,' he explained to Frances. 'I should not mention these things before her.'

'I do hate niggers,' Honoria said quietly to Frances as the men talked across the table. 'I wonder you can bear to teach them. I won't have them near me.'

'Do you have no black servants?'

'Most of them are half-castes,' Honoria replied. 'Mulattos. We prefer to use them in the house.'

'Half-caste?' Frances repeated the unfamiliar word.

'Yes,' Honoria said calmly. 'Papa likes to mix the stock.'

Frances heard the genteel euphemism; but she would not examine what it might mean. 'And what is it like?' she asked. 'Living on the plantation?'

Honoria glanced at her father and at Josiah and Sarah who were listening only to him. 'Dreadfully slow,' she complained. 'There's hardly any society unless we go into Jamestown and even then there are only two balls a year. We've come home for me to buy some gowns and . . .' she gave a small smile '. . . make acquaintances.'

'Young gentlemen?' Frances hazarded, and was rewarded with another small smile.

'I have nothing to do all day except watch the sugar grow and torment the housegirls,' Honoria said. 'Mama spends all day in bed. She's delicate, she's dreadfully delicate. She has Nanny – my old black Nanny – running up and down for her every half hour with one thing or another, sending dishes back to the cook, and complaining and carrying-on.'

Frances nodded, trying to imagine the large white house amid a sea of lush green forest, with three discontented whites, drinking rum or nursing hypochondria in the shade while outside two hundred exiles worked under the merciless sun, whipped if they went slow, mourning for their homes and their families.

Brown removed the soup and loaded the table with dishes: cutlets, a haunch of beef, a venison pie, and sweetbreads.

'You Bristol merchants spread a good table!' Sir Charles exclaimed. 'I always enjoy a visit to your house, Miss Cole.'

Miss Cole smiled her acid smile and asked for how long the Fairleys would be visiting Bristol. Sir Charles outlined an itinerary designed to net Miss Honoria a husband. They were to go shopping for clothes in Bath, attend the Pump Room, visit in the country during summer and then stay with friends for the London Season in the winter.

'We hope to be setting sail again by next spring,' he concluded. 'Unless Honoria here surprises me with other plans!'

Honoria turned her eyes down to the table and tried to blush. 'Oh, Papa!'

'And who runs your place while you are away?' Josiah enquired. 'D'you have a manager you can trust?'

'An overseer,' Sir Charles nodded. 'He's a man from Jamestown, working his way up. He's a brute but I can trust

141

him with a shipful. He knows how to handle them and he'll give no quarter. I'll come home and there will be some sad faces in the slave quarters, and some new mounds in the graveyard; but there will have been no trouble.'

'Surely on Clearwater you never have trouble?' Miss Cole remarked.

Sir Charles shook his head as his plate was cleared away. 'I never sleep without a gun at my bedside,' he said. 'You never know where you are with them, Miss Cole. You have to remember the numbers you are facing, all the time you have to be wary. Remember that there are only three of us, Lady Fairley, Honoria and myself, and there are two hundred of them, and more if you count the visitors in the slave cabins that I don't know about, and the runaways hiding in the forests around. I have to keep the upper hand night and day. They're always waiting – waiting for their chance. Who next, eh? Where next?'

He nodded at Frances. 'If you have the management of them you had best remember my warning, Mrs Cole. They are killers. They are all born killers. Never let your guard down.'

'Our slave driver watches the lessons and he has a whip,' Miss Cole said. 'And they are manacled.'

'Keep them that way!' Sir Charles recommended. 'Keep them that way until their spirit is broken, until their very will to live is under your feet. They have to long for death. If they are attached to their lives then they want to better them-selves – that's when your trouble starts.'

Miss Cole looked thoughtful. 'We have perhaps already been too kind . . .'

Sir Charles shook his head. Brown put a large portion of syllabub before him and poured cream. 'Break their spirit and keep them low,' he advised. 'Separate the bucks from the women, keep them underfed, watch them losing weight. Keep their minds on pleasing you for little rewards, and if you see

142

the least sign of unwillingness beat them near to death – or beat one to death if need be. The others will note it, I assure you.'

Miss Cole smiled at him. 'You are so kind,' she said. 'I will consider it very carefully.'

He beamed back. 'A sensible woman,' he proclaimed with pleasure. 'Josiah, you are to be congratulated with helpers such as these. Beauty, and brains. You will go far, I know it!'

Josiah smiled and raised his glass. Frances pushed aside her untouched dessert. She had a sour taste in her mouth, the conversation was making her nauseous.

The men talked of the Trade while the fruit and sweet-meats were brought in. Honoria nibbled a sugar plum, her pale brown eyes blank with boredom. Frances sat very still, her hands in her lap, her face a mask of polite interest, willing herself to be deaf to them both.

When Josiah nodded to her, she rose from the table and led the way for the ladies to sit at the fireside. It was a pathetic parody of the rituals of gentry life. Frances's face revealed nothing, she conducted Honoria to a place at the fireside as if Lady Scott herself always dined and sat in the same room.

'We'll go to my office,' Josiah announced. 'We'll take a glass there and join you later, ladies.'

They went unsteadily from the room, having already drunk the best part of four bottles. Honoria, Sarah, and Frances made thin conversation at the fireside and ordered tea. The men did not return. The conversation dwindled and died. Honoria openly watched the hands of the clock on the mantelpiece. When it chimed nine she asked if the maid might tell her Papa that she wished to go home.

Sir Charles appeared in the doorway, woefully drunk. 'So sorry, my dear,' he said, speaking with meticulous care. 'I shall send you home in a chair, don't you know. A chair. Brown has gone out to fetch you one and she shall see you home. I'll see you in the morning, my dear. In the morning.

Josiah and I are setting the world to rights and finishing a very pretty port. A very pretty port indeed. I shall take my supper here.'

Honoria nodded and let Frances help her with her cape.

'I shall go to bed,' Frances said quietly to Josiah.

'Do,' he said pleasantly. 'We will make a night of it. No need to wait up.'

The men retreated to Josiah's study again, broached another bottle and ordered some supper. By midnight they were thoroughly drunk.

'Let's have one of the slave girls brought in,' Sir Charles suggested. 'Have a little sport.'

Josiah peered at him owlishly. 'We're not at Clearwater now,' he observed. 'There are the servants to think of, and the ladies.'

Sir Charles laughed his rich happy laugh. 'Servants be damned. And the ladies know when to look the other way. Lady Fairley knows when she'd better look aside, you can depend on it.'

'I cannot,' Josiah protested. 'I don't keep the keys and anyway Mrs Cole would not like it.'

'She need never know,' Sir Charles said. 'Go on, Josiah. Don't be such a damned Methodist.'

Josiah was drunk but still reluctant. 'It's not the done thing in England,' he said. 'Assure you, my dear fellow. Let's go out and get a woman if you wish . . . but slaves in your own home . . . not done.'

'I know what the done thing is!' Sir Charles was starting to get unpleasant. 'I'm a damned baronet . . . a baronet! I should know the done thing, I hope. I'm good enough to buy your slaves at a handsome profit to you, and good enough to sell you sugar on the quayside at knock-down prices. I know the done thing then, don't I?'

'I just meant . . .'

'And here am I, offering to take a share in one of your

ships, one thousand pounds' worth, I remind you, Josiah! I should have thought I know the done thing!'

'No offence, no offence,' Josiah said quickly.

'Well, none taken,' Sir Charles replied, his mood swinging back into sunshine. 'None taken. But let's have a girl, Josiah! Let's stir the stock.'

'They're in the cellar,' Josiah said. 'And my wife has charge of all the household keys.'

'Send her a message, tell her we want to see the slaves!' Sir Charles had the characteristic stubbornness of the drunkard. 'Come on, man! You can't be under the cat's paw in your first year of marriage! Who rules the roast here?'

'I do!' Josiah said stung.

'Then get us a damned woman!'

Josiah touched the bell rope and Brown came wearily to see what he wanted now. 'Tell Mrs Cole we want to see one of the slave women,' Josiah ordered. 'Ask her to send me the keys.'

Brown curtseyed and went out.

Sir Charles smiled in anticipation and poured himself another glass of port. 'I assure you,' he beamed, 'once you get the taste for it, you are spoiled for anything else. At home I take them whenever I fancy.'

Josiah hid his distaste. 'Do you not take African diseases, Sir Charles? African illness?'

The man nodded. 'Aye, and pass them on too! But I'm grown very reckless, you know. There is something about being master, complete master, of so many. There is something which stirs you, to know that every woman has to do your bidding, and that the others can do nothing but watch.' He blew out a plume of cigar smoke with a shaky little laugh. 'There is nothing like it. This empire of ours is a glorious thing, Josiah. It makes us Englishmen like gods.'

Josiah nodded, took a small sip of port and swallowed down

his distaste. There was a tap on the door and Frances stood in the doorway, wearing a loose gown and with her cap hastily pinned on her hair. 'May I speak with you, husband?' she said.

Josiah rose and went to the door, half-closing it to shield their conversation from the guest. 'What are you doing downstairs dressed like this?'

Frances glanced at her wrapper, the usual morning dress for ladies in their homes. 'I had gone to bed,' she said reasonably.

'You come before a guest half-dressed?'

Frances gave a little laugh, and then looking into Josiah's face saw that he was serious. 'Excuse me, husband,' she said carefully. 'I had no idea that you would object.'

The gulf between his world and hers suddenly opened before them. Josiah knew that on all matters of etiquette she was bound to be in the right; but he was an ambitious man, anxious about his respectability. 'I do object,' he said, knowing himself to be in the wrong, knowing himself to sound foolish. 'I do.'

Frances bowed her head, wary of his drunken irritability. 'Shall I go and change my dress?' she asked.

'No. Tell me now what it is that you wanted.'

'Brown brought me a message.' Frances had been distracted by his disapproval; she tried to regain the initiative. 'I came to ask you ... it seems so strange at this time of night ... may I ask what you want to see a woman for?'

'No, you may not, madam! Sir Charles wishes to inspect the slaves. I sent for the keys which should be in your safe-keeping. There was no need for you to come downstairs at all and no call for you to question me.'

'It is just for him to see a woman?' Frances broke off. 'To look at her? It is not to – er – to trouble her?'

Josiah flushed dark red. 'I beg your pardon, Mrs Cole! You amaze me with your boldness! Please give me the keys and go to your chamber. I do not want Sir Charles to see you like this, nor hear such slander spoken against him!'

Frances stood her ground, scarlet with embarrassment. 'I cannot give you the keys,' she maintained, her voice shaking slightly. 'I beg of you, sir, not to ask me. I am supposed to be teaching them, they are in my care. You are speaking of my pupils. I cannot permit it. I have to have an undertaking from you.'

Josiah came out into the hall and shut the door behind him. He was trembling with drunken anger, his spittle flew as he hissed at her. 'You are shameless! Your insinuations are shameless! This is an honoured guest! A man who has done many years of very profitable business with me and my house. If he wishes to look at one of our slaves then of course we will allow it. Why not? Why on earth not? Go and fetch one of the women, Mrs Cole!'

Frances backed away from him until she reached the newel post at the foot of the stairs. She had the keys in her hand behind her back. 'I must ask for your assurance . . .' she insisted weakly.

'My assurance?' he repeated, ready to explode with anger.

She collapsed before his bluster, her breath coming short, her hand to her thudding heart. 'Very well. But you will just look at her, won't you?'

'Fetch one of the slave women, Mrs Cole,' he said angrily. 'You should have stayed where you were and sent the keys to me by Brown. I am much displeased. Since you insist on coming down you can fetch the woman yourself, and then go to bed!'

Frances's face was white as she turned from him and went slowly, very slowly, down the stairs to the kitchen.

Brown and John Bates were sitting either side of the kitchen range, waiting for the family to go to their beds so that they could lock up. At her step they rose to their feet.

'I am sorry to trouble you,' she said. Her lips were cold

and stiff, she found it hard to speak. 'Bates, could you come with me to the cellar? Your master wishes to see one of the women slaves.'

Bates thrust his hands into the armholes of his jacket and straightened his stock. Frances went to the cellar door and turned her key in the lock.

The cellar below her was shadowy. As she went down the steps she heard the chink of the chains. One or two of the slaves had been sleeping, but as they heard the door open they stirred nervously and woke. Mehuru rose slowly to his feet, looking from John Bates to Frances, trying to read their faces.

She did not meet his eyes. She looked around the cellar in the shadowy unreliable light of the lantern and then pointed to the biggest woman, the one who seemed the most robust. 'Her,' she said.

John stepped forward and unchained the woman from her handcuffs. She flinched away from him as he came towards her and shot a look at Frances – a look which was both a question, and an appeal. Frances's face gave nothing away, she was like a cold stone statue.

'What does she want of me?' the woman demanded of Mehuru.

He shook his head, his eyes on Frances. He could sense her powerlessness. He could feel her sense of defeat and something more . . . a deep sense of shame.

'I don't know,' he said softly. 'Have courage, Sister.'

The woman trembled and would have fallen but John Bates grabbed her around the waist and pushed her towards the steps. Her knees buckled beneath her and she crouched at the foot of the steps. 'They will eat me,' she whispered. 'Look at her face. She has come for me and she will eat me.'

Mehuru glanced swiftly towards Frances and saw her horrid narrow lips bitten even thinner. 'No,' he said certainly. 'It's not her choice.'

148

'Save me,' the woman begged softly. 'Mehuru, save me!'

Mehuru stood very still and felt the depths of his helplessness wash through him and over him. He knew that she would be raped and all that he could do was watch her be taken. He was unmanned, perhaps forever. 'Have courage, Sister,' he said tightly. 'We are a proud people. Bear this proudly.' He heard the hollow bravado in his voice, even as he spoke. He was a proud man no more; he was less than an animal for he did not have even a safe lair.

She found her feet, managed to stand.

Bates, growing impatient, asked Frances: 'Shall I carry her upstairs? I don't think she can climb them.'

'Yes,' Frances said shortly. She did not dare to look at Mehuru. She kept her eyes on her feet. She had dainty grey silk sandals to match the gown she had worn at dinner. She pointed her toe to look at the sheen on the silk, and the twinkle of the paste buckle.

John Bates caught the woman up. She grunted as his meaty shoulder butted into her emaciated belly, but she was silent as he climbed the steps. She seemed to have fainted from her fear, her head lolled at each step, her arms dangled down. 'Shall I carry her to Mr Cole's office?' he asked.

'Yes.' Frances followed him up the steps and carefully locked the door behind them. Slowly Bates walked through the kitchen with Frances behind him. Brown watched them pass in silence. Frances kept her eyes on the worn heels of Bates's boots.

When they left the warmth and light of the kitchen and went into the dark hall the woman started muttering the prayers for death. Over and over again she called the name of her husband, who was still waiting for her, still hoping for news of her. Over and over again she called to her ancestors to prepare a place for her, and begged them to forgive her for whatever wrongs she had done that she had been sent away from her home to die in dishonour in exile.

Frances heard the babble of pleas without understanding. She did not know the woman was calling on her, demanding of her what was wanted, what they wanted her to do, if there was any way she might be spared. Frances walked behind Bates, nursing her ignorance, deaf and blind to pain.

She tapped on Josiah's door and then swung it open, her face impassive. Bates marched in with his burden and Frances closed the door on them all, and went steadily up the stairs to her bedroom. Through the closed office door she heard the woman call out suddenly and clearly: 'Day-bull! Day-bull!'

She was trying desperately to please them. To say 'table' as they had wanted her to say this morning. To do whatever it was they wanted.

Frances hesitated for a moment at that one despairing cry, and then she went on, slowly, slowly up the stairs, her face set and grim. She was seated before her dressing table looking at her white face in the pier glass when she heard one scream of pure pain, quickly muffled by a heavy hand.

Frances unpinned her cap and plaited her hair, pulled on her nightgown and got into bed. 'I made an agreement,' she said to herself. 'I knew it would not always be to my liking.'

She pulled the cold white sheets up to her chin and lay very still. She closed her eyes. From the floor below came a rhythmic grunting which went on and on like a clumsy machine at work, and at last, a loud satisfied groan.

Frances put both her hands over her face and pressed down as if she would suffocate herself, block out the air as well as the noise. 'I made an agreement,' she whispered. 'I was warned that it would not be like home. But I made an agreement. That was my Trade.'

There was silence from downstairs. Then Frances heard her husband's study door open, and someone walk downstairs heavily, carrying a burden back to the caves. No expression crossed Frances's white face, she did not move. She lay as still and as cold as an effigy of a lady in white marble and she heard nothing, she saw nothing, and she thought of nothing at all.

Chapter Eleven

John Bates heaved her down the stairs like a lumper on the quayside, and dumped her ungently back in her place. He felt the accusing wide eyes of all the others on him.

'Well, I did nothing,' he muttered, half to himself.

She crouched on the straw with her head between her hands, doubled up over the pain in her belly. Bates had trouble making her straighten up so that he could bolt on the neck-collar.

The little children, the two-year-old and the five-year-old, looked at him with big frightened eyes but they were too wise to cry aloud.

'Oh damnation,' John Bates said irritably, and took the lantern off the hook and stamped up the stairs, leaving them alone in the dark and silence.

In the office Sir Charles and Josiah broached another bottle of port. Sir Charles was sated and at peace with the world, and Josiah hid his discomfort. He had made his fortune from the Trade but he had never before abused an individual. All the pain and grief had happened far away, out of sight, out of earshot. Seeing a woman raped on the hearthrug of his office made him uneasy. He had sat in the window and pretended to watch the pitch-black quayside while Sir Charles had laboured over her, but he could not help but hear her half-suffocated whimper of pain, and he could not avoid the smell of her fear, and the dirty clotted smell of Sir Charles's unwashed body.

He reminded himself that she was an animal, with only animal feelings, but he had not liked her agonised face when they had finally lifted her from the floor. Not even his best port could wash away the unpleasant taste from his mouth. He dared say nothing. Sir Charles was an important customer to Cole and Sons and, besides, Josiah feared that he himself was less of a man for his absence of desire.

It was nearly dawn, a grey sunless winter dawn, before the men parted. Josiah bade farewell to Sir Charles, climbed the stairs to his room and got into his bed.

Frances, lying awake, cold, and with her head buzzing with pain, heard him get into bed in the next room and the little puff as he blew out his candle. She did not know that he was lonelier than he had ever been in his life, and that he would have given a ship's cargo to be able to get into bed beside her and feel a little human warmth.

Frances woke later to the dark of a cold morning with her head a raging storm of pain. Small pinpricks of light danced against her eyelids. Her shoulders were rigidly tense, her neck was tight. The very skin of her face and the bones in her cheeks ached as if she had an ague.

The adjoining door to Josiah's bedroom opened. 'I owe you an apology,' Josiah began without preamble.

Frances barely opened her eyes. 'I am ill,' she said. 'Forgive me.'

Josiah checked. 'I wanted to speak with you,' he persisted.

'I cannot.' Frances's voice was a thin determined thread.

'Can I fetch you something?'

'My laudanum, in my writing table.'

He opened the lid of the little box. In the shelf at the back was a small bottle. 'How many drops?'

'Three.'

He measured three drops into the glass of water at her bedside and gave it to her. She drank without opening her eyes and lay back on the pillow, waiting for the pain to ease.

'Sir Charles's behaviour was not fitting for an English home,' Josiah said precisely. 'You were right to object. I had taken a little too much drink and, moreover, I was bound to be hospitable. But when I awoke this morning I thought your objection should have been heeded. I apologise.'

'You need say no more,' Frances said. She turned her head away and closed her eyes.

'The woman took no hurt,' Josiah said. 'And Sir Charles returned to his hotel in the early hours of the morning. I fear that too long a stay in the Sugar Islands has made him forgetful of English courtesies.'

He waited, looking at Frances as if she should say something.

'I have apologised,' he said with increased sharpness.

'I am sorry,' Frances whispered weakly. 'My head . . .'

'You will feel better when you are up and dressed, no doubt,' he said without sympathy. 'I will leave you now for my work. I shall be home for dinner at the usual time. The maid will bring you your chocolate – my sister will expect you in the parlour at nine.'

'In the parlour?'

'For their lesson,' he said levelly. 'The slaves will be waiting for their lesson. Today. It is my wish that they be taught all together, every day. It will take too long otherwise.'

'I cannot do it,' Frances protested stubbornly. 'I am too unwell to see them.'

'Then do not work overlong,' Josiah replied promptly. 'But start at nine, teach them all together, and then send them away after an hour or so. I do not wish them to miss a day of their training. Sir Charles was convinced that they have to work daily or they will become unruly.'

Frances searched for grounds for refusal and could not think of one. 'I wish you had not fetched her to your office,' she said pettishly.

'I did nothing,' Josiah said awkwardly. He paused. Neither of them could discuss exactly what had taken place. 'The woman was not harmed,' he repeated. 'Indeed, at Clearwater, or any plantation, these things happen almost every day.' He hesitated, seeking refuge in generalities. 'It is not as if she were hurt. She would expect nothing else.'

There was a silence. Josiah went towards the door.

'I feel ashamed,' Frances said suddenly. Her headache thumped as if in recognition of a truth spoken aloud at last.

Josiah, closing the door softly behind him, was careful not to hear her.

They filed into the parlour, all thirteen, and took their seats at the table without looking at her. They were crowded. Frances was already at her place and did not look up as they came in quietly, but she sensed Mehuru's presence when he drew out his chair and sat on her right. Looking down at the polished table top, she could see his gently clasped hands. She longed for him to put his hand on her forehead where it throbbed and tightened. She longed for him to lay his hands on her hot eyes and tell her that he forgave her; that she might forgive herself.

She shot a swift painful glance at him. His dark dark eyes met hers in one long judging look and then turned away. He would not look at her, though Frances waited. The other slaves sat in silence around the polished table and watched her. Tentatively, Frances put out her hand and gently touched his clasped fingers with her forefinger. It was the lightest of touches, but one which lingered with her, the warmth of his slim strong hand under her fingertip.

'Mehuru,' she said softly.

He looked up at her. She put her hand on the base of her throat. 'Frances,' she said aloud, and then, very softly, too softly for Miss Cole or the driver John Bates, or any of the other slaves to hear, she said, 'I'm very sorry. I could not stop them.'

Mehuru looked at her with a hard, unforgiving glare, and would not hear her whisper; and if he had heard it, would not have understood.

The lesson went badly. Miss Cole sighed in the windowseat and picked her teeth with a silver toothpick which clicked against the stained enamel. She had painful indigestion from the night before and every now and then she shifted in her seat with a little grunt of discomfort. John Bates stood like a statue with his back to the door and his whip held across him. Mehuru would not meet Frances's eyes again. The woman who had been raped sat in complete silence, her head bowed so low that her face nearly rested on the table, hiding the dark bruise on her temple and the dead look in her eyes. The smallest boy cried continually, little half-smothered heartbroken sobs. He sat still on his seat, leaning forward, and his tears fell on his bare black knees where they peeped from his breeches. He was only two, he did not know how to endure in silence. Frances did not know how to teach simple nouns while the child shook with silent grief.

'Get them to say their names,' Miss Cole suggested, moving from her place in the window. 'That's where you left off yesterday. What is wrong with them today?'

Frances looked at her. 'Sir Charles disturbed them in the night,' she said.

There was a brief silence. Miss Cole understood perfectly. 'What for?' she asked, daring Frances to speak the truth.

'I don't know,' Frances replied, deliberately ignorant. Behind the words was Miss Cole's sharp comprehension of what had happened, and Frances's shame.

'Well, that is no reason for them to be dull,' Sarah said briskly. 'They should not object to being looked at. Ask them their names, all of them.' She pointed to Mehuru. 'He said his name last time. Ask the others what they are called.'

Frances nodded. She put her hand to the warm cambric of her gown at the neck and said her name, and then she pointed at one, and then at another. Today they would not speak. They shifted uneasily in their seats and stared at her with frightened eyes. When she pointed at the woman that Sir Charles had taken from the cave the others gave a soft groan, as low as the creak of bending trees in a forest.

Frances touched the back of Mehuru's hand again. The warmth of the dark skin under her fingers encouraged her. 'Mehuru,' she said quietly. 'That woman. What is her name?' She pointed to herself. 'Frances.' She pointed to him. 'Mehuru.' She pointed to the woman. 'What name?' she asked.

'She wants your name,' Mehuru said to the woman. His voice was tender, as one would speak to a sister mortally injured. But his resentment burned beneath the quiet tone and Frances could hear it.

'My name is Shame,' the woman said quietly. 'My name is Shame. My name is Died of Shame.'

Frances frowned at the quick low exchange and then turned enquiringly to Mehuru.

'Shame,' he said in Yoruban. 'Died of Shame.'

Frances's stupid white face brightened, she nodded. 'Died of Shame,' she repeated, pleased. She pointed to the next. 'And who is this?'

Kbara did not raise his head. 'Despair,' he said in his language, Mandinka.

'Despair,' Frances repeated happily. 'Now we are getting on! And who is this?'

'Homeless,' the girl said in Wolof.

'Homeless!' Frances repeated carefully, mimicking the sound.

Mehuru closed his eyes for a moment at the horror of Frances's encouraging bright voice mouthing curses.

'And this?'

'Grief.'

'And this?'

'Accursed.'

'And this?'

'Lost.'

'You'd much better give them English names,' Miss Cole interrupted. 'No-one will be able to say this gibberish. It doesn't mean anything. Tell them some new names, Christian names.'

Frances hesitated. 'I will, when I've learned their African names.' She smiled at them. Mehuru recoiled from the horrid paleness of her mouth and the white teeth against the pale bloodless lips. 'They need to trust me,' Frances said. 'We need to be friends.'

She rose from her seat at the table and went to the sideboard and rapped on the polished top. 'Sideboard.' She waited for Mehuru's response, sensing his unwillingness. 'Sideboard,' she said again.

There was a glass bowl in the centre of the sideboard, piled with expensive hot-house fruit from last night's dinner. Frances took a warm apricot in her hand. She brought the fruit to the table. She laid it before Mehuru like a woman of a village might lay a gift before the shrine of a difficult god. She had the same supplicating deferential smile.

'Apricot,' she said.

Mehuru looked from the fruit to her intent face. There was a ripple of unease from the others. Frances did not notice, she did not even see them. 'Mehuru.' She spoke his name like a caress. 'This is an apricot. Apricot.'

He could not bear the appeal in her face. He dropped his gaze to the polished surface of the table. 'Apricot,' he said, very low.

Frances exhaled slowly as if he had made some private long-sought agreement with her. She took the apricot up to her mouth and bit a little piece from it. She took the mouthful from between her lips and offered it in silence to Mehuru. Their eyes met, then his hand came up and took the piece of golden fruit from her hand and put it in his own mouth.

'Good,' she said and nodded at him.

'Good,' he repeated obediently. Then his eyes fell back to watching the table. His face revealed nothing.

Frances took a knife from the sideboard and cut the apricot into small slices for the rest of the class. 'Apricot,' she said to each of them. When they repeated the word she gave each one a piece. They ate their share delicately and in silence.

'Good,' she said.

They repeated the word like automata, without understanding. They kept shooting glances to Mehuru for cues as to how to respond to this strange dangerous woman who could come for them like Ayelala the goddess of death and judgement in the night; but during the day was a supplicant, begging for forgiveness, speaking one nonsensical word at a time.

Frances pointed to the fruit plate. 'Plate,' she said. 'Knife.'

'Plade,' they said nervously. 'Knigh.'

Mehuru felt his consciousness back away from reality, like a wounded animal will retreat into its lair, lie in the darkness and long for death.

'Plade. Knigh.'

Frances looked around the table at the shuttered faces. 'Smile!' she suddenly commanded. She bared her teeth at them. 'Smile!'

They shrank back from her dreadful white face and the huge gaping mouth. 'Oh my fathers, save us!' one boy muttered. A woman gave a sob of fear.

'Steady,' Mehuru warned softly. He was still in his lair, his dark eyes watching Frances, his soul tucked safely away from her.

Frances turned to him, her eyes – dark like his own –

imploring. 'I'm trying to help you,' she said. 'You have to learn and I have to teach you. Smile.'

'Mile,' Mehuru said softly to her. With dead unfeeling eyes he curved his lips up in a ghastly parody of joy. 'Mile,' he said.

Chapter Twelve

When the lesson stopped at half-past ten and the slaves were sent away Frances remained seated at the parlour table.

'Would you like a dish of tea before breakfast?' Sarah offered.

Frances shook her head. 'I shall not be eating breakfast,' she said.

There was a short silence. 'Frances...' Sarah warned. 'I hope you are not getting vapourish.'

Frances's head came up. 'Vapourish!' she exclaimed. 'I am not vapourish, I am sick to my heart! I don't believe I can do this, Sarah. I don't believe it should have been asked of me. I shall speak to Josiah. I don't think this scheme can work. They cannot be taught and certainly I cannot teach them.'

Sarah moved from the windowseat and took a chair opposite. 'You do not wish to work,' she said bluntly.

'I cannot do this,' Frances said. 'I cannot prepare them for a life of slavery where any master can abuse them as he wishes.'

'Not in England,' Sarah said quickly. 'They would not be abused in England. They would be treated as servants.'

'Then let them be servants,' Frances replied. 'With wages and the right to leave if they find themselves in a disagreeable position.'

There was a pause. 'Where would be the profit in that?' Sarah asked simply. 'You have forgotten why we are doing this, Frances. We are doing it to sell them, as we sell sugar and tobacco. We are here to sell them at a profit.'

Frances dropped her head into her hands and clasped her thudding skull through the tight curls. 'I cannot do it,' she said miserably.

Sarah watched her for a moment. 'But you have no objection to slavery in principle,' she remarked quietly.

'Of course not,' Frances said.

'You have no objection to taking the profits and enjoying the goods which slavery brings us?'

'No.'

'Then your only reservation is that you do not want to do the work yourself.'

Frances raised her head. 'Yes,' she said.

Sarah shrugged and rose from the table. 'This is not principle, this is laziness. I warned my brother that a fine lady would not be prepared to work for his business as he works and as I work. But he believed that you understood the trade you were making. You wanted a family and a house of your own, and he wanted a working wife. You brought him aristocratic connections and he gave you a handsome settlement. He is keeping his side of the bargain, the house at Queens Square will be yours. But you wish to renege.'

'I am not lazy,' Frances replied, stung.

'Then keep your side of the bargain,' Sarah Cole said firmly. 'As we are keeping ours.'

Downstairs two women slaves were watched by John Bates as they took out the pail and slopped it on the midden. The girl who had named herself Died of Shame fell back as they went through the yard, snatched up handfuls of earth from the foot of the wall, and pushed them down the bodice of her dress.

When they were back in the gloomy light of the cellar John Bates brought them a pail of food – some bread, some potato peelings, the scraps and the bone from Sir Charles's roast dinner. They ate right-handed from the pail, taking it in turns to choose a piece of food and then putting it on the tin plates before them.

Mehuru took the piece of fruit out of his mouth where he had held it under his tongue ever since Frances had given it to him in the lesson. Squatting, he put it carefully on the floor between his bare feet and looked at it for long minutes. The other slaves sat in silence around him. He was the obalawa, he could be talking with the fathers.

'Apricot,' Mehuru said softly.

At the thought of her saliva on the piece of fruit that had gone into his mouth his throat tightened with terror.

'Will you not eat?' one of the women asked softly.

He shook his head. He would not touch Sir Charles's leavings. He drank only water and watched the woman who called herself Died of Shame. When it was her turn to take her pick from the breakfast pail she tipped the earth from her bodice on her plate and ate mouthful for mouthful with them until her face was stained with mud and her breath smelled of death.

Mehuru did not stop her. He could not ask her to live. He could not reassure her that no harm had been done, that the husband who loved her would never know of it. That the little baby she had left behind her in Africa would never be insulted because his mother was dishonoured. That it was a new life, and new and dreadful ways were facing them all, but that they might survive. He had no right to persuade her against her own wisdom. And besides, he had no hope to give her, and no hope for himself. They sat in the half-darkness, all of them with their faces buried in their hands. When she started moaning very softly, they moaned quietly with her, in a gentle chorus of lament.

'Here,' Cook said upstairs. 'What's that?' She was making pastry for a pie.

'It's them!' the scullery maid said nervously. 'Groaning.'

'Mr Bates! Mr Bates!' Cook cried. 'What are they doing down there?'

John Bates listened at the cellar door. 'They're just singing,' he said. 'And sighing.'

'Why?' Cook demanded irritably. 'They never have before. I can't work in a kitchen with sighing and singing in the cellar. I shouldn't be asked to.'

John paused. 'I'll beat them,' he offered. He took his whip, unlocked the door and surged down the steps. The slaves raised themselves up at the noise of his boots, their faces turned towards him and the light and the good smell of baking. He slashed the whip at random in the small space and heard it sing and crack as it found an arm, a face, an ear. Kbara cried out, a woman screamed. John Bates looked around for any challenge. They huddled together and watched his scarlet angry face and his popping eyes. 'That'll do,' he shouted at them, incomprehensible threatening words. 'Stop that noise.' He turned on his heel and marched up the steps again. They heard the door at the top of the steps bang and the key turn in the lock.

They sat in darkness and silence for a while and then Died of Shame put her hands over her mouth and groaned out her pain as quietly as she could. The other women drew closer to her, and they moaned with her, as soft as the cooing of plantain-eaters.

Mehuru started to recite, very softly, the prayers for the dead, calling on the forefathers of Died of Shame to take their daughter home, back over that long wide sea, so that she might feel the sun on her face again and lie on the fertile earth.

'They've started again,' Cook said sharply.

John listened. 'You can hardly hear them.'

'But I can hear them! I think I'd better tell Miss Cole I'm no longer suited. I could walk into any place tomorrow, the

Cole table is well known in this city. I can't keep my pastry light with savages groaning in the cellar. They shouldn't ask it of me.'

John Bates turned in irritation to the kitchen maid. 'Find Brown and tell her to tell Mrs Cole that the slaves are moaning. She's supposed to be teaching them to speak. She can teach them to be silent too!'

The kitchen maid peeled off her grimy hessian apron, revealing a cotton pinny underneath, only marginally cleaner. She scurried for the stairs and found Brown polishing the little table in the hall. Brown thrust the duster into her hand, went up to the parlour and tapped on the door.

'Beg pardon, Mrs Cole,' she said. 'The slaves are moaning in the cellar.'

Frances looked to Miss Cole. 'Moaning?'

Sarah waited. 'Do you wish them to be left, Frances?' she challenged. 'If you will not care for them and I do not have the time then they will have to moan in their cave until my brother comes home.'

'Bates says he could beat them,' Brown volunteered.

'I'll come,' Frances said. She led the way down the backstairs, Sarah following behind her. Cook was standing behind the kitchen table, banging the rolling pin down on a lump of pastry. There was a low soft sound from the cellar, like the panting of a hurt beast.

'I gave them nothing more than a little clip,' Bates protested. 'But they started again. They were quieter for a while. They know they're doing wrong. Shall I beat them again?'

'No,' Frances said quickly.

'Did they start for any reason?' Miss Cole asked. 'Have they been fed?'

'They had the pig pail,' Cook answered without turning around, her broad back expressing her total disapproval. 'And good food there was in it too. Then they started this noise.

It's not right for a Christian kitchen. It's not what I'm used to.'

'Of course,' Miss Cole said rapidly. 'We'll stop them, Cook. We'll stop them at once. Frances, go down and see what is wrong.'

Frances shrugged resentfully. 'How should I know? I've had no experience.'

'I could beat them, ma'am,' John offered. 'That's what we always did in Jamaica. Beat them till they were quiet.'

'No,' Frances said. 'I don't want them whipped.'

'Then you must silence them some other way,' Miss Cole demanded. 'Either by teaching or beating, Frances, they must be quiet.'

Reluctantly Frances went to the head of the stairs. John unlocked the door, uncurled his whip. 'Perhaps I had best go first,' he cautioned her. Frances heard the note of fear in his voice.

'Are they chained?'

'Yes, ma'am.'

He preceded her down the stairs. Frances blinked, accustoming herself to the gloom. She saw the food pail in the centre of the cellar ringed with plates. On one plate she saw a dark smear, like mud.

'Fetch me that,' she said to John.

He stepped towards the four women who leaned away from him, like a field of rustling sugar cane leaning away from the wind. The woman called Died of Shame had tipped earth over her head, had covered her face, and was moaning, as soft as a breath, into her cupped hands.

John proffered the plate to Frances. 'Looks like earth, ma'am.'

Frances looked across at Mehuru. He met her eyes without expression. He had neither smile nor scowl for her. He looked at her as one might look at a cheating market trader – with a distant scorn.

'She is eating earth?' Frances asked. 'Why should she eat earth?'

Bates shrugged. The movement uncoiled the whip and the long tail of it hissed on the straw of the floor. The women shifted in one small movement, farther back against the wall, farther away from him.

Frances showed the plate to Mehuru. 'Died of Shame?' she queried, repeating the girl's name in her strange stupid voice.

Mehuru nodded.

'She is eating earth?' Frances asked.

Mehuru's face was impassive.

'I don't understand,' said Frances, who understood all too well. She turned to John Bates. 'I *don't* understand,' she insisted.

'They're savages,' he volunteered. 'Perhaps they eat it all the time in their own country. Perhaps she fancied a bit of Bristol dirt for a change.' He gave a little chuckle and then straightened his face when Frances scowled at him.

She turned and went back up the steps to the kitchen, taking the plate with her. 'It's the girl called Shame.' She carefully pronounced the African name. 'She has been eating earth. I think she may be sick.'

'Which is she? You know I can't remember their names.'

Frances flushed scarlet. 'She is the one . . . she is the one . . .' Frances could not say that she was the one she herself had sent to Sir Charles last night. Frances could not say such a thing before the servants.

'Oh.' Miss Cole understood at once. 'Well, that's no reason. It must be something else.'

'Should we call a doctor?' Frances asked.

Miss Cole shook her head. 'No, too expensive. Besides, how would a white person's doctor know what to do?'

'The farrier might know, ma'am,' Bates offered. 'A horse will eat earth sometimes. A farrier might know.'

Miss Cole tapped her teeth with her toothpick. 'Sir Charles,' she said finally. She turned to John Bates. 'Go to his hotel and see if he is at home. Give him my compliments and ask him if he would step over. We need his advice.'

John Bates gave a little bow, reached for his hat on the chair and went out of the back door. Miss Cole turned her attention to Cook. 'All this will be swiftly settled,' she assured her. 'Sir Charles is very experienced in the handling of slaves. It will be all over by dinner. And I shall see that my brother knows that you have worked through some disruption.'

Cook slapped the pastry on a brimming pie and abruptly trimmed the rim. 'I hope so indeed, Miss Cole,' she said ominously. 'I must say it's not what I am accustomed to.'

Miss Cole nodded to Frances to lead the way up the stairs to the parlour. She returned to her seat in the window and looked down at the quay, watching Bates as he waited for the little ferryboat to take him across the river to Sir Charles's hotel on the opposite side of the Avon. 'I hope Sir Charles is at home,' she said. 'Or we will have to send for my brother.'

Frances did not answer. She knew that they should not have sent for Sir Charles with his tainted expertise. She knew why the woman who had named herself Died of Shame was eating earth and pouring earth on her head, and streaking her face with it. Frances knew that she was inviting a rapist to order how his victim should be managed. She knew that she was being slowly and effectively corrupted by a system over which she had no control.

'How will he know what to do?' she asked.

'Clearwater is one of the best-run plantations on Jamaica.'

'But he said that a quarter of their slaves died within the first year, and another quarter within the next four, just through illness. He loses even more by punishments and selling on.'

'That's quite good actually,' Miss Cole remarked. 'Some plantations, especially those that are low-lying in fever country, lose every single slave within a couple of seasons.'

Frances seated herself at the table, and picked up the sheet she had been darning. 'Sir Charles said that of every ten slaves shipped out of Africa, two die on the voyage, two more die the first year, and then another two are dead by the fourth year,' she said, her voice carefully neutral. 'So for every ten that have been caught and shipped, only four are left alive by the end of five years.'

Miss Cole nodded. 'And this is why it is such a reliable trade,' she observed. 'That is why it is such good business for us.'

Frances inclined her head. 'I see.'

The two women sat in silence until Miss Cole, looking down at the quay, said, 'Here he is,' as Sir Charles strolled up to the front door and hammered on it with his pearl-handled stick.

He came into the parlour behind Brown. He kissed Miss Cole's hand, he bowed low over Frances's hand and kissed it gently. He straightened up and gave her a little intimate roguish smile. He looked like a charming boy caught in an apple orchard with bulging pockets. He very nearly winked.

'Forgive me,' he said in his warm flirtatious tone. 'I should have presented myself with my compliments this morning. My daughter and I enjoyed a most excellent evening with you. Alas! I overslept – your wine was very fine!'

'We sent for you because we have some difficulty with one of the slaves,' Miss Cole interrupted.

He turned from scanning Frances's face and smiled at her. 'Anything I can do to assist – you only have to command me.'

'Frances has the managing of them,' Miss Cole said, allocating blame where it was due. 'And now one of them is behaving very strangely. They are all moaning and it is disturbing Cook.'

Sir Charles gave a little seductive laugh and flickered a

smile at Frances. 'We cannot have that excellent cook disturbed for one moment. Would you like me to see them?'

'It is just one,' Frances said quietly. 'She will not eat food ... She is eating...'

'Earth?' he guessed.

Frances's glance flew to his face. 'You knew?'

He shrugged. 'It's not unusual. A foul habit, isn't it? The women do it often. It makes them sick as dogs, they get the yaws and they will eat it till they die sometimes. It is their mad spite. They know they are robbing you of their purchase price. They are insane with spite. You will need to use a bridle, ma'am.'

'A bridle?'

He tutted in irritation. 'Of course, you will not have one to hand. I had thought myself at home! We put a bridle on them when they eat soil. A metal cage which goes around the face, under the jaw, with a gag of metal across the mouth. Their driver must take it off at mealtimes and watch her to make sure she eats her food. She must wear it all the rest of the time. They are cunning as monkeys. If they want to eat dirt they will get their hands on it somehow. The only way is to gag their mouths.'

'And you frequently use these devices?' Miss Cole asked, interested.

'We could not run the plantations without them. We use it on those who eat earth, and many people put their cooks and kitchen maids in bridles to stop them tasting as they work. This is a common problem for us, ma'am, and a common solution. I could draw one for you and a farrier could make it up. It looks like a scold's bridle from olden times – it has the advantage of making them dumb as well! Which one is causing the trouble, what size is she?'

Miss Cole looked at Frances. Frances wanted to say, 'the one you raped', but she found she could not. The man stood before her, smiling, assured, charming. She could not name him as a rapist. He had assaulted a woman and now she ate dirt and heaped dirt on her head, and Frances was dumb.

'The largest woman,' she said, cowardly.

'Well, you'll just want a medium-sized one then,' Sir Charles said comfortably. 'It has to be tight enough to cut into the mouth, to press against the lips, against the teeth and gums. They learn the lesson well that way. If she bleeds a little around the mouth it is no great loss. Here, I'll sketch one out for you.'

Miss Cole gestured to the parlour table and put paper and a pen before him. With swift confident sweeps of the pen he drew a little helmet with an open socket for the nose and a smooth plate which blocked the mouth, fastening behind the head with leather straps.

'Don't be discouraged,' he said kindly to Frances. 'One little setback means nothing. I am sure you are making good progress.'

'Thank you,' Frances said stiltedly.

'Now, come back with me to my hotel!' he commanded. 'And take a glass of wine and a little luncheon with me there! Honoria will join us, she is longing to improve her friendship with you, Mrs Cole.'

Frances glanced at Miss Cole, who was flustered and flattered. 'You must give us a moment to put on our bonnets. Shall I need a cape or a shawl?'

'It's as cold as ever but it has stopped raining, thank God!' Sir Charles exclaimed. 'I shall wait for as long as you need to get ready, Miss Cole. It's not often I have the honour of a beauty on either arm. I would wait all day for the privilege.' He smiled at her and Miss Cole flushed with pleasure. His sideways gleam to Frances gave the compliment to her. His powerful maleness, his confidence of his own desirability filled the little room.

Frances went slowly to the door. She did not want to put her hand on Sir Charles's arm. She did not want to have luncheon with him. She did not want to see his knowing little smile or hear his half-shamed, half-bragging chuckle. She thought of him taking the black woman against her consent, and of all the other black women he had used, against their wills. She paused at the door, nerving herself to refuse.

'This is a great pleasure for me,' Sir Charles beamed. 'I have such little occasion for the society of English ladies. I can feel myself becoming more civilised minute by minute.'

Frances felt the traitorous weakness of her polite smile. 'Oh good,' she said.

Chapter Thirteen

The lunch party was not a great success although Sir Charles was a charming and expansive host and Miss Cole was delighted to be in his company. Honoria was as coldly polite as she had been the previous night. Frances could feel the sick thudding of her headache coming back.

'You are pale, Mrs Cole,' Honoria said in her rich languid accent. 'You are so lucky. I have to shield my face from the sun all the time at home. Mama is terrified of me getting brown – brown like the girls.'

'I don't feel very well,' Frances said quietly.

'The strains of new married life, eh?' Sir Charles interrupted, smiling intimately down the table at Frances. 'Running a house, teaching the slaves. You must tell Josiah that he must not work you too hard!'

'It is not the work,' Frances said. 'I worked harder when I was at home.' She felt a sudden pang of homesickness for the rectory and the little village where she and her father were well-known along every lane and track, and where she enjoyed a constant sense of self-righteousness. 'I used to walk in all weathers. I used to visit the poor, my father was the rector, and my uncle, Lord Scott, the landlord. It is the countryside I miss. My home was in the hills outside Bath.'

'And now you are cooped up in town!' Sir Charles exclaimed sympathetically. 'I wish I could take you ladies to Clearwater.' He included Sarah in his smile, but his eyes were on Frances. 'You could rest in a hammock and look out over two hundred acres to the sea, Mrs Cole! As lush and as thick and as fruitful as your heart could desire, and a dozen slaves to do your bidding, whatever you might want! That would bring the colour to your cheeks. And I myself should make you rum punch which would make your heart beat a little faster.' His voice held a caress. Frances glanced uncomfortably at Sarah.

'My sister is happy where she is,' Sarah said. 'And within a month we will be living at Queens Square. There is some delay with the purchase of the house but when it goes through we shall have the Queens Square garden for our enjoyment.'

'An excellent address,' Sir Charles agreed. 'But had you not thought of the heights of Park Street? I barely recognised the city, there has been so much building since I was last here. The whole town seems to be sprouting terraces.'

Miss Cole shook her head decidedly. 'No. We prefer to live in the town. My brother says that a merchant is happiest where he can see the masts of his ships.'

'I am sure he knows best,' Sir Charles said pleasantly. 'And so the next time I come to visit you I shall see you in a beautiful town house, Mrs Cole.'

'Yes,' Frances said thinly.

Sir Charles nodded at the black slave who stood behind him for more wine and the man stepped forward and poured. Frances shook her head. 'I drink only water at noon.'

'Why, that is why you are so pale!' Sir Charles exclaimed. 'You must let me give you a little of my own rum, in a punch of my own devising.' He nodded to the slave. 'Punch, Sammy. Punch. Quick-quick.'

The man bowed, unsmilingly. 'Yassuh.'

'Please don't bother,' Frances protested. 'I assure you, Sir Charles . . .'

He smiled and leaned towards her. He put out his hand and rested it over hers. Unseen by Miss Cole, his little finger slid beneath her wrist and caressed the delicate skin. 'You must indulge me,' he said. His voice was very warm. 'I have been spoiled in the Sugar Islands and I bring my luxurious ways home with me. You must indulge me, Mrs Cole.'

Frances, thinking of his indulgences last night, and the woman who today smeared earth on her face and filled her mouth with dirt, took her hand away.

'You are a fine host,' Miss Cole said sharply, keeping a critical watch on Frances. 'My sister will be delighted to taste your punch and then we must go home. We have much to do in the afternoon, as you will understand. My sister is no longer a lady of leisure, she is the wife of a working merchant. She has duties now.'

Sir Charles shot a sympathetic look at Frances, then his slave came in with a silver punch bowl and he turned his attention to the drink.

'I must speak with Mr Cole on business this day,' he said, after he had squeezed the lemons and added the sugar. He nodded to the slave and watched him carefully as he handed around the silver cups of punch.

'My brother will be delighted,' Sarah replied instantly. 'Is there any way that I can be of assistance?'

'You can advise me, ma'am,' Sir Charles said pleasantly. 'I am dogged by the troubles of getting my moneys to England. There are investments I wish to make, I wish to buy land here. I shall return to live here one day, of course, and there is Honoria's dowry to think about. I don't like to send bullion on a strange ship and I have no agent in England to handle notes of credit for me. I even have some gold with me now, but I need the name of someone whom I can trust to handle it for me, to invest it.'

Miss Cole thought for a moment. 'You have no family here?'

He shook his head. 'It was all done by my brother, he was my factor. But he died two years ago, and I have no-one to take his place.'

Miss Cole cleared her throat. 'If I might be so bold as to offer our services . . .' she began tentatively. 'We have had a long and successful trading relationship, Sir Charles. I know that both my brother and I would be honoured . . . You could place your moneys with us and we could serve as your agents in England. We could purchase what things you needed and send them out to you on our ships. You could give us notes of credit for all the slaves you purchase from other traders, and we could pay them when they were presented to us.'

Sir Charles hesitated. 'I know trading companies do this. But mostly in London and, forgive me, they are all larger concerns.'

Sarah touched her tongue to her dry lips. 'We are expanding, as you know,' she persisted. 'And we have reserves of our own capital to draw on. We are experienced in the Trade.'

'But the purchase of land . . .' Sir Charles let his doubt trail into silence. He implied, but did not say, that a self-made Bristol trader would hardly know how to buy good agricultural land.

'You would want to choose your own estate, of course,' Sarah continued desperately. 'But we could collect the rents for you.'

'Yes,' Sir Charles said slowly. 'But land is a very different thing from the Trade, my dear Miss Cole.'

'I am sure my uncle Lord Scott would be happy to assist,' Frances interrupted suddenly.

Both Sir Charles and Sarah looked towards her, surprised. Frances felt irritated that they should assume that she had nothing to say in a conversation about business, that she was as much of a parasite as Honoria, who was gazing blankly out of the window.

'He told me that Josiah was to call on him at any time,' Frances said. 'And he owns much land in Somerset, and he also has a large estate in Scotland and a lot of land in Ireland.'

'Lord Scott himself would be prepared to advise me?' Sir Charles asked. He glanced towards Honoria. 'You would introduce us?'

Frances, who might know nothing of business, knew a great deal about social values. 'My uncle Lord Scott would be delighted to assist you, and to welcome you and Miss Honoria to Scott House in London. My aunt and uncle are there for the Season. My aunt generally gives a ball. I could ask her for tickets.'

Honoria, who had been daydreaming during the business discussion, straightened in her chair and fixed her father with a meaningful glare.

'Well, well,' Sir Charles smiled. 'What an excellent idea! I should be honoured with Lord Scott's acquaintance. I should be happy to enter into an agreement with you, if Lord Scott were our advisor. It might be a very good idea indeed.' He beamed at Frances and shot an indiscreet wink at Honoria. 'I should be grateful,' he said. 'Grateful to make his lordship's acquaintance. And Miss Honoria would be glad of a ticket to the ball, I don't doubt! You are obliging, Mrs Cole. I appreciate it.'

'It is my pleasure,' Frances said coldly. She knew that she was a fool to be led into favours for Sir Charles, but her pride had been piqued at being neglected at the luncheon table, she had been driven by an unworthy desire to outshine Sarah, and by irritation at being excluded from the conversation. She did not know how to be his guest and yet keep her distance from him. And she had longed to put Miss Honoria in her place.

Sir Charles sent them home in his hired carriage as it had come on to rain. As they drew near to the quay Frances could smell the sweet nauseating stench of the river. The rain was washing smuts down out of the heavy sky. The dark dirty clouds of smoke from the glass furnace and from the lead-works hung around the spire of St Mary's, staining the intricate carvings and trailing tears of soot down the faces of the stone saints. It was growing dark with the early dusk of mid-winter. Sarah was bubbling with suppressed elation. 'You did very well, Frances,' she said. 'Very well indeed. Sir Charles is a fine man to have as a friend.'

Frances felt her momentary excitement drain away. 'I do not like Sir Charles,' she said in a small voice. 'And I have a headache.'

'He is a most important man to us,' Sarah snapped. 'And your mention of Lord Scott was very helpful. Will you be able to bring his lordship up to scratch, d'you think?'

Frances stepped out of the carriage and went to the front door. A new ship was in port near to the Cole dock, and the Merchant Venturers' great crane was screeching as it swung out and hauled barrels up from the hold. The noise jarred on Frances's taut nerves. She was sorry that she had been persuaded to go to lunch, and angry with herself at her complaisance to Sir Charles. She had wanted to enter into the world of persuasion and business. With the return to the dirty little house on the quayside she realised that she had been exercising her social charm on a rapist to benefit a petty dockside trading company.

'Lord Scott has my interests at heart,' Frances said distantly. 'I am sure he will do anything I ask him.'

'If we can get him to come in then we can be Sir Charles's agents, and our problems of cash will be over.'

The door opened. Frances stepped inside before her sister-in-law. 'I hope so, indeed,' she replied, smothering a cough.

Sarah clicked her teeth together. 'You did offer,' she reminded Frances. 'You will have to come up to scratch. You cannot promise something and then renege. These are business matters, your word must be sacred.'

'It is not a religion,' Frances said tartly. 'You speak as if a contract was one of the ten commandments.'

Sarah nodded. 'It is. That is exactly what you must learn

as a merchant's wife. You should break one of the commandments before you break your word. Everything this house has been built on depends on the reliability of our word.'

'I will try and understand,' Frances said with dull resentment. 'I am teaching the slaves, Sister. I will do everything else that is in my power to further our business. And if Josiah wishes it, I will ask Lord Scott for his advice, and ask him to invite Sir Charles and Miss Honoria to Scott House.'

'He is a fine gentleman,' Sarah insisted. 'He would be perfectly at home in Scott House, I don't doubt.'

'I do not share your confidence. But Lord Scott will understand, and make allowances.'

Sarah knew herself to be snubbed, but let it pass without comment. Brown closed the front door behind them as Frances started to climb the stairs.

'You will teach the slaves this afternoon,' Sarah reminded her.

'I will have a rest, and teach them at four o'clock.'

'I hope you will feel better then,' Sarah said grudgingly. 'You have done well today, Sister. I do recognise it.'

Frances nodded and went into her room, closed the door and leaned back against it. If it had been furnished with a bolt she would have locked it against her sister-in-law, and against the claustrophobic house, and against the imposing vulgarity of Sir Charles.

Sarah had not seen that tiny distasteful caress of his finger on her wrist and Frances did not know what would have been said. In her world – the world of the country aristocracy – a flirtation after marriage was a normal state of affairs. But in this anxious world of Bristol merchants where a fortune hung on appearances Frances did not know how she should behave.

She had no feelings to guide her. Even as a girl Frances had never fallen in love. She had watched her cousins' passing infatuations and agonies at balls and dances and picnics with mild amusement. When they declared that she was cold, she had not denied it. She lacked passion, and the years had made her cool and distant – even from herself. The death of her mother, and then a year later of her father, had taught her that the price of love is vulnerability, and she never wanted to feel the grief of loss again. She thought that all her feelings had died with her father, that she had wept them out of her heart, and that for the rest of her life she would see everything through a thick pane of glass, and feel everything as though through gloves.

Frances rubbed her face, pressing her fingers against her temples where her headache drummed. She lay down on the bed and stared up at the ceiling. In the street outside her window someone was rolling barrels; the rumble of the wood against the cobbles seemed to shake the very house. She shifted her head on the pillow, seeking comfort but finding none, then she closed her eyes and slept.

Her bedroom door opened and Brown came in. 'Miss Cole said to wake you,' she said apologetically. 'She has ordered the slaves up from the cellar. Bates will take them to the parlour when you say.'

Frances yawned. 'I slept.'

'You'd have been tired out, late last night with Sir Charles at dinner, and then lunch with him today.' Brown moved around the room deftly folding laundry and putting it into the drawers, straightening Frances's silver-backed brush and comb on the ponderous chest of drawers. 'Even Miss Cole took a rest, and that's not a thing which happens often.'

Frances sat up in bed. 'I'll change my gown,' she decided, glancing down at the creased muslin. Nothing stayed clean in this city. At home she would wear the same gown all the day but in Bristol the continual drift of smuts and ash covered everything with a fine dark grit which soiled white linen within hours.

'There's the sprigged muslin, with a green silk sash, that's pretty. But rather fine for staying home,' Brown suggested.

'I'll wear it,' Frances said.

Brown shook the gown by the shoulders and spread it out for Frances to see. It was tightly fitted over a silk bodice with smooth close-fitting sleeves. The sprig in the white muslin was in the pattern of little flowers and the green sash was embroidered with matching flowers. It was a dress for springtime, a dress for walking on a warm well-clipped lawn in the country.

Frances nodded and stood with her arms out while Brown unhooked her at the back, helped her step from her old gown and then threw the afternoon gown over her head.

'Just tie my hair back,' Frances ordered. 'I'll wear it in a knot.'

'You have such pretty hair,' Brown said. 'I could put a little curl in it. There's the kitchen fire lit, I could have the tongs heated in a moment.'

'No,' Frances said, reaching for a warm shawl against the chill of the bedroom. She did not want to confide in a servant but she thought to herself that it was hardly worth curling her hair when there was no-one to see her but her sister-in-law and her husband. Mehuru would see her, of course. But Mehuru was hardly interested in whether her hair was curled or straight. For a moment she wondered if he saw her as a woman at all, or only as a slave driver, as an enemy. She hoped very much that he knew she was not his enemy. 'Tell Bates to take the slaves to the parlour. We can start at once,' she said.

She waited while Brown went downstairs and then she heard the slaves slowly coming up the backstairs from the kitchen. She heard their low frightened whispers from the hall before she went to the head of the stairs and walked down.

Mehuru, looking up at the noise of her bedroom door closing behind her, saw her coming down, almost floating, down the stairs, gliding like a ghost in a white mist of a gown. Frances, seeing his face upturned and watching her, paused on the stairs and put her hand to the base of her throat where her pulse was suddenly thudding. Mehuru saw the colour rise into her face and go again, leaving her even whiter than before.

'Mehuru,' she said.

'France-sess.'

She followed them into the parlour and watched them sit in their usual places. She gave them a small smile. 'Hello,' she said.

Their faces were smooth and unchanging, like ebony.

For once, Frances and the slaves were virtually alone. Bates stood at the door holding the whip across him, but he was not listening nor watching. He was a bored sentinel, standing at his post. Miss Cole's windowseat was empty. Frances gazed at Mehuru, disregarding the others. She felt restless and light-headed. 'Mehuru,' she repeated. He looked at her but said nothing.

She glanced around the room, wondering what she could teach them. She went to the window, took a handful of the curtain material and showed it to them. 'Curtain,' Frances said.

She looked at Mehuru. 'Curtain,' she said again. She nodded at him. 'Curtain,' she said more firmly.

Mehuru suppressed a small unhappy sigh. 'Curt-dane.'

'That's right!' Frances said brightly. 'Curtain.'

She tapped on the window. 'Window,' she told them. 'Win-dow.'

She took her seat at the head of the table and pointed to the back of her chair. 'Chair,' she said. They repeated it dully. Then she slapped the table before her.

'What's this?' she asked Mehuru. 'What's this?'

'Table,' he said easily.

She pointed to the curtain and the window and the chair.

He repeated all the names, he had learned them instantly, he did not need a second reminder. He was learning nouns with the facility and speed of a linguist. He had always known a good deal of Portuguese; another European language was not difficult for him. He listened to the orders from John-bates, he eavesdropped while he waited in the kitchen. He was putting together words and meanings all the time. Frances was teaching him single words like a child, while he was stringing together sentences and guessing at their meaning every time he was taken from the cellar.

Frances rose from her seat and went to the window. He watched her carefully, without seeming to watch her, as a man will watch an animal when he is not certain if it is tame or wild.

'Come here,' she beckoned him. He rose and went carefully towards her, his bare feet silent on the boards and the rugs. She liked to command him. She liked the way he came silently to her side. In all her life she had been powerless before men; and now here was a man who moved like a dancer, in complete obedience to her smallest gesture.

'Look,' she said. She pointed out of the window. 'See, a ship. A ship.'

Mehuru had not seen the view from the front of the house before. He had seen nothing beyond the backyard but a small patch of dirty sky. Looking down from the parlour window, he could see, lying on the mud of the harbour at low tide, the ship that had brought them on the long long journey from home. She did not look so fearsome now, he thought. Beached and unloaded she looked vulnerable, not like the smooth devouring monster of his nightmare.

He could see the gratings in the deck, which had been his sky for those long months, lifted out and leaning on the railed side of the ship. He could see the hold, which had been his world, scoured clean and ready for re-loading. The sails were stripped from the masts. They were being re-sewn and repaired in sail lofts on the top floors of the warehouses. There were sailors seated on the dockside retying the ropes and cables. Mehuru recognised the cycle of preparation and readiness. Soon the ship would sail again, he thought. Sail that long journey over those grey dangerous seas and then wait off the coast of his homeland for people, his people, to be snatched in their twos and threes and gathered together in a dreadful poaching expedition and taken away to their death, or to a life so cruel that they would wish themselves dead many and many times.

'Ship,' Frances smiled. 'Ship. You know that ship, that is the *Daisy*, which brought you here.'

Mehuru nodded. He knew that ship. He knew it better than any sailor could know it, for it was the blood from his back in the timbers of the hold and his bare feet that had danced on deck, and his pride and his joy and his manhood that had drained down into the stinking bilges. He knew that ship.

'Ship,' he said coldly.

'Excuse me, ma'am,' John Bates said from the doorway. 'But the little ones are crying again.'

The smallest child was hunched in his seat, rocking himself. Unstoppable tears poured down his face. The little boy next to him, only five years old, was holding the sleeve of the Fulani woman to his face. His shoulders were shaking as he sobbed. The two seven-year-old children, the girl and the boy, were dry-eyed but anxious; they looked ready to weep at any moment. Frances looked around at them.

'Now!' she said brightly, taking up a plate from the sideboard. 'What is this?'

The lesson continued with the naming of things until Brown tapped on the parlour door and peeped in. 'It's the farrier, ma'am,' she said. 'He's brought the thing you ordered.'

'That will be the bridle,' Frances said. She glanced

nervously at Mehuru. He listened carefully, trying to follow the inflections of her speech. He did not understand the words but he saw her quick guilty look.

'What?' Kbara tapped on the table urgently.

'Don't know,' he tapped back.

'Perhaps you had better take them away,' Frances said to John Bates. 'Put the bridle on her in the cellar.'

'I'll do it when they're chained,' he said. 'That big one, the pagan, he might cause trouble.'

'Very well,' Frances agreed. She wanted nothing to do with it. She did not want to see the bridle being fitted. She did not want to hear of any struggle.

'I'll take the lad down with me, and I'll wear my pistols,' Bates told her. 'If she struggles I may have to whip her.'

Frances hesitated. She looked at the woman. She was lifeless, she had taken no part in the lesson, she had said nothing and made no sound. Her eyes were sunk in her head, she was blind with despair. She seemed to hear nothing and know nothing. 'Very well,' Frances said, abandoning her. 'Whatever you think best.'

Bates nodded and opened the door. He jerked the chain on the neck rings and the slaves formed up into a line. There was a spatter of rain on the parlour windows. Mehuru shivered at the sound of it. At home there was a short season of rains and a long season of dry hot weather. He could not understand a country where it rained chilly, damp rain every day. He thought he would never be warm again. Even if he were miraculously transported home, sprawled by the side of the river in the middle of the day, he thought he would still feel this deathly chill in his bones and smell this stink of decay.

He stumbled as he went down the steps into the cellar and jerked the chain on the neck ring of the smallest child who was following. The child did not even cry out against the pain. He seemed to be in a deep silence, too deep and too filled with despair for any protest. Mehuru put a hand down to him but the child did not look up. He was still crying silently.

The lad secured them to the wall, running the chain from each collar through the rings fixed on the wall. Then Bates and the lad came and unfastened the chain for Died of Shame. She did not protest. She did not look to Mehuru for help. She went dully with them, not knowing what they wanted of her, no longer caring what they might do.

'We could have her and no-one would know,' the lad said. He giggled, an odd lively sound in the quiet cave.

'Go on then,' Bates said, uncaringly. 'The gentlemen did, why not us?'

They laid the woman down on the floor and she lay still and turned her head away from them and closed her eyes. The lad took her first, quickly and fumblingly; then Bates followed him roughly. The woman said nothing except a grunt when Bates first thrust inside her. Mehuru, watching this tableau of cruelty as it was enacted before him at his very feet, felt himself dizzy with rage, dizzy with pain, dizzy at his own helplessness.

The men got to their feet but Died of Shame lay still.

'Is she all right?' the lad asked.

Bates kicked her experimentally with the toe of his boot. She did not move.

'Sister,' Mehuru said. Slowly, slowly she turned her face and looked at him. He saw her eyes were glazed. She had gone to somewhere they could not reach her and it would be cruelty to call her back.

'You are in the keeping of your fathers,' Mehuru said to her blank unseeing face. 'They love you still.'

'Let's get on with it,' Bates said. 'I don't like him.' He jerked his head towards Mehuru. 'He's learning fast. It's not natural. She shouldn't be teaching them like this. It's not right.'

He picked up the bridle from the ground. 'You hold her down,' he ordered. 'Stand on the chains of her wrist and neck, and beat her with the butt end of the whip if she fights me.'

He knelt at the woman's head and forced her face roughly inside the mask. It was a plate of metal with a triangular hole cut away for her nose. A broad band ran across her mouth. The whole device was fastened behind her head with thick leather straps and buckles. Bates fitted it on her face and then pushed her head to one side to tighten the straps. She said nothing, she made no move to resist. Mehuru, watching them handle her as if she were a doll, wondered if she had fainted, her neck was so slack. But then they dropped her head back on the floor and he saw, gleaming on either side of the metal band, her blank black eyes.

'Chain her up,' Bates said.

They had to drag her to her feet and prop her against the wall so that they could pass the chain for the collar through the ring on the wall. It was long enough for all of the slaves to stand or lie as they wished.

'Now go and fetch their dinner pail,' Bates said.

'What about her? She won't be able to get anything to eat.'

'She can do without tonight, she'll be hungry tomorrow and then she can eat. Teach her a lesson.'

The boy sped away and came back as Bates put a new candle in the lantern, lit it and hung it on the high hook. Bates watched the lad put the food pail, thirteen plates and the pitcher of water with the tin mugs within reach of the slaves then he went out, locking the door behind him.

Chapter Fourteen

The candle had guttered into darkness and the smallest children had been asleep for some time. The women had gathered the crying babies into their arms for comfort and slept with them held close. Mehuru had been waiting and listening a long while for Snake but he did not come. He leaned back against the cold wall of the cave, closed his eyes and readied himself for sleep.

Something touched his foot. 'Obalawa,' a muffled voice said.

It was the woman who called herself Died of Shame. She was sleepless, her face half-hidden by the bridle they had put on her. It covered her mouth completely and her nose was bleeding on either side where it poked through the sharp edges of the roughly made hole. She had to speak through clamped lips, her speech distorted by the plate over her mouth. 'You are an obalawa, a powerful priest.'

'I have been trained,' Mehuru said carefully. 'I have dedicated my life. But I am losing my vision, Sister. This country is making me blind.' He could hardly make out her speech, but he knew what she would want.

'They have gagged me like a dog. They have shamed me and now they starve me.'

'I know, Sister,' Mehuru replied gently. 'I grieve for you.'

'Wish me dead, Obalawa,' she said simply. 'I must go to my fathers. They may forgive me.'

He paused. 'They may not allow us to bury you rightly.

With your things . . .' He broke off. She had no things here. No cooking pot, no piece of chalk, no beads for her hair, no bowl, no spoon, no sharp knife, no hoeing stick, no purse with coins or cowrie shells, no comb. No little pretty women's things that a young wife should have laid in her grave beside her, none of these things could go with Died of Shame to the other world. And her son, her young son who should be the first to say farewell to her, who should wash her face in the funeral rites and kiss her goodbye – she had left him before he could say more than her name, before he could do more than call and call for her, and never hear an answer.

She nodded. 'The fathers may forgive me.'

'It might get better,' Mehuru said. 'We might be freed. We might find a way home. To choose death is often a mistake as well as a sin against the breast of the earth.'

In the darkness her eyes gleamed alongside the gleam of the metal plate. She looked like a masked dancer summoned to dance at a funeral, she looked eerie, mysterious. 'What do you see, Obalawa?'

Mehuru fixed his eyes on the gleam of the metal bridle that gagged her mouth. He looked into its dull light as if he might picture some future for them in the leaden sheen. Then he shook his head. 'I do not see us going home,' he admitted.

'And I could not go,' she said simply. 'Look again. Look at me. Look into me.'

Mehuru leaned forward and took her in, the blank strange shapes of her masked face, the hunched shoulders of a woman in deep pain, the shapeless clothes which hid her round smooth breasts and the pure line of her hips, and then he leaned a little closer, sensing the start of new life. He sighed a small hidden breath. He could see Sir Charles's baby.

The woman nodded, but Mehuru did not let the sense of the embryo slide away from him. There was something wrong. He breathed a little deeper; if he had the smoke, if he had the water, if he had the polished tray and the cowrie shells for the complicated arithmetical divination he would have been able to know what was wrong.

'The baby,' he said. 'I think it is sick.'

'The man was diseased,' she answered. 'He was thick with illness, he smelled foul, like death.'

Mehuru nodded. The baby would not go full term, he would not be taking a viable life when he wished the woman dead with a baby inside her. And Died of Shame did not have a life worth living now.

'Can you wish me dead?' she asked. 'Without pain, but quickly?'

Mehuru waited for guidance, closing his eyes. Patiently, the woman sat beside him, watching his face. They were silent together for nearly an hour until Mehuru hissed a long slow hiss 'Yes.'

'The goddess will not eat you,' she said generously, freeing him of any guilt, absolving him of blame so that Ayelala the goddess who punishes lawbreakers would not come for him.

'Or you.' Mehuru returned the blessing.

He took one last look at her before she went back to her place beside the other women and lay down. He saw that his wishing would only complement her own desire. Her eyes were already dead, they were as dull as the metal plate across her mouth.

He heard her moving softly in the darkness, lying down and wrapping her arms around herself. He heard her muffled lips name the people she loved, her little son, her husband, her mother, and then the ancestors who might come to her, who might, despite all that was wrong in her life, forgive her. And then he heard the long long silence of a woman waiting for death.

Mehuru sat up and stared into the darkness and started the wishing.

* * *

In the morning in the darkness of the cave he heard the women stirring and then an abrupt exclamation. 'Aiee! She is dead.'

'Mehuru! Did you know? Died of Shame is dead!'

He rose to his feet and staggered a little from the stiffness in his legs. 'I knew,' he said.

Kbara, chained to the wall at the other end of the line, was awake. 'What shall we do? She needs to be buried here.'

One woman pushed back the straw and tapped on the cave floor. It was sandstone. 'Do they have no earth in this damned country?' she asked. 'How are we to bury our sister where she should be buried, under the floor of her own hut?'

'She knew,' Mehuru told them. 'She was prepared for it to be done wrongly.'

The woman who named herself Grief drew a little closer to him. 'She spoke to you?'

Mehuru said nothing.

'So how will we manage?' Kbara demanded. 'Shall we shout out for them?'

'Don't make them bring the whip,' the girl called Homeless said hastily. 'When we shout they bring the whip.'

'We'll sing to her very quietly,' Grief decided. 'And make her ready as much as we can. Then Mehuru can tell them. Mehuru, you will ask for Frances and tell her.'

He nodded. It was a relief to see a woman taking command. They knew what they should do, it was their business. They gathered around her. He heard their soft lament, a whispered song, and he heard the shuffle of their feet in the straw as they moved, straightening her torn clothes and washing the parts of her face they could reach around the metal bridle.

'It is not right,' the girl called Lost cried despairingly. 'How can we do it right here?'

Kbara, Mehuru and the older boy Accursed stood uneasily waiting. They should have been digging the grave for the woman, inside the door of the hut, at her own hearthside so that she might always be with her family. They should have been walking to outlying houses to tell them of the death. They should have been making a gift, or doing some task for the bereaved family. They should have been helping to prepare a feast to say farewell, they should have been priming their guns to celebrate her passing with gunshots, they should have been practising their steps and preparing the grim masks to dance for her funeral. There was so much to do when there was a death, especially that of a young woman. And now they stood around like fools, like idle fools.

The opening of the door was a relief. John Bates came in, carrying a big pan of porridge. He recoiled as Mehuru went to the length of his chain to greet him.

'Now then, now then,' he said nervously. 'Shush shush shush, stay quiet.'

'Frances,' Mehuru said quietly. 'See . . . Frances.'

John Bates nearly dropped the pan in amazement.

'Johnbates,' Mehuru said gently. 'I . . . want . . . Frances.'

'My God, he's talking,' John exclaimed. 'He said my name!' He turned his head and yelled up the stairs. 'The darkie's talking. The big one! He's talking words!'

Cook appeared at the top of the steps. 'If you've finished I'll shut this door,' she said crossly. 'I won't have it open all day. Shall I shut you in?'

'Wait a minute, if you please.' He thrust the bowl into Mehuru's arms.

'See Frances,' Mehuru repeated.

'Frances,' the driver nodded. 'Mrs Cole. But I know what you mean. I'll tell her.' He opened his mouth and suddenly shouted very loudly. Spittle flew from his red lips into the porridge, Mehuru could feel it on his face. 'I'll tell her!'

He turned and went back up the stairs. 'Remarkable,' he said as he closed the door and went into the kitchen. 'Here,

Mrs Brown, tell Mrs Cole that the big nigger is asking for her. He's never done that before. He said her name.'

Brown sniffed disapprovingly. 'She's not even awake yet,' she snorted. She was laying the tray with Frances's drink of hot chocolate and a bread roll with fresh-churned butter and plum jam.

'Well, tell her when you take her breakfast in,' Bates said. 'She'll want to know. She takes a deal of trouble over them.'

Brown picked up the tray without answering and swept from the kitchen. But by the time she had woken Frances, drawn her curtains and set her tray before her on the bed, she knew that Bates was right.

'The big slave was asking for you,' she said.

Frances paused with the cup halfway to her lips. 'He asked for me?'

'He said, "see Frances", according to John Bates. I said I'd tell you. I hope I did right.'

'Yes, of course,' Frances said. 'I'd better see him at once.'

'You'll have your chocolate first?'

Frances pushed the tray to one side and got out of bed. 'No, you can make me some more later.' She was now accustomed to ordering what she wanted. 'Fetch me a wrapper and tie back my hair. I'll see him now. Is Mr Cole at home?'

'No, ma'am. He's gone out. He went over on the ferry to see Sir Charles Fairley at his hotel.'

'Then I'll come down in my wrapper.'

Frances brushed her own hair, scrupulously pinned her cap and tied her loose gown. 'Tell Cook I'm on my way,' Frances said, mindful of the protocol of Cook's kitchen.

There was a stony silence as she went into the kitchen but John was waiting by the cellar door. 'He said your name, Mrs Cole, clear as a bell. Shall I come down with you? Shall I bring my whip?'

Frances was about to refuse but then she hesitated.

'You don't know what he's doing,' John warned. 'It could

193

be a trap, ma'am. I'll fetch my pistols as well before you go down.'

An old dark fear touched Frances. The fear of a woman outnumbered by men, the fear of one species among several of another, the master's fear when he is surrounded by slaves, the driver's fear when he knows himself hated, the slaver's fear when he knows he is a criminal. She tasted the sharp tang at the back of her throat which is the taste of power over others, and the fear that they, in turn, will take power over you. Then she thought of Mehuru and the darkness of his eyes and her vision of him as an individual – not as one of a dangerous crowd. She had absolute trust in him.

'I'll go down alone,' she said lightly, opening the door and descending the stairs.

Mehuru stepped forward to greet her and she knew from his face that something important had happened.

'Frances.'

'Mehuru.'

He said simply: 'Died of Shame,' and Frances in her ignorance did not know that his words were more than a name – the name the woman had given herself – but also a diagnosis of her sickness; and now, finally, her epitaph.

'Is she ill?'

He shook his head slowly. He leaned his head to one side in a mime of intense weariness, and then he shut his eyes.

'Dead?'

He looked at her questioningly.

Frances repeated his mime, closing her eyes. 'Dead?'

Mehuru nodded. 'Dead,' he said in his low steady voice, the word added to his growing English vocabulary. 'She is dead.'

He stepped to one side so that Frances could see the still body and the women who sat at her head and feet singing very softly.

Frances went forward and recoiled. She had forgotten the

194

bridle. The young woman's face was encased in metal. Blood and saliva stained her neck from where the gag had cut her mouth and gums. She looked like a victim of some barbaric mediaeval torture. And Frances had ordered this. And now the woman was dead. There was a stillness about her which was very final. She looked peaceful; even in the strange helmet with a collar and chain, manacles and shackles, she looked at rest. For the first time she looked as if she were free, as if she had escaped from all the constraints they had put on her.

Frances shook her head, denying the truth, denying her responsibility. 'But she was well,' she said. 'Except for . . .' She broke off. She could not bring herself to claim that Died of Shame had ever been well. She had been a captive in a strange land, she had been the victim of a rape, she had been in such great despair that she had filled her mouth and her belly with earth, and then, despite the cruelty of the bridle, she had escaped her tormentors and fled to her death.

Frances suddenly did not want to excuse herself, not even to Mehuru. She knew that she was culpable, that she was guilty of this woman's capture and her death. She had colluded with her capture and her ill-treatment, with her rape. Frances, by trading her prestige for Josiah's wealth and comfort, had been a party to bringing this young woman far from her home to her death. She had been raped and Frances had lunched with her rapist and promised him tickets for a society ball.

'I am sorry,' Frances said. Her voice was low. Mehuru did not recognise the words, but thought it was the first honest tone he had ever heard from her.

He bowed his head in a strange formal gesture. In his own language he said: 'We all have guilt to bear.'

Frances said nothing, and they stood, facing each other in silence. When she raised her face to him he was shocked, her dark eyes were filled with tears. He watched, fascinated, as one spilled over and rolled down her cheek. He put his hand out and touched it, almost as if he wanted to know if it was real. The skin of her cheek was warm, the tear was real. Frances stayed very still as he touched her, his fingertip soft and tentative against her cheekbone, as light as the brush of a feather.

Slowly he took his fingertip, wet with her tear, and put it to his lips. It was salty and wet, like a real tear. He tasted it on his tongue and gazed into her eyes as if he would read her like the oracle of Ifa.

'I am so very, very sorry,' she said again.

Chapter Fifteen

≈≋≈

They took the body of Died of Shame away. There was a ripple of distress when Bates came into the cellar and took her by the wrists and dragged her like a doll up the steps.

'Mehuru, she should be washed and wrapped in cloth,' Grief accused him. 'You did not tell Frances!'

'How could I tell her?' he asked. 'I do not know the words for a proper burial. I told her that our sister was dead. I thought she would know what to do. I thought she would do the right things.'

They watched anxiously but the door at the head of the steps banged shut.

'Perhaps they will bury her as they bury their own people,' Kbara said. 'They may treat her with respect. It may not be our way but it could still be a good way.'

The girl called Homeless looked at him with anger. 'She is our sister,' she said. 'Of course she should be buried in our way. How else can she find her fathers?'

Kbara caught the sense of the Wolof words and was about to answer but Mehuru shook his head. At home they had the Gelede festival – the festival for soothing the mothers – designed solely to direct the awesome power of women for good. For ten days they would feast and dance, and watch ritual theatre to harness the magical power of women. Here in this dark cave, ominously like a grave, ominously like a womb, the women would seethe with their suppressed desires. Missing their children, missing their mothers, anything could focus their grief and anger. In any case the girl was right. Mehuru had failed Died of Shame in her death as he had failed her in her life.

'It is I who am at fault, Homeless,' he said gently in her language. 'Not Kbara. We are not men here, we have no power. I cannot provide for you, or hunt, or farm, or even guard. I could not tell Frances what was needed. She seemed grieved, and I thought she would do the right things for our sister. I had not realised that these people can feel one thing and do another. They are strangers indeed.'

'Was she grieved for Died of Shame?' the youth called Accursed asked him.

'She had tears in her eyes,' Mehuru said. 'I trusted her. I thought she must care.'

The woman called Grief shook her head. 'She is a dreadful woman. She had tears in her eyes and yet she sent that rapist to bury his victim?'

'Yes,' Mehuru said. 'Exactly.' He sat on the stone bench, drew his knees up under his chin and wrapped his arms around them, isolating himself from the world, from the others.

'Are you praying, Obalawa?' Accursed asked in his endearing husky voice which was just breaking into the male depths and yet could still go unreliably squeaky.

Mehuru shook his head. 'I can summon no god,' he confessed. 'He comes to me no longer. I am waiting for him but he does not come. I am waiting for understanding, but it does not come either. Perhaps some day something will come to make sense of all this pain. Perhaps some day I will understand why we suffer this.'

The death of Died of Shame was to make no difference to the routine of the day, Sarah Cole decreed. The corpse was taken up to the Redclift graveyard and buried in an unmarked grave. It was not a pauper burial; Sarah paid threepence for

198

the site and entered the sum in the company ledger as a loss. She looked accusingly at Frances as she dusted sand on the ink and closed the ledger. 'A loss,' she said reproachfully. 'You had better start teaching them to obey commands. We need to show a profit on this.'

They came into the parlour in silence and sat in their accustomed places. The two youngest children were not crying today, they were too shocked. Frances saw their little faces at table-top height as blank and as empty as new black slates.

She had brought her sketch and watercolour books for today's lesson, and she put up the easel at the head of the table. The first picture was the long view down the avenue of elms to the house at Whiteleaze.

'This is a house,' she said. She nodded at Mehuru. 'House.'

They knew now what she wanted of them and they repeated the word without emphasis, without interest. She might mean the paper, she might mean the easel. She might mean the artist or the gods who made it possible for men and women to dream and create art. They did not care. They repeated the word as she wished.

'This was my house,' Frances explained to Mehuru. 'Well, it was my uncle's house. I stayed here very often, and we dined here two or three times a week.'

Sarah Cole in the windowseat leaned forward to look at the easel, her curiosity overcoming her irritation with her sister-in-law.

Frances gestured to herself and then pointed to the picture. She said to Mehuru, 'This was my house. My house.'

So she was an exile too, Mehuru thought. That accounted for the strange sense of loss which hung around her. It accounted for her powerlessness in this place. She was a new arrival, she had not yet made it her home. He thought of his country and the careful arrangements of introducing a bride to a new home. The senior wife would fetch the new bride and take her to her husband's house. They would wash her legs and send her to his room. She would live in the senior wife's house as her apprentice, to learn what should be done and the right way to do things. For three months she would visit her parents only at night, when the work of the day was done. It was almost a game, the sneaking back home to mother, and any troubles in the early months could be whispered in the darkness. After three months the girl had served her apprenticeship and knew her rights. But in any case, there were few troubles. It was a world where men and women knew their duties to each other, and where the gods were kind. Before the slavers had come, before the slaving nations had been armed and set upon their neighbours, it had been a world of particular good fortune: fertile, with good weather, and long, long-established political stability.

Frances turned a page to show a competent watercolour of a still life. 'These are fruits,' she said. 'Fruits.'

She pointed to the painted fruits and they named them after her. 'Apple, pear, grapes, peach.'

She turned another page. It was a picture of a King Charles spaniel sitting at the edge of a cornfield. The pale green corn was bright with flowers, scarlet poppies and blue love-in-a-mist. The hedgerows around the field were spotted with dog roses and the nodding heads of foxgloves.

'This was my dog,' Frances said. 'My little dog.' Her voice quavered slightly. 'I had to give her away when I went to work. She was a spaniel.'

Mehuru heard the distress in her voice and looked from the picture to Frances's face. She tried to smile at him. 'My little dog,' she said. 'My companion.' Her eyes were bright with tears. 'I know it's very silly.' She pulled a small handkerchief from her pocket. 'But she was a wonderful little dog, she used to go everywhere with me. And I lost her, and lost my home, and lost my Papa . . .'

The women glared at Mehuru. 'Her tears do not mean

much, then,' Grief remarked bitterly. 'One tear for Died of Shame, raped three times and dead in a cave, and a dozen tears for a picture of a monkey.'

'No,' Mehuru said. 'I was a fool to trust her. Her tears do not mean much at all.'

'They are chattering amongst themselves,' Miss Cole interrupted from the windowseat. 'How will they learn if they go on talking their own language and don't even listen to you?'

Frances cleared her throat and dabbed at her eyes. 'I beg your pardon,' she said to the sullen black faces. She turned a page of the easel and showed a picture of a church. 'This is my father's church,' she said. She looked at Mehuru and pointed to the building. 'Church,' she said. 'Jesus. Church.'

The slaves repeated the words in a sulky murmur. Frances smiled, pleased. 'Later on I shall teach you stories from the bible,' she promised.

She turned another page. 'And these are flowers.' She pointed to sketches of flower heads and named each one. They named them as she did.

Frances left the easel and sat down at the head of the table. 'Now,' she said brightly. 'My name is Frances. I come from England.' She pointed to Mehuru. 'Your name is Mehuru, you come from Africa.'

He stared at her in dull resentment.

'Go on,' Grief taunted him. 'You are her favourite. You tasted her tear. You trusted her. Speak as she bids you.'

'Say: "My name is Mehuru, I come from Africa".' Frances repeated her command.

He stared at her, a long burning stare filled with reproach. Frances stammered, and lost the thread of the lesson. 'What is it?' she asked him in an undertone, glancing quickly towards Miss Cole. 'What is the matter?'

He turned his head away from her, there was no mistaking the snub.

'Mehuru!' she whispered urgently. 'What is it?'

'My name is Mehuru,' he repeated in clear perfect English, mimicking her precisely, his accent sharp with anger, his very obedience an insult. 'My name is Mehuru. I come from Africa.'

Josiah Cole came home in time for dinner in a sunny mood. Frances, changing into yet another gown, heard him talking with his sister as he climbed the stairs.

'Two pieces of good work today. Sir Charles is considering placing money with us for us to act as his agents. You did well to suggest it, my dear, and Frances is a credit to us. If she can get him and Miss Honoria tickets for the Scott ball I will be obliged to her. And even better – Waring has closed the sale of his house with me at last! I was beginning to wonder if he meant to let me down.'

'I was beginning to wonder if it were not better to pull out from the deal altogether,' Sarah said. 'Brown told me that number 31 is to come on the market. Two for sale in such a short time must mean that both will be cheapened.'

'Queens Square will always be Queens Square,' Josiah declared firmly. 'Prices may fluctuate from time to time but it will always be the best area of Bristol.'

'It may be,' Sarah said urgently. 'But have a little patience, Brother, and think! With two houses on the square you could bargain with Waring, you could force his price down.'

'The deal is done,' Josiah said stubbornly. 'And I have shaken on it. My word is my bond, everyone knows that. I have agreed a price. I don't go running back to ask for a discount.'

'And when do we move? When do you have to pay the rest of the money?'

Frances opened her bedroom door and the two broke off.

'Excuse me.' She felt suddenly shy, as if she had been eavesdropping on a private agreement. 'But I heard you mention the house. Have we bought it at last?'

Josiah beamed at her, came up the last few steps, caught her hand and kissed it. 'Yes indeed, it is ours!' he said. 'You can move in tomorrow!'

'Tomorrow!'

'My brother exaggerates,' Sarah said. 'It is his way.'

'I do not!' he contradicted her. 'The house is being emptied now. When Mr Waring moves, at least he moves swiftly. He and his wife have moved out to stay in a hotel and their servants are ordered to move all their goods. He sent me a note to tell me that we can have the keys and call the place our own from tomorrow.'

'And the money?' Sarah demanded urgently over Frances's cry of delight. 'When is it due? We do not have it in hand, Josiah, you know.'

Josiah took her hand. 'Have confidence, Sarah,' he urged her. 'You do not buy a house like Queens Square outright with saved shillings. I have a long-term loan, against *Rose*'s profits. I do not have to repay until *Rose* comes in at the end of next year. This is my first great investment. And I have others in my mind. I have been waiting for this chance for a long time.'

'You have forestalled on a cargo?' Sarah was shocked. 'We have never done such a thing before, Josiah! The risk . . .'

'But how wonderful!' Frances interrupted. 'Will we not have to buy a great deal of furniture? Does the house need wallhangings renewing, and repainting? Is there not a lot to be done before we can move in?'

'You shall see for yourself,' Josiah said happily. 'We will go first thing in the morning and you shall judge for yourself. But I believe that there is very little that wants doing. Mrs Waring had it done throughout in Chinese fashion only last year. If the style is agreeable to you then we can simply move in our furniture and take up our residence.'

Frances inwardly swore that however dreadful Chinese

fashion proved to be she would not complain. 'I am certain it will be delightful! I so long to live on the square.'

'We are taking a risk,' Sarah interrupted. 'I *will* be heard. We are taking a risk in doing business in this way. We are trading on credit and we have never done such a thing before.'

Frances was quenched. She looked to Josiah.

'We have traded small,' he said firmly. 'We had small beginnings, Sarah, and we had to keep to our limits. But there are great profits to be made for men who dare to take a risk. It is my judgement that it is worth it.'

Sarah clutched her hands together in an odd involuntary movement. 'It is too great a risk,' she said. Frances looked at her curiously. The woman was near to tears. 'If *Rose* founders then we are ruined overnight. We cannot stake the survival of this trading house on such a gamble.'

Josiah hesitated, thinking for a moment that he would tell her of the further risks he had taken with *Rose* – uninsured for the middle passage, overloaded and ordered to smuggle slaves to the Spanish colonies; but Sarah's white anxious face dissuaded him. He could not face her anger and distress. He stretched out and stilled her wringing hands. 'Peace, Sister,' he urged her gently. 'There is no need for this worry.'

She looked at him as if he did not understand at all. 'I was born on the floor of a miner's hovel,' she said. 'I have been poor, Josiah, as you were not. You were born when we were on the rise; you know nothing about hardship.' She looked at Frances. 'You neither. You think that having to work and living here, over the warehouse, is poverty. I know you do, I have seen you looking down your nose at our ways and thinking them very mean. But I have known hardship that neither of you can understand. I have gone barefoot for lack of shoes and hungry for lack of food and I cannot *bear* to hear you talking, Josiah, about gambling with our livelihood. As if poverty were not waiting beneath our feet every day of our lives, waiting longing to gobble us up.' She was flushed, her eyes were bright with tears. 'We are in a little trow on a great river of poverty,' she cried. 'And your debts and your gambles, Josiah, will overturn us!'

He was taken aback by her vehemence. 'Sarah . . . I . . .'

'Promise me you will not run us into debt,' she demanded. 'Promise me that we will make an agreement with Mr Waring and pay him what we owe from our profits, not from forestalling on our cargoes.'

Josiah looked uncomfortable. 'Be still, Sister,' he said awkwardly. 'I am sorry to see you so distressed . . .'

'Promise me!'

'It is too late,' Josiah admitted. 'I have agreed to pay Waring a lump sum, some borrowed, some from *Daisy*'s profits, and I have sold *Rose*'s cargo already. The gamble has been laid, Sarah. You will have to accept it.' The rest of the gamble – the missing insurance, the smuggling – he left to silence.

She lost her colour at once, and swayed as if she might faint with fear. Frances, a silent observer between the two of them, thought that the older woman looked as if she had lost the love of her life. Sarah was obsessed with financial security. Nothing frightened her more than debt.

She took a deep breath and rallied. 'I am sorry to hear it.'

'It is signed and sealed and done,' Josiah said, impressing her with the finality of the deal.

'Then I can say nothing more,' she said with dignity. 'Except that I wish you had talked it over with me first, Josiah.' She carefully avoided looking at Frances. 'You would have discussed it with me, in the old days. You should have discussed it with me, even now.'

'I would have discussed it with you,' Josiah placated her. 'But it all took place in the coffee shop, it was quickly and easily done. And there is no great risk, Sarah. *Rose* is a good ship. There is no reason to think she will not come home safe.'

Sarah at once knocked on the wooden banister and Frances

saw Josiah tap his foot involuntarily on the wooden tread of the stair.

'We had to buy the Queens Square house or throw away the deposit,' he reminded her. 'And I had promised a new house to Frances in the marriage settlement.'

'This house was our father's pride,' Sarah observed.

Josiah turned on the stair and smiled at her. 'It has been a good house for us,' he agreed. 'We have made our start from here. But now we must go upwards in the world.' He stopped himself and laughed. 'Here! I must go upwards to my bedchamber and wash before dinner. I am famished. I did not stop to eat at noon, I have been so busy this day.'

'Why?' Sarah asked, following him up the stairs. 'Have you found partners for *Daisy*?'

'Sir Charles is in for his share, of a thousand pounds, of course; and I have other partners to hand,' Josiah said happily. 'Money breeds money. Now it is known that Sir Charles has bought a share the others want to come in too. And when we are living in Queens Square it will be even easier. Have you had a good day?'

'We have done badly,' Sarah told him. 'Frances has lost one of the new slaves.'

Josiah looked quickly at Frances and saw her stricken face. 'One here or there does not matter,' he said kindly. 'Sarah, you must not reproach her. We are bound to lose two or three from a batch. It does not matter.'

He came up the last few steps, took Frances's hand and led her into her room.

'I am sorry,' Frances said. 'I do not think I should have the care of them. It was a woman, it was the woman . . .' She wanted to put the blame on Sir Charles, but she could not bring herself to speak of what he had done. 'It was one of the women. She ate earth and I let her be put in a bridle and now she is dead.'

Josiah seated her gently before her looking glass and stood

behind her, his hands on her shoulders. 'It does not matter,' he said gently. 'I promise you, my dear, do not fret. One here or there makes no difference. This is an experiment. If we do well and sell at a profit we will repeat it on a grander scale. If they all die tomorrow then we will have learned that it cannot be done. Don't fret, my dear, you are doing the best you can and it is a difficult business, breaking slaves.'

He loosened the pins in the back of her head and Frances's coils of hair started to tumble down around her shoulders.

Frances felt lulled, as if she were a little girl again with her mother plaiting her hair. 'I do not know that I can teach them, Josiah. It is not like teaching children. They are so different from us, and the man who understands the most, Mehuru . . .' She broke off. 'He is not like a slave,' she said inadequately. 'I cannot think of him as a slave. I keep thinking of him as a civilised man.'

Josiah took up her silver brushes and gently brushed her hair. 'This is nonsense,' he said gently. 'You are overtired. Just do your best, my dear, it is nothing more than an experiment. We have to try, and we have to take chances. I cannot make the life for us which we desire without taking chances. We have to learn to take risks. I am a venturer, Frances! Not a shopkeeper!'

He swept the hair back from her forehead and from her temples where her pulse throbbed. It was a soothing gentle caress, the pressure of the soft bristles on her head and then the clean sweep.

'It makes me uneasy,' Frances confessed. 'To think of them all in my charge.'

'It is the nature of the Trade,' Josiah comforted her. 'You must not think of them as people or you will get distressed. They are commodities, my dear, they are goods, and English merchants have been trading in them for more than a hundred years.'

'So long? I did not know it had been so long! Why, how many slaves have we taken?'

'Oh, my dear! Who can say? English ships have grown bigger every year. The Trade has doubled and quadrupled.'

Frances saw in the mirror that her face was shocked. 'Hundreds of slaves? Thousands?' she asked.

Josiah shrugged. 'More. Many many more. Millions. It is an enormous business – three million slaves taken by the English in this century alone, and all the other European countries are slavers too.' He smoothed her hair away from her face. 'I see you are surprised,' he said. 'It is a mighty Trade, it is the very backbone of Britain, there is not a port that does not deal in it. There is no family in the country that does not feel the benefit. We all profit from it. It is the greatest trade that the world has ever known. It crosses and recrosses the Atlantic, it makes massive fortunes. We *all* profit.'

'I did not know,' Frances said. She thought of the light easy conversation at her uncle's dining table, of her father's gently reproachful sermons against the sin of laziness, or gluttony. No-one had ever questioned the ethics of the slave trade in her hearing. No-one had even thought about it. She had heard nothing but complaints of radicals and abolitionists who wanted to threaten the prosperity of Britain, ruin the colonies and overpay idle working men. 'But it must have destroyed Africa,' she exclaimed suddenly. 'Taking so many people, and all of them young, and most of them men. It must have emptied villages, it must have ravaged whole countries.'

She tried to imagine what it would be like in England if three million young men and women had been stolen away in only a hundred years. The country would be devastated. There would be no wealth, no farms, no industries, no roads. It would be a blow to the very heart of a nation. And the absence of three million people would mean that children were not conceived, that babies were not born. In the next generation seven million would be missing, in the next fifteen. There would be a gap, a gulf into which poverty and despair would flood. Inventions would not be made, industries would not develop, farms would lie idle, the whole fabric of society and order would collapse.

Josiah nodded. 'Africa is our farm, my dear. The farm produces the stock, we ship the stock to where it is needed. Africa is a slave-farm to serve the civilised world. It is a most elegant and efficient system.'

Frances leaned forward and let her hair hide her face from Josiah's easy smile. She felt dizzy with the view of the world suddenly opened before her. She could not imagine how she had known none of this, how successfully it had been gilded over. And now her livelihood depended on its successful continuance. 'It must be wrong,' she said. But she spoke without conviction. 'It cannot be right for us to farm a whole continent for our own use. And they are not stock, Josiah. The men and women I am teaching, they are not stock. They are people and they feel as we do – at least I think they do.'

'Who knows?' Josiah asked comfortably. 'When you have taught them to speak and civilised them perhaps you will teach them Christian feelings too, Frances. That would be a fine thing to do. I am sure you are doing well, far better than most ladies could.'

Josiah brushed softly and steadily and then his hand came under her hair and caressed the back of her neck. Frances sat still and let him do what he wished. She thought of the thousands of deaths he must have caused and the heartbreak in those hundred, thousand, million homes. She looked up and met his kind face in the mirror.

'I fear it is not right Josiah,' she said.

He smiled at her. 'You're looking very pretty,' he said gently. 'I love your hair let down.'

Chapter Sixteen

~~~

Josiah awoke Frances early. He came into her room himself and drew back the window curtain and the half-curtain at the head of her bed. The fire had been lit in skilful silence by the scullery maid before dawn and the room was warm.

'Up and awake, Mrs Cole!' Josiah cried joyfully. 'I have a carriage ordered for us at eight. I am taking you to see your new house today!'

Frances sat up in bed and laughed at his eagerness. 'But the Warings will still be packing their goods!'

'I shall throw them out of the back door when you enter the front!' Josiah exclaimed.

There was a tap on the door and Brown stood hesitantly in the doorway with Frances's tray in her hands.

'I'll take that!' Josiah said, bustling forward. He put the tray on Frances's knees. 'Now eat up, Wife, and meet me downstairs in an hour. No later, mind!'

Frances smiled at him. 'I shall be prompt,' she promised.

Josiah bent to kiss her forehead. Obeying an impulse, Frances lifted her face and their lips met. Josiah's kiss was very gentle. Frances felt tender towards him, he was so exuberant, like a little boy about to open a gift. In Lady Scott's eyes he might be nothing more than a vulgar trader, but Frances acknowledged that he was her husband and that her future wealth and happiness depended on him. And besides, she was coming to like him.

'An hour,' Josiah said ebulliently, and went from her room.

* * *

The carriage was waiting on the cobbled quay outside. Frances was dressed in her best dark blue velvet gown and pelisse with matching blue hat and muff.

'You look very fine,' Josiah said. He did not know that it was an old gown, carefully unpicked and resewn with the bald patches of the velvet folded inside where they would not show. 'You look very grand. You look like a proper lady.'

Frances winced at that. 'I should hope so, indeed.'

Josiah heard the slight reproof in her voice. 'Of course, of course,' he said hastily. 'Shall we go?'

Sarah was at the top of the stairs. Frances hesitated. 'Are you not coming, Sarah?'

'There are things that have to be done to ensure that the *Daisy* sails on time. Cargo to be ordered and checked, papers to be made ready. All the permits have to be entered. I shall spend this morning at work.'

Frances wavered a little at the reproach but Josiah was cheery. 'Excellent!' he exclaimed. 'And do not think that we are gallivanting, Sister. There are many ways to make money in this town and one of them is to be seen to be prosperous. This move will be the making of us, I swear it!'

'And will she teach the slaves this afternoon?' Sarah asked rudely.

'Yes, yes,' Josiah said. He opened the door, led Frances to the coach, and handed her in. 'And tell Brown that the slaves can start to help packing. I want us to move in as soon as possible. They can start today.'

Frances settled herself in the carriage and smiled half-apologetically at the dark house and Sarah's irritable glare. Josiah swung himself into the seat beside her as the carriage jolted on the cobbles and lurched forward. 'Sour as lemons,' Josiah said cheerfully under his breath. 'Now, Mrs Cole, you shall see something!'

* * *

The house was indeed furnished in Chinese fashion. Frances had to close her eyes when she first saw the best parlour, which was gloriously ornamented with plasterwork that sprawled magnificently from the top third of the walls to the central rose in the middle of the ceiling, rich with dragons, cherubs, swirling leaves, wild vines and the ultimate vulgarity of long-beaked ho-ho birds. The walls were lined with plush red silk – an eccentric choice given that the carpet, all twining vine leaves and fruit, was blue, and the curtains were green.

'Very grand,' Josiah said with satisfaction. 'Very fashionable. Colourful! I doubt there is another house like it in Bristol!'

'I doubt it too,' Frances said. She stepped from the room and peeped into the second parlour opposite, which was slightly smaller and plainer. 'And this is a very pretty room.'

'You won't sit here,' Josiah ruled. 'The best room is surely the morning room at the front of the house? This back room will be my office, and tradesmen can come and see me and enter from the back door. We shall have two doors now, Mrs Cole! No more working men tapping at your front door! No more tradesmen marching through your hall.'

Frances smiled. Despite the excesses of the plasterwork and the exuberant colour schemes it was a fine house, built in simple rectangle shapes; four rooms on the ground floor, four above, four above them, and then the attic rooms fitted into the roof. The kitchen and domestic rooms were crammed into the rear courtyard, the cellar stored wine and goods. As they stood in the hall they heard a crash and muffled oath from above as one of the Warings' servants dropped something.

'We will need to take on more staff,' Frances thought aloud. 'There is too much to be done for Brown and the scullery maid in a big house like this.'

'Aye,' Josiah said with satisfaction. 'We will use the slaves for now. And we will have to buy furniture to fill the place up a bit. Shall we buy all Chinese goods, my dear? I have a man in mind who imports very good copies from India, I swear you would not tell the difference.'

Frances managed to smile. 'I think I would prefer some simple English furniture.'

'But Chinoiserie is all the rage!' Josiah expostulated. 'It is the very thing! And with the house already so designed!'

Frances gave him a small sideways glance.

'Is it a little ornate for your taste?' he asked. He was immediately unsure. 'I thought it very fine? Is it not any good?'

Frances touched his bare hand with her gloved finger. 'Mr Cole, it is very fine indeed,' she said. 'And it is the very height of fashion. But I think we will look a little less . . .' she hesitated, trying to find a word that would not hurt his feelings '. . . a little less new if we buy some furniture which is not at the very top of fashion but which will give us a little background.'

'Background, is it?' Josiah asked. 'But not second-hand. I'm not having other people's goods furnishing my house. I'm not a bailiff to sit on other men's chairs.'

'My parents' furniture was kept at Whiteleaze,' Frances offered. 'They had some very fine pieces and it is good to have things in a house which are not all new. They give a house a sense of . . . belonging.'

'Old stuff?' Josiah said, still ready to argue. 'We don't want old stuff.'

'From the Scott family,' Frances added quickly. 'Heirlooms.'

'Oh, heirlooms!' Josiah cheered immediately. 'I thought you meant old rubbishy stuff. Heirlooms is excellent. And with the Scott crest? Does it all have the Scott crest? Or we could put the Scott crest on anything we buy, couldn't we?'

Frances was about to refuse but then she saw the eagerness

213

in his face. 'Oh well,' she said, thinking that no-one who would matter would ever know. 'Why not?'

'But we'll buy some China stuff as well,' Josiah persisted. 'Great vases and that.'

'Yes,' Frances said. 'I shall write to Lady Scott for my father's furniture this afternoon. When we see what we still lack, we can buy it.'

'But we will have a great vase or two,' Josiah insisted. 'Whatever furniture you have. We will have a great Chinese vase or two. And porcelain dragons. I have seen them in red porcelain. We will have a pair of dragons!'

Frances giggled. 'I could not live here without!' she told him. 'I am depending on it.'

Josiah gave her his half-ashamed rueful smile. 'You think I am a fool. But I am assured that China stuff is the thing.'

'It is,' Frances agreed. 'And as long as we do not have too much then the house will look very lovely.'

'You will make it nice?'

For the second time that day Frances was prompted to show him affection. She reached up and put a dry kiss on his cheek. 'I will,' she promised. 'I will make it lovely for us.'

He was surprised at her caress, and they stood in embarrassed silence for a moment.

'I should like to see the upstairs rooms.' Frances moved away and up the stairs, Josiah following.

Only when she had seen all over the house, from the attic bedrooms to the kitchen with the new-designed range for cooking, did Josiah agree that they could leave the Warings' servants to take the last of their things out and close the big front door behind them.

Just as they were leaving, a carriage drew up. It was Mrs Waring.

'Mrs Cole.' She stepped down to shake Frances's hand. 'You must forgive my informality but I so wanted to see you and wish you well in your new house. It has been a happy house for us, I trust it will be good for you too.'

'You're very kind,' Frances replied, taking the rather grimy kid glove in her hand. 'May I present my husband? Mr Cole.'

Mrs Waring turned to smile at him and gave him two fingers to shake. 'And will you be moving in at once?' she asked. 'And will you be entertaining? Shall we see Lord and Lady Scott here soon?'

Frances nodded. 'We shall move in the New Year. My uncle and aunt will be constant visitors, I don't doubt. Perhaps you would like to come to tea when we are settled?'

Mrs Waring smiled. 'I shall be delighted.'

'Thursday is our day at home,' Frances said easily. Josiah, who had not known that he had a day at home until this moment, opened his mouth to say something and then closed it again. It was apparent to him that Frances was as skilled at this, her work, as he was on the dockside.

'And Mr Waring?' Frances enquired smoothly.

'He is very well. He will be delighted to accompany me. And your sister-in-law is well?'

'Miss Cole is in excellent health,' Frances replied. 'But I must not keep you talking here in the street.' Her tone implied the slightest of reproofs.

Mrs Waring bustled at once towards her carriage. 'Oh no! Of course! Thursdays, then!'

'I shall be so pleased to see you,' Frances said sweetly. 'Good day.'

The carriage moved off and Frances raised a hand in a very small wave. 'By George,' Josiah said, impressed. 'You handled her very sweetly, my dear, you handled her like a tickled trout.'

Frances tried to look at him reprovingly but for the second time that day she could not contain a giggle. '*Not* a tickled trout,' she said. 'Please don't say that, Josiah. Not ever. Not a tickled trout.'

He grinned. 'Oh aye. Now come away, Mrs Cole. I have something else to show you before we go home.'

Frances climbed back into the carriage and Josiah ordered the driver to go once again to the Hot Well. They drove up Park Street, and then dropped down to the road which ran alongside the river. The tide was in and the bright sunshine danced on the water. The air was warm and smelled salty. Seagulls wheeled over the river, the sunshine bright on their white plumage as they dived for garbage in the water. Frances let down the window of the carriage and looked out over the river to the Rownham ferry on the far side.

'In summer I should like to cross the river and go for a picnic,' she said.

'You may have work which keeps you this side of the river,' Josiah warned her portentously.

The carriage rolled up before the little colonnade of shops which led to the Hot Well Pump Room.

'The Merchant Venturers who own the Pump Room, this row of shops and indeed half the lodging houses, are looking for a tenant to take the whole lot off their hands,' Josiah said.

Frances gasped. 'Not you?'

Josiah gave her a little conspiratorial smile. 'Now not a word to Sarah, who would rather die. But I think that I might venture it. Not the whole of the property, not by a long way. But I think I might make some money from the Pump Room and the spa, don't you?'

'You have planned this for some time,' Frances observed acutely. 'When we came here on my first visit you were thinking of it then.'

'I heard rumours, but the whole property is owned by the Merchant Venturers,' Josiah said. 'I cannot buy in to the lease without their consent. There is no way to get into the business without their blessing.'

Frances nodded, staring out at the pretty diminutive row of new shops and the towering square Pump Room building.

'If I got it, d'you think we could make it a great success?'
Josiah asked. 'I thought that if you advised me on the fashionable world and things that we needed to do, and if Lord Scott
could be prevailed to come, and Lady Scott . . . if we made
it as grand a place as Bath?'

Frances nibbled the tip of her glove, thinking.

'It would have to be as good as Bath,' Josiah went on.
'People visit here but the season is too short, and we need
to draw in more customers. It is dead in winter, we need
local Bristol society to come too. And I do not know what it
lacks. Would you know?'

'Yes,' Frances said finally. 'I think I know what we would
need and how it could be done. And certainly I know the
people that we would invite to make it fashionable. All of
that I could do. But it would take a lot of money, Josiah, I
don't know how much.'

He nodded. 'With the lease in my pocket I could borrow.
But I have to buy the lease from the Merchant Venturers'
association.' He gritted his teeth and then, in a sudden ges-
ture of frustration, thumped his fist into his open palm.
'Everywhere I go in this town they confront me,' he groaned.
'I cannot get insurance at their rates and on their terms.
I cannot get my ship unloaded without hiring their crane.
Everything I do, I need their blessing. I *have* to be in with
them, Frances. I have to have it.'

'I see it,' Frances concurred. 'I have seen it from the beginning. But will they not invite you? Surely now you are a big
enough trader?'

'With the house in Queens Square, and with you, and with
Lord Scott backing us, and with Sir Charles investing with
us, surely then they will ask me?'

'Mrs Waring.' Frances named the key to their social
success.

'Her, and her friends, and their husbands,' Josiah agreed.
'It is all part of a pattern which we have to make around us.

217

We have to make ourselves one with them. We have to get in.'

Frances nodded and then smiled at him. 'I can do that,' she declared. 'I can do that for you, Mr Cole. Mrs Waring, her friends and their husbands can be managed. I can get us on the inside, as you wish.'

Sarah remained silent and sulky for the rest of the month of December. The festival of Christmas came and went in the little house on the quay with no greater acknowledgement than an extra visit to church, a day off for Cook and Brown – so a cold collation was laid at midday for them to eat at dinner time – and an early night. Frances, eating cold dried-up ham for her Christmas dinner, with cold boiled potatoes and a cold chicken pie, consoled herself with the thought that next month they would be in the house on the square, and she would have the ordering of dinner. She tried not to think of the noisy jolly dinners at Whiteleaze and at the little parsonage when her mother and father had been alive. She went to bed with a shawl wrapped tight around her, and found in the morning that she had been clinging to her pillow for comfort. There were stars and flowers of frost on her window on the morning of Boxing Day, and they did not melt until long after breakfast. At Whiteleaze they would be hunting, the hounds meeting on the lawn before the house and Lord Scott resplendent in his pink coat. Or the family might be in London, and there would be a continual parade of morning callers showing off their winter furs and smart boots.

Frances wore her warmest gown and sat as close as she could to the parlour fire. Inside her boots, her toes stung and burned with scarlet chilblains. In the stuffy room she felt her breath come short and laboured. On the other side of the fire, Sarah sat straight-backed, wreathed in woollen shawls, nursing a cold. She sniffed. Frances estimated that she sniffed three times every minute. They spent the long winter evening sewing, reading sermons, and waiting for the clock to show nine o'clock so that the tea tray could come in, and then they could go to bed.

The move to the new house in January was not as smooth as Josiah had confidently predicted. The house on the quayside was turned upside down with the confusion of packing, and then unpacking things that were needed at once. The plan was to move everything, furniture, goods, wine, food, and all the stored letters and papers of years over the bridge to the square on the other side of the river. But even with the slaves working under the command of John Bates and his lad, it took several days before the furniture and the goods were shifted, and in the two nights of confusion Frances slept in a bedroom bare of anything but her bed, and took her breakfast off kitchen china.

Frances selected only the very best pieces of furniture from the warehouse to send across the river. The Coles' furniture was old and shabby, most of it badly made. Frances left almost all of Josiah's office furniture; his worn desk and the captain's chair were riddled with woodworm. Sarah took a pride in insisting that all the bedroom furniture should be moved, and the parlour table and chairs. 'I chose it myself,' she told Frances, smoothing the cheap walnut wood. 'In the year that we bought the *Lily*.'

'Lovely,' Frances said.

The carters came from Whiteleaze with Frances's stored furniture and a note from Lord Scott wishing Frances every happiness in her new house. Lady Scott sent her card and Frances, who expected little affection from her ladyship, blessed her for that chill courtesy and put the card on the silver tray in the hall so that other visitors leaving their cards would be sure to see it.

In all the business and confusion Frances remembered to

order a livery and shoes for the slaves. 'They cannot go bare-foot up and down the road to Queens Square,' she insisted when Sarah complained of the expense. 'They will get sick if they are too cold, and their feet are already bad with chil-blains. It will do us no good if they are ill, but it will help us a great deal if they are seen smartly dressed and looking the part.'

The slaves were to have two attic rooms at the top of the house, one for the women and girls and young children, and one for the men and boys. They were to have straw pallets and blankets. They were to have jugs and ewers for washing, and proper chamber pots for their use. They were to be treated as servants and to be freed from their manacles and chains.

'But locked in at night,' Miss Cole specified. 'And stout bars on the windows.'

Frances nodded. The move to the new house had conferred on her, at last, the status of the senior woman in the house. She took the decisions for the new place, and only conferred with Sarah out of courtesy. 'We would have to release them sooner or later,' she pointed out. 'We would have to trust them not to run away. Besides, where would they run to?'

'There are many people who would be only too pleased to kidnap them for sale,' Miss Cole said. 'Captains on their way back to the West Indies, visitors to England. Or English families who see the chance of getting a servant for free. Or they might simply escape and live free.'

'Are they free men – those black men who work on the quayside?' Frances asked.

'Most of them,' Sarah replied. 'Their masters may have died and freed them in their wills, or they may have earned enough to buy their freedom. Or they may have escaped. There are many free blacks now; in London there are tens of thousands. And every port has more and more of them.'

'So our slaves could be free one day.' Frances spoke her

thoughts aloud. She was thinking of what Mehuru would do with his freedom if he were one day to be released. She did not know what he wanted, his dark face was inscrutable now when he turned it to her. In the hurry of moving there had been only short lessons most days, and some not at all.

Even without lessons they were learning many words, words of command and words of abuse. Mehuru in particular listened intently to all the conversation around him and Frances, watching him as he took the weight of a load of bedding on his back, could see the comprehension in his face. But however fluent Mehuru might become, Frances could not command his speech. Nothing could make him want to talk to her. His gaze was veiled, he could act incomprehension. It was his final defence. It was a problem Frances had not anticipated: that Mehuru might understand almost everything but refuse to speak. When she asked him a question his face would become deliberately dull and stolid. Sometimes she thought he might know a million words of English, might speak as fluently as Josiah, and still hide behind an assumed ignorance, and act dumb.

She knew he had not forgiven her for the death of Died of Shame. She knew he blamed her for betraying the woman to Sir Charles. But as the days went on and Frances ran from the top of the house to the kitchens several times a day, supervising the unpacking and the placing of furniture in the new rooms, she put it into a corner of her mind and began to forget all about it. As Josiah had said, it was only one slave among many, and they had always known that they would be likely to lose two or three within the first year. If the woman had not died in the cave she might have died of the cold, or of some disease. There was much for Frances to do, it was easy for her to forget her sense of guilt. It was easier for her to forget than to remember.

Mehuru did not forget Died of Shame and the others did not forget either. The bustle around the new house they regarded with anxious suspicion, not knowing what it might mean. The stockings and shoes were intolerably uncomfortable for the first few days; feet hardened by walking barefoot did not fit into the stiff cheap leather. But after a few days they learned to like the comfort of warm feet, and when they walked along the Redclift quay up to the bridge and back again on the greasy cold cobbles around frozen middens, they were glad to be dry-shod.

Without the weight of the collar and the constant clink clink of the chains, Mehuru tried to straighten up and look about him. But he found the muscles of his neck were knotted tight, he was used to the weight of the collar. For days he could not teach himself to walk like a man, he could not rid himself of the slavish shuffle of a dog whose neck has always been chained to a tether. In his shoes and stockings, in his warm breeches and grubby shirt, Mehuru crept from the dockside to the new house, carrying goods and pushing a cart, and knew himself to be walking head bowed, neck bent, like a man without pride, like a man without hope, like the slave he was.

Chapter Seventeen

They completed the move to the house on Queens Square by the end of January and Frances was able to preside over her first day 'at home' on the following Thursday.

Mr and Mrs Waring came, and Mrs Waring brought her sister, Mrs Shore, who was married to one of the senior traders in the Bristol Merchant Venturers. While they were taking a dish of tea Mr Woolwick was announced, calling to present his compliments to his new neighbour.

'You'll forgive me bursting in on you,' he apologised. 'But since we live next door I thought I might intrude when I saw the carriages.'

'Of course,' Frances said. She nodded at Brown to bring another teacup. 'I am delighted that you have called. Do you know Mr and Mrs Waring and Mrs Shore?'

Mr Woolwick nodded at Mr Waring and bowed to the ladies. 'Aye. I'm afraid we are a tight-knit little group. Mrs Shore's husband is my cousin.'

Frances smiled. 'Then it is you who should introduce me,' she said pleasantly. 'For I am likely to be the only stranger here.'

'Newcomers are very welcome,' Mr Waring declared gallantly. 'Especially such a lady as yourself. Do you have no friends in Bristol, Mrs Cole?'

'Only my dear sister-in-law,' Frances said tactfully. Sarah Cole, sitting behind the tea tray, smiled thinly. 'I was born and bred in the country near Bath.'

'At Whiteleaze?' Mr Woolwick enquired.

'Oh, do you know my uncle, Lord Scott?'

'I have heard of him, of course. And we are members of the same club in London, but we are not personally acquainted.'

'I hope he will call soon with Lady Scott,' Frances said. 'And my cousins, the Miss Scotts.'

'Is Mr Cole not at home?' Mrs Waring asked.

Frances smiled at her. 'I do not know about Mr Waring, but I find that my husband is curiously reluctant to take tea. It is as well that he is not a tea importer.'

Mr Waring and Mr Woolwick chuckled ruefully.

'I, for one, take tea under protest,' Mr Waring admitted. 'But on this occasion, and with this hostess, I was easily persuaded!'

'Well, I hope I can tempt you to supper on another day,' Frances said easily, turning her head to look up at him. 'I find I can command my husband with the promise of a good table more easily than I can summon him to tea.'

'Gentlemen often prefer to work during the day,' Mrs Waring agreed. 'Though what they find to do in the coffee house all day long is a mystery to me.'

'Why, they drink coffee and we drink tea, and we all of us use sugar!' Frances exclaimed.

'Mrs Cole, you have learned all there is to know of trade.' Mr Woolwick beamed at her. 'Mr Cole is a fortunate man.'

Frances suppressed any thoughts of what her parents would say at such a compliment to their daughter. Their one concern in life had been to cling to the precarious status of intimacy with Whiteleaze and keep a distance from trade, and now their daughter was seated in a parlour flirting daintily with Bristol merchants and being complimented on her grasp of business.

The door opened and Josiah came in. He was looking very smart, dressed as Frances had requested in buff riding breeches and highly polished boots with a well-cut brown coat with deep dark brown cuffs and collar. He had wanted to wear his best suit but Frances had dissuaded him. He looked better in riding clothes, he looked more established, he looked more at ease. 'But I don't have a horse,' he protested.

'You don't have one yet,' Frances corrected him. 'Anyway, they are not to know that you have not been riding for pleasure.'

'On a working day?' he demanded.

Frances held up one admonitory finger. 'Riding breeches,' she said, and Josiah had obeyed.

'Why, here is Mr Cole now!' Frances exclaimed in well-simulated surprise. She introduced him to the ladies, and he greeted the men. 'And I was complaining that I could not tempt you to tea, Mr Cole!'

'Indeed you cannot,' he said. 'But I have ordered punch for the gentlemen in my parlour if they would like to take a glass?'

Stephen Waring and George Woolwick rose to their feet at once.

'Well, run along,' Frances said indulgently. 'But do not kidnap my guests for long, Mr Cole!' She turned and smiled at the ladies. 'At least we can have a comfortable gossip on our own. You must tell me all the people I must meet in Bristol, and, if I may ask, Mrs Waring, would you tell me who does your hats? I thought you wore such a pretty bonnet the other day, and that cap is enchanting!'

Under Sarah's amazed gaze Frances slipped easily from charming the men to charming the ladies. Josiah abstracted the men from the room as easily as a pickpocket dipping for shillings, and led them off to drink punch and talk business. No-one could have suspected that the whole campaign had been planned and executed by Frances, but when Brown closed the front door on the last of their guests Josiah called for a bottle of champagne, popped the cork in the best parlour and spilled it on the hearthrug.

'Here's to you, Mrs Cole!' he cried, pouring Frances a brimming glass. 'And here's to you, Sarah! And here's to me, because I have just been offered insurance for *Daisy* at the Merchant Venturer rates. I was afraid I would have to send her out uninsured. Now she can sail, and *Lily* is due in any day, and they will insure her too. And I am well on the way to being invited to join the Venturers.'

'Not already?' Frances asked, taking a glass and sipping.

'In the parlour just now!' Josiah confirmed. 'I could hardly believe it myself. They had a glass of punch with me, they asked me about Lord Scott and Sir Charles and I was just as you said I should be – discreet. I said nothing at all and they understood far more than is the truth. They are certain that both his lordship and Sir Charles are my partners, and the next thing I know is, do I need an insurer for my vessels? – yes please, says I – and then would I like to go to a little supper party – just for gentlemen – at the Custom House next week? – yes please, says I!'

Frances crowed with delight and clinked her glass against his. 'What a campaign! And so quick!'

Josiah shook his head. 'I knew we would do it,' he said. 'I knew you could do it. But I never thought it would tumble into our laps on our first night!'

Frances found herself laughing for joy, for the first time in long long years. 'And all I have to do is to buy a dreadful bonnet from Mrs Waring's milliner!'

'I shall reimburse you,' Josiah promised swiftly. 'I will buy it for you myself and you can fling it in the dock.'

'I do not understand,' Sarah said slowly. 'I thought you did not want to attend Frances's tea party.'

'A ruse! A ruse!' Josiah huzzahed. 'Frances thought of it all, tea for the ladies and punch in another room for the gentlemen. And now you see how right she is, Sister. We

226

have made more progress in one afternoon than we made in a lifetime of trading.'

Sarah put down her glass of champagne with unnecessary force. 'I see that we are pretending to be what we are not,' she said sharply. 'I see that we are pretending to partners we do not have. I see that we are trying to live above our station in life and claiming kinship and partnership where they do not exist. I am the daughter of a man who was not ashamed to be a collier, and proud to own one little trow. Now I find I have to pretend that I am on calling terms with Lady Scott of Whiteleaze whom I met once, and did not much care for.'

Frances turned a shocked face to Josiah.

'Sarah . . .' he began.

'We were traders,' she said fiercely. 'Frances is making us over into mountebanks.'

'You are tired with the move and all the changes . . .'

'I am not tired,' Sarah contradicted him. 'I was never tired when I worked all the hours of the day on the company papers and accounts. But when I have to sit in the parlour and tell a string of lies to women who know nothing – yes! then I am weary of the turn our business has taken. I have been clerk, and factor, and ship's husband in this trading house. And now you expect me to simper in the parlour among a gaggle of women!'

Josiah was stunned. 'You still have your place in the company, Sarah.'

'I cannot lie and chatter about bonnets,' she said bitterly. 'I cannot do the pretty as Frances does.'

'I don't ask you to . . .'

'You do! You do!' she exclaimed passionately. 'I have sat here listening to nonsense all afternoon while you have been talking business in your study. It is *my* business too! It is *my* inheritance too! Da never spent a penny without checking with me. I knew every transaction in the books. I knew every guinea we made. And now you leave me with the women while you talk business with the men.'

'It has to be done!' Josiah exclaimed. 'We can't stay as we were. We can't be a little dockside trading house with you at the books and me on the quayside. We'll employ proper clerks, we'll open an office. We have to rise,' Josiah said exasperatedly. 'We have to be ladies and gentlemen.'

'I am not a lady!' Sarah screamed at him. 'I am the daughter of a working man, and I am proud of it.'

There was a stunned silence.

'I am so sorry,' Frances said feebly. She swallowed down her fear at Sarah's anger and choked. Her nervous consumptive little cough sounded very loud in the room. 'I did not mean to offend you, Sarah. I did not mean to embarrass you.'

Sarah shrugged her shoulders rudely, her face still trembling with anger. 'You can't help it. It's the way you were reared. But I can't pretend to it. And I won't pretend to it. I am the daughter of a trader and the sister of a trader. This is the business I was brought up to do. This is the business I understand; an honourable business done by hard-working merchants. Pushing in among our betters, mixing with the gentlemen of the Corporation, claiming kinship with lords and ladies and trading on their name . . . that is not my business and I cannot do it.'

Josiah said nothing. Both women waited for him to speak. 'It has to be done,' he said at last. 'I have to join the Venturers, you know this, Sarah. I cannot get the capital, I cannot get insured, I cannot get the trade unless I am in.'

'They would have invited you on your own merits in the end,' she replied, not looking towards Frances. 'You did not have to marry and claim kinship with lords.'

'Never,' he said bluntly. 'You do not know what it was like, Sarah, in the coffee house and on the quay. They would never have had me without this house, without Frances. We would have stayed there forever.'

'There are worse places,' she said bitterly. 'You don't remember, Josiah, you don't remember where our family came from. There are worse places to be than the storehouse of a prosperous trader.'

'And there are better,' he argued stubbornly. 'We are on the rise, Sarah. Frances knows how to do it. I know how to profit from it. You must be glad of it. You *must* learn to be glad of it.'

Her bony face was white and stubborn. 'I fear it,' she said bleakly.

Josiah made no reply.

'I bid you both goodnight.' Sarah moved to the door. 'I shall dine in my room.'

At the doorway she hesitated, as if she expected Josiah would call her back, but he stood with his back to the fire and let her go.

The door closed behind her with a firm click. Josiah and Frances were silent.

'I am sorry . . .' Frances repeated awkwardly.

'It is not your fault,' Josiah said. 'We have moved too fast for her, we have got on too quick. And she is old-fashioned and stubborn as a grandma.'

'But this *is* the right thing?' Frances confirmed. 'This is the way ahead for you? You do not risk springing up too fast?'

'This is not a bubble which will burst,' Josiah said, his confidence returning. 'This is the direction in which I have aimed for years. Even my father would have been a Merchant Venturer if he could have had the chance. My family is on the rise and this is where the crest of our wave will take us. Drink up your champagne, Frances, we have done good work this afternoon. Whatever Sarah says!'

It was strange dining together. It was the first meal they had eaten alone in six months of married life. It was the first time they had ever been without Sarah's critical observation.

Frances, looking down the long table at Josiah seated at the head, thought that for the first time she felt truly married to him. They had plans and ambitions in common, they had shared the excitement of their first success. They had chosen a house together and it was furnished by them both. The rooms might fluctuate violently, sometimes garish, sometimes elegant, but this reflected the nature of the marriage, and the compromises they had both made for the sake of harmony.

She saw him seated at the head of her father's dining table and for once she did not fear what her father might have thought. If anything, she was irritated by her father's imagined distress. This was not the son-in-law he would have chosen; but Frances thought that her father had been reckless with her life. He had made no provision for her – neither a suitor of his choice, nor an independent fortune. Josiah was the only man who had offered. He might not be situated as her father would have wished, he might not speak correctly, he might wear the wrong clothes and his taste in furniture and decorations might be garish, even by Bristol standards; but he was working, he was trying as hard as he could to make them a proper place in the world. And she could not help but respect him for his dogged determination to rise, and to take her up with him. Her father had failed to provide for her and she had been forced to accept Josiah. Josiah's single-minded vision of wealth and prosperity for them both inspired Frances to gratitude. At last she had someone who would care for her.

She smiled down the table at him and Josiah, always responsive to her approval, smiled back.

And so that night, when Josiah came to her room, Frances turned back the sheets of her bed to invite him in beside her, and for the first time she did not flinch as he moved towards her. Josiah blew out the candle before he reached for her and for once his embarrassment did not eclipse his ability and he was able to do his duty with less pain for Frances and less awkwardness for himself.

It was not love, it was still a very long way from love; but it was better than it had been, and better by far than either of them had ever expected.

Mehuru in the attic room above them was sleepless. The room was lit by a little window set square into the slates of the roof, barred over by stout nailed planks. Lying on his back he could see the stars, like silver pin heads against indigo silk. If he had been a woman he would have wept for loneliness.

His three companions were asleep: Kbara, the youth who had named himself Accursed, and the boy called Sad. The two little pickins were next door with the women and the girls. Mehuru called to Snake to give him sight for the future and tell him what would become of them all.

Nothing came. Mehuru thought that the coldness of the air had entered his body, and the dark mornings and grey afternoons had bleached the colours from his imagination, and would bleach the pigment from his very skin. Every day Snake slid further away from him, until one day he feared he would be an Englishman, as dull and as slow as any of them, and not an African at all.

He thought of his house in Oyo: its coolness in the morning and the way the sun gilded the walls and the paving stones of the street, the scarlet and black Barbary shrikes gathered around the well, waiting for Siko to spill water for them to bathe and drink. He thought of the cool interior of his home, shadowy and restful even when the sun outside was burning hot, and the comfortable warmth of the outside stones when he came home from a journey and leaned back against them. He thought of his wardrobe of clothes, the intricately embroidered court robes of billowing bright silk, the smooth cotton house robes, the softness of the pure wool travelling capes. He went over every stone in the door lintel in his mind, counting each one with a passionate homesickness. He reviewed the skyline of Oyo, the high walls of the palace, the imposing towers, the great proud sweep of the city wall which guarded every citizen and encircled a city that a man could be proud of.

He turned it all over in his mind, loving every stone, every corner. He thought of it as a man will think of the woman he adores, every little detail of her. And he fixed his gaze on the little distant star which he could see through the skylight and wished that this new life was a dream and that he could wake at home and find himself in his own bed, and Siko coming in with a brass cup of mint tea, and everything in the world to look forward to.

Insured, and with her full complement of partners, *Daisy* was at last ready to sail. Josiah went to see her off on the twentieth day of February. Captain Lisle was on board, going downriver with the ship.

'I will bring you back another two dozen slaves for your wife to train,' he promised. 'Are you sure you don't want more?'

Josiah shook his head and laughed. 'This is a little venture, not my whole business,' he said. 'Sell the slaves and bring me good sugar!'

'I will,' Captain Lisle promised. Josiah shook his hand and stepped down the gangplank.

They ran it ashore and cast the ropes off as the rowing boats took the strain. Josiah raised his hand to his departing ship. She had brought him in a profit of a thousand pounds on her last voyage and she was likely to do as well again. He owed more money than his father had earned in all his lifetime; but he was confident. He was investing large sums and he was earning large sums.

'God speed,' Josiah called over the widening grey water.

Daisy dipped as the rowing boats pulled her away from the quayside, as if she were saying farewell. Josiah watched the wedge-shaped stern of his ship move slowly away from him. Above her, a flock of seagulls wheeled, hoping for scraps from the galley. Josiah's last sight of her as she went round the curve of the river was a silhouette of clean rigging, the strong workmanlike shape in the water, and the cloud of seagulls wheeling and calling like mourning angels around her.

In the handsome town house the slaves were working as domestic servants. There was much for them to do. Every day the big rooms needed sweeping, the large windows needed dusting, the panes of glass had to be washed daily to rid them of the grease and grit of the constant Bristol smog. Curtains, carpets, all the linen of the house had to be continually laundered against the filth of the uncontrolled industries.

Every room was heated by an open coal fire, and every morning Kbara and Mehuru heaved full scuttles of coal from the cellar at the back of the house to each room where the women, under the scullery maid's nervous supervision, cleaned the grates, laid the fires, and struggled with a tinder box to light them. Frances liked to have a fire lit in her bedroom before she woke, and the fires were lit in all the downstairs rooms by mid-morning. The slaves swept the floors and scrubbed them with buckets of cold water and thick slabs of soap. They got down on their hands and knees and scattered used tea leaves and brushed the carpets clean. Kbara and Mehuru carried Frances's handsome Turkish rugs into the yard and beat them with cane sticks. Mehuru looked carefully at the quality of the weave. They were vastly inferior to the carpets on the stone floors and walls of his home. He guessed they had been bought from Arab traders and, in his opinion, the white people had been robbed.

Mehuru took to domestic work like a thoroughbred horse

harnessed to a cart. He could manage it with ease, but he felt himself ground down by the dirt and the drudgery of labour. He had to take out the kitchen garbage and burn it in the backyard. He had to pour the slops from the chamber pots into the night-soil cart when it came to the backs of the houses every morning. He did tasks which his own slave Siko would not have done. He felt his hands harden and grow callused and his fingernails, which had once been so carefully manicured, split and broke down to workmanlike stubs rimmed with grime.

His English improved daily. He learned a dozen curses from John Bates, he learned streams of scolding from the cook. He even learned to distinguish one English accent from another: the affected gentility of Brown's parlour voice, and the Somerset burr of the kitchen and at the back door.

Lessons with Frances were resumed. Morning and afternoon the slaves were summoned to the dining room and seated around the large table under the ornate ceiling. All the slaves could now name things, and understand short clear sentences. In one lesson Frances surrendered to Sarah's demand and all of them were given new names, English names. Frances chose them without any care, almost at random, from Bible stories. She started with the children. The two smallest boys she called James and John, the three girls were named Susan, Ruth and Naomi. The two young boys were Matthew and Mark. The three women were Mary, Martha, and Elizabeth. Kbara, she called Julius, then she looked at Mehuru.

'I shall call you Cicero,' she smiled. She reminded him of a little girl naming her dolls.

Mehuru felt a slow burn of anger, an unusual emotion for him in these days of servitude and endurance.

'My name is Mehuru, I come from Africa,' he said, reminding her of the lesson she had taught him. He would not take a strange name. It was as if she was robbing him of the last thing he had been able to bring from his home, his name, his identity.

Frances nodded. 'That's very good,' she said. She was still light-hearted, she did not realise the depth of his opposition. 'Very good indeed. But all of you are to have new names, English names. That will be nice for you. And you and Julius have special, classical names. It is the fashion. Julius will be Julius and you will be Cicero.'

Mehuru shook his head. 'My name is Mehuru,' he repeated. His voice was soft but there was a warning note to it. Frances's smile died. She turned to the others. 'You can go,' she said. She nodded to John Bates. 'Take them to the kitchen and see what work Cook has for them,' she ordered.

'I should perhaps stay with you here, ma'am,' Bates said. 'If he gets cheeky I could whip him.'

Mehuru looked at Bates, his face like stone.

'Just because he can speak proper doesn't mean he can't be whipped,' Bates said, aiming the words at Mehuru. 'There's no law that says he can't be whipped even if he can speak Chinese!'

'I know,' Frances said. 'But I don't need you, Bates. Take the others downstairs.'

The slaves shuffled out, leaving the two of them alone, still seated side by side at the dining table.

'I want you to be called Cicero,' Frances told him quietly.

Mehuru measured her determination. 'Not my name,' he said. 'I have a name. I will not take other.'

'English people do not like African names,' Frances said.

'Then they should not ... take African slaves.'

She gave a little sigh of impatience. 'Slaves have to do as they are ordered.'

Mehuru said nothing.

'I want to call you Cicero,' she continued. 'He was an admirable man, a very fine Roman. It is a compliment to you to name you after him.'

She had spoken too fast for him to follow and he did not understand what she meant by 'admirable', 'Roman' or 'compliment'. But her meaning was clear.

'My name is Mehuru,' he repeated.

Frances reached out and slapped his hand as it rested on the polished table, an impetuous, playful gesture. 'Cicero! I want to call you Cicero!'

He caught her hand the moment she struck at him, snatched at it in the air, and she gasped in shock. The very room seemed to freeze, and she was suddenly still, her lips slightly parted, her eyes alert.

He thought she would scream but she was frozen. He did not move, he did not release her. His face was close to hers, his eyes black with anger. They were as close as lovers, caught in a lovers' quarrel. Her eyes were dilated. When she breathed out he could feel the warm sigh on his cheek. Slowly, slowly, Mehuru exhaled and the tension left his face and his neck and his shoulders. His fingers uncurled and he let go.

Frances sprang to her feet and fled to the closed door, but she did not fling it open and call for John Bates. She stood before it, her face turned from him, her hand wrapped around her wrist where he had held her.

'Please,' he said, as humbly as she could wish. 'You steal all. Leave my name.'

Frances turned slowly and met his eyes. He did not look suppliant, he looked very grave. She went back to the table where he was still seated, and put her hand gently on his shoulder. He looked up at her; but still there was no pleading in his face nor in the tilt of his head. He looked steadily at her, without fear or tenderness.

'You *are* my slave,' Frances said, as if to remind them both. 'I can call you what I wish.'

'Yes.'

'Then I shall call you Cicero. It is a lovely name.'

236

Mehuru rose to his feet and Frances took an involuntary step backwards.

'Very well.'

He waited before her, his hands by his sides, his eyes on her face. The plain dark green livery which Frances had chosen enhanced the darkness of his skin and the blue tattoos around his mouth and eyes.

Frances's colour flowed into her cheeks and drained away again. She put her hand out to him.

'I *shall* call you Cicero,' she repeated. It was as if she were asking some kind of permission from him.

Her finger touched the inside of his palm. He did not respond at all. Frances looked down and saw the contrast of her white hand against the smooth darkness of his skin.

'Cicero,' she whispered.

His hand did not clasp hers, he moved no closer. He stood like a rock before her and though she took a step, a tiny half-step, towards him he did not respond at all. He did not even look at her but stared over her head at the blankness of the wall, as if he were trying to see the open free plains of his home in the silk wall covering.

Frances turned away from him and went to the window. 'You can go, Cicero,' she said abruptly.

He went towards the door without looking back.

'We will have another lesson tomorrow,' Frances continued, trying to make him acknowledge her. 'Cicero? You will come to another lesson tomorrow.'

Mehuru bowed his head, and went silently from the room.

Chapter Eighteen

Josiah took the ferry back to the north bank after he had seen his ship slip away downriver, but he did not go home for breakfast. Instead, he went to the coffee house where the traders met. Although it was early the place was already crowded. Josiah glanced around for a friendly face and started to make his way to his usual table.

'Josiah Cole! Hey! Josiah!'

He turned. At the top table Stephen Waring nodded to him and George Woolwick beckoned him. 'There's a place for you here!' he called.

Josiah, his heart swelling, nodded casually to his friends at his old table and strolled as nonchalantly as he could manage through the busy room to the best table in the coffee shop: the table laid with white linen, the table served first, and served with the very best of things.

'Cousin, this is Josiah Cole,' George Woolwick said to his neighbour. 'Josiah, this is my cousin, John Shore. You met his wife at your wife's tea table the other day.'

'Of course.' Josiah nodded to the man, who moved his chair over to make space for Josiah.

'Mrs Shore told me all about it,' John Shore said. 'She had her eye on that house, I have not heard the last of it I know. She said that your wife had some very fine furniture and would I ask you where she got it.'

'The Chinese pieces?'

John Shore frowned slightly. 'No, she didn't mention Chinese. I thought she said old stuff. But I wasn't properly listening.'

'Oh.' Josiah thought fondly of Frances's resistance to Chinese. 'I think the best pieces come from Whiteleaze. My wife was a Miss Scott of Whiteleaze and she has some pretty things.'

'No chance of buying them then?' John asked gloomily.

Josiah shook his head. 'They're heirlooms,' he said. 'Priceless, I should think. You know what these old families are like, priceless heirlooms with the Scott crest on them.'

'Well, I shall tell Mrs Shore that we can't buy that,' John Shore said with finality. 'But she won't thank me for it!'

Josiah managed a commiserating smile. 'The ladies like to have things just so,' he said. 'Mrs Cole would have the ordering of her house whatever I might say to her.'

'And it's a devil of a house to run,' Stephen Waring interrupted. 'Have you had to take on many new servants?'

'Not a one,' Josiah said smugly. 'I imported some niggers for domestic work a little while ago, and my wife has been training them. They are doing the work to perfection.'

'By jove, that's a good idea,' Stephen Waring exclaimed. 'But I thought your maid was English?'

'Oh, I have kept her on for now,' Josiah said airily. 'But if my wife has her way we will employ none but slaves. They are quick and obedient and if they are well-trained they are better than English girls.'

'What race are they?' George Woolwick asked. 'I always think that men from Dahomey are very unruly.'

'Bonny slaves *will* kill themselves,' Stephen Waring said. 'They get melancholy and just die, just lie down and die.'

'These are hand-picked, mostly Yoruban, two Fulani

women, a Mandinko, and a Wolof,' Josiah said. 'But the skill is in their education. They are not melancholy and they are not suicidal because they have been continually trained in England by my wife. They've never seen a plantation, they've no idea of anything but the way we do things here. These plantation house servants are spoiled by the time they come to England. But my slaves are fresh from the coast, they have been broken as I want them.'

'And you say your wife trains them?' Stephen Waring confirmed.

Josiah hesitated. Frances had coached him in what he had to say until he was able to sound convincing. She had warned him never to mention her period of work as a governess. 'She has had the ordering of very large houses,' he explained easily. 'At Whiteleaze, and at her father's rectory. She is experienced in handling a large number of servants. A dozen slaves are no difficulty at all to her.'

Stephen Waring nodded and the other men looked impressed. Josiah glanced around and signalled to the waiter to bring him a pint of small beer and a plate of bread, ham and beef for his breakfast.

'And will you keep these slaves for your personal use?' George Woolwick asked.

'I shall sell most of them,' Josiah said. 'When we are established in the new house, and when they are completely trained, I shall sell them as English servants. The men will be footmen, or even butlers. The women can serve as upper servants or ladies' maids.'

'Mrs Shore would want one,' John Shore said hastily. 'Please reserve your best manservant for her. I know that she would want one.'

Josiah nodded. 'I will make a note of it,' he said. 'The best one is to be called Cicero, I think. I will reserve him for you.'

'Any children?' Stephen Waring asked.

'Two little boys, two youths of about seven and fifteen, and three girls,' Josiah replied.

'I'll take one of the little boys,' Stephen Waring said. 'My wife wants a little playmate for our children, and when he grows he can be a pageboy.'

'One of them is a very pretty child,' Josiah said.

'No diseases?'

Josiah shook his head. 'They have been in my house for more than a quarter,' he said. 'By the time they are ready for sale they will be as fit as English children. As I say, bringing them from the coast and training them in my house, I can vet them before I sell them on.'

'By God! It's a pretty piece of business,' John Shore said enthusiastically. 'How much are you charging, Cole? I did not think to ask.'

'One hundred and ten each.' Josiah named Frances's astronomic price.

There was a stunned silence. 'Good God,' said Stephen Waring. 'Where did you get that price from, man?'

'From my wife,' Josiah confessed simply. 'She tells me that is what Lady Scott expects to pay for the slave we are training for her. These are the best prices for the very best slaves.' He hesitated, measuring their eagerness. 'Each is, in every respect, an English servant; but one which never asks for wages, or time off, or can move to another employer. Think what you pay in wages to your servants – and how they behave! Then think what value a slave is!' He paused and shrugged lightly. 'But if you wish to cancel your orders, gentlemen, there will be no hard feelings. I can sell them over and over again as you will imagine. The London ladies are wild for them.'

'No, Mrs Shore is bound to want one,' John Shore said with even greater certainty. 'If Lady Scott herself has ordered one, you say?'

'Yes.' The waiter put a mug of ale before Josiah and

brought the joint of beef to the table and started to carve succulent pink-hearted slices and arrange them, fanned out on the plate. Josiah glanced past him to the table where he used to sit. His old friends were gazing at him in his new elevated position. Josiah grinned at them.

'And Mrs Waring must have her pageboy,' Stephen Waring agreed. 'One hundred and ten, I think you said?'

'Guineas.' Josiah took a gulp from his ale and smiled over the top of the mug at Stephen Waring. 'Guineas if you please.'

'You are an astute businessman,' Stephen said pleasantly. 'I wonder if you would be interested in a venture I am proposing. I want to sink a deep shaft at my colliery at Bedminster and I need some extra capital to finance the work. It would be a loan at, say, four per cent over two years.'

Josiah accepted his plate from the waiter and bent over it to hide his elated face. 'Possibly,' he said. 'What sort of capital sum?'

Stephen shrugged. 'Not more than five thousand pounds. I don't know if you have that sort of sum by you?'

Josiah lifted his head and his expression was calm. 'I could have,' he said steadily. 'It would depend on the project, of course.'

'Indeed!' Stephen nodded. 'Perhaps you would like to ride out with me and see the mine. It's good quality coal, if we can get down to reach it. Are you at liberty this afternoon?'

Josiah buttered a slice of bread and loaded it with meat. 'Perfectly, Mr Waring. I should be glad to come out and see it.'

'Very well,' Stephen Waring said. 'And now let us have a look at these figures for the port charges. The town clerk suggests that we raise the harbour dues to amass some capital to build a floating dock. Of course we have needed a floating dock for years but nothing has yet been done. Here are the plans.' He pulled a sheet of paper from a roll beside his chair. 'It will mean that the port charges have to go up again . . .'

'But not for us,' John Shore added rapidly. 'Not for Merchant Venturers.'

'Not for us,' Stephen Waring confirmed. 'The smaller men can carry the cost. There will be no additional charges for us.'

Josiah came home at midday to change into his riding coat and breeches. Frances had ordered a horse to be waiting for him at the livery stables and she saw him off from the front door.

'I shall not invest,' Josiah said. Frances handed him his gloves and held his hat. 'Unless it is very advantageous indeed. I would have to borrow it all and I doubt I could get a rate to make it worthwhile.'

'Don't say one way or another,' Frances advised him. She did not understand about interest rates but she knew that it was wise not to disappoint a new acquaintance. 'Leave it until he has made you a member of the Venturers. Leave it until your supper party and then see which way the wind is blowing.'

'I do not have the capital,' Josiah said. 'I would have to borrow to invest it with him. But I have not said that. I spoke as if I had thousands sitting under my bed.'

'That is the way to do it,' Frances said encouragingly.

'I wish you could have seen me in the coffee house,' Josiah grinned. 'Sitting at the top table and taking my breakfast with them all. And then I saw the plan for the new dock, and discussed port charges with them. And selling the slaves – why, I made more than two hundred guineas this morning before breakfast!'

Frances smiled, catching his enthusiasm. 'We are on our way,' she assured him. 'But do not spend your two hundred guineas before you have it!'

'It is your two hundred,' he said fairly. 'They were bought with your dowry, and they have been trained by you. You are their owner. They are Miss Scott's slaves.'

'Then keep my two hundred guineas safe for me! I am not sure that I want a mine shaft!'

'Anyway, I do not think it would pay. I would not want us to be overstretched. And he was a fast customer over this house. I will not forget that. I heard today that there are two other houses coming up for sale on this square. I would have done a better deal if I had waited.'

'Two more houses for sale?' Frances was instantly on the alert. 'Why?'

'Oh, different reasons. There is nothing wrong with the buildings, my dear, never fear.'

'No, I did not think that there was. But why are the other houses for sale?'

'One family is moving to Clifton, and the other is building off Park Street, I think.'

Frances looked thoughtful. Josiah took his hat from her. 'They are foolish,' he said easily. 'This will always be Bristol's best address. Clifton is too far away and the Park Street houses are a jumble of designs, there is no elegant square like this one.'

'No,' Frances agreed politely. Then she saw a shadow of self-doubt pass over his face. Josiah was not always as confident as he seemed, and he trusted in her judgement more and more. 'I know you are right,' she reassured him. 'And this is a beautiful house! I would not live anywhere else!'

'It *is* the best,' Josiah repeated. 'The biggest and best on the square. There is not another of better proportions. It is a very good investment.'

Frances nodded. 'I know it.'

Josiah opened the door and nodded his farewell. 'I'll be back before dusk,' he said. 'By five.'

'We will dine late then. Enjoy your ride.' Frances waved him off and went indoors to sit in the best parlour.

Sarah was seated at the table with the book for *Daisy*'s accounts laid out before her. Frances hesitated in the doorway, but Sarah looked up. 'Come in,' she said. 'I wanted to speak with you.' Sarah closed the book and waited while Frances pulled out a chair and sat, rather nervously, opposite her.

'I am about to start the afternoon lesson,' Frances began defensively.

'It's not that.'

'Is it still the tea party?'

'No, it's more important than that.'

There was a little silence.

'You are a powerful influence on my brother,' Sarah started. 'Since we moved to this house especially. He admires your taste, he takes your advice.'

Frances nodded, saying nothing.

'You should be aware of our situation,' Sarah said.

'Is it no better?'

'How can it be, when we have trebled and quadrupled our expenses by moving to this house and our earnings have remained the same?'

'Is it very much more expensive here?'

Sarah bit her lip to contain her temper. 'Instead of one fire burning during the day we have four,' she said. 'You have bought curtains and wallhangings for five rooms. You have bought chinaware – those Chinese vases, and the porcelain dragons – and much furniture. I am aware that you brought many of your own things to furnish the house, but even so, the carters had to be paid. Today Josiah has hired a horse, three times this week you have hired a carriage. I imagine that soon you will want to buy a carriage and then we shall have to buy horses and set up stables, and pay a coachman to drive them for you.'

245

'Josiah hired the horse to ride to Mr Waring's coal mines to look at an investment,' Frances observed. 'We are not wasting money, Sister. We are keeping a house in the style that Josiah's station in life demands.'

Sarah folded her lips together, and placed her hands gently in her lap. She was determined not to lose her temper. 'I am aware of my brother's ambition,' she said quietly. 'And I know that you support him. But I must remind you, Frances, that we do not have the money to spend on high living. The housekeeping bills have more than doubled. Your dress-maker's bill arrived today. You have spent more in a month than I spend in a year. The business cannot support this kind of spending.'

'Josiah has taken two orders for the slaves only today,' Frances countered. 'From men who were at my tea party. At one hundred and ten guineas each!'

'Then let them be sold at once. And let us have the two hundred and twenty guineas without delay. I have bills at the chandler's for *Daisy*'s stores, and a bill at the sailmaker for her sails which I cannot meet.'

Frances shook her head. 'They are not ready,' she said reluctantly. 'They can do simple tasks but only Mehuru – Cicero – is fluent.'

'They must be sold as soon as possible,' Sarah said. 'All but two women. Now we have such a large house we will have to keep two of the women to do our work. After Easter, I shall let Brown and the scullery maid go. We cannot afford a staff of so many.'

'Yes.' Frances suddenly thought of Mehuru's hand, the warmth of his palm under her finger, the fascinating tracery of brown lines against the paler skin of his palm, the turn of his head, and that charged moment between them when he had snatched her hand. 'I wish . . .'

'What?'

'I wish we could keep them longer. There is so much

that they will have to learn. It is such a strange world to them.'

'You are not teaching them for their convenience,' Sarah said. 'You are teaching them to increase their value. And *Daisy* will bring you a dozen more on her return.'

'It won't be the same,' Frances murmured half to herself.

'You have not forgotten that they are slaves?' Sarah reminded her sharply. 'They are Trade goods, Sister, the same as sugar or brass kettles.'

'I have not forgotten,' Frances said quickly. 'I am not likely to forget my place with them. I have commanded servants all my life.'

'These are not servants. These are goods.'

'I don't forget it,' Frances said.

Josiah stood with his hands thrust deep into the pockets of his new winter coat and watched his ship, the *Lily*, sail into port on the last day of February.

It was a cold raw day, but nothing could shift the beaming smile from Josiah's round face. The rowing boats brought her carefully to the side, the quayside workers fended her off and caught the ropes to make her fast. The gangplank came down and Josiah strolled on board.

'You made good time,' he said to the captain.

'We did,' the captain replied. 'And a good profit also. Slave prices are high in the West Indies again, for a couple of the best of them I got seventy pounds!'

Josiah's grin broadened even further. 'And the sugar price? And tobacco?'

'Fair,' the man said. 'I think you will be pleased. I have the books to hand.'

'Do you carry much gold?'

The captain nodded to his cabin. 'I have three hundred pounds' worth in my strongbox. It's all accounted for.'

'Unload it now,' Josiah said. 'I'll have it at once.'

'There's the crew to pay, and the bonuses,' the man demurred.

'Pay them tomorrow,' Josiah said. 'I'll see to it. You'll get your share, don't worry.' He whistled for one of the sailors and the captain let him take the strongbox down the gangplank to the old empty warehouse.

'I've never seen him do that before,' the captain said to himself. 'Usually it's the books or the cargo he wants. I've never seen him rush the strongbox ashore before he's even tasted the tobacco.'

He shrugged his shoulders and yelled to the crew to start the unloading. They lashed a wheel to the mast and began to haul the heavy hogsheads of tobacco out of the hold and on to the dock. The hold was foul with the stink of slaves; the men wore their scarves pulled up over their mouths. Not even the powerful scent of new tobacco and the rich heavy smell of molasses could overcome it.

Josiah in his office was counting the money and setting it into heaps of coins balanced on bills. He had not yet settled all the *Daisy*'s bills, though she was more than a week out of port. He owed the carpenter and the plasterer for the Queens Square house. He owed the sweep and he had not yet paid for the new curtains and carpets. The profits of *Lily*'s voyage – which usually paid for her refitting and victualling – would be spread among Josiah's debtors, and he would seek extra partners for her next trip to meet her costs.

'Damnation!' Josiah had rung a coin on his desk and found it to be false. It did not ring true. It was lightweight base metal, gilded to look like gold. He was only a guinea short, the strongbox held more than three hundred pounds and his ship was well loaded with sugar and tobacco; but for a moment, knowing himself to have been cheated, Josiah looked absolutely afraid.

* * *

Friday 20th March 1789

My dear niece,

This letter is to bring you my very Best compliments and
to inform you that the Family will be arriving at Whiteleaze
at the end of May.

You will be pleased to hear that your Sir Charles Fairley
and Miss Honoria presented their Cards to Lady Scott and
– as you asked – were invited to our Ball. Despite some little
roughness of tone they Acquitted themselves Moderately well
and Sir Charles in particular Endeared himself to my Guests
by Losing heavily at Piquet. I have introduced him to my
Club where his inability to Win makes him a Constant
favourite.

On a more Serious note he tells me that he is considering
Cole and Sons as his agent and I have Promised him that I
will make myself Busy in seeking out a Suitable house for
him and Consult with you. He has described to me the size of
Establishment and the Extent of land and I am Certain that I
can Find him such a place – and under terms which are
Advantageous to all of us. I am Delighted to find that you
have Become such a shrewd Woman of Business – since
Your destiny has called you to be such. In Sir Charles you
have a Customer to be Proud of, Generous and Indeed, feck-
less. I think we will all benefit from the Association. He is
Extremely wealthy.

Forgive my speaking plainly but I know you will not

'Take offence. You have done your husband a Good turn
Indeed by winning Sir Charles's fortune to your 'Trading
house. I am happy to do all I can to help Yourselves – and
indeed to help Myself to the Benefits of such an association.
'That Sir Charles benefits also Cannot be in 'Doubt. I will
keep you Informed of all opportunities of Investment which
come my way and of which you should be Informed. My
favourite project at the moment is a building scheme in
London of 'Which I shall reserve a Share for Cole and Sons,
if I think fit. Also, there is a New scheme for 'Wet Docks at
Liverpool which is seeking investors. I will keep you
informed.

Forgive me this Odd mixture of Business and family
Matters, but I am anxious that you and your Husband continue to Prosper. I imagine that it 'Would help your standing
with your New neighbours if Lady Scott were to 'Drive over
for 'Tea? I will take the Liberty of promising her Attendance
on you as soon as she is in the Country.

You will have heard that the Abolitionists, headed by Mr
'Wilberforce, are planning to bring a Bill before Parliament
in this session to Abolish the 'Trading of Slaves. I am assured
that he will 'Fail. There are 'Too many men in the House
whose fortunes depend on the 'Trade. However, for the
'Future, you would be well Advised to move Some of your
Business away from shipping Slaves. A Law to limit the
Numbers of Niggers packed into the Holds is almost
Certain to pass which must make Shipping less profitable. If
you could find Another such as Sir Charles you could move
your 'Business from Shipping to Agenting – 'The movement

of Money, my dear, is So much Easier than that of Goods, or even People!

I Trust you are well Established in your new House and that the furniture all Arrived safely. I think of you Often and your Happiness and Prospects are always Dear to my heart.

  Your loving Uncle

  Scott of Whiteleaze.

Frances put down the letter and looked into the red embers of the fire. Josiah was home late. It was a supper party of the Bristol merchants; they rarely finished before midnight, and Josiah was rarely home sober. The excesses of the Corporation were legendary even in a hard-drinking city. Josiah would return red-faced and smelling of strong roast meat and sweet rum, hoarse from singing bawdy songs and shouting jests.

Sarah might be tight-lipped with disapproval at breakfast, but Frances believed Josiah was carousing his way into the very inner circle of the Bristol Corporation and Merchant Venturer power – the unholy alliance which ruled Bristol completely. Besides, however drunk Josiah had been the night before, he was never late to work. He was always on the quayside at the usual time, before any other trader. He was always last in the coffee house for breakfast, he was always alert and ready for the small sale, for the little investor with a bandbox of money.

Frances looked at her uncle's letter again. If he was right, and if their business could develop, then Josiah's scramble for the capital of small men might be over. The ceaseless worry of insurance and ships, of storms and broken masts might be replaced by the easy transition of capital from one money-making scheme to another. She shook her head.

Nothing would wholly wean the Coles away from trade, nothing would make them feel as secure as their bond house full of tobacco, their storeroom full of barrels of rum, of sugar. The handling of notes of hand was too distant for them. They liked goods they could taste and wealth they could weigh.

The rest of Bristol had moved away from the slave trade – abandoned it to the quicker, more efficient Liverpool ships. But the Coles had clung to it, and clung to it still. Even Josiah's dream of buying the Hot Well was not to replace his main business as a trader, but to supplement it.

Sir Charles's money left with them for safe-keeping when he had gone to London had not been fully used. If Josiah had had his own way he would have stowed it all securely in a locked chest under his bed, bought only those goods Sir Charles required, paid Sir Charles's bills from it, and kept it safe for him. He would have invested only on his own ships, borrowed from it with his own note of hand. It was Frances who insisted that it be used to buy a share in a ship leaving for the Americas for cotton, and Josiah had watched unhappily as another trader left port with Sir Charles's money invested in a rival voyage.

Josiah was as jealous of Sir Charles's capital as of his own. But Frances would be proved right. The good ship *Endeavour* would show a profit of more than fifty per cent and a handsome forty per cent of that could go straight into the coffers of Cole and Sons.

Frances heard Josiah's knock on the front door, and Kbara going wearily down the hall to open it.

'Mrs Cole is there,' Kbara said.

Josiah came down the hall and put his head around the parlour door. 'My dear,' he said, blinking owlishly at the light. 'I am so glad you are still awake. I am obliged,' he nodded. 'Obliged to you.'

Frances stifled a giggle. 'I think, Husband, you have been drinking well.'

'A little punch,' he said seriously. 'And port, and wine, and sherry and a good deal of my own excellent rum, and a little brandy as well.'

'Would you like tea?'

'Certainly not,' he said. 'I fear it would give me a headache tomorrow.'

Frances laughed aloud. 'You are cautious.'

'As a Methodist,' he confirmed. 'Now, madam, cease laughing at a poor man, I have news for you which will make you wish to drink my health many times over too.'

Frances half-rose from her chair. 'The Venturers?' she asked. 'You are invited to be a member?'

Josiah opened his arms wide. 'At last!' he exclaimed.

Frances rushed across the room and hugged him. His warm breath reeked of alcohol. 'I am so glad!'

'I feel as if I have waited a hundred years,' he exclaimed. 'At last! And now I am excused dock charges, and lighthouse charges, and I can take a share of the fees and fines for others using the port. Now I can see the private plans for the new docks and know where to build a warehouse. Now I am privy to the very heartbeat of the town. At last, Frances! At last!'

Frances hugged him close, his rumpled stock under her cheek.

'And it is thanks to you,' he said in her ear. 'Your name, your position, the way you played them, your training of the slaves, Frances, you have made me!'

'I've done nothing . . .'

'You've made me!' he insisted. 'I knew where I wanted to be, but not how to get there. You knew how we could do it, and together we have done it. From now on, my dear, there is nothing that we cannot achieve. I shall buy you a carriage and pair, I shall buy you a riding horse. We can take a house in London for the Season, we can buy a house in the country. I can buy the lease for the Hot Well and you can work your magic there too. You are a ruby, my Frances, your price is above rubies!'

'Josiah!' Frances was smiling, overwhelmed with praise.

'We shall have sons,' he announced grandly. 'And leave them a fortune, a fortune apiece! We shall found a family! I shall buy a baronetcy and we shall have a title! You will not be humbled by marrying beneath you. I shall rise, Frances, and you will be where you belong again!'

'I did not feel humbled . . .'

There was no stopping Josiah. 'I shall build new ships,' he predicted. 'As big as the Liverpool ships and faster. And the first ship I shall call *Frances* and the second ship I shall call *Ruby* and the third ship I shall call *Virtue* and the fourth ship I shall call *Wife*.'

'Josiah,' Frances said fondly.

He dropped to the sofa. 'I shall close my eyes for a moment. And then you shall make me a glass of punch and we will drink your health.'

'I think you had far better go to bed,' Frances suggested hesitantly.

'Lemons,' Josiah ordered sleepily. 'Fresh lemons and lots of my sugar . . .'

Frances moved slowly to the bell, but by the time she put her hand out to ring for Kbara, Josiah was already asleep.

Chapter Nineteen

Even Sarah was pleased with the news when Frances met her at breakfast. But the promises from Lord Scott threw her into spinsterish anxiety again. 'We should not be too hasty to spend,' Sarah fretted anxiously. 'Sir Charles's money is for safe investment, not for risks. We know the risks of the Trade. What do we know of London buildings? And Liverpool docks?'

'That is why Lord Scott must advise us,' Frances said patiently. 'Sir Charles has chosen us as agents and Lord Scott as his advisor. Sir Charles wants us to invest in schemes for him.'

'We know the Trade,' Sarah said stubbornly. 'I can find him good investments in Bristol. I can find him voyages that pay five, even ten, per cent!'

It was pointless to argue that Lord Scott's investments might pay thirty or forty per cent. The prospect of huge profits frightened Sarah almost as much as the prospect of insolvency. Frances nodded. 'I shall write to Sir Charles for his instructions.'

There was a clatter from the sideboard. One of the slaves, Mary, had dropped a cup.

'Tell her to be more careful,' Sarah said.

'She understands perfectly well,' Frances replied. 'You can tell her yourself if you wish.'

'Careful!' Sarah ordered loudly. 'You! Be careful!'

The woman dropped a curtsey, as she had been taught to do. 'Sorry,' she said. 'Sorry.'

Frances looked at her. For a brief moment she did not see her as a careless slave who should be corrected, but as a woman, a little younger than Frances herself, uncomfortable in a plain green dress with a white cap on her head, always too cold, always hovering between exhaustion from the constant drudgery of her work, and the boredom of repeated meaningless tasks.

She was a Fulani, one of the nomadic people of Western Africa. If she had been at home she would have been gathering firewood and roots, beans and berries, watching the cattle, pounding millet in the big stone churn, hauling water from the well. She would have lived in a hut, set in a circle of huts, carelessly made; because next year, or the year after, the family would move to new pastures and build again. But inside the humble round hut would be her bed, draped in deepdyed cotton, gorgeous with colour, and a woven palm-leaf basket carrying her clothes. At the foot of the bed would be a hand-carved cradle and a fine-boned chocolate-coloured baby blissfully asleep. It was a life that any English country-man would have recognised – a herdsman's life. It was a life that followed a seasonal round of moving across a broad plain, as light and as free as a herd of antelope. It was a life that turned in tune with the earth, that followed the rains, that chimed with the seasons. It was as alien to slavery as a silver-winged flight of cattle egrets to a moulting hen in a coop.

'Shall we keep that one, or the other?' Sarah enquired.

Frances was shocked from her reverie. 'We'll sell them both,' she decided. 'We'll keep Elizabeth. She is in the kitchen now. She is Yoruban like Cicero and some of the others. I think it is easier if they can speak amongst themselves.'

'But we'll only keep three,' Sarah said. 'A lad and two women.'

'Yes,' Frances said. 'They will be sold in summer. As soon as they can speak properly and follow orders.' She turned and smiled at the woman. 'Tell the others to go to the dining room,' she said and pointed to the door. 'I will come and teach them.'

The slaves were waiting for her when she entered, seated in silence around the table. Frances was alone in the room with them. John Bates had been dismissed. They no longer needed watching with a whip, they were thought to be safe. They no longer needed teaching domestic tasks, they had learned how to run a house.

Indeed, they were safe. They no longer spoke of walking back to their home, they no longer tested their imprisonment. Mehuru had not even checked the strength of the bars on the skylight window. They had ceased plotting for freedom. They were too overworked and weary to think of anything more than their survival. And also, fatally, they had lost their courage. They did not plot to escape because they feared the sprawling streets more than the drudgery of the house. They were very far from happiness, but they felt safer staying in slavery than running away into the unknown.

Mehuru was tired and drawn. He woke at five every morning and by six he had emptied the great bath tubs, brought coal for the fires and the kitchen range, cleaned the grates and emptied out the ashes, laid the fires afresh and taken out garbage for the cook. He was given no breakfast until the cook was ready and she made a policy of feeding the slaves last, with the leavings of the family food. He was cold when he woke in the morning, and cold while he worked all the day. Not even the heavy labour of house and yard warmed him through. He was losing weight though his muscles were leaner and harder than they had ever been before. The women were overworked too, and even the little children were set to sweep the floors and tidy the rooms. One of the children had a dry nagging cough which kept them all awake.

'Very soon,' Frances said clearly and slowly, 'we will have the feast of Easter. This is the day when we celebrate the death and the rising from death of Our Lord. He is our god.'

She looked around the table. The slaves looked blankly back at her. She directed her speech to Mehuru. 'We worship the Lord Jesus,' she said. 'He was born on earth to save us from our sins.'

'A man?'

'He was a man, he lived many years ago. He died for our sins and after he died he went to heaven. He lives now and cares for us all.'

There was a silence as Mehuru took in the words, and tested them against his own certainties. 'Where is heaven?'

Frances glowed with pleasure at his interest. 'Heaven is not a place on earth,' she explained. 'It is the best of everything. The best of places. If you are good,' she said carefully, 'you go to heaven when you die.'

'Another place?'

She nodded. 'Far away.'

'How is this?' Mehuru asked. He searched for the simple words to express the complexity of his concept. 'The best is home.'

Frances shook her head. 'Your home is not important. Not compared to the love of God. Your home, your family, nothing matters as much as obeying Jesus and going to heaven.'

Mehuru paused, thinking. If Frances thought that the love of your home and the company of your family mattered less than a man who had died long ago then she was more of a fool than he had imagined. If she thought that the best of all places was exile, then no wonder she could take slaves from the heart of their country and expect them to sing and dance on the voyage. 'Do you all think this?' he asked incredulously. 'All white people?'

Frances nodded. 'And I hope you will come to think it too.

258

Then you will be free from the burden of sin and death.'

'I will be free?' Mehuru asked, tasting the word.

Frances saw her mistake. 'You will still be a slave,' she corrected him. 'But you will be free of sin.'

'A free slave?'

'Yes, I mean . . . in a way . . . yes.'

Mehuru looked at her and she saw a sudden springing laughter in his eyes. Despite himself he smiled and then he laughed. 'Oh, Frances!'

Frances found she was smiling in return. In the face of his pagan wrong-headedness it was almost impossible to explain as she should explain. 'I am serious,' she protested. 'This is serious.'

Mehuru's rich chuckle was infectious. The others, not understanding all that was being said, but hearing the triumph of Mehuru's common sense over Frances's garbled theology, smiled too. Mehuru reached forward and put his hand over Frances's hand as it lay on the table.

'First make me free,' he said, still smiling.

Lord Scott sent a box of daffodils from the woods at Whiteleaze as an Easter gift for Frances. She arranged them in a large crystal bowl in the hall and they scented the stairs and the whole of the house with their clean green fragrance. Mehuru brought the water in a large enamel jug.

'These smell sweet,' he said.

Frances hung over the bowl, inhaling the perfume. 'They smell of spring,' she said dreamily. 'When I was a little girl we always had a big bowl of these flowers on the breakfast table on Easter morning. I used to get up early and pick them for my mother. They smell like hope, like being young and hopeful.'

'They are free flowers?'

Frances hesitated. 'You mean wild flowers? Yes. That's the great beauty of them. They grow in floods along river banks and under the trees, and every year there are always more.'

He smiled a little, watching her face. It was the first time he had seen her enjoying a sensual experience. He was oddly touched to see how rapt she was in the scent of the flowers. Her face above them was golden with their reflected colour. She had a smudge of yellow pollen on her cheek. He had a sudden insight into her joy at the free richness of the flowers: that every year there were always more. The flowers were a complete contradiction to the house, to the Company, to the Trade itself which depended on scarcity and hunger. The earth itself was a generous giver of wealth, of this river of gold. It was the Trade which was mistaken, it was the Trade which was unnatural.

'Always more?' he asked and had the reward of seeing her dark dreamy eyes turned towards him.

'Yes,' she replied. 'Isn't that wonderful? When they grow from the ground they are just leaves, and then slowly you see the thicker leaves, fat little buds, and then suddenly the flowers have burst through and the ground is alive and bobbing with gold. And the wild cherry trees have thick white blossoms which bob in the wind and rain down white petals, and the birds start singing and singing, and the cuckoo calls.'

'Mmm,' he said. Many of the words she used were unfamiliar, but he could understand her tone of delight. Suddenly she looked years younger. The greyness had gone from her face, the daffodil glow was all around her. He put his hand to her cheek to brush away the pollen.

At his touch she froze, almost as if she were afraid, her face still turned towards him. His black finger lightly touched the smudge of yellow, and he showed her the dust on his fingertip. Her colour rose, he thought she looked young and desirable, and he wondered if she knew it.

Frances stepped back. 'You may go, Cicero,' she said.

* * *

Easter Day itself was a disappointment. Josiah and Sarah had no plans other than to eat goose instead of mutton at four o'clock and leave the company account books closed for the one day. There was no tradition in the Cole family of foolish sports like rolling coloured boiled eggs down hills, or egg hunts, or even a walk in the country.

'Do you receive no company?' Frances asked.

'No,' Josiah said uncertainly. 'We always spent Easter in the house on the quay. And no-one called on us there.'

'Did you not visit your friends or your family?'

'Our family live in Wales,' Sarah explained. 'And when we moved to Bristol we lost touch with them. They were a colliery family, in the coal mines of South Wales. My father did well to leave the valley; he never wanted to go back.'

'So what shall we do today?' Frances demanded.

Brother and sister looked equally bereft of ideas. They exchanged an uncomfortable look.

'I assumed you would go to church, to take communion,' Sarah volunteered. 'I shall attend chapel.' Both women looked to Josiah. Before his marriage he had always gone with Sarah to the Unitarian chapel. The cold clean walls and the simple creed suited many of the men in the Trade. There was no pretension in the chapel. A good straight sermon and a few bawled hymns. Frances, daughter of a Church of England rector, regarded the chapels with some disdain as the haunt of enthusiasm, evangelism, and labouring people. She had tried unsuccessfully to conceal this from Sarah, while Sarah had made little secret that she saw the richness and beauty of St Mary's church on the Redclift as being halfway to idolatry and papacy.

Josiah, caught between the convictions of the two women, sometimes went to church twice on a Sunday, accompanying Sarah in the morning and Frances in the evening. But he found, as Frances had shrewdly predicted, that the ambitious men in the Venturers attended the cathedral on the green, north of the river.

'Of course I will go to the cathedral,' Frances said. 'But shall we take a holiday for the rest of the day? We could drive out into the country?'

'I would not drive on a Sunday,' Sarah said piously. 'You must do as you please. I shall go to chapel, eat my dinner, then read my Bible, and then eat my supper and go to bed. I see no reason for excessive expenditure on a day which is set aside for thought and prayer.'

Frances closed her lips on a retort.

'The servants take a holiday after they have served us dinner,' Josiah intervened. 'We have a cold supper so that Cook can take the evening off. They have their own Easter dinner.'

'Brown and the scullery maid used to go home to see their mothers,' Sarah said. 'But since they are leaving tomorrow anyway I expect they will eat at our expense tonight.'

Frances nodded. When she had been a girl the Whiteleaze rectory was full of company for the Easter season. Her father and mother would invite friends from London to stay for a week. They would walk in the hills around Bath and pick armfuls of wild daffodils. They would sketch the trees, just thickening and budding into leaf. If the Whiteleaze family were at home they would ride out, far into the countryside, taking advantage of the warmer days and the lighter evenings. Even after her father's death and the gradual slow chilling of her happiness Frances still found her spirits lifting when the sky was light when she woke in the morning, and dinner was served in the yellow glow of sunset.

'I should have planned some treat for us,' Josiah said unhappily. 'Next year I shall do it better. I am sorry, Frances, it is not a season we have paid much attention to, in the past.'

'My father did not believe in it,' Sarah stated. 'He said the Lord's ascension should be celebrated with thoughtfulness and gravity.'

'Well, *my* father was a rector, and I suppose he should know!' Frances snapped. 'Next year I shall plan a party.'

Sarah raised her thin eyebrows and said nothing more.

The day was as thin of joy as she had feared. Josiah attended the cathedral with Frances, and Frances wore her new bonnet from Mrs Waring's milliner. The Easter Day service was longer than usual and the worshippers, leaving the gloom of the building with relief, gathered on the green outside in the sunshine. Frances was pleased to be greeted by all the major figures of Bristol society and saw that Josiah was at ease with the important men.

That little elation did not last long, and when the goose had been cleared from the table, and the puddings and sweetmeats were gone, the afternoon seemed very long and dark and dreary. The sun had gone in and it was starting to rain, a steady misty drizzle which created a premature twilight, as cold and dark as winter. Sarah settled herself before the parlour fire with a book of sermons and seemed well content. Josiah dozed on the sofa. Frances sat on a chair facing them both, feeling as lonely as she had ever felt in her life.

Very faintly, from the very floorboards beneath her feet, came a soft insistent thudding, and then the half-heard snatch of song. Frances glanced across at her husband. He was fast asleep. Behind her book of sermons Sarah's head was nodding. Frances got to her feet and went to the door.

With the parlour door open a crack she could hear better. There was a patter of drumming, like rain, coming from the kitchen. Frances went into the hall and then pushed the green baize door which led down the corridor to the kitchen. As soon as she stepped through the sound hit her like a dark fast-moving wave.

It was a thud-thud-thud of drumming, and above the deep rhythm a patter, an exciting patter, of a contrapuntal rhythm. The two sounds chased each other, like laughter, like play, and Frances felt her feet tapping to the insistent dancy rhythm of the noise. A voice started a song, a deep confident voice – Mehuru – singing in Yoruban, a song about love, a song about the wantonness of young women and the pleasure there is in satisfying them. It was a song about magic – the magic of a woman's hair and the dark sideways glance of her smile. And at every verse-break, at every line-break there was a chorus of assent, in half a dozen tuned voices.

Frances crept slowly down the corridor and peeped around the half-open door, like a little child trying to watch a party.

Mehuru was seated at the kitchen table with an upturned wooden washtub and a couple of wooden spoons before him, a hastily improvised bass drum. He had thrown the spoons aside, their hardness gave no resonance, and he was drumming barehanded, using his strong fingers to call out a deep echoing rhythm, almost a tune, from the hollow bell of the wood. Kbara, beside him, standing barefoot on the stone floor and swaying in time, was pounding on a brass saucepan, sometimes using a metal fork, sometimes the flat of his hand. Mehuru was singing, his head thrown back, his eyes half-shut to hear the music, his wide sensual lips smiling and his whole face happy, in a way which Frances had never seen before.

It was a transformation. He was changed from a powerful brooding unhappy man into a man at ease with himself, singing from the depths of his belly, smiling at the joy of the rhythm and the excitement of the pounding noise.

And the women! Frances craned forward. The women were like a chorus in a Greek play. They were grouped together, swaying and singing, drawn by Mehuru, entranced by him. Every now and then one of them would step forward and dance towards him, for herself alone; and also completely at his bidding, and for him. When one of them stepped forward Kbara's treble drum would pound invitingly, the tone sharper and sharper as the fork rattled on the brass, piercing notes raining around her. Mehuru would speed his drumming, faster and faster, as if he were calling to her to dance and dance and dance for him. And the woman – Mary or Martha or Elizabeth – bunched up her skirt in her hand to show her bare feet and lovely black legs and pounded the floor with feet moving so fast that they were a blur to Frances, peeping around the door. Bent over, haunches moving, the women hammered into the floor, their feet making a new beat, a new quick erotic rhythm of their own, and then they would drop the hem of their skirts and sway back to the others, laughing and disclaiming praise, and Mehuru and Kbara would shout applause, and resume the slower pace of their song.

Frances stared disbelievingly at this explosion of strangeness into her English kitchen. She looked around for the other servants and then saw that the heady potency of the drumming had caught them too. As she watched, Cook, who had waged a campaign of bullying against the slaves since their arrival, was dragged forward by two of the little children and she too held her skirt from her feet and jiggled from one foot to another. And for her too Kbara and Mehuru speeded the music, called encouragement, pounded the rhythm.

Cook flushed rosily with a sudden sense of her own desirability. 'No, no!' she said, pulling her hands from the grasp of the two little boys. 'My dancing days are over!'

Mehuru shook his head and pounded his drum. 'You are a fine woman!' he called. 'A fine woman!'

Cook beamed at him. 'You ask Brown to dance a jig for you!' she said. 'She had an Irish mother!'

Mehuru rose to his feet and hefted the washtub under his arm. He snatched up a wooden spoon and walked towards Brown, smiling, drumming as he advanced. Frances thought that there was not a woman in the world who could have resisted him.

'I can't dance,' Brown protested, but she looked up at Mehuru as if he were a god, and she could not stop her colour rising.

265

He said nothing, he let his music call her. Brown's feet were tapping. 'I can't,' she repeated. 'I can't dance like you do.'

Mehuru stepped back, his long slim feet drumming on the ground in time to the music, his body swaying. Brown rose to her feet, stood before him and followed his movements like a thin white mirror of his potent image. He shuffled and stamped, and she followed him, he drifted to the right and she moved as he did. He turned and strode forward and she was behind him, then he whirled and hammered on the drum and called out to her and Brown hitched her skirts up in both hands and let her feet pound into the rhythm of an Irish jig, as wild a dance as could ever be – the deep irresistible drumming of Africa with the lightning heel-tapping toe-stamping dance of a Celt.

Mehuru laughed aloud at Brown's sudden abandon and pounded the drum in her praise as he turned to the other women. Cook rose up from her seat again, the scullery maid danced behind her, the slaves clapped rhythmically, swayed and sang in a compelling unending melody, in an incomprehensible promising language.

And Frances, watching this sudden explosion of joy and sensuality and passion on the stone floor of her cold empty house, sprang from her hiding place and whirled away from them, from the rich seductive drumming and song. She dashed to the hall, and then up the stairs to her chilly bedroom, with loud unladylike sobs choked back until she could slam her door and fling herself face down on her bed and cry out against her coldness and her loneliness. As she pushed her face into her pillow to weep without restraint for the first time in her life she acknowledged at last her vision of Mehuru as the only man in the world who could save her from the icy death-in-life of ladylike English behaviour, and she knew that for the first time in her life she had fallen, irretrievably and completely, in love.

Chapter Twenty

Next morning, Mehuru tapped on the parlour door. Frances was sitting at the round walnut table, another chair placed opposite her. A bowl of hyacinths stood in the centre of the table, their white waxy flowers scenting the room. Mehuru saw in one quick glance that this was not a lesson, when the table was swept bare; but he could not read Frances's set face. She was very pale and there was a bluish shade under her eyes as if she had lain sleepless. He wondered if she were ill. A second child had taken the nagging cough; they were all finding the slow turn to warm weather arduous and long. Maybe even white people, whose skin was suited to sodden days of mist and long grey afternoons, dreaded the long darkness and the pale disappointing coolness of the midday sun?

'Please sit down,' Frances said. Her voice quavered slightly.

Mehuru drew back the chair and sat before her, his hands clasped lightly on the table before him.

'I realise . . . I realise . . .' Frances started and then broke off. 'I have taught you for months, and I hardly know you at all,' she faltered. 'I have taught you to speak and never asked you anything about yourself, about your life before you came here.'

Mehuru's face was an ebony mask, carefully held from expression. He could not follow Frances's train of thought. He did not know she had heard his drumming. He did not know that for the first time and painfully, Frances was feeling emotions stir and warm into life.

'You want to know about me?'

'Will you tell me about your home, Cicero?'

He flashed a look at her at once. 'Cicero is an English slave,' he said precisely. 'Cicero was born here, in this room. You named him then.'

She bit at her upper lip, sucking it down so that her face was momentarily distorted and ugly. 'Very well. Just for now I will call you Mehuru. Where were you born, Mehuru? And where did you live? And what did you do?'

He hesitated, thinking to refuse this sudden, surprising curiosity. Then he relented. He could not resist the pleasure of talking of his home, even to Frances. 'I was born in the city of Oyo,' he said. 'My mother was a companion to the mother of the king, my father was one of the Eso –' he broke off, searching for the English word. 'I don't know what you call it –'

'What did he do?' Frances was smiling, thinking that the 'Eso' might be a little band of singers, or farmers, or some primitive group.

'He leads fighting men,' Mehuru replied. 'Those on horses.'

'Cavalry?' Frances asked, surprised. 'You had horses?'

'Yes. An army of horses.' Mehuru hesitated, gathering the words. 'A hundred horses to a lord, each lord obeys a higher. At the top a commander, and he reports to the Alafin – the king.'

Frances blinked. It all sounded rather complicated for a tribe of naked cannibals. 'Who else reported to the Alafin?'

'The prime minister and the council of nobles.' Mehuru thought. 'Seven lords who choose the Alafin. And then there is our church – a chief priest who keeps the oracle with chiefs under him. I worked for him.'

'You were a priest?'

Mehuru nodded. There was a distant look in his eyes as if he could barely remember. 'I was a diviner of the oracle, I spoke on grave matters. The oracle spoke against slavery. I took the message.'

'But niggers are slavers. You keep slaves yourself,' Frances protested.

'Not like you,' Mehuru told her gently. 'A criminal may be sentenced to work as a slave, or a free man may sell himself . . .' He had an abrupt vision of Siko who had sold himself into Mehuru's protection, and had been betrayed. He would never find the boy now, he was far away in the Sugar Islands. It was most likely that he was already dead. He had been a slight boy, not strong enough for back-breakingly cruel work in the fields or in the sweltering heat of the boiler houses, or feeding the roaring cane-crushing machines for ten, twelve hours a day. Mehuru looked away, his throat suddenly tight. 'I cannot tell you.'

'But human sacrifice . . . you do human sacrifice with your slaves . . .'

Mehuru stared blankly at her. 'I don't know what you mean,' he said with immense dignity. 'I think you must be thinking of another country. Murder is a crime in any of the Yoruban countries.'

Frances felt snubbed. 'I was told that all of Africa was a pagan country, practising human sacrifice and . . .' She paused. She could not mention bestial sexual practices. She flushed scarlet. 'And . . . impropriety.'

'Africa is a very large country,' Mehuru explained patiently, as a man might speak to a stubborn and stupid child. 'There are many different nations and many different ways of doing things. In Yoruba we live in cities cleaner than this one, we have laws which forbid actions which your laws allow, we trade, we farm, we hunt, our brassware is famous, our gold mines are wealthy, our leather and art goods are sold miles away, even across the Sahel desert. Why, you have some of our leatherwork here.'

'African leather?' Frances queried disbelievingly.

'Mr Cole's leather slippers,' Mehuru replied.

Frances thought of Josiah's beautifully worked leather slippers. 'Those are Moroccan,' she corrected him. 'From an Arab country.'

Mehuru shrugged. 'We sell leatherwork to the Arabs and they sell it on. You have named it for the trader, not the makers. That leather is certainly Yoruban work.'

'It's not possible,' Frances protested. 'For Yoruban leather to get to North Africa would be a most tremendous journey. Thousands of miles across Africa, and across the desert.'

Mehuru nodded. 'We have very great trade routes. And mighty cities along the routes.' A shadow crossed his face. 'We *had*,' he corrected himself, his voice very low. 'When the slavers came the routes became unsafe. I am afraid that all that may be finished.'

He paused. Frances was looking down at her hands, pleating the fabric of her gown between her fingers and then smoothing it out. She was wearing a morning gown of muslin threaded with a blue velvet ribbon with a matching blue velvet jacket. It was one of her prettiest dresses, she rarely wore it. The skirt was creased from her fiddling, and as he watched she spread it out and put a hot hand on it.

'Mehuru,' she said very softly.

'What is the matter?'

She looked up quickly at the kindness in his tone and he saw her lip was trembling, and her face was filled with some suppressed emotion, her hands, her whole body was shaking. 'Mehuru,' she whispered.

'Are you ill, Frances? Shall I call one of the women?'

He got to his feet and she put out a hand to stop him. He checked at the touch on his arm, suddenly understanding her. Drawing in a breath, he froze, looking at her intently.

Mutely, she raised her white face to him, her trembling lips were pitiful. He scanned her expression from her dark eyes to the neck of her gown where he could see the thudding of her pulse in the hollow of her collarbone. And as he looked her breath came faster, the colour rose and rose into her cheeks and her eyes filled inexplicably with tears.

Silently he drew back. 'I shall call one of the women for you,' he said and left the room.

Josiah took his breakfast in an expansive mood at the top table of the coffee shop. He had a message from *Rose* who had passed a Bristol privateer off Africa. Captain Smedley wrote that they had made good speed and were off Goree Island, on the coast of West Africa. He was too discreet to refer to Josiah's illegal order to sell slaves to the Spanish colonies, he merely promised that he would ship as many as he could buy and pack them tight. Already the holds were half-filled. Josiah was to repose every faith in him and to know that he understood exactly what was required.

'You're early, Josiah,' Stephen Waring remarked, taking a seat beside him.

'The early bird . . .' Josiah said.

'Have you thought any more about my colliery?'

Josiah shook his head. 'It's a likely venture, I agree, but I have another project that must have first call of my capital. And you are the man to advise me if you will.'

Stephen nodded, snapping his fingers for a plate of ham and a pint of ale. 'If I can,' he said, smiling his sharp smile. 'You are a Merchant Venturer now. You have only to ask and there are a dozen men who will assist you.'

Josiah glowed slightly. 'I don't forget it. And it is that which makes me bold enough to ask you what the Venturers plan for the Hot Well. I hear that you seek a tenant to take over the lease. Is that right?'

'Indeed,' Stephen said cautiously. 'I don't know for sure. I have heard some rumour to that effect but I don't know. Would you be interested in the lease?'

'I would!' Josiah said. 'On the right terms, of course. But

I think that with a little investment and with the advice of my wife and her family, I could venture to take the lease on.'

'I had no idea that you would ever shift from shipping, Josiah.'

'A man can spread his investments,' Josiah proclaimed boldly. 'It makes sense to spread your investment in these days.'

Stephen nodded. 'I shall enquire,' he promised. 'And then, if you wish to pursue it you could bring it up at the monthly dinner. I would be prepared to support your bid to buy the lease.'

'You would?'

'My dear fellow, why not?' Stephen smiled. 'A new member, and a new colleague? I would be delighted to be of service to you.'

'I would certainly make a bid,' Josiah said, abandoning his usual caution. 'I would need to see the figures of the investment in the Well, and the profits.'

'Very misleading,' Stephen murmured. 'I can tell you in confidence, Josiah. The Venturers have poured money into the premises and left no capital to run it. We have built a magnificent building, established an excellent name, there is now every reason in the world for it to prosper. The Venturers want rid of it, they want nothing more than a return for their money and someone else to take on the day-to-day expenses.'

'And so a man coming in fresh . . .' Josiah said excitedly.

'Would find all the work done for him,' Stephen supplemented. 'All of the rebuilding, the new colonnade of shops, the new pumping station, the filtering of the water, all done, all ready to run at a profit. The one thing against it is the ready funds. If you have those – you have only to pay your wages and you will make money in your second month of trading.'

'Just wages and trading money?' Josiah confirmed.

Stephen smiled. 'I would do it myself but it is so far out of my usual line of business. And I lack a wife with the friends and acquaintances of yours. You are a lucky man, Cole. This opportunity could have been made for you.'

'Will no-one else take it up?'

Stephen shrugged. 'They will snap it up as soon as they see it. But if you had the money to put down on it and my support, I would think it would go to you. There will be the lease to buy, of course, and an annual rent.'

'How much would that be?'

'As I say, I have not seen the figures. I should think you would need about two thousand pounds.'

Josiah looked aghast. 'So much?'

'It's an expensive purchase. And a handsome profit. But I would not advise it, Josiah, unless you have substantial sums to hand.'

'I do have,' Josiah said stubbornly. 'I do have substantial sums. If the terms are right.'

Stephen speared a forkful of ham and ate. 'Your judgement is sound. Shall I get the figures for you to look at?'

'Yes,' Josiah said. 'I would be interested if the terms were right.'

'Of course,' he smiled pleasantly. 'I only wish I had the skill to take it on myself.'

The cook had mellowed towards the slaves since their Easter party. The kitchen seemed very empty after Brown and the scullery maid had left, and Cook had only the slaves for company. In the evenings they all sat together in the kitchen and Mehuru, Kbara and the three women dined at the kitchen table with the children seated at a smaller table by the fire. Since John Bates had left Cook ordered all the work in the kitchen, now that Brown had gone Elizabeth ordered the work which needed to be done in the house, and Mehuru took overall responsibility for the security of the house and backyard.

Slowly, the division between enslaved and free was melting, and the kitchen was a home and a workplace to them all. The warmth of the kitchen range made it more comfortable than the cold attic bedrooms and after supper the boys would clear the plates, the girls would wash them and the children would put them away while Kbara, the three women and Cook drew up their stools to the fire and talked. Mehuru stayed at the kitchen table, reading. Frances had joined the circulating library at the Hot Well and once a week she sent Mehuru to change her books. He brought back the novels she wanted, and for himself he brought back histories and studies in geography and long difficult books on political economy. He was desperate to learn more about the world than Frances could tell him; and he suspected the glib simplicity of Frances's explanations.

The little boy who had been named James coughed constantly, and Elizabeth called him from his work to sit at her feet at the fireside. He had been only two when he was taken from Africa. He could not remember the warmth. He thought now that he had been cold forever, and he had forgotten his mother's face.

'You should tell Mrs Cole about his cough,' Cook said to Martha. 'Tell Mrs – boy sick.'

Elizabeth nodded. 'Both boys,' she said. 'I will tell.'

'Could be nasty,' Cook said. She looked thoughtfully at the child whose eyelids were heavy. 'Course you can't tell if he's pale or not under the black.'

'I can tell.' Mehuru looked up with a half-smile. 'He is pale and he is very hot in the evenings, and he coughs often.'

'Better tell Mrs Cole,' Cook repeated. 'She won't want to lose him. Not when he's learning to talk and waiting on her in the morning so prettily.'

'Yes. He has to be fit for sale,' Mehuru said coldly.

Cook looked down at the boy. He was sitting on the floor staring into the range, leaning back against Elizabeth's knees. The door of the firebox was open and the embers made a dream landscape, as intricate and lovely as the winding path of a river at home.

'Doesn't seem right,' Cook said, suddenly dissatisfied. 'I wager his mother misses him.'

'It will be as if he is dead for her,' Elizabeth said suddenly. Her English was slow and stilted, but they could understand her. 'He was her only child, he told me.'

The little boy was not listening to them, far away in a dream of a place where it was always warm, where he could remember a taste, a haunting taste: the sweet bland softness of mango. His eyelids drooped, his head nodded. Elizabeth bent down and lifted him into her lap. His body lolled in the sweet collapse of childhood.

'Doesn't seem right,' Cook repeated. 'Shall you all be sold?'

'I don't know,' Mehuru replied. 'They will need some of us to work in the house. She has not said which she will keep.'

'I don't want a new set,' Cook grumbled, getting to her feet. She shut the fire door and untied her apron. 'I'm for my bed,' she said.

Elizabeth gathered the little boy closer. He was half-asleep, limp with his fever, his forehead hot and dry. Mary picked up the other little boy and they walked together to the kitchen door, each one with a child on their hip. Mehuru watched them go, walking as easily and as steadily as if they were in their own country, on their own earth, with their own babies held close.

'It's not right,' Cook said. She looked at Mehuru and saw his face set with bitterness. 'Aye,' she said. 'It's not right.'

Frances lay on her back in bed and watched the cold light of the moon walk slowly from one side of the room to the other as the hours slid away. There were no clouds to shield the sharp sickle of the spring moon. The fire in the grate had died into soft white ash. The house was still and silent.

She could not sleep. She lay without moving, listening to the steady thud of her heartbeat. She thought that she would never sleep again. She knew that on the floor above, in the attic, Mehuru was asleep. If she called out, he might wake. If she crept from her bed and went softly up the stairs and opened his door she would see him. For a moment she let herself imagine that she could go to him – imagined her feet on the cold floorboards, on the creaking attic stairs, imagined the door swinging open and him sitting up in bed, his dark eyes opening and saying to her – 'Frances?'

And there she stopped – she could not think what she could say to him. She could not acknowledge to herself what need, what absorbing need could take her, a married woman, in the middle of the night to the bedroom of a servant – lower than a servant, a slave.

Frances stared, as blank as a corpse, at the ceiling. There could be no reason that could take her looking for Mehuru. Not the moonlight, not the coldness of the night, not her growing awareness of his own tragedy – of the urbane cultivated society which he had exchanged for this drudgery in her house – not her own loneliness, not her own inexplicable desire to hear his drumming, to hear his laugh, to see his smile. Frances lay in her own bed, imprisoned by her code of behaviour, by the powerful habit of denying her own desires, still and sleepless and waited for the morning when she might see him again.

Chapter Twenty-one

29 Queens Square.

2nd May 1789

Dear Uncle,

Thank you for your daffodils, we enjoyed them very much. Of all the things I miss most, living here in the Town, it is the trees and the Flowers of Whiteleaze. I hardly notice One season change to Another. Now it is Spring and soon it will be Summer and only One little Plane tree to show me! Josiah and Miss Cole are well and send their compliments.

The Weather here has been very grey and cold and the society here is very Quiet. Neither Josiah nor Miss Cole Dance, and apart from the Assemblies there is little Society. For some reason, I am not as Satisfied as I should be with my Situation. Since Easter I have felt Restless and Unsettled.

I am sure you will wish to remind me of my Duty of Obedience to my husband and Loyalty to his Life and his Business. I do not forget my Duty. Ours was a Marriage of convenience and I do not Regret it. I have promised myself that I will never Regret it. In the Trade a man's word is his

277

bond – and I gave my word to Josiah. Fancies may come
and go but Duty and Loyalty Remain Forever.
I remain your devoted niece,

Frances Cole.

Frances re-read the letter, crumpled it up, and added it to the others in the wastepaper bin beside her little writing desk, one of Josiah's Chinese purchases, elaborately carved with dragons breathing fire and little drawers hidden by sampans, bridges, and sinuous rivers. Frances leaned forward and put her head on her hands.

'You warned me,' she whispered. 'But I did not listen. Anyway . . .' Her voice trailed away as she thought of what her life would have been if she had refused Josiah's proposal.

She sat down and drew a piece of the hot-pressed note-paper towards her again, dipped her pen in the ink and wrote in plain spiky letters, quite unlike her usual elegant hand.

Dear Uncle,
*   I have made the Dreadful mistake of falling in love with a*
man who is, in all probability, quite indifferent to Me. He is
worse than a Servant, he is a Slave. He is in my Employ and
I am bound to sell him for a profit to Another owner.
'Everything I have ever been taught about the Behaviour and
natural Feelings of a lady tell me that this Cannot Happen. It
cannot happen. It Cannot happen to me.

She crumpled the letter and took it, with the others, to the fireplace which was laid with kindling and small pieces of coal. Frances scattered the letters on the top and then fetched the sealing-wax candle from her desk. She put the flame to the half-dozen pieces of paper and watched the pages darken, crinkle, and then burst into flame. She stayed on her knees on the hearthrug, watching them crumple into fragile ribbons of ash, watching the words drift up the chimney in harmless smoke to gather with the smog which hung always in the skies above Bristol.

'I can never tell anyone,' she said softly. 'I shall never again acknowledge it even to myself. This is where it ends. It is over. It must be over.'

She got up from the hearthrug wearily, as if she were very very tired. She turned back to her desk, blew out the candle, and closed up the drawers. She turned the little key in the lock as if she were shutting away forever her youth, her new desire, and her hopes.

'Over,' she said with finality. And then she sat down in the chair, before the dirty cold grate, and took up some handkerchiefs to hem, and worked as if she could see her stitches through her blurred eyes.

Josiah found her there when he came in for his breakfast. Something in her frigid composure aroused his notice. 'Are you well, Mrs Cole?' he asked.

Frances smiled. 'I am perfectly well, thank you. Were you looking for me?'

'I have booked a little treat for you, my dear,' Josiah said. 'I remembered you telling me that you used to ride at Whiteleaze, and the stables have a lady's horse to hire. I have booked it for you this afternoon. One of the servants can go with you. One of the men can ride, can he not?'

'I think Cicero can ride.' Frances's voice was level. 'But I will ask Julius.'

'And you would enjoy it?' Josiah asked. 'You are looking a little pale today.'

Frances nodded. 'I thank you for a kind thought,' she said

calmly. 'I should enjoy riding again very much. I will ask Julius if he can ride now.'

She went out into the hall. Kbara was coming downstairs with a heavy tray in his hands.

'Julius, can you ride a horse?' Frances asked.

He frowned. 'A horse?' he repeated. 'No, Mrs Cole. I never do.'

'Oh.' Frances turned. Mehuru was behind her. He had a scuttle full of coal in one hand and his livery was shielded from the dirt with a coarse hessian apron.

'Can you ride, Cicero?'

'Yes,' he said shortly.

'You should say, "Yes, Mrs Cole",' Frances corrected him.

Mehuru nodded at the information but did not repeat the sentence.

'I am going riding this afternoon,' she said. 'You will accompany me. You must go to the stables and pick out a riding horse for yourself, and borrow some riding clothes. You will need boots also.'

He did not look grateful. He stood leaning against the weight of the heavy bucket of coal, waiting for her to dismiss him.

'We will ride out on the Downs,' she said. 'In the sunshine. It will be like a holiday.'

Still he said nothing.

'Do you not want to ride with me?' she asked, suddenly impatient of his silence. 'I should have thought you would welcome a change from your work, from the continual drudgery here?'

Mehuru inclined his head only slightly. 'Yes, Mrs Cole,' he said.

The stable sent two fine hunters around to Queens Square. Frances, coming out of the front door in her old grey riding habit, saw Mehuru standing at the animals' heads, talking to the groom. She had to shield her eyes from the bright sunlight; the profile of his tall slim body was like a black cameo. It was just after noon and the square was bright and warm. The branches of the little trees were nodding with the bursting weight of new shoots. The grass of the gardens was springing green and ripe and was starred with white daisies in pink-tipped buds. One of the houses had a cherry tree in a tub at the doorway and the blossom was like a pink gauze scarf flung across the golden sandstone. The birds on the rooftops and in the saplings were singing and singing at the sunshine, a long ripple of sound. Frances bit her lip against the sudden welling of joy.

The stable had loaned Mehuru a pair of breeches and boots. He looked very tall and English in the handsome high boots and fawn breeches, the white shirt and stock and the dark brown hacking jacket. Against the high white stock at his throat his face was very black. When he saw Frances at the door he turned and smiled, and held her horse as the stable lad cupped his hands to help her mount and threw her up into the side-saddle.

Mehuru mounted and moved with the horse as it side-stepped and curvetted. 'He is . . . dancing,' he said. 'I do not know the word.'

'Dancing is a good word,' Frances agreed, watching Mehuru seated easily on the animal. 'We would say – he is fresh – meaning that he is eager.'

'I thought fresh was food?' Mehuru brought the horse under control and rode alongside her as she moved off, out of the square towards Park Street.

Frances found she could not think straight with him so close at her side. 'Sometimes,' she said unhelpfully. She gathered her thoughts and explained, 'Fresh food is new, prime food. A fresh horse is new out of the stable and in prime condition.'

'I see,' he said. 'It is an interesting language.'

Frances, who knew only conversational French and a lady-like smattering of Italian, had thought English the only language in all the world – not an option. 'How is it different from your language?'

A wagon went past them and Mehuru's horse threw up its head and sidled. He held it firmly and stroked its neck, murmuring softly until the wagon had passed. 'You have some words we do not know. And we have shades of meaning you do not have.'

'Like what?' Her voice was cool. She had herself under control.

'Oh, you have a word "beauty" – we do not have that.'

'You don't believe in beauty?'

'We believe in it, anyone can see it. But we don't have a word for it as you do. We have words which mean that something is good, or the rightness of things, the right thing for the right place, the right colours. We have a word that you do not have – it means – that it lacks nothing. But we don't call a thing beautiful, we call it complete.'

Frances shot a small flirtatious smile at him. 'So if you loved a lady would you not tell her she was beautiful?'

He looked away from her, refusing to see the line of her cheek or the downward sweep of her eyelashes. 'No,' he said shortly.

They were riding side by side up Park Street. On either side of the street wooden scaffolding had sprung up, pale yellow stone houses were growing from foundations which marched like ascending steps up the hill. Gaps in terraces where a site had not been bought or where a builder had stopped work, short of cash, gaped like missing teeth. The city was being built piecemeal, all planning and order thrown aside in the rush for profit.

'So what would you say?' Frances persisted. 'If you wanted to tell a lady that you loved her, that you thought she was beautiful?'

'A man would tell her that he wanted her as his wife,' Mehuru said simply. 'He would not tell her that she looked as well as another woman. What would that mean? He would not tell her that she was enjoyable – like a statue or a picture. He would tell her that he longed to lie with her. He would tell her that he would have no peace until she was in his arms, until she was beneath him, beside him, on top of him, until her mouth was his lake for drinking, and her body was his garden. Desire is not about "beauty", as if a woman is a work of art. Desire is about having a woman, because she can be as plain as an earthenware pot and still make you sick with longing for her.'

Frances choked on a cry of outrage. She kicked her horse forward and rode ahead of him in shocked silence, looking straight ahead, her cheeks burning, her colour high.

Mehuru came up alongside. 'What now?' he demanded, exasperated. 'What's the matter now?'

'You should not speak to me like that,' Frances said, muffled. She would not turn her head to look at him.

'You asked!' Mehuru exclaimed. 'You asked me how I feel desire. And so I told you.'

'You should not speak like that,' Frances repeated in a small voice, her face still turned away.

'And how should I feel?' he demanded. 'You order everything. How should I feel, Mrs Cole?' He reined his horse back and rode a little behind her, like a servant.

They rode up the length of Park Street in single file in silence. Frances held her head high, she could feel her heart pounding with anger and desire: a breathless mixture of passions. Mehuru raged on his horse, watching her slim straight back leading the way. At the top of the hill the road petered out into a cart track and on either side there were builders' sheds and store yards of stone and piping and wood. There were stone cutters working under temporary wooden shelters, shaping stones to size and carving ornamental friezes and decorative heads and pillars. For long sprawling acres at the top of the hill it was nothing but a series of builders' yards for a city gripped with building fever. The sense of the city growing and re-making itself was almost tangible.

Frances and Mehuru rode on, Frances holding a handkerchief to her mouth to keep out the pervasive dust from the stone cutters, until they left the yards behind and the track became lined with little market gardens, and then fields with dairy cattle. Mehuru gazed around him as he rode, looking at the thick glossy coats of the cows, the incredible lush greenness of the grass. Even the hedges in this warm springing month of May seemed to glow with the sweetness of the constant rainfall. Bushes trembled with catkins as yellow as the primroses at the foot of the hedge. Whitebeam, hornbeam, and hawthorn flowered in a white mist. The beech trees were hazy with the greenness of their buds and the silver birch coppice at the edge of one field was a brilliant luminous budding green.

In Mehuru's home it was only in the brief spell of the wet season that trees glowed and dripped and oozed sweetness like this. He knew from Cook that this country was always wet. It always rained. No wonder they had fields as rich as forests and cows with pelts as glossy as lions. He glanced at Frances. In a country so ripe and rich and easy, how could a woman be taught to be sour and dry, so punitively cold to herself?

Frances felt his eyes on her. 'I am sorry. I should not have asked,' she said.

He waved it away. 'It does not matter. Do the cows always stay in these little fields? Do they not walk out to feed?'

Frances threw him a sideways look, amused and half-mocking herself. 'You are more interested in the cows than in my apology?'

He moved his horse close so that his knee was brushing

her horse's flank. She could have reached out and touched him. He answered her with a smile which was singularly sweet. 'Frances,' he said gently. 'How can we speak truly one to another, when I am your slave and you can order me as you wish? Anything you say can mean everything or mean nothing. If I offend you, you can beat me or sell me. If I please you, you can give me a sweetmeat or a word of praise. I am your dog, I am your horse. You do not say "I am sorry" to a dog or a horse. You behave as you wish and they suffer as you please. Nothing else between us is true.'

'I do not wish it to be so,' Frances answered, her voice very low. 'You are not a dog, you are a gentleman, a nobleman in your own country, high in the government. I do not wish you to be my slave. I should like you . . .' She broke off. 'I should like you to be my friend.'

There was silence for a moment. The horses pulled gently on their bits and pricked their ears forwards as the country opened out before them, a little hill and the track curving upwards, an avenue of trees and from somewhere the faint salt smell of the sea.

'Then set me free,' Mehuru said simply. 'Only a free man can give his friendship. If you wish us to be friends I have to be free. Anything else is slavish devotion – it means nothing. You have to set me free, Frances.'

She let her horse trot and then ease into a gentle canter. Mehuru's horse followed, speeding up. Mehuru sat easily in the saddle and watched Frances lean forward and let her horse go faster. They breasted the hill side by side and burst out at the top of the Downs. Frances's horse lengthened its pace from a canter into a gallop across the close-cropped green turf. The sun was bright and the wind was light and keen, smelling of salt and the early buds of wild thyme. Mehuru let out a wild hunter's yell and his horse caught his sense of excitement and sudden feeling of freedom. Its ears came forward and it chased after Frances's hunter. Neck and neck they thundered on until Frances pulled her horse up and shouted, 'Woah! Woah!' and called out: 'Be careful! Be careful! The cliff edge!'

Mehuru pulled his horse over beside hers. There was a rough wooden fence marking the edge of the cliff and then a precipitous drop of white limestone rocks hundreds of feet down to the sluggish curves of the dirty river below, winding between banks of slime. On the far side equally high cliffs were tumbled with woodland and white dramatic outcrops, right down to the river edge. It was a staggering sight, a mighty gorge leading onward, westward, out to the distant sea.

'Is this the way we came in?' Mehuru asked. 'Our boat, up the river?'

Frances nodded. 'They have barges to tow the boats. It's very difficult to sail up the gorge. The winds are uncertain and the channel is very narrow.'

He nodded, looking down the deep chasm to the river below. 'I am glad it was night and I was below and did not see it,' he said. 'I would have thought it the entrance to a prison for life – these high walls.'

'I cannot set you free,' she suddenly said.

'Who is my owner?'

'I am. But I cannot set you free.'

He was gazing westward. The river curved out of sight, he could not see where it flowed into the sea. He wanted very much to see the waves and the clean water of the sea and know that on the other side of that ocean, miles and miles away, the waves of the same water were breaking on the white beaches of his home.

'What would you do, if you were free?' Frances asked.

'I should go home,' he replied instantly. 'I am needed there.' He thought how much he could tell them about the white men, how much he knew. He thought how much they needed his skills and now his grasp of the English language to keep them safe through these most perilous times. 'And I need to be there,' he added, his voice very low.

Frances, watching the longing on his face, said nothing. He glanced across at her. 'I can never be happy until I am home,' he said simply.

'I cannot let you go,' she repeated, and for a moment he thought she sounded more like a possessive woman deeply in love than the owner of a slave. 'I cannot possibly let you go.'

Josiah had the figures of the Hot Well before him in his office, the back parlour at Queens Square. Stephen Waring had obtained them for him and told him, with a wink, to read them and return them quickly before the May monthly meeting. Josiah understood that they had been borrowed for his benefit, that he was already gaining from Stephen's friendship and from his membership of the Merchant Venturers.

The figures went back to the earliest days a century before when the spring was first discovered. It was underwater for all the day except for a brief hour at low tide when it could be seen bubbling out, hot and sparkling, showing a clean ripple of water in the brown of the river. A businessman had opened a bath-house and later bottled the water. Josiah nodded; as soon as the site started to show a profit the Merchant Venturers took an interest. They bought it, and started to lease it out to speculative tenants.

The last tenant, Mr James, had seen the boom of interest in spas and mineral waters and determined on capturing the gentry trade from Bath. He had done well. The spa was now running in parallel with Bath. Convalescents were notoriously restless and many would decamp from Bath to the Hot Well. Desperately ill people would pay anything for a cure and the Hot Well's reputation for curing diabetes, skin complaints, stomach troubles, and even pains in the heart and lungs, gave them hope. The Methodist preacher John Wesley himself had been cured by the treatment. Endorsed by him and by other more worldly invalids, the business was thriving and the Merchant Venturers decided to expand it yet further.

The figures showed the spending – a two-thousand-pound investment in the Pump Room, making it the largest assembly room in the country. A thousand pounds on the pretty colonnade of nearby shops. A double avenue of trees leading to the rooms, and a complicated system of pumps and filters to get the water away from the contaminating river which was daily more of a threat to the health of the spring as the river water grew dirtier and dirtier with the outfall from Bristol sewage and industries. The Venturers had done everything to establish a thriving business, but they did not want the trouble of running the spa themselves. They wanted to hand it over and to see a return on their investment.

Josiah chuckled and rang the bell. Kbara came, light-footed and smart in his livery. 'Yes, sir?' he asked.

'Rum and water,' Josiah ordered.

He pulled a sheet of paper towards him and scribbled down some figures. He thought he could borrow two thousand pounds for the lease against the cargo of *Daisy*, who should be loading at the efficient Africa Company ports and due back in December. If Josiah's captain bought well and crammed on sail Josiah would make a small fortune on her.

He would need it. The vagaries of the Trade meant that sometimes all three of his ships were away from Bristol at the same time. There was a fallow period in which Josiah could do nothing but wait. From April to July all his ships were loading off Africa while the debts mounted steadily at home. He could not clear a penny until they came back into port again. The Hot Well's profits would smooth over the dramatic fluctuations of the Trade in which a man could be bankrupt one day and then see his ship sail, heavy-laden, into port the next.

Josiah had a loan outstanding of a thousand pounds for

the Queens Square house and five hundred for furnishing. He had borrowed a thousand pounds against the *Rose* herself and he owed for half the cargo instead of splitting the risk with equal partners. By deciding to take women and children, pack them tight and sell them to the Spanish, Josiah had made the voyage at once more risky and more profitable. Selling to the Spanish plantations was smuggling, breaking the laws which limited trade with the competing plantations of Spain. But since it was contraband cargo it was paid for in gold. Josiah would not have to offer credit to the planters which could not be redeemed until a year or two later. *Rose* would come home in November and bring him sellable sugar and gold. She would reward one of the greatest risks he had taken in his commercial life – sailing without a full complement of partners, and without full insurance – with the greatest profit he had ever seen. She would be followed into port by *Daisy* in December, and two months later by *Lily*, and Josiah would be acclaimed as a wealthy man.

He needed that public success. Even with Merchant Venturer friends Josiah found his ships were not attracting investors. The returns on the slave trade were too risky compared with the guaranteed profits of land. The three markets where a profit or a loss might be made, in Africa, in the West Indies, and in England, no longer fired men's imaginations. The men who used to gamble on the slave trade to give them a triple profit now preferred to buy and sell sugar direct – trading to and from the West Indies. Prices were easier to calculate, and profits came quicker. By cutting out two legs of the three-way journey they diminished the risk by two thirds, they speeded the return of the ship – and thus the profits. Only the traditionalists, who had always dealt in the Atlantic trade, and the little savers who were welcome nowhere else, were still investing in slavery and Josiah's ships.

But Josiah was confident. His membership of the Merchant Venturers was already showing him benefits. Through the

Company he would obtain full insurance on all future voyages, even including the loss of slaves except by death through illness. He could reassure future investors that their money was safe, completely insured.

Best of all, as a member of the Merchant Venturers he was a member of the Royal Africa Company. For the first time ever Cole and Sons ships would not have to trade up and down the fever-sodden coast, searching for individual slaves, bartering with coastal chiefs, haggling for one man here, for another there, exposed to illness, threats from the shore, and mutiny on board. From now onwards a Cole and Sons ship would moor at a Company fort, where she would take on supplies of food and clean water. Slaves would be waiting for purchase in the huge dungeons. The captain could take his pick of the prisoners, and if he wanted more, he could send a message to the Company warehouses further upriver to send down as many as he wished. The turn-around of the ship could be as swift as if she were in the dock at Bristol. The gathering of the slaves was as efficient as an industry. At last Josiah would leave the uncertain, chancy old days behind. As long as the seas were kind, he could guarantee a profit on each and every voyage. When the investors saw the account books of his ships under these new circumstances Josiah was certain they would put their money with him again.

Against all these fair omens were only Josiah's debts on the house and on *Rose* – three thousand pounds altogether – and his soaring living costs. Neither of them troubled him yet. The value of the house justified his debt, the loan on *Rose* was investment capital, and living costs were bound to increase. He thought that a man aspiring to the status of a gentleman had to be generous about his housekeeping bills.

He drew a sheet of paper towards him and wrote to Stephen Waring.

'Dear Waring,

I return these papers to you at Speed, as you requested, and with my Thanks. I shall certainly bid for the Hot Well lease Provided that I can have an Undertaking that the Rent for the lease will be Agreed for a Minimum of Ten years and not be increased During that time. I thank you for your support in this Matter. I shall see you at the Dinner when I will Make this offer to the Honourable company.

Yours etc.

Cole.

Josiah dripped sealing wax on to the fold of the letter and pressed his ring into the hot liquid, rang the bell and told Mehuru to send one of the boys round to Mr Waring's accounting house with the letter and the parcel of papers.

Mehuru hesitated.

'What is it?'

'I shall go myself.'

'Very well, very well,' Josiah said impatiently. 'As long as one of you goes and comes straight home.'

Still the man hesitated. 'If I see a seller of flowers shall I buy some for Mrs Cole?'

Josiah turned in his chair. 'What?'

'The flowers in the hall are dead. Mrs Cole loves flowers. There are flower sellers outside the house every day. Shall I buy some flowers for her?'

'Oh!' Josiah was genuinely surprised. He heard the cries of flower sellers as he heard the cries of knife grinders or muffin men. He had never thought that they might be selling a commodity he would want. 'She likes flowers, does she?'

Mehuru thought of Frances's dreamy sensual delight over the daffodils and kept his eyes down so that her husband would not see his amusement. 'Yes, she does.'

'I'll give you a penny, get her a bunch.'

Mehuru took the coin. 'She would prefer many,' he said carefully. 'For the big bowl in the hall.'

Josiah tutted, thrust his hand in his pocket and threw a handful of coins at Mehuru. 'Here! Take half a crown, take a crown and bring me the change! Make sure you bring me the change, mind!'

Mehuru bowed swiftly, took the letter and vanished from the room before Josiah's innate caution with money could defeat his grand gesture.

He put on his hat and coat and slipped out of the back door, walked briskly to Mr Waring's warehouse on the northern, Bristol side of the dock, delivered the letter and then found a flower seller shouting her wares on the quayside near the bridge over to Redclift.

She had a tray hung from her neck filled with flowers. She had fat bunches of wood violets, picked in Rownham woods that morning, with their leaves still damp and their scent potent. And she had late-flowering daffodils by the hundred with their fat buds bursting into pale yellow petals and the trumpets opening in the morning sunshine.

'How much?' Mehuru asked.

'Ha'penny a bunch.'

Her Bristol accent was so strong that he could hardly understand her. 'Where do you come from?' he asked curiously.

She made an impertinent face at him. 'Closer to home than you,' she said.

He smiled at her. 'I don't want a bunch. How much for all?'

Startled, she stared at Mehuru. 'All of them?'

'Yes, quickly, I have to be home.'

'I've never sold all of them at once.'

'I want the tray too, to carry them.'

She stared at him open-mouthed. Mehuru had to laugh.

She was as slow and as stupid as any peasant in a village in his own country. 'No-one has ever bought them all before,' she said.

'I see,' Mehuru said patiently. 'But *I* want to buy them all. How much would they all be?'

'Are you from London?' she asked, as if only that could explain his eccentricity.

'It doesn't matter,' Mehuru said. 'Look. When you get home in the evening and you have had a good day and sold nearly all, how much do you have?'

'Half a crown,' she answered promptly. 'But I never have.'

'Well, I give you three shillings for all the flowers, and you can come with me to my home, carrying the tray, and then I will take the flowers into the house,' Mehuru said patiently. 'Then you get some more flowers to sell, or you take the rest of the day off.'

She blinked at the concept. 'If you gave me four shillings I could buy a good dinner,' she said hopefully.

'Why not?' Mehuru declared, generous with Josiah's hard-won cash. 'But now!'

'All right,' she suddenly decided.

Mehuru set off at a brisk pace, the flower seller trotting behind him.

'Is it for a lady?' she asked slyly. 'A lady that loves flowers?'

'Yes,' Mehuru said, without turning his head.

'And do you love her?' She bumped into him as he stopped at the backyard gate.

Mehuru hesitated on his denial. He thought of Frances and the contradictory feelings which were growing between them. He knew it would be easier for him if he did not love her and safer for him if the word was never mentioned between them. 'I don't love her,' he denied stoutly. 'I am just getting flowers.'

He tipped Josiah's coins into the flower seller's hands and

gathered up the armfuls of daffodils. The bunches of violets he packed carefully into the deep pockets of his coat.

'You'll smell like spring,' the flower seller said, looking at him and noticing for the first time his broad shoulders, his lean well-muscled body, and the deep soft blackness of his skin. 'Does she love you?'

Mehuru shook his head at her and smiled. 'Goodbye,' he said firmly. 'Enjoy your dinner.'

The kitchen was empty except for Cook, who was stirring a pan on the stove and did not turn round and see him, his arms full of buds, his pockets bulging with posies.

He slipped into the hall and then up the stairs to Frances's bedroom. Her bed was made, the room was tidy. He was struck by the cold elegance of it all. The hairbrush and comb were precisely positioned on the dressing table, the small pictures hung carefully on the pale silk walls, the pale blue carpet, the little blue silk chair placed at a right angle to the empty grate. He had meant to put the flowers in vases around her room, but something in the spinsterish tidiness of the bedroom made him feel anarchic and playful. He thought of the trickster god dressed in dark indigo blue studded with white cowrie shells who throws the destinies of men and women into gambling disorder. He laughed at the thought, and at the madness of flooding Frances with flowers.

He ripped back the covers of the newly made bed, and flung down the daffodils pell-mell on the white linen sheets. He studded the pillows with violets, dozens and dozens of bunches, and then he stood back and surveyed the disorder with delight.

Already the room was smelling sweet as the crushed violets poured out their essence and the opening daffodils exhaled their subtle insidious perfume. Mehuru gave another little laugh and crept from the room, closing the door behind him with a sense of having released something troubling and dangerous and wild in the orderly house.

So it was that when Frances came upstairs at noon to change from her morning gown, she found her room filled with a heady golden powerful scent and her bed drenched with flowers.

She did not think, she did not hesitate for a moment. In some archaic, intuitive part of her mind, as yet unfrozen and untamed, she knew precisely who had brought her the flowers. No-one else in the house would have bought them with such spendthrift abandon. No-one else in the house knew that she loved daffodils and that this spring had released her wild young greening desire. She stripped off her dress and her shift, recklessly, like a young girl, and fell, naked, into bed with them. She buried her face in their cool passionate greenness, and bathed in the watery pale scent of them. She rolled around on them and among them, swimming like a diver in a green pool, until her body was slick with the juice and her hair was tumbled over her bare shoulders and filled with petals. White sap from the daffodils smeared on her skin and was slick on her lips, sharp and bitter to the taste, staining the white purity of her sheets – and Frances was laughing and breathless and wanton, at last.

Chapter Twenty-two

~=~

Josiah was at his desk waiting to be called for dinner but whiling away the time in adding figures. He had half a dozen sheets of paper before him and each displayed a different calculation. *Rose* was due home first, but Josiah had already borrowed against her cargo to buy the Queens Square house. She should bring an extra profit in gold from her smuggled slaves; but Josiah could not borrow against contraband goods; they must remain a closely guarded secret. *Daisy* should only be a month behind her. Loading and unloading with the efficiency of a Merchant Venturer vessel, she should come into Bristol at the end of December, and *Lily* would be only two months behind.

Josiah hoped to raise money against *Daisy*'s expected profits. He wanted to offer them as security for a loan on the Hot Well. On each page he calculated how much the repayment would be if he could borrow at three per cent, and then the further calculation if *Daisy* came in late . . . a week late, two weeks late, a month. The difficulty of Josiah's work as a long-distance shipper was its unpredictability. The voyage took, on average, fourteen months. But storms could delay a ship, a wrecked mast could mean that she put into a strange port for repairs and was delayed for months. The captain was authorised to buy repairs in such a crisis, but he could be cheated, or the work expensively done, and he could come home carrying no gold at all, forced to sell cargo to cover his costs.

Josiah never knew, until his ship docked, whether he had made a fortune or lost one. There was no way for a captain to get a message home unless he met another Bristol ship on the voyage and it got home before him, and that happened only rarely. There was never anything to do but wait, and try not to borrow against profits which even now might be tossing in a storm on a sinking ship.

There was a tap on the door and Frances looked in.

'Am I disturbing you, Josiah?' She was wearing her hair in a new way, combed simply over her shoulders. Her face was radiant, and she looked pretty in a way that Josiah had never noticed before.

'New gown?' he asked.

'No.'

'Oh.'

'Is it you I must thank for my flowers?' she asked carefully.

'I sent Cicero to buy you a bunch,' Josiah said. 'Did he find a pretty bunch for you?'

Surprisingly the colour rushed into Frances's cheeks. 'He bought a lot,' she said. 'They are beautiful. Thank you.'

Josiah waved his hand. 'What can I do for you, Mrs Cole? It's not dinner time, is it?'

Frances shook her head gravely. 'I wish to send for a doctor for one of the children. The smallest boy is very feverish. He has had a cough since before Easter and he is getting worse.'

Josiah looked thoughtful. 'Can we not give him a poultice or something? A few days' rest in bed?'

'He has been resting,' Frances said. 'And Cook has done all that she can. She wants him to be seen by the doctor, and I think she is right.'

'I'm very sorry for the boy,' Josiah said awkwardly. 'But we are running a business here, Frances. We cannot care for him as if he were our son. The doctor charges for every visit and then there are medicines to buy as well. I would rather we waited until we were sure it was essential.'

'The child is very ill,' Frances insisted.

'I daresay, and I wish him well. But a couple of visits from the doctor and we will start to run at a loss on him.'

Frances turned to go, the prettiness drained from her face. 'But I may send for him if the child gets worse? It will be a greater loss if the little boy dies, after all, Josiah.'

'I don't wish him to be neglected,' Josiah said. 'But we have to measure our costs against our likely profits. Otherwise it is not a business venture but a mission. We are not in business to take little children from Africa and bring them up in civilised homes and spend a fortune on medicines for them. They have to earn their keep.'

'I know,' Frances conceded. 'But I cannot help but feel for him.'

Josiah smiled at her. 'You have a tender heart. Oh, send for the doctor if you insist; send if it worries you! But remember that we must keep costs down.'

'I will,' Frances said. She gave him a quick smile and slipped from the room. She went upstairs to the top floor where the slaves slept. James, the smallest boy, was on his pallet bed, Elizabeth beside him. She was sponging his hot face with vinegar and water. He was tossing his little head from side to side, his black eyes glazed, seeing nothing.

'Very sick,' Elizabeth said as Frances came into the room. 'No better?'

'No.'

Frances bent down and put her hand against the child's forehead. His skin burned under her touch. His little close-cropped curls were damp with sweat, his smooth black skin flushed darker with the fever.

'I will send for the doctor this evening if he is no better,' Frances said.

Elizabeth shook her head. 'No better.'

'You do not understand,' Frances said, irritated. 'I said: "I will send for a doctor if he does not get better".'

Elizabeth shook her head again. 'No better.'

'It is you who do not understand,' Mehuru said softly from the doorway. 'She is saying he is no better, and he will not get better.'

Frances looked shocked. 'Of course he will,' she cried. 'This is just a fever. Children get fevers all the time. By later today he will have probably sweated it out and the fever will have gone. In a few days he will be up and running around playing.'

'He did not do much playing,' Mehuru observed. 'Even when he was well.'

Frances flushed. 'If he had gone to the plantations he would have been weeding in the sugar cane every day from dawn to sunset,' she pointed out. 'He has an easier life here.'

Mehuru nodded. 'And if he had stayed in Africa he would have been safe on his mother's back while she worked in the fields. And in the evening when she cooked his supper he would have played in the dust with the other children. And at night she would have tucked him up in bed beside her.'

Frances said nothing. In the silence they could hear the hoarse sound of James's breath, rasping through his closing throat. 'I know he would have been better left at home,' Frances said very quietly.

James turned his head restlessly on the pillow, seeking a cool place. Frances leaned forward and lifted his little head. Elizabeth turned the pillow over and Frances let him lie down again on the cool new cotton. 'I'll send for the doctor now,' she decided.

'I'll go,' Mehuru said. 'Where is his house?'

'Trenchard Lane, near the hospital. Dr Hadley. Wait, I will give you one of my cards to take.'

Frances went downstairs to the parlour for a card from her case, Mehuru following. She scribbled a note on the back of it. 'There,' she said. 'Ask him to come as soon as he can.'

Mehuru took the card, went down to the kitchen to throw

on his jacket and snatch up his hat, went out through the back door and set off at a steady jogging run along the quayside of the Frome to John's Bridge.

The doctor was not at home. Mehuru tracked him around the city from one fashionable address to another and found him, coming from a lying-in at Culver Street. He was a young fair-headed Scotsman, notoriously free-thinking and politically radical. He was only tolerated by the conservative citizens of Bristol because of his remarkable abilities and his degree in medicine from Edinburgh University. He took Mehuru up in his phaeton and drove down to Queens Square.

'Are you a free man?' he asked curiously.

'No,' Mehuru said. 'Mrs Cole owns me.'

'You seem to be a man of education. You speak well.'

'Mrs Cole taught me to speak and I have taught myself to read.'

'Read, eh? Do you read the newspapers?'

'When I can see them. I have no money to buy newspapers or books.'

'You could go to a reading room or a coffee house.'

'I have no money,' Mehuru pointed out. 'And no time off. I am not a servant, I am a slave. I am not allowed out of the house.'

The doctor muttered something brief and impolite. 'Ever heard of Granville Sharp?' he asked.

'No.'

'He's a Londoner. He lives in London. He's made a bit of a name for himself, championing the people of your race.'

'Slaves or free?'

The doctor clicked to his horse as they turned into the square. 'Slaves,' he said. 'He defended a black runaway slave – what was his name now? Strong, Jonathan Strong, and another, James Somerset – their cases went to court and the judge ruled they could not be sent out of the country against their wishes. If they try to send you to the plantations you can refuse to go, slave or not. Did you know that?'

Mehuru jumped down from the seat and ran to the horse's head. 'I did not! I thought they owned me completely.'

'Not completely,' the doctor said with sharp irony. 'Even in Britain, in the land of freedom, you have some few rights. For instance, they can beat you but not to death.'

'Can I speak with you again?' Mehuru asked urgently.

'I dine at the Crossways coffee shop on Mondays,' the doctor told him. 'I talk to a number of friends there. We would be pleased to see you, if you could get there.'

'I'll get there,' Mehuru said.

'Don't get yourself shipped out before Monday,' the doctor warned wryly, lifting his bag out of the carriage. 'There's always a ship going to the West Indies and you won't be the first negro stolen away.'

'I'll be there Monday,' Mehuru promised.

The doctor nodded and ran up the steps.

The door opened at once, as Martha had been watching for him. She took him to James's little room at once. When he came down again Frances was at the foot of the stairs.

'Is he very ill?' she asked.

'He may pull through,' Dr Hadley replied. 'It's a violent fever and a putrid sore throat. But he's underweight and very sick. I've given the woman some pastilles to burn in his room, and some syrup to bring down the fever.'

'I did not know he was so ill.' Frances could hear the exculpatory tone in her voice.

'He's only a little boy,' Dr Hadley said abruptly. 'What is he? Three? Scarcely more than a baby. He should be with his mother. What's he doing here anyway?'

'It is a scheme of my sister-in-law's,' Frances explained. 'We import slaves direct from Africa and train them here for domestic work . . .' Under his sharp blue stare her voice died away. 'It is better work for them and a better life than on the plantations,' she finished feebly.

'I am sure of it,' he said ironically. 'I should think death itself is preferable to work on the plantations.'

'You are against slavery,' Frances accused him. 'You are an abolitionist.'

'In this town?' He raised his sandy-coloured eyebrows. 'A man would be lynched if he acknowledged such beliefs. I am a professional man, a doctor. I attend where I am summoned and I generally keep my opinions to myself.'

'Shall you come again?'

'I will call later to see how he is. The woman tells me that there is another little boy who is also unwell.'

'I did not know,' Frances said. 'Will you please see him too?'

'When I come tonight. He has gone out now to carry a message for your husband.' Dr Hadley glanced out of the window at the scudding clouds. 'A nasty day for a little boy with a fever to be running errands around town,' he observed. 'I will not delay you any more, Mrs Cole.' He made her a brief bow and strode to the front door. 'Good day.'

Stephen Waring was in his accounting house discussing his colliery with two other men. As they turned to go he called one of them back into the room as if he had suddenly remembered something.

'Oh! Green! I had forgotten to ask you. You are planning to give up your houses at the Hot Well, are you not? And move your business to Clifton?'

The man closed the door swiftly behind him to prevent eavesdroppers. 'Why yes, I am going to sell the lodging houses in Dowry Parade at the Hot Well. I am sure that Clifton is the coming place; such pretty buildings and such good company.'

'Perhaps you are right,' Stephen Waring said smoothly.

'But I know of a man who might be interested in taking on the Hot Well. He might be prepared to buy your place also.'

'Does he know what the lease for the Well will cost?'

'I believe so. But he thinks he can make it pay.'

'I thought they would never get someone to take that lease,' Green exclaimed incautiously.

'The Merchant Venturers have too much money tied up in the Hot Well,' Stephen said smoothly. 'I for one should like to see that money released for other projects. And if the Hot Well can be made to pay we would all benefit. The debt should be cleared, and this is the man to clear it for us.'

Mr Green hesitated. 'If it can be made to pay,' he said. There was a hint of warning in his voice. 'Fashionable society is moving up to the heights of Clifton, not down along the river. However elegant the Assembly Room – it is in the wrong place. If he is a friend of yours, you may wish to warn him. It is a fine building but I think Clifton is the place to be.'

'It is a venture like any other,' Stephen observed pleasantly. 'There is always risk where there is profit to be had. He is a trader – he should know that.'

When Dr Hadley came back to visit James late that night the child was worse. His fever had broken but the boy was no better. He was cold now, instead of hot. He lay very still and quiet on the little bed, his rasping breath coming slowly and sluggishly. When the doctor took the little dark wrist he could hardly find the pulse. The doctor looked at the black woman sitting at the head of the bed. She had the soft fringe of her shawl in her hand and she was leaning forward and gently stroking it against the boy's cheek. His head was turned to her and his eyes were shut.

The doctor raised an eyebrow to her.

'No better,' she said softly.

He opened his bag and took a small bottle of laudanum

and mixed four drops in a glass of water. 'If he cries,' he said simply, 'if he cries for pain he can have this, a little at a time. I can do no more for him. He's sinking fast. He's going now.'

'Going home,' she said simply.

Stuart Hadley found that his eyes were smarting. He bent down and put his hand against the damp little cheek. The boy was so small that the white hand cupped his entire face from curly hair to rounded chin. He was little more than a baby.

'Going home,' he agreed softly.

He snapped his bag shut and went from the room.

Frances was waiting for him in the hall. 'Is he better?' she asked.

He looked at her coldly. 'He is dying, ma'am. He will be dead by tomorrow.'

She staggered slightly and went white.

'It is a risk you will have to carry,' he said precisely. 'If you bring slaves into England. They are susceptible to English diseases, just as white men quickly die in Africa. They are susceptible to the English cold and damp. Is this the first one you have lost?'

'No,' Frances admitted. She remembered the woman called Died of Shame, and the unmarked grave in the Redclift churchyard.

'What did that one die of?'

Frances shook her head wordlessly.

'Was she sick?'

'She ate earth,' Frances said, her voice very low. 'And she was found dead one morning. She died in her sleep.'

'How awkward,' he observed savagely. 'Well, I must be getting on. I send my bill to Cole and Sons, do I? It is a commercial loss, is it not?'

Frances flushed. 'I shall pay.'

The doctor bowed and went to the door.

'You despise me because we own slaves,' Frances accused.

He looked into her face. Her eyes were filled with tears and she was trembling.

'No,' he said with sudden honesty. 'That would not be fair of me. I used to take sugar in my tea, and I still love sweet puddings. I smoke tobacco, I wear cotton. I benefit from the Trade as much as you do but I manage to keep my hands clean, I take my profits from the Trade at a distance. How can I measure what good it does me? My university is endowed by rich men who draw their wealth from the colonies. My patients are all Traders. We all profit from the thieving in Africa. If we stopped it tomorrow we would still be rich from their loss.'

'Would you wish to see slavery abolished?'

'I believe the Trade will be ended,' he said certainly. 'And I pray to God that I will see it ended this very month in Parliament. But the cruelty we have learned will poison us forever.'

The parlour door behind Frances opened and she gave a guilty start. 'Oh! Sister! This is Dr Hadley, he is just leaving.'

'Is the boy better?' Sarah asked.

Frances shook her head. 'Dr Hadley thinks he will die.'

Sarah nodded brusquely. 'Thank you for calling anyway, Doctor.'

Doctor Hadley bowed to them both and let himself out of the front door.

Sarah looked crossly at Frances. 'Another burial,' she said pointedly. 'They all cost money, you know. I shall order the undertakers to call tomorrow morning.'

'When the undertakers come I will see them,' Frances said.

'It's not necessary.' Sarah went around the parlour blowing out the candles, without asking Frances if she were ready to go to bed.

'I know it is not necessary; but I want the little boy to be buried as he should be buried.'

Sarah took her cup and threw the dregs of the tea on the

fire to damp down the last smouldering small piece of coal which she had been sitting over since supper. 'They know their business. You can leave it to them.'

'He is an African boy,' Frances protested. 'There will be things which they will want to do for him. The woman who has been sitting with him, Elizabeth, she nursed him as if he were her own child. She will not want him taken from her and thrown into a grave. She will want to say farewell to him, in her own way.'

Sarah straightened up, her face full of suppressed anger. 'You can make a big parade of your feelings over this,' she snapped. 'I heard you talking with that doctor. You can attend the funeral, you can hire a hearse. It is throwing bad money after good. The child is dying, and you knew when you started this that at least two or three would die during the first year. It is natural wastage. It is the natural loss of stock. If we have to go into mourning every time a slave dies we might as well grieve for a broken barrel of sugar.'

'He is a child,' Frances cried passionately. 'A little boy . . .'

'He is our Trade,' Sarah said. 'And if we cannot make this Trade pay then we are on the way to ruin. Wear black crepe if you like, Sister. But get those slaves trained and ready for sale.'

Chapter Twenty-three

In the morning Frances did not summon Mehuru to ask him how the slaves would want to say farewell to little James. She went down the corridor to the kitchen and found Elizabeth, her head in her arms, half-asleep on the kitchen table.

'May I come in, Cook? I want to speak to Elizabeth.'

Cook bobbed a stiff unwelcoming curtsey. 'Of course, Mrs Cole. This poor girl is worn out. I don't think she's slept for more than a few hours in these last two days.'

Frances pulled up a stool and touched Elizabeth gently on the arm. Elizabeth started awake at once. Frances saw that her eyelids were swollen from lack of sleep and from weeping.

'The men are coming to bury James,' Frances said, speaking slowly and carefully, watching Elizabeth's face. 'But I have said that you may make him ready and see it done as you wish. Would you like that?'

Elizabeth nodded.

'I shall tell Mehuru to spend the morning with you and the men to make sure it is done as you wish,' Frances promised. She rose up from the stool. 'I am very sorry,' she said softly. Her eyes were on Elizabeth's face as if she were asking for forgiveness. 'I am very sorry that James was ill, and that we lost him in the end.'

Elizabeth nodded, her face grave.

Frances went to the hall to find Mehuru. He was on his hands and knees in the parlour, sweeping the grate.

'Cicero, the men are coming to bury James. You are to

stay with Elizabeth and see that they do what she wants. He is to be buried as she wishes, as far as it is possible. You can tell them that I will pay for anything extra.'

Mehuru rose to his feet and wiped his hands on the rough apron protecting his livery. 'How do you want it done?' he asked.

Frances looked into his face for the first time. 'In your way,' she stumbled. 'However you wish. In the African way.'

He shook his head, his eyes on her face. 'Elizabeth is Yoruban, as am I, James was Sonke. Kbara is Mandinka. How do you wish him to be buried?'

Frances shook her head in frustration and clapped her hands together. 'I don't know!' she cried. 'I was just trying to make it better, Mehuru! I was just trying to make it right!'

He caught her hand and held it gently. Coal dust smeared her hand as black as his. 'There is no little way to make this right,' he said gently, almost tenderly. 'It is as wrong as it could be. But I will see him buried with care.'

Frances stepped back, their hands parted. 'Thank you,' she whispered, and slipped from the room.

Mehuru chose not to ask for permission to go out on the Monday night, a few days after the funeral. Instead he put his arm around Cook's broad waist while she was bolting the back door and whispered in her ear. She slapped his hand away. 'Impertinence!'

'I'll be in by midnight,' he cajoled. 'And I promise to lock up safely.'

'And what if we are all murdered in our beds between now and then?' she demanded. 'With the back door left open for any passing thief?'

'I'll ask Kbara to sit in the kitchen and wait up for me,' he said. 'You'll be safe enough.'

'And what if Master comes down and finds you gone and Julius out of his bed and waiting for you?'

'He never comes down to the kitchen, Cook. You feed him too well for him to hunt for food in the night. Such a wonderful cook that you are.'

She slapped him again. 'That'll do. Where d'you want to go anyway?'

'Just to a coffee house for some talk,' Mehuru said. 'You get a night off, why not me?'

She nodded. 'All right then,' she agreed reluctantly. 'But mind you don't get press-ganged, or kidnapped. The slaver captains will steal anyone away to serve on their ships, remember! And the press-gangs for the Navy are not choosy! And don't get drunk! And don't go with a woman, half of them are diseased and the other half will take you round a corner and hand you over to be beaten.'

Mehuru threw up his hands, laughing. 'I will go to the coffee house and come straight home. I swear it.'

She opened the back door a crack for him to slip through. 'You have no money,' she said. 'Here.' She rummaged under her apron in her pocket and drew out a purse. She offered him a sixpence.

'I cannot repay you.' Mehuru hesitated. 'I have no money at all, and no chance of earning.'

'I know,' she said. Her powerful sense of dissatisfaction with the Coles made her push the coin, and then another, into his hand. 'It isn't right. It can't be right to work a man all day as hard as you do, and then not even have the price of a drink in the evening.'

The coffee shop was noisy and crowded, a pall of smoke hung at head height, the windows were running with condensation. When the door was opened steam and smoke billowed out into the dark street. Mehuru paused in the doorway, uncertain. But then he saw that a number of the men inside were black-faced like him. With a surprised exclamation he stepped over the threshold and saw Dr Hadley seated at a table with four other men, one of them a negro.

'Dr Hadley,' he called. 'I have come.'

'Cicero! Sit down,' the doctor said. He looked rumpled and informal with his jacket off and his hair tied carelessly back and unpowdered. 'Here is a countryman of yours, Caesar Peters, and Edgar Long, and James Stephenson.'

Mehuru hesitated. For a moment he could not believe the sudden joy of meeting men as an equal, of being among men who looked him in the face and nodded a casual greeting. For long months now he had been invisible, a piece of cargo, an animal to be tethered and fed and trained. Only among his fellow slaves and the women – Cook and Frances – was he seen as a man, a real man. What he had missed was the casual company of strangers, the easy conviviality of free men. The constant pain of homesickness and the constant ache of injustice was suddenly lifted from him. He felt that he stood taller, his shoulders square. He remembered that when the weight of the slave collar was taken off he had learned to walk again, to free himself of the slavish shuffle.

He pulled up a stool to the table and smiled around at the men. 'Good evening,' he said. 'I am glad to be with you. My name is Mehuru, Cicero is a slave name.' He glanced at the black man. 'Are you Mandinka?' he asked.

The man smiled. 'I am Jamaican,' he said with a little irony. He spoke with a lilt to his voice, a rhythm almost like music. Mehuru found him hard to understand. 'I was born and bred on a plantation, and taken from my mother when I was small. I have never seen Africa. I cannot speak any African language. I'm told I look like a Mandinko – but it means nothing to me.'

'Are you free now?'

He nodded. 'I was press-ganged on to a ship. They didn't care whether I was a slave or free, they needed crew. I was paid off at the end of the voyage in London, and I now work there for a printer. I have brought these gentlemen some pamphlets.'

'Are there many free black people?' Mehuru was trying to adjust his view of England. He had thought it a country inhabited solely by white people.

'Thousands,' the man said. 'There are more than ten thousand in London alone. I live in a house owned by a black landlord with black neighbours.'

'Thousands?' Mehuru was astounded.

The man nodded.

'But what are they – what are *we* all doing here?'

The man chuckled, a deep rich chuckle. 'Some are slaves, brought from Jamaica and the West Indies when their owners came home to England. Some are free men, who have bought themselves free. Most have escaped. A good many are American slaves, freed or escaped during the war.'

'Don't you want to go home?' Mehuru asked incredulously.

'Home? My home is Jamaica and there's nothing there for a black man but beatings and labour. I'd rather stay here and earn a living.'

Mehuru shook his head and Dr Hadley laughed at his bewildered expression. 'Did you think yourself the only black man in England?'

'Very nearly,' Mehuru said ruefully. 'I have seen one or two men working at the docks but only from the window of the warehouse.'

'You must have been very lonely.'

Mehuru nodded.

'Well, you're among friends now. We're a radical society.' He lowered his voice, but no-one could have eavesdropped above the hubbub of the coffee house. 'Mr Stephenson here is a wheelwright and Mr Long writes for a newspaper. We are the Bristol Society for Constitutional Information – committed to the reform of Parliament. We're in touch with societies all around the country. We're collecting names for a petition to Parliament. The time has come for the suffrage to be widened, every man should have a vote to choose his government. The laws are made by the landed gentry and they oppress the working men. And –' he nodded at Caesar and Mehuru '– we *must* abolish slavery in Britain and in the British colonies. How can we progress towards true liberty when we are a nation of slave takers and slave users? Black or white, men must be free.'

'The pace of the abolition campaign is increasing,' Caesar said. 'They are holding meetings everywhere in the country and preparing petitions. The debate has been postponed once, but Wilberforce will bring a bill before Parliament on the eleventh – next week. Pitt, Burke, Fox all support it.'

'But the government is very fearful,' Edgar Long cautioned. 'We will have to take care to stay inside the law. First the Americans and now the French have grown so radical – they are making our masters uneasy.'

'We are outside the law already,' Dr Hadley said briskly. 'With so many offences on the statute books, just being in company with more than two other men is a crime if you criticise the government.'

'The London Society is being watched,' Caesar said. 'There is no doubt that our letters are opened.'

'It is not the government I fear but the mob.' Edgar drained his pot of beer and called for another round. 'The gentry call out the mob against us, get them drunk and set them on us. These are dangerous times.'

'They are times of opportunity.' Dr Hadley disagreed. 'America, France, change is in the air and we are in the thick of it. The world is changing, and we are at the head of it. I am not afraid of the mob. More and more the people will come to see that Reform is the way ahead. Proper wages, proper conditions will follow the vote. Look at France! It is a fine and noble thing they are doing there, bringing the power of the people to bear on a dissolute and tyrannical regime. I tell you, the work I do in the City Hospital would make a radical out of the king himself.'

A serving man came over and dumped five pint pots of ale down on the table. Mehuru realised that it was the first time anyone had served him since he had lost Siko. For a moment the warmth of the coffee house and the cheerful noise faded away. He thought of Siko, and his quick smile and his impertinence. Mehuru grimaced, and took up the tankard and tasted the beer. It was warm and watery but it made a pleasant change from the slop of the small ale of the kitchen and Cook's unending pots of weak tea.

'And the bill for the abolition of the Trade?' demanded Edgar Long. 'What do they say are the chances of the bill?'

'It must come,' Caesar said. 'It cannot fail. The mood of the country is with us, the leaders in the Parliament are with us. Wilberforce has twelve resolutions to put to the house to ban the capture and shipping of slaves.'

'They will oppose,' Edgar Long warned. 'There is a lot of money in this country tied up in the Trade. The opposition is hidden because it is ashamed – but it is there nonetheless.'

'It is not ashamed,' Stuart argued. 'I meet these people, Edgar, as you do not. They are shameless. They live off the profits and they dine off gold, and they manage to forget that every penny they earn is paid for in torture and blood.'

'It cannot fail,' Caesar repeated. 'There is a majority in favour. We have canvassed the members of Parliament and they have faithfully promised their support. Slave trading will be abolished, and then we can go on to abolish the whole business of slavery, and my people . . .' he glanced at Mehuru with a smile '. . . *our* people, Brother, will be free.'

Mehuru had no reply, the man had taken his breath away. 'I did not know . . .'

'You shall see your home again,' Caesar said. 'And have an African son.'

Mehuru's face suddenly crumpled and he put his hand over his eyes. 'Forgive me,' he said softly. 'I had almost given up hoping.'

Stuart slapped him on the back. 'We are on the turn of the tide. You will be free to come and go as you please.'

At the thought of coming and going Mehuru glanced at the clock. 'I cannot stay now,' he exclaimed. 'Though for the first time in this country I feel that I am among friends. I promised the woman who works in the kitchen that I would be home to bolt the back door before midnight and I will not break my word to her.'

'Can you come out again?' Edgar Long asked him.

'It is difficult,' Mehuru said. 'I would take the risk willingly, but the cook is responsible for locking the doors and she is a good woman. If they found I was missing she would be in grave trouble.' He downed his beer in four greedy gulps. 'But I will try. You can be assured that I will try. Are you here every week?'

'They are here every week,' Caesar confirmed. 'I am here once a month or so.'

'I'll walk home with you,' Dr Hadley said. 'Gentlemen, I'll see you next week, when we have had a chance to read Caesar's pamphlets. And we will meet on Tuesday night for news of the debate.'

The night air was cold when they stepped out into the street. Mehuru shivered and drew his cloak closer around him.

'I brought these for you.' Dr Hadley produced a handful of pamphlets from under his cloak. 'Abolitionist pamphlets. One of them is written by a countryman of yours, Equiano – a freed slave.'

'How did he gain his freedom?'

'He bought himself out. He is married to an English woman, he has written a fine book which I can lend you, if you wish.'

'He is married to a white woman?' Mehuru demanded. 'I had not thought it was possible.'

'There's no law against it. Most of your countrymen marry

white women. How else are they to find companions?'

'There are no freed African women?'

'Most of the slaves brought back from the Sugar Islands are pageboys or footmen. And of course only men are press-ganged, or serve as soldiers. So only a few black women come here to England. But your countrymen marry well enough with white women. They have very pretty children, of a pale colour.' Stuart Hadley gave a short laugh. 'In a couple of hundred years you will not be able to trace the African descendants. But every Englishman with black hair or black eyes will have to wonder if his great-grandfather was a slave. Perhaps that will be your revenge on us – by the year 1900 there will be no pure white men at all.'

'I don't want revenge,' Mehuru said softly. 'I want to go home. I am needed at my home, and if I wanted to marry, the women of my nation would be my first choice.' He thought for a moment of the line of Frances's pale cheek and the way her skin gleamed like buttermilk.

'There is a scheme to take men back to Africa,' Dr Hadley said. 'Some land on the coast has been bought and named Sierra Leone. There are many black men in London who feel as you do, who want to go home to Africa. They are pioneers, they have grants of land to farm.'

'No,' Mehuru chuckled. 'You misunderstand me. I am not a farmer, I am not a pioneer. When I say I want to go home I did not mean that I wanted to camp out in the bush. I want to go home to my house, to my work, to my own country.'

Dr Hadley hesitated. 'Forgive me,' he said. 'I had thought of all Africans as living off the land, in – er – I suppose mud huts.'

Mehuru thought of the great high stone walls of Oyo and the architecture of the great houses and the palaces. 'I might as well suppose that all Englishmen lived in warehouses beside stinking rivers,' he said bitingly.

They were at the back of Queens Square. The Merchant

Venturers' great crane threw a shadow like a giant gibbet over the quayside.

'You are right to correct me,' Stuart Hadley said. 'It is hard for white men to imagine your country.'

'That's all right,' Mehuru replied bleakly. 'Sometimes it is hard for me to remember it too.'

Kbara was dozing in the chair when Mehuru slipped in through the back door. He started awake and Mehuru clapped his hand over his mouth. 'Sshhh! Fool!' Mehuru said swiftly in Mandinka. 'Is everything quiet?'

'The little boy is sick.'

'Like James?'

'The same.'

'Is he as bad?'

'Elizabeth says not yet, but she is worried for him.'

Mehuru thought. 'Should we fetch the doctor now?'

'Elizabeth said you were to go to her when you came in.'

Mehuru stepped out of his shoes, took them in his hand and crept up the stairs. Kbara stayed behind to lock the kitchen door and shoot the oiled bolts.

Mehuru hesitated on the landing. The two grand front bedrooms were Josiah's and Frances's. From the one on the left came a rumbling snore – Josiah – which meant that Frances was sleeping alone. Mehuru paused. He had a great desire to see her asleep. He wanted to see her without her knowing he was there, standing at the foot of the bed. He wanted to see her as a sleeping woman, innocent of her power as his slave owner. He wanted to see her warm and half-naked in her bed. He went towards her door, his feet silent on the Turkish rugs. He turned the handle and took one step inside her room.

Her window curtains were only partly drawn and the moonlight bathed the room in pale colours. Mehuru came a little closer to the bed. Frances was asleep on her back, one hand outflung. Her long hair was twisted into a careless plait. She was wearing a white nightgown of pure lawn, embroidered and pin-tucked around the neck. In her sleep one of the buttons had come undone and he could see the long pale column of her throat and the two smooth lines of her collar bones.

Mehuru swallowed. She was a lovely woman in the moonlight. Pale as a woman made of white flour, pale as a woman sculpted from frozen cream. He thought of what Dr Hadley had told him – that many black men had married white women – and he wondered if he would ever lie with a woman again. He could not believe that he must not go closer to Frances, he could not believe that he was not allowed to touch her outstretched hand nor put his lips to where the pulse beat slowly and steadily at the base of her throat.

He heard Kbara's stealthy tread on the stairs and he slipped back out of the door, closing it quietly behind him, and met him on the landing. They went up the next flight of stairs together and tapped softly on the women's door. It was locked, of course. One of Cook's jobs before she bolted the back and front doors was to lock the slaves in their rooms. Kbara took down the key from its hook, unfastened the door and Elizabeth opened it from the inside. Her face was strained and tired. She had grieved for the death of James, her little foster-son, and watched them take him away and bury him in the cold alien ground. Now John was coughing as badly and his fever was rising.

'Should we fetch a doctor tonight?'

She nodded. 'He is a good man. Ask him to come.'

'I shall have to ask Frances,' Mehuru said.

'Do we have to wait until she is awake?' Kbara asked. 'Wait till the morning?'

The temptation to wake Frances was too much for him. 'I will wake her now to ask her,' he decided. 'I will go. Kbara, you go to bed. I will fetch the doctor. Frances will give me the front-door key.'

He went quickly down the stairs before they could argue, tapped very softly on Frances's door and went into the room. She opened her eyes as he came in and for a moment she thought she was dreaming, and that he had come to her in a dream of desire. Then she blinked herself awake, and there was no mistaking the expression on her face. 'Mehuru!' she said and her voice was full of joy.

He touched her outstretched hand and in a movement too quick for either of them to consider they clasped hands and he bent down to her bed, snatching her to him. Her arms went around his neck, he kissed her throat, the warm hollow where the pulse was now thudding, a line of kisses up to her mouth which was warm and sweet and opened under his. Her skin smelled of rosewater. He rubbed his face against her neck and felt beneath his moving lips the smooth swell of her breasts.

Her hands pulled at his stock, at his jacket, and he moved to throw his jacket aside but suddenly checked. 'Frances! No . . .'

'What is it? What is it, Mehuru?'

'I must not – I came to tell you – it's John. He's sick.'

Her eyelids fluttered for a moment, and then a cold closed look spread over her face. Her years of training shut down upon her desires like a trap. Her hand went to the open neck of her nightgown and pulled it close. 'Oh. Oh. I see.'

'Elizabeth wants him to see the doctor. May I go for him?'

She threw back the covers of the bed. He had a brief glimpse of her pale long legs. 'Frances . . .'

But she had herself under control. She would not even look at him. She threw a shawl around her shoulders and when she finally turned to him her face was icy. 'Mr Cole does not want the doctor called except in an emergency.'

'The child is sick.'

'Is he seriously ill?'

Mehuru exclaimed with impatience and reached out to her but she stepped back. The coldness of her face forbade him to come closer. He felt his quick anger rise at once.

'I beg your pardon,' he said bitingly. 'Excuse me, Mrs Cole. Yes, he is sick. He is sick like little James. Do you want him to be left to die, or shall I fetch the doctor?'

She flushed at the insult in his voice. 'You can fetch the doctor.'

He went to the door and hesitated, wondering if she would call him back. His mouth was still hot with her passionate kisses. He could not understand how she could suddenly summon such iciness and distance.

'The front-door key is in the drawer in the table in the hall,' Frances said precisely.

'Yes, Mrs Cole.'

Stuart Hadley was reading in his study when Mehuru arrived, breathless and hatless. He grabbed his bag and washed his face while Mehuru put his horse between the shafts of the phaeton and drove it around to the front door.

'Same symptoms?'

'Symptoms? I don't know that word.'

'Signs, signs of illness.'

'Yes. I think so.'

Hadley nodded. 'Better pray it's not typhoid.'

The clock in St Mary Redclift struck two and was answered by the cathedral clock on the other side of the city.

'Get into the house all right?'

'Yes.'

The carriage wheels rattled over John's Bridge and Mehuru turned the horse sharply to the right to drive down the bumping cobbles of the quay. The tide was out and the mud steamed with fresh sewage. Even in the cool night air the smell was overpowering.

'It's a wonder anyone survives,' Hadley said shortly.

Mehuru turned the carriage away from the quay and into the clean white enclosure of Queens Square.

'Will the horse stand?'

'He's used to it.'

Mehuru looped the reins over a railing and led the way into the house, up the stairs, past Frances's bedroom and up to the servants' rooms.

Stuart Hadley took in the overcrowding at one quick glance. The other women and girls had pulled their blankets over their heads, from tiredness and modesty, and were sleeping. Only Elizabeth watched by the bedside of the little boy, so like her own baby who had been left in Africa and now could not remember his mother at all. She looked up when the doctor came in.

'John,' she said, pointing to the little boy.

He was hot but fully conscious. He looked up in surprise as the white man came in and Mehuru whispered quickly that this was a good man come to make him well. Stuart smiled at him, took his pulse, and touched a hand to his forehead and his cheek.

'Not too bad yet,' he observed. He opened his bag. 'Here are the pastilles to burn again. They should stop the rest of you catching the illness. I wish that you were better housed. I will speak to Mrs Cole in the morning. There should be no more than four in a room of this size. And here is something to help him sleep. Keep sponging him with vinegar and water to keep the fever down and let him drink all he wants of clean water.'

Mehuru nodded and translated for Elizabeth.

'If anyone else feels sick you are to call me at once,' Stuart said to Mehuru. They closed the door of the women's room and went quietly down the stairs together. 'I do not think it is typhoid but I cannot be sure.'

'What is typhoid?'

'A very bad illness, a high fever, many people die.'

Mehuru nodded. They walked quietly along the landing, past Frances's closed bedroom door, and on down the stairs.

'I'll call tomorrow, in the morning, to see how the boy does,' Stuart Hadley promised on the doorstep.

'She may not want you to call,' Mehuru said tightly. 'They don't want to pay.'

The two men exchanged a look of mutual anger. 'She'll want me quick enough if she's got typhoid in the house,' Stuart replied. 'I'll call.'

He swung himself into the phaeton and gathered up the reins. 'Good night again,' he said softly, and turned the horse out of the square towards home.

Mehuru watched the carriage go, enjoying the silence of the night-time square and his rare sense of freedom. Overhead the blue-black sky was rich with stars, hundreds and thousands of them. Mehuru slowly turned to go back inside and closed and locked the front door and returned the key to its place.

He went quietly up the stairs and paused outside Frances's bedroom. He could not tell if she were sleeping or awake. He felt an irresistible temptation to open her door and see if she would again come to his arms, but then he thought of the sudden coldness of her face, and how, whether she was warm or cold, he could never reproach her. She could be exactly as the whim took her, and he could do nothing but obey. At night, in her bedroom, with Josiah sleeping next door, he would not dare to speak louder than a whisper.

He made a muffled exclamation of anger and turned from her door. At once it opened, silently, and she was standing before him.

Her long dark hair was brushed over her shoulders, in the half-light of the hall her eyes were dark pools of shadow. He turned and stepped towards her and saw that she was smiling. He knew at once that for some reason, inexplicably, they had

321

broken through the many boundaries which separated them, and that Frances had plunged through the restraint of her training. For this night, they were free to love each other as equals.

Frances, waiting for him to move, half-afraid and half-delighted, stood quite still. She thought for a moment of her bed of daffodils and whether being held by Mehuru would be like that sudden abandoned dive into freedom and sensuality.

He reached out his hand to her and put his finger against her cheek. Frances closed her eyes and leaned towards him. His desire for her rose up and he caught her to him and held her, feeling the warmth of her body against him, and the pleasure of her lips under his as she returned and sought his kisses. Mehuru lifted her easily in his arms, went into her bedroom and tumbled her on to the bed as recklessly as he had thrown the flowers.

Chapter Twenty-four

Early next morning, Stuart Hadley's phaeton drew up outside 29 Queens Square. Frances was waiting for him in the hall, her hair piled high, wearing a rich peach gown. 'I think he is better,' she greeted him.

'You have seen him yourself?'

Frances gave him a small sideways smile. 'I am not completely a slave driver. Of course I have seen him. And I think he is much better. Elizabeth is with him now, do you want to go up?'

Mehuru came halfway down the stairs. Frances glanced up at him and quickly looked away.

Mehuru made a little bow, his eyes on her face.

'Take the doctor to the room, Cicero,' she said carefully.

Mehuru bowed with meticulous politeness and led the way up the stairs. Stuart Hadley quickly glanced back at Frances and caught such a radiant smile from her as she looked up at the two men that he checked on the stairs, and hesitated. 'Mrs Cole?'

Frances blushed a deep rosy red. 'I am sorry,' she said. 'I was thinking . . . I was thinking . . .'

Mehuru too had paused. 'What were you thinking of, Mrs Cole?' he asked, his voice warm with suppressed laughter.

Frances blushed rosily, tried to say something, and then ran into the parlour and shut the door.

The two men were silent for a moment. 'I see,' Stuart said, understanding everything.

Mehuru glanced at him. 'You see nothing.'

They climbed the stairs to the attic bedroom in silence. Stuart put his hand on Mehuru's arm before he opened the door.

'I hope you are not putting yourself in very great danger, my friend,' Stuart said quietly. 'This is a perilous road for you and for her.'

Mehuru nodded. 'I cannot help but walk it. It is my Ifa – my fate.' He stepped back to let the doctor precede him into the bedroom. The little boy was seated on Elizabeth's lap and taking gruel from a spoon. She looked up and smiled as the doctor came in.

'Well, this is very much better!' he exclaimed. 'The fever broke in the night, did it?'

She nodded and put her hand against John's face. 'Cool,' she said. 'John is well.'

'Keep him in for the next few days,' Stuart advised. 'And don't let him go running errands in the rain. Plenty of food to build him up again. I think we have been lucky this time.'

Elizabeth smiled.

'And you get some rest,' Dr Hadley said gently. 'No point you getting overtired and making yourself ill too. Sleep.'

Her glance slid to Mehuru. They both knew that a slave only rested with permission. 'I will tell Frances,' he said. 'You rest with John today. I will tell Mrs Cole. She will allow it.'

The two men left the room together and went downstairs. Mehuru tapped on the parlour door and stepped to one side.

'The fever has broken,' Stuart reported briefly. He did not step into the room, he stood on the threshold and addressed Frances and Sarah without preference. 'It is not typhoid. You were lucky with this one.'

Frances smiled. 'I am glad,' she said.

'The woman who has been caring for him should have a rest today,' Stuart continued. 'She was at his bedside all night.'

Sarah looked as if she might argue but Frances nodded. 'Of course,' she said. 'And thank you for coming out in the middle of the night, Doctor.'

He bowed briefly to them both and went out into the hall. Mehuru, who was waiting, handed him his hat and went with him to his phaeton.

'I want my freedom,' Mehuru said suddenly. 'Whatever else. It makes no difference. I still want my freedom.'

The doctor nodded. 'I agree. You have no future here, like this. And slavery corrupts you all, spoils all your lives, hers as well as yours. That's what they can't see, the traders, the owners. When you use another person you are both enslaved, both corrupted. And by next week, by Tuesday when Wilberforce's bill is agreed, you will all be on the way to freedom!'

He climbed into the driving seat. 'Tuesday night!' he said softly to Mehuru, and the horse moved on.

29 Queens Square,
Bristol.

7th May 1789

'Dear Uncle,

I have Heard this day from Sir Charles. He is coming to See us on his Way to stay at the Home of Lord Bartlet. He has Decided to Buy Shelby Manor from You and he wishes to Sign the Lease here. We are to Act as his Agents in this Matter also: Investing his Rents and settling Debts at the Manor. I understand there is a Land Agent to Manage the Day-to-Day running of the Farms. I therefore Await the lease from You and will Return it to You signed, and with the money for the Purchase Price.

The Weather here is still very uncertain, the winter seems

325

to have lasted forever. The City is Prone to Fogs and low-lying clouds and the Smell from the Manufactories is very Bad. Josiah and Miss Cole do not Notice it, being Accustomed. I Drive out on fine Days to enjoy the Cleaner air of the Downs. Despite this I am very happy. I feel so Full of joy and I have Never been in stronger Health. I Wake every morning so Easily and I am Never tired.

An Acquaintance of Mine has asked Me for some Advice on which I Should like your Opinion. She has made a Marriage with a Bristol Merchant but Finds herself very Attracted to a Visitor to Bristol – a Nobleman in his Own Country, and most Handsome and Tender to her. He tells her that he Loves her and She Believes it is the Truth. She tells me that she has Never felt Happier, as if her Life depends on him. She has Asked me What she Should do. I Wonder what Your Opinion is? There Can be no Future for them, of Course? I have told her My opinion: that the Bonds of Matrimony can never be Loosed.

I Hope you are in Good Health, my Dear Uncle. I remain your loving niece,

Frances.

Mehuru tapped on the parlour door and came into the room as Frances blotted her letter and sealed it.

'May I speak with you?'

Her quick colour rose at once, she smiled at him and whispered: 'Shut the door.'

He pushed it closed, but came no nearer.

'I wonder if we might be paid a wage,' he said.

'What?' She recoiled as if he had slapped her. 'A wage?'

'We work as Cook works,' he went on persuasively. 'She

is paid wages and has time off. We are servants as she is.'

'But you are slaves!'

'I wish we could be servants. I could be content as your servant. I could serve you and have my pride.'

'It's not possible . . .'

'No, Frances,' he said quickly. 'It is *this* which is not possible. I cannot be owned by you any longer. I have to have my freedom. I cannot be with you as I want to be with you, unless I am a free man. Anything else shames us both. I want you to pay me, to pay all of us, and then at least I would be here by my own choice, I would be my own man.'

'Josiah would never agree . . . Sarah would never allow it.'

'If you paid me enough, I could rent a room and you could come to me. We could be together under my roof, not hidden, not secret.'

She shook her head. 'It is not possible, my dear. It is not possible.'

'You are the owner.'

'In name alone. Everything I own, from my clothes to my father's dining table, became Josiah's when we married. It is his scheme, he bought you and the others. If you and the others were freed who would pay? Sarah keeps the accounts, there are the shipping costs and your food and livery . . .'

'We could pay you back, out of our wages.'

She shook her head. 'Mehuru – you have been sold and John has been sold for a hundred and ten guineas each! You could never earn that amount! Cook is paid only thirteen pounds a year, and she is trained. This is all part of a scheme, you are the first consignment and then there will be other slaves coming and they . . .' She trailed off at the thunder-struck look on his face. 'What is the matter? What is it?'

'Did you say I am sold? And the little boy John is sold?'

She nodded.

'You have sold me?'

Her eyes flickered from him to the door as if she wished someone would interrupt them. 'Cicero, I –'

'Don't call me that!'

'What?'

'Don't call me Cicero!' he said in a sharp undertone. 'In your bedroom you called me Mehuru! I won't be a free man in your bed and a slave in your parlour.'

'Mehuru . . . the sale has not gone through. It was an offer only, and Josiah has accepted it. It was before Easter . . . before I knew . . . It was before we . . . I did not think . . .'

He turned sharply, strode over to the window and glared out into the backyard. It was a warm sunny morning. A rose bush, sprawling over the backyard wall, was slowly opening its buds. He watched a bee land and struggle through the rich parcel of petals to the orange centre.

'You will sell me?'

She could not see his face, and did not know what the tight tone in his voice might mean.

'No,' she protested. She could feel a sense of panic rising. She had never argued with a man before, she had never faced a man's anger. 'Please, Mehuru, be patient. You know I could not bear to be without you. You know that. I will tell Josiah that we have to keep you, and we will sell Julius in your place.'

He turned on his heel. 'Until you are tired of me,' he said bitingly. 'When you have had your fill of me you can sell me then. You could sell me to a woman who wanted a man, with a special recommendation. You could tell her I am not fit to be paid a wage for a decent day's work but that I can be played with and . . .' in his anger he stumbled over the English words, but he made an obscene gesture with his hand '. . . used like a bull to a cow.'

Frances went white and dropped into a chair. 'It isn't like that . . . it isn't like that . . .'

He stalked to the door. 'Excuse me. I have not carried the

328

nightsoil pail down from the women's room. It will be stinking. I have work to do.'

'Mehuru!' she called. But the door had slammed behind him and he was gone.

Frances rose from her chair, ran to the door and flung it open. But in the empty hall she hesitated, her hand on her heart to still its painful racing. She could not cry out for him, she could not chase him around the house. He was her servant, he was lower than her servant; he was her slave. To betray for one instant that she had forgotten her position and his would be a disgrace so total that death itself could not be worse. If Josiah knew, if Sarah knew . . . Frances shuddered at the thought and went back into the parlour. She seated herself again at the table and stared unseeingly at the notepaper.

Anyone coming into the parlour would have seen a Lady of Quality, fashionably dressed, writing letters. Frances, as still and as elegant as if she were sitting for her portrait, listened, in case Mehuru relented and came back into the parlour. She listened and she waited all morning. The rapid fluctuating beat of her heart raced every time she heard a footstep in the hall; but he did not come.

Chapter Twenty-five

At midday Josiah came home from the coffee house where he had been forward selling the cargo of *Daisy*. She had been seen loading off Africa and should be home in December. Josiah wanted to raise money to give him some ready cash for the housekeeping costs. He was gambling that she would be home on time and with a good cargo of sugar. He met a friend of Stephen Waring's, Mr Green, who was enthusiastic about the Hot Well lease. He assured Josiah that it was a fine piece of business, and only his commitment to building in Clifton meant that he himself was not in the running for it. In the meantime, he offered Josiah a Hot Well lodging house at a price which anyone could see was attractive. He complimented Josiah in seeing the opportunity of the Hot Well for what it was, a potential gold mine. Josiah came home excitable, and with a sense of moving in the circles of the highest power in Bristol where a whisper could make or break a man.

Frances hastily sent down a message to Cook that Josiah was home and wanted some luncheon. Within half an hour a cold collation was laid in the morning room. Sarah joined them.

'You are pale, Frances,' she observed. 'Are you unwell again?'

Frances shook her head. 'I am perfectly well,' she said. A small niggling pain at her heart contradicted her but she ignored it.

'Will you take a little rum and water?' Josiah offered.

Frances refused. 'No. I will have a glass of ratafia and just a piece of bread and butter.'

He helped her to her place and rang the bell. 'I had an enquiry for one of our boys. The surviving one is promised to Mr Waring. He is well enough to be sold now, is he not?'

Frances caught her breath. 'Oh no,' she said hastily. 'Not yet. I don't think so. And he is very little.' She glanced over at Mary who was serving them from the sideboard and who knew enough English to follow the conversation.

'How old d'you think he is?' Josiah asked around a mouthful of bread and ham.

'About four years, perhaps five,' Frances answered.

'Old enough then to run errands. He could go as a pageboy.'

'I am not yet happy about his health,' Frances said desperately. 'It would look very bad if we sold him and then he was sick or even died. We must make sure he is well before we let him go.'

'Yes,' Josiah agreed. 'But we could use the money, Frances.'

'What news of *Rose*?' Sarah demanded. 'Have you had bad news, Josiah?'

He shook his head. 'No, no news at all, Sister. I was thinking merely that it is time that the slaves were sold. We have had them for more than half a year. We always thought they would go within six months.'

'Their training was so interrupted, with moving house and everything,' Frances insisted breathlessly. 'You must give me longer. If they are to be a credit to us ... They don't all speak well ... and we have to keep Mehuru, I mean Cicero, to run the house and train the others ...'

'Very well,' Josiah said pacifically. 'No matter. Whenever you think fit, my dear.'

Unseen under the table, Frances pushed her fist against her ribcage where she could feel a sharp, growing pain.

'And what have you been doing this morning?' Josiah asked, making ponderous conversation.

'I have written to my Uncle Scott,' Frances said. 'He is staying with some friends in Yorkshire.'

'Yorkshire, eh?' Josiah exclaimed. 'I have no friends in Yorkshire, I am sure. That's where that blackguard Wilberforce comes from, they're very hot on Abolition in Yorkshire, it is a nest of agitators.' Josiah nodded at Sarah. 'I think we have no cause for concern as yet. The Venturers say that it will all blow over. Wilberforce has the support of only a few men, and we are a powerful lobby. All the main cities of the kingdom and all the manufacturers are against him.'

'When is the vote?' Frances asked. 'It is this month, is it not?'

'The eleventh,' Josiah replied heavily.

'What would we do if the Trade were to be abolished?'

Josiah gave her a small smile. 'Beg, borrow or buy ships and do as many voyages as we could. The profits on slaves would go through the roof.'

'If it were banned?'

'No ban would be immediate,' Sarah explained. 'Any ban on the Trade would take several years to come in, and during that time prices would be at a premium. Everyone would want to stock up while they could.'

'And compensation would be paid to slavers,' Josiah supplemented. 'The greater profits one could show the greater the compensation. But in any case, I am not afraid of Abolition. We have too much power. This is our Parliament chosen by our electorate and stuffed with our placemen. Of course it will serve the interests of honest Traders and landlords.'

Frances nodded.

'I shall drive out to the Hot Well this afternoon,' Josiah said. 'Will you come with me, Frances? I want to see how busy it is mid-week. This is the prime season, it should be coining money.'

'Certainly,' Frances replied. She had a swift thought that now she would not be able to see Mehuru until the evening. But Josiah's wishes must come first. 'I would like to see it.'

'You can take a glass of the water,' Josiah said cheerfully. 'Will you come, Sister? You must come and see it. I am serious about buying the lease, I have had sight of the books and they show that the major expenditure has all been made. Stephen Waring is sure that we can earn a return from it.'

'A return such as a voyage to Africa and the West Indies will make?' Sarah demanded. 'I doubt it.'

'A different business with different costs and different benefits,' Josiah assured her. 'We have to move with the times, Sarah. All the great Merchant Venturer companies have shipping but they have land and collieries and building interests too. We have to be like them – we have to have some of our money out at sea and some of it safe home here on shore. And it is steady, Sarah. There is not the long wait for your profit. Now that we have high and steady expenses we need a business which pays us every month, not once every two years.'

Sarah cleared her throat. 'You can go, Mary,' she said. Mary curtseyed and left the room. Sarah waited until the door had closed behind her. 'I did not want to speak before her but, Brother, I must speak to you and Frances frankly.'

Josiah looked deeply unhappy. 'Speak, Sarah. You know I always value your advice. This is your company as much as it is mine, and your fortune as well as mine depends on it.'

Sarah glanced at Frances. 'I am not against Frances, or you, Brother,' she began. 'But I must question what is happening to the company. In my father's day and in the early days when you and I ran the company we took a pride in trading with cash in hand. We bought trade goods with cash, we bought slaves with trade goods, we sold slaves for gold,

333

we bought sugar with gold, and we sold sugar at a profit on the quayside for more gold which then paid for the next voyage.'

Josiah nodded.

'When we realised that the Trade was slipping away, that fewer and fewer large investors were taking a share on our voyages, we decided to sell slaves direct into England. You married Frances to obtain her dowry to finance their purchase and so that she should teach them for free and sell them to her friends.'

Frances, who had never before heard Josiah's proposal explained in such bald terms, blinked, but could not disagree.

'Why do we now think of changing everything?' Sarah demanded passionately. 'The money we earn from the sale of these slaves should buy more slaves. The money we earn from each voyage should equip another voyage. But instead it is being wasted on this house and high living, and all I hear from you is one scheme after another. We do not need schemes. We already know how to make a profit. Trade is what we have always done and trade is what we should do – trade with cash in hand.'

Josiah and Frances were silent.

'There is another thing,' Sarah continued more quietly. 'I know that you have longed all your life to be a Merchant Venturer and I congratulate you on your election to the Company. I believe it was bound to come to you in time, as an honest, profitable Bristol Trader. But I would remind you, Brother, that these are new friends, they are not tried and tested. If Mr Waring advises you of an opportunity or wants to borrow money, you should treat him with as much suspicion as an out-of-work captain in the coffee house. He cheated us over this house . . .'

'Now, Sarah! He never did!' Josiah exclaimed.

'He did! He did!' she cried passionately. 'Three houses on the market the moment we paid him the deposit. All of them friends and neighbours of his! All of them cheaper than this! He told them to hold off until he had landed his fish, Josiah. And you are so besotted with becoming gentry you will not see it.'

She had caught him on the raw. His voice rose to match hers. 'How dare you say such a thing! In all my years trading I have never been bested but I have always seen chances which you would have missed. You've never moved on, Sarah. You've always looked back. You were happiest living with Da over the warehouse and with one racked old boat. You think small, Sarah, and you want to cut me down to your size!'

Frances ducked her head down and sliced bread and butter into tiny slivers, longing to be out of the room and away from the loud voices.

'I think as you should think,' Sarah hissed. 'I think that you are a small trader and now you are swimming in a large pond with greedy men who will gobble you up, Josiah. I do not trust Stephen Waring. I do not trust his ideas. And I certainly do not trust the Hot Well if it comes with his recommendation! Why can you not see that! Why can you not keep to the Trade you know?'

Josiah pushed his plate away and strode to the window, his face flushed, his feet stamping on the floor in anger. He glared out of the window and a street seller who had been about to set up his pitch and sing his ballads picked up his tray and hastily moved on.

Josiah gripped the windowsill until his knuckles showed white. He fought his anger until he had it under control. Then he cleared his throat and turned back to the table. 'Now, Sarah,' he said kindly. 'Don't rant at me. I am trying to do my best. Let me explain my thinking to you and let us be friends.'

She was still quivering but she nodded that she would listen. Brother and sister glanced down the table to Frances.

Her head bent low, she was pleating and re-pleating the napkin in her lap. Brother and sister regarded her with mild irritation, and then returned their attention to each other.

'When we buy goods – trade, slaves, whatever – we move them to make our profit. We take them to another market where they command a better price.'

Sarah nodded.

'And it costs us to move them. We can never be sure what damage a ship will suffer. It can lose a mast, it can lose its sails. If the worst occurs we can lose the whole ship and the crew and cargo.'

Sarah nodded again. 'So?'

'But when we buy land – such as the Hot Well spring – we can work it where it is. We know the risks. Nothing can go wrong with it. It's not like a ship tossed about by the wind and the weather. The water comes out of the ground hot and bubbling and we bottle it and sell it, or we sell it at the spa. It's safe money, Sarah. Safer than your ships. And there's another profit, a hidden profit.'

'How?' she asked reluctantly.

'Everything is costing more,' Josiah said. 'It was his lordship, Lord Scott himself, who showed it to me. We were talking about his rent rolls when Frances's dowry was to be paid and he showed me. They are using new methods to farm, the land is yielding more, and so every farm, every farm in England, is more valuable than it was twenty years ago. The ground beneath our feet, even here in the city, is more valuable. When we come to sell this house we will get more than we paid for it. When we come to sell the Hot Well we will get more than we paid for it. Every day, everything we own becomes more valuable.'

Sarah shook her head at the incredible concept.

'It is like a miracle,' Josiah breathed. 'A miracle, Sarah. Everything we own is becoming more valuable. Even the warehouse, even the rock of the caves. Everything is growing in profit. All we have to do is to turn the warehouse, the rock, the land under our feet into cash.'

Sarah would have interrupted but Josiah was entranced by the prospect of self-generating wealth. 'Look at the prices for land on Park Street. If we had bought land either side of the street ten, twenty years ago we could have had it for ten pounds an acre. Do you know what it is worth now?'

Sarah shook her head.

'Hundreds,' Josiah said. 'You could name your price.'

'But we did not buy it,' Sarah maintained stubbornly. 'Because we did not know that it was going to become fashionable. We did not know it would be valuable. We could not have predicted it. You have never looked beyond a house here, in this square.'

'Yes, but now we can make predictions,' Josiah said. 'We did not guess that people like the Warings would move up the hill to Park Street because we did not know them. I did not hear them speak of it, I was not invited to their table in the coffee house. But now I *am* there, Sarah, and I *do* hear the rumours. Now I *know* where the fashion is taking hold. And I tell you, it is the Hot Well, it is Park Street. We are too late for Park Street. But we can snatch at the Hot Well and in ten years' time we can sell it for ten times what we have paid for it, as well as running it at a profit now.'

Sarah was almost convinced. 'But if this is so,' she asked slowly, 'if it is such an excellent deal then why are the Merchant Venturers selling it? Why is Mr Waring not buying it himself?'

Josiah slammed his fist into his cupped palm. 'Because I have hit it right! I have! Me! This is my moment! This is my time! Waring is buying land in Clifton – but there will be no development of Clifton for fifty years, he is in too early. James – the tenant of the Hot Well – was in too soon. The Company has done all the improvements and want their money repaid. I have caught this fashion on the bough –

337

Clifton may be the very place in twenty years' time, Park Street was tempting ten years ago – but the time for the Hot Well is now! And here I am now! I am ready to buy in now!'

'What with?' Sarah demanded. As ever she went to the very heart of the question.

'I shall borrow against *Daisy*'s cargo, and two thousand pounds against *Rose*.'

She nearly moaned. 'Borrow more against *Rose*? You have forestalled her cargo already to buy this house. If she fails we will be ruined!'

'I own half the cargo,' he confessed. 'I could not get partners for her and now I am glad of it. I shall borrow every penny I can against her profits, and *Daisy*'s too.'

'Two ships carrying debt?' she demanded.

'Yes,' Josiah said defiantly. 'Look around you, Sarah! No-one trades with their own money any more. All the big schemes are done with loaned money. All the coal mines, all the foundries, all the industries are launched on borrowed money. You know that is the truth.'

'It is not our way.'

'No, and our way has been slow and sure. But I want to go faster, Sarah. I want the Hot Well. I can show you the figures and you will know I am right. We have to borrow to buy into the lease. I am determined that we should do it.'

Sarah turned from his stubborn face. 'Frances!' she appealed. 'This is your fortune too. Do you want to see Josiah borrow against a ship which has not even docked?'

Frances had relaxed when Josiah had controlled his anger and they had stopped shouting. She was thinking of Mehuru and wondering when she could see him again and how she could divert him from his demand for wages. She gave a little start and used her usual excuse. 'I am sorry. I know so little about business.'

Sarah turned back to her brother. 'I see you are determined,' she said. The colour had drained from her face.

338

'I am.'

'You will go ahead with this scheme, whatever I say?'

He nodded.

Sarah paused for a moment, measuring her will against his. 'You promised my father that I should share in the running of his business,' she reminded him bitterly. 'You made a deathbed promise, Josiah.'

'I did, and I have never broken it.'

She glared at him. 'You are breaking it now, when you will not listen to my advice, when you run headlong into debt and into schemes that we know nothing about.'

'I promised you should share in the running of the business,' he said. 'I never promised that you should rule the roast. I never promised that you should stand in my way and so ruin me.'

'I!' she exclaimed. 'I! Ruin *you*!'

He was quick and biting. 'Yes, you. You still keep the household books, you see how much money we spend every month. Where is it to come from, Sarah? We will be ruined if we do not find new ways to make money, new ventures. Not even you can wish us sold up and back at the dockside.'

She was silenced.

'We have to go forward,' Josiah insisted stubbornly. 'To hesitate is to be wrecked.'

They were both silent. 'I have not seen the ships' books since we moved house,' Sarah said. 'I have not brought them up to date. I shall need to enter these debts you are incurring, I shall need to show that you have sold their cargoes.'

'They are at the warehouse,' Josiah told her. He rose to his feet and went to the door. 'I have opened my office down there. I have taken on a clerk. He will keep the books for me. It is more convenient so.'

He did not dare face her. He opened the door and slipped away from her before he could see her stricken face.

Chapter Twenty-six

~~~

The drive to the Hot Well was not a great success. The day had clouded over and under the dark bellies of storm clouds the little colonnade of shops and the Pump Room did not look pretty and inviting, but seemed overwhelmed by the lowering cliffs above. The tide was out, the river oozed between greasy banks of brown mud and the sweet sickly smell of sewage lingered. Every day that the sun grew hotter increased the stench. The wind ruffling the low-tide river was heavy with it.

The Pump Room was built on an imposing scale but it had the inescapable appearance of a warehouse. Frances, looking at the blank wall fronting the river, and the windows set square in the three-storey-high stonework without any relief or decoration, thought that in every corner the city of Bristol was dominated by trade. Even this most important building had an uneven roof, odd-numbered chimneys, and faced the river as blankly and as plainly as a tide mill for grinding corn.

At the back of the Pump Room, at the free pump which dispensed the spa water without charge, there was a collection of sickly paupers. When they saw the carriage they came forward with their hands out, begging for pennies. Josiah waved them away and the hired coachman gestured with his whip. One of them, a young woman, raised her face blotched livid with a skin disease. Frances shrank back into the carriage.

'Aye, they're off-putting,' Josiah conceded. 'Get back, you!' he shouted. 'You're upsetting my wife.'

They stepped back but Frances heard a muffled curse as she hurried out of the road and into the assembly room. The place was busy. Josiah looked around, visibly counting the number of customers while Frances swallowed a glass of the water. She was hoping that it would quiet the fluttering in her chest which had pained her ever since the quarrel with Mehuru in the morning. Josiah noted the white faces of the invalids with consumption, and heard the dry racking coughs of those with chest complaints. There were fashionable people visiting for the day and taking tea, or expensive hot-house strawberries with cream, but there were not enough.

'Can we make it more fashionable?' he asked. 'What would you do?'

Frances thought. 'I would rent consulting rooms cheaply to good doctors,' she said. 'They will bring the patients in. And perhaps build a bath house, with beautiful mosaics, and plants, and furniture, like a winter garden.'

Josiah nodded. 'The bath house,' he said. 'What would it be like?'

Frances considered. 'What about large windows and a terrace overlooking the river? And build it like a hot house, like the hot house at Whiteleaze. Oh! I forgot you have never seen it. But it is a fine large room and very light. Very well-heated with many plants. It is a pleasant place to sit in winter. And when the fruit comes into season it is like sitting in a garden. We could call it the Bristol Winter Garden! So that the Hot Well was popular all the year round.'

'That's it!' Josiah exclaimed. 'Frances, you are a genius! Do you know who should design it for us? Who is the finest architect?'

'We need someone who designs follies and grottoes,' she said. 'Something charming and romantic and out of the ordinary.'

Josiah shook his head. 'I don't mix with such people. There's a grotto at Goldney House, in Clifton, I know. But I've heard it is very strange. Full of shells and pagan statues, and a fountain.'

'That's the very thing,' Frances said decidedly. 'A fountain and classical statues. We want a Gothic bath house. Lord Scott will know the best man to design it.'

'Gothic!' Josiah exclaimed. 'Will it not look very strange?'

'A little strange.' Frances smiled at his uneasy face. 'But it has to be a little strange to draw people from Bath. Bath is such an established place, everyone knows of it, everyone goes there. We need to create something very fanciful, something that will draw people who love a novelty.'

'You know best,' Josiah said firmly, reassuring himself. 'Will you write to his lordship and ask him?'

'Yes,' Frances agreed. 'I was writing to him this morning, I have not yet sealed and posted it. I was telling him that Sir Charles Fairley wishes to buy Shelby Manor. He will come to us to sign the papers and he wishes us to hold his capital for his house and deal with his land agent.'

Josiah grimaced. 'Will it not take a lot of letter writing and bother?' he asked.

'Josiah!' Frances exclaimed. 'We are to hold his capital! We can invest it as we wish! I should have thought that it was worth a good deal of letter writing and bother!'

'I have always done my business face to face,' he excused himself. 'I hate writing letters.'

'It is very little effort,' Frances said. 'I can do it, and my uncle advises on investments for Sir Charles. All I have to do is to keep a note and render him an account.'

'Will you do it? Or ask Sarah?'

'I can do it,' Frances said easily. 'Sarah prefers ships.'

'She should have been a captain,' Josiah agreed. 'Did you hear her at lunch today? She cannot tolerate the thought of spending money on anything which does not float.'

'She has your interests at heart,' Frances said pacifically. 'And it has been a big change for her, moving house, and my arrival.'

Josiah nodded, and glanced once more around the room. 'Does it get busier later on?' he asked the woman serving the water. 'What is the trade like in winter?'

'On a weekday in winter it is like the death house,' she said cheerfully. 'Sometimes no-one is here at all, and sometimes the only visitors are the incurables. Very gloomy, sir. If you want a jolly place you had better go to Bath.'

'Why, I thank you,' Josiah snapped, instantly irritated. 'We were going anyway.' He offered his arm to Frances and swept her from the room. 'As soon as we purchase the lease that woman is sacked,' he said. 'Telling paying customers that the place is like a death house!'

The skies outside were darker than ever. As they got into the carriage there was a low warning rumble of thunder and a few drops of rain started to fall. The horses were restless. 'Here!' Josiah said to the coachman. 'Put the hood up, please.'

The man called to a lad and ordered him to hold the horses. He got down from the driving box and came to the back of the carriage to try to lift the folding roof, which was made of canvas, folded back on wooden hoops. It should have unfolded easily from both the back and front of the carriage and stretched over the seats to lock together in the middle. But the joints were rusted and would not shift. The coachman pulled at them. The rain started to fall more heavily. Frances seated herself in the carriage and pulled a rug over her knees.

A cold wind blew down the gorge. The tide was on the turn and little waves slapped against the mud, the wind whipping them into white-crested ripples. The thunder was blown in with the incoming tide; there was a loud roar immediately overhead and the rain fell harder and faster. Frances shrank back into the carriage and tried to wrap the rug tighter

343

around her knees. She was wearing only a light coat and a silk gown underneath. Her bonnet flapped dangerously in the wind.

'My wife is getting soaked!' Josiah exclaimed. 'Can you not get the hood up?'

'I am sorry, sir, it is stuck,' the man apologised. 'I am trying.' His words were drowned out by a tremendous thunderclap. Frances screamed as the whole world went brilliantly white for a moment and then black.

Josiah leaped down from the carriage and pulled at the other side, trying to free the rusty catches. The horses moved uneasily, and Frances called, 'Hold the horses, Josiah! They will bolt!'

There was a sudden scud of bitterly cold rain. 'This is hopeless!' Josiah shouted. 'Get down, Frances, and we will wait for it to pass.'

'I'm so wet,' she cried. 'Let us just drive home as quick as we can.'

'Drive then!' Josiah shouted at the coachman. 'But I shall not pay for this hire!'

The coachman swung himself on to the box and let the frightened horses go forward. They sprang into a trot and he had to steady them. The speed of the coach whipped rain into Frances's face, tumbled her hair, blew her bonnet. She had the driving rug clutched around her legs but it was quickly soaked through. Rain collected on the brim of her bonnet and then poured down her neck. She was shivering and chilled.

The rain pelted down on them. There was no shelter at all. The rug around Frances's legs was sodden in moments and she could feel the damp seeping through her skirt and through the thin soles of her shoes.

By the time they drew up outside the house she was wet through to the skin and her teeth were chattering from the cold. Martha, who had been on the watch for them, threw open the door and Mehuru came running down the steps, opened the carriage door and pulled the folding steps out so that Frances could step down and he could rush her into the warmth of the house.

Elizabeth swept her upstairs and within moments Frances was stripped of her wet clothes, wrapped in warm blankets and seated by the fire. But still she shivered and the colour was drained from her face and her lips were pale.

'You cold, Mrs Cole?' Elizabeth asked, looking anxiously at her. 'You sick?'

'Just chilled,' Frances said, trying to smile and hold her chattering teeth still. 'Fetch me some hot tea. I am quite well.'

Elizabeth nodded and went from the room. Mehuru was lingering outside. 'Is she all right?' he asked in Yoruban. 'Can I go in and see her? Is she all right?'

Elizabeth shook her head. 'You cannot go in, she is undressed. She says she is well. She does not look well to me. You are the healer, what can you see?'

Mehuru hesitated. It had been so long since he had used his priestly gifts, they were like a tool he had mislaid. He had watched Frances as a lover, not as a healer. He paused for a moment and brought her face into his imagination, noted the heavy sweep of dark hair and the shadows which were always there under her eyes, the transparent skin and the frequent rosy blushes. He sensed a pain in his chest which he knew was her pain, a permanent squirm of discomfort like a murmur in the heart. He felt a tightness across the lungs, and thought of Frances's continual gesture of putting her hand to her throat when she was breathless. 'She is a white woman,' he said, trying to reassure himself, discounting his insight. 'They all look sick to me.'

Josiah treated himself to a bowl of steaming punch and called Kbara to light a fire in his study. As he warmed the seat of his dressing gown there was a tap at the door and Sarah came in.

'I heard that you and Frances were caught in the storm,' she said. 'The slave Elizabeth thinks we should send for Dr Hadley for Frances. Should you see him, Brother?'

He noted her controlled tone. 'No, I am well. What's amiss with Frances?'

Sarah did not hide her lack of concern. 'She's always ill with something.'

'What do you want, Sarah?' he asked.

She took a deep breath and faced him. 'I want sight of the books,' she said. 'The ships' accounts. I have done them all my life, Brother. Even if you have a clerk he will still need to be overseen. Let me check his work for you. Let me see the ships' books.'

Josiah turned his back to her to warm his hands at the fire. He could not let her see them. *Rose* had gone out uninsured for the middle passage and Sarah would spot the discrepancy at once. Sarah had no idea of the household debts, nor the interest Josiah was paying on his borrowings. He could not face her distress if she saw the full figures.

'Certainly,' he said. 'I will bring them home for you to see. At the moment the clerk is studying them, to make sure he does things your way.'

'I could teach him . . .' Sarah volunteered hastily.

'In a week or two,' Josiah interrupted. 'You shall see him and go through the books with him.'

'It is not just the work,' Sarah said hesitantly. 'Though it is hard for me to do nothing, to do worse than nothing, when I have been so busy for all my life.'

Josiah glanced at her over his shoulder. Her mouth was working, she was biting back rare tears.

'I do not feel at home here,' she said pitifully. 'It is not what I am used to.'

'You cannot miss the noise and the stink of the quayside, Sarah!'

She nodded. 'Even the smell of the dock at low tide,' she confessed. 'I have nothing to do here. And I am of no use to you. Frances runs the house, and you talk to her about your schemes.'

He almost turned and held out his arms to her, he almost showed his deep abiding love for her, the sister who had mothered him through a harsh loveless childhood. But the habits of coldness were too strong for them both. He gave an awkward shrug and cleared his throat. He could think of nothing to say.

She stood for a few moments, waiting to see if he would reply. Then when he said nothing she turned and went to the door. 'I shall send for the doctor if you insist,' she said unpleasantly. 'I imagine Frances will want to linger in bed for weeks.'

Chapter Twenty-seven

Frances was seriously ill after her soaking at the Hot Well and Mehuru could not see her for several days. He had to hand over the coal scuttle for her bedroom fire at the door to Elizabeth or to one of the other women, and the hot water for her washbasin was taken from him by Martha, Mary or Elizabeth. One of the women carried her meals up to her on a tray, and Elizabeth was ordered to sleep at the foot of her bed on a little truckle bed in case she was ill in the night.

With Josiah absorbed in his plans for the Hot Well and Frances sick, the slaves were freer than they had ever been. In the afternoons the women would take the children to play in the gardens of the square. No-one complained, people soon became used to seeing little John, and eight-year-old Susan and Matthew on the grass beneath the young trees playing the tiny intricate children's games of Africa which Elizabeth taught them.

They became a new kind of family, an invention all of their own. An African family which mostly spoke English, a black family clothed in cotton and heavy serge, a community with two men but headed unquestionably by the women. And – less comfortably – a family that snatched at a little space and a little time, and could be torn apart and sold away from each other at any moment.

They never forgot that they were slaves and that their happiness and security depended completely on the slender thread of their owner's whim. In the evening, when they sat around the kitchen table, the boys and girls painstakingly reading, or the girls sewing while the boys played jacks, the adults would talk softly about what they could do to secure their freedom, how they could gain their liberty and stay together.

Dr Hadley came and said that Frances was suffering from an inflammation of the lungs brought on by the chill. He prescribed rest and warmth. Mehuru waited outside the house and held the horse to create an opportunity to speak to him.

'She's not desperately ill,' Hadley said cheerfully. 'But she's not strong. She's one of these delicate highly strung women. She cannot bear much anxiety and anger, and there are weak hearts in her family. Her mother died when her heart failed and Mrs Cole has that pale, dark-eyed look. She needs a calm life. She should be living in the country. She has delicate lungs and the air here is poison.'

'Would she be well in the country?' Mehuru asked. He had a sudden vision of Frances seated at her leisure on the terrace of a little farmhouse in the hot reliable sunshine of his home. He imagined a parasol of silk shading her from the sun, and her skin flushed with heat and health.

'She'd be better,' Hadley said. 'Will we see you on Tuesday night? We are hoping for news of the Abolition debate. Wilberforce will speak on Monday night to the house. Caesar has promised to send us a messenger.'

'I would not miss it for anything,' Mehuru declared. He glanced at the windows of the house. 'But I had better go now.'

Hadley pressed a coin into his hand. Mehuru instantly recoiled. 'I don't want this!'

'For holding my horse,' Hadley said patiently. 'I would give it to anyone who held my horse for me.'

Pride and necessity fought across Mehuru's face. 'Very well,' he agreed unwillingly. 'I thank you.'

Stuart gave him a quick boyish grin. 'Well, I thank you for taking it. I thought you were about to throw it back at me.'

Mehuru smiled reluctantly. 'I am not used to being in service,' he said. 'I do not wish to become used to it, either.'

'Have you had a chance to read those pamphlets?' Dr Hadley asked, climbing into the driving seat.

Mehuru released the horse and stood back. 'I have read them. And I am reading them aloud to my friends. We talk in the kitchen at night.'

'Excellent,' Hadley said. 'The more who understand the better! These are times of great change and you and I can play our part.'

Mehuru nodded. 'I am a radical,' he observed, experimenting with a new word.

Stuart shot a nervous look up and down the street. 'Well, for pity's sake keep it to yourself,' he warned. 'Or you will be a dead radical and I will be blacklisted among the Bristol merchants.'

Mehuru grinned. 'Being black is not such a bad thing.'

'And when you start punning in English you have learned too much,' Stuart said. He waved his whip. 'Good day!'

Scott House.

9th May 1789

'*Dear Niece,*

I Enclose the lease for Sir Charles's Signature. It is a handsome Property and I have sold it to him at a Fair price. You will note that I have Not sold him the Mineral rights to the land. He did not Ask for these and I would rather they 'Remained in my Keeping. You will Oblige Me if you do not draw his attention to this slight Omission.

In reply to Josiah's question about the Agitation for the Abolition of the Slave Trade, I am assured that Wilberforce

350

has only Pitt's support and Few others. But Outside the House there is a Rising mood of Radicalism in the Country which can only Dismay all men of True patriotism.

As I Understand it – and this News is for you and Josiah Alone – the plan is to Affect to go along with Wilberforce and to Adjourn the debate, For ever. I am assured that No Slave Trader need fear for his Income during the life of this Parliament. Liverpool, Bristol, and the London merchants are Pouring money into the pockets of their Placemen to Stall the Debate and there can be No Doubt that the Abolitionists are A Small minority in the Commons. In the House of Lords of course, There are None, and Never Will be. Every Lord and most Gentlemen have Some part of their Fortune invested in slavery, be it Sugar, Rum, Cotton, or Tobacco – or Even, Shipping, Canals, and House Building – all of Which Depend on General Prosperity.

There is a Powerful Unity among the working Men and the Free Negroes in London. They see their Cause as One and the Same. Our Interest, as Employers of the One and Owners of the Other, must be to Separate them. If we can Persuade white working Men that Negroes are an Inferior Animal then we will Sever this Inconvenient unity. For the meantime – do not Fear. Negroes and Working men will always have one thing in common: they Lack All power. They have neither Money, nor the Ear of the country, nor a Vote to change their Masters. We are Secure.

I have a very Pretty investment in Mind at the moment and if your Holdings for Sir Charles could Advance one thousand pounds I could buy him a share. Let me know by

351

Return of post. It is a proposed Colliery in Kent.

Family news is that Lady Scott is expecting Another child, and she is Confident that this time she will bear me an Heir. You can imagine how Dearly I hope that she is right. She will Remain in her Lodgings at the Sea until Autumn and then I shall Expect her to stay Quietly at Whiteleaze until my Son is born.

As to your question about your Acquaintance who finds herself attracted to A Nobleman. I will speak frankly to You, my dear. I do not like these mixed marriages between the Ranks of Society. A Lady cannot be Satisfied with a man who is in every way, except Financial, her Inferior. She is bound to meet a man of her own Rank whose company she Prefers. However she has Married into a class which does not tolerate Freedom in these matters and an Indiscretion would be fatal. A Lady has to put Aside her own Inclinations and remain Faithful to her husband. Any other Choice is Disaster for her and for her Family. Her Dishonour Shames all – Family and friends. I heartily Pity the woman who finds herself in this Plight but there is no way Open to her. She has made her Choice and she has to endure it. Please make this Clear to Your Friend. She has No Choice. She must Forget the Gentleman she loves and follow her Duty and her Marriage Vows. She has No other Choice.

I am Very Very sorry my dear.

I look forward to receiving your Speedy Reply about the Business matters. I remain your Loving uncle,

Scott.

Frances slipped the letter into the drawer of the little writing table which was balanced on the covers of her bed. She felt too exhausted to reply at once and his advice confirmed what she already knew. She had allowed herself to dream, for a moment only, that he might have written telling her that if a person is lucky enough to find a love that transforms the world around them, then nothing should stand in her way. She smiled wearily. Her uncle was hardly likely to advise her to defy the conventions, and her own life had taught her nothing but caution and fear.

All day Tuesday Mehuru haunted Josiah's study, hoping for news of the Abolition debate. Josiah also was restless. For half of the morning he waited for news from London, and then he could bear it no longer and went out to prowl around the quayside.

All along the quays there were knots of men discussing the situation. All sorts of rumours were starting: Wilberforce had been shouted down and left the House of Commons in tears. No! Not at all! Wilberforce had been acclaimed and had wept with joy. The Trade was to be banned outright, as of tomorrow. Josiah and the other men, buoyed up by hope and then flung into despair, spent an uneasy and unhappy day.

They collected in the evening in the coffee house. Stephen Waring was there.

'Cole!' he called pleasantly. 'Come and have a bowl of punch with me! I am awaiting my messenger from London with the news of the debate.'

Josiah wound his way through the gossiping men to the top table. 'I shall be glad to take a glass,' he admitted. 'This is an anxious day.'

'I am confident,' Stephen said easily. He squeezed an extra lemon into the bowl of punch, tasted it, and poured Josiah a glass.

'Yes, but you have investments all over the country,' Josiah growled irritably. 'I have three ships at sea even as I speak. What happens to men like me if they abolish overnight?'

Stephen Waring gave Josiah a long slow smile. 'They abolish!' he snorted contemptuously. 'Do cats abolish cream? Do pigs abolish the trough? The government will never abolish slavery until they cease making money from it. They are milkmaids and Africa is their cow. Slavery will flourish until it ceases to make money, Josiah. You know that.'

Josiah was warmed by the punch, and by Stephen's arrogant certainty. 'You sound very sure indeed.'

'Take another glass,' Stephen said genially. 'Business brings risk, Josiah. Who should know better than you and I? And tell me, are you determined to have the Hot Well?'

Josiah accepted the glass and took another fortifying gulp. He was diverted to his plans for the Hot Well, his fears slid away. Outside over the Redclift and Bristol quays the sun was slowly going down. Coming up the channel on the evening tide was a Bristol slaver, her decks burnished gold, her rigging like threads of brass. Seagulls whirled away from her masts like flying pennants, crying and crying. The wind blew to port the smell of death and despair. It had been an average voyage: four hundred men, women and children stacked on shelves for six months while loading and then a three-month voyage of terror, sickness, and torment. Some had gone mad, some had killed themselves, many had died of disease. Eighty had died on the voyage and been dropped overboard as carelessly as garbage from the galley. Nearly all of them sold at a profit in Jamaica would be dead within four years.

'That's a grand sight,' Josiah said, catching a glimpse of the ship from the windows of the coffee house, and thinking fondly of *Rose* and *Lily* and *Daisy*, loading off Africa.

'Beautiful,' Stephen Waring agreed.

* * *

354

Mehuru slipped out of the back door at nine o'clock. With Frances ill in her room, Josiah waiting for news from London at the quayside, and Sarah reading sermons in the parlour he would not be missed. He ran through the darkening streets to the coffee house and arrived there as Stuart Hadley's phaeton drew up outside.

'Any news?' Mehuru demanded.

'None yet,' Stuart said. He looked grave and excited, like a man who cannot believe that his battle has been won. 'Caesar promised to send word as soon as he knew which way the debate is going. He will not fail us.'

They went in together, ordered ale, and sat in the corner. Edgar Long drifted over to join them, and a couple of other men. Another freed black man came over to meet Mehuru. He was a Zulu, from the far south of Africa. To their mutual amusement they found their easiest shared language was English.

'I am getting a white tongue,' Mehuru remarked with distaste. 'Soon I will forget everything I ever knew.'

The atmosphere was edgy and nervous. Edgar Long had some predictions as to the way that the MPs would vote. He was certain that the Abolition of the Trade would be handsomely and rapidly passed. 'And then the banning of slavery altogether,' he said hungrily.

The evening dragged on. At midnight, many men muttered that they had to be at work in less than six hours, and left. Stuart, Edgar and Mehuru clung on. 'Caesar said he would send me news as soon as he could see which way it was going,' Stuart said. 'Surely there cannot be a difficulty. Everyone knows where they stand. There has been discussion enough, God knows.'

'Unless the Trade has bought more men than we knew,' Edgar suggested.

'It cannot be,' Stuart protested. 'It cannot possibly fail.'

At two in the morning a travel-stained man came into the

coffee house and glanced around. 'Over here!' Stuart shouted. The man came to their table and they pulled him down into a seat. Other men gathered around, waiting.

'What news?'

'Nothing,' he said bitterly.

'What?'

'There is no news worth the bringing,' he said savagely. 'I waited till the debate was adjourned, I slept for six hours, and then I rode down to tell you, as I promised to do. I have ridden all day to bring you the news – there is no news.'

'Here,' Mehuru said hastily and pushed a mug of ale towards the man.

He drained it and set it down on the table. 'Wilberforce started speaking in the afternoon,' he told them. 'He was simple and clear. He said that they were all guilty, himself as well, and that they should put the matter right.'

There was a murmur from the listening men. 'He had twelve resolutions to end the Trade,' the messenger said. 'And he was ready to put it to the vote.'

'And?' Stuart demanded, anguished.

'And nothing,' the man said.

'Then what?' Stuart shouted with impatience.

'Nothing,' the man said stubbornly. 'They refused to put it to the vote and half a dozen of them leaped up to speak. They never debate after midnight – you can be sure that they'll none of them lose sleep for the likes of him . . .' He jerked his thumb at Mehuru's scowling face. 'All of the placemen of the Trade were there in their fine coats and gold watches. All waiting to speak. They're going to drag it on, they're going to drag it out.'

'It will be adjourned?'

'They chattered on like fat starlings till eleven o'clock and then they adjourned it for ten days.'

'They will vote then?'

'You may think that,' the man replied scathingly. 'But I

356

wager that they chatter and chatter until the cause is lost and Wilberforce defeated, and this country as far from freedom and justice as ever, as it ever will be.'

Stuart slumped into his chair, put his head in his hands and groaned.

The men exchanged shocked looks. Mehuru felt sick.

'We fight on,' Stuart said, muffled. 'But I am going to bed now.' He looked up. 'I thank you for bringing us the news, however bad. Shall you stay the night at my house?'

'I'd be grateful,' the man said. 'I am as tired as a dog.'

'So what happens now?' Mehuru demanded.

Stuart gave him a crooked smile. 'We fight on. Next week, ten days' time, next month, next year. Shall I give you a lift to your door?'

'I'll walk,' Mehuru said miserably. 'I'm in no hurry to get back there.'

'See you next Monday,' Stuart said. 'We'll have more news then.'

Mehuru nodded and stepped out into the darkness of the May night.

In the next week Frances grew no better. The inflammation of the lungs brought on by the chill she had caught at the Hot Well had left her feeling weak and tired, and she seemed unable to throw off her fatigue. She had been convalescing for a fortnight in her room. For the first week she had seen no-one but the maids and the doctor. Now she was a little better and Josiah would sometimes sit with her after dinner, and he had agreed that Mehuru could come into her bedroom for reading lessons in the afternoon.

Frances wore her prettiest cap for his lesson, and her white embroidered robe. Elizabeth was ordered to sit in the window and darn table linen, acting as chaperone. Mehuru had a seat at the foot of Frances's bed and now and then she would lean forward and point to a passage in his book which he should read, and under cover of the book Mehuru could touch her finger with his.

It was not much of a courtship, but for Frances it was restful. She liked having Mehuru near at hand without his sudden unpredictable flashes of temper. She loved him being close to her.

Mehuru found the intimacy deeply disturbing. When his finger brushed against her hand he could hardly stop himself from seizing it and kissing her palm. When she leaned forward she was close enough for him to smell the light lavender scent of her linen. When she said, 'Catalogue, that word is catalogue, it means a list of things', he watched her lips and listened to the cadences of her voice and hardly heard the meaning of her words at all.

The afternoon was hazy with unfulfilled desire. Even Elizabeth, stitching slowly in the windowseat, was affected by the atmosphere. She rested her hands in her lap and gazed out of the window at the square where the trees were in full green leaf and the birds were criss-crossing the sky with their beaks full of food for nestlings.

Frances leaned back against her pillows and listened to Mehuru reading. She had set him a passage from the *London Magazine* about the prevalence of circulating libraries. Mehuru read fluently and easily, stumbling only once or twice over unknown words.

'How ever have you learned so quickly?' she interrupted him.

He looked up and their eyes met for long wordless moments. They were drenched in desire for each other, there was nothing to say. Elizabeth, daydreaming in the window-seat, was blind to their silent communication.

'I like different languages,' Mehuru explained slowly, the words forming and shaping in his mind while he watched Frances's face, scanning her dark eyes and her soft mouth. He thought she looked quite different from the woman he

358

had seen in the cellar of the warehouse all those months ago. She was alive now in a way she had never been before. Her pulse was more rapid, her skin as clear and light as a girl's. He thought that she had been half-dead when he first met her, and that his desire for her, and her passion for him, had brought her back, back from the very brink of coldness and a death-in-life where all these English women seemed to live.

'You have learned much quicker than the others,' Frances observed.

She was fascinated at the way his eyes could smile at her while his lips spoke of ordinary things. It was a most delicious sensual game, this speaking and listening while all the time his eyes were eating her up, his desire for her showing in every line of his body. His glance over the top of his book was a caress, when his gaze lingered on the neck of her nightgown she could almost feel his touch.

'I speak four African languages, and a little Portuguese,' Mehuru said. 'Until I came to England I thought that all white men spoke Portuguese. English is not very different from Portuguese. Some of the words are the same, as you must know.'

'I don't speak Portuguese,' Frances confessed. 'Just French, and a little Italian.'

'You are very ignorant then,' Mehuru said with provocative impertinence.

Frances reached forwards to slap his hand and only just checked herself in time.

The flirtation in his voice could not be hidden. Elizabeth in the windowseat suddenly turned her attention to the room and looked in surprise at them. Frances blushed scarlet.

'What do you think of the demands for the vote?' Mehuru asked, diplomatically changing the subject.

'I think that it is wrong,' Frances said seriously, repeating her family's received wisdom. 'It cannot be right for people who have no investment in the society to want to run it. The only people who should have power in a country are the people who own the land, they have a genuine interest.'

'In my country no-one owns land at all,' Mehuru said.

'How can that be?'

He smiled at her surprised face. 'Because there is so much land. More than you could imagine. More than all the families could claim. You could ride or walk for days and days and never see anyone. If you want a field for your own, you mark it out, and plough it and water it, and it can be called yours. We are rich in a way you could not imagine, you in this little country where everyone has to own everything for fear that someone else takes it.'

Frances was tired, she closed her eyes. 'Tell me about it,' she murmured. 'Tell me all about it.'

'The capital city is a great walled town, much bigger than Bristol,' Mehuru said. 'It is called Oyo – and the Alafin lives in the palace at the heart of the city. He is like a king, except he takes advice from the people, and acts on their wishes. He is confirmed in his place every year. It is his task to bring their wishes all together, to make an agreement. I was a diviner, I served the Ifa oracle. My patron's task was to read the oracle for the king and I served him.'

'Oh, can you tell fortunes?' Frances asked, not opening her eyes.

Mehuru looked at her pale face with tenderness. 'I can,' he said. 'I tell fortunes for silly girls like you who want to know who will love them.'

Elizabeth could follow most of the words. She put her hand over her mouth to smother a giggle. Mehuru glanced at her and winked.

'And who will love me?' Frances demanded recklessly, her eyes still tight shut.

'I shall,' he breathed.

'And how will we be together?'

'I have to see the palm of your hand.'

360

Frances blindly stretched out her hand to him and he uncurled her fingers and stroked the soft white skin of her wrist and her palm. 'What does it say?' she whispered.

'It says that we will go together to my home and you shall live in my house,' he said. Frances smiled, and snuggled down in the bed like a child listening to a bedtime story.

'And what else?'

'You shall wear gowns of indigo silk and a deep blue head-dress pinned with gold. You will be my wife and you will bear me many beautiful children.'

Frances gave a scandalised chuckle. 'Hush!'

'You will grow well in the sunshine and the hot winds from the plains,' he promised. 'You will like the countryside. The trees on the plains are so broad and strong, their shade is sweet. When the wind is high in the palm trees they rattle and roar, like a rainstorm. When it is calm you can hear a hundred, a thousand birds singing. The rivers are deep and very green, they carry the reflection of the forest so clearly that it is like two forests – one above the water growing to the sky, one below the water growing down. I shall take you to swim in the river where the sand is white and clear and when you lie in the water the little fish will swim around you and nibble at your white skin. There are white and pink lilies which float on the water like little boats, and their roots are sweet and good to eat.

'I shall take you into the forests and you can eat all sorts of sweet fruits that are just growing for free, Frances. No-one owns them, you can eat them all, you can eat all day if you want. You will see the monkeys in the treetops, you will hear the roar of the lions at night, you will see the elephants moving in great herds across the plain, and antelope and deer like a sea of tawny brown hides and sharp pretty horns.' His voice fell silent.

'She is asleep,' Elizabeth said softly in their own language. He nodded.

'You are in love with her.' It was a statement, not a question.

He nodded again.

'And she loves you?'

'I think so.'

Elizabeth rose from the windowseat and put her hand on his shoulder. 'You poor foolish man,' she said, and there was a world of pity in her voice. 'Mehuru, it was bad for you already. You have made it a hundred times worse.'

Chapter Twenty-eight

House of Lords,
Westminster.

29th May 1789

Dear Josiah,

   Just a Note written in Haste from the House to tell you
that We – the owners, the Masters, the landlords – have
Won, as I promised. The bill for the abolition of Trading in
Slaves is Talked to Death. There will be a committee which
can run forever. There will be much Hand-wringing and
Agitation which will change nothing. You can Ship all of
Africa into Slavery if you wish and No-one in England can
prevent you. This is a great Day for men of property.
Wilberforce is Sick with grief, There are some who say his
Health cannot stand the Disappointment. My Regards to
Miss Cole and to my niece,

Scott.

Mehuru read the letter left open on Josiah's desk, his face
grim. He turned to the door and felt himself shrug, philo-
sophically, slavishly – a man who expects little and receives

less. He knew that Stuart would despair and would then launch into a frenzy of pamphletting, and writing, and secret agitation. But Mehuru thought that his own anger had been sapped. You had to be a free man to feel spontaneous anger, he thought. You had to have power in your own life to feel rage. When you were a household drudge you thought no farther than the next floor to wash, the next grate to clean. When the messenger from London had told Stuart that Wilberforce had not even reached a vote, Mehuru had known then that the white men would not let him go. They would not throw away their investments, they would not give away their profits. Why should they?

Mehuru heaved the heavy coal scuttle and dumped it on the marble grate. If he wanted his freedom, he thought, he would have to run.

The Merchant Venturers were at their June supper. The cloth had been taken away and the port and rum were being passed around. Josiah was seated in the middle of a long dinner table, taking a little rum and water and smoking a pipe. His fresh aromatic tobacco leaf was passed around for others to sniff.

'Your tobacco, Cole?' someone asked him, and he nodded.

'Can you send me round a hogshead?' the man asked and then dropped his voice as the man at the head of the table tapped the heel of his knife on the wood.

'Shall we get to business?' asked Sir Henry Lord, at the head of the table. 'Before the evening begins in earnest?'

There was a roar of appreciation. Sir Henry nodded at the clerk, who quickly ran through a list of decisions which the Company had to make. All of them went through on the nod. The Bristol merchants moved with one accord, knowing their own interests, and working as a team. When they came to the issue of the Hot Well lease, Stephen Waring spoke up for Josiah's bid.

'May I say, Sir Henry, that I support this bid for the lease by my friend Josiah Cole – a new member of the Company and a merchant of enterprise whose business is well known to us all. He has asked for an assurance that the present rent for the Hot Well lease of nine hundred pounds per annum should remain the same for ten years to enable him to plan his investment.'

Sir Henry peered down the table to where Josiah was sitting. 'Are you planning new buildings at the site?' he asked.

'I plan a winter garden,' Josiah said. 'A bath house designed on romantic lines with a view over the river and plants. Like a conservatory, Sir Henry.'

'You had best take your profits first,' Sir Henry observed.

'I want to see the Hot Well as the best spa in Britain,' Josiah declared.

Sir Henry nodded like a man prepared to keep his opinion to himself, and said nothing.

'M'friend Cole is prepared to pay two thousand pounds entry to the lease, payable at once, and the rent for the first year at once,' Stephen Waring reminded him.

Mr James, the previous tenant who had resigned from the lease when the Company made their improvements, raised his glass to Josiah in a gesture which could have been seen as a tribute to superior financial acumen. Josiah smiled and bowed his head at him.

'Very well,' Sir Henry said. He looked towards the clerk. 'You have the papers, Browning?'

The clerk produced a lease, and took it to Sir Henry. 'Sign on, then,' Sir Henry said. He scrawled his signature at the foot of the papers and waved them away. The clerk took them down to Josiah with a pen and a standish of ink. Josiah, beaming with triumph, signed his name in his round honest script at the foot of the document and knew that his career as an entrepreneur had truly begun.

'I wish you the best of luck with it, the very best of luck!' Mr James drawled from the other side of the table.

Josiah tried not to look superior.

'You will make a handsome profit from it, I don't doubt,' Mr James went on. 'I should have stayed in longer, I know. But I had to free my capital for other schemes. It should be a little gold mine for you.'

'I hope so,' Josiah said modestly.

'Is it your only investment?'

'My first, not my only, my first on land.'

'I am surprised you are not buying leases and building,' Mr James said. 'I thought everyone was buying building land.'

'I have connections which make the Hot Well particularly attractive,' Josiah said discreetly. 'And I have no knowledge of the building trade.'

'Oh, that does not seem to stop anyone. Half of the men I know are building. It is like a plague and we have all caught it!'

Josiah nodded. 'Timing is everything. Clifton and the Downs is a long-term prospect. The Hot Well is more immediate. It suits my plans.'

'Well, the best of luck,' Mr James said. 'It is a high rent, that, a crippling rent, you know. How will you ever meet it?'

'I shall increase charges, of course,' Josiah said. 'No more family rates, no discounts for local people, no free water given away. And I hope to attract more trade from London. The fashionable crowd, you know. My wife's friends and family.'

The Company settled down into their places again and the chairman went on with other business. They set a new levy on the dock, they set a new rent for the use of the great crane. There was some joke which Josiah did not quite understand about the aldermen of the city, but he smiled and laughed with the others. He had an exhilarating sense of breaking unknown ground. He was mixing at last with the men who controlled everything in Bristol. The jokes, the cliquish references were not yet clear to him, but he felt that he was on the threshold of belonging. In a year, in two, he would be seated farther up the table, he would be party to the private discussions which were now ratified. Josiah had penetrated the Company only to find a further cabal, hidden behind it. Next year, the year after, he would understand all the references, he would be one of the decision makers. For this year he was happy to be one of the new boys who could roar out 'Aye' to decisions he did not fully understand, who could trust his leaders to make the right judgements. Josiah felt he was among friends who would safeguard his interests.

At the other side of town in a dingy coffee house, Mehuru was also attending a meeting. Poorly financed but infinitely more ambitious, he was at a formal meeting of the Bristol Society for Constitutional Information, one of a network of societies committed to reforming the corrupt political structure and bringing in the right to vote for all men. It was Stuart's response to the disappointment of the Wilberforce bill. He was determined to widen their campaign, to bring in the freedom for black men as part of the freedom for white workers. Seated at the head of the table with the door tightly shut and guarded against eavesdroppers, Stuart was chairing a discussion of a motion brought by one of the more radical members: 'This Society should ally itself with our brothers engaged in the struggle for their rights in France, in America, and in the colonies.'

Mehuru was listening carefully, trying to follow the passionate interruptions to the debate. The Society had divided into two broad camps: those that feared that an association with the foreign reformers would invoke a patriotic backlash against them, and those who saw the reform movement as naturally international.

'These are great days,' Dr Hadley summed up. 'These are times for great change. The people taking power in France, the people taking power in America, slaves rising against their masters in every colony – who can doubt that the people will take power in England too? Is the English tyranny of king and church and landlords immune? Can anyone doubt that a hundred years from the last bloodless English revolution we are heading towards another?

'All over the country men are coming together to demand that they be truly represented in Parliament, that their leaders be men of their choice and not some pretty puppets set at their head. In the new industrial towns, even in the quiet market villages, all men of sense are demanding a change and a right to be heard. And in the ports of Britain and in her colonies the black citizens are asking for their rights too. They demand a living wage, they demand their freedom. And they demand the right to return to their homeland. This is a glorious crusade! I am proud to put this matter to the vote. All those in favour say "Aye".'

'Aye,' said Mehuru, along with the other two dozen men in the crowded room. He felt that Stuart was right, that he was at the forefront of a powerful international movement which could not fail. The logic of it was too strong, and its moral power was irresistible. 'Aye,' said Mehuru, from the heart.

Stuart carefully noted the vote in the Society's new ledger and closed the meeting. The men called for drinks, coffee or small ale. Mehuru noticed that all of them were following the self-imposed ban: refusing sugar in their coffee, and rejecting rum. They were all signatories of the petitions to support the banning of the slave trade, they were all refusing to support the plantation trade until slavery was abolished.

'Have you had a chance to read those pamphlets I gave you?' Stuart asked. He took a drink from his pint pot. 'What d'you think now of the Sierra Leone scheme?'

'I think it is a risk,' Mehuru answered. 'The men who planned it seem to have no idea what it is like on that coast.

Since the coming of the slavers all order has been destroyed. You have to realise that you are not planting a settlement in a desert, in an empty space; there are people living there now, and they are not people at peace in an ordered nation. The whole coast of Africa and for miles into the interior is in a state of perpetual uproar and warfare. Each bandit is paid and licensed by white men to make war on each other and capture slaves. Every village is like a fort, except for those which are already destroyed and the survivors hiding in the forests and scavenging for food. It is a wild lawless country now, you cannot draw a line on a map and say that inside this line it will be different.'

'They have negotiated treaties . . .'

Mehuru gave a short bitter laugh. 'I was envoy for the kingdom of Yoruba. The mightiest kingdom in Africa. I spoke three of the neighbouring languages and enough Portuguese to make myself understood. On a mission for my king, and with his protection, I was captured, my servant was stolen from me, and I was chucked into a canoe like a sack. I was left naked, I was force fed, I was manacled in the bottom of a ship and left to roll in my own vomit and excrement. If slavers can do that to me, why should they respect a group of poor farmers who have nothing but a piece of paper signed in London, two months' voyage away?'

Stuart Hadley nodded. 'I am sorry to hear you talk like this,' he said. 'I am friend to one of the directors and we urgently need African leaders to live there. Someone like you who could speak many languages would have been ideal. And it worries me if you think it is so risky.'

'Only the ending of the trade in slaves could make it safe,' Mehuru declared.

'And that will come soon,' Stuart promised. 'Next spring in Parliament Wilberforce will speak for it again. Then they *must* agree. And then Sierra Leone would have a future. We could make it a crown colony, give it the protection of the

Navy...' Stuart broke off as he saw Mehuru's sarcastic smile.

'Oh! I had no idea! We are talking of a new colony for Britain! I thought we were freeing black men to return to their own lands, but we are planning new plantations!'

'I did not mean a colony like a plantation,' Stuart protested. 'And you know that would never be my intention.'

'It is the danger though,' Mehuru said thoughtfully. 'If the European states stop slaving will they also stop seeing Africa as their market? Will they leave us to get our country back into order, to re-establish our own laws?'

'Of course there is a strong feeling that Africa should be converted to Christianity and to civilisation.'

There was a little silence. 'They plan to convert Africa to Christianity and civilisation?' Mehuru asked.

Stuart Hadley nodded.

'Then Africa is lost,' Mehuru said simply.

Stephen Waring stood in the doorway of the Custom House, breathing the warm night air. Other members of the Merchant Venturers' Company went past him into the dark gardens, some of them weaving unsteadily from the wines at dinner and the heavy drinking which had followed.

Sir Henry came up behind him and took his arm. 'Walking home?' he enquired.

'Why not?' Stephen replied easily. He tossed his cigar away and whistled for a linkboy to light their way. As they drew away from the others he said, 'A pleasant evening, I thought.'

'Very.'

'I am sorry for that little Josiah Cole,' Sir Henry said suddenly.

'Oh, why so?' Stephen asked. 'He wants his Hot Well and he has bought it.'

'He's paid a high price for it,' Sir Henry said. 'And we both know he will regret it.'

'It's his choice,' Stephen said comfortably. They strolled slowly over the lowered drawbridge. The tide was on the ebb and the river bank was starting to stink. The dark mud and water reflected the boy's moving light.

'Still, he might get his money back,' Sir Henry predicted cheerfully. 'If he can hang on.'

'More importantly, the Venturers have got *their* money back,' Stephen said. 'Anything he pays in rent hereafter represents a profit to us.'

'Where d'you want it invested?' Sir Henry asked. 'Clifton? The Downs?'

'I think we should spend money on the port,' Stephen said. 'We lose trade to Liverpool every day. We must straighten the river and make some deep-water anchorage. It is madness trying to run a commercial port out of a tidal harbour.'

'Oh aye,' Sir Henry agreed lazily. 'But you won't see a profit inside fifty years.'

'Still, it should be done.'

'I'd have thought you would have wanted some investment in Clifton,' Sir Henry teased. 'I heard that you had plans for terraces and assembly rooms and all sorts of grand projects.'

'Did you?'

'But I said that Clifton would never be anything more than a pretty little out-of-the-way place.'

'D'you think so?' Stephen asked interestedly.

'It won't grow until it can be supplied with water,' Sir Henry assured him. 'Limestone. You can't have a town on limestone. It's dry, bone dry. To reach the water you'd have to drill – oh – three hundred feet.'

Stephen nodded. The bobbing light of the linkboy's torch lit his face and then hid it again. 'Would it be that deep?' he asked pensively.

'But *if* you hit water then prices in Clifton would go through the roof,' Sir Henry pointed out.

'Lucky then that we all own land there,' Stephen said

371

simply. 'And that the Company owns the whole manor, Clifton, and Durham Down too.'

'Satisfactory,' Sir Henry said. He paused at his doorway on College Street. 'I like talking to you, Waring. You are always so uninformative.'

Stephen laughed shortly. 'I thought we had understood each other very well,' he said.

By July Frances was well enough to get out of bed but was still easily tired and short of breath. Dr Hadley called once every week and one day detained Josiah for a quiet word as he walked to his waiting phaeton. 'The air does not suit her,' Stuart said. 'It is low-lying here and the river mists are very unhealthy. You can smell the diseases like a fog. Any day now I expect to hear that we have cholera in the old town. Already there is typhoid fever not half a mile from this house. And all the drains from the old town flow into the river which surrounds you. She has a weak heart, she could not survive a major illness.'

Mehuru was holding Stuart's horse, straining to hear.

'I cannot move house,' Josiah exclaimed. 'We have only just bought this one!'

'That is a pity,' Stuart said carefully. 'Could Mrs Cole perhaps go away to the country for a visit once a year, especially now in midsummer?'

'She could go to the Hot Well spa every day,' Josiah offered. 'I have just bought the Hot Well spa, you know, Doctor. She could go there daily.'

'No, that is not what I mean. She needs a more airy situation in summer, and a warmer climate in winter like France, or Italy. She needs warm dry air, especially in winter time.'

Josiah shook his head. 'We have never travelled abroad, I would not know how to manage it.'

Mehuru's face was like stone, his impatience burning inside him.

'It could be managed,' Stuart said earnestly. 'And I do fear for her if she spends the next winter in Bristol. She is delicate, I am afraid, and another serious chill and inflammation like this one could even be fatal.'

Josiah looked shocked. 'Frances might die?'

'She could live for years,' Stuart said quickly. 'But these delicate lungs are very difficult to predict. If it is possible for her to go somewhere warm every winter then she would grow stronger.'

Josiah was badly shaken. 'I will consider it,' he assured Stuart. 'It is just that we have never thought of such a thing. My sister and I have never even taken more than a day's holiday. We have never been away from Bristol. I would not know how to set about it.'

Mehuru fidgeted at the horse's head, unable to stand still for anger.

'Arrangements are easily made,' Stuart said. 'No doubt Mrs Cole would know people who travel abroad. She has many friends and family, does she not?'

'But she would be away from Bristol for such a long time,' Josiah protested. 'I bought this house for her enjoyment and only she knows how it should be run. I thought this house would suit her very well.'

'I am sure it does,' Stuart soothed him. 'But in very hot weather such as these last few weeks it is not salubrious for anyone. And it may be that next winter she will need a little time in the sun. That is all.'

'I will consider it,' Josiah assured him. 'I would spare no expense to keep Frances in the best of health. Whatever a trip abroad would cost I would be prepared to pay. Anything that I can do, shall be done.'

He shook Stuart's hand and turned back into the house.

'Fool,' Mehuru spat through his teeth, released at last. 'What a fool!'

'I pity him,' Stuart said shortly. 'He chose a woman to

bring him money and connections and he finds himself obliged to provide things for her which he does not even understand.'

'He runs a shipping company.' Mehuru's voice was an angry mutter where he wanted to roar. 'He has three damned ships going anywhere in the world. He could put her on a ship, couldn't he? He could send her to Africa, couldn't he? Or to the Sugar Islands? Good God, if she were my wife and you told me she needed sunshine I would carry her on my back if there was no other way.'

Stuart smiled wearily at Mehuru's rage. 'Do you love her so much?'

Mehuru checked, looked at Stuart's face for any signs of mockery and saw none. 'Yes,' he said shortly.

Stuart shook his head and climbed up into the high perch seat of the phaeton. 'Then I am sorry for you,' he said conversationally. 'And for her too.'

Mehuru would not release the horse, but held the rein, forcing Stuart to wait. His expression was sharp, as if with a pain held inside. 'Because she is ill? Is it worse than you told Mr Cole? Do you pity me because she will die?'

Stuart kept his true opinion of Frances's health to himself. 'I pity you because there is nowhere for you,' he answered. 'She cannot leave him, you cannot freely love her. If I were you, my friend, I would rather go to Sierra Leone with all the risks that entails, than fall in love with a married woman, the niece of a peer of the realm, and my owner.'

Mehuru's face lightened, his smile started at his eyes and then his whole face lit up into an irresistible beam. 'When you express it like that,' he said ruefully, 'it does not sound like a very good idea. But Stuart, when I touch her hand, it is more than the whole world to me.'

The two men were silent for a moment.

'Have you any news from France?' Mehuru asked. 'I read

in Josiah's newspaper that the Bastille had fallen. How far do you think they will go?'

Stuart was instantly animated. 'Who knows? It is great news for all lovers of liberty. They will be sick with fear in Westminster. People are taking their power all around the world. The future must belong to us.'

'They will free the slaves?'

'Certainly. I imagine they will make their colonies departments of France and we will see black Frenchmen representing white constituencies.'

Mehuru smiled. 'It is like a miracle.'

'And so fast!' Stuart said. 'They will bring the king to realise that he must consult the people. And our king,' he lowered his voice, 'God help him, the poor madman, will become a people's king also. The Trade will end, slavery will be abolished, working men will get the vote. These are great times.'

'There must be a place for me,' Mehuru said determinedly. 'In these times of change. I must have a voice.' He thought for a moment. 'And I must have Frances,' he continued. 'If prisons can be opened then marriages can be ended. If we are to be free we must be free to love as well.'

'She surely could not leave him for you?' Stuart asked. 'It would be her ruin.'

'In an age of miracles?' Mehuru reminded him. 'Why should it not be possible?'

Stuart shrugged. He could not bring himself to tell Mehuru that he thought Frances would not live long enough to see the freeing of English slaves. He could not tell Mehuru that to free a lady such as Frances from her loveless marriage would be a harder task than to free Mehuru from slavery.

'Will you let my horse go now?' Stuart asked. 'If it is all the same to you, I have other patients to visit.'

'I was thinking of my home and how good the sun is there,'

Mehuru said absently. 'If I could take Frances there, how well she would be!'

'Look, here's someone calling on you,' Stuart said.

A large travelling carriage with a crest emblazoned on the door was drawing up behind the phaeton. Stuart glanced from it to Mehuru's face and was surprised to see a look of coldness and hatred such as he had never seen before. All at once Mehuru's charm and warmth had frozen into a grimace of absolute distaste.

'Who is it?'

'A man called Sir Charles Fairley,' Mehuru said. His voice was sharp with contempt. 'When he visited before he raped a woman, a Yoruban slave, and when she ate earth he had her bolted into a bridle. She is dead now. He was poxed and he made a baby on her.'

Stuart covertly glanced across at the carriage. The footman was putting down the steps and a black slave got out first to assist Sir Charles.

'A slave owner,' Stuart observed quietly.

'A Sugar Island nabob,' Mehuru said. 'He should be hanged.'

Stuart could not disagree. 'And soon he will come home to retire and buy a borough and stand for Parliament,' he predicted. 'Truly, we have to cleanse England. But next spring . . . Mehuru! Next spring!'

Mehuru's face was dark. 'You are hopeful,' he said curtly. 'But I saw how sure you were last time, and your man was talked into silence.'

'This time it will happen. We must keep up the campaign to support it. We are wiser now, we know our enemies. And then your fine friend will find his business is very much changed.'

Mehuru watched Sir Charles swagger past them up the steps to the house and nod to his slave to hammer on the door.

'I wish his business could be ended completely,' Mehuru said. 'And his slaves freed.'

'I too. But we have to move in small stages. First we ban the trade in slaves and that will force them to treat their slaves better. Then slavery is abolished altogether, it will just wither away, Mehuru. Slowly they will pay wages and your brothers will earn their freedom. We will see it. In our lifetime we will see it.'

Mehuru gave him a wry smile. 'You are confident.'

'I am certain! Now let me go, Mehuru, I have work to do.'

Mehuru nodded and stood back from the phaeton. Stuart clicked to his horse and drove off as the black slave preceded his master up the steps to the front door and hammered on the knocker.

Mary answered and Mehuru saw her look of shock when she recognised Sir Charles, before she drew back to allow him and his slave into the house. Mehuru followed them in.

Frances was seated in the morning room embroidering Josiah's waistcoat but when Sir Charles came in she put it aside and held out both her hands. 'Sir Charles! How delightful!' she said. 'And you are so early! The roads must have been very good.'

He kissed both her hands and thought privately that she looked very pale and drawn. 'The roads were filthy with dust,' he told her. 'But at least they were passable. I do not know how I shall tolerate them in wintertime!'

Frances laughed and nodded to Mary. 'Fetch the tea tray, Mary, and tell Miss Cole that Sir Charles is here. Will you have tea, Sir Charles? Or in this hot weather would you like some lemonade? Or shall you have some punch? I remember your preferences!'

'I will take some punch,' he decided.

Frances sat down and gestured to Sir Charles to take a chair but he stood before the window gazing out over the square.

'And how do you like your new home, ma'am?' he asked. 'You are very grand here. Quite a change!'

Frances kept her smile fixed on her face. 'It is a little small after Whiteleaze,' she remarked, as if she had never served dinner and then withdrawn to the fireplace in the same poky parlour over the warehouse. 'But we are very comfortable here.'

'And in the height of fashion,' Sir Charles commented, looking at the corner of the room where two red porcelain dragons glared at each other in a fixed snarl.

'Do you stay in Bristol for long?' Frances asked.

'No, I shall drive on to Lord Bartlet when I have signed my paper with you,' Sir Charles said. 'Miss Honoria is already there. Between you and me, Mrs Cole, I think there may be a match of it between her and Lord Bartlet's son.'

'Not Sir Frederick!' Frances exclaimed, thinking swiftly that Lord Bartlet must be hard-pressed indeed if he had let his son and heir be caught by such a one as Miss Honoria, whatever her fortune.

'No, his second son, Nicholas.'

'Ah, Nicholas,' Frances said. Good for neither church nor army, Nicholas would do very nicely with a Sugar Island heiress. 'He is such a pleasant young man.'

'A good match,' Sir Charles said with satisfaction. 'Nothing is settled, mind, but Lord Bartlet and I have tipped each other the wink.'

Frances smiled politely but inwardly shuddered at the thought of the impoverished old gamester winking his red-veined eye at Sir Charles. Compared with that crude bartering, her own marriage to Josiah seemed a love-match.

'I will not delay you then,' Frances said. 'I have the lease to hand.'

She went to her writing table, took out the lease and spread it before Sir Charles on the parlour table. He seated himself

378

and read through the clauses. He did not notice that he had not bought the mineral rights.

'You sign here,' she said politely.

Sir Charles signed.

'And here are the accounts for your capital laid with us,' she said. 'There is no interest to show yet, for it is paid annually. But you can see what investments I have made on your behalf, and Lord Scott has suggested a colliery in Kent for an investment of one thousand pounds.'

'Excellent, excellent,' Sir Charles beamed. 'His lordship is most kind, and I am very glad to have you take care of my capital. I should not have found my new house without your good offices, Mrs Cole! I am indebted to you!'

Frances smiled. The parlour door opened and Sarah came in followed by Mary with the tea tray and Mehuru carrying the punch bowl on a silver tray which he set down before Sir Charles.

Frances was instantly aware of Mehuru's anger. It was present in the precise way that he placed rum, water, sugar and lemons within Sir Charles's reach. It was present in the way he looked at her with his eyes like a black frost and said, 'Will that be all, Mrs Cole?'

'I say, he speaks well!' Sir Charles exclaimed, swinging around in his chair and inspecting Mehuru as if he were some exotic pet.

'We have made much progress since you were last here,' Sarah said pleasantly. 'My sister has been tireless. They can all speak and understand English now, and the two younger men, and this one can even read.'

'Well, that is remarkable,' Sir Charles said, staring frankly at Mehuru. Mehuru stared back, his face blank and insolent. 'Make him read for me.'

Frances drew a breath. 'He has other duties now. He will read for you another time.'

'A handsome buck,' Sir Charles commented.

'You can go, Cicero,' Frances said quickly.

His bow was an insult.

'I tell you what I shall send you,' Sir Charles exclaimed. 'Little slave collars, very pretty.'

Mehuru checked in the doorway and looked back to meet Frances's anguished glance.

'They're the very thing,' Sir Charles went on. 'Like a dog collar, you know, but finely made. A little chain and on the front a little metal tag, I like silver myself, with the slave's name engraved. They all wear them in London. They look very smart. You shall jot down their names, all of them, and I will send you a set.'

'You are very kind,' Frances said. She could feel her breath becoming shorter in her anxiety that Mehuru would make a scene.

Mehuru wheeled around in the doorway and suddenly strode into the room. Frances started up and her workbox spilled to the floor with a clatter, shedding silks and ribbons and bobbins of cotton. 'Oh, how careless!' she cried. 'How careless of me! How silly I am! Cicero, fetch Martha, or one of the girls. Go at once, please! Go!'

For a moment he hesitated as if he would defy her.

'At once!' Frances insisted, her voice sharp with fear. 'Go and fetch one of the girls at once, please.'

He turned unwillingly and obeyed her, stalking from the room, prickly with anger.

'I do apologise,' Frances said. She could hardly breathe at all. 'So silly of me.'

Miss Cole regarded her with suppressed irritation. 'Shall I pour the tea, Sister?'

'Oh, please do! And Sir Charles, do make your punch and tell us all about London. And the Scott Ball in the winter! Did Miss Honoria enjoy herself?'

The girl Ruth came in to clear up Frances's workbox. As she entered the room and saw Sir Charles she recoiled and her face went a grey sick colour. Frances knew that she was taking tea with a rapist and that she was commanding the people who had witnessed his crime to serve him.

'Hurry up, Ruth,' she ordered. 'Is the punch to your liking, Sir Charles?'

It took all her carefully learned social skills to chatter through Ruth's slow resentful tidying. It took all her charm to divert Sir Charles, and to distract Sarah from Mary's sullenly reluctant service at tea. She heard her voice, a little breathless, but still light and frivolous, and she despised herself for the facade she presented. She longed to tell Sir Charles that she knew him for what he was, that she loathed him, and that she would never forgive him for the abuse of a woman who had been in her charge. But her social self, which always had the upper hand, stirred the tea, passed cakes, and laughed at his jokes, just as she had been trained to do. Just like a little pet dog, she thought miserably, which sits to order, and begs when told, and barks a little, and perhaps has forgotten altogether that it was ever a real dog.

The visit was mercifully short. Sir Charles wanted to be on his way to Lord Bartlet's country seat at Kings Weston.

'My brother will be sorry to have missed you,' Sarah observed.

'I shall have the pleasure of his company another time,' Sir Charles said gallantly. 'This was a business visit, merely.'

Sarah nodded, a little surprised. 'I am glad that Frances can transact your business. I had thought you would want to go over the figures with my brother.'

Sir Charles smiled. 'Mrs Cole is an excellent agent for my little fund. I need no other!'

'As long as you are satisfied,' Sarah said doubtfully.

'I am indeed. My only regret is that I cannot stay to dine, but I hope to be at Lord Bartlet's in time for supper.'

Frances rang the bell and Sir Charles's own slave came with his cloak, hat and cane.

'Will you have a hot brick for your feet in the carriage, Sir Charles?' Sarah asked. 'Despite the season it can get cool at night.'

'I hope my boy has placed one there already,' Sir Charles said. 'Done hot brickee? Sammy?'

The man glanced at him with one weary look. 'Yassuh,' he said.

Frances closed her eyes for a moment to shut out the man's bowed head and empty eyes.

'Here, Sammy has a collar,' Sir Charles said. 'Sammy! Show chain! Show chain!'

The man's hand went to his neck to open the collar of his jacket. Tight around his throat was a silver chain and a plaque. In elegant flowing script it was engraved with the name 'Sammy'. 'Charming, ain't it?' Sir Charles demanded. 'You jot down the names of your slaves and I will send you a set.'

Frances held on to her smile as if it were a mask in a carnival ball. She took a page of paper from her writing desk and wrote down carefully the eleven names, from Cicero to little five-year-old John.

'Charming,' Sir Charles said. 'Eleven now, eh? You have eleven?'

'From an original consignment of twenty,' Sarah said. 'We have had only nine deaths. Seven in transit but only two here. We are pleased.'

Frances's hand trembled and the pen made a blot on the page. She wanted to tell him that the woman he had raped had died. She wanted to accuse him. Instead, she handed him the page of names and looked at his slave, Sammy. The man would not meet her gaze. She did not know that at home in Jamaica he would be beaten for looking at a white woman. It was considered to be impertinent. Under her stare he ducked his head and gazed at his boots. On the delicate skin at the back of his neck and curving up behind his ear Frances could see the puckering of a deep scar from an old misplaced lash.

'I'll bid you goodbye,' Sir Charles said, throwing his cloak around him and bowing over Sarah's hand and then lingering his kiss on Frances's hand with moist lips.

'Safe journey,' Frances said quietly.

They escorted him to the front door and stood on the doorstep in the late afternoon sunshine, waving him farewell as the carriage pulled away.

'Isn't he a *charming* man,' Sarah sighed with pleasure as the carriage rolled out of the square and disappeared.

'Delightful,' Frances replied. Her lips were very stiff on the lie. 'Quite delightful.'

Chapter Twenty-nine

Next morning Sarah woke early and was dressed and out of the house even before Josiah. She called Mehuru to the hall and told him to put on his green livery coat, and attend her for a walk. Mehuru bowed, hiding the curiosity in his face, and followed her at a polite distance as she walked from the square towards the river.

He called the ferry for her and held her parasol as she stepped from the greasy steps into the little boat. The dock was stinking in the heat of midsummer but Sarah did not seem to notice it. Mehuru was first out of the boat on the other side and handed Sarah up the steps to the Redclift quay.

The warehouse door was shut; Josiah's clerk had not yet arrived. Sarah stood with calm patience on the doorstep of her old home. Mehuru waited beside her. She did not speak to him, she never spoke to any of the slaves except to give them orders.

Just as the bells of St Mary Redclift struck eight o'clock Mehuru saw the clerk hurrying down the quayside. At once he sensed Sarah's attention sharpen.

'Good morning,' she said. 'I am Miss Cole. I wish to see the ships' logs and the company accounts. Please let me into the office.'

The man hesitated, glancing at Mehuru. Mehuru's face was impassive.

'I don't know . . .' the clerk began.

'Thank you,' Sarah said magisterially. She took the key from his hand, let herself into the warehouse and walked upstairs to Josiah's office. As she had hoped, the books were in their usual place, on his desk. She nodded over her shoulder at Mehuru. 'You can wait outside,' she told him.

Mehuru and the clerk retreated over the threshold. Sarah shut the door on them and then they heard the key turn firmly in the lock. The clerk looked at Mehuru as if for advice. Mehuru shrugged and waited, as Sarah had ordered him to do.

Inside the room Sarah seated herself at Josiah's desk and drew the company books towards her. She did not like the clerk's handwriting but his work was adequate. She turned to the other page, the debits, and frowned. There was a massive £5400 outstanding to Hibbard and Sons, a small banking house, including £2000 for the lease of the Hot Well and £1000 for the Queens Square house. Josiah had given them a note of hand of £500 to pay for the furniture and fittings. Sarah thought of the red Chinese dragons and put her hand to her mouth. Josiah had borrowed the first year's rent for the Hot Well of £900 as well. He had borrowed £1000 to equip *Rose* and £500 to buy cargo. Sarah's face trembled. There had never been such amounts in the debit column of Cole and Sons in all their years of trading. She did not curse Josiah, she did not feel anger. She felt icy cold and nauseous with fear. It would take a miracle voyage to clear such a debt, and profits were falling, not increasing.

She knew the debt was a long-term loan, negotiated and managed by Josiah. The first payment was not even due until November, when the *Rose* was due, with *Daisy* close behind her; but the books had always been Sarah's work and she resented any entry into the debit column. To see them in a state of permanent debt made her as uncomfortable as other women would be with a dress done up wrongly at the back. And this was no small debt. Greater merchants than Cole and Sons had been ruined for less. The *Rose* alone would not clear it. It would take four, perhaps five, voyages to clear it over at least two years.

They would have to borrow to repair and refurbish *Rose* as soon as she arrived, and there was no money to hand. They would not be able to take a large share in her next voyage. 'We will be sailing the ship for the benefit of the partners,' Sarah muttered miserably to herself.

Sarah drew *Rose*'s account book towards her and ran her eye down the cargo list. The usual goods were listed for sale to the African slave traders – brass cooking pots and kettles, knives, necklaces of paste polished to sparkle like diamonds, special poor-quality cotton known as negro linen, negro looking glasses, and negro guns. Then Sarah looked at the account again. For a moment she thought Josiah had made a mistake and entered the goods twice for the total cash value was almost double. She checked the amounts of goods against the previous pages. The amounts were almost double too. Josiah had sent the ship out equipped to double the African trade.

Sarah frowned slightly and pulled towards her the account book of the *Lily*, which was their last ship out. No, *Lily* had sailed as usual. It was just *Rose* which Josiah had laden with goods and sent out to trade. Sarah scanned through the other totals for the voyage. The accounts had been made up in Josiah's neat hand, they were easy to read. She had wondered at the time why he had insisted on doing them himself; usually he was very ready to hand over a fistful of cargo manifests to her and let her copy out the totals into the ledger. But this time Josiah had done them, and this time they were different.

She could see nothing untoward elsewhere in the ledger until she came to the cost of insurance. It was unusually low. Sarah's finger traced the row across the page to Josiah's clearly written entry.

For insurance, the ship Rose and her cargo outbound to Africa, and homebound from West Indies to England...

Sarah sat very still, her mind reeling. Josiah had not insured the ship or the cargo for the perilous middle passage, the transport of slaves on the long, stormy, sickly, mutinous journey from Africa across the vast dangerous sweep of the Atlantic Ocean to the shelter of the West Indies. He had not insured the precious cargo of slaves on their single dangerous voyage.

She nodded, piecing it all together: Josiah's difficulty in getting insurance; his complaints about the ruling on the ship *Zong* which had made all insurers suspect that slavers simply tipped slaves over the side to claim on their policy; his acceptance of too few partners. Josiah had taken on his new wife and a massive gamble together. He had been so determined to rise in the world, he had been so determined to make a fortune for his family, that he had doubled the number of slaves he was carrying, and he had gone out without insurance. He had not even shared his potential loss among a full complement of partners. He wanted to keep the risk, and the profits, all to himself.

Sarah pinched her lips together, her face looked gaunt and old. She hated risk, she hated expenditure. The lesson of her childhood had been the amassing of a small fortune by steady laborious work. She had watched her father make one little voyage after another, ferrying goods up and down the Severn. It was Josiah's childhood that had been fired by the prospect of great wealth. It had been Josiah's formative moment when their Da brought the French brig the *Marguerite* into port. Ever since then Josiah had loved the grand risk, the great gamble. Sarah, ten years older, scarred by early poverty and always more conservative, preferred the security of steady earnings.

A noise from downstairs distracted her. She took her hand from her mouth. She had been biting her fingernails while reading the account books, and her index finger was nibbled bloody and raw.

'What the devil is going on?' came Josiah's voice on the stairs.

'It's Miss Cole,' the clerk replied. 'And she has locked herself into your office.'

Sarah crossed to the door, turned the key, and opened up. 'Come in, Josiah,' she said.

Josiah was prepared to bluster but one look at her face silenced him. She closed the door on the waiting clerk and took her seat at Josiah's desk once more, leaving him standing, looking like the little brother that she used to smack and scold for naughtiness.

Josiah looked from her face to the account book emblazoned with the name *Rose*.

'Oh,' he said.

'Yes,' Sarah said bleakly. 'You have no insurance for the middle passage.'

'I could not get it, Sarah. Before God, I tried. It was impossible.'

'You have insured the others?'

'Sarah, once I was inside the Merchant Venturers it was easy. We all insure each other, we all take a little of the risk. But *Rose* sailed before I was invited to join. I went all around Bristol. No-one would take me for the middle passage. She was covered from here to Africa, and she is covered for the voyage home.'

Sarah took a little shuddering breath. 'But the risk . . .'

He shrugged. 'What could I do? She had to sail. She was costing me money sitting on the quayside. I thought when she was at sea I might be able to get insurance for her then. But I could not.'

'Have you heard from her captain?' Sarah asked. The longing in her voice was like a woman asking for her lover. 'Is *Rose* safe?'

'I have heard nothing since he was off the coast of Africa, loading. But I would expect to hear nothing until he is in Jamaica. He would only send to me if he happened to meet a Bristol ship homeward bound. Compose yourself, Sarah. It may all be very well with him and we hear nothing until he docks.'

She nodded. 'I know,' she said. 'I know.'

'I am sorry,' Josiah apologised awkwardly. 'The insurers left me no choice.'

'And the trade goods? You are carrying so much?'

Josiah glanced at the door, as if a spy might be hidden outside. 'You will not like this, Sarah, but I had to earn capital quickly.'

She understood him at once. 'Oh God! You are smuggling.'

'One load,' he said. 'One load only. I have ordered them to be packed as tight as they can go and Captain Smedley is under orders to sell them to the Spanish plantations. He will take no notes of credit, he will take only gold or sugar at the best prices. No-one will know and I will make a small fortune.'

'You have spent a small fortune,' she answered bitterly. 'And that is why we are in this strait.'

'This one voyage will pull us clear,' he said. 'When *Rose* comes home in November I shall pay off my debts and we will have cash to spare. It is a gamble, Sarah; but they are familiar odds. Why should we lose a ship now? We have done the voyage a hundred times and never lost a ship yet.' He tapped his hand against the wooden door frame for luck. Josiah was talking confidently but he never forgot to touch wood.

'How much should we make?' Sarah asked. She was reluctantly tempted by the thought of a shipload of gold.

389

'Say he carries six hundred slaves . . .'

'Six hundred!' Sarah exclaimed. 'But *Rose* has room only for three hundred!'

Josiah gleamed at her. 'I told him to pack tight. He will. Say he carries six hundred and lands four hundred and fifty.'

'A hundred and fifty die during the voyage?'

'Packed so tight they are bound to get sick,' Josiah reasoned. 'And with so many he will have to ration water and food. Maybe it will not be so bad. Anyway, say he lands four hundred and fifty and sells them for fifty pounds each . . .'

'Not more?' Sarah demanded.

'Many of them will be only little children . . . that is £22500.'

She opened the account book. 'Less £8732 paid in trade goods.'

Josiah beamed. 'A profit of nearly £14000.'

'A fortune,' she said. 'It will clear your debt on the house, and on the Hot Well. It will pull us clear.'

Josiah nodded. 'I owe a thousand on the house, and I borrowed my deposit of two thousand on the Hot Well. I have debts for the furniture and carpets for Queens Square, and I have borrowed to start the season at the Hot Well. I borrowed more than a thousand to equip *Rose*. Altogether I owe more than £5000, call it £6000 with interest. I plan to pay it off, all at once, in November when *Rose* arrives. It is only four months.'

Sarah nodded. 'It all rests on the *Rose* then. If she comes in safe, we will have made a fortune worthy of a nabob. But if she fails . . .'

'It is as near a certainty as you can get in the Trade,' Josiah said. 'I am confident, Sarah. Be confident too. You are a trader's daughter and sister to a Bristol merchant. We have to take risks. And we will show such profits!'

'She is sailing without insurance,' Sarah said heavily. 'In the most dangerous seas in the world, overloaded, and bound for an illegal destination. If we lose her we are ruined, Josiah. Not even the new house is safe. We own nothing outright but our two remaining ships and this warehouse, and we would have to sell the ships.'

Josiah hammered on the wood of the door frame again. 'I know! I know this, Sarah! Why d'you think I am so desperate to see the Hot Well pay? Why d'you think I am here on the quayside every morning, selling and dealing in barrels of other ships' cargoes? Why d'you think I draw on every ounce of credit I can get from the Merchant Venturers? I know how close to the wind I am sailing! No-one knows better than me! But if I succeed then we are wealthy and established. It is a risk, Sarah! It is the nature of the Trade!'

Her hand was at her mouth again, biting the cuticle around her fingernail. She tasted her own blood.

'Don't, Sarah,' Josiah begged. 'I hoped to spare you this.'

'It is better that I should know,' she said, her voice low. 'I was fearing worse.'

'Well, you know now,' Josiah said.

'You will not deceive me again?'

'You will not stand in my way?'

'Josiah . . .'

'I will be master in my house, I will run Cole and Sons in my own way, Sarah.'

'This is all Frances's fault!' she suddenly burst out. 'If you had not married her you would have been content!'

'I was not content!' Josiah exclaimed. 'I married her because I was not content with the warehouse. I wanted more, and I am getting more. You will not stand against me, Sarah, I will not allow it.'

She turned away and looked out of the window. Below them a rival's ship was safely docked, swarming with sail-makers come to collect the sails for repair, half a dozen sailors crawling over the deck caulking the planks with tar and hemp rope.

'We used to stand together,' she said.

'I know.'

There was a silence. Sarah sighed. 'I will not go against you. So trust me, Josiah. Don't keep things from me. I am not a silly girl. I am not a lady of leisure. I was brought up to this business, I can help you.'

He nodded and came across the room to her. He put his arm around her waist and held her for a brief moment. 'I know,' he repeated. 'I have been miserably lonely with this worry.'

They stood still for a moment, watching the ship, as bereft parents will watch someone else's baby in a cradle.

'I must go,' Josiah said briskly. 'I have a horse waiting.'

'You have hired a horse again?'

Josiah laughed. 'Sarah, I have bought the Hot Well. I have to check on my business! Of course I have hired a horse and as soon as I can find one that suits me I shall buy one! I need to ride out and see that my business is thriving. I would not be doing my work if I were *not* riding out to look at it. Surely you see that!'

She smiled unwillingly at him. 'Yes. It is the expense which worries me.'

'It would cost me more if I did not inspect it,' he said briskly. 'Now let me go.'

She watched him from the window. Mehuru held the horse's head for him as he mounted. It seemed odd to see Josiah setting off for his work on horseback. All his life he had gone no further than the quayside outside their house. Now he looked like a gentleman, in riding boots and with a cape on his shoulders. Sarah thought that if she saw him at a distance she would not recognise him. The little brother she had reared was going far away from her and she did not understand him, nor his business, any more. The figures in the ledgers were no longer small manageable amounts, easily understood, added and subtracted. They were dangerous sums, perilous debts. And Josiah was no longer her little brother who came to her for advice and never sent out a ship without her checking the figures. He was a man prepared to take great risks, to take a massive gamble to win the home he wanted for the wife he had chosen.

Unseen by Josiah, she put up her hand to wave goodbye in a gesture which looked more as if she were calling him back.

Josiah's heart lifted a little as he rode along the riverside to the Hot Well. The tide was coming in and the sunshine sparkled on the water. The woods on either side of the river had lost their lush greenness, the leaves dulling in the heat and glare of the July sun. Josiah felt better for confiding in Sarah. She had been his business advisor for so long that any secret from her made him uneasy. And in reassuring her, he convinced himself.

The Merchant Venturers' expensive avenue of trees were dusty after months of carriages going to and fro beneath their spreading branches. The waves were slapping the river wall of the Pump Room in a pretty irregular sound. An onshore breeze had lifted the constant smoke away from the city, and the sky was blue with fleecy strips of white cloud. Josiah rode down the little avenue with his hand on his hip and felt the novel pleasure of being a proprietor of land. He inspected the building with smug care, he took in the sky above it and the circling birds as if they too were part of his investment and a credit to his acumen.

At the back of the building the tap, which had traditionally dispensed water for free, was being bolted off. The workmen looked up as Josiah rode past and pulled at their caps. Josiah responded with a small jaunty gesture.

He could have hitched his horse to one of the posts outside the Pump Room. There were others there, bearing the traditional Bristol saddle – a two-seater – for a lady to sit behind the groom. Instead Josiah chose to whistle up a loitering urchin and promise him a penny to hold the horse. It was not that the animal was too high-bred or skittish to be left unattended. The stable knew Josiah was not a confident rider and they always sent him a placid slow-moving hack. But Josiah was learning the pleasure of spending money. A penny was a little enough sum, but to Josiah hiring a child to hold a horse when there was a hitching ring for free was an extravagance. It excited him to be extravagant. He foresaw a future when he would become a liberal tipper, a spendthrift in small, enjoyable ways, a man who carried loose change in his pocket and had spent it all on trifles by the end of the day.

He strolled into his Pump Room and looked around. The perennial invalids were in their usual places, drinking water or loitering under the roof of the colonnade, taking their prescribed exercise. Josiah hardly glanced at them. These were not the people whose custom would determine the success of the Well. He needed the fashionable crowd, the London pleasure-seekers, the day-visitors from Bath. They had come here in their hundreds in previous years and Josiah had been at pains to advertise that the spa was under new management and offering advantageous rates for this first season. Surely, with a sky so blue, and an outlook from the large windows of the rooms so beguiling, they would come in their hundreds again?

'Ah, Mr Cole.' The Master of Ceremonies, newly appointed by Josiah but chosen by Frances, came forward and bowed to him. 'Mr Cole, our proprietor! We are all prepared, as you see! All ready for the launch of the new management. I have already received several cards notifying me of the arrival of Ladies of Quality. I think we shall have an enjoyable year! I do indeed! We are starting a little late, a little late in our season to be sure. But people do not go to London till October or November, and I am confident we can charm them from their country houses to here. We have the rest of this month and all of August and September, after all!'

Josiah smiled. He could not help but be uneasy with the man who wore such tightly strapped stays under his clothes that his waistcoat fitted without a wrinkle and his coat was one smooth line from padded shoulders to stiffened hem. 'Good,' he said shortly. 'I see they are shutting off the free tap at the back of the building.'

'Certainly,' the Master confirmed. 'It would be fatal to our atmosphere of elegance to have the back of the building crowded with dirty and sickly people. Besides – how can we charge for water inside the building if we are giving it away free outside?'

'Yes,' Josiah agreed curtly. 'The room looks well. I will take the attendance book and the cash register home with me.'

'Certainly, certainly,' the man said sweetly. 'But I think you will be happy. *I* am content enough with how it is going. We have our poor little invalids here as usual but also a fair number of pleasure-seekers, and it is they who give the spa the air of fashion that it needs.'

'Yes,' Josiah said, rather at a loss.

'There are a few little improvements I would suggest?' the Master of Ceremonies continued archly. 'I would have put them in hand but they *do* cost money and I wanted to speak to the holder of the purse strings. I cannot have you thinking me extravagant, now!'

'What are they?'

The man held up his slender hand and ticked the items off on well-manicured fingers. 'One: the quartet only plays in the summer season and I think it is a shame. In the winter when it is grey outside we so badly want music and light and laughter inside, don't you think, Mr Cole? Don't you agree, sir?'

'Yes,' Josiah said, goaded. 'Keep them on.'

395

'And I want to hire a little woman, a pretty little woman to stand behind an urn and make tea in the afternoons. You can *order* tea but I want it here, visible, so you can see it, and want it, and have it in a flash. In a flash! D'you see?'

Josiah shook his head at the volubility of the man. 'Do as you think best,' he said. 'But check any expenditure with me of more than ten pounds.'

'Now that is a reasonable way to do business!' the man cried. 'But how silly of me, you are a businessman first and foremost, aren't you, Mr Cole? Now is there anything else I wanted to ask you?' He put his head on one side. His wig released a little puff of scented powder. 'No! Not a single thing! Now, can I tempt you to a glass of your own water?'

Josiah recoiled hastily. 'No, no. No need. The men bring bottles for my wife to drink when they deliver in town. She likes it. I – er – I do not take it. I am in perfect health, thank God.'

The man laid a gloved hand on Josiah's sleeve. A faint but unmistakable scent of geraniums blew sweetly and powerfully into Josiah's rigid face. 'Are you sure I can't tempt you?' he cooed.

'No, no.' Josiah nearly choked in discomfort. 'I have to go! Business, you know, business.'

He got himself out of the room at speed, mounted his horse and threw a penny at the boy. But once he was safely out of reach he turned his head and looked back. He chuckled. He could not help but wonder what his Da – the son of a collier – would have made of the family's meteoric rise, and this new fanciful trade.

Chapter Thirty

~~~~~

'I have been thinking what we can do,' Mehuru said to Frances. She was sitting on the bench in the central garden of Queens Square, with him standing beside her. Frances had just walked around the square, obeying Stuart Hadley's instructions to take light exercise in the open air.

Frances turned to look at him, shading her pale face from the sun with her little parasol. The August day was hot; she was wearing a muslin gown flecked with pink and a pink shawl over her shoulders. Mehuru had to curb his desire to straighten the shawl and wrap her tighter. Ever since Stuart had warned him of her health he found he was desperate to keep her warm, as if she were some rare African plant which would wither and die under the cool damp skies of England.

'We,' she repeated with a little smile. She did not say whether or not she recognised his right to speak of them as a couple.

'Has the doctor spoken to you about your health?'

'No,' she said. 'I am well now.'

Mehuru made a little grimace. 'He thinks that you have weak lungs.'

'Oh, I knew that,' Frances said. 'It was my mother's complaint too.'

'He told Josiah that you should go abroad in wintertime.'

'Josiah never said.'

'Josiah cannot see how it can be done,' Mehuru replied

grimly. 'Three ships of his own and he cannot see how you can be sent somewhere warm for the winter.'

Frances twirled her parasol and peeped up at Mehuru from under the fringe. 'Don't be unkind about Josiah,' she reproved him. 'It is not fair to criticise him.'

'Mmm.' Mehuru suppressed his disagreement. 'The point is, the doctor thinks you should be in a better climate than here for the winter months.'

'How do you know all this?' Frances suddenly demanded.

'I was holding the doctor's horse and listening,' Mehuru said without embarrassment. 'Servants always know everything, Frances, you know that.'

'But not about us? They don't know about us?'

'Frances,' Mehuru said patiently. 'I am trying to make plans.'

'My reputation . . .'

'They know nothing about us,' Mehuru lied quickly. 'I want to plan . . .'

'To plan what?'

'The doctor says that you should go away in the winter for your health. This is not a light matter. He means it. He is afraid that your lungs are damaged and the wet and cold weather is bad for you. This house is low-lying, too near the river. And the air of this city is unbreathable!'

Frances nodded more seriously. 'I have never felt well since I came to Bristol.'

'I want you to come away with me.' Mehuru finally took the plunge. 'I want us to go to Italy, or better than that, to France. I think that the political situation in France is perfect for us. I want us to live in France together, as man and wife.'

Frances was stunned. She sat bolt upright and snapped the parasol shut. 'France!' she exclaimed.

'They will have a parliament governed by the will of the people,' Mehuru predicted. 'And negroes from the French colonies will sit side by side with white representatives. They will free the slaves in the colonies and black men and white men will be equal under the new French law. It is the ideal place for us. I will work as a journalist, I will earn a living as a writer.'

She shook her head. The cluster of pink silk flowers on her bonnet quivered as if they were afraid.

'Why not?'

'They cannot free the slaves,' she said disbelievingly. 'They will not.'

'I am assured they will, and France would be the very place for us to live together.'

She shook her head. 'I could not live in France,' she said in a small voice.

'Italy then.'

'I could not live abroad. The only family I have is in England, I could not go abroad.'

'But you never see your family.'

'My family name is important to me.' She looked at him as if she could never explain. 'People know who I am in England. This is where I belong.'

He curbed his impatience. 'Let's walk,' he suggested. He could not bear to stand behind her seat and not be allowed to touch her while she threw away her chance of health and their only chance of happiness. She rose up obediently and they went down the path to the centre of the square; he walked a scant half-pace behind her.

'Very well then,' he said. 'Let us find a house with good healthy air, perhaps near your old home. You liked it there, did you not? At Bath?'

Frances felt her heart speeding and her breath coming short.

'You don't understand. We could not live together, Mehuru, I would be ruined.'

'I understand that Josiah's friends and family would not

recognise you,' he said carefully. 'But your own family would surely still care for you?'

She put her hand at the base of her throat, trying to still her panting. 'No,' she said. 'I would be ruined, Mehuru. They would cut me off. I would never see any of them again.'

'What about your uncle, the one who writes to you, Lord Scott?'

Frances, thinking of his lordship's unequivocal advice about the fatal results of infidelity, gave a shaky laugh. 'Him least of all!' she said. 'If I left Josiah at all it would be the end for me, Mehuru! If I left him for you I would be outlawed by my family. They would never speak of me again.'

He had a growing, painful sense that he was defeated before he had even started. 'Frances,' he said. 'I have lost everything. My house, my family, my country, my work which was the greatest joy of all, and I am beginning again. Why cannot you and I begin again together?'

She shook her head. 'It's not possible, not possible. You do not understand.' She turned away and started to walk, a little quicker, down the westward path towards her house.

'Why not?' he demanded, catching her up.

'We would have no money,' she said. She was breathless from walking too quickly. 'I have nothing except what Josiah gives me, and you have nothing at all. We could not take a house, we could not even rent a room. The only work I can do is governessing, and you cannot earn at all.'

'People would help us,' he argued. 'We could go to London. I already have made friends with some Englishmen, members of a Constitutional Society. These people would be our friends, we could live near them. There is a place in London called Wapping where a friend of mine lives. We could leave Bristol and stay there.'

The look she turned on him was simply incredulous. 'You have been to radical meetings?' She was stunned. 'Mehuru, how could you? How could you even get to them?'

'I crept out. I have been to several.'

She gasped. 'But these are dreadful people! They threaten the whole nation. These are dangerous radical agitators!'

He tried to laugh at her alarm but he felt a growing fear at the gulf which was opening between them. 'You have not met these people, Frances, and I have. They are not dangerous agitators, they are quiet sensible men who wish to see sensible changes made in this country and the ending of the slave trade. Two or three of them are my countrymen and they understand my position.'

She was quite white with horror. 'You have been plotting with runaway slaves?'

'They are not runaway slaves,' he snapped. 'They are free men.'

Frances put her gloved hand to her cheek as she tried to catch her breath. 'Mehuru, this is awful. I had no idea that you were doing this. They are dangerous agitators and they will be arrested and hanged or transported. If they catch you, they will send you to Australia or to the plantations. You must promise me never, never to go again.'

'Or what?'

She did not hear the warning note in his voice, she was too absorbed in her fears for his safety. 'I shall tell Josiah that the doors have to be locked at night. You must not meet with these people.'

'Or you could chain me up,' he suggested bitingly. 'Or have me whipped.'

She suddenly realised what she had said. 'I don't mean that,' she recanted swiftly. 'I meant that you are a foreigner, you do not speak the language, you do not understand the people you are mixing with. I want to protect you.'

'I think I do not need the kind of protection that locks up a grown man and forbids him to choose his friends.' He was toweringly angry. 'I think I do not want a woman who threatens me with imprisonment. And I do not want a woman who

401

desires me but will not acknowledge that she desires me and still plans to spend the rest of her life with her husband.'

He spun on his heel and was walking away from her when Frances, reckless of who might see her, ran after him and caught at the sleeve of his coat. 'Don't!' she cried. She was panting for air. 'Please! Mehuru!'

He stopped when he saw the whiteness of her face and heard her breath coming so short.

'Oh!' he sighed, and turned back to her. 'Sit down, breathe slowly.' He pressed her into a seat. 'Come, Frances, breathe properly. I will not be angry with you. Breathe!'

With his hand on her back she took three shaky breaths and he watched as the colour came back into her face.

'I am very sorry,' she said as soon as she could speak. 'Please don't be angry, Mehuru.'

'It is I who am sorry,' he said. 'I should have remembered your health.' He glanced around at all the windows facing the square, longing to take her into his arms but knowing he did not dare. He waited until her breathing steadied. 'Now,' he said. 'Frances, I must tell you that these are good men and friends of mine. Anything you have heard against the societies is not true.'

She nodded, anxious to avoid a quarrel. 'Perhaps.'

'And they tell me that English women often marry men of my colour,' he continued. 'And they live happily with them.'

She nodded. 'I have heard of that.' She did not tell him that she had heard of it because of an article in a newspaper deploring the tendency of white women to marry freed slaves and accusing them of the grossest immorality.

'These would be our friends,' he said. 'Our neighbours. We would make a new life for the two of us.'

Frances drew a breath and tried to speak calmly. 'Mehuru, I know that you mean well but it could not happen,' she said quietly. 'These are working women, they are not ladies.

Wapping is a poor part of London, it is not like Queens Square, it is even worse than the Redclift quay. It is dirty and unhealthy, and all the people there are poor people, labouring men and women. They would despise me, I would hardly understand their speech. I could not possibly live there. I would be miserable living in poverty and so would you.'

He gave her a swift unhappy look and straightened up.

'Josiah might pursue us,' Frances said. 'He could have you arrested as a runaway and then I would be there on my own.' Her voice trembled. 'There is a pit of poverty underneath me. You never saw me before my marriage. I had to work or tumble downward into charity, and I was never very good at my work. I dare not leave Josiah, I dare not leave my family. It is their name and their wealth that feed me and house me and clothe me. Without them I would be ruined.'

Mehuru said nothing. He stood behind her, as a slave should stand, alert for her command but detached from her. He looked over her head, over the bonnet with the small bobbing flowers, and he felt his heart ache for her, and for the unlikely romantic future he had dreamed for them. She turned her head and looked up at him. She looked very small and vulnerable, like a scolded child. Her eyes, as dark as his own, were huge, shadowed with blue bruises from her illness.

'What are we to do then?' he asked tenderly. 'What do you want to do?'

She shook her head. 'I don't know.'

Josiah was on the quayside, watching his rival's ship preparing to set sail, his own berth achingly empty. The sailmakers dragged heavily laden sledges across the cobbles and the runners screamed in protest. When one of the sailmakers saw him, he hesitated and then came over.

'Your bill, Mr Cole,' the sailmaker said. 'From *Lily*, in March. I would appreciate it if you could settle it now.'

Josiah put his hand to his pocket and then checked. 'I am sorry, George,' he said. 'I have left my purse at my house.'

George looked uncomfortable. 'Do you have nothing at your office, Mr Cole?'

'No,' Josiah said. 'I keep no gold here, it is not safe with no-one living here any more. I shall send one of my slaves to your loft this evening to pay what I owe.'

The man made a little bow and shouted to his lad to unload the sails. Josiah went down the steps to the ferry over to the Bristol side of the river. He sat in the bow and looked back at the ship. She was sailing direct to and from the West Indies. Josiah's neighbour and rival had given up the trade of slaving. Josiah hawked and spat in the filthy water – he knew better. When *Rose* came home in November, when *Daisy* followed her into port with *Lily* not far behind, they would all know that Josiah had been right to cleave to his own trade – the only trade he knew. The ferry nudged against the steps of the quay and Josiah tossed a ha'penny to the lad and stepped ashore, heading for the traders' coffee shop.

Stephen Waring was at the top table taking breakfast when Josiah came in. He raised his head and nodded an invitation. As Josiah came over Stephen regarded him rather grimly, without his usual smile.

Josiah ordered a plate of meat and bread and a pint of porter.

'I have heard some news which I hope you will not take amiss,' Stephen began. He finished the last of his meat and took a piece of bread to wipe around his plate, sopping up the juices of the rare beef and the remains of the mustard.

Josiah cocked an eyebrow at him.

'The Company has been told that you have shut off the tap for free water at the Hot Well.'

Josiah nodded. 'I have.'

'Why is that?'

Josiah smiled. 'I should have thought it would be obvious.

I have leased that Hot Well from the Company and it has cost me two thousand pounds deposit and nine hundred pounds a year. I have staff to pay, and I have this very day spent two hundred pounds on an architect's drawing for a winter garden. I am hardly likely to give water away. At your colliery, Waring, do you give away coal to anyone who calls?'

Stephen nodded at the jest but still did not smile. 'I do not have a lease,' he said slowly. 'I own my colliery outright.'

'So?'

'I do not have a lease which says that I am bound to give away my coal to anyone who calls for it.'

Josiah looked a little flustered. His breakfast came but he pushed it to one side. 'You are not telling me that my lease says I have to give away the water?'

'I am afraid that it makes clear that the poor and sick of Bristol have a right to draw water from the Hot Well,' Stephen said smoothly. 'That was the agreement when the spring was first walled in and enclosed in the building. There is a general feeling that you have to abide by it.'

Josiah took a long draught from his drink. 'That is the letter of the lease,' he expostulated. 'But surely no-one seriously expects me to give water away! After all that has been spent on the Well? After all the work we have done to make it more fashionable, to make it more exclusive?'

Waring pushed back his chair from the table and shrugged slightly. 'That is the lease,' he said easily. 'I wanted to warn you – as a friend – that the Company would wish to see the conditions of the lease fulfilled, including this one.'

'But this is preposterous!' Josiah exclaimed, still disbelieving. 'We cannot have the riff-raff of Bristol turning up night and day and queuing at the tap with their kettles and their pots, wanting the water! There is no place for them! There is no provision! They will be in the way of the carriages, they will spit and soil in the gardens! The Company cannot want that!'

Stephen Waring shrugged again. 'You signed the lease, Josiah,' he said. 'It makes it clear that water shall be provided free to the needy poor of Bristol. I think you will have to obey.' He rose from his seat. 'I must go. I am expecting a ship in port any day now. It is a worrying time waiting, isn't it? Where are your ships now?'

'God knows!' Josiah snapped irritably. '*Lily* may be loading off Africa, *Daisy* should be in the middle passage and the *Rose* in the West Indies by now. And I would be a richer man today if I had stayed in shipping. At least with my ships I know my rights. No-one has yet told me that I have to give away half my cargo. I must tell you, Waring, I cannot see my way clear to opening the tap. There is no room for the needy poor at the Hot Well!'

Stephen Waring nodded. 'As you wish, Cole,' he said equably and walked out of the coffee shop. Outside he put his hat on his head and strolled towards the quay. 'I think you will find that you are wrong,' he said thoughtfully to the wheeling gulls in the clear sky. 'I think you will find that the Company knows what it is doing.'

Frances and Sarah rose from the dinner table to leave Josiah alone with his port.

'I wish Lady Scott could have come to the Hot Well,' Josiah said uneasily. 'I was counting on your family to visit, and to tell others.'

Frances raised her eyebrows. 'She is not allowed to travel in her condition,' she said. 'They have been much at the sea this year. My uncle says he will come later. And Lady Scott will certainly come in the spring.'

'But now is the important time,' Josiah insisted. 'This is the middle of our season, we are far busier in summer than in the winter. In the winter people go to London. Summer is the time for the country and the spas. People must come *now*. If they don't come now they may not come for another year.'

'I can ask my cousins,' Frances suggested.

'What good are your cousins to me?' Josiah demanded rudely. 'You can ask your father's parishioners, but if they are not lords and ladies they will not bring in the Quality and they are no good to me.'

Frances flinched at his hectoring tone. 'I am sorry, Josiah,' she said, her voice affected, unnaturally calm. 'I am sure that Lady Scott did not wish to disoblige you.'

'I thought you would bring in the Quality patrons,' Josiah said. 'I was counting on it, Frances.'

'I *have* invited several ladies,' Frances pointed out. She could feel her breath coming short and uncertain. 'And at least two of them have promised they will come and bring their families too.'

'We've put the price of a subscription up so much,' Josiah said. 'It was ten shillings for an entire family, whatever the size, and now it is twenty-six shillings per person for the month.'

'Will that not drive away trade?' Sarah demanded.

Josiah flushed at her tone. 'Not at all. What are shillings to these people? We have to think grandly! I am just concerned for these first few weeks.'

Sarah scrutinised his face. 'We should not be too greedy,' she observed.

'I have to meet the Merchant Venturer rent,' Josiah said. 'I owe a year's rent in advance, I have to pay them. But when *Rose* is docked and I can pay off my creditors for the purchase price of the Hot Well I will be easier. I am known to be credit-worthy and I expect to see a large profit on the *Rose* voyage.'

'The sugar crop is so good at this time of year?' Frances asked.

It was nothing to do with the price of sugar, but Josiah

could not tell her about the slaves, double the usual number loaded into the small space, or the Spanish preference for women and children workers who were more obedient and less likely to rebel against the particular cruelty of those plantations. 'Oh. Yes,' he said simply. 'Very good.'

'And what day will the *Rose* arrive?' Frances asked.

'She is not a wagon,' Sarah answered acidly. 'You cannot say what day and what hour.'

'She is due in November,' Josiah said. 'But please God she will come in early and my worries will be over.'

'I am sorry you are worried,' Frances said pleasantly.

Josiah nodded unsmilingly. 'You could reduce your expenses,' he remarked.

Frances glanced swiftly at Sarah. Her sister-in-law was staring at them with avid curiosity. Frances realised that it would not occur to Josiah that such a conversation should take place in private.

'I will certainly do so,' she said with quiet dignity. 'I had no idea that matters were not as prosperous as they seem. If you had told me earlier, Josiah, I would not have ordered my autumn gowns. I shall cancel them.'

Josiah's anxiety warred briefly with his ambition. 'Oh, keep them! Keep them!' he said irritably. 'I can't have it said that my wife goes around in last season's dresses. Keep your gowns, Frances. But save on things that don't show. Underwear or shoes or something.'

Frances flushed scarlet at his indelicacy and went to the door. 'Certainly. I shall be in the morning room if you wish to continue this conversation in private.'

Sarah gave a snort of laughter as Frances closed the door on the two of them. Frances crossed the hall to the morning room, shut the door and leaned back on the white-painted panels with a sigh of relief.

Mehuru was there before her, lighting the fire. Although the September days were bright there was a chill in the air, and so Mehuru always lit a fire when Frances was sitting in a room. The children were to be brought to her at six o'clock; she was teaching them their catechism. Frances's smile was immediate and delighted. 'Oh! Cicero!' she cried.

'Call me by my name.'

'Mehuru,' she said, her voice low and passionate.

He wanted to draw her to him and kiss her, but he heard footsteps in the hall and stayed still. They looked at each other across the room.

'Frances,' he said tenderly. 'Are you well today?'

'I am perfectly well,' she replied. She sat down near the fire and smiled at him. He scanned her face for any trace of pain.

'Truly I am,' she assured him. 'Perfectly.'

He knelt at the fire to put coal on it, and sat back on his heels to look at her.

'I *am* well,' Frances said softly. 'If you wished it . . .' She broke off. He looked carefully at her. She was flushed but smiling, her eyes were bright.

'If I wished what?' he asked, half-guessing what she might say.

'If you wished to come to my room . . .' she whispered so softly that he could hardly hear her.

He was silent for a moment. 'You know I desire you,' he said hesitantly.

She took up some embroidery, as if she wanted to avoid his gaze. He watched the dark sweep of her eyelashes on her cheeks. 'I think so,' she said. 'I thought so . . .'

'But I cannot . . .' He stopped. 'Not here. Not in Josiah's house with him asleep next door. He could wake and come in at any moment.'

She nodded briefly and stole a quick glance at him. 'I was afraid . . .'

'What?'

'That you did not . . .'

409

'Desire you?'

She looked down at her embroidery and her colour rose again. 'Yes.'

He gave a short laugh. 'Frances, I lie awake every night burning up for you. All these long weeks of your illness I have thought of nothing else but holding you again. I am sleepless for you, I am hungry for you. Sometimes I think I shall go mad for you.'

'Oh,' she breathed.

'I see you are not worried about my lack of sleep,' he said.

She gave a delicious gurgle of laughter. 'I am sorry, I suppose I should be.'

'But I cannot come to you, with him in the room next door,' he said more seriously. 'I should feel a fool. I should feel . . . shamed.'

'You did once,' she reminded him in a whisper.

'I don't forget it,' he said. 'I was mad for you, we were both mad that night. But I cannot creep around the house every night like a thief, Frances.'

She nodded. 'I understand how you feel. I am glad that you told me.'

He laid the long poker and tongs either side of the grate and swept up the coal dust. He rose to his feet. 'So what shall we do?' he asked. 'Are we never to be together again? Will you not leave him and come to me? Or set me free so that I can make a place for us to be together?'

At once the joy was wiped from her face. 'I have been thinking,' she said. 'I have been thinking all the time. We will find a way. Somehow we must surely find a way.'

'I will wait,' he said. 'Not forever. But for a little while. Perhaps Wilberforce will win the vote next spring and slavery will be ended. Perhaps I will be freed by law, free to leave here, and you will be forced to choose then.'

She nodded, still grave. 'Perhaps.'

'And how would you vote?' Mehuru asked. 'Your whole

fortune depends on the Trade. Josiah's wealth, this house, everything you own. Would you end the Trade if it was your choice?'

Frances looked up. It was a question she had never put to herself. On the one hand was her tenderness for Mehuru and her recognition of the terrible wrong done to him and to the other millions, tens of millions, of Africans. But on the other hand was Frances's determination to cling to gentry status and her deep fear of poverty. Anything which could endanger her prosperity was bound to be her enemy.

She hesitated, and then she did not dare to tell him the truth: that she did not know. That she would not force herself to decide. 'I wish it had never started,' she said, taking the easy way out. 'I wish with all my heart that we had left Africa alone. I wish they had never taken you, nor all the others. I do wish it, Mehuru.'

He nodded, put the coal scuttle carefully in its place, and left the room.

In the kitchen Cook was slicing a pie for the servants' dinner and Mary and Elizabeth were hulling bowls of late rosy Cheddar strawberries for Frances's supper.

'Mehuru,' Mary said hesitantly. 'We have been thinking, Elizabeth and Martha and me . . .'

'Yes?'

'We have been thinking of running away,' she said.

Chapter Thirty-one

The Vessle Rose,
at Sea between Africa and the West Indies.

4th July 1789

Dear Mr Cole,

I Send this to you by a Reliable friend who Hove-to beside us Today to exchange News. He is First mate Stephens, travelling in the Bright Guinea to Bristol and likely to be in port In early September some two months Ahead of us who have yet to make Landfall in the West Indies. I have told him to put this into Your hands and None other and he is a Trustworthy man.

Firstly you will be Happy to hear that we are making good time in the middle passage with Clear skies and favourable winds. I Expect to see the Spanish Islands within a month, please God. According to your Orders in the letter I have shipped mainly Women and children and packed them Tighter than I would have believed Possible. We are carrying nearly Double the usual number and have had a Quieter voyage than I have Ever made, on account of the fact that they have Never mutinied nor threatened to fight but are simply Dying very quiet and Melancholy. I do assure you that I am doing everything you might wish to keep them Bright and lively, but to No avail. I have let the Youngest children stay with their Mothers and I have them up on Deck as much as I can, I am keeping them Clean, and the sailors have Not Molested them overmuch. But despite my Best endeavours there is a Great loss of life on the voyage from their Temperament which is the Worst I have ever experienced. We have Nets rigged to prevent them Throwing themselves off but when I tell you that One woman squeezed her Infant through the net and threw him Overboard to Drown him rather than Keep him with us you will understand what a Reckless bunch they are.

Of the Load of five hundred and seventy-three I have lost only ten by them drowning themselves, and in a long voyage with most of them Unchained you will know that Shows my care. One of them managed to Pierce a vein in her Arm by hammering her spoon flat and Stabbing until she was through the skin and I lost near a dozen this way, who Learned the trick and Bled to death during the Nights, and another Twenty whose cuts oozed and turned Black and thus poisoned themselves. Twenty-two of them Starved themselves to death and Vomited up when we got the brace on them and forced Slabber down their throats, and could not be saved, and near a Dozen are being fed by force now. Four made a party to Hang themselves and made their own Rope for the purpose from their clothes. In the haste of Loading, according to your Orders, some were taken on with the Flux and it is spreading to the others. Thirty have already died from the *illness, and 'Four of my crewmen whom I sorely miss.'Four babies have died in their Mothers' arms but we do not know 'Why.*

Altogether then we have near five hundred for Sale and we will start preparing them for inspection and auction next Month. Nearly a hundred look poorly, some are Old with drooping breasts and others sick. But we will 'Bung up the ones with the 'Flux, and 'Boot-black those with sores.'Trust me – I will be rid of them.

'The ones I cannot Clear I will sell in a Scramble, and any I cannot be rid of I will 'Drown on my way to Jamaica.

I will buy as much 'Top-grade sugar as I can conveniently obtain and Load and make all Speed home. I hope this meets with your Satisfaction, Sir. 'For my own 'Pride I regret the loss of so Many but that was a 'Risk we ran as you yourself acknowledged at the 'Time. 'The profit will no doubt console Us both.

I remain your obdt. servant,

Stephen Smedley
(Capt).

Josiah read the letter from Captain Smedley in the back parlour which Frances had furnished as an office for him. He read it through once again and then he drew a sheet of paper towards him. He estimated that there would be about four hundred and fifty slaves who could pass as fit once Captain Smedley had finished painting their sores and blocking their anuses. They could be sold for a total of about £22000. A scramble – when greedy or poor planters paid an entrance fee at the gangway and were allowed down into the hold to take pot-luck in the dark, grabbing as many slaves as they could and only finding if they had sick or even dying workers when they dragged them out into the daylight – would earn no more than a couple of hundred pounds.

Once *Rose* docked and Josiah shared the profits with his partners he should be left with little more than ten thousand pounds. He nodded. He had over-calculated the amounts as a man always does, speaking grandly to Sarah of profits of £14000. But even this would clear all his debts and leave him with a profit greater than Cole and Sons had ever shown before.

More slaves had died than he would have believed possible and there were more sick and unsellable slaves than Cole and Sons usually carried. Never before had a captain written in a matter-of-fact tone about dumping sick women and children over the side. Josiah shrugged. He would come out of the venture with enough profit to settle all his debts and still show a handsome margin.

He went to the fireplace where coal and kindling were laid. He took a tinderbox to the incriminating letter, carefully lit the corner and sat back on his heels to watch it flame up and then crumple to ash. The letter had taken two months to reach him. He might confidently predict that the sale of slaves had now gone through, and *Rose* was even now on the seas, headed for home, rich with sugar in her hold and bullion locked safe in the captain's cabin. On this leg of the voyage she was insured, over-insured. Josiah's gamble – overloaded slaves smuggled to the Spanish colonies – had paid off.

'Two more months and I am clear,' he said softly to himself. 'Two more months and it will be November and she will be home laden with gold and sugar.'

He went back to his desk and looked at his other letters. One was addressed to him in an unfamiliar hand. He opened it and read, then re-read, the letter.

It was a summons to appear before the Bristol magistrates.

He had been summonsed by the Merchant Venturers' Company for failing to comply with the terms of their lease – namely, to provide water from the famous healing spa the Hot Well for the needy poor of Bristol.

For a moment, Josiah was too stunned to take in the meaning, and then he felt himself gripped by a rage so total that he could not see the letter in his hand, nor the desk, nor the window before him overlooking the little backyard where Kbara was slowly sweeping.

'My God,' he said. He was almost awed by the passion which shook him. 'My God.'

He could not think why they should persecute him for the little tap, why they, who had grown rich on the sweat of the Bristol poor and on the blood of the slaves of Africa, should suddenly suffer a crisis of conscience about one little tap. He had heard Stephen Waring's warning but he had never dreamed that the Merchant Venturers' Company – his own club, his own new-found friends – would take action against him.

He rose from his chair, he almost staggered and, clasping the letter to his chest, went to find Frances.

She was seated in the ornate parlour, with some sewing in her hands. She put it down as soon as she saw his face.

'Josiah?'

'Read this,' he said and thrust the letter at her.

He watched her face as she read it through, and read it through again. He saw her grow suddenly wary, as if she had found something to fear.

'What do you make of it?' he asked her. 'Waring warned me but I had no idea they would go so far. Why should they take me to court for such a trifle?'

Frances frowned. 'Did he warn you that they would take you to court?'

'No! I would not have believed it if he had! He told me only that he had heard that the Company wanted the tap open. I had no idea . . .' Josiah trailed off. 'I would have opened it if they had insisted. But why should they insist? Why should they want to spoil the spa with sickly paupers hanging around and collecting water in buckets? Why should they want beggars at the Hot Well?'

Frances shook her head. 'I don't know. It makes no sense. I thought their whole idea was that it should be elegant and exclusive.' She thought for a moment. 'When is the hearing?'

'Next week.'

'Can you open the tap before then? Prevent this case getting to court?'

'I should think so. It is only bolted off. But I don't see why I *should*! Why should anyone ask it of me?'

'Do you have a lawyer, Josiah?'

He shook his head miserably. 'I have never needed one before,' he said. 'All my dealings, all my father's dealings, were done on a handshake. You can ask anyone; when I give my word that is as good as a bond. I have never used a lawyer. I have always thought them more trouble and expense than they were worth.'

'I think we need a lawyer now,' Frances decided. 'There is something happening here and we need a friend who can tell us what is going on.' She opened the summons again. 'Who is the presiding magistrate? Mr John Shore?'

'That is Stephen Waring's brother-in-law,' Josiah said. 'And his partner.'

Frances's face was grave. 'I think we need a lawyer.'

The lawyer's advice was simple. Even Josiah conceded that he had given value for money. The tap was to be opened at pre-arranged times every day and only then could the needy of Bristol disturb the gentility of the spa by queuing for their water. There was no fine to pay, and aside from the lawyer's fee there were no costs incurred. Josiah went before the magistrate, John Shore, who nodded pleasantly to him from the bench, while Josiah explained that there had been an oversight and that all was remedied now. It turned out to be a simple little matter.

Josiah would have kept it from Sarah if he could, but the week after the court hearing she read of it in the newspaper. A journalist made a great to-do over it, writing as if a moral victory had been won over the grasping new tenant of the Hot Well. It appeared as if the Merchant Venturers had stood firm for the rights of the poor and defended their health. The Merchant Venturers had protected the defence-less paupers' right to the miracle of the spa water. The Mer-chant Venturers had saved the Hot Well for the people of Bristol. Someone had given the journalist a great deal of information and none of it reflected very well on Josiah. Someone had gone to a deal of trouble to show Josiah as a newly rich, grasping landlord who had tried to ride rough-shod over the rights of the common people. The water from the Hot Well was said to be the saviour of the Bristol paupers – the only water they could safely drink in the whole contami-nated, dirty city. It was a miracle water which had cured countless patients of skin ailments, digestive troubles, lung and heart complaints; and now the new landlord, a self-made man, a Trader, would snatch this natural boon from the mouths of the needy.

'It means nothing, Sarah,' Josiah said. She had brought a copy of the newspaper to his office.

'We have never appeared in a newspaper before,' she said, her voice throbbing with suppressed emotion. 'And they are calling you an upstart.'

Josiah flushed. 'It means nothing.'

'You did not tell me,' Sarah reproached him.

'It was not ships' business, I did not want to worry you. I saw a lawyer and took advice. It is a storm in a teacup.'

'We are all out of our depths in these matters. The

418

Merchant Venturers' Company was your new-found friend only last month, and this month they take you to court.'

Josiah nodded. 'They surprised me,' he acknowledged frankly. 'I will take it as a warning shot across my bows, Sarah. Things are not always as they seem.'

'In this town they are never as they seem,' Sarah said.

Josiah smiled. 'You are prejudiced. You are a Welsh girl at heart, Sarah.'

She shook her head. 'I am the daughter of a self-made man,' she said simply. 'I will never trust the gentry.'

Josiah was teased very roundly at the October Company dinner for oppressing the poor and he took it with a small grim smile. No-one saw fit to tell him why the Company should have gone to the length of threatening one of its own members with prosecution, and Josiah did not find himself confident enough to demand an explanation. When the decisions were nodded through he heard to his surprise that Cole and Sons would be excused charges at the light-houses all the way down the Bristol channel for the next two years.

A smiling nod from Stephen Waring suggested that it was a favour from him. Josiah raised his glass in thanks and hid his confusion. In the roaring bonhomie of the songs and the toasts there was no opportunity to draw Stephen to one side and ask why he was so unexpectedly favoured. When he woke up the next morning with a nauseating headache he merely assumed that the Merchant Venturers had brought the case against him to demonstrate their care for the people of Bristol and had paid him for his embarrassment with an easing of their charges. It seemed a reasonably fair exchange.

The publicity about the re-opening of the tap did not damage the reputation of the Hot Well at all. It made it appear even more exclusive. Another London paper reprinted the story, emphasising the increased elegance of the spa, which certainly led to a couple of extra bookings. Then the story died away and was forgotten.

Only Frances wondered why the Merchant Venturers' Company had taken such pains to appear as heroes and defenders of the common people. She wondered why they had taken the deposit for the lease and a full year's rent from Josiah and then threatened his business in its first season. And she wondered why they had cast Josiah, their new tenant, the newest member of their company, as the villain of the piece.

When she mentioned her worries to Josiah he snapped at her and ordered her to go and look at the Hot Well herself and tell him what he could do to make the spa more profitable. Frances and Sarah drove out together, on a bright sunny day towards the end of October.

The avenue was bare and stark, the broad yellow leaves blown away from the little plane trees. On the far side of the river Rownham Woods glowed with autumn colours, reds, yellows and golds. Frances was wearing one of her new gowns and a pretty fur-lined jacket, but when she saw the saddle horses standing idle outside the Pump Room, and the places for the waiting carriages standing empty, she felt that she should have taken Josiah's angry demand to heart and cancelled all her new outfits.

'It looks quiet,' she remarked uneasily to Sarah.

Sarah said nothing.

The two women dismounted from the carriage and went inside.

'Mrs Cole! Miss Cole!' The Master of Ceremonies surged forward. 'What a pleasure to see you both. You will take a dish of tea, I know!'

Sarah nodded and Frances allowed him to draw them to one of the little tables. A smart maid came forward and gave them tea.

Frances looked around the room. A few invalids were

reclining in seats around the echoing room. The quartet played brightly. The card tables stood empty, new packs of cards still in their wrappings at each corner. A few people walked slowly up and down the room, undertaking their exercise with mournful expressions. It was deeply depressing.

'I did not know you had so little company here,' Frances said.

'Today *is* a little thin,' the man said, as if he had suddenly noticed. 'But in the middle of the week it is often quiet. We don't have the local trade that we used to enjoy. We still have our residents though.'

'Because it is too expensive,' Sarah said abruptly.

'Let us say – too select!' he replied sweetly.

'If it is too select for the Bristol merchants and their families then it is too select to succeed.'

'Sarah!' Frances whispered. To the Master of Ceremonies she said: 'I hope it will improve. Do you think it will improve, Mr Tucker?'

'I am certain,' he said. 'When our new winter garden room is built we will be packed every winter. And in summer we always succeed. These are the worst months for the Hot Well – autumn, and of course winter. You can see it in the records. These are the months when the Quality are in Town. We have to be patient and wait until spring. More tea, Miss Cole?'

'No thank you,' Sarah replied, containing her irritation with some difficulty.

'Perhaps we had better go,' Frances suggested. 'Mr Cole asked us to call and see how things were.'

'Tell him they are well,' Mr Tucker said with breezy confidence. 'A little slow today of course, but busier every day the sun shines. And all of us here, all of this little team are ready and confident for spring.'

'But it is October now,' Sarah hissed through her teeth as

they got into the carriage. 'How does the booby think we will manage until spring?'

'Perhaps the *Rose* will come in early,' Frances said. Both women turned and looked towards the mouth of the river. Seagulls wheeled and cried over the empty water.

'She must come in next month,' Sarah said. 'She must come in when she is due. It is not long to wait now. Only four weeks if she is on time. With so much riding on her, she *must* come home on time.'

Chapter Thirty-two

On the first of November Josiah's debt to Hibbard and Sons fell due. He had planned to pay them out of the profit which *Rose* would bring home. But *Rose* had not yet returned. He wrote a brief letter to Hibbard and Sons explaining that his ship was slightly overdue and that he would be obliged if they would extend the life of his loan for another month.

Hibbard and Sons wrote an equally brief note back within the week, saying simply that they did not wish to extend the loan for another month. Josiah would oblige them by clearing his debt of £5400 plus interest at once.

Josiah stared at the letter for a long time in silence. He did not know what he should do next. He opened the front door and looked down the street to the river. His dock was empty, and the tide was coming in. The *Rose* could sail in on this tide, or the next, or the next after that.

He called for Kbara and told him to go round to the stable and hire a horse. Perhaps takings at the Hot Well had increased.

He rode along the river with little pleasure. There were no large boats, the tide was too shallow and uncertain. A single trow, like Josiah's father's first ship, was sailing up the river, moving swiftly on the flowing tide. Josiah had an odd fanciful notion that he would have been a happier man today if he had stuck to a single trow to sail up and down the river carrying little loads, and coming home at night to Sarah.

He hitched his horse to the ring in the wall of the Hot

Well and strode into the room. The beautiful long assembly room, newly whitewashed since his purchase, was all but deserted. The string quartet played mechanically without spirit in one corner of the room, the card tables were still empty with new unopened packs of cards laid invitingly on the green baize. A silver urn hissed in the corner with a smartly liveried maid beside it waiting to serve tea. The visitors' book, prominently displayed at the doorway, was empty of any new names.

Only the invalids, sick and pale as ever, were slumped in the chairs around the room. Josiah glared at them as if he wished they would relapse and die rather than linger and give the place its depressing atmosphere of a hospital.

'Where is everyone?' he demanded of the Master of Ceremonies. 'It may be mid-November but the place should be busier than this. I've seen last year's attendance book. It should be better than this. It's not midsummer but there should be people on repairing leases from the London Season. Where is everyone?'

'Most disappointing,' the man replied. 'I too am most disappointed.'

'I am sorry for it,' Josiah said grimly. 'I shall add your disappointment to my other worries. Why is no-one here?'

The man shook his bewigged head. 'I can't say. I don't know.'

'Very well,' Josiah said carefully. 'What is your opinion? Do you have any opinion? Would you venture a guess?'

The man regarded him warily. 'I think it is a number of things,' he offered cautiously. 'A number. Shall we take tea?'

'No. What number of things?'

'Well, the charges,' the man said delicately, looking longingly at the urn and the maid and the diversion of teacups. 'They are rather high now. Higher than Bath, I believe. Perhaps too high, you know, Mr Cole. People don't want to pay them. I think they won't pay them, in fact. No-one from

Bristol comes at all now, the spa has a reputation in the town of being too expensive, of being too fashionable.' He simpered slightly. 'Perhaps we have been too successful?'

Josiah nodded. 'And what other things?'

'Well, the atmosphere,' the man went on. He waved his hand exquisitely gloved in white kid at the row of desperately sick people. 'Very dreary. Not quite the place you want to come for amusement.'

'It's a spa!' Josiah exclaimed. 'Of course there are sick people here. You're supposed to come here for your health. That is rather bound to attract ill people.'

'Of course. But it's just that they all seem so very ill indeed, don't they? They are calling Dowry Parade "Death Row", you know.'

'What?'

'Mmm, lowering, isn't it? You can see that it would put people off.'

Josiah clenched his teeth together. 'Anything else?'

'France, I'm afraid.'

Josiah felt his teeth grind. He carefully relaxed his jaw. 'France?'

'A lot of the younger, wilder fashionable set are off to the French spas. They're interested in France this year. The French, you know.'

'What?'

'The French, sir, the Jacobins! You know, *Liberté, Egalité . . .*'

'What the devil has this to do with my Hot Well?' Josiah bellowed. The quartet died into silence. Josiah flushed scarlet with suppressed rage and embarrassment. 'Tell them to play on,' he muttered.

The MC waved an airy hand at them. The quartet bowed to Josiah and started their little rippling tune again.

'What has the fall of the Bastille to do with my Hot Well?' Josiah demanded through his teeth.

425

'There is a great enthusiasm for liberty and France and so on. They are all rushing off to France this year. We cannot make poor little Bristol appeal at all.'

Josiah sighed. 'I can make no sense of this. Anything else?'

The man shrugged. 'I don't know. It is a shame. I *do* think it's a shame.'

'So all we have to do,' Josiah said bitterly, 'is drop our subscription, stop sick people coming here, and put an end to the revolution in France and our worries will be over.'

The Master of Ceremonies looked at him coyly. 'Rather a task, isn't it?' he smiled.

'It's damnable,' Josiah said. He strode from the room. The Master of Ceremonies fluttered behind him.

'But don't be disheartened, I implore you. It's only November. Anything could happen! Once the winter is over – and I so *dread* the winter, don't you? Once the winter is over and the spring comes I am sure anything could happen . . .'

Josiah turned to face him and the man skidded to a standstill, his high-heeled shoes slipping on the polished floor.

'Anything *is* happening!' Josiah cried sharply. 'This place costs me nigh on one thousand pounds a year for the lease alone, and the running costs are near a hundred pounds a week. Anything and everything is happening with the sole exception of this place earning a living.'

'Oh! Money worries! Money worries!' the man exclaimed. 'They are so wearisome, aren't they?'

'How much do I pay you?' Josiah demanded unpleasantly.

'Why, by the Season, you pay me eighty guineas a Season, Mr Cole.'

'At least I can save that!' Josiah said. 'You are fired.'

'I?' The Master of Ceremonies was genuinely amazed. 'You cannot fire me, sir. You are making a mistake.'

Josiah trudged to his horse, his head down. 'I have fired you,' he said grimly. 'You can pack your bags.'

'I? Pack?'

'Or leave 'em here. But you are out of this place by the end of this week, so help me God! You were hired to bring in the fashionable set. I don't see one of them. So you are fired!'

'Well, I doubt very much that it will help you.' The Master of Ceremonies teetered to a halt and flung the words after Josiah's back.

Josiah unhitched his horse from the ring and mounted it in surly silence.

'The Hot Well will not pay because you bought it at too high a price!' the Master of Ceremonies called up at him. 'You can blame me but it is your own fault! Blame me all you like! But everyone knows it is your own fault!'

Josiah's face went so black that the man sprang back, half-fearing him, but Josiah dragged the horse's head round and headed away, down the track to the docks where *Rose* with her cargo of gold and sugar was due this month and soon would surely arrive.

He did not go home, though it was nearly dinner time. He returned the horse to the stable and walked, rather uncomfortable in his riding boots, down to the quayside. The lad in the ferryboat was moored on the far side but at Josiah's shout he rowed over.

'Been riding, Mr Cole?' he asked.

Josiah scowled at him and made no reply.

The lad rowed in silence, slightly surprised. Josiah's good nature was well-known on the quayside. But the rumour that he was over-extended had been growing lately. The boy took his ha'penny in silence and pulled his cap as Josiah went up the slimy steps to his quay.

The familiar noise and bustle comforted him. The porters' sledges screeched on the greasy cobbles, the men swearing and cursing as they pulled heavy loads. The quay next to Cole and Sons was again busy with a ship newly in from the

West Indies. As Josiah watched they ran a gangplank up to her and the captain came down and greeted the owner. Josiah hung back until they had spoken and the owner gone on board to see for himself the full sweet-smelling hold, then he called to the captain.

'Holloa! Captain Smythe?'

The man turned. 'Oh! Mr Cole, is it?'

'Good crossing?'

'Moderate.'

'How long did it take you?'

'Eight and a half weeks from quayside to quayside.'

'You will have seen my ship, *Rose*?'

'*Rose*? No, I have not seen her.'

Josiah tried to smile but he knew his face was strained. 'Come now, you must have done. I had a letter from her writ in July. She was just off the Sugar Islands then. She will have bought sugar and set sail for England. Surely you will have passed her in the channel. I cannot think why she is not ahead of you.'

The man shook his head gravely. 'I have not seen her, Mr Cole. Not sailing home, nor in the West Indies. No-one spoke of her either. I hope she has not gone astray.'

Josiah laughed mirthlessly. 'Not *Rose*! She is the luckiest ship that ever was and she is commanded by Captain Smedley. If he does not know the way home then no man at sea knows it! She will be home within the sennight, I am certain.'

'Indeed I hope so,' the captain said. 'And we had some black storms. I could have passed within inches of her and not seen her on some of the nights.'

'Exactly!' Josiah exclaimed. 'No. I shall not worry. She will be home any day now.'

The owner came out of the hold, his face bright. 'There's no better sight in the world, is there, Cole?' he demanded. 'A full hold and the smell of fresh sugar!'

Josiah found a weak smile. 'No,' he said with difficulty.

'Here is Mr Cole asking me after his ship *Rose*,' the captain said indiscreetly.

'Is she late?'

'No!' Josiah replied quickly. 'She's just due. I just thought that they might have passed her.'

'Well, I daresay it does not matter to you now,' the owner said jealously. 'With your other interests. Your fine house, and your membership of the Venturers, and your Hot Well. I daresay *Rose* late or early matters very little.'

Josiah's smile was ghastly. 'Very little.'

He went into his warehouse to avoid their stares and up into his old parlour. It was empty and dusty. Only the pieces of furniture which were too shabby to move had been left. He found his father's old broken-seated chair and dragged it to the parlour window.

He sat, looking out over the quay, over the dock, down-river. The tide was going out and the new ship at the quayside would have to be unloaded tomorrow. They were loosening her ropes to let her drop down on the ebbing water to settle on the mud. She would not split her sides, even with her heavy cargo, she was built 'Bristol fashion', strong enough to withstand the stress of the tidal port which dumped all the ships on to their keels in the mud twice a day.

There was no point looking for *Rose*. She would not come into port against the tide. He would have to wait until tomorrow for her now. For a moment Josiah imagined her, riding easily in the water with her cargo of sugar stowed evenly in the hold, moored for the night safely in the Kings-road anchorage with her lanterns lit fore and aft. He sat still, his eyes on the swiftly draining water, picturing his ship so passionately that it was almost as if he could call her into life.

'*Rose*,' he said.

When Josiah arrived home at five o'clock, late for his dinner, he was irritated to see a travelling coach emblazoned with the Scott arms waiting outside his door. In the morning room Lord Scott was sitting with Frances and Sarah. Josiah came in reluctantly.

'Why, Cole!' Lord Scott exclaimed. 'We thought you had gone down with one of your ships.'

Josiah flinched at the image of a sinking ship. 'I was working,' he said irritably.

Frances glanced at his riding breeches and boots. 'You have been to the Hot Well! Is everything as it should be?'

'No,' Josiah answered shortly.

There was an embarrassed silence. Frances gave her breathless society laugh. 'I am sorry to hear it,' she said. 'You must tell us about it over dinner. Shall I ask them to delay dinner while you change your clothes, Mr Cole?'

'No,' Josiah said stubbornly. 'I can dine like this.'

A shadow crossed Frances's face. 'Whatever you wish,' she said smoothly.

'You are kind to keep me in countenance,' Lord Scott smiled. 'Here I am in my travelling clothes but my niece insisted I stay for dinner. I only called for tea on my way to Whiteleaze.' Lord Scott's travelling clothes were an immaculate suit of light grey cloth with a matching light grey cloak. He looked as if he had never seen a dusty road in his life.

Josiah nodded curtly. 'I hope you will come back to visit the Hot Well and bring your wife.'

Lord Scott shot a quick look at Frances as if to see how he should respond to such a brusque invitation. 'Well, of course we shall come,' he said smoothly. 'As soon as Lady Scott is strong enough to go visiting again. And sorry I am to hear that it is not going well for you there. But these are early days, surely. And it is a new line of business for you.'

'What is wrong, Josiah?' Sarah cut through the light patter of conventional pleasantry.

430

He looked directly at her. 'Hibbard and Sons are pressing me, the Hot Well is losing money and I am still waiting for *Rose*.'

She nodded, her eyes never leaving his face. 'Early days yet,' she said bravely. 'We've had many a ship come in later than this and bring us nothing but good news.'

Her calmness was like a sheet anchor in a storm. His face cleared a little. 'Yes,' he said. 'You are right.'

There was a short silence.

'I have brought you a gift,' Lord Scott announced, bridging an awkward moment. 'Not of my own choosing, I am sorry to say. I am a messenger for Sir Charles Fairley. He ordered some slave collars for you after his last visit here and had them delivered to me. They are in the hall. Would you like to see them?'

'Of course,' Frances said. She reached out and rang the bell. Mary came and Lord Scott asked her to tell his coachman to bring in the boxes.

'What are these things?' Josiah asked as the coachman carried in eleven narrow boxes and put them on the table at Lord Scott's elbow.

'Slave collars,' Lord Scott replied pleasantly. 'They are very much in fashion in London for slaves. Sir Charles has ordered you a most pretty set, each one engraved with your slaves' names.'

He opened the first box and held one up. It was a light decorative silver chain, carrying a label at the front, also of silver. Engraved on the label was the name 'Julius'.

'Which are you?' Lord Scott asked Mary.

'Mary,' she answered, unsmiling.

He opened a couple of the boxes. 'Ah yes! Here it is.' He turned the black woman around as if she were a doll and fastened the chain around her neck. 'You get a blacksmith to forge the final link,' he told Frances. 'So they are fixed on. They are of ornamental value only, symbolic, if you like.

431

If a slave runs off and wants to be free he can break the chain if he tries hard enough. It is a fancy, merely.'

'Very pretty,' Sarah said. 'Mary, fetch the others. They can all have them on.'

Frances put her hand out to stop her, but could think of no excuse. The other slaves came into the room one by one. Mehuru came in with the little boy John and glanced across at Frances. She met his eyes with a look of veiled warning.

Sarah had taken a few of the boxes and Lord Scott had the others. Without explaining to the slaves what they were doing, they ordered them to stand still and then fastened the chains around their necks and sent them back to the kitchen. Mehuru was the last of the line, left alone in the room with the white people. When Lord Scott held out the chain, Mehuru recoiled. 'I will not have that thing on me.'

Lord Scott hesitated. 'I do not think you have a choice,' he said with a little smile. 'Come here.'

Mehuru took another step backwards. 'I will not have that on me,' he repeated.

'Cicero . . .' Frances said quietly.

He threw her a look which demanded her support. 'It is not my name,' he said desperately.

Lord Scott turned the label around. 'Cicero,' he read. 'It is your name. It is. See the "C"? That means Cicero.'

'I can read,' Mehuru exclaimed. 'My name is not Cicero. My name is Mehuru. I am an envoy of the Yoruba Federation. I will not be labelled like a dog.'

Josiah's temper, which had been on the edge of breaking all day, suddenly snapped. 'You will wear what you are bid!' he shouted, his voice horribly loud in the pretty room. 'You will wear what you are bid and damned well do as you are told!'

With a bound he launched himself across the room and pounded his fist into Mehuru's face, thumping him in the eye. Frances screamed and leaped to her feet. Mehuru,

432

stepping back from Josiah's onslaught, stumbled against a table and fell. In a moment Josiah was on him, forcing him to the ground, pummelling his face and his shoulders. The coachman, at a swift nod from Lord Scott, grabbed Josiah from behind, pinning his arms and dragging him off.

'Josiah! Josiah!' Lord Scott said swiftly. 'Not here. Not before ladies!'

The coachman released him and Josiah felt for the back of a chair to haul himself to his feet, pulling at his neckcloth. The coachman had fallen on Mehuru as soon as Josiah was off him and turned him face down on the floor, twisting his arms behind his back. Mehuru did not struggle; he lay still, his face forced into the carpet.

'Please . . .' Frances said. She was ashen, her hand at her throat, she was gasping for air, 'Please . . .'

'Sit down, Frances, and calm yourself,' Lord Scott said, glancing towards her. The habits of her childhood obedience were very strong. She sank into a seat but did not take her eyes from Mehuru.

'Put it on him.' Lord Scott handed the chain and label to the coachman. 'I advise you to be still,' he said quietly to Mehuru. 'Or you will be taken and beaten.'

Mehuru gave no sign of hearing. He lay completely still. Even when they put the chain around his neck, and fastened it, and crushed the soft metal clasp together so that it could not be undone, he did not move.

'Let him up,' Lord Scott ordered the coachman. The man released Mehuru but stepped quickly back, ready to knock him down at the least sign of disobedience.

Mehuru climbed slowly to his feet. His eye was badly bruised and was swelling fast, the eyelid closing. Frances gave a little cry, hastily suppressed, and turned her face away from him. He looked towards her and his mouth twisted at being shamed before her. Lord Scott thought he had never seen a man brought so low.

433

'You had better go to your room and wash your face,' he suggested gently.

Mehuru gave him one burning look and stalked from the room. His slave collar caught the light as he turned. The lettering said clearly: 'Cicero'.

Josiah raised his head. 'Lock him in,' he said shortly.

Lord Scott hesitated. 'Is that necessary?' he asked. 'You were not cruel. He surely would not go running to a magistrate with a complaint of cruelty. And this is Bristol after all, no-one would listen to a slave.'

'I don't want him running anywhere,' Josiah retorted crudely. 'Order your man to lock him into his room for the night and bring me the key.'

'Very well.' Lord Scott nodded at his man who bowed and quietly followed Mehuru. 'You are perhaps right to take care.'

'That is a hundred and ten guineas of bloodstock walking round,' Josiah said sullenly. 'I don't want it walking into the Avon and drowning itself for despair.'

Dinner was late and served with sulky unwillingness. Kbara and the boys had tucked their slave collars under their high neckcloths; but the lower necklines of the women's dresses meant they could not conceal them. Their chains glinted in the candlelight as they moved around the table, each one labelled like a decanter of drink. Frances thought that at last they were clearly marked for all to see, a Bristol commodity, as much goods of the city as sherry or port wine.

Josiah drank heavily at dinner and ate little. Lord Scott, seated on Frances's right and opposite Sarah, kept up an easy flow of talk. He had news of Frances's cousins, and of the health of Lady Scott, banished to Whiteleaze for her lying-in. And he had news of London and the gossip from the City and from Parliament.

'The Abolition debate is rather subdued at the moment,' he reported. 'But there is no doubt that it will rise up again

434

next year. They cannot succeed, not while the gentry is against them, but they can stir up a lot of bad feeling.'

'It will never come to anything,' Sarah said firmly. 'Mr Wilberforce knows nothing of what he is talking about. He should turn his attention to the conditions in the northern cotton mills, that is nearer to his home! But no, he is one of these meddling minds who has to see things at a distance. Why, he has even been party to the setting up of a school for farm labourers' children near Cheddar. There have been many complaints from farmers that they cannot get the children to work as they should, they are forever running off to Mr Wilberforce's school. I should like to see how he would like it if we meddled in his business and started trying to pass laws to ban it.'

'No,' Lord Scott said, smiling at Sarah's indignation. 'I do not think he would like it at all. But surely we cannot hope to avoid Abolition forever. Your company might do well to perhaps consider another venture.'

'I do consider it,' Josiah said grimly. 'I consider my land-based venture every day, and every day it costs me more.' There was a brief embarrassed silence. Lord Scott glanced across at Frances.

'I was sorry to hear that you were unwell, Frances,' he said. 'Are you quite recovered? Bristol suited you so well. I was so pleased when you wrote to me that you were feeling so strong and so happy.'

Frances started, she had not been following the conversation at all. 'I am quite well,' she replied. She was desperate to know if Mehuru was badly hurt, and she was still shocked at the explosion of violence in her own parlour. She could not look at Josiah. Brought up in a vicarage and shielded from the reality of life both by her status and her sex, she was frightened by the least sign of violence. Josiah's anger, erupting in her own morning room, was enough to make him a monster in her eyes.

435

At the end of the meal when the ladies withdrew, Frances whispered to her uncle that she felt unwell and that she would bid him farewell. He rose from his seat, drew her to him and kissed her on the forehead. 'I am sorry to see you thus,' he said and the phrase took in the whole evening: Frances's sick pallor, and Josiah's despairing rage.

'Such a thing has never happened before . . .'

'I will call again,' he soothed her. 'As soon as Lady Scott has been brought to bed. And you must come and stay with us.' He turned to Sarah and Josiah. 'And you too, Miss Cole, and Josiah. Lady Scott would be delighted to have your company.'

Sarah looked frankly disbelieving, and Josiah hardly heard the invitation. He was slumped in his chair, staring at his glass. Lord Scott's quick assessing gaze passed over him.

'Goodnight,' Frances said, and slipped from the room.

Chapter Thirty-three

As soon as the family had gone to bed the slaves had unlocked Mehuru's door with Cook's spare set of keys and brought him down to the kitchen. He sat, with the children at his feet, in the fireside chair. The women slaves were seated on the kitchen bench, facing him in a solemn row. Kbara sat at the kitchen table. Cook, her feet on the fender, was seated in the opposite chair and clasped her hands in her lap, controlling her sense of outrage. In the flickering light from the fire the slave collars on the women's necks gleamed.

'It isn't right,' Cook said softly. 'I want no part in it. I won't order you. I won't work for them any more if they treat you so. There are many kitchens where I would be welcome. I don't have to stay here and be a party to this.' She rose to her feet and stirred the coals with a poker through the door of the range. 'It isn't right,' she repeated.

Mehuru nodded. He was reminded for a moment of the lengthy counsels of the villages at home. To an outsider it might look as if no-one was capable of any decision, to an outsider it might look as if the men were sitting around idly, chattering. But what was happening was the difficult stages of discussion, working through to a hard-won consensus. What was primitive, Mehuru thought, was the notion of government as a state of permanent warfare – first one side having the upper hand and then the other. The English justice system was no better – a battle between two opposing points of view. The African way was slower and harder but it worked on the belief that agreement was possible, that men and women could come together and find a course to suit them all. It was neither victory nor defeat.

Kbara was in favour of them taking all that they could carry and running away this very night. But the women, especially Elizabeth, were afraid of what might happen. The newspapers were full of advertisements for runaway slaves and the rewards offered would tempt anyone.

'But don't you see,' Mehuru argued, 'that the rewards show that slaves are hidden by English people. The owners have to offer a high reward to make English people betray the runaway slaves. The rewards should make us more confident, not less. We could not stay in Bristol, of course. We would have to go to London and there are thousands of people of our colour living there.'

'Maybe,' Mary said slowly. 'But they would offer a high reward for all of us, and if we stay together, as we want, we would be easy to find. Besides, what could we do?'

'Mehuru and I could work,' Kbara said.

'Doing what?'

'On the quayside, there are lots of black men working at the port.'

'And we could work as house servants,' Martha suggested. 'Laundry, or waiting tables, or housework. We've been trained well enough. Elizabeth could be a parlourmaid or even a lady's maid. I could try out as a cook.'

'Could we get the boys apprenticed to a trade?' Elizabeth asked. 'They need proper work. I don't want them working down at the docks. It is rough and it is dangerous, and besides, anyone who wants a slave can just come by and thieve them away from us.'

Mehuru's face was hard. 'They can't get an apprenticeship in London. The Lord Mayor himself has ordered that no black boys can be trained for work. They passed a special law to ban black boys from being trained.' He gave a bitter little smile. 'They must think us very skilful, if the white men have to be protected against our apprentices.'

'And what about the girls?' Elizabeth pressed. 'The girls need work too. I don't want them growing up with nothing to do but dirty work. Little Susan is as bright as any child I've ever known. She should be sent to school, if we were at home ...' She broke off. At home a bright girl could find herself a training, she could work in the palace and rise as high as her skills took her. 'It seems a long way away now,' Elizabeth said sadly.

'What about going home?' Kbara asked. 'What about this Sierra Leone? We could go to London and take a ship to Sierra Leone. It's not Yoruba, it's not my people, but at least we're in the right place. At least we're in Africa. And we could maybe travel overland, back to our homes.'

Mehuru shook his head. 'We can't travel home. The trading routes have been destroyed, there are no caravans we could join. There are no villages we could visit. Inland from the coast for miles and miles the country has been wrecked. The people are enslaved or in hiding, the fields are growing weeds. No-one travels down the rivers unless they are hunting for slaves. The country is unsafe.

'And I doubt very much that this Sierra Leone is safe either. I've seen the pamphlets, I read them to you all, but I also heard from a man at the Constitution Society. He says that it is not a proper colony at all but just somewhere for England to dump unwanted freed slaves. They got volunteers for the first settlement by refusing black beggars their dole unless they signed on and went. When the ships were blown ashore at Plymouth the captains battened down the hatches and wouldn't let the black people go ashore. They had to eat the rations they had for the trip while they were waiting, so they were hungry on the voyage. They would not let them have stoves or candles. What does that remind you of? A long sea

439

journey with not enough to eat and cold all the time? What does it remind you of, Kbara?'

'But if Africa is at the end of it? Africa and freedom?'

'What if at the end of it there is a couple of farms, a stockade fence, and the whole of the country from north and south making war to take slaves, selling slaves at a profit? How long do you think we would last? And these little children would be taken by slavers again. Do you think they would survive that journey twice?'

Kbara was silent for a moment. 'So what shall we do?' he demanded. 'What shall we do? We have to do something now, while Josiah is away from the house all day and Sarah is too worried about the business to watch us. And we will not bear these collars. This is our chance, Mehuru.'

'I know,' Mehuru said gently. 'You are right. Our chance is now and we should take it. I don't think we can go back to Africa and I don't think we should stay in Bristol. But there are other cities and towns. There are places where we could get work, perhaps send the children to school, teach them trades. Stuart Hadley would help us get away, he would advise us where to go.

'I cannot stay here.' He touched his shirt where the silver collar rubbed against the skin of his neck. It was smooth and well-made but he flinched as though it scratched him with every move he made. 'I cannot bear it,' he said.

'We stay together,' Mary decided. 'I want to stay with you, all of you.'

Elizabeth dropped her hand on Mary's. 'You are like my sister. I could not bear to be without you.'

'I will ask Stuart to advise us,' Mehuru said. 'I will creep out and find him tomorrow.'

Josiah wakened in the morning with a thick head and a foul taste in his mouth. He washed quickly and dressed without care. He brushed past Kbara in the hall and his silent sulky step to one side reminded Josiah that Mehuru was still locked away.

He turned, ran up the stairs and tapped on Frances's bedroom door. She was awake but still in her bed. When she saw him she shrank back against her pillows and her hand went to her throat. She was afraid of him. She remembered the sullen rage of his drinking through dinner, and the sudden explosion of violence when he had pummelled Mehuru to the ground. Frances flinched at the sight of him and underneath her fear was resentment.

Josiah did not even notice. He was too anxious about his business – too absorbed in the disaster which was building every day. He had forgotten the slow growth of confidence and ease between them, he had forgotten the pleasure of making Frances smile. He had forgotten the ease and sense of plenty in the luxurious house and the slowly blooming beauty of his expensively bought wife. All he could see now was the mounting weight of his debts and the steady tick-tick of accruing interest. All he saw when he looked at Frances, pale and defensive in her bed, was another expense.

'The slaves are supposed to be in your keeping,' he said brusquely. 'See that Cicero is fit to be released this morning, and have him ready for sale. If I can speak with Stephen Waring I shall close the sale today. And the little boy. I will sell the others as soon as they can be advertised. We are desperate for money and I am sick of having the house cluttered up with their idle bodies.' He tossed the key to Mehuru's room on the bed where it fell with a weighty clink.

'He cannot be sold,' Frances protested. Her voice was a little thread against Josiah's angry gruffness.

'Why the devil not?'

He had never sworn in her presence before. Frances flinched. 'I . . . He is promised to my Uncle Scott,' she lied quickly. 'You can sell Julius to Mr Waring. He will not know

441

the one from the other but my Uncle Scott specifically asked for Cicero.'

'He's a fool then,' Josiah snapped. 'After the man's behaviour he should be shipped out to the plantations.'

'You would not . . .'

'Only because it would not pay,' Josiah said spitefully. 'If I could sell him for hounds' meat at a profit I would do so. Now get up, madam, and set the house to rights. You are idling here while everything is going wrong. The slaves are your charge and they are running wild, God knows how much they cost me. God knows how much you all cost me.'

He stamped from her bedroom, leaving the door carelessly ajar. Frances stayed very still in her bed, frozen with fear, until she heard his feet thunder down the stairs and across the hall, and the front door slam.

It was a brisk November morning in the square. A gardener was sweeping the fallen leaves into large damp piles. Josiah did not look up at the pale sky nor enjoy the fresh cold air on his face. He could smell the tang of the incoming tide as it washed the flotsam and garbage back into the heart of the city. This tide should bring in *Rose*, he thought, and strode down to the quayside to scan the splashing water for his ship. He looked along the length of his quay in all its neat lonely emptiness. He looked downriver to where the gorge started to rear up. There was no ocean-weary ship being towed inland. There was no sign of her. There was still no sign of her.

In the house in Queens Square Frances dressed quickly and then climbed the stairs to Mehuru's room, the key in her hand. She tapped on his door.

'Yes?' he answered in Yoruban.

'It is me,' Frances said. 'I have the key.'

She fitted it in the lock and opened the door. Mehuru had washed and shaved and changed his linen. He looked elegant

442

and impassive. His eye was bruised, a dark shadow against the darkness of his skin. 'I am sorry,' Frances said inadequately.

'Will you take my collar off?'

She looked down at his feet. 'I don't dare,' she admitted shortly. 'I don't dare go against him.'

'I will run away,' he warned. 'I will run and you will never see me again.'

She stole a quick glance at his face and then looked away again. 'Indeed I think you should go,' she said, her voice very low. 'He wants to sell you, he said he would close the sale today. I have delayed him with a lie and so he will sell Julius instead. I cannot keep you safe, Mehuru. I cannot keep any of you safe. I am sorry, I am so sorry.'

'We will go tonight,' he said.

She nodded without looking at him. 'Very well.'

'We will never come back.'

They stood, a foot apart, neither touching nor looking at each other.

'I know I will never see you again,' she whispered. 'I wish you God speed.'

'Won't you come with me?' he asked. 'Take the chance now, Frances. Now while there is nothing to stay here for. Josiah is in trouble, Sarah openly dislikes you. Come away with me, we will find somewhere to live, we will find somewhere that we can be together.'

She shrugged her shoulders, a small unhappy gesture of defeat. 'I cannot,' she said. 'I dare not. I have no money and I cannot work. I am ill, Mehuru. You would not get very far with a sick woman. And I have no courage.' She looked up at him honestly. 'I have no courage at all. I saw him strike you last night and I did nothing but jump to my feet and say, "Josiah!" and then I poured him his tea. I am ashamed.'

He shrugged. 'There was little you could do,' he said tightly. 'And I have had worse beatings.'

'But I did nothing,' she persisted. 'Nothing to save you,

nothing to save Died of Shame. I lack courage, Mehuru. When I was a girl I was full of spirit, but I have been made into the very essence of an English lady – all I can do is watch and wring my hands, and pour the tea.'

'You could run away from it all,' he suggested. 'Run away to be the wife of an African, be an African woman.'

'I dare not.'

There was a noise of a door opening below them. 'Frances?' Sarah called, her voice sharp.

The colour rushed into Frances's face as she turned to go at once, instantly obedient. Mehuru put his black hand on the white sleeve of her gown.

'Hire a carriage,' he said quickly and insistently. 'Let us drive out together this afternoon, for the last time, Frances. Let us be together this afternoon for we will never see each other again.'

She kept her head turned away, she could not bear to look at him, she did not dare to risk looking into his intent face and seeing the longing in his eyes.

'Yes,' she whispered and went downstairs.

Josiah went for his breakfast to the quayside coffee house. The door was swinging open and shut as busy men pushed in and out. The cold draughts billowed in and the sweet smell of rum, tobacco smoke and sugar billowed out. There was a small silence as the traders saw Josiah – a pause no longer than a heartbeat – but Josiah heard it. It was the silence of the herd when they notice an animal mortally sick. They were ready to turn on him and drive him out. They were ready to eat him alive. Their own survival was a stronger force than any friendship or loyalty. The word was out that Josiah was over-extended and that *Rose* was two weeks overdue.

A man rose from a table in his path and put a hand on his sleeve. 'Josiah,' he said pleasantly. 'A word with you.'

444

Josiah was on his way to the top table, to the Merchant Venturers' table. He hesitated, scowling at the man from under his brows. 'Yes?'

'A little bill overdue, a trifle,' the man said. 'From fitting out *Lily* when she was last in port.'

Josiah nodded. 'An oversight,' he said gruffly. 'I'll see to it. Send it in again, it must have been mislaid.'

'I *have* sent it in,' the man said. 'Twice. I would trouble you for the money now. It is thirty guineas.'

Josiah twitched his sleeve from the man's grasp. 'D'you think I settle my bills at my breakfast?' he demanded. 'Come to my warehouse at noon and I will pay you then.'

'I knew you when you paid your bills at breakfast, and when you touted for business at dinner,' the man replied angrily. 'And I have been to your warehouse twice yesterday and once today and there was no-one there to give me satisfaction. If it's no trouble to you, Josiah, I'll take my thirty guineas now.'

'Oh, for God's sake!' Josiah exclaimed. He plunged his hand into the big pocket of his cape and drew out a leather purse, which he tossed at the man. 'Take that, and if it is not enough I will settle up with you later, it is all I have on me. Unless you would like the buttons off my coat? They are solid brass.'

The man stood his ground. 'I am sorry if I offend you, Josiah, but it has been a long time. I cannot give you more credit. I dare not take the risk.'

'I do not trade on credit!' Josiah exclaimed, goaded beyond endurance. 'I am not a bad risk.'

The man said nothing. The whole coffee shop was silent, listening to the exchange. Josiah glared around and the men, who had been staring, at once turned to each other and chattered noisily or applied themselves to their breakfast plates. They all recognised the anger of a man cornered, whose luck is running out.

'I bid you good day,' Josiah muttered and strode to the top table.

The man turned and rejoined his friends. Under cover of the table he tipped the contents of Josiah's purse out into his hand. There was £23. 10s. 8d. He counted it quickly, returned it to the purse and tucked it in his pocket.

'It's not the full amount,' he said quietly to his neighbour. 'But I think it's the most I'm going to get.'

'He owes me for some stores,' the man replied uneasily. 'I had not thought to press my bill.' He glanced up at the top table. 'And there's nothing to be had from him now. You've picked the bones clean this morning, Tobias.'

The man nodded. 'Catch him another morning. It's the only way you will get your bills met, I believe. There will be no more credit for Cole and Sons from my business. Take my word for it: he's going down.'

Chapter Thirty-four

Frances changed into her driving gown and waited at her bedroom window for the hired carriage to come round to the door. When she heard the rattle of the wheels and the ring of the horses' metal-shod hooves in the street she ran downstairs. Sarah was in the hall. 'You hired the carriage?' she demanded, outraged.

'I wanted to drive out,' Frances said.

'We cannot afford your extravagance,' Sarah said bitterly. 'Do you know how much we owe the stable already?'

'I won't do it again.' Frances pulled on her gloves and would not meet Sarah's accusing stare. 'Just this time, Sarah.'

'This time, and then another time, and then another. We cannot afford it,' Sarah maintained. 'Do you not understand? We have no money to pay for such luxuries. We cannot afford it. You must send it back.'

Mehuru came into the hall and opened the front door for Frances.

'Wait!' Sarah snapped at him.

'I have to go!' Frances breathed and slipped out of the door and down the steps before Sarah could catch her.

Mehuru bowed to Sarah and swiftly followed Frances to the carriage and handed her into the driving seat.

'Sit beside me,' Frances said breathlessly. Mehuru nodded to the lad from the stables to let the horses go, and swung himself up beside her. 'You must fold your arms and sit very straight,' she said. He gave a wry smile and did as he was bid. Frances flicked the reins to make the horses go forward.

When they were clear of the square she relaxed a little. 'I thought she would stop me.' She gave a quavery little laugh. 'I thought she would lock me in my room rather than see me spend money.'

'They are getting desperate,' Mehuru observed.

'I would have insisted, however angry she was.' Frances flicked out her whip and feathered it neatly back. 'Shall we drive up to the Downs?' she asked.

'Anywhere,' he said. 'Let's drive to Africa.'

She caught her breath on a little sound halfway between a laugh and a sob. 'You know I wish I could,' she said.

He nodded. 'This is our last time together, Frances. I will not ask and you need not refuse. Let us just be together for this afternoon. At least we have these hours, and the sun is warm, and you are well, and I am going to be free.'

'Perhaps we can be happy just for this afternoon,' she said doubtfully.

'Yes we can.'

She steadied the horses over the little bridge and then let them walk up the steep hill of Park Street. Even in the short time since they had last ridden out more building work had started and foundations were outlined where new houses would rise.

The workmen were stripped down to their breeches and torn ragged shirts in the cold November sunshine. Mehuru looked at their skinny muscled backs and weary faces. 'It is a cruel country,' he said. 'I have yet to see a working man or woman who looks properly fed and rested.'

Frances did not turn her eyes from the road between the jogging ears of the offside horse.

'Do you not see?' he asked.

'There is much hardship,' she conceded but still she did not look round.

448

'I am talking about these men,' Mehuru prompted her again. 'These, working here, digging this trench.'

Still she did not look round.

'Will you not look at them?' he demanded.

She glanced at him and he could see her face was pink with embarrassment. 'They are half-naked, Mehuru!' she said with quiet indignation. 'I cannot stare at them!'

He gave a shout of laughter. 'Oh, Frances!' he exclaimed. 'If I live here until I am an old man I will never understand. You are a married woman, you see Josiah, don't you? You saw me.'

Frances caught her breath. The memory of Mehuru in her bedroom with the moonlight cascading down the darkness of his body was too vivid.

'Why cannot you look at some poor working man in his breeches?'

'Because I am a lady,' Frances snapped, goaded to reply. 'There are things I should not see. There are things I should not discuss – even with you.'

'I wish I could hold you,' he said softly. 'And kiss this nonsense from you.'

At once her face softened. 'I wish it too,' she whispered.

He smiled at her profile. 'Sometimes I think you are two women, not one,' he said. 'The stiff cold lady with her strict manners and rules, and sometimes you are my love, my little love, and as natural and easy as an African woman.'

She nodded. 'I have been brought up to be an English lady, I think it is too late to change now.'

'I don't think so,' he muttered stubbornly under his breath. But she just shook her head and would not say any more.

At the top of Park Street, the buildings petered out into rough yards and the road became a mud track through the fields. Frances took the left-hand fork for Clifton, skirting the round mound of Brandon Hill. High up on the hillside

449

washerwomen were spreading out their linen to dry on the grass.

Frances clicked to the horses and they went forward at a brisk trot.

'These are good horses,' she said approvingly. 'Josiah promised to buy me a pair and a carriage of my own when the Trade mends . . . if the Trade mends.'

'Why did you ever marry him?' Mehuru demanded.

Frances was silent for a moment. 'I don't know if I can explain it to you,' she said. She slowed the horses and pulled them over to let a wagon pass by which was carrying glass bottles carefully packed in straw. Ahead of them they could see the pretty hills and valleys of the approach to Clifton. On their left was the boggy ground of Rownham Meads. Migrant birds crossed and recrossed the sky, searching for homes for the long cold winter ahead. Higher above them the seagulls soared and circled, their white wings gleaming like silver in the bright sunshine. In the pools of standing water and the marshy mud a tall grey heron was fishing.

'What you must realise is that there was nothing for me,' Frances began. 'Absolutely nothing. I had no money, I did not even have a home. My home had been the rectory and then the new rector and his family moved in. I did not want to be a poor relation living on charity in Scott House.'

She paused and glanced at Mehuru, who was listening carefully and trying to make sense of what she was saying. In his country a girl without money or a husband would still be an honoured member of a family. They would naturally take her in and she would help with the work of the family and eat with them, and play with the children. The idea of a person being redundant was impossible to his way of thinking.

'Was there nowhere that you could go?' he asked.

Frances shook her head. 'I took employment,' she said. 'As a governess.'

'Like a servant?'

Frances made a little grimace. 'In some ways worse. The pay is very poor but you dare not complain. The children can treat you as they wish, they can be cruel –' She broke off. 'I had not known how cruel children could be,' she said. 'I could not make them mind me and their mother laughed at me. Every morning I used to wake up and dread the day ahead. I was unhappy every moment of the day.' She paused. 'I am not exaggerating. Every single moment of the day.'

Mehuru was silent. The horses walked briskly along the track away from the river up the hill towards Clifton, where they could hear the rumble of wagons and the sound of chisels on stone.

'Josiah advertised for a governess. I applied for the post and met him. He did not tell me what the work was, but said he would write to me. Then, when he wrote proposing marriage, it was as if my prayers had been answered. In return for being his wife I am fed, I am clothed, and when I get old I will *still* be fed and clothed and live in a fine house. I would do anything rather than go back to governessing again, Mehuru. It was worse than slavery –' She stopped. 'I am sorry, that is a foolish thing to say to you; but it was a little like slavery in some ways. I was not free to do as I wished. I could not come and go as I wished. And they were free to get rid of me whenever they wanted.'

'You are not free now,' Mehuru pointed out.

'But neither is Josiah,' she replied. 'We are both bound by our agreement. He has to keep me, whatever else happens.'

They drove in silence for a little while, the horses straining in their collars to climb the hill away from the river. They were driving along the edge of the rising gorge to the heights of Clifton. To their left, and far below, hidden by the overhang of the cliff, was the riverside and Josiah's colonnade of shops and the Hot Well. A pretty track, too steep for anything but the most nimble of the Bristol saddle horses, zig-zagged in sharp hairpin bends down the cliffside to the Hot Well at its foot. The few healthy clients of the Hot Well would sometimes climb up to Clifton to enjoy the view and walk in the woods.

Before them was a handsome street, built as a terrace, in pretty uniformity but stepped irregularly to match the mounting ground. They started along a terrace marked 'Granby Place' which deteriorated at the far end to a pile of builder's stones and an earth track. Frances laughed and pulled up the horses. 'We should have brought a guide,' she said. 'I have got us hopelessly lost.'

They looked to their right. There were thick woodlands tumbling down the hills to the track, cleared here and there by the lime burners, whose stone kilns could sometimes be seen among the thinning foliage of the trees. Above them there was a large attractive stone building and a high scaffolding of some kind of winding gear.

'That can't be a mine,' Frances said. 'There are surely no collieries here in Clifton?'

'Do you want to walk up and see?' Mehuru asked. 'Someone can hold the horses.'

'Why not?' Frances replied. Mehuru whistled at an urchin who had been sitting on a wall observing them and the lad came forward to hold the reins.

Mehuru got down from the box, helped Frances to the ground and took her arm. They strolled together up the grassy track to the new building. In a sea of dust and dirt workmen were drilling a hole with the winding gear screeching above their heads. To the right of them other men were setting square-cut stones on the foundations of what would be a grand and imposing building.

'Ask them what building this will be,' Frances said. 'It looks big enough for a town hall.'

Mehuru went over to speak to one of the men who had a

paper plan pinned to a board. The man looked back at Frances, pulled off his cap and came over.

'Good day, madam,' he said. 'The darkie said you were asking about the building.'

'Yes.'

He held the plan before her. It showed the outline of a large square building subdivided into small rooms at one end with a large assembly room or ballroom at the other. Over the top of the plan in handsome script was the legend: 'The New Hot Well: Pump Room and Bath Houses.'

Frances read it, and then read it again. 'What is this?' she demanded.

'The new Hot Well,' the man replied.

'What d'you mean?'

'It is a new Hot Well, madam. A new spa. Here we are drilling down for the hot water, and here will be the spa building. You can see it here, on the plan. It will be a handsome assembly room, and here you see bath rooms for immersion in the hot water. There will be houses built on each side as well and they will be supplied with hot water from the spa. Hot running water! Think of it!'

Frances put her hand to her throat which felt as if it were closing tight. 'I don't understand. There must be some mistake!'

'I hope not!' The man's broad face grinned. 'For we have drilled down nearly two hundred feet and we will hit the spring soon.'

'But what spring is it?' Frances demanded. 'You must be near the Hot Well, at the foot of this cliff.'

'We are straight above it, madam,' the foreman said. 'It is directly below us. That is why we know that we will hit a hot water spring. The old Hot Well is sited on it. We will tap the Hot Well spring.'

Frances recoiled and staggered. At once Mehuru's arm was around her waist, but she did not even feel his touch. 'Who knows of this?' she asked, her voice sharp. 'Who gave permission? Whose land is this? How can you just drill here without permission?'

The man was offended. 'You'll have to take all that up with the landlord. I am just ordered to supervise the men. I am sorry if I have given you offence, madam. You did ask.' He bowed and turned to walk away from her.

Frances tore herself from Mehuru's support and ran after him. 'But who is the landlord?' She snatched at his arm to detain him. 'You must stop your men working! They have no right to do this! My husband will hear of it!'

He pulled himself free and glanced at Mehuru, hoping he would take her away. Frances's face was white and agonised, and the man feared a scene. 'I suppose a man can do what he wants on his own land, madam,' he said defensively. 'I have to do my work, I have my orders; you must forgive me.' He walked away from her, holding his plans.

'It is not possible!' Frances screamed. Again she ran after him and caught his hand. 'You *will* tell me who has ordered this! Who is the owner? You *must* tell me! My husband is an important man. He is a member of the Merchant Venturers. He will stop them!'

'Why, it is owned by the Merchant Venturers of Bristol!' he shouted impatiently. He pulled himself from her grasp and turned away. 'It is their project, sub-let by them to Mr Stephen Waring and Mr James of the old Hot Well,' he threw over his shoulder. 'You must speak to them if you have a complaint, madam, it is nothing to do with me.'

Frances stumbled back to the carriage, staggering blindly on the uneven ground and Mehuru had to lift her back on the driving box.

'What is the matter? What is it?' he demanded.

'Get me home,' she gasped.

Mehuru drove while Frances clung on to the box seat, her hat askew, her face white.

'What is it? Are you ill, Frances?'

She gave a little moan. 'I want Josiah.'

'What the devil is wrong?' he nearly shouted at her. He flicked the horses and let them rattle down the hill.

'I think we are ruined,' she said through numb lips. 'I want Josiah.' And she would say nothing more.

'Tell me,' he said. 'Tell me what the matter is. I don't understand.'

She looked at him but she did not see him, he was irrelevant to her. 'I want Josiah,' she whispered. 'Take me home.'

He set his jaw and drove as fast as he dared on the rough track. He saw Frances was clinging to the rail on the carriage, and was badly jolted, but he did not pull up the horses, and she did not ask him to drive slower. He glanced sideways at her once, and saw that her face was set and agonised. They rumbled down the hill of Park Street and she clung to the rail and looked straight ahead. A carriage coming up the other way paused, and Mrs Waring waved to her. Frances went by, unseeing, her face ugly and blank.

'Get me home,' she said as he pulled the horses up to let another carriage come across the bridge. 'I want Josiah.'

As soon as they were at the door, she clambered down, not waiting for him to come round and lift her for that precious little moment of intimacy. She had forgotten that this was their last time together. Everything was pushed aside by her need to see Josiah. She jumped down from the carriage step, lifted the hem of her driving gown and raced to the front door, her little kid boots pounding up the steps. She snatched the knocker and hammered it until she heard someone coming.

Kbara hurried to let her in. She pushed past him without explanation and whirled down the hall to Josiah's study. She flung open the door without knocking as Josiah turned in surprise from company ledgers.

'Why, Frances!'

455

'Do you know of a new Hot Well?' she demanded, the words tumbling over each other. 'Do you know of a new Hot Well in Clifton?'

'What?' he asked. He took in her white face and her dishevelled appearance. 'Frances, what is the matter? Sit down, let me ring for Elizabeth. You look ill.'

She nearly screamed at him. 'Josiah! For God's sake answer me! Do you know that there is a new Hot Well being built in Clifton?'

Her meaning slowly sank in. 'A new Hot Well?' he asked. 'A new Hot Well? In Clifton? That is not possible. There is no spring in Clifton. It is on limestone. It is dry.'

She dropped into a chair and wrenched at the ribbons on her bonnet, and stripped off her gloves. 'I drove up to Clifton,' she recounted, her voice low. It struck Josiah she was like a woman who has seen a fatal accident, who has to set the scene, who has to describe the surroundings.

'I saw a new building and beside it some winding gear. I was curious so I walked towards it.'

'Yes,' he said. He could feel himself growing cold, as if the sun were not streaming in through the window, as if there were not a good cheerful fire in the grate. 'Yes. Go on.'

'Mehuru spoke to the foreman and he brought me the plans of the building,' she went on. 'It is to be an assembly room, a big ballroom and promenading room, and bath houses. They are drilling down through the cliff above our Hot Well. They are going to take the water from our spring. Do you hear me? They are taking the water from our Hot Well. They are even planning to pump the water to new houses to be built in Clifton. It will be a great spa resort, with a terrace of houses each with their own hot mineral baths.' She licked her dry lips and swallowed down the lump in her throat. 'He showed me the plan,' she said helplessly. 'And the foundations are dug and the walls going up.'

'This is not possible,' Josiah said weakly. 'There must be some dreadful mistake. I shall go up there at once. D'you still have the carriage out? Cicero shall drive me up there at once. It is not possible, Frances. You must have made a mistake.'

She shook her head. 'I saw the winding gear. I saw the winding gear where they are drilling. The foreman told me they have gone down two hundred feet, but they know they will find hot water, because they are drilling down to the Hot Well.'

Josiah refused to believe it. 'It cannot be. How could such a thing happen without the permission of the Corporation? Without the consent of the Merchant Venturers? It must be a mistake.'

'It *has* the consent of the Merchant Venturers!' Frances cried out with sudden passion. 'Don't you see! Don't you see, Josiah? It is their land! They are the landlords. That is why they are buying land in Clifton! Why they own the freehold for Clifton and all the Downs up to the very cliff edge! They own everything! And they are developing Clifton as a new spa. They have cheated you, Josiah. They have cheated you of everything and now you own a spa with no water, and you have signed a ten-year lease!'

He stared at her open-mouthed. 'Who said this?' he cried angrily. 'This is a calumny! They are my friends. It is a mistake!'

'Who advised you to buy into the Hot Well and gave you sight of the account books and sponsored you at the Merchant Venturers' dinner?' Frances hissed at him, her teeth bared. Her hair was falling down, her face was ashen and bony.

Josiah hated her at that moment. 'Waring,' he answered. 'My friend Stephen Waring.'

She sunk back in the chair as if he had knifed her in the heart. 'He is the landlord of the new Hot Well.' She could hardly speak through her cold lips. She could hardly breathe. 'Him and Mr James, the old tenant of the Hot Well. They have sold you a pup, Josiah. They have taken your money and now they will take your spring water too.'

Josiah staggered and felt behind him for his chair. His knees buckled and he dropped into it. 'It is not possible,' he whispered, his face grey. 'I have borrowed and borrowed against the profits I thought to make. I paid two thousand pounds for the purchase alone. And I have to find near a thousand pounds a year for ten years for the lease, and the interest on the borrowing and the wages and the furnishings.'

Frances moved her head restlessly, her eyes closed.

Josiah looked at his desk, put his hand on the papers before him, stroked the page of his ship's accounts. 'I am ruined,' he said disbelievingly. 'They took me in and ruined me.'

Frances put her hand to her throat, pulling at her collar, gasping for breath. Her face was even whiter than before. 'Josiah,' she gasped. She could hardly catch her breath to say his name.

'I am ruined,' he said again. 'They have ruined me.'

'Josiah . . .' she began and then she gave a sharp cry of pain.

Mehuru, who had been loitering in the hall, could not stop himself. He burst into the room in time to see Frances pitch forward out of her chair. He caught her up but her head had hit the fender and she was bleeding from her temple. Her lips were blue, she was not breathing.

'Fetch the doctor!' Mehuru shouted. 'Fetch Stuart Hadley!' He gathered her to him, trying to warm her. Her neck lolled as limp as a broken doll. Not knowing what to do, Mehuru rocked her, holding her tight. 'Frances!' he cried urgently. 'Frances!'

She was not breathing. Mehuru sprung to his feet.

'I am ruined,' Josiah repeated quietly. He had not moved from his desk.

Mehuru threw a quick contemptuous look at him and then ran for the hall. 'Kbara!' he yelled.

Kbara came running up from the kitchen. 'Take a horse from the carriage shafts and ride and find Stuart Hadley the doctor!' Mehuru commanded. 'Tell him Frances is ill, she is like a dead woman. Go at once!'

Kbara nodded and dashed out of the front door.

Mehuru turned with Frances still in his arms and strode towards the stairs. Sarah Cole appeared in the parlour door. 'What on earth is happening?' she demanded.

'Fetch the women,' Mehuru threw over his shoulder. 'Frances is ill.'

Sarah looked incredulously at him, carrying Frances in his arms and then ran up the stairs behind him. 'Put her down!' she ordered. 'At once.'

Mehuru strode up the stairs without even hearing her. He kicked open the door to Frances's bedroom and laid her gently down on the bed. He took the high neat-buttoned neck of her driving gown and ripped it open, sending buttons spinning across the room.

'How dare you!' Sarah exclaimed.

He caught Frances up and shook her gently. 'Breathe!' he urged her, passionately low-voiced in his own language. 'Breathe! What is there to stop breathing for? Breathe, you little fool!'

Sarah recoiled from his passion. Elizabeth dodged around her and came into the room with a tumbler of brandy in one hand and a bottle of water in the other. She dashed the water in Frances's blue face and then Mehuru held Frances's limp shoulders while Elizabeth dribbled brandy into her mouth.

Frances choked then struggled against their hold and sat up whooping and gasping for air.

Mehuru nodded and ripped her dress further, pulling the wet cloth away from her skin. Elizabeth snatched up a warm

459

comforter from the foot of the bed and Mehuru put it around Frances's naked shoulders and held her tight.

'Don't try to speak,' he said urgently. 'Stuart will be here in a moment. Just breathe, Frances. Breathe!'

The dreadful blue was fading from her lips though her skin was still waxy white.

'Get a warming pan,' Mehuru directed Elizabeth. 'She is too cold.'

Elizabeth pushed past Sarah in the doorway and shouted down the stairs in a string of incomprehensible Yoruban. There was an answering shout from the kitchen, and one of the boys came running upstairs with a tinder box. He dodged under Sarah's elbow and knelt to light the fire. Elizabeth came back into the room and started to remove Frances's skirt.

'Cicero, leave the room,' Sarah demanded, coming forward, trying to reclaim some order.

He gave her a look which threw her back on her heels, and raised Frances as if she were a little girl. He picked up a pair of scissors from her dressing table and cut the laces of her stays. Elizabeth pulled the skirt away and turned back the covers of the bed. Mehuru lifted Frances, wrapped in the comforter and wearing only her shift, into the bed as Martha came into the room, pushed around Sarah's back to thrust the warming pan under the covers at the foot of the bed and take the chill off the sheets.

The fire blazed into life as the kindling caught and then the little pieces of coal. Frances opened her eyes and managed a weak smile at Mehuru. He caught her hand and crushed it to his mouth. 'Little fool,' he said. 'Lie still. And don't speak.'

She closed her eyes again. 'I hurt,' she whispered in a small voice. She put her hand between the swell of her breasts. 'In here,' she said. 'My heart.'

'Shall I open the window?' Elizabeth asked Mehuru.

460

He glanced at Frances's pinched face. 'No,' he said, fearful of the cold English air. 'Let us keep her warm until Stuart comes.'

He turned around. 'Now go,' he said to the boy. 'Martha – out.' He was suddenly aware of Sarah, standing like a stone in the middle of the room, taking in everything, his easy air of command, the instinctive obedience of the others, and his loving intimacy with Frances. He did not hesitate for a moment. 'Please leave, Miss Cole,' he said. 'Frances needs to rest.'

'What *do* you think you are doing?' she demanded and her voice was like a blade.

He stepped forward and swept her, physically swept her from the room. 'I said, she needs to rest,' he repeated as soon as the door was shut behind them both, and Frances could not hear. 'Her health is the most important thing. You can speak with me later.'

'I shall have you whipped,' she promised. 'What do you think . . .'

'Your brother is sick too,' he interrupted her. 'You should go to him.'

She checked, half-disbelieving, half-alarmed, but he turned from her and went back into Frances's bedroom. 'I have noted this,' she said threateningly to the closing door. 'My brother shall know of this!' She stood irresolute for a moment but then her anxiety for Josiah overcame her and she ran down the stairs to his room.

He was sitting at his desk, flicking the pages of the big account book forward, and then flicking them back again. Something in that careless, almost childlike movement arrested Sarah on the threshold.

'Josiah?'

When he turned to look at her the years had fallen away from his face and he had the open innocent gaze of a child. 'They have gulled me, Sarah,' he said. His voice was small, like a little boy shocked by some hurt. 'They took me in and played me along and they have gulled me for all of our money.'

She could feel herself chilled all through. 'How so?' she asked very steadily. 'How so, Josiah? What have they done to you?'

'They sold me the Hot Well and a ten-year lease, nine thousand pounds over ten years and two thousand pounds down,' Josiah said.

Sarah closed her eyes, briefly repelled by the large capital sums. 'But you saw the books, it will pay,' she said. 'We knew this, we knew we could manage it. When the *Rose* comes in . . .'

Josiah nodded. 'It looked like safe investment. And I borrowed money to buy it.'

'But it *is* a good investment,' Sarah repeated. 'You saw the books. It will run at a profit. You would not take a risk. Not with those sums!'

Josiah cleared his throat. 'It would have done,' he said. 'And I was out daily to inspect the business. You know how often I have been down there, Sarah. You know I hired an architect to draw up plans, I was not careless. I was not careless with our business.'

Sarah nodded. 'I know, Brother. I know.'

'Then they sued me, to make me keep the tap open,' he continued softly. 'I could not think why they did that . . . but now it seems . . . it seems to me . . .' He broke off. 'If I complain of them there will be no-one on my side. The people of the city, the Corporation, the Company . . . every-one thinks that I am in the wrong. The Merchant Venturers have the interests of the city at heart and I am – what did they call me? – an upstart.'

Sarah nodded silently.

'They have destroyed my reputation,' Josiah went on in a thin little voice. 'No-one will defend me now. They made me look like a mountebank. No-one will speak up for me now.'

'But the Hot Well will still earn money . . .' Sarah started.

'I did not think to look up,' Josiah said inconsequently. 'On the cliff top high above my Hot Well . . .'

'Why?' Sarah prompted urgently. 'Why should you have looked up?'

'Because they are drilling down,' he said simply. His face was ghastly. 'They are drilling down into my spring. They are building a new assembly rooms, new bath houses, they are piping the water away from my spa. And they are calling it the new Hot Well. They have not even chosen another name. They are advertising to everyone that my Hot Well is the old one. Soon it will be dry. They are calling theirs the new Hot Well.'

Sarah hissed like a snake through her gritted teeth. 'The new Hot Well? Are you sure?'

He nodded. 'Frances has seen the building. The foreman showed her the plans.'

Sarah strode over to the window and gazed out into the backyard, seeing nothing. She turned back to him. 'Can we do nothing?' she demanded. 'Have you looked at your lease? Do you not own the rights to the water? Surely one cannot buy a spa without buying the water?'

He shook his head, still numb with shock. 'I bought the buildings, and the furnishings,' he said. 'I did not know. I did not think. I was too foolish to foresee this. I did not think to buy the water. I am a trader, I sail my ships on the sea – I do not buy the sea. Water is always there.'

'Who has done this?' Sarah cried passionately. 'Who has done this to you? Who owns the new buildings?'

He could not meet her eyes. 'Stephen Waring,' he answered dully. 'He will have done well from us, first and last. He has plucked me like a little pigeon.'

She did not reproach him. Her shoulders went back as if

to strain against a weight. 'We still have the ships,' she said. 'We still have the ships and we still have the slaves, and the warehouse. We are not ruined yet, Brother.'

He riffled lightly through the pages of the account book. 'We will have to see,' he said idly. 'But I do not know what will be left when all the debts on this are paid. If I shut down the Hot Well and sack all the staff and sell the furnishings . . . I do not know, Sarah. I used to know to a penny, didn't I? When you kept the books and the Trade was good. But I have such interest charges to meet, and they will not defer payment . . . I have quite lost track, Sarah.'

He rose on unsteady legs. 'I think I'll go now.' He looked at her vaguely. '*Rose* could come in any day, you know. Come in full of gold and smelling of rum. I like to be on the quayside when my ship comes in. She is late already, perhaps she will come in today. On the next tide. Or the tide after that.'

Sarah put a hand out to stop him, but he went past her quietly, as if he had not seen her, as if he did not know she was there. He took up his hat from the table in the hall. He did not wear a coat, he went out like a labouring man in his shirtsleeves into the grey twilight and the sharp evening air.

'When *Rose* comes in, we will be laughing about this,' he said uncertainly. 'We will be rich.'

Only when he was gone, and the front door shut behind him, did Sarah sink into the chair, gaze blankly at the empty hearth, and let herself wonder if they were ruined indeed.

Chapter Thirty-five

Sarah heard the hammering on the front door but she did not turn her head. The noise of it came from a long way away. She heard Stuart Hadley's pleasant voice; but she did not go out to greet him. She let Elizabeth show him upstairs.

He went into Frances's bedroom and sent Mehuru outside while he examined her. She had regained a little colour but she was hunched with pain. The cut on her forehead had dried and a small bluish bruise was spreading over her temple.

She answered his questions in a strained little voice, hardly able to catch her breath, and she could not move readily for the pain. He thought that her weak heart had taken a seizure from the shock, and her damaged lungs were in spasm also. He gave her a large dose of laudanum and watched the colour slowly come back into her cheeks as the drug worked its way into her body.

Stuart Hadley had never before seen her without her tightly laced stays. For the first time he was able to see the outlines of her body, only half-hidden by the sheet and blankets. He asked her permission and pressed gently on the round of her belly. It was solid and hard. For a moment he feared a growth of some sort and then a smile came to his face.

'How long have you been with child?'

The look she gave him was shocked. 'Child?' she repeated in her thin rasping voice.

'I think so,' he said. He pressed her belly again. The firmness was unmistakable. 'Yes.'

Her face gave h∴r away, the burning flush of colour rising from her neck to her forehead. She closed her eyes and turned her head on the pillow away from his gaze. 'Oh my God,' she murmured softly.

'Did you not realise?'

Numbly she shook her head. 'I have not been unwell for these past six months,' she said. 'But I thought . . . I thought . . . I have never been regular . . .'

He nodded. Few ladies of her class understood about conception. Virgins on marriage, they were rarely told either by mothers or husbands about pregnancy or childbirth. Even if they lived in the country they were shielded from the cycle of birth and death of farm animals, and Frances had seen the countryside only through the rectory windows. She was not the first lady he had attended who had been advanced in a pregnancy and not known.

'I had been so ill,' she said. 'With that cold. I thought that it had just stopped. And I am not grown much fatter.'

'There is no doubt that you are with child,' he said. He cleared his throat. 'Forgive me, Mrs Cole. This must be a shock.' He hardly knew how to ask the question, but opted for blunt honesty. 'I suppose you are certain that the child is Mr Cole's?'

She opened her eyes at that, and then turned her head away from him to the wall. He was afraid that she was mortally offended. But when she spoke her voice was level and clear. 'There *is* a doubt,' she said steadily, gazing resolutely at the wall. 'Mr Cole is . . .' She broke off, partly through embarrassment and partly because she simply did not know the words. 'I think it unlikely that Mr Cole would make a child,' she explained very softly.

There was a long silence. Stuart took a seat on the side of her bed without permission and took her thin hand in his.

She was cold, despite the fire. He did not know if she could tolerate this shock тɔ an already vulnerable system. 'Do not be afraid,' he encouraged her. 'We will find a way to manage this. Do not be afraid, Mrs Cole.'

She said nothing.

'Mehuru is a friend of mine,' he said quietly. 'I honour and respect him. He is a gentleman.' He smiled inwardly at hearing himself repeat the cant of their class. 'A gentleman,' he said firmly.

She shot a quick look at him. 'Is it you who has taken him to radical clubs?' she demanded bitterly. 'Who persuaded him that he must be free?'

Stuart bit back an angry reply. This woman was a patient, he must care for her. 'What I wanted to say,' he went on, his voice very low, 'is that a child of his, even with a white-skinned mother, would be dark-skinned, would be noticeably dark.'

She looked at him so blankly he thought that perhaps she did not understand, that the seizure of her heart had damaged her comprehension. He feared for a moment that he was making the most enormous and foolish mistake. He had assumed that Mehuru and Frances were lovers. He was assuming that the baby was Mehuru's child.

'Any baby of his will show its parentage,' he said carefully. 'Any baby of his would be dark-skinned.'

'Black like him?'

'They call them mulattos in the Sugar Islands,' he told her. 'They are brown-skinned, very beautiful babies, enchanting children.'

She blinked. She remembered, it seemed a lifetime away, Miss Honoria telling her that they always preferred mulattos in the house as servants. She remembered Honoria's easy gliding over unpalatable facts: 'Papa likes to mix the stock'.

She opened her mouth, her face blank as stone, and laughed, a high shrieking laugh. Stuart recoiled, but she did

467

not stop, she laughed and laughed as if nothing would stop her.

'Enough,' Stuart ordered and his voice cut through her screaming laughter.

She looked wide-eyed at him. 'What shall I do?' she asked simply. 'I shall be ruined.'

'Do you know when it is due?'

'Yes,' she said quietly. 'It was conceived in May.' Her face softened as she thought of the daffodils in her bed, and the darkness of the May night.

'It will be born in January then,' he said.

'It might die,' she said coldly, but her hand crept down to her belly and she spread her palm over where the little head was lying.

'Do you want it to die?'

Her face quivered into life and her colour rose. 'No,' she replied with sudden surprising conviction. 'It is a love-child. It is my child. It is Mehuru's child. I want it to live. Oh!' She gave a small gasp of desire. 'Oh! I want it to live very much!'

'Then we must be very careful with your health,' Stuart said. 'Avoid all excitement and disturbance, and rest as much as you can. For yourself, and also for your baby.'

She nodded. 'But if my heart is too weak . . .'

'You *must* rest,' he insisted. 'We may get you safely through this, and your little baby too.'

She was silent for a moment, and then she turned to him and faced him honestly. 'I don't care for myself,' she said quietly. 'I have not been very lucky, you see, Mr Hadley. Not in my girlhood, and not in my marriage, and not even in my love for Mehuru. Oh! It was not his fault! But the gulf between us was so great that I don't think we could ever have bridged it. And I have not been good to him.' She paused, thinking. 'So if I am ill, and if you ever have to choose . . . you will save the baby, won't you?'

468

Stuart grimaced. 'I hope never to make that choice.'

'But if I am dying and you can save the baby, you will do that – won't you?'

'If it is your wish,' he said slowly.

'It is,' she said. 'Mehuru's baby. Think what a precious child that will be.'

'Could you sleep now?' he asked.

'Yes,' she said. 'The laudanum has made me drowsy.'

He held her hand. 'I will stay with you until you sleep,' he said gently.

She opened her eyes for a moment. 'Don't tell Mehuru.'

He hesitated. 'You want to tell him yourself?'

Her eyelids were drooping. 'He has to be free to go,' she whispered so softly that he could hardly hear her. 'He has to be free. I have to set him free.' She glanced at him for a moment, in jealousy. 'You want him free,' she said.

'Yes, I do.'

'And you will advise him where he could go, where they can all go so that Josiah cannot find them and enslave them again?'

'I will.'

'Then he must be free to leave now,' she said simply. 'He cannot stay with me.'

When her eyelids fluttered shut the doctor sat with her a little while, looking at her white face. The bedroom door opened quietly and Mehuru stood there.

'You can come in,' Stuart said quietly. 'She is sleeping.'

Mehuru came in as light-footed as a cat. He checked when he saw Frances, the slight rise and fall of her breasts as she breathed slowly and painfully, the waxy white colour of her face.

'She will need someone to watch her,' Stuart told him. 'Night and day. Her heart is very weak. She needs to be kept quiet. She must have nothing to trouble her at all.'

Mehuru remained silent, his eyes never leaving her face.

469

'She will need someone to watch over her. I can find a nurse for the first few days, but they are not reliable women. Will Miss Cole care for her?'

'I will watch her,' Mehuru decided.

'You cannot . . .'

Mehuru shook his head. 'It is my right,' he said with gentle dignity. 'I will watch her sleep, and be here when she wakes.'

Josiah did not come home that night, nor did he return the next day. Sarah, walking alone down to the old warehouse on the quay in the wintry dawn, with a shawl over her head like a trader's daughter, found that he had spent the night in their old home, and was sitting in his old office, looking out over the dock, waiting for *Rose*.

In the following week he did not come home to the expensive house in Queens Square at all. He chose to stay in his little warehouse, sleeping on a pallet on the floor wrapped in his cloak at night and sitting in his old place at the window overlooking his empty quay from the first grey light of the morning. He spent his day bargaining and dealing in tiny, pitiful amounts of cash on the quayside; while the bigger debts in the account books at Queens Square grew fat like maggots in the dark of the ledgers, and the letters from Hibbard and Sons warning that they would prosecute for non-payment collected, unopened, on his desk.

He chose to dine in the coffee shop, sitting once again far from the top table. He might have claimed his place and been still tolerated. There were a few men who might have greeted him with sympathy; but Josiah did not try. He no longer wanted to be with them. He sat, neither with his new friends, nor with his old, but at a little table on his own, near the window where he could see his dock and the entrance to the harbour every time he lifted his eyes. He never stopped looking for *Rose* and whenever he saw the shape of a travel-weary brig silhouetted against the sparkle of the incoming water he would rise a little in his seat, drop his napkin on the floor, and start forward. But it was never the *Rose*. Despite Josiah's faith in her, in the short grey days of November she never came.

In the silent house in Queens Square Frances lay all day in her room, with the curtains open, looking out at the squares of sky in the panes of her window. The thick glass made little ripples and whorls of the grey. She tried to get up once or twice but she was so breathless and her colour became so white that Stuart Hadley insisted that she lie in her bed, or at the most on a day bed in her room.

The weather was against her. The bright autumn days had slipped away under a blanket of fog. When Elizabeth opened the windows on Frances's insistence, the yellow smog crept into the room like the coils of a thick snake. The rich dirty stink of the river filtered up the backs of the houses and penetrated even the front windows of the square. Elizabeth closed the windows, and burned scented candles, trying to cleanse the air. Nothing could rid the city of its choking fumes and every draught which came into the room was icy and as dirty as stale smoke from a burning midden.

Sarah sat with her in the afternoons but the women were no company for each other. Frances lay quite still, her colour waxy and her breath short. Her thickening body was concealed completely by the drapes of her robe and the sheets and blankets on the bed. She had no desire to confide in Sarah, nor in anyone else; and Sarah had nothing to say to her. She had never wanted a sister-in-law; she had tolerated her for the sake of the business and because Josiah was determined to have her. Now that Frances lay sick and silent in her bed Sarah could see no use for her at all. Frances's connections with the aristocratic families had not brought visitors for the Hot Well spa, and anyway, the water was cooling and dying away to a hopeless trickle. The new Hot

Well in Clifton had tapped into the spring and already they were pumping out gallons every day to the bright fashionable houses high on the cliff above. The only visitors to the old Hot Well were those too poor or too weak to move anywhere else. In Josiah's absence and without the ebullient Master of Ceremonies the business was slipping from bad to worse. Every day the spa took less and less money, and still the wages and the lease had to be paid. Only the paupers still came, on their set days. The new Hot Well was too inaccessible for them, too far from the city, and besides, the Merchant Venturers had made sure that there was no agreement to provide them with a free tap in Clifton.

Sarah brought plain darning with her when she came to sit in Frances's room and stitched irritably, small neat angry stitches, while Frances lay, her eyes half-closed, enduring the soft insistent sound of Sarah's breathing and the puncturing noise of her needle through linen, sensing her scorn.

Frances hardly spoke to Mehuru although he made a point of serving her. He would allow no-one else to carry the jug of hot water to her room in the morning or bring her dinner tray to her room in the afternoon. He would put the tray beside her bed and ask her how she felt and if she were better. But she would not speak to him, she turned her face to the wall and would not reply. She would not tell him about the child. She remembered too clearly her desperate need to see Josiah and her panic-stricken flight for her home. She had showed him, in that moment, where her loyalty lay: with her husband. She felt that she had betrayed him and she was ashamed.

And she was steeling herself for his disappearance. He had said that he would go and she had warned him that she could not protect him in the house in Queens Square. She did not want to hold him back. She did not want his child, their child, to hold him back. She had made up her mind to keep the baby a secret from him, so that he would be free to leave.

472

'Are you better today, Frances?' Mehuru asked softly, setting her dinner tray on the table at her bedside.

'Yes, thank you,' she said quietly. But when he left, Elizabeth, coming to straighten the sheets, found that Frances's pillow was wet with tears.

'Now what's the matter?' she would ask kindly. 'What's he said to you to make you cry so?'

But Frances would only shake her head and say nothing.

Elizabeth stopped Mehuru on the stairs as she carried Frances's dinner tray down to the kitchen. 'She cries when she sees you,' she said accusingly. 'What have you done to her?'

Mehuru spread his hands. 'I? I've done nothing! I've told her that I love her, and I asked her to come away with me. But ever since that day when she found that they were building the new Hot Well she has not spoken to me. She's Josiah's wife, not mine. She's telling me that in the cruellest way.'

'Well, it's breaking her heart, whatever she's doing,' Elizabeth observed.

'What can I do?' Mehuru demanded. 'I can't be her pet, Elizabeth. I am hers till death, but if she turns her face away when I speak to her, what can I do?'

'You could ask her, instead of standing on your pride,' Elizabeth said sharply. 'You could ask her what is wrong, instead of assuming you know everything. Everything! Or you could use the eyes in your head. You have the Sight! I should think you could see what ails her.' She stamped down the stairs away from him, cursing the stupidity of men as she went through the door to the kitchen. Mehuru scowled at her disappearing back, and then followed her. The others were seated around the kitchen table at their dinner. Mehuru took his place at the head of the table and bowed his head and took a brief moment to thank the Earth for the richness of her goods, and for the breath to eat them.

Kbara nodded to him when he raised his head. 'We have

473

been thinking,' he said in the liquid warm accents of their home. 'We have been thinking we should go soon. We have delayed for Frances's illness, but we dare not wait much longer.'

Mehuru took a piece of bread and broke it. One of the girls set a bowl of soup before him. He nodded. 'I have spoken to Stuart and he knows where you should go,' he said. 'He will give you money for the journey and he has friends who will greet you. Of course, now is the time for you to go.'

'For us to go,' Kbara interrupted quickly. 'We do not want to be parted.'

'We are a family now,' Mary said. 'We cannot go and leave you behind, Mehuru.'

He shook his head. 'I am sorry. But I cannot leave Frances like this.'

There was an instant murmur of dissent. 'You must come,' Martha insisted, and the others nodded. 'We have agreed that we should all stay together. You *must* want to be with us, Mehuru.'

'I love her,' he said simply. 'And she is very sick, she could die. I can't leave her to die alone with that sister of hers. Who will hold her with love? Who will wash her face and body when she is cold? You must see that I cannot go until I know what she wants.'

'But she will not speak to you,' Elizabeth argued. 'You say yourself she loves her husband and not you.'

Mehuru shook his head. 'It does not matter. It is not easy for us to love each other. It never could be easy. It does not matter that she will not speak to me, nor that she is his wife. What matters is that in spite of all these things – all these things which have stood like walls between us – she has loved me and I love her still. I will not leave her until I have said goodbye.'

'What if she gets better and sells you?' Kbara demanded

unkindly. 'She has already agreed a price for you and for John. What if she sells you and John tomorrow? They need the money. They are in debt.'

Mehuru nodded. 'You must go. For the safety of little John, and for all of your sakes. I will wait until she sends me away. When she tells me to leave I will come and find you. I love you. I love the children as if they were my own, and I love you, my brother, and you, my sisters. But I love Frances as if she were my wife. I cannot run away from her. When she sends me away I will come and find you. But I will not leave her until she herself tells me to go.'

'What if we get separated and can never find each other again?' Mary asked.

'I have to take that risk,' Mehuru replied. 'But Stuart knows a safe place for us all. You can go now, and I will follow you later. We have been through too much, we have survived this far. Surely we will find somewhere to live, and some way of living together!'

Kbara looked unhappy. 'I had thought you would come with us. I thought you would put your own people first.'

'I am torn two ways,' Mehuru admitted. 'You are my people. But look at Frances, she is almost certain to die. How can I leave her?'

'And I'll stay too,' Elizabeth said suddenly.

Mary turned on her in amazement. 'You as well?'

Elizabeth made a small gesture to Mary, under cover of the table. 'I have work to do here,' she said with simple dignity. She faced the disapproving faces of the two men. 'You would not understand. There is work for me here, woman's work. I have to stay and see Frances through to the end of her illness.'

'I don't think . . .' Mehuru started.

'I know,' Elizabeth said with finality.

Both of the men looked defeated by her certainty. Mehuru was reminded of the small village councils at home where the men might talk all day but if one of the senior women came in and said that a thing *must* be done, then that was the end of the discussion.

'I should be glad for Frances's sake,' he said. 'I am not allowed to nurse her, and Miss Cole is cold and hard.'

'I shall care for her until she dies,' Elizabeth declared. 'And the moment she is dead and washed and ready for their burial I shall come after you.' She nodded round the table. 'And I will bring Mehuru with me. They will not catch us and keep us just because we stay now.'

'Very well then,' Kbara said. He looked at Mehuru, who in the old days would have known with his priest's Sight how long a sick woman might live. 'It will not be very long, I don't think? The doctor said it will not be long. You must be able to see?'

'I don't know,' Mehuru said, deliberately choosing blindness rather than foreseeing Frances's death. 'How should I know? I don't know.'

Chapter Thirty-six

Josiah sat in his old chair, at his old desk, in the window of his office overlooking the quay. He had forgotten the house in Queens Square that he had struggled so hard to win and that had cost him so much to buy. He had forgotten his Hot Well, and his ambitions and his plans. He sat at his desk as if the years had never been, as if at any moment Sarah, or even his father, might call him to eat his dinner in the parlour next door.

At a casual glance it looked as if he were working. He had the ledgers of all his ships spread before him and he was carefully going down the profits column, adding them up, and then adding one to another. On another piece of paper he had a note of the debts he had to service, and every now and then he would transfer the total from his profits and subtract it from the money he owed. It was a nonsensical task: a piece of fairytale arithmetic. Every time he did it, the amount of the debt was hardly diminished at all. Josiah was looking at ruin, and he was too shocked to see it.

Only the sale of his ships themselves, his warehouse, and his lease of the quay would settle his debts. Over and over again Josiah added up the value of the tobacco in his bond, the value of the rum in his cellar and the sugar in his store. Again and again he subtracted it from the debt on the *Rose*, on the Hot Well lease and on his house in Queens Square, and saw that thousands and thousands of pounds were still owing.

The room was cold, the rain pattered against the grimy windows making tracks in the greasy dirt on the unwashed panes. The windows rattled when the wind blew up the gorge and the draughts whistled around Josiah's bowed head as he puzzled over the arithmetic of loss. He was not conscious of the cold on his bare head. He could see nothing but the dazzling whiteness of the page and feel the paper smooth under his hands. However he added it, however he subtracted it and then added it again, he could not make it come right. Whatever he did with the figures they came out at a loss.

Only *Rose* could save him if she came home soon, smelling sweetly of sugar, potent with rum and filled with bullion. Only *Rose* could save him if she came home in time, before the next payment on the Hot Well spa fell due, if she came home before Hibbard and Sons closed his loan and demanded the overpriced house at Queens Square, or the failed Hot Well spa and all his ships against his debt. If she did not come soon then Josiah would have to hand over his house, and come back to the little quay and the warehouse which Josiah's father had been proud to call his home and which Josiah had left with such pride just ten short months ago.

Frances woke from light sleep with a sensation akin to someone tugging at her sleeve. Or was it a noise that had woken her? She rested, halfway between waking and sleeping, wondering what it was – a noise in the street outside perhaps, or someone calling her name.

Then she felt it again. A small distinct movement, a squirm, a touch, a caress. Inside her belly her baby had moved and she, lying quietly in sleep, had felt it. It was the strangest feeling in the world and as distinctive as a child's call for his mother. She put her hand on her swelling belly and felt the child kick out. He was alive, and strong. She had been sensing him move and felt that she had learned to love him, this little exuberant swimming kicking being.

478

'Not long now,' she whispered.

There was a gentle knock on her door. She turned her head and said, 'Come in!', thinking it was Elizabeth.

But it was not Elizabeth who came quietly in the door but Mehuru, and his face was grave.

Frances snatched the bedcovers higher, shielding the round shape of her belly.

'May I come in?' he asked humbly. He paused at the threshold of the room, awaiting her permission.

'Yes,' Frances said. She could not meet his eyes. She felt as if she had betrayed him on the very day which was to be their last together, which was to be a day of farewell, filled with love; and then all she had thought of was Josiah, and the wreck of his fortune. 'Of course you can come in,' she said quietly. 'What is it?'

'There is a difficulty,' he began.

For a moment she thought that Stuart had broken her confidence and told him about the pregnancy. Stuart was sworn to secrecy and besides, there was his professional oath, but still he was Mehuru's friend and he might think that a man had a right to know that a woman was carrying his child. Unconsciously she put her hand to shield her belly; beneath her touch she could feel her baby kick again.

'What difficulty?'

Mehuru's mind was on how to tell her that the slaves had gone without precipitating one of her breathless attacks. But some wisdom, some old awareness in the back of his mind, noted the gesture she made. In Africa he would have read her at once. But Mehuru was becoming more and more of an Englishman. He concentrated on the topic in hand, and made himself blind to other impressions.

'Do you have some medicine the doctor left you?'

She gestured quickly to her bedside table where her laudanum bottle stood. 'But I don't need it,' she said, though she could feel her heart pound warningly. 'What difficulty? Is it Josiah? Is he ill?'

'No, your husband is well, as far as I know. Please do not be distressed.'

'Tell me quickly.'

'It is your slaves,' he said softly. 'All except Elizabeth. They have run away, Frances. They are all gone.'

For a moment she did not understand. She looked at him as if his words were meaningless. 'Gone?'

'They went last night,' he explained. 'After Cook locked up. Cook knows nothing about it. They must not blame her.'

'But you knew,' she said.

He nodded. 'I knew.'

There was a little silence. Frances raised herself up in bed. 'And yet you did not go too?'

He came further into the room. 'I decided to stay.'

'Do you know where they are?'

'On a farm, in a place called Yorkshire. We hope that we can farm the land.' His sudden smile broke up the gravity of his face. 'I am sure nothing will grow in this cold soil! But two are Fulani and they can rear cattle. I think we can make a life for ourselves.'

'You are going to join them?'

'It is up to you.' He paused for a moment, carefully measuring what he might say to her. 'I have not changed, Frances. I told you that day that I loved you, and I love you still. I know that you are ill and I know that Josiah is ruined, and that everything here is now different. But if you will come with me, we can go to Yorkshire together. Or I will stay with you. Or you can send me away. You have only to tell me what it is that you wish.'

He stepped forward and took her hand. Something in the way that her other hand rested below her ribs tugged at a memory in his mind. He paused, looking at her, and then saw for the first time the lovely curve of her swelling belly under the concealing drapery of her robe and the coverings of the bed.

'You are pregnant,' he said.

She looked as if she might deny it, but then she nodded.

'Josiah's child.' His mouth had a bitter twist. 'You are risking your life for Josiah's child.'

Frances nodded again, not trusting herself to lie to him in words.

He turned from her pale strained face and went to the window and looked out over the square. The trees were leafless now, their bright colours stripped away and the grey colour of the grass reminded Mehuru of home, at the end of the dry season. 'I still wish that we could go to Africa,' he said, half to himself.

'You go,' Frances whispered softly. She could not bring herself to send him away, she could only give him permission, and tell him nothing that would bind him to her. He had been ready to run and she had seen him humiliated too many times before her. She felt she owed him his freedom, even though he was the father of her child – especially since he was the father of her child.

He shook his head. 'It makes no difference,' he said finally. 'It makes no difference to how I feel for you – whether you are carrying Josiah's child or not. You are ill, and your husband is never at home. I love you and I have promised myself that I will stay with you until you tell me to leave.'

'I never asked you for a promise,' she interrupted. 'I will not keep you here.'

'I promised myself,' he replied. 'You are the first woman I have ever loved in my life, Frances, and I know now that it was a mistake for me. There is too much that separates us. Our colour is less important than everything else.' His gesture took in their politics, their culture, their expectations, and their sense of what was important. 'But it does not matter. None of it matters now with you so ill, and your life ruined.

481

I love you and I will stay with you until you tell me to go.'

'And if I say go?'

'Then I will join my people.'

'And if I say stay?'

'Then I stay.'

She looked across the room at him and into his open tender face. She thought that she should let him go, let him run while he could and make a new life with his people. She did not doubt that they would make a success of their farm. They were all dogged survivors, and they were in touch with the reality of the earth and with their own tenderness in a way that she and Josiah and Sarah had never been. They would court and marry and bear children, and the children would grow up as English men and women, only knowing Africa as a deep memory, hidden in their souls.

She put a hand out to him. 'I will not ask you to stay,' she said stubbornly. 'I think it would be safer for you to go. Josiah could still sell you and I could not save you and . . .' She broke off. 'I am ill,' she told him honestly. 'I am fatally ill, Mehuru. I saw my mother die like this. There is nothing to stay for.'

He crossed the room and took her hand. She was as small-boned as the skeleton of a little bird. The flesh had wasted from her hand in the short time of her illness; he could feel the light bones of her wrist. He turned her hand palm upwards and gently pressed a kiss into it.

'I will stay for as long as you need me,' he promised.

They both knew that it would not be very long.

Frances did not see Sarah until she came to her room before dinner in the afternoon. The two women now lived almost separate lives. Sarah still dined downstairs in solitary state in the ornate dining room. Frances had her meal on a tray in her bedroom. Neither woman ate very much. Josiah never came home at all. Sarah did not disturb him. She had a faint hope, a trace of wishful optimism, that Josiah's struggles with his debts would suddenly come right and he would swagger home again with his hat set jauntily on his head and another scheme in his hand to right them all. She knew it was not likely, but she could not keep herself from hoping.

In the meantime she could not bear to see his demented concentration. The third night he had not come home for dinner she had walked down to the quayside to fetch him. She had seen the light burning at his window and looked up. She had seen him hunched over his desk, she had seen him move the papers from one pile to another and then shuffle them and move them back again. For half an hour Sarah had waited on the quayside, trying to find the courage to go to Josiah and bid him come home. But the habits of coldness and distance were too strong for her to break. In the end she had left him to his pointless vigil over debts, and gone back alone.

Sarah blamed Frances completely and entirely for their ruin. She could not speak to her except with the coldest courtesy. She saw Frances grow weaker and she could find no pity for her at all. Stuart Hadley advised her that Frances's heart was fatally weak and vulnerable to shock; and Sarah merely nodded and said, 'We are none of us as strong as we appear,' as if the news meant nothing to her.

Stuart had said, 'Perhaps I did not make myself clear. Another shock could kill her.'

Sarah had merely looked at him and said: 'She was always weakly.' She spoke as if Frances were a bale of shoddy cotton, sold as good, and indeed she felt as if the Scotts had joined with the rest of the world in gulling her and Josiah, in selling them substandard goods and trapping them into ruin.

The only time she could bring herself to see Frances was for a once-a-day ritual before dinner when she came to her sister-in-law's room and enquired glacially if Frances felt any better.

'No better,' Frances replied. 'But I have had some very bad news today.'

Sarah raised an eyebrow. She did not sit down. She paused at the foot of Frances's bed, ready to leave as soon as the courtesies had been paid.

'The slaves have gone,' Frances said baldly.

'What?'

'Run away,' Frances said.

'But I saw Cicero just now!'

'He and Elizabeth are the only ones left.'

Sarah moved away from the bed and sank into the pretty blue chair at the fireside. 'I don't understand,' she said.

'They went last night,' Frances reported. 'Cicero told me this morning.'

'Why did you not tell me then?' Sarah demanded. 'We could have informed the magistrates . . .'

'I daresay they had it well planned,' Frances said dryly.

'Have they stolen our goods?'

'I don't know.'

'Why did you not tell me at once?'

Frances looked at her wearily. 'It did not seem to matter much,' she said coldly. 'Not now.'

The gulf of their loss opened up before them. Sarah's protests were stilled. Soon, she thought, they would have neither home nor business. If they had made as much as fifteen hundred pounds on the slaves it would only have gone to pay creditors.

'They were your dowry,' she said sullenly. 'And much good they have done us.'

Frances nodded at the implied criticism. 'It has not been a success,' she observed. 'Not the slaves, not the business, and not the marriage. When did you last see Josiah?'

'Last night. He is living down on the quay. He did not see me, I saw him through the window.'

'Is he ill?'

'He is trying to save his business,' Sarah said loyally. 'He is working all day and all night.' She would not tell Frances that he was working ˙s a madman works, little detailed actions which change nothing.

Frances nodded. 'Will you tell him about the slaves?'

Sarah shook her head. 'I will advertise for them. And if we cannot get them back I will tell him then. There is no point in running towards bad news. Josiah has enough to worry him.'

She rose from the chair as if she were achingly weary. 'That Cicero and Elizabeth,' she said. 'Do they know where the others are gone? Will they help us fetch them back?'

'They do not know, but even if they did they would not tell us.'

'If they know we could make them tell us. We could have them whipped.'

Frances sighed with impatience. 'All of them have run away except these two. Is this how we reward loyalty? With a beating?'

'Why did they stay?'

Frances looked away from Sarah. 'I don't know,' she said. 'But I am glad that they did. We cannot afford to pay anyone to do the work, I suppose.'

Sarah shook her head. 'There is no cash for the housekeeping books. All the tradesmen are giving us credit but soon they will know that there is no money to pay them. I do not know if anything is left from the profits of the *Lily*. I have avoided asking Josiah, but I will have to find out soon. I think it has all gone into this house, and into the Hot Well. I think it has all gone and there is nothing left at all.'

Chapter Thirty-seven

There was a loud hammering on the door knocker at seven o'clock on a cold December morning, hard with white frost. Mehuru, carrying hot water to the bedrooms on the first floor, put down the heavy jugs and went to the front door.

A round-faced man in brown serge, followed by two others, stepped into the house and put his hand on Mehuru's arm.

'Bailiffs,' he said abruptly. 'Is your master at home? Savee? Big boss? Savee?'

Mehuru jerked his arm away. 'Mr Cole is at the warehouse.'

The big man blinked in surprise at the perfectly spoken English. 'Here, we'll have you straight away,' he said, tightening his grip.

'What's this?' Cook asked, surging up the passageway from the kitchen.

'Bailiffs,' the man said shortly. 'Come to distrain goods to the value of more than two thousand pounds.'

Cook squared up to him. 'And what d'you think you're doing with him?' she demanded, plucking Mehuru's sleeve away.

'He's goods,' the man said. 'And worth a lot, I should think.'

'He's free,' Cook lied instantly. 'He's a free man, a servant.'

'We'll see about that,' the bailiff replied. 'I've got authority to seize household goods here.'

'You wait there,' Cook ordered. She nodded Mehuru to go upstairs. 'Wake Miss Cole and tell her,' she said.

486

Mehuru nodded and went up to Sarah's bedroom. He tapped lightly on the door. At Sarah's sharp command he opened the door and spoke from the threshold.

'A man is here called Bailiffs.'

He heard an abrupt exclamation from inside the room and the noise of Sarah getting hastily out of bed and throwing a shawl around her shoulders. She peered around the door at him. 'Bailiffs?' she asked.

'Yes,' he confirmed.

Her face was more pinched and angry than ever. 'Go out of the back door,' she hissed. 'Run to the warehouse. Find Mr Cole. Tell him to come home at once. Tell him he must come at once and bring everything he has, all the money he has to hand, all the notes of credit, a note of what we still hold in bond.'

Mehuru nodded.

'Go without them seeing you,' Sarah cautioned. 'And be quick.'

Mehuru went quietly downstairs. In the hall Cook was blocking the way. Another man with a handcart had arrived, and a pony and cart behind him. Mehuru slipped like a shadow down the hall and out through the back door into the yard.

He ran down to the dockside and whistled for the ferryboat to take him across.

'Ha'penny,' the lad said.

'Mr Cole will pay on the way back,' Mehuru promised. He still had no money in his pockets.

The lad nodded. 'He better had.'

The prow of the little boat nosed against the green slimy steps. Mehuru jumped ashore, clearing the tidemark of garbage and filth and ran up the steps to the Cole warehouse. He hammered on the front door and shouted until the window above opened and Josiah stuck his head out.

'Oh, it's you,' he said. 'What's the matter?'

'Bailiffs,' Mehuru told him. 'Miss Cole said to come home at once. She said to bring everything you have, all the money and all the notes of credit, and a note of what you have in bond.'

Josiah laughed shortly, a cold mirthless sound, staring down at Mehuru below him. 'I'll come,' he said. 'But I've nothing to bring. Nothing. D'you hear?'

Mehuru waited. There was a bitter wind blowing up the gorge and a cold frost on the quayside. The garbage in the dock was rimmed with white. The door before him opened and Josiah came out. He was wearing an old suit of home-spun brown and his linen was dirty. His stock was badly tied and his jacket pulled on carelessly with one pocket flap tucked in. The two men went side by side to the ferry, the immaculately dressed black man in livery and his shabby master.

'Do you have a penny for the boy?' Mehuru asked.

Josiah bared his stained teeth. 'It's about all I do have,' he said. 'And I suppose I have to pay for you too, good money to bring me bad news. You should have run around the long way and not cost me your fare.'

The boat edged against the steps on the Bristol side of the river. Mehuru got out first and gave Josiah his hand. The older man moved as if he were stiff and tired, but at the entrance to Queens Square, as he took in the waiting carts and the bailiff's men, his pace grew swifter.

'What's this?' he cried as soon as he was at his front door. 'What authority?'

The bailiff turned to him. 'Are you Josiah Cole?'

'Who wants to know?' Josiah demanded with pointless cunning.

'Bailiffs. I have a warrant here for the distraint of goods.'

Josiah looked indoors to the shadowy hall. Sarah, coming downstairs in her plainest gown, nodded at him. Brother and sister's eyes met. Neither of them smiled but there was a grim recognition o. mutual need and a promise of mutual support. Mehuru thought of the warriors of Oyo who sing that only those who fear nothing, not even the hornbill who feasts on the eyes of dead men, can march with them. The taut readiness for disaster was there in Sarah and Josiah. Upstairs, Frances still slept.

'How much?' Josiah said evenly. He thought he might part with some of the more extravagant pieces of porcelain and keep the basic goods.

The bailiff looked at his list. 'It's £2300. 17s.,' he said.

Josiah staggered as if he had been knifed in the belly. Sarah came swiftly forwards and drew him into the hall, half-supporting him with her arm around his back.

'Show me,' Josiah said. 'Who has done this?'

The bailiff handed over the warrant with the bills and signatories attached. Josiah read them with minute attention, as if he hoped to spot an error of a few pence. His lips moved as he scanned the words but Mehuru could tell that he was not seeing them at all. He was turning the pages, one after another, but his eyes were sightless.

'Let me see.' Sarah's voice was gentle. She took the papers from Josiah's hand and looked from one bill to another. They were the bills for the wallhangings, for the carpets, for the curtains, for the pictures. The plasterer, who had repaired the broken beak of one of Josiah's beloved ornamental plasterwork ho-ho birds, the carpenter for a new step on the stair. The chimney sweep who had cleaned all the chimneys before they had moved in, the coal merchant for the last delivery. Not a bill had been settled since they had moved into Josiah's great house. While Sarah had been balancing the housekeeping books for butcher and baker, Josiah had been letting the costs of the house double and re-double, with one eye on the Hot Well and the other on his ships.

The second set of papers were the bills for the Hot Well: wages, new furnishings, running costs. Sarah turned page after page as the bailiff looked at her, his stolid face carefully impassive.

There was a third set of papers from the chandlers, the sailmakers and the ropewalk, unpaid since *Lily* had sailed, still owing from *Daisy*'s sailing nearly a year ago.

'You will have to give us a few days to settle these,' she said.

The bailiff shook his head. 'I am sorry, Missis,' he said. 'My orders are to take goods to the value for sale. They are to be taken today.'

'I don't believe we have goods to the value of two thousand pounds,' Sarah said, her voice sharp and unemotional. 'Much of the furniture belongs to my sister-in-law.'

'Married to Mr Cole?'

'Of course.'

'Her goods are his, then,' he said. 'If they're married.'

'Even so,' Sarah maintained, 'we do not have goods to the value of these bills.'

The bailiff nodded. 'Then I have to ask you to vacate the premises, Missis. I have instructions to claim the property itself. You can take your personal clothes and belongings.'

'Go back to the warehouse?' Josiah was suddenly roused from his daydream. 'Back to the warehouse? But we've only just come from there!'

Sarah turned to him. 'It doesn't matter, Josiah,' she said urgently. 'We can go back for now, while we get this sorted out. The house will not be sold for weeks. *Rose* could come in any day and then we will settle our debts. We can go back for now.'

'No!' Josiah yelled. He suddenly plunged towards the bailiff, his hands snatching for his throat. The bailiff side-stepped him easily and his man, waiting behind, seized Josiah and wrestled him away. The man with the handcart raced up the steps and the three of them bent Josiah's arms behind his back and held him. 'No!' Josiah yelled again.

Mehuru hesitated, then he heard Frances's bedroom door open. At once he turned for the stairs and ran up to her. He saw a glimpse of her pale face and her tumbling dark hair.

'Not so fast, you!' the bailiff called. He took three swift steps up the stairs behind Mehuru and flung his arms around him. 'Here! Sam! Help me with this!'

Mehuru twisted in his grip. 'Let me go,' he said steadily. 'I must go to Mrs Cole . . . she is ill . . .'

'You're goods,' the man said with sudden abrupt viciousness. 'And I'm distraining you along with everything else.'

The second man raced up the stairs towards them. Frances from above could see Mehuru's danger. 'Mehuru!' she screamed. 'Run! Run!'

At the sound of her voice Mehuru kicked out and threw the bailiff backwards against the banister. There was a splintering sound and the banister creaked outwards, away from the stairs. He stumbled against the other man and Mehuru punched him straight-fingered into his round belly. The man slumped down, whooping and gasping for breath, knocking the other man off balance. Mehuru tore out of his grip and raced up the stairs to Frances.

She was clinging to the door frame. 'What is happening? Who are those men?'

Mehuru swept her off her feet and carried her back into her bedroom, kicking the door shut behind them. 'It is nothing, nothing. Be calm, Frances!'

She struggled out of his arms and stood unsteadily before him. 'Mehuru! Tell me! What do they want?'

He could feel her rapid pulse thudding in her fingers.

'Please,' he said. 'Please, Frances, be still. They have come for money. That's all. They want money.'

'Bailiffs?'

He nodded. 'That is what they said.'

Her face was wax-white. 'We will lose the house. We will lose everything.'

There was a loud bang on the door and then it was thrown open. The bailiff stepped into the room. 'Beg pardon,' he said heavily. 'But I'm distraining him for sale.'

Frances staggered. 'He is sold,' she improvised swiftly. Her face was ashen. 'You cannot have him, he is the property of Mr Waring.'

The man hesitated. 'Mr Waring?'

Frances held her hand to her heart. She could feel its erratic pounding. 'Ask him!' she said. 'And he will be angry if you touch his servant.'

The bailiff recoiled. 'Leave my room,' Frances said. 'How dare you come in here?'

He was impressed by her frosty air of command. 'Beg pardon, ma'am. Just trying to do my job, and he struck me.'

'Mr Waring will compensate you,' Frances assured him. 'You must complain to him.'

He nodded and left. They were silent as they heard his heavy tread going down the stairs.

Frances gave a little gasp. Her face was ashen. 'You must run,' she whispered breathlessly. 'Get out of the back door, Mehuru. And take Elizabeth.'

'I won't leave you,' he said stubbornly. 'He won't touch me. He thinks I am Mr Waring's slave.'

'That won't save you. Mr Waring could come and claim you. You must go.'

He caught her in his arms. 'I promised that I would stay with you.'

'Look at me!' she cried in sudden passion. 'I am dying, Mehuru! And you have a life before you! Go! I want to know you are free!' She gathered her strength and pushed him away from her, thrust him to the door. But as she did so, her face suddenly changed and went into a spasm of pain. She doubled up. 'Oh God, Mehuru! The baby is coming! The baby!'

He scooped her up and laid her on the bed. She screamed a sharp cry of pain and then gasped for breath.

Mehuru recklessly flung open the door and shouted for Elizabeth. She came running down the stairs. 'The baby is coming,' he said. 'Go to her, I will fetch Stuart. Lock the bedroom door and let no-one in but me.'

He glanced down to the hall. The bailiffs had given up on him for the time being, they were arguing with Josiah. Brother and sister were blocking the doorway, shoulder to shoulder and insisting on seeing one bill after another, haggling as if a reduction of a few pounds would make all the difference. Mehuru thought that the two worlds of the house had split off from each other completely. Downstairs Sarah and Josiah still struggled for money, upstairs the slaves and Frances struggled to bring life into the house, and to cheat death.

Mehuru went quietly down the hall, slipped out of the back door and then took to his heels towards Stuart's house.

He was lucky, he saw the doctor's phaeton waiting outside the Merchant Venturer almshouses at the back of the square. 'Stuart!' he shouted to the squat white-painted facade intersected with black beams, and was rewarded by the sight of his face at a small leaded upstairs window.

'It's Frances! The baby is coming!'

Stuart made a grimace at Mehuru's crashing lack of discretion, vanished from the window and then appeared at the little door.

'She's in pain! Come!'

Stuart swung into the driving seat and Mehuru leaped for the footman's hold behind the carriage.

'Did something bring it on?' Stuart shouted over his shoulder.

'Bailiffs in the house,' Mehuru said. 'A fight. They tried to catch me.'

Stuart scowled.

'You knew of the baby,' Mehuru accused.

'I am her doctor.'

'You did not tell me.'

'Why should I have told you?' Stuart hedged. He steered the horse carefully around the square and pulled it up well clear of the bailiff's cart.

'Because I was caring for her,' Mehuru said. 'I needed to know. She needs my protection with Josiah away all the time. You should have told me.'

'And who do you think is the father?' Stuart asked conversationally. He reached into the phaeton and pulled out his bag.

'Come on! Hurry!' Mehuru was dancing on the pavement with impatience. He had forgotten all about the bailiffs.

Stuart gave him a brief quizzical look and let himself be rushed towards the house. Inside the hall they could hear Josiah and Sarah conducting the bailiffs from room to room.

'That is porcelain, it is worth a hundred pounds,' Josiah was saying in the morning room. 'And that is an heirloom, you can see the crest, the Scott crest.'

Mehuru led the way up the stairs, taking the steps three at a time, Stuart behind him. At Frances's door he suddenly checked, listening to the low moaning noise from inside.

'The father?' he suddenly demanded, at last registering Stuart's look and his question. 'The father of her child?'

Stuart put him carefully to one side and tapped on the door. 'I will call you when she can see you,' he promised. 'But, Mehuru, don't expect too much. She is not strong.'

'Let me see her now.'

'In a moment.' The door opened and Stuart went in, firmly closing it behind him. Mehuru collapsed on the stairs outside and listened.

He could hear Frances gasping for breath when the pains crushed her. He heard Sarah draw Josiah out into the hall leaving the bailiffs in the morning room, pricing the furniture.

'Let it go, Josiah,' she begged urgently. 'Let it go!'

'The heirlooms . . .' Josiah said. 'And the dragons.'

Sarah grasped the lapels of his jacket. 'Josiah, listen to me,' she said. 'We have a chance, we have a good chance.'

Josiah looked at her with his old keen attention. 'How?'

'They can have it,' she said recklessly. 'The house, the furniture, the Hot Well spa, everything. They can even have a ship! They can even have two! We can deal! Don't you see? We can deal on the debts.'

'We lose the house?' Josiah asked.

'Let it go!' Sarah repeated. 'As long as we have the quay and the warehouse, and one ship. That's all we need, Josiah! We can start again. The warehouse and the quay and one ship!'

'Frances cannot live there,' Josiah said suddenly.

'Frances can go too. Along with the other luxuries.'

'She is my wife . . .' Josiah protested weakly.

'We are not suited for marriage, you and I,' she ruled. 'You have forgotten how our mother died. She died alone while Da was out trading on the trow. He said then that business and love do not mix. D'you remember?'

Josiah shook his head.

'He did,' Sarah said convincingly. 'And we chose the Trade. We chose the cruellest business that ever has been. That ever will be. You cannot make your money as we have made ours and still be tender-hearted, Josiah. Your wife is sick and dying upstairs. Down here we can bargain with the bailiffs and take our kitchenware to the warehouse and start again. Tell me what it is you wish.'

Josiah hesitated for only a moment. 'If *Rose* comes in tomorrow . . .'

'Then we are rich. If she never comes in at all then there is still *Daisy* and *Lily*. One of them will come in, and both of them could come 'n at a profit.'

He nodded. 'Pack up the kitchenware and everything you think we can get away with,' he said softly. 'I will get the best price I can for these things. Those dragons should be worth something. I always said they were the thing.'

'And her furniture,' Sarah said. 'Sell her furniture. She cost us enough from first to last. She can pay now.'

Mehuru sat at the top of the stairs listening half to them, half to the painful hard gasps of breath from Frances's room. As he sat he gathered his old skills around him. He sat quite still, focusing his mind to give her ease. He closed his eyes. The noise of Josiah going protestingly from room to room downstairs faded away like the chatter of parrots. All he could hear was the rasp of Frances's breath and then slowly, slowly, she grew quieter.

Mehuru felt himself drawing her pain from her, and watched it flow through his own body, the griping pain at the heart, the hot rasp of breath in the labouring lungs, and the powerful, unimaginable vice-like grip of childbirth. He opened his body like a cave, like a cavern, and let the pain flow through him like a fast deep river, scarcely touching the sides. His conscious mind heard Frances's sharp breathing ease as the pain left her, and he held the river of pain close to him, to keep her safe.

The bedroom door opened and Stuart looked out, his face drawn. 'You had better come in,' he said. 'I am losing her.'

Mehuru straightened up and went slowly into the room. Frances was lying back on the fine linen pillow, her face as white as her sheet and her hair stuck with sweat to her forehead and neck.

When she saw him she managed a little half-smile. 'Mehuru,' she said, and the way she spoke his name sounded like 'water'.

He knelt beside her bed and gathered her gently into his arms, cradling her head on his shoulder, holding her close. She closed her eyes and clung to him, one hand around his shoulders and the other reaching up to touch his throat. 'Oh God, Mehuru. I have been a fool.'

'We both have been fools,' he said. He could feel a deep slow pain in his own chest which he thought was probably heartbreak.

'I've been such a fool,' she said, snatching a little gasp of air. 'All the time I was trying . . .' she lost her breath and stuttered as she tried to inhale '. . . t . . . t . . . trying to keep a position . . .'

He nodded. 'I know.'

'To be a lady!' She gave another little gasp. 'At such cost!'

He held her very close, willing the pain to pass. 'I know,' he said softly. 'I understood from the very beginning.'

'All your pain . . . and the wreck of Africa . . .' He rocked her gently, letting her speak, letting her finally speak honestly to him from her heart. 'And you . . . and I . . . Such a waste, Mehuru!'

He laid her back on her bed and buried his dark head into the warm curve of her neck. She put her arms around him and held him close. 'I love you,' she said quietly.

He pulled back and looked at her face. The twisted frantic look had gone and she was smiling slightly. Mehuru looked into her eyes. He had watched men and women die and he knew that nothing could keep Frances now. 'I never said so before,' she whispered. 'But I loved you from the moment I first saw you.'

'Stay,' he begged urgently. 'Stay with me, Frances.'

She smiled almost lazily. 'Look in my writing box. Later. Hold me now.'

'Stay . . .' He was speaking like a man and not an obalawa.

'Maybe one day,' she said very softly. 'Maybe one day there

will be a world where a man and woman like us might love each other, d'you think?'

'Stay now . . .'

She suddenly lunged forward, her eyes black with the grip of sudden pain, and she cried out, once. He caught her to save her from falling, calling her name. When her body went limp and he laid her back on her pillows, she was gone.

Stuart dragged him from her bedside and pushed him to the window. 'Don't look,' he said forcibly. 'Look out of the window.'

Mehuru stumbled to the window and leaned his head against the cold pane of glass and looked without seeing at the frost under the trees and the white incised blades of grass.

Then Stuart said, 'And here we are!' and Mehuru heard a strange little noise, a cry, a tiny breath, and then another cry.

He turned to see Elizabeth wrapping a tiny thing, smaller than a doll, in soft white cloth, and dabbing at its head.

'See?' she smiled, though her eyes were still running with tears. 'Your son, Mehuru. You have a son.'

Hardly knowing what he was doing, he put out his hands and she gently put the little bundle into his arms. The baby looked up at him. It had black black eyes, as dark as Frances's, as dark as his own. Its little face was a rich colour like rum and milk, like the colour of the palms of Mehuru's tender hands. Mehuru staggered for a moment, as the truth finally hit him. The child's smooth skin was a rich brown colour, a mixture of Frances and himself. It was not Josiah's child, it had never been Josiah's child. It was his own son.

'My son,' he said incredulously. 'My son.'

The baby looked at him with his wise dark eyes as if he could understand everything, everything that was in the world. He opened his little mouth and yawned, a complete thorough yawn, as precise as a kitten.

'Hello, my son,' Mehuru said in English, and then in Yoruban: *'Baa woo ne o moo me.'*

498

The baby's eyes widened as he solemnly considered his father, and then his little face constricted. He squeezed his eyes shut and began to cry.

'He will be hungry,' Elizabeth said. 'Give him to me.'

'Can you feed him?' Mehuru asked.

The look she gave him was rich with love. 'I have been waiting and preparing for him for months,' she said. 'Frances knew. She knew I would care for him.'

Stuart turned from the bed. 'I am sorry, Mehuru. I could not save her. I will send a woman to lay her out.'

'I will do it,' he said instantly. 'I have stayed here, all this time, to do it as it should be done. She is an African woman now. She is the wife of a Yoruban, she is the mother of my child.'

Stuart nodded. 'I will wait for you in the kitchen. I will take Elizabeth there, with the baby, and make sure they are safe. We should go from here, as soon as you are ready. You can join the others now.'

Mehuru nodded. He held the door for them and watched Elizabeth take his son downstairs. She was holding him close, tucked into the curve of her neck, and all he could see was the crown of the little black head. His son had inherited his hair; it was as tight and as curly as the fleece of a little black lamb.

Mehuru shut the door on them. Downstairs he could hear the bailiff's men taking furniture out to the cart, he could hear Josiah's baffled arguing and Sarah's sharp complaints. He heard it all as if it came from many miles away.

He straightened Frances in her bed and took the blood-stained sheets away. He poured the warm water from the jug into the ewer and sponged her body, her face, her arms, and her thin white fingers. He combed her hair and he braided it close to her head in the manner of his people. She looked very beautiful with her hair in African braids, he thought. They showed the fine structure of her face, and she no longer looked weary. She no longer looked as if she were warring with herself. She looked at peace, she looked as if she finally had understood ·hat there was no need to hunger and struggle.

He went to her chest of clothes and drew out a blue gown, blue the colour of coolness, of *itutu*: composure. Carefully he put it on her, drawing it around her, and holding her close as he fastened it. Into the pockets of the gown he slipped the things that she should take with her when they put her in the earth: her comb, a teaspoon from her breakfast tray, a pinch of salt. He opened her sewing basket and took out her little silver embroidery scissors. He cut one of the tight black curls of hair from his head and tucked it under her handkerchief. He closed her eyes and kissed her, her cool eyelids, her lips, and the still-warm hollow at her collarbone. Then he drew the white counterpane over her.

At the doorway he hesitated. She had told him to look in her writing box. He took it to the windowseat and opened it. Laid neatly on the top was a single sheet of paper. At the foot was Frances's seal and name and two other signatures: Stuart Hadley, and Mary Allen, the cook. It read:

'This is the Last Will and Testament of Me, Frances Jane Scott Cole, signed this 29th day of November 1789 before Stuart Hadley and Mary Allen.

'To my Sister-in-law Sarah Cole I do Bequeath all my 'Dresses and Gowns and Jewellery. 'To my 'Dear husband Josiah I bequeath all my 'Furniture and Heirlooms.

I 'Direct their attention to my 'Work as Agent for Sir Charles 'Fairley. 'They will see that the Agency is now of a size that it could be registered as a 'Bank and I do bequeath to my Sister-in-law and to my Husband Jointly all my Interest in these Matters, and 'Recommend to them that 'They develop this Bank as their Business, Abandoning the Slave Trade.

For my Own Slaves I hereby Grant them their Complete and Absolute Freedom: Julius, Mary, Martha, Elizabeth, John, Susan, Ruth, Naomi, Matthew, and Mark are hereby all Freed. The man Mehuru, once known as Cicero, is also Completely and Absolutely Free.

I send them my Dearest Blessing and the hope that they may make a Home in England and Find it in their hearts to Forgive me – and all English people – for the Very great wrong that we have done to Them and to their Country. It has taken me a Long Long time to realise what we did to you, I am sorry, I am Sorry. Perhaps one day we can learn to live together in Love and Respect?

Author's Note

There were Africans in Britain before the English were here – that's the opinion of Peter Fryer, the great historian of the black presence in England. In his history *Staying Power* he quotes the record of an African legion stationed on Hadrian's Wall in the third century. Before the coming of the Vikings, before the invasion of the Normans at the Battle of Hastings, before Elizabethan England, before everything we think of as English, there were black men here then. We even have a record of one individual. He sounds as if he was a bit of a trouble-maker; he barracked Caesar when he came to visit. He was popular with the other soldiers and a bit of a comedian. The record of the time says: 'He was of great fame among clowns and good for a laugh at any time.'

If we skip forward to James VI's court in Scotland, we come across a number of black court entertainers, including a drummer, a choreographer of the court dances and masques, a black knight, and a lady who was famed for her beauty: 'A black lady – a skin that shone like soap. In her rich costume she gleamed as bright as a barrel of tar. When she was born the sun had to suffer an eclipse.'

All through the sixteenth century, in the records of English history, there were men and women arriving from Africa – and going home after a visit to England. In 1555 John Lok brought five Africans from Ghana to Britain to learn English. When they got home they acted as interpreters to the growing trade in ivory, spices and gold. As the trade grew more important in the African economy, enterprising merchants and princes sent their sons to be educated in England so that they could develop commercial contacts. We know that there were African children educated in London, Bristol and Liverpool, who came for their schooling and then went safely home again.

But the trade and these trading relationships changed. From 1570 onwards the slave trade developed. For more than two centuries, for generation after generation, ships sailed from British and European ports loaded with gold, trinkets and, more than anything else, guns. They traded these goods along the African coast with African slavers who were commissioned and armed by the Europeans to go deep into the African countryside and hunt for slaves.

When the slave traders from the most popular west coast penetrated so deeply that they met the slavers from the east coast, there was no place safe for a black man in Africa. African slavers had been taking slaves for generations, but the scale of this was unprecedented: millions rather than thousands, a slavery which extended over generations so that their children would be born enslaved. And these people, enslaved and then taken overseas, would never see their homes again.

I don't think that we will ever know how many men, women and children were kidnapped from Africa and sold into slavery. Most historians think about fifteen or twenty million slaves were shipped across the Atlantic. We cannot know how many millions died in the slave wars that were an inevitable part of the slave trade, some people have estimated that it was as many as one hundred million. Of those who survived to be shipped to the colonies it is thought that a quarter of them died on the voyage, a quarter on landing and a further quarter within the first couple of years. That was why it was such a big business. The slave stocks had to be replenished constantly; the plantations were a death sentence for three-quarters of the enslaved.

As Josiah Cole says: 'It is the greatest trade that the world has ever known. We all profit.' It was the first and the greatest global trade. It launched Britain as a maritime power, as an industrial power, and as a centre for capitalism. Most of the British banks started as finance houses for the distant plantations. Lloyds of London insured the slave ships. Modern weapons designers started out as gunsmiths for the Africa trade, the industrial revolution would not have been possible without the massive injection of capital that came from the profits of slavery and the plantation goods. And the very fabric of eighteenth-century English society that we love to see now in stately homes and in historical dramas on television was built on the profits of slavery. In Jane Austen's *Mansfield Park*, Sir Bertram is away from home because he has to go to his plantation. Sir Thomas Bertram is a slave owner, and dear little Fanny Price will find true happiness as the daughter-in-law of a slaver, her elegant life financed by terrible suffering.

A tiny fraction of this holocaust did not end their journey in the New World, but were brought on to Britain. Some of them came as the ships' captain's perks – some captains liked to be served by a slave on board and brought their slaves home. Returning planters, accustomed to being waited on hand and foot, brought their house slaves back to Britain when they retired. Wealthy sugar planters on visits brought their slaves with them to show off. It was tremendously fashionable to have a little black page boy to carry a lady's fan or her gloves or to stand behind her in a drawing room. Black horn players were employed at deluxe foxhunts, black footmen ran behind the richest carriages. Black laundresses starched white linen and black prostitutes were brought in to serve white men. Black slaves were imported and sold in the newspaper columns, alongside advertisements for dogs and horses – as luxury items.

Many of these slaves did not stay with these masters and

mistresses who bought them. Many of them took to their heels and we meet them again in the lost-and-found columns as their masters advertised in the newspapers for their return, sometimes remarking that they had run away again, sometimes identifying them as being scarred from previous beatings. Even now we must feel admiration for the young people – mostly young men – who survived the ordeal of kidnap, the horror of the two-month voyage across the Atlantic, the terror of the next two-month voyage to England, then sale to an English owner in a strange country; and still had the courage to run for it as soon as possible.

What is remarkable about their stories is that they found freedom, running away from white masters to hide among white working-class people. White people living in the roughest areas of towns saw that a black man enslaved by a cruel master was in the same situation as themselves – also working for cruel masters. The early struggle by white workers for their rights, the earliest associations and unions, were linked to the battle against slavery. They thought that their struggle was the same as the right of freedom for black slaves. And when black slaves ran to white working-class communities they were welcomed and sheltered and hidden.

Of course, they all fell in love. One ex-slave Ukasaw Gronisaw wrote: 'The morning after I came to my new lodgings, as I was at breakfast with the gentlewoman of the house, I heard the noise of some looms over our heads, and upon inquiring what it was, she told me that a person was weaving silk. I expressed a great desire to see it, and asked if I might. She told me that she would go up with me, for she was sure that I should be very welcome; and she was as good as her word. As soon as we entered the room, the person that was weaving looked about and smiled upon us, and I loved her from that moment.'

Marriages between black men and white women produced children who, living in predominantly white communities, met and married white partners. The family's skin grew paler with each generation until after about four or five generations, the great-great-great-grandson or -daughter might never know that their ancestor had been an enslaved black man. It is this disappearance that caused the loss of the story. Until very recently there were few historians researching the history of slaves in England simply because people were not aware that there were significant numbers of them. But a London court case in the middle of the eighteenth century was told that there were more than fifteen thousand runaway slaves living freely in London. One contemporary commentator said that there was a black face in every village in England.

What is so surprising about the individual stories of individual slaves is their courage in going on to make lives which were worth living and which were even filled with joy and love. The story of the slaves in England is a story of a crime against humanity but it is also a story of triumph – of people who set themselves free and made new lives for themselves and sought their own happiness.

The history of these most courageous people can be read in a number of accessible books. I particularly enjoyed James Walvin's *Black Ivory*, HarperCollins, 1992. For the long and honourable history of black Britons, I recommend Peter Fryer, *The History of Black People in Britain*, Pluto Press, 1984. But the last word should be with the African peoples themselves, in an anthology edited by Paul Edwards and David Dabydeen, *Black Writers in Britain, 1760-1890*, Edinburgh University Press, 1991.

Philippa Gregory, England, 2005

Gardens for The Gambia

Ten years ago I was in The Gambia, researching *A Respectable Trade*, which would become a book and also a four-part BBC drama serial. I met a headmaster, Ismaila Sisay, who showed me around his small country school, and then asked me, would I consider making a contribution to his most important project – a well for the school yard? He told me that a garden in the school yard, watered by the well, would supplement the children's diet of rice from the World Health Organisation, would teach them sustainable agriculture, and might even make a small profit which could be used to buy books and stationary for the school.

I decided to take a chance on this stranger and gave him the full cost of the well: three hundred pounds. A fortnight later, when I was back in England, he sent me a fax to confirm the well was dug, and filled with water, and the children were watering their garden. It seemed like a small successful miracle of trust. Then he told me that the next-door school had asked, could they have a well too? It seemed an utterly reasonable request, and I wrote an article in a women's magazine, asking for donations. They poured in, in small and larger amounts and Ismaila and I started a partnership that has now gone on for ten years, building wells in Gambian primary schools and community gardens.

We started in 1994 and we have, to date, dug more than sixty wells to provide water to irrigate school and community gardens. In the school gardens the children learn the skills of sustainable agriculture. The vegetables they grow supplement the rice dinner for the poorest children who would otherwise have nothing to eat all day, the surplus produce is sold, and stationary and educational equipment is bought with the profit.

The gardens are planted rather like an English allotment. They grow all sorts of pulses, root and salad vegetables. Usually the school also plants citrus and walnut trees. Often pupils from the senior class of these primary schools will be made responsible for the health of their particular tree. They fence it to protect it from straying animals and they water it every day from the well. It is wonderful to see the enthusiasm the children feel for their garden.

The wells are deliberately low-technology, low-budget. Basically they are circular holes dug down to the water table by a hired well digger. Usually we have to go down to about sixteen metres. When the soil is very dry then the well has to be lined with concrete pipes. To keep the children safe, a small wall is built around the top, and a pulley, rope and bucket are provided. Once the well is built and handed over, then the headmaster of the school and the school committee is responsible for its maintenance. We don't put a well in a school without their enthusiastic support. For some schools the experience has been transformational. Some schools have financed adult-education programmes with the surplus cash; others have started community businesses.

We are starting to expand from schools to community projects. Two have been particularly successful. The first was a well we put into a women's communal garden. The women were so successful in producing vegetables in the garden based around our well that the Gambian Agricultural Research Authority asked them to trial some rice strains. The women hand-dug earthworks around a massive forty acres, an extraordinary achievement, and used our well and the annual rains to flood the area to grow rice. They brought off a magnificent crop, and now they are responsible for the biggest paddy field in The Gambia. They produce and sell good yields of early rice, they feed their own villages and they distribute seeds to other farmers. It is a tremendous success story and it started with one three-hundred-pound well given by us.

The other great success story of this year is at the remote village of Njawarra, in the far north of the country. It took us nearly all day to drive to it going almost cross-country on roads that are nothing more than sandy tracks. The farmers were aware that their lands were getting drier and their yields poorer. On their own initiative they agreed that they should form an agricultural college and try to improve their farming. A few years ago they asked us for a well. That was just the start of it. With our well at the centre of their fields they applied to the Canadian and European governments for aid. They now have a residential block for visiting trainees, a seed bank, a centre for alternative technology, tutors, a restaurant, an orchard, a vegetable plot, an explosion of projects and enthusiasm which is rolling out across the country – all based on our first little well.

Since my last visit to The Gambia, just before Christmas 2004, we have started a whole programme of new wells, and I am determined that this project will go on. It has directly fed thousands of school children and taught them methods of farming which will make them and their own children safer from hunger in the future. I have seen how the benefits of one well can transform adult farming projects too – the women's rice field and the Njawarra agricultural college are major sources of change in this poor country. I foresee that we will continue to invest in schools and well-organised groups.

I do ask you to contribute anything that you can readily afford to Gardens for The Gambia. The country is the poorest in Africa (excluding those damaged by war) and the people work tremendously hard and effectively with the little help they get. The climate is getting drier and the Sahara desert is encroaching. Any sum of money you wish to donate will go direct to The Gambia; I take no administration fees in this country. Your donation will make a tremendous amount of difference to people who really deserve a chance. If you can help at all, I thank you very, very much.

Philippa Gregory

Cheques, or postal orders should be sent to:
Gardens for The Gambia
PO Box 165
Carlton in Cleveland
Middlesbrough
TS9 7WX

Gardens for The Gambia is applying for charitable status in the UK, and is a registered charity and non-governmental organisation in The Gambia. In an official survey it is the biggest donor of wells for primary schools in the country.

All donations will be acknowledged. Please look at my website www.PhilippaGregory.com for future news. There is a special section about Gardens for The Gambia.